D0936249

Reading Prophetic Narratives

Indiana Studies in Biblical Literature

Herbert Marks and Robert Polzin, general editors

Reading Prophetic Narratives

Uriel
Simon

*Translated from the Hebrew
by Lenn J. Schramm*

INDIANA UNIVERSITY PRESS
BLOOMINGTON AND INDIANAPOLIS

KNIGHT-CAPRON LIBRARY
LYNCHBURG COLLEGE
LYNCHBURG, VIRGINIA 24501
WITHDRAWN

Originally published as
קריאה ספרותית במקרא - סיפורי נביאים by the Bialik Institute,
Jerusalem and Bar-Ilan University Press, Ramat-Gan, 1997

Translation © 1997 by Uriel Simon

All rights reserved

No part of this book may be reproduced or utilized in any form or by any
means, electronic or mechanical, including photocopying and recording, or
any information storage and retrieval system, without permission in writing
from the publisher. The Association of American University Presses'
Resolution on Permissions constitutes the only exception to this prohibition.

The paper used in this publication meets the minimum requirements of
American National Standard for Information Sciences—Permanence of
Paper for Printed Library Materials, ANSI Z39.48-1984.

Manufactured in the United States of America

Library of Congress Cataloging-in-Publication Data

Simon, Uriel.
[Ḳeri 'ah sifrutit ba-Miḳra, sipure Nevi 'im. English]
Reading prophetic narratives / Uriel Simon ; translated from the
Hebrew by Lenn J. Schramm.
p.   cm. — (Indiana studies in biblical literature)
Includes bibliographical references and indexes.
ISBN 0–253–33227–3 (alk. paper). — ISBN 0–253–21093–3
(pbk. : alk. paper)
1. Bible. O.T. Prophets (Nevi 'im)—Criticism, Narrative.
I. Title. II. Series.
BS1286.S5613   1997
222'.06—dc21   96–40267

1 2 3 4 5   02 01 00 99 98 97

For
Itamar and Ariella
Michal and Yakov
with love

.

KNIGHT-CAPRON LIBRARY
LYNCHBURG COLLEGE
LYNCHBURG, VIRGINIA 24501

R. Aha said: "The conversation of the servants of the fathers is more precious to God than the laws given to the sons: The episode of Eliezer is recounted twice in the Torah, but many important points of law are only alluded to."

Rashi on Gen. 24:42, drawing on
Genesis Rabba 60,8

KNIGHT-CAPRON LIBRARY
LYNCHBURG COLLEGE
LYNCHBURG, VIRGINIA 24501

CONTENTS

LIST OF TABLES

PREFACE

Things we have heard and known, that our
fathers have narrated to us, we will not
withhold from their children, . . . that a
future generation might know—children yet
to be born—and in turn narrate to their
children.

Ps. 78:3–6

Biblical stories were meant for readers, not critics; hence any criticism must
be based on reading. The inner significance of a great work is apparent
only to someone who is willing and able to read it as part of its target audience. Because of our great distance from Scripture and its world, however,
we cannot attain an unmediated and naive reading of it. Just as the language
of Scripture cannot be properly understood without philological research,
so must the norms of scriptural narrative be investigated in order to reduce
the gap between our own reading habits and those of the readers of antiquity. A systematic study of narrative modes is thus a prerequisite for understanding a story. Everything we learn through such comprehensive and
external scrutiny can then be applied to a profound and integrative reading
of the individual story and must withstand that test. The relationship between reading and criticism is reciprocal—the two stages follow and build
on each other. Yet they cannot be practiced simultaneously, because they
have different goals: criticism seeks whatever the various stories have in
common and aspires to generalize and explain; reading looks for what is
unique about a particular story and tries to distinguish and understand.
Many scholars who have attempted to combine these two disciplines, with
their contrary orientations, wind up subjugating reading to the needs of
criticism; as a result, the precision of the former is lost and the force of the
second undercut. In the present volume I have maintained a scrupulous
distinction between the two: the chapters of this book are devoted to a
literary reading of seven prophetic stories, whereas the appendix investi-
gates a literary problem—the role of secondary characters in scriptural stories—which must be clarified to enhance reading.

An oral or written narration of prophetic deeds perpetuates those deeds and extends their influence beyond their original time and place. All the stories dealt with in this book are narratives of impressive feats performed by prophets, in which their humanity is emphasized by the depiction of their mistakes and hesitations, anger and despair, loneliness and alienation. The prophets' own personality is thus an essential part of their teaching. From the theological point of view, this means that the prophet is not presented to us as God's representative on earth but as His human emissary. From the literary standpoint, this concept is reflected in the characterization of the prophet standing before the Lord as a sort of representative of those to whom the prophecy is addressed. Elijah is instructed to cover his face with his mantle when confronting the awesome revelation; Samuel is warned that his ears will ring when he hears the bitter decree. The epithet "man of God" expresses the tension between the fact that even though the prophet is a man he comes into contact with the divine. Despite his intimacy with God, Elijah must be cautioned not to find Him in wind, earthquake, and fire. Even though Samuel is privy to God's counsels, he must be reminded that he sees only what is visible, not into the heart. Of all people, only the prophet hears the word of God and is thus its first recipient. As the first believer who withstood the test of faith he is sent to blaze a trail for God's word to the hearts of those who find it more difficult to believe. In this way, the prophet's humanity serves both as evidence of the existential gulf between the sender and the messenger and as an exemplum of human obedience to the Creator.

A literary reading deals with the story and not with the event related. Unlike historical research, its goal is to listen to what the narrator has to say, not to reconstruct what actually happened. The narrator's explicit and implicit assumptions are an integral part of his story. Understanding them is a necessary part of reading and is incompatible with a historical analysis of the events recounted in the light of external assumptions about the nature of reality, the validity of natural laws, and the nature of history. For the reader, the most important question is that of the literary genre: does the narrator present his story as the relation of an actual event or as a fictional story? The answer to this question is likely to be found within the story itself, in its style, and in its depiction of the situation. In this respect, Jonah and the frame story of Job are quite different from the seven prophetic stories discussed here. Whereas the former are "theological narratives" that use a nonrealistic story to express a religious truth, the latter derive part of their religious force from the fact that they tell of a prophet who actually lived and experienced these events. There is no recognizable difference in the degree of reality of the words of Samuel raised from the grave as against his words while still alive, or in Elijah's miraculous sustenance by the ravens as against his drinking from a stream until its water dried up.

The objective of reading is to understand the story, not to reconstruct the process of its composition and revision. The diachronic study of the stages in the evolution of an individual story and the editing of the book in which it has been included is incompatible with a reading of the story as a work of rhetorical art. Such inquiry is not interested in the story as we have it before us but in what preceded it and what is outside it. (In addition, it frequently suffers the defect of literary obtuseness and an ignorance of the unique features of biblical poetics.) There is consequently a growing tendency today to prefer a synchronic reading, which posits the unity of the story and finds some way or other to resolve the questions that served as anchors for the critical undermining of this unity. Nevertheless, just as the reconstruction of the original text is a legitimate part of reading a story when it is indeed impossible to arrive at a reasonable understanding without it, so too is there justification for reconstructing the stages through which the story passed, when such reconstruction serves a pressing exegetical need. The genetic explanation can be pressed into the service of literary reading when it exempts us from the penalties imposed by forced harmonization and an apologetic leveling of genuine tensions, and permits us to distinguish between the meaning of the conjectured original story and the changes this meaning underwent due to additions or editing.

"New literal meanings are revealed every day," stated the medieval commentator Rabbi Samuel ben Meir. Every generation is rooted in its own existential situation, searches Scripture for answers to its specific spiritual needs, and reads it through the exegetical methods it considers to be reliable. In this way, every authentic exegetical method opens a door to another one of the "seventy facets" of Scripture. The method adopted in the present volume is rhetorical criticism, and it can be characterized as a combination of three disciplines—close reading, form criticism, and structural analysis. Close reading asks the following question of all the elements of the text and of the entire literary unit: What is the text saying? How does it express this? What is it trying to convey? It answers these questions through philological, stylistic, and rhetorical investigations. But close reading is inadequate if it does not draw on form criticism: the same elements have different meanings in different genres. In addition, without a definition of the genre (which the readers of antiquity recognized at once), we cannot distinguish many of the literary conventions on which the genre is based. The structure of the story, the hidden scaffolding that binds the elements of the plot in a tight, formal structure, is one of the narrator's most obvious rhetorical devices. Hence laying it bare is a prerequisite for understanding the story. Uncovering the structure begins by clarifying the scope of the literary unit (exactly where the story begins and ends), continues by distinguishing among its major parts and the scenes in each part (based on the distinguishing markers used in biblical narrative), and concludes with an analysis of the links among the various subunits (such as symmetrical parallelism and contrasting analogy). To facilitate a comprehensive investigation of these structural elements they will be presented, when possible, in a schematic table that provides a basis for the main goal—determining the rhetorical significance of the structure. I have endeavored to reflect faithfully the sequence of the plot as it is and to avoid overly sophisticated structures—frequently built by imposing a formal Procrustean bed on the literary material and giving arbitrary titles to the elements of the structure—that are intended to enhance the artistry of the biblical story. Unlike the sacrificial laws in the Book of Leviticus, which are demarcated explicitly by titles and summary verses (such as 1:2, 3a, 9b; 10a, 13b; 14a and 17b), in biblical narrative the division into subunits is inherent in the plot. Even though I consider it most unlikely that the structure we discover was overtly apprehended by readers of antiquity, it seems that this method of organizing the narrative material is not imposed from the outside but was implanted there by its creator, knowingly or unknowingly. To me, in any case, clarifying the structure has been of great assistance in identifying the theme of a story, tracing the internal dynamic through which the plot develops, and locating the message it embodies.

"The gates of exegesis have not been locked," wrote Maimonides. Every generation has the right, and even the obligation, to add its own link to the long chain of biblical exegesis. This link is necessarily connected with those that preceded it, for the new is in large measure a product of the old—whether it continues it or rejects it. Knowledge of the history of exegesis not only fertilizes our own interpretations with the achievements of our predecessors, it also deepens our understanding and hones our sensitivity to the complex and twisting nature of the exegetical process. The commentator's labor is replete with large and small exegetical decisions. For readers to judge their plausibility, they must be accompanied not only by proofs and demonstrations, but also by an awareness of alternative glosses and reasons for rejecting them. My reading has been nurtured by two exegetical schools—the medieval Jewish tradition of contextual exegesis, and the international biblical scholarship of the modern era. The combination of these two is natural for me as a contemporary Jewish student of the Bible. I believe it to be an extremely useful combination, precisely because it crosses two different and at times even contradictory perspectives. Readers will note that disagreements frequently transcend the boundaries of the schools, and that different approaches often yield similar results.

For one who considers Scripture to be Holy Writ, a literary reading of the Bible is also a religious reading. It is clear and undeniable that modern biblical criticism is based, in large measure, on the rejection of religious dogma. When we come to balance the one-sidedness of the overtly secular reading of Scripture, we find lurking in ambush the danger that we may be led to defend religious truth at the price of an apologetic compromise of scholarly rigor. Still, to the extent that a religious reading suits the biblical texts and has an advantage for understanding them, it has significant scholarly contributions to make. The glory of the religious reading of Scripture is not a search for some quasi-scientific confirmation of traditional verities but the exposition of religious questions that have been neglected by biblical scholarship. Questions that are genuine produce answers that are true. For me, this is the ultimate test of the present volume.

Chapter 7 (Elisha and the woman of Shunem) and the last part of chapter 6 (Elijah on Mount Horeb) were written especially for this book. The other chapters and the appendix are revised and updated versions of the following articles:

Chapter 1: "The Story of Samuel's Birth: Structure, Genre and Meaning." In U. Simon, ed., *Studies in Bible and Exegesis* 2, pp. 57–110 (Ramat-Gan, 1986) (Hebrew).

Chapter 2: "Samuel's Call to Prophecy: Form Criticism with Close Reading." *Prooftexts* 1 (1981): 119–32.

Chapter 3: "A Balanced Story: The Stern Prophet and the Kind Witch (1 Samuel 28:3–25)." *Prooftexts* 8 (1988): 159–71.

Chapter 4: "The Poor Man's Ewe-Lamb: An Example of a Juridical Parable." *Biblica* 48 (1967): 207–42.

Chapter 5: "1 Kings 13: A Prophetic Sign—Denial and Persistence." *HUCA* 47 (1976): 81–117.

Chapter 6: "Elijah's Fight against Baal Worship: Unity and Structure of the Story (1 Kings 17–18)." In U. Simon and M. Goshen-Gottstein, eds., *Studies in Bible and Exegesis* 1, pp. 51–118 (Ramat-Gan, 1980) (Hebrew).

Chapter 7: No prior publication.

Appendix: "Minor Characters in Biblical Narrative." *Journal for the Study of the Old Testament* 46 (1990): 11–19.

The Book of Jonah fits into the subject of this volume in all aspects, and I originally planned an eighth chapter, to be based on my article, "The Story of Jonah: Structure and Meaning," which appeared in A. Rofé and Y. Zakovitch, eds., *Isaac Leo Seeligmann* vol. 2, pp. 291–318 (Jerusalem, 1983) (Hebrew). But since my Hebrew commentary on Jonah (Tel Aviv and Jerusalem, 1992) is to appear shortly in English translation under the imprint of the Jewish Publication Society, I decided to avoid duplication. Interested readers are referred to that volume.

Not only have the original articles been revised, expanded, and updated, they have also been unified with regard to method and presentation. My literary reading has become more sophisticated over the years, terminology has crystallized, and it has become increasingly clear that there are major benefits from combining the three disciplines. Nevertheless, I have avoided imposing a single format on all the chapters because differences in the characters of the stories and the severity of the problems that must be solved require that the order and scope of the discussion be adapted to suit each individual story. An important tool for unifying the chapters into a single unit is the detailed index, designed to help readers quickly find all the places where a particular literary issue or exegetical approach is discussed so that they can derive a more comprehensive picture and reach more general methodological conclusions. One question—the role of minor characters in scriptural narrative—has been treated separately in an appendix.

Any translation is inherently a gloss, favoring one possible interpretation of a verse over all others. Clearly, no standard version of the Bible could always be used, then, in the English translation of this book. The procedure adopted was to start with the New Jewish Publication Society Translation (1985), to interpolate readings from the Revised Standard Version when the former strayed too far from the reading advanced here, and, when neither of these versions proved satisfactory, to modify them in accordance with the interpretation presented by me.

The late Benjamin Zev Emmanuel endowed the Rabbi Mordechai Nurok Chair of Bible at Bar-Ilan University as a mark of esteem and gratitude to the late Rabbi Nurok, who saved his life and that of many other Jews during the Holocaust. Rabbi Nurok's wife and two sons were murdered during the destruction of Latvian Jewry. The name of Rabbi Mordechai, son of Rabbi Zvi Nurok, of blessed memory, will be perpetuated in Israel thanks also to Mr. Emmanuel, who established this monument for him in the halls of Torah learning. As the incumbent of the Rabbi Nurok chair, I received assistance in preparing this book for the printer and in funding its translation into English.

I am permanently indebted to Esther Cohen for everything she has done, professionally and faithfully, to permit this book to see the light of day. I would also like to thank Yael Shemesh, who read the entire manuscript, corrected mistakes, and made many helpful comments. I am very grateful to Herbert Marks and Robert Polzin for their many years of long patience.

Special thanks are due to Lenn Schramm, the translator of this book, for his accurate and fluent English translation and for his critical scrutiny of the Hebrew original, which resulted in a number of very helpful suggestions.

I dedicate this book to my son Itamar and his wife Ariella, and to my daughter Michal and her husband Yakov. May the verses from Psalm 78 that serve as the epigraph to this preface continue to be valid for all of us throughout the generations.

Bar-Ilan University   Uriel Simon

GUIDE TO TRANSLITERATION

א	alef	ʾ
בּ	bet	b
ב	vet	v
ג	gimel	g
ד	daleth	d
ה	heh	h
הּ	heh-mapiq	ĥ
ו	waw	w
ז	zayin	z
ח	ḥet	ḥ
ט	tet	ṭ
י	yod	y (i)
כּ	kaf	k
כ	khaf	k̲
ל	lamed	l
מ	mem	m
נ	nun	n
ס	samekh	s
ע	ayin	ʿ
פּ	peh	p
פ	feh	f
צ	tsade	ṣ
ק	qof	q
ר	resh	r
שׁ	shin	š

שׂ	sin	ś
ת	tav	t
ת	thav	th
ְ	mobile schwa	e

·1·

THE BIRTH OF SAMUEL

Miracle and Vow, Divine Gift and Maternal Consecration

All is from You, and it is Your
gift that we have given to You.

1 Chron. 29:14

The Compass of the Story

Clarifying the extent of a story is the first step in discovering its structure, determining its literary genre, and understanding its meaning. The account of Samuel's birth obviously begins with his father's genealogy in the first verse of the first book of Samuel; but it is far from clear where it ends. Hannah, Samuel's mother, is the only character who is present throughout chapter 1 as well as in 2:18–21, which is separated from the account of Samuel's birth by a description of the iniquities of the sons of Eli (2:12–17). Despite this separation, verses 18 to 21 are clearly the end of our story. The last verse in this section (2:21) repeats, in reverse, the exposition at the beginning of the story, thereby constituting an *inclusio.* "For the Lord took note of Hannah" (2:21a) is the utter antithesis of "the Lord had closed her womb" (1:5), just as "she conceived and bore three *sons* and two *daughters*" (2:21b) is the opposite of "Hannah was childless" (1:2) and underscores the happy ending of the story, wherein Hannah has both sons and daughters, just like her cowife at its beginning ("He used to give portions to his wife Peninnah and to all her *sons and daughters*" [1:4]). In addition to this closure of the plot, attained by the total reversal in the fate of the main character, many themes and phrases in this passage in chapter 2 link it intimately with the previous scenes: (1) The mention of the yearly pilgrimage to Shiloh to offer the annual sacrifice (2:19) repeats the language of 1:3 and 21; (2) the priest's blessing of Elkanah and his wife (2:20) refers both to his first blessing (1:17) and to the vow and the wordplay on the name Samuel that accompany it (1:27–28); (3) the description of the cele-

1

bration at Shiloh, just like the previous scenes (1:19; 2:11), concludes with
the return to Ramah ("Then they would return home" [2:20]).

Thus the account of Samuel's birth, which opens with Hannah's barrenness, ends with a description of the abundant blessings showered upon her
as a reward for fulfilling her vow and dedicating him to serve in the sanctuary of the Lord. But why is the conclusion of the story separated from
the rest of it and, instead of following immediately after the fulfillment of
her vow (which ends at 2:11), interpolated between the description of the
sins of Hophni and Phinehas and Eli's rebuke of his sons? The concluding
passage must originally have been joined directly to the body of the story;
the separation in our text is the result of a later interweaving of the account
of the youth of the prophet Samuel (the stories of his birth and dedication
in chapters 1 and 3) with the story of the fall of the house of Eli (the description of his sons' corruption, his rebuke, the prophecy of the destruction of Shiloh, and the first stages in the fulfillment of the prophecy at the
battle of Aphek in chapters 2 and 4–6). It is extremely difficult to ascribe
these two narratives to a single literary source: first, because the prophecy
of destruction speaks of the replacement of the house of Eli by another
priestly house rather than of the substitution of prophetic for priestly leadership (as follows from chapter 3); second, because in the three chapters
about the Philistine war—in which the two sons of Eli are killed on the
same day, as foretold by the anonymous man of God—Samuel is never mentioned.[1] These two sources were not arranged consecutively but interwoven,
so that we read alternately about the birth of Samuel, the moral decline of
Eli's sons, the consecration of Samuel, and the death of Eli's sons. This
alternation is intensified by the relocation of the concluding passage of
Samuel's birth and its incorporation within the story of the sons of Eli.

This placement has two advantages: it reinforces the melding of the two
stories,[2] and it also creates a twofold contrast between the concluding passage and what immediately precedes and follows it. On the one hand, there
is the sharp opposition between the sin of the priests, who are always taking
(the consecrated meat), and the righteousness of Hannah, who continues
to give (a "little robe" every year); between the importunate demands of
the young priestly servitor with his three-pronged fork and the loyalty of
the young Samuel, who serves the Lord in his linen ephod. On the other
hand, there is the contrast of Eli's blessing of Hannah and her great reward
(many children) with his rebuke of his sons and their anticipated punishment (death). In addition, and more significantly, the juxtaposition of the
priest's blessing and rebuke intensifies the reader's astonishment at the appalling contrast between the priest's abundant capacity to call down blessings on the house of Elkanah and his powerlessness to avert calamity from
his errant sons. This endows his words to his sons with additional poi-
gnancy—"if a man offends against God, who can obtain pardon for him?"

(2:25). Thus we learn that the virtue of the priestly blessing applies only to one who truly deserves it, such as Hannah or Elkanah, whereas priestly prayers are unable to save sinners such as Hophni and Phinehas.

From the perspective of the integrated text that we have before us, the cost paid on account of the separation is compensated for by the reward of the contrast. Nevertheless, we must read the concluding passage as a direct sequel to the body of the story if we would uncover the structure of the original account of Samuel's birth and consider its meaning and message. In addition, we must endeavor to clarify which of the five verses about Samuel's service in Shiloh are original elements of the account of his birth and consecration and which were added—when it was merged with the story of the fall of the house of Eli—in order to create a stronger interface between the alternating passages and sharpen the contrast between them. The repetitiousness of these verses and the paltry informational contribution that each adds to its predecessors is evident if we transcribe them sequentially:

> 2:11b: "The boy *(ha-na‘ar)* served the Lord before the priest Eli."
> 2:18: "Samuel served the Lord as an attendant *(na‘ar)*, girded with a linen ephod."
> 2:21b: "The boy *(ha-na‘ar)* Samuel grew up before the Lord."
> 2:26: "Now the boy *(ha-na‘ar)* Samuel continued to grow in esteem and favor both with God and with men."
> 3:1a: "Now the boy *(ha-na‘ar)* Samuel served the Lord before Eli."

From the compositional point of view, what all these sentences have in common is that each intervenes at a seam between the two interwoven accounts. They differ in that two of them (2:18 and 3:1a) are expositions at the beginning of passages, whereas the other three (2:11b, 2:21b, and 2:26) come at the end of passages. It is clear that the two expositive sentences belonged to the original account of Samuel's birth, because they are prerequisites to understanding what follows. That Samuel serves while girded in a linen ephod (2:18) is required, as informational and syntactic background, for the dependent verse that follows: "His mother would make a little robe *for him*" (2:19). Similarly, the verse that defines his status and role as a boy "who served the Lord before Eli" is an essential preamble to the account of his consecration, which describes how, overnight, the servitor became a prophet with the assistance and guidance of his master, Eli.[3]

On the other hand, the three closing sentences are clearly secondary. The first of them—"the boy served the Lord before the priest Eli" (2:11b)— seemingly continues what comes before (the account of Hannah's fulfillment of her vow), as shown by the anonymity of "the boy." It is quite superfluous, however, when attached to the final passage of the birth story, which begins with an almost identical exposition: "Samuel served the Lord as an attendant, girded with a linen ephod" (2:18); what is more, it seems to be copied from 3:1a. The same applies to "The boy Samuel grew up before the Lord" (2:21b), which ends the final passage and is superfluous when attached to the exposition of the consecration story—"The boy Samuel served the Lord before Eli" (3:1a); it too seems to be copied from 3:19a—"Samuel grew up and the Lord was with him." The third concluding sentence also seems to be secondary, coming as it does not in a passage dealing with Samuel but within Eli's rebuke of his sons, where it provides a chiastic contrast:

> If a *man* sins against a *man*, the Lord may pardon him; but if a man offends against *God*, who can obtain pardon for him? (2:25a)

> Now the boy Samuel continued to grow in stature and in favor both with *God* and with *men*. (2:26)

We see, then, that a literary commentary on the original account of Samuel's birth must disregard 2:11b and 2:21b, which were evidently added to it when it was combined with the story of the house of Eli. The same applies to Hannah's psalm (2:1–10), which I do not think can be reconciled with Hannah's character as described in the body of the story. Because this assertion can be grounded only on a close reading of the entire story, we must defer consideration of the psalm until later (see below, pp. 30ff.). To sum up, if our various arguments are on the mark, the original account of Samuel's birth consists of 1:1–28, 2:11a, and 2:18–21a.

The Division of the Story into Parts and Scenes

The scene changes in our story are clearly indicated by two interrelated elements: a change in the personae, and a change in location. The break between parts is indicated by unmistakable formal signs. Because a part generally consists of more than one scene, the division into parts ought to be more conspicuous than that into scenes. The Book of Ruth, for example, is divided into four parts (coterminous with its chapters), each of which has three scenes. The end of the fourth part is of course also the end of the story and requires no special indication. Each of the other three parts, however, ends at a lull in the course of the plot, with formal unity provided by the repeated use of the roots *š.w.b* or *y.š.b*, accompanied by indications of time: "at the beginning of the barley harvest" (1:22); "until the barley harvest and the wheat harvest were finished" (2:23); "until you learn how the matter turns out" (3:18).[4]

Similarly, the account of Samuel's birth is divided into two parts plus an epilogue: 1:1–19a, 1:19b–2:11a, and 2:18–21a (for simplicity's sake, we shall speak below of three parts). At the end of each of the first two parts the plot comes to a temporary standstill, when Elkanah and his family return home. Both concluding verses contain two elements—the valedictory prostration at Shiloh and the trip home to Ramah—phrased in similar terms:

> End of part I: "They bowed low before the Lord, and they went back home to Ramah" (1:19a).[5]
> End of part II: "They bowed low there before the Lord. Then Elkanah went home to Ramah (and the boy served the Lord before the priest Eli)" (1:28b + 2:11).[6]

The epilogue also has this concluding phraseology, but with two important differences: first, it is truncated—"then they would return home";[7] second, it does not come at the very end of the story but one verse earlier. Below we shall attempt to explain the rhetorical significance of this deviation.

Each of the two main parts is divided into two scenes. The second scene of each part is clearly marked off from the first by indications of a change in the whereabouts of the protagonist:

> Beginning of I,2: "After they had eaten and drunk at Shiloh, Hannah rose" (1:9a).
> Beginning of II,2: "When she had weaned him, she took him up with her" (1:24a).

In I,2 the change of venue is within Shiloh itself—Hannah leaves the place where Elkanah's family ate the sacrificial meal and goes to pray at the gate of the sanctuary, near where Eli is sitting. In II,2 she leaves her house in Ramah and makes the pilgrimage to Shiloh. In both opening sentences the change of place is accompanied by an indication of time: in I,2 Hannah gets up from the table after her family has finished eating and drinking; in II,2 she goes to Shiloh after Samuel has been weaned.

The conclusions of the second scenes are of course identical with the ends of the parts. In addition, these two scenes also have an internal *inclusio* that highlights the end. Before the closing sentences about the return to Ramah, each scene contains a specific reference to its opening:

> Beginning of I,2: "After they had *eaten* and drunk at Shiloh, *Hannah rose*" (1:9a).
> Penultimate sentence of I,2: "*So the woman went her way and ate*" (1:18b).

Beginning of II,2: "When she had weaned him, *she took him up* with her" (1:24a).

First words of last sentence of II,2: "*[She left] him there* and bowed low [before the Lord . . .]" (1:28, according to 4QSam[a]); *She left him there before the Lord* and went to Ramah (2:11, according to the Septuagint).[8]

These statements about Hannah's leaving her family and returning to it are merely external and formal expressions of the change of the supporting cast, which is one of the basic components of the subdivision of the story as well as of its symmetrical structure, as can be clearly seen from the following schematic division of the personae in the five scenes:

I,1:	Hannah	II,1:	Hannah	Epilogue:	Hannah
	Elkanah		Elkanah		Elkanah
	Peninnah				Eli
I,2:	Hannah	II,2:	Hannah		
	Eli		Eli		

Unlike the two main parts, the epilogue—which consists of only four verses—is not subdivided into scenes. The first three verses describe what happened at Shiloh year after year—the repeated gift of a new robe for Samuel and Eli's repeated blessing of Elkanah and Hannah. After that comes the standard closing phrase, "then they would return home," and, finally, one verse about the five other children born to Hannah in Ramah. Even though Eli's benediction is recounted in direct speech, this is not a dramatic scene but rather a report of recurring actions. As was mentioned above and as we shall see below, there is a close thematic and linguistic bond between the elements of the epilogue and both the description of Hannah's status in the exposition and the description of her two earlier encounters with Eli. Thus, in principle, part III parallels the first two parts; what is shown in the corresponding scenes there is here condensed into a brief report. This abridgment is also expressed in the fact that here Elkanah (the deuteragonist in I,1 and II,1) and Eli (the supporting actor in I,2 and II,2) appear together alongside Hannah, while the truncation of the change-of-place formula, "then they would return home," weakens the impact of the geographical distinction between Shiloh and Ramah. From a structural perspective, this condensation expresses the harmony at the end of the story: not only is there no allusion to Peninnah's participation in the yearly pilgrimage, there is no reason for Hannah to experience friction with Elkanah and Eli. The temporal generalization also contributes to this—the blessing received by Elkanah and Hannah in Shiloh and the births of her children in Ramah are repeated year after year.

Three Structural Principles

The first structural principle—*the* inclusio *that ties the end of the story with its beginning* (see above pp. 1–2)—gave us solid grounds for assigning 2:18–21 to the story. The contrast between the happy ending and the despairing beginning is further reinforced (in addition to the parallel phrasing mentioned above) by identical temporal references. The main thrust of the opening (1:1–7a) is the misery that Hannah faced every year when the family made its pilgrimage to Shiloh, while the end is devoted entirely to her good fortune in Shiloh and in Ramah, year after year, once she had fulfilled her vow. Hence in both places the narrator uses verbal forms that indicate repeated action—the future (*yiqtol*) and the inverted perfect (*w-qatal*)—and explicit generalization, while using the same verb (*ʿ.ś.h*) in both places:

1:7a: "This he used to do (*yaʿaśeh*) [Peshitta: she used to do] year after year: Every time she went up to the House of the Lord, her cowife would taunt her."

2:19: "His mother would make (*taʿaśeh*) a little robe for him and bring it up to him every year, when she went up with her husband. . . . "

Hannah's humiliation by Peninnah at the yearly sacrifice is here contrasted with her noble deed, henceforth repeated each year at the annual sacrifice.

The second structural principle is *the division of the story into three parts, each dealing with a different basic situation.* Each part begins with a succinct description of the situation in which Hannah finds herself: part I—protracted barrenness; part II—pregnancy and the birth of a son; part III—a son who serves in the House of the Lord. Each part unfolds a sequence of events that develops from the basic situation described at its beginning. I have attempted to express this tension between the ever-different challenges and the appropriate response to them in the following précis:

Part I: *Barrenness and vow*—Hannah wrestles with human beings and with God to obtain a son (she responds to the challenge of *distress and frustration* with a capacity not to despair and not to give up).

Part II: *Birth of a son and fulfillment of the vow*—Hannah faithfully keeps her commitment (she responds to the challenge of *good fortune and success* with a capacity to fulfill her obligation despite the changed circumstances).

Part III: *The reward*—Hannah's reward for giving up her son—the birth of other sons and daughters (this time there is no challenge and Hannah is blessed without having to struggle).

This tripartite division does not impair the unity of the plot, because each part clearly builds upon its predecessor. The resolution of part I (the vow) is the problem of part II (will it be fulfilled?), and the resolution of part II (the fulfillment of the vow) is the basis for the unexpected dénouement of part III (the reward for fulfilling the vow). In extremely basic terms we can express the structure of the story as follows:

Part I: The effort to *receive* a son from God;
Part II: The effort to *give* the son to God;
Part III: *Receiving* sons and daughters from God without any effort.

This schematic arrangement of the structure does not reflect the unequal lengths of the parts. The expressive correlative of the fact that part I is twice as long as part II is that the internal and external struggle to have a child is incomparably more difficult than the internal struggle to give him up. The extreme brevity of part III (it is only half as long as part II) reinforces the reader's impression that now everything is attained without a struggle.

The intimate association of these three themes is also reflected in the three references to the name of the newborn child. The first (homiletical) explanation of the name—"I asked him (*šᵉʾiltiw*) of the Lord" (1:20)—expresses her gratitude at *receiving* him from the Lord. The second explanation—"I, in turn, hereby donate him (*hišʾiltihu*) to the Lord" (1:28)—accompanies his *dedication* to the service of God. Eli's later reference to the second explanation—"in place of the donation she made (reading with 4QSamᵃ: *hišʾilah*) to the Lord" (2:20)—is the basis of his blessing that she *receive* again: the Lord will repay Hannah for what she has given to Him. This striking correlation between the three plays on the name Samuel and the three themes of the story is another expression of the second structural principle.[9]

Going beyond the division into parts and the unfolding of the plot, the entire story can be subsumed in the three facets of the child's name— Samuel is the son of the barren woman who was remembered by the Lord because of her prayer and vow; Samuel is the lad who was pledged and given to the Lord by his mother; and Samuel is the servitor in the holy place, by virtue of whose consecration to the Lord his parents are blessed with additional children.

The third structural principle is the *uniform format of all five scenes*:[10] each scene has the identical elements and in the same order. Each section of table 1.1, "The Birth of Samuel—Structure of the Story," presents the plot elements in the right columns and their function in the left columns (for each scene). The first element in each scene defines the point of departure for ensuing developments. But whereas the beginning of the first scene of each part is the exposition of a particular *situation*, the second scenes, which are more dynamic, begin with a decisive *act* performed by the heroine. Each scene, except for the fifth and last, follows the first element with two trials that Hannah must endure (these are the second and third elements). The severity and intensity of these trials diminish as the plot advances from distress to good fortune. Accordingly, while I have designated all four of the trials in part I as "tests," the second trial in each scene of part II is designated "perfect fulfillment," whereas the lone element in part III (the harmonious and truncated epilogue) is characterized as "full contentment."

Beyond this common core, the second scenes of the first two parts and the only scene of part III share an additional element, which describes the climax attained by the plot at the end of each part. In the table, the fourth element of I,2 is designated "great hope," of II,2—"thanksgiving," and of the epilogue—"new hopes." Thus there is a conspicuous structural difference between the first scenes of each part as opposed to the scenes that conclude each part and the entire story. In the first scenes (I,1 and II,1), only the preparations are described; hence they begin with a given "situation" and conclude, after the third element, with an open ending (leaving the reader in suspense—what will Hannah do on an empty stomach? what will she do after weaning the child?). By contrast, the second scenes contain the heroine's great deeds; hence they begin with a "decisive act," include a fourth element—a climax—and have a closed ending (the characters return home to Ramah).[11]

The epilogue, too, has four elements. The first of these ("new circumstances") resembles the first element in I,1 and II,1 in all respects; the second element (the annual gift of a little robe) seems to parallel the first and second elements in II,2 (the delivery of the child to the sanctuary, accompanied by many sacrifices). The third element ("Eli blesses Elkanah and Hannah every year") clearly corresponds to the last element in each of the two second scenes (the priest's blessing and Hannah's thanksgiving). This striking conflation of preparatory scene and implementation scene is followed by the truncated closing formula, "they would go home" (2:20), and after that, to round off and conclude the entire story, a single verse reporting the radical change in the situation of Elkanah and Hannah. As a "reversal of circumstances" this finale corresponds to the first element in each of the three parts, especially the beginning of part I, with which it creates a contrasting *inclusio*.

TABLE 1.1: The Birth of Samuel—Structure of the Story

I. Barrenness and vow: "I asked the Lord for Him."	
I,1 (1:1–8) In Shiloh, with the family: Barrenness, disgrace, and refusal to be comforted	
Situation	Protracted barrenness: "the Lord had closed her womb."
Test: Will she break?	The disgrace of barrenness exacerbated by her cowife: "she would taunt her that the Lord had closed her womb."
Test: Will she acquiesce?	(Silent) refusal to accept vain comfort from Elkanah: "she wept and would not eat."
I,2 (1:9–19a) In Shiloh, with Eli: Prayer, vow, and metamorphosis of a chastiser into a patron	
[Introduction: "After they had eaten and drunk at Shiloh, Hannah rose."]	
Decisive act	Vigorous prayer and exceptional vow
Test: Will she break?	Additional shame—the priest's rebuke: "How long will you make a drunken spectacle of yourself?"
Test: Will she win out?	Overcoming Eli's false indictment: "Oh no, my lord!"
Great hope	The priest's blessing and Hannah takes comfort: "she ate, and was no longer downcast."
[Conclusion: "they bowed low before the Lord, and they went back home to Ramah."]	
II. Birth and fulfillment of the vow: "I, in turn, hereby give him to the Lord."	
II,1 (1:19b–23) In Ramah with the family: Birth, naming, and avoidance of error	
Change of circumstances	Pregnancy and birth of a son: "the Lord remembered her."
Test: Will she forget?	A name that expresses her gratitude: "I asked the Lord for him."
Perfect fulfillment	(Explicit) refusal to accept Elkanah's advice: "Hannah did not go up."
II,2 (1:24–28, 2:11a) In Shiloh, with Eli: Generous and wholehearted fulfillment of the vow	
[Introduction: "When she had weaned him she took him up with her."]	
Decisive act	Bringing the lad to the sanctuary ˙
Test: Will she be sorry?	Three-year-old bull, ephah of flour, and a jar of wine
Perfect fulfillment	Overcoming Eli's forgetfulness: "Please, my lord!"
Thanksgiving	The prayer is accepted, the blessing realized, and what the Lord gave is given back to him.
[Conclusion: "he bowed low there before the Lord. . . . Then Elkanah (and Hannah) went home to Ramah."]	

TABLE 1.1—*continued*

Epilogue. The reward: Many children, "in place of the gift she made to the Lord."	
Epilogue (2:18–21) **In Shiloh and Ramah: Plenitude and peace**	
New circumstances	In Shiloh: "Samuel was in the service of the Lord."
Full contentment	Annual gift of a little robe
New hopes	Eli blesses Elkanah and Hannah every year
Reversal of circumstances (*inclusio*, inversion of the opening)	In Ramah: Birth of sons and daughters—"the Lord took note of Hannah."

Everything said thus far remains a mere hypothesis until we can show, by means of a close reading, that the actual content and meaning of these elements does in fact coincide with our abstract descriptions. Before we do this, however, we ought to wind up our discussion of structural principles with one last question: what narrative purpose is served by giving all five scenes the same basic format? The answer seems to be that the uniform pattern is intended to create two sets of symmetrical parallels. On the one hand, there is a "vertical" parallel between the first and second scenes of each part, and, on the other hand, a "horizontal" parallel between the two first scenes and the two second scenes, and the "condensed" fifth scene with both scenes of both earlier parts. This matrix of parallelisms permits an implicit contrast and comparison of different situations and reactions. From the vertical perspective, we are invited to draw parallels between the forging of an emotional stance and the pangs of realization, as we follow the heroine's progress from a refusal to acquiesce to a refusal to break (in part I), and from an unwillingness to compromise to the complete fulfillment of her obligations (in part II). From the horizontal perspective, we are invited to draw parallels between how the barren woman copes with her misery (in part I) and how the new mother copes with her good fortune (in part II), and between Hannah's silence out of pain at the beginning of the story (I,1) and her silence out of plenitude at its end (part III).

A Close Reading

Part I, scene 1 (1:1–8): Barrenness, humiliation, and a refusal to be comforted

The first two verses of the story are a static exposition of the situation of Elkanah's family. There are no action verbs, and the predicates all involve existence and ownership—Elkanah of Ramah has an impressive genealogy that goes back four generations and a family constellation that hints at the direction in which the plot will develop: he has two wives, one fruitful and the other barren. The next five verses (3–7a) continue the exposition, but with a distinctly dynamic character: we read of recurring actions and events—the yearly pilgrimage to Shiloh and the bitter intrafamilial contention that accompanies the annual sacrifice. The description of the tensions between the husband and his two wives has great narrative interest, but the narrator, wishing to keep it in the background, avoids protracting the exposition and even incorporates the beginning of the plot into it: "One day, Elkanah offered a sacrifice" (v. 4a).[12] After these few words, from which we learn only that the story will center on incidents that occur in Shiloh in close connection with the sacrifice, the narrator immediately returns to the exposition. In a longish parenthesis (vv. 4b–7a) we are informed about what happened every year at the time of the sacrifice. The listener of antiquity had no trouble distinguishing between the one-time acts, expressed by the inverted future (*wa-yiqṭal*) or perfect (*qaṭal*), and repeated acts, expressed by the future (*yiqṭol*) or inverted perfect (*wᵊ-qaṭal*).[13] Nevertheless, the exposition concludes, for the sake of clarity and emphasis, with an explicit generalization—"This he used to do year after year: Every time she went up to the House of the Lord, her cowife would taunt her" (v. 7a). Only at this point do we dispose of all the information needed to understand what happened for the first time on the day that the plot commences—"she wept and would not eat" (v. 7b).

The accumulated misery that led Hannah to refuse to partake of the sacrificial feast on this occasion is described in dramatic terms. While Peninnah and her children are receiving many portions, in accordance with their number, Elkanah gives Hannah only one portion. This single portion is described by the obscure adjective *ʾappayim*. To understand its signification, we must look at the end of the verse, where the narrator explains the motives of the male lead—"for Hannah was his favorite, even though the Lord had closed her womb" (v. 5b);[14] and consequently he gave her "*mana ʾaḥat ʾappayim*" (v. 5a). In spite of the enigmatic word *ʾappayim*, it is clear that because of his unconditional love for Hannah, he wanted to compensate her by the special quality of her single portion. The context requires us to understand *ʾappayim* as a positive adjective modifying "one portion" (on the model of the series of adjectives in "a fine Shinar mantle"

[Josh. 7:21]). The Targum, too, translates our verse on the basis of the context ("one choice portion"), ignoring the etymology of *ʾappayim*. In fact, the many strange glosses suggested for this hapax legomenon attest how remote we still are from a satisfactory interpretation.[15]

What the loving husband attempts to amend by means of the special quality of the portion he gives Hannah, her cowife Peninnah wishes to exacerbate by infuriating her. Here, too, the narrator adds an explanation—not of Peninnah's motives in angering Hannah but rather of her intent: "in order to vex [?] her *(harrʿimah)*, [she] would taunt her that the Lord had closed her womb" (v. 6). The few occurrences of the verb *r.ʿ.m* with an emotional or quasi-emotional sense do not help us understand the difficult word *harrʿimah* (rendered above, provisionally, as 'vex her'). In poetic parallelism, the equivalents to "let the sea thunder *(yirʿam)*" (Ps. 96:11 and 98:7; 1 Chron. 16:32) suggest that it always connotes a joyous sound, while the context of "their faces are contorted *(raʿamu)*" (Ezek. 27:35) requires that the root indicate surprise and astonishment. Thus we are forced to rely on comparative etymology: Driver (*Notes*, ad loc.) remarks that in Aramaic the *ethpaʿal* of the root *r.ʿ.m* denotes complaint (Onkelos renders in Exod. 16:2 the Hebrew equivalent of 'grumbled' by *w-ʾithraʿamu*). In Mishnaic Hebrew the *hithpaʿel* form has this sense, as does *ragâmu* in Akkadian. Hence the meaning of the *hiphʿil* form would be 'to get Hannah to utter a complaint against her husband or against the Lord'. (This was the interpretation of R. Tanḥum bar Abba: "The Master of the Universe said to [Peninnah]: You are causing her to rage against me? By your life, there is no thunder [*raʿam*] without rain following it, and I shall remember her [i.e., cause her to become pregnant] immediately" [*Yalquṭ Shimoni* 2,77].) We might also refer to the Arabic verb *raʿima*, 'to be humiliated and scorned', and say that Peninnah got Hannah angry in order to humiliate and depress her at her childlessness.

Both glosses are possible, but the context clearly inclines toward the second: "in order to humiliate her." If Peninnah really did want to make Hannah rebel against her husband or against God, it is rather astonishing that her efforts to this end have no strong connection either with what preceded them in the story or with what follows. But if we assume that Peninnah wanted to humiliate Hannah, her taunting alludes directly to Elkanah's attempt to lift the spirits of his beloved wife. Barrenness was a grave reproach for a biblical woman, as Rachel attested when she finally gave birth: "God has taken away my shame" (Gen. 30:23). The factual shame could be blurred and alleviated by expressions of respect and love (like Elkanah's), or it could be intensified by a deprecatory and scornful attitude (Hagar's treatment of Sarah—"when she saw that she had conceived, her mistress was lowered in her esteem" [Gen. 16:4]). The scriptural root for accentuating another's shame by underscoring that person's failing or blemish is *ḥ.r.p*: the people of Succot "taunted" *(ḥerfu)* Gideon that he had not captured the two Midianite kings (Judg. 8:15); Goliath the Philistine cast "disgrace" (*herpah*) upon the arrayed hosts of the Israelite army by emphasizing, over a period of forty days, that not a single man among them dared contend with him (1 Sam. 17:26); and Rabshakeh did the same (*heref*) to besieged Jerusalem and its God in the days of Hezekiah (2 Kings 19:4). The words Peninnah used to taunt Hannah are not quoted directly; we are probably meant to see the narrator's explanatory "that the Lord had closed her womb" as a paraphrastic summary of what she actually said. Note that the words "the Lord had closed her womb" appeared in the previous verse to explain Elkanah's motives, implying that Hannah was trapped between her husband, who wanted to dispel her shame by a public expression of his love for her despite her barrenness, and her jealous cowife, who wanted to depress her by verbalizing her shame.[16]

This contest took place year in and year out, as the narrator generalizes and stresses—"This he used to do [Peshitta: she used to do][17] year after year: Every time she went up to the House of the Lord, her cowife would taunt her" (v. 7a). The hopes that Hannah attached to the yearly pilgrimage were disappointed time and again, and her cowife rubbed salt into her wounds every time she received her single portion of the sacrifice. This time, however, the cumulative influence of the protracted disappointment at God's lack of response and of the recurrent needling by her cowife plunges her into a crisis—"she wept and would not eat" (v. 7b). On the particular pilgrimage during which the plot begins, Peninnah has the upper hand—Hannah weeps from a surfeit of frustration and shame and refuses to eat her portion. Her husband Elkanah rushes to help her, and with soft words endeavors to persuade her that there is no point in crying, fasting, and being despondent, since his love for her is better than ten sons. This consolation also provides an indirect reply to Peninnah's taunts: it is true that as a mother your cowife's situation is better; but not only does Hannah, as the favorite, outrank her cowife, even if Peninnah had ten children they would still not outweigh a husband's love. Note that Elkanah does not say that Hannah is better *for him* than ten sons, that is, that he, the paterfamilias who stands at the center of the family, loves her despite her barrenness,[18] but that he is worth more *to her* than ten sons, that his love for her can satisfy her emotionally just like full motherhood.[19]

This should be Elkanah's great moment, and the reader wonders whether true love can heal the pangs of barrenness. But Hannah neither replies nor complies. The scene has an open ending; for the moment we have no idea what will happen next. Elkanah surely tried his best, but is his implied advice really good? True, the husband's solicitude can alleviate the shame of barrenness and help her contend with her cowife. Given the magnitude of her pain, it is most tempting to do what Elkanah says, to accept what is within her reach and forget about what she cannot achieve. If she acquiesces in her fate, however, she will be sealing her destiny with her own hands. Have the gates of prayer already been closed before her? Has she truly done everything in her power to get the Lord to remember her? Thus the protagonist[20] stands at a crossroads: it is hard to say which is more difficult for her—to be calmed by one who truly cares for her and rest content with what she already has, or to be provoked further by her bitter rival and make a desperate attempt to change her situation.

Part I, scene 2 (1:9–19a):
Prayer, vow, and the transformation of one who scolds into one who blesses

Hannah does not listen to Elkanah, but neither does she rebel against him. Unlike Jonathan, who in passionate protest rose from the table of his father the king in the middle of the feast (1 Sam. 20:34), Hannah does not get up until Elkanah, Peninnah, and their children have finished their sacred meal. Despite the difficulty presented by the Masoretic text of verse 9,[21] it is clear from the sequel that Hannah herself neither ate nor drank. In verse 15 she tells Eli, "I have drunk no wine or other strong drink," and in verse 18 we learn that only after Hannah has been blessed by the priest can she do what her husband had asked: "So the woman left, and she ate, and her countenance was no longer sad." Not only does she not heed her husband's advice to eat, she remains oblivious to his two other pressing questions: he asked, "why are you weeping?" (v. 8) but she was "weeping all the while" (v. 10) as she prayed; he asked, "why is your heart so sad?" (v. 8), but she continued to be "desperate" (v. 10).

Hannah goes to the gate of the sanctuary without revealing her intentions to her husband or asking for his assistance.[22] Ignoring the presence of Eli (v. 9b), she stands solitary and alone before her God.[23] Before we learn what she does, however, the narrator delves into her innermost thoughts and reveals what we ought to have realized long since—"she was desperate" (v. 10a). *Marath nefeš* can hardly be intended to highlight her misery (along the lines of Prov. 14:10 and 31:6; Job 3:20 and 27:2), but rather to prime us to expect an extreme act of despair on the part of one whose distress and affliction have sundered the chains of convention (like the Danites in the house of Micah [Judg. 18:25], David's men in Ziklag [1 Sam. 30:6], and the Shunammite lady with Elisha [2 Kings 4:27]) and unleashed an explosion of emotional energy (like the "bear in the wild robbed of her whelps" to which David and his men are compared in their flight from Absalom [2 Sam. 17:8]). This desperate act is not her prayer, whose words are not quoted, but her vow, which is, in direct speech and quasi-poetic phrasing in verse 11:

O Lord of Hosts,
if You will look upon the suffering of Your *maidservant*
and will remember me and not forget Your *maidservant*,

and if You will grant a male child to Your *maidservant,*
I will dedicate him to the Lord for all the days of his life;
and no razor shall ever touch his head.

The vow has a clear poetic structure—a vocative, a triplet of parallel
lines, followed by a pair of parallel lines (AAABB), along with a fairly regular meter (4/4/4//4/4). We find this same structure in Elkanah's words
of consolation in verse 8:

Hannah,
why are you weeping?
and *why* aren't you eating?
and *why* is your heart so sad?
Am I not better for you than ten sons?

Here too there is a vocative and three parallel lines, followed by one
longer line (AAAB). From the metrical point of view the fourth line should
perhaps be divided into two ("Am I not better for you / than ten sons?"),
again producing a fairly regular meter (2/3/3//3/2). A third poetical
device, found in both speeches, is the repeated ending (*epiphora*) in Hannah's vow and the repeated opening (*anaphora*) in Elkanah's questions.
This triple repetition of the humble "your maidservant" on the one hand,
and the triple repetition of the interrogative "why" on the other, strengthen
and reinforce the parallelism of the first three lines in each passage. In
addition, Hannah's vow has a thematic and linguistic link between "I will
dedicate" (*uf-nathattiw*) in the fourth line and "if You grant" (*uf-nathattah*)
in the third line; we find this also in Elkanah's speech: "better than" (*tov*)
in the fourth line is an inversion of "sad" (*yeraᶜ lᵉvavek,* literally: 'your heart is
bad', in the sense of 'in pain') in the third. The extensive formal parallelism
between Elkanah's speech to Hannah and Hannah's speech to the Lord
must be intended to create a close thematic connection between them.[24]
Before we consider this, however, we ought to offer additional examples of
these phenomena to buttress our argument about the quasi-poetic nature
of these two speeches and the link between them.

Quasi-poetic speech is of crucial importance for the story, with a similar
reliance on the pattern AAAB and a threefold *epiphora* (although without
parallelism) that is found in the Israelites' lamentation over the imminent
extinction of the tribe of Benjamin after its crushing defeat and their oath
not to intermarry with it (Judg. 21:3):

Why, O Lord God of *Israel,*
has this happened in *Israel,*
that henceforth there will be missing from *Israel*
one tribe?

Here too the meter is almost regular (3/3/3//2), and here too the fourth line is clearly set off from its predecessors—though by virtue of its brevity rather than its length. A similar AAAB structure based on a triple *epiphora* is found in the central sentence of Nathan's prophecy to David (2 Sam. 7:7), although the length of its four lines, which lack parallelism and meter, bring it very close to prose:[25]

> In all the places I have moved with the people of *Israel*,
> did I ever reproach any of the tribes of *Israel*
> whom I appointed to shepherd My people *Israel*:
> Why have you not built Me a house of cedar?[26]

Other patterns, too, can give a quasi-poetic nature to speeches that play a central role in a story. We shall offer a single example of the pattern AABB, reinforced by a fourfold *anaphora* and an almost uniform meter (3/3//3/4) but divided into two by parallelism. When David speaks to Saul near the cave in the wilderness of Ein Gedi, the ancient poetic parable is followed by the following quasi-poetic speech (1 Sam. 24:15):

> *After whom* has the king of Israel come out?
> *After whom* are you pursuing?
> *After* a dead dog!
> *After* a single flea!

For our present purposes it is important to demonstrate how the thematic link between a speech and the response to it is intensified by the quasi-poetic design of both and by the formal resemblance between them. Their form and language make them stand out against the background of the underlying prose narrative, and their shared pattern augments and sharpens their interrelationship. The northern tribes' demand that Rehoboam lighten their tax burden is couched in prose (1 Kings 12:4), but later in the story his youthful counselors summarize it in a quasi-poetic fashion (v. 10):

> *Your father* made our yoke heavy,
> now *you* make it lighter for us.

The expectation of a change in corvée and tax policy is expressed by the antithesis "your father"/"you" and "made heavy"/"make lighter," as well as by the play on words *ʿullenu*, 'our yoke'/*meʿalenu*, 'for us'. Rehoboam borrows the same pattern (and even the opening line almost word for word), but with an unexpected change of the antiparallelism into a true parallelism (which is also an amplification), while also adding two lines that link up with their predecessors via two antithetical anaphoras (v. 14):

My father made your yoke heavy,
but *I* will add to your yoke;
my father flogged you with whips,
but *I* will flog you with scorpions.

Whenever there is a dialogue, as here, there is obviously a thematic link between the speeches. However, the elegant formal analogy between the people's demand (A A-) and its rejection by the king (A A+BB+) deepens and enhances this dialogue of the deaf (inter alia, by endowing the king's cynical irony and catastrophic court wisdom with additional dimensions).[27] The situation is somewhat different in the story of Samuel's birth, where Elkanah's words of consolation remain unanswered, and Hannah's speech is directed to heaven rather than to him. In the absence of an open and direct discussion between the two main characters, the formal analogy reveals the latent association between the otherwise unconnected speeches. We are thus impelled to consider whether the phrasing of the vow makes some sort of indirect reference to what Elkanah had said.

Let us begin with the anaphoras. Elkanah wants to restore Hannah's dignity to her; his triple repetition of the interrogative "why" signifies that her reactions are exaggerated, since, in view of his great love for her, her situation is not all that terrible. Elkanah's words fail to calm Hannah or comfort her. But how can she retort that his love for her is not better than ten sons without wounding and humiliating him? Hence she pours out her soul before God; her threefold reference to herself as "Your maidservant" indicates that she does not petition the Lord God of Hosts with the pride and dignity of a woman beloved of her husband who wishes to obtain what her cowife has received in abundance, but as a maidservant forsaken by her God, who tearfully beseeches Him to take note of her misery and ignore her no more. Elkanah said, "is better for you," and she says, "the suffering of Your maidservant"; he used the hyperbolic "ten sons," and she uses the understated "a male child." He counseled her to be realistic about her situation and understand that her destiny is actually better than Peninnah's, whereas she recognizes her inferiority vis-à-vis her cowife and understands that the only way she can have a son is to demand no more than the experience of pregnancy and childbirth while waiving in advance any pleasure or benefit from her son.[28] He urged her to acquiesce in her fate, and she vows to pay a high price to transmute it. He suggested that her sadness be weighed against and counterbalanced by his devotion, whereas she is willing to strike a bargain of "I will dedicate him" in return for "if You grant Your maidservant."

Eli's vocal anger intrudes upon her prayer. The priest's rebuke is reported verbatim; but before quoting it the narrator explains how the priest could make so gross an error. Eli thought she was drunk because, unlike the normal practice, she was praying silently and because her prayer went on for so long (and also perhaps because she did not ask for his blessing despite his presence). In the context of the characterization of the protagonist, Eli's error serves as a faithful mirror of the extraordinary nature of Hannah's prayer—the priest, despite his vast experience, has never encountered a prayer that is simultaneously so intense and so internalized: hence he believes Hannah to be intoxicated.[29] From the perspective of the plot, however, the priest's unwarranted rebuke is yet another trial that Hannah must endure. Peninnah taunted and enraged her by deriding her as a God-forsaken barren woman; now the priest rebukes her as a God-forgetting drunkard. Peninnah humiliated her by referring to her true disgrace; now Eli reproaches her with an undeserved stigma. When her cowife proclaimed her shame, Hannah's only possible reply was that Elkanah's love was better than ten sons. But she chose to remain silent rather than say this, because the sole true remedy for a real blemish is to eliminate it. Hence Hannah faced a cruel dilemma—to break under the weight of her bitter heart or build upon it by enlisting it in her bold prayer and desperate vow. On the other hand, nothing now prevents her from finding an appropriate answer to the priest's false aspersion. Here the trial is not one of substance (how to reply to one who has mortified her) but of situation (why has the priest been added to the roster of those who humiliate her?). She did not respond to her husband's importunities to eat and participate in the sacrificial feast (which involved drinking, as verse 9 informs us); now the priest demands that she stop drinking wine so as not to defile the holy place! Does the fact that the priest has so negative a perception of her sincere prayer and momentous vow indicate that they have not been accepted in heaven, just as they were rejected on earth?

Hannah's confrontation with Eli thus has two facets—it parallels her confrontation with Peninnah (since both deal with her shame), and it also parallels her confrontation with Elkanah (since both stem from a fundamental misunderstanding). The two rhetorical questions addressed to Hannah on the same day contradict each other in content and intent. Elkanah's question—"why aren't you eating?"—was an attempt to draw her closer, in the name of love, while Eli's question—"how long will you make a drunken spectacle of yourself?"—is meant to push her away in the name of holiness. But these contradictory questions share a common root: neither of these good men feel the depth of her pain. Isolated and alone, Hannah is in the throes of a struggle on two fronts—with her cowife and with her God. As such she must ward off both her husband's praise and the priest's condemnation. Elkanah exalts her as his beloved, and she must reject his assistance; Eli denounces her as a worthless woman, and she must overcome his misapprehension.

The greater the magnitude of an error, the easier it is to correct it on the factual level; but by the same token, it is more difficult to get the one who made it to acknowledge his mistake, especially when he occupies a lofty position and is sensitive about his own dignity and that of his office. Hannah, who kept her mouth shut in the first scene because she had nothing meaningful to say to Peninnah and Elkanah, now finds just the right answer for Eli. The tone of her answer is one of noble restraint and true humility. Just as she did not leave the festal table in anger, and just as, in her desperation, she did not accuse heaven of causing her distress, so now she neither feels nor voices the slightest hostility or bitterness when she endeavors to refute the absurd accusation of the reverend priest.[30]

The expression *q̄šath ruaḥ* ("of hard spirit"?) is a hapax legomenon; furthermore, it is hard to fathom its psychological meaning. It is not surprising that the Septuagint reads instead *q̄šath yom*, which has a parallel in Job 30:25—*q̄šeh yom*, 'unfortunate'—clearly referring to those on whom fate has frowned.[31] On the other hand, the prophet's description of the barren woman who has been remembered by God (Isaiah 54) uses the intelligible phrase *ʿaṣuvath ruaḥ*, 'grieved' (v. 6), which is to a certain extent synonymous with *marath nefeš*, 'of bitter soul', that is, desperate, applied to Hannah in verse 10. In any case, it is clear that Hannah describes her situation with this vague term because she still has no intention of telling Eli about her barrenness and humiliation. She wants to make him aware of his error but not to awaken his pity. She does not begin with a factual denial—"I have drunk no wine or other strong drink"—but with another explanation for her extraordinary conduct, which in fact augments the credibility and persuasive force of this denial when she does voice it. By the same token, delaying the denial to the second sentence allows its juxtaposition with the continuation of her explanation: true, "I have *drunk* no wine or other strong drink," but at the same time, "I have been *pouring* out my heart to the Lord." Hannah's prayer can indeed be interpreted as intoxication, because of its intensity and because of an element the two share, albeit in inversion: rather than pouring wine down her throat, she has poured out her heart before the Lord. What the priest apprehends as conduct totally lacking in self-control stems not from the consumption of some intoxicating beverage but from the fact that in pouring out her soul before God she attains total self-oblivion. Hence Hannah generously confirms that someone who knows nothing about her might easily misunderstand her conduct. She adds that in principle the priest is essentially correct to denounce a drunken woman and expel her from the sanctuary as a worthless creature. But she, his maidservant, has not done this, she says, because "I have only been speaking all this time out of my great anguish and distress." On the face of it this last sentence merely repeats the explanation given in the opening sentence, and the repetition endows her speech with greater ceremoniousness and emphasis (even without it her speech abounds in repetition and is probably quasi-metrical). In fact, though, these closing words do something more. The words *ʿad hennah*, 'all this time,' are a direct response to Eli's *ʿad mathai*, 'how long': what appeared to be habitual drunkenness was merely a protracted appeal to the Lord, and its duration reflects the magnitude of her anguish and distress. Note that whereas "my great anguish *(kaʿsi)*" could not remind Eli of any particular act, for the reader it clearly echoes "her rival would taunt *(uⁱ-kiⁱasattah . . . kaʿas)* her" (1:6). This association is intended to express, inter alia, that it was Peninnah's taunts that instigated Hannah's unique prayer.

Now Eli's unjustified condemnation undergoes a similar metamorphosis from evil to good. Hannah intended only to ward off the priest's anger; in fact, her rebuttal transforms him from one who scolds into one who blesses. Eli does not hesitate to rectify his error and makes no attempt to justify it. He tactfully refrains from attempting to discover what she has concealed and does not interrogate her about her troubles. The cocksure suspicion of the priestly guardian of the sanctuary is replaced by the full confidence of the priestly bestower of blessings. Eli senses that Hannah not only poured forth her distress before the Lord, she also entreated for relief; his blessing is that the Lord grant what she requested of Him. To this blessing he prefaces the words "go in peace,"[32] expressing his confidence that now she can go her way and cease praying, because her prayer—to which he now adds his own—will be answered.

With humble thanks Hannah takes her leave of Eli. Thus far she has been meekly designating herself "your maidservant *(ʾamathʿka)*," both in her prayer to the Lord God of Hosts and in her address to Eli the priest. When she leaves Eli, though, she uses the synonymous "handmaid *(šifhathʿka)*," evidently for the sake of elegant variation.[33] This humble title is incorporated in the formulaic phrase, "may your handmaid find favor in your eyes" (v. 18a), whereby Hannah expresses her thanks for the blessing that Eli has bestowed upon her and her hope that his kind disposition toward her will continue (cf. similar expressions of gratitude for unexpected favors: Gen. 47:25; 2 Sam. 16:4; Ruth 2:13). Next we read that "the woman went her way and ate, and her countenance was no longer sad" (v. 18b).[34] By these three actions Hannah complies not only with the instructions of the priest, who has just told her to "go in peace," but also with her husband's earlier urgings: "why are you weeping, and why aren't you eating, and why are you so sad?" In fact, nothing has changed, but Hannah can now return to the bosom of her family and break her fast, and the expression on her face clearly attests that her misery is past. Thanks to her despairing prayer and solemn vow, and thanks to the priest's blessing and gesture, she is now radiant with her quiet trust in divine assistance.

The scene that began with Hannah going away from her family ("Hannah rose" [v. 9]) concludes with her return to it ("the woman went her way" [v. 18b]). The end of the scene does not precisely coincide with the end of the first part of the story, which also ends with a reversal of its beginning. Echoing the pilgrimage by Elkanah and his family to prostrate themselves and sacrifice to the Lord in Shiloh, at the beginning of the story (v. 3), we are now told about the valedictory prostration and the return to Ramah (v. 19a). The plural form of the concluding sentence ("they bowed low before the Lord, and they went back home") expresses that the family is once again acting as a unit; the crisis that erupted with Hannah's refusal to eat has blown over. True, Hannah is still childless, and her conflict with Peninnah has not been resolved; but thanks to the tranquil ending of part I, the reader shares Hannah's confidence that this homecoming will not be like previous ones, that this time there is hope for her.

Part II, scene 1 (1:19b–23): Birth, naming, and avoidance of error

The longed-for change occurs quickly. Going beyond a bare account of events, the narrator interposes between "Elkanah knew his wife Hannah" and "Hannah conceived" the words "the Lord remembered her."[35] In such bald factual language Hannah's pregnancy is presented as the result of her being remembered by the giver of all life. Moreover, the words "the Lord remembered her" clearly echo the protasis of Hannah's vow—"if You . . . will remember me and not forget Your maidservant" (v. 11); this association depicts her pregnancy as the direct result of the vow. When Hannah gives birth to a son, the link acquires an additional dimension, because it also realizes the continuation of the condition—"and if You will grant Your maidservant a male child." The child is born "at the turn of the year," that is, twelve months after the annual sacrifice at Shiloh. This temporal information stresses the rapidity of God's response to Hannah's prayer and Eli's blessing (along the lines of "next year your wife Sarah shall have a son"—Gen. 18:10; cf. 2 Kings 4:16).

In addition to the causal association that presents this scene as the direct outcome of the previous one, the symmetrical structure creates a contrasting link between this scene and its parallel in the first part. "The Lord remembered her" is the antithesis of "the Lord had closed her womb" (v. 5), not only as a matter of fact but also—and chiefly—as a matter of theology. Against the background of scene I,1, the significance of the Lord's remembering Hannah is that henceforth she will be spared both the shame of having to make do with "one portion only" as well as her cowife's humiliating insinuations. At the same time, the glorious transformation in her life poses a new trial: is she truly prepared to bear the far-reaching implications of the view—so far expressed only by the narrator—that not only evil, but also good, comes from the Lord, and that it was her vow that wrought the change? Or will she ignore the link between her vow and the infant in her arms so as not to be separated from him? It is true that Hannah—as we know her from part I of the story—is suspected neither of ingratitude (against which the psalmist cautions: "Bless the Lord, O my soul, and do not forget all His bounties" [Ps. 103:2]) nor of reneging on vows (against which the Law warns—"You must fulfill what has crossed your lips and perform what you have voluntarily vowed to the Lord your God" [Deut. 23:24; cf. Eccles. 5:1–6]. Hence the story, rather than describing the trial itself, tells us how she passed it. When Hannah names her newborn child Samuel, which she explains as meaning, "I asked the Lord for him" (v. 20), she is announcing in the most obligatory and public fashion that this son is the fruit of her request; his very name attests that had the Lord not answered her prayer, he would not have been born. This grateful acknowledgment that the condition of her vow has been realized by the Lord is tantamount to a renewed affirmation of her commitment to fulfill what she vowed to do in return.

Samuel is born close to the time of the annual pilgrimage. Elkanah and "all his household" (this is the only allusion to the presence of Peninnah, whose claws have been blunted) go to Shiloh "to offer to the Lord the annual sacrifice and his votive sacrifice" (v. 21). There was no mention of Elkanah's vows with regard to previous pilgrimages, nor has anything yet been said about this vow. Obviously the reader of antiquity could be relied upon to understand that not only had Elkanah not nullified his wife's vow on the day he heard about it (cf. Num. 30:11–17), he had even reinforced it by means of his own vow. Whether his was uttered by way of a request before Hannah became pregnant, or in gratitude afterward (like the sailors' vows after the storm in Jonah 1:16), clearly what is involved here is a thanksgiving offering, since the verb "to offer" also applies to "his votive sacrifice." This adds another line to the contrasting character sketches of the woman and her husband: she grapples to change her destiny, while he acquiesces in it; she vows to give up her son, and he pledged a sacrificial animal!

On the face of it, Hannah too should be included in "all his household." Hence we are quite surprised when the next verse begins with the adversative *waw*—"But Hannah did not go up" (v. 22). Once again she separates herself from her family at the time of the annual sacrifice and presents her husband with a fait accompli that cannot be altered by his arguments and warnings. The similarity in the situation is underscored by the repetition of the negative word: in I,1 we read, "she wept and would *not* eat," and in II,1, "Hannah did *not* go up." The fundamental change in her situation has not—surprisingly enough—led to a corresponding alteration in her conduct. But before we have a chance to suspect her of trying to evade the fulfillment of her vow, she explains her motives to her husband.[36] As long as the child still needs its mother's milk, the time to fulfill the vow has not yet arrived; or, in positive terms, fulfilling the vow appropriately requires that the child first be weaned. Elat ("History and Historiography," pp. 8–11), relying on two neo-Assyrian legal documents of the seventh century, which contain the binding legal endorsement for the consecration of children to lifelong service in the sanctuary, has demonstrated that this is the correct understanding of "when the child is weaned, I will bring him." The first document, from Nineveh, refers to the son of a sacred prostitute, dedicated to the sanctuary by her two brothers and two other men; it is stressed that they had "raised" him before they conveyed him to the priests. This is made even clearer in the second document, from Calah, which deals with a man who had dedicated his sister's two sons to the god Nevo after he had "fed them and sustained [them], weaned them from their [mother's] breast, raised them and consecrated them to the god Nevo who is in Calah."[37]

All the same, what prevents Hannah from making the pilgrimage now with the infant and then bringing him back to Ramah until he is weaned? She answers this question herself: "For when he has appeared before the Lord, he must remain there for good." Her heart tells her that bringing him home from Shiloh is not allowed, even if it is necessary and temporary.[38] Hannah's two arguments have a single root (which we have designated in the table as "perfect fulfillment"): a full gift of her son means not conveying him to the House of the Lord while he still requires his mother, lest he be a burden there; and perfect fulfillment implies not bringing him to the sanctuary so long as it is impossible to leave him there forever, lest she appear to be violating her vow.[39]

Elkanah lacked Hannah's sensitivity. This time too he has difficulty understanding her, and even more difficulty in persuading her. The narrator expresses this difficulty by prefacing the husband's remarks, both here and previously, with the same longish introduction—"Her husband Elkanah said to her" (vv. 8 and 23). In fact, in both places their disagreement as to what should be done is presented as a dispute concerning the nature of what is "good." There he concludes his attempts to convince her with, "Am I not better for you *(tov)* than ten sons?" (v. 8); now, having learned from experience, he begins, "do as seems best *(ha-tov)* in your eyes." Given the thematic and verbal links, it is hard to see his words as expressing genuine acquiescence in her decision and identification with her motives; they should rather be read as evincing a willingness to honor her decision post factum, while putting his reservations on record and making her responsible for any untoward results. When he says, "stay home until you have weaned him" (v. 23), he is borrowing her own words: "When the child is weaned, I will bring him" (v. 22). It is likely that he repeats her condition in order to fix the day when the child is weaned as an explicit and agreed-upon final date for her to stay home in Ramah and skip the annual pilgrimage. Even though we have no evidence from Scripture as to the duration of nursing in those days, it is clear from later and external evidence that it was a matter of some years.[40] Hannah's staying home thus means that she will not partake of the annual sacrifice not only this year but during the coming years as well. It is rather farfetched to assume that Elkanah did not trust her motives and suspected that she was merely attempting to postpone fulfilling her vow. It is more plausible to assume that a man who was so strict about paying his own vow on time felt that her refusal to make the pilgrimage after the birth of her son had a whiff of ingratitude about it, liable to be punished by cancellation of the favor, as he says—"Only may the Lord fulfill [literally: make stand] His word" (v. 23). Because there is no prophecy in the story, and because it is difficult to say that Elkanah relates to Eli's blessing as the word of God (the interpretation of Rashi, R. Joseph Kara, and Kimchi), it seems that by "His word" he means the Lord's will as manifested by the birth of a son in the wake of Hannah's prayer and vow (for God's will referred to as "His word," see: "let her be a wife to your master's son, as the Lord has spoken" [Gen. 24:51]; "then I knew it was indeed the word of the Lord" [Jer. 32:8]; and 2 Sam. 15:26]). Another possibility is to adopt the version of 4QSam^a and of the Septuagint—may the Lord fulfill "what has crossed your lips" (based on the language of the laws of vows in Num. 30:3), a reading supported by the Peshitta. In this case, Elkanah is referring to Hannah's vow and giving vent to his fear that the Lord may prevent her from fulfilling it (as, "her husband will uphold [literally: make stand] or annul it" [Num. 30:14]). Whichever reading we adopt, Elkanah is expressing his apprehension that Hannah's conduct may cause harm to the still-helpless infant.[41] Hannah, on the other hand, imbued with faith in her path, thanks to the miraculous response she has received and the destiny imposed on her child as a holy obligation, has no such fears (like the wife of Manoah—Judg. 13:22–23). She does exactly what the two agree upon: "So the woman *stayed home* and nursed her son *until she weaned him*" (v. 23b). Her success is the clearest evidence that this time, too, she is right and he is wrong.

Unlike Peninnah, Elkanah and Eli are not negative characters. Both of Elkanah's mistakes, as well as Eli's, stem not from some flaw in their moral make-up but from a misapprehension caused by the unique situation and personality of the heroine. Thus these supporting characters provide a realistic contrast against which Hannah's great virtues stand out and have greater verisimilitude.[42]

Part II, scene 2 (1:24–28; 2:11a):
Generous and wholehearted fulfillment of the vow

The third pilgrimage described in our story is not made at the annual festival, but "when she had weaned him" (v. 24). Unlike its predecessors, this special pilgrimage, devoted to fulfilling Hannah's vow, is not described as a family event led by the paterfamilias; only at the end of the scene do we learn of Elkanah's presence, from the reference to his return home (2:11a). Hannah does not hold on to the child: she brings him to the House of the Lord as soon as he is weaned, without waiting for the annual pilgrimage to Shiloh. Yet we may wonder in what spirit she will pay her vow: will she (like Jephthah) grieve that her pledge was excessive and that she was not clever enough to volunteer some less painful offering? Or will she crow in triumph over Peninnah her cowife, who can no longer taunt her in this place? The narrator answers these questions indirectly, by listing the many additional donations that Hannah adds to the gift of her son and by omitting any mention of conflict between her and Peninnah. With wholehearted generosity Hannah brings her son to the Lord's House—with a three-year-old bullock (that is, at the peak of its economic value),[43] an ephah of flour (worth much more than the ephah of unmilled barley that it took Ruth an entire day to gather [Ruth 2:17]), and a flask of wine.

The description of Samuel's arrival in Shiloh concludes with the crux, "the lad was a lad (*uf-ha-naʿar naʿar*)"; logic suggests that this continues the description of the perfection of Hannah's gift. The doubts about the tautological nature of this statement have been dispelled by Tsevat,[44] who cites similar statements—both from ancient Assyrian ("the year was a year"— that is, a full twelve months) and from the Mishna and Gemara ("his gift is a gift" [*Mishna Peʾah* 3,7], which parallels "his gift is valid" [JT Baba Batra 9,6])—in which a predicate that at first glance adds nothing to the subject actually reaffirms and clarifies it.[45] Accordingly, the text is telling us that the lad Samuel is truly a "lad," not a toddler recently weaned from his mother's milk but mature enough to take care of himself and, perhaps, even ready to be a servitor (*naʿar*) in the sanctuary (just as the bullock brought with him is at its best).

The sacrifice itself and the accompanying feast are dismissed in a few words—"they slaughtered the bullock"—to convey that there is no place for the retrospective contrast—on the face of it required by the repetitive structure of the story—between the three-year-old bullock and "one portion only," between the ephah of flour and "she would not eat," and between the flask of wine and "put away your wine from you." Not only does the narrator avoid any hint of sentimentality and melodrama, but by skimming lightly over the slaughter of the bullock he indicates that Hannah's mind is on fulfilling her vow and not on the alteration in her situation. In other words, Hannah is described here not as receiving but as giving, as someone whose link with the past is based not on remedying the discrimination of many years but on fulfilling her obligation to the Lord who heard her prayer. Once again Hannah has faced a trial, and once again she has passed it admirably.

Only after the sacrifice is the lad brought to Eli. To our astonishment, Hannah once again must convince the priest of something. The similarity between this scene and its analog (I,2) is underscored by the close parallelism between her opening words to him there—"Oh no, my lord!" (1:15) and her prefatory address here—"Please, my lord! As you live, my lord" (1:26). The sequel reveals that Eli has not recognized her, so she must persuade him by her oath that she is the very same woman who some years before prayed an unusual prayer in his presence, and that "this lad" who stands alongside her today is the fulfillment of the petition she made then. We do not suspect that Hannah may exploit Eli's forgetfulness as a pretext for reneging on her vow, especially since the priest knew nothing about her vow and the object of her prayer. Nevertheless, her efforts to remind Eli of that forgotten scene and her oath about her identity and that of her son are intended to make it clear that Samuel's dedication to the sanctuary is a direct result of past events. Just as in the previous scene she insisted that the lad not be brought to the Lord's House before he was weaned, now too she insists that he be accepted by Eli as the fruit of her prayer, which was answered, and as the fruit of his blessing, which was fulfilled. To this end she stresses that "the Lord has granted me what I asked of Him" (v. 27), clearly echoing the language of Eli's blessing: "may the God of Israel grant you what you have asked of Him" (v. 17). Again we are in for a surprise: instead of telling Eli about the vow that accompanied her prayer, she prefers to represent the gift of her son as an obligation stemming directly from God's response to her prayer—"I, in turn, hereby give him to the Lord." God has given her what she requested, and she ought to repay Him by donating to Him what He has granted her. Hannah does not see herself as surrendering her son because of a commitment made in the past but as giving him with a grateful heart that rejoices in her present fortune. The child's very life is the result of the Lord's bounty; hence he is given to the Lord "for as long as he lives" (this renders the Septuagint and Peshitta, whose text is preferable to the Masoretic "for as long as he will be").[46]

In addition to placing this donation of her son to serve in the sanctuary in the proper light, Hannah's words have another dimension, which can be characterized as "loud thanksgiving" (Jon. 2:10). Someone who has benefited from a miracle and recognizes the fact feels a sacred obligation to do more than simply offer a thanksgiving sacrifice; there is also a duty to publicize the miracle "in the presence of all His people" (Ps. 116:14 and 18), so that all may be made aware of it. In her address to Eli, Hannah does indeed express a number of the fundamental ideas of the thanksgiving Psalms. When she says, "It was this boy I prayed for, and the Lord has granted me what I asked of Him" (v. 27), she is proclaiming the Lord's total response to her entreaty, just as the psalmists do: "O Lord, my God, I cried out to You and You healed me" (Ps. 30:3); "I turned to the Lord, and He answered me; He saved me from all my terrors" (Ps. 34:5 as well as 7 and 18; see also 21:3 and 5; 61:6; 66:16–20; 102:18). When she says, "I, in turn (w^e-gam ʾanoki) . . . " (v. 28), she is using the very same terms with which the psalmists preface their own statements of obligation: "then I too (gam ʾani) will acclaim You to the music of the lyre for Your faithfulness, O my God; I will sing a hymn to You with a harp, O Holy One of Israel" (Ps. 71:22); "As for me, I will declare forever, I will sing a hymn to the God of Jacob" (Ps. 75:10; and cf. 79:13). When she relies on paronomasia to associate "what I asked (šaʾalti) of Him" with "I give him (hišʾiltihu) to the Lord," she is expressing her aspiration to repay the Lord in a manner befitting His favor to her, an aspiration expressed by the psalmist in the rhetorical question, "How can I repay the Lord for all His bounties to me?" (Ps. 116:12).

As a preliminary contribution to our consideration of whether Hannah's psalm (2:1–10) belongs to the original story (the actual discussion is better postponed until we conclude our close reading of the entire account), we can say that "loud thanksgiving" is by no means absent from the story itself. Moreover, not only does Hannah's prose express several of the fundamental elements of the thanksgiving psalms, it also glorifies and exalts the Lord's great deeds, just as her lyrical prayer does. When Hannah presents herself to Eli as a barren woman who has finally given birth because the Lord answered her prayer, she not only thanks the Lord for His favor to her, she also bears public witness to His mighty deeds, of which she has personal experience.

Hannah's speech is followed by the words, "they bowed low there before the Lord" (1:28b). If we skip over the psalm, the continuation of this sentence follows at once: "then Elkanah went home to Ramah" (2:11a). In fact, the Septuagint makes all of this into a single verse, placed after the psalm, thereby supporting the theory that the verse was originally one but was sundered in two when the psalm was interpolated. The Septuagint's rendering of this verse also explicates the two cruxes of the verb "bowed low." The first difficulty is that even though the verb refers to Hannah or to her entire family, it is inflected in the masculine singular (*wa-yištaḥu*). The second difficulty is that the adverb "there" is not really needed after "they bowed low," since they must obviously have bowed low "there." Hence it is plausible to adopt the Septuagint reading (Vatican MS): "she left him there," which seems to be supported by the fragmentary 4QSam^a. From a literary point of view this version has a decided advantage—the scene that opens with "she took him up with her" concludes by way of *inclusio* with "she left him there." Furthermore, these words give explicit yet fairly low-key expression to the concrete act that implements her vow. So far Hannah has spoken of giving the child to the Lord; now she actually parts company with him when she leaves him "there" (cf. Gen. 44:22 and Ruth 1:16).

As for the rest of this verse, the textual evidence is so varied that we ought to give up any attempt to determine whether Elkanah was mentioned in the original text:

> *Masoretic text:* "He bowed low there before the Lord; then Elkanah went home to Ramah" (the first clause before the psalm, the second one after it);
> *4QSam^a:* "[She left] him there and she bowed low [. . .]" (the first clause before the psalm, the second clause missing);
> *Septuagint* (Vatican MS): "She left him there before the Lord and went to Ramah" (everything after the psalm);

Septuagint (Lucian version): "They left him there before the Lord and bowed low before the Lord and went to Ramah" (everything after the psalm).

It is clear in any case that this is the closing sentence of part II,[47] since it concludes the special pilgrimage in which the vow was fulfilled. If the reference to Elkanah is indeed original, it tells us that the hegemony of the paterfamilias has now been restored, along with family harmony. Hitherto it had been otherwise: the vow was fulfilled from start to finish by Hannah, in accordance with her own understanding of it, and accompanied by serious tension with her husband Elkanah (in II,1) and by a strenuous effort to gain Eli's cooperation (in II,2). By contrast, Peninnah is conspicuous by her absence: not only is she never mentioned in these two scenes, there is not the slightest echo of any conflict with her. We learn thereby that even though Hannah leaves her only son in Shiloh, the shame of her barrenness has ceased to torment her.

Epilogue (2:18–21): The reward—many children

The epilogue begins with a description of the situation in Shiloh: Samuel, having been entrusted to Eli the priest, has meanwhile become a servitor in the sanctuary, "an attendant girded with a linen ephod" (2:18). The narrator's attention, here for the first time diverted from Hannah, returns to her immediately—"His mother would make a little robe for him" (2:19). Evidently the narrator mentions the lad's holy apparel so that he can juxtapose it to the little robe, thus suggesting that the robe, too, is one of his sacred garments.[48] If this is true, Hannah's motivation for making her son a new robe every year is not concern that he be well-dressed but a desire to continue her act of giving. For her, the dedication of her son to service in the sanctuary is not a one-time deed, but one renewed each year by the recurrent donation of a sacred robe to the lad who serves in the sanctuary.

This third part of the story, too, revolves around the pilgrimage to Shiloh, but without referring to the specific pilgrimage of a particular year. Instead, we read in general terms of what henceforth transpired each year at the time of the annual sacrifice. In symmetrical parallelism with the exposition in I,1 (1:4b–7a), here too all the verbs are in the future or the inverted perfect—that is, forms that indicate recurrent action. This conjunction of language and narrative modes underscores the thematic contrast: now all is harmonious and there is no longer any opportunity for Peninnah's taunts, just as there is no longer any cause for tension between Hannah and Elkanah.[49] Again the narrator avoids a dramatic contrast between the distribution of portions of the sacrifice now with the painful distribution then. Instead, he juxtaposes with great finesse Hannah's recurrent elevating acts of generosity after she became a mother ("His mother would also make [*ta'aseh*] a little robe for him and bring it up to him *every year*") with the humiliating situation that kept repeating itself when she was barren ("this he used to do [*ya'aseh*; Peshitta: *ta'aseh* = she used to do] *year after year*").

Moreover, in contrast with Hannah's encounter with the priest in I,2, by which his rebuke becomes a blessing, and in contrast with her efforts to overcome his forgetfulness in II,2 so that he will see the lad as that which his name expresses, here there is no need to remind him who Hannah is; he blesses her on his own initiative. While the first blessing was given to Hannah alone and was phrased in nonspecific terms, every year now Eli gives "Elkanah and his wife" a direct and explicit blessing that they have children. In this way Eli also helps reinforce Elkanah's status as paterfamilias and Hannah's husband. Hannah herself is a partner in this. Whereas in the past she did not heed Elkanah's urgings, acted without his knowledge, and even imposed her own ideas upon him, now she stands alongside him before the priest and is blessed through him—"May the Lord grant you offspring by this woman in place of the gift she made to the Lord" (2:20). At first sight there is a slight in Eli's anonymous reference to "this woman," but it is clear that he adopts this tone in order to create a gentle and indirect contrast with that other woman, her cowife (who is not mentioned in this scene either).[50] The blessing of children is given to the husband, but the merit is explicitly that of "this woman." In his first blessing, by virtue of which Hannah became pregnant, Eli referred to her *request:* "may the God of Israel grant you what you have asked of Him." In his annual blessing, though, he refers to her *gift* and to the homiletical explanation of the child's name that accompanied it: "in place of the gift she made (reading with 4QSam[a]: *his'ilah*) to the Lord."

Eli's blessings instill new hopes that will be realized at home in Ramah. Thus in this scene, too, the blessing is followed by a reference to the home; this time, in accordance with the abridged nature of the scene (see above, p. 5), it too is abridged—"then they would return home."[51] Immediately afterward the narrator reports in summary fashion that Hannah had five more children—"For the Lord took note of Hannah; she conceived and bore three sons and two daughters" (2:21a).[52] Thus the story concludes with the great reward granted to that desperate, barren woman, whom the Lord lavishly recompensed with sons and daughters for having asked for Samuel and giving him back to the Lord, for the bold faith that inspired her vow, and for her utter fidelity in fulfilling it.

The Problem of the Psalm

Two conclusions regarding the link between Hannah's lyrical prayer and the original story follow from our close reading of the story and analysis of its structure. First, the account has a complete and independent existence without the psalm. Second, the absence of Peninnah from parts II and III means that the conflict between the two cowives (so important in part I) is significant only in connection with the struggle over birth; once Samuel was born it ceased to engage both the heroine and the narrator. Were this conflict the linchpin of the story (as in the story of Jacob and his two wives) the narrator would contrast Hannah's distress and humiliation during the earlier pilgrimages with her proud carriage and ready retorts to her cowife on the later pilgrimages, instead of dealing exclusively with the fulfillment of the vow and Hannah's reward for her faithfulness. Nor is the tension between Hannah and her husband the crux of the story. Although it does continue into part II, it is explicitly resolved in part III (and, according to the Masoretic version of 2:11a, immediately after the fulfillment of the vow). This strengthens the reader's impression that Hannah contended not for dominance within the family, but for motherhood itself. Hence the narrator deals with these two conflicts in different ways (ignoring one when it ceases to be acute, and resolving the other). In both, however, his purpose is the same—to sketch the character of Hannah as a woman whose sole aim is to become a mother and to pay the full price for achieving her wish.

By contrast, the first part of the psalm (2:1–3) is given over to thanks to God the redeemer and to a cry of triumph over the enemies whose mouths have been sealed:

> My heart exults in the Lord;
> My strength is exalted in the Lord.
> I gloat over my enemies;
> I rejoice in Your deliverance.
> There is no holy one like the Lord,
> Truly, there is none beside You;
> There is no rock like our God.
> Talk no more with lofty pride,
> Let no arrogance cross your lips!
> For the Lord is an all-knowing God;
> By Him actions are measured.

The question before us is not merely "the incongruity between the psalm and the occasion on which it is uttered" (Kaufmann, *Religion of Israel*, p. 310). The narrator could have described Hannah as giving thanks by reciting an existing psalm (as does everyone today who recites a psalm or a prayer from the prayerbook). The question is much more serious and is one of the contrast between Hannah's emotional attitude toward her co-wife, as sketched in the story, and that reflected in the psalm. To Hannah's noble silence in the face of Peninnah's infuriating words we must add the strong impact of the narrator's silence about the changes in Peninnah's status and feelings after Hannah had given birth. In the thanksgiving psalm that accompanies the fulfillment of the vow, however, Hannah suddenly gloats over her rival. Is this the same Hannah? Is this the same narrator? It is hard to ascribe to a narrator who is so scrupulous about every jot and tittle of his story such a radical displacement of the center of gravity of the story, from a description of a bold yet restrained contention with God and man for a son, to the exultation of the weak person who has been saved from powerful enemies by the intervention of the omnipotent God.

Furthermore, and more acutely, it is precisely the verse that ostensibly bridges psalm and plot that sunders them more than anything else: "While the barren woman bears seven, the mother of many has languished [i.e., become downcast]" (v. 2:5b). In Scripture, *ʾumlal*, 'languish,' is synonymous with "mourn" (Isa. 19:8; Jer. 14:2; Hos. 4:3; Lam. 2:8), and generally indicates not only the pain involved in loss but also the loss itself—"She who bore seven has languished, she has swooned away; her sun has set while it is still day" (Jer. 15:9). Hence the meaning of "languished" is not that the woman with many children is unfortunate in light of the pregnancy of the once-barren woman, but that the destinies of the two women have been interchanged: the barren woman has given birth to seven, whereas the woman with many children has lost all of them. In the psalm, this twofold change provides tangible proof that nothing is beyond the Lord's capacity, and hence that neither strength nor frailty is forever. But when uttered by a woman in Hannah's situation, this verse is tantamount to cursing her cowife that she lose her children (or mercilessly gloating at her tragedy after she has lost them). In fact, the significance of "the mother of many has languished," when spoken by Hannah, is so drastic that it is quite impossible to make the words compatible with her character without first somehow extracting their sting. This is what R. Nehemiah did in his midrashic interpretation, which is also intended to explain the discrepancy between "she who bore seven" in the psalm and the reported fact that Hannah had only five children:

> R. Nehemiah said: Peninnah had ten sons. Hannah gave birth to her first, and Peninnah buried two; Hannah gave birth to her second, and Peninnah buried her fourth; her third, and Peninnah buried her sixth; her fourth, and Peninnah buried her eighth. When she became pregnant for the fifth time, Peninnah came and *prostrated herself before her* and said to her: "Please, I beseech you, pray for my two that they live!" *Hannah prayed for them*, and they were thereafter referred to as her children. (Midrash Samuel 5,10)

The italicized words illuminate the problematic nature of the psalm when it is understood as an integral part of the story: the song of thanks becomes a paean of victory, and the wonder at God's intervention in man's fate turns into a sort of curse that is so foreign to Hannah's nature that it must be turned on its head and viewed as a generous prayer![53]

What the midrashic interpretation seeks to do by divorcing the psalm from its philological meaning, our interpretation tries to do by divorcing the psalm from its narrative context. For the meaning of the psalm varies according to whether we assume that it was placed in Hannah's mouth by the author of the account of Samuel's birth, or that the psalm was later interpolated into the story to magnify the expression of gratitude by means of a psalm and to give explicit and direct expression to the abstract lesson. Divine remembrance of the despondent barren woman by virtue of her prayer and vow is a classic example, not only of the Lord's power over nature, society, and history, but also of His justice. We seem to be ruled by natural, social, and political forces; but the psalm asserts that the Creator imposes upon them His own religious and moral laws—"He guards the steps of His *faithful,* / But the *wicked* perish in darkness / For *not by strength* shall man prevail" (2:9). There is something self-righteous and haughty in this when spoken by Hannah, who triumphs over her cowife; but there is no such ugliness if the intention is to encourage the wretched of the earth to cleave to God's path and hope for His salvation by setting before them the deliverance of that righteous woman as a sign and a model.[54]

The Literary Genre and Meaning of the Story

The identity of the hero of a story does not necessarily determine its theme. Abraham's servant is the protagonist of Genesis 24 (he is on stage throughout, except for one short interlude in verses 28–30a), but the theme of the story is Rebekah—the appropriate wife whom the Lord has ordained for Isaac. The husband of the concubine who is molested and murdered at Gibeah is the main character in the first half of that story (he is continuously present throughout Judges 19, except for verses 25b–26), but the subject of the story is the abominable deed performed in Gibeah and its disastrous results, for the tribe of Benjamin, in the prevailing anarchy of the period. The same applies to Hannah; although she is undoubtedly the heroine of our narrative, and even though Samuel's role in it is secondary and passive, the story ultimately focuses not on her but on him. We reach this conclusion not from reading the story itself but from examining it in the context of the literary genre to which it belongs.[55] In fact, in a different literary tradition, one in which many stories do not necessarily deal with characters or events of public importance, we would say that the theme of this story is the exemplary struggle of a believing woman to attain motherhood. But in Scripture we find such a nonbiographical approach only in wisdom stories such as those of Jonah and Job (though these too focus on characters who have a distinctly public status), while the personal accounts tend to deal with the mothers and fathers of humanity, the nation, the tribe, and the family, or with prophets and other spiritual, political, military, and judicial leaders. Accordingly, all of the birth stories in Scripture are about important persons, with the one exception that indirectly confirms the rule—the birth of the anonymous son of the matron of Shunem and his resurrection, recounted only because it involves an important man: the true subject of that story is the miracle-working power of the prophet Elisha. If, however, our story really is the first chapter in the biography of the prophet Samuel, why does it go to such extremes in praising his mother (and this to no little extent at the expense of his father Elkanah)? If the actions of Samuel's parents are not presented as a model for their son the prophet, why does the story devote so much space to an artistic portrayal of Hannah's character, traits, and attributes?

In order to understand the significance of the account of Samuel's birth as the introduction to his biography, as well as the attention lavished on his mother's deeds and character, we must consider the other stories of miraculous births related in Scripture.[56] Because the death of an infant (or of a child who has not attained maturity) is equivalent to nullifying his birth, rescuing children from death is tantamount to giving birth to them. It is this idea that led the Shunammite woman to demand so vehemently that Elisha restore her child, who had been born only thanks to the miracle he had wrought (2 Kings 4:27–30). Hence, in addition to the stories about childless women who were ultimately remembered by God and gave birth, we should also examine those about children saved by God from death, whether this miraculous survival is the immediate sequel to a miraculous birth (as in the story of the Shunammite) or not (as in the rescues of Ishmael, Moses, and the son of the widow of Zarephath).

There are seven stories of miraculous birth in Scripture, of which two refer to the birth of the same person (the annunciation of Isaac's birth occurs in both Genesis 17 and Genesis 18, and their common continuation is the account of the birth itself, in chapter 21). I have compared these seven with the four stories of miraculous survival found in Scripture (one of which, that of the resurrection of the Shunammite's son, is the sequel to the story of his birth). In order to gain a nonscriptural perspective (partial but illuminating), I have also examined the account of the birth of a son to the barren Danel, which opens the Ugaritic epic of Aqhat.[57] What is common to all of these stories can define a literary genre with distinct lineaments and a specific theme—the birth (or rescue in youth) of an important person whose unique destiny is closely linked with the fact that without the intervention of the Lord he would not have lived.[58]

The inquiry—whose findings are summarized in tables 1.2 and 1.3—reveals that most or all of the ten components that define the genre are found in each of the twelve stories. All ten are found in the account of Samuel's birth, only five in the resurrection of the son of the widow of Zarephath, and six to nine in the other stories. The genre rests on three fundamental elements found in all of the birth stories and two of the survival stories: first, the *affliction* (the inability to have a child because of barrenness or old age, and/or the threat hanging over the child's life); second, the *miracle* (the Lord alleviates the affliction—the birth of a son and/or his rescue from death); third, the *destiny* for whose sake life was granted to the child (this is stated explicitly in seven of the stories, receives strong expression in the sequel to two of them, and is of course absent from the stories about the widow of Zarephath and the matron of Shunem, where the focus is on the prophet who restores the child to life and not on the child).[59] In the stories of the patriarchs, the destiny of the newborn is to carry on the existence of the nation. About Isaac we read: "I will maintain My covenant with him as an everlasting covenant for his offspring to come" (Gen. 17:19); about Ishmael: "As for the son of the slave-woman, I will make a nation of him too, for he is your seed" (Gen. 21:13); and about Jacob and Esau: "Two nations are in your womb" (Gen. 25:23). The same applies, implicitly, to Joseph, ancestor of the tribes of Ephraim and Manasseh, who was moreover destined by his extraordinary powers (as a dreamer and interpreter of dreams and as a wise man nonpareil) to provide food for his brethren and to arrange their settlement in Egypt. Moses, Samson, and Samuel are all destined to save and lead Israel and are consequently endowed with the spirit of prophecy (Moses and Samuel) or might (Samson). It is true that, on the face of it, the son born to Danel by the grace of El, the chief deity of the Ugaritic pantheon, lacks any specific destiny. Danel, who "unlike his brothers has no son / and no root like his relatives" (*Aqhat* A,1:19–20), will be rewarded: "he will have a son in his house / and a root in his sanctuary" (ibid., 26) who will faithfully fulfill all the obligations incumbent upon a son who honors his father as he ought to (these are spelled out no fewer than four times in the passages that have survived from the account of Aqhat's birth).[60] Still, because of the extremely fragmentary nature of the text, we obtain only a partial picture. Just as we cannot know whether the naming of the newborn son was accompanied by an explanation of his name (because the lines that relate Aqhat's birth are missing), we cannot know whether the description of Aqhat as a mighty hunter armed with a heaven-fashioned bow (the axis on which the entire plot revolves) explicitly associates this with his miraculous birth. In any case, it is clear that in retrospect, looking back from the end of the epic, the link between the hero's destiny and the unique circumstances of his birth is quite evident.

The logical connection among these three fundamental elements is clear enough—a severe affliction requires the miraculous intervention of the deity (because it cannot be remedied without a miracle); and the miraculous granting of life creates a link of destiny between the deity and the newborn child. The miraculous origin of his life explains how the bearer

TABLE 1.2: Miraculous Birth Stories

Active parent	Affliction	Worthiness of the miracle		Attitude toward the affliction		The woman's wisdom and resourcefulness
		Good deeds	Prayer	Acquies-cence	Refusal to acquiesce	
Abraham (Gen. 17+21)	Woman's barrenness; couple's advanced age	Circumci-sion		"O that Ishmael might live by Your favor."		
Abraham and Sarah (Gen. 18+21)	Couple's advanced age	Hospitality				
Isaac and Rebekah	Barrenness followed by a difficult pregnancy		"Isaac pleaded with the Lord."	"If so, why do I exist."	["Isaac pleaded with the Lord."]	
Rachel	Barrenness and disgrace		["Now God remembered Rachel; God heeded her."]		"Give me children or I shall die."	Giving Bilhah to Jacob and buying the mandrakes (in vain)
Manoah's wife	Barrenness					Identifies and understands the angel (better than her husband does)
Hannah	Barrenness and disgrace		Prayer and vow in Shiloh		"she wept and would not eat"; "she was desperate."	Vows and accomplishes (better than her husband and the priest)
Woman of Shunem (2 Kings 4:8–17	Elderly husband	Hospitality				Recognizes the holiness of the prophet better than her husband does
Danel father of Aqhat	No son		Seven days of offering sacrifices in the temple; Baal(?) prays on his behalf		"Desolate and sigh-ing."	

Note: Motifs that occur with in the broader context of the story rather than in the specific episode are enclosed in square brackets.

TABLE 1.2—*continued*

The herald and his message	Attitude toward the annunciation		The child's destiny	The miracle	Midrashic explanation of the name	Thanks-giving
	Disbelief	Belief				
God: "I will give you a son by her."	"Abraham . . . laughed . . . 'Can a child be born to a man a hundred years old?'"		"I will maintain My covenant with him as an everlasting covenant."	"a son in his old age, at the set time of which God had spoken. . . ."	"you shall name him Isaac." (Gen. 17:19)	"God has brought me laugh-ter . . . Who would have said to Abra-ham. . . . " (Gen. 21:6)
The angel: "I will return to you next year, and your wife Sarah shall have a son!"	"Sarah laughed."		"it is through Isaac that off-spring shall be continued for you."		"God has brought me laughter." (Gen. 21:6)	
God: "Two nations are in your womb."			"Two nations are in your womb . . . the older shall serve the younger."	"The Lord responded to his plea."	"like a hairy mantle"; "holding on to the heel."	
			[Provider for his brothers and father of his tribes]	"God . . . opened her womb."	"May the Lord add . . . ."	"God has taken away my disgrace."
The angel: "you shall conceive and bear a son."		She tells Manoah: "He . . . made such an announce-ment to us."	"He shall be the first to deliver Israel from the Philistines."	"The woman bore a son."		
The priest: "May the God of Israel grant you what you have asked of Him."		"The woman . . . was no longer down-cast."	A Nazirite dedicated to the Lord [and a prophet]	"The Lord remembered her."	"I asked the Lord for him"; "I . . . give him to the Lord."	"the Lord has granted me what I asked of him."
The prophet: "At this season next year, you will be embracing a son."	"Do not delude your maidservant."			"The woman conceived and bore a son at the same season the follow-ing year."		
Baal (?) announces El's favorable response.		Triumphal laugh	Performs the duties of a son [a hunter with a heav-enly bow]	The birth of the son	?	[Cry of joy]

TABLE 1.3: Miraculous Survival Stories

Active parent	Affliction	Worthiness of the miracle		Attitude toward the affliction		The woman's wisdom and resourcefulness
		Good deeds	Prayer	Acquiescence	Refusal to acquiesce	
Hagar (Genesis 21)	Lost in the wilderness with no water	[Abraham's son ("for he is your seed.")]		"she left the child."		
Moses' mother	Drowning of newborns				"she saw how beautiful he was."	Concealment, the basket, and Miriam's advice to Pharaoh's daughter
Widow of Zarephath (1 Kings 17)	Death of the child	Hospitality		"to . . . cause the death of my son."		
Woman of Shunem (2 Kings 4:18–37)	Death of the child	[Hospitality]	Vigorous request for the prophet's assistance		"she is desperate."	Saves the boy (better than her husband, Elisha, and Gehazi)

Note: Motifs that occur within the broader context of the story rather than in the specific episode are

of this destiny acquired the supernatural powers that permit him to realize his destiny and why he enjoys the divine favor. In several stories it even underlies the obligation to remain loyal to that destiny. The idea that rescue by Heaven imposes special obligations to the Lord is clearly expressed with regard to the first-borns of Israel—"For every first-born is Mine: at the time that I smote every first-born in the land of Egypt, I consecrated every first-born in Israel, man and beast, to Myself, to be Mine, I am the Lord" (Num. 3:13; see also Exod. 13:14–15). Whereas the compelling idea of their providential birth was revealed to such men as Moses and Samson indirectly, through their miraculous birth and/or delivery, it is stated explicitly to Jeremiah at his consecration: "Before I created you in the womb, *I selected you;*

TABLE 1.3—*continued*

The herald and his message	Attitude toward the annunciation		The child's destiny	The miracle	Midrashic explanation of the name	Thanksgiving
	Disbelief	Belief				
The angel: "Lift up the boy."		"She . . . let the boy drink."	"I will make a great nation of him."	"she saw a well of water."	"for God has heeded."	
			[Prophet and savior]	The encounter with Pharaoh's daughter— "she took pity on it."	"I drew him out of the water."	
				"the child's life returned to his body and he revived."		"Now I know that you are a man of God."
				"The boy opened his eyes."		"She . . . fell at his feet and bowed low to the ground."

Before you were born, *I consecrated you; I appointed you* a prophet concerning the nations" (Jer. 1:5).[61]

This is the perspective from which we must understand Hannah's vow as well. She accepts the obligation not only to repay God for His bounties to her, but also to give practical expression to her understanding of the obligation imposed on the child himself by his miraculous birth: "If You will grant (*wǝ-nathatta*) Your maidservant a male child, I will dedicate him (*wǝ-nathattiw*) to the Lord for all the days of his life" (1:11). Hannah dedicates Samuel to serve in the sanctuary and reside in the Lord's House "forever" (1:22), but the subsequent destruction of Shiloh by the Philistines will, at least on the surface, interrupt the fulfillment of this destiny. Nevertheless, even before the destruction God will transmute the Temple servitor into a prophet, so that both the destiny expressed by his miraculous birth and the destiny defined by his mother can be realized: "For as long as he lives he is lent to the Lord" (1:28). She prophesies, but does not know what she speaks.[62]

Without the three fundamental components—affliction, miracle, and destiny—the genre does not exist; but by themselves they cannot provide verisimilitude to the story. First of all, it is essential that the beneficiary of the miracle (and in his wake also the reader) recognize the miracle as such. Just as Moses warned Pharaoh about the impending plague and even announced when it would pass, eight of these stories feature heralds who announce the imminent blessed event. In addition to the basic role played by the annunciation in all the stories where it occurs, it also plays other roles: instilling hope in despairing parents (Hagar—so she will look for water; Abraham and Sarah, the lady of Shunem and her husband, Danel and his wife Danati—so that they will renew sexual relations);[63] an explanation for the painful pregnancy (Rebekah); instructions about raising the child to be born (Samson's parents); and, most important of all, the trial of faith for the recipients of the unexpected message (Abraham and Sarah, Hagar, Manoah and his wife, Hannah, the Shunammite lady, Danel). The contrasting reactions to the annunciation—laughter of disbelief at one extreme, total belief expressed in a change of countenance at the other—require a separate discussion (see below, pp. 43–45).

In contrast to the internal literary explication proposed here for the varied role fulfilled by the element of annunciation in all the birth stories (except with Rachel) and in one of the survival stories (that about Hagar), Zakovitch (*Life of Samson,* pp. 74–84) suggested a largely external polemic explanation. In his opinion, the main thrust of the scriptural accounts of barren women who become pregnant (Sarah, Rebekah, Rachel, Samson's mother, Hannah, and the lady of Shunem) is to counter the pagan traditions that explain the birth of the superhuman hero (e.g., Hercules) as the result of a coupling between a god and a mortal woman with an alternative, nonmythological conception. To this end, the scriptural birth stories underscore the human nature of the hero whose birth is recounted; and they stress that the role of God is miraculous (remembering a barren woman) and not sexual. Zakovitch presents this demythologization as a gradual process: initially the Lord Himself serves as the herald (Gen. 17:15–21), to be replaced later—in descending order—by an angel (Gen. 18 and Judg. 13), a man of God (2 Kings 4), and a priest (1 Sam. 1)—until finally the herald vanishes from the story (Gen. 25:19–26 and 30:1–24), probably because the struggle against the pagan myth has already been won.

However, this hypothetical development does not accord with the fact that the Aqhat epic—whose great antiquity is certain, whose mythological nature is undeniable, and whose influence on the Bible, because of the similarity of language and geographical proximity, is clear—lacks two of the supporting pillars of mythological birth stories—the intercourse between divinity and mortal woman on the one hand, and the birth of the superhuman son on the other. The role of El, the chief god of the Ugaritic pantheon, in the birth of Aqhat is fundamentally no different from what we find in Scripture: he responds to the sacrifices offered by Danel during his seven-day pilgrimage to the sanctuary and to Baal's prayers on his behalf, and announces this with great ceremony to Baal or some other messenger (this point is not clear because of lacunae in the text), telling him to inform Danel that a son will be born to him. This concludes the direct intervention of El; the annunciation scenes include a mildly erotic description of Danel's future intercourse with his wife, as a result of which she will become pregnant and give birth to a son (1:39–42). Moreover, the totally human nature of this son is also stressed in his dialogue with the goddess Anath, who covets the heavenly bow he has acquired and offers him eternal life in exchange for it. Aqhat rejects the deal, advancing the decisive argument that as a mortal he cannot attain eternal life (4:33–39). If in a prescriptural pagan epic, whose heroes are both gods and men, the birth of the hero is related from a distinctly nonmythological perspective, we must not only avoid ranking the scriptural birth stories according to their relative distance from myth, but also guard against exaggerating the importance of the polemic against myth as the foundation of the genre. Hence the rejection of the mythological concept by setting a clear boundary between the divine and the human is at best one of many aspects of the divine annunciation (direct or indirect) whose main literary function, both in the Aqhat epic and the scriptural birth and survival stories, is to guarantee that everyone (parents, son, and audience) be fully aware of the great miracle involved.

The birth of Aqhat affords us a proper perspective not only on the literary genre to which, along with certain scriptural narratives, it belongs, but also on many details in the account of Samuel's birth, because there are so many impressive points of contact between them (as can be seen from tables 1.2 and 1.3). In both stories we find an acute opposition between the initial misery of the protagonists, because of their barrenness, and the total change that occurs in their feelings and appearance when they hear the good news. Danel is initially described as "forlorn and sighing" (1:18–19); but when El's favorable response is announced to him, "he opens wide his mouth and laughs and places his foot on the footstool" (2:10–11). Similarly, at the beginning Hannah "in her wretchedness . . . was weeping all the while" (1:10), whereas after receiving Eli's blessing, which promises that the God of Israel will answer her prayers, "her countenance was no longer sad" (v. 18). In fact, the similarity is also the difference. The priest's blessing has vastly inferior force to El's promise; nevertheless, Hannah believes in it with no less intensity than Danel believes in the promise: her demeanor changes completely, just as his does. They are both joyous but express this in quite different fashions: he adopts a triumphant pose and expresses his pride that the shame of barrenness has been removed from him, whereas she takes humble leave of Eli and serenely returns to the bosom of her family; he breaks out in ecstatic song and celebrates the impending realization of his desires, whereas she keeps silent until the day when she can accompany the fulfillment of her vow with a song of thanks to her God. Furthermore, in both stories the hero's struggle to be remembered by the deity takes place during a pilgrimage to a sanctuary, so that both accounts mention the offering of sacrifices. But again the difference is great: during his seven days at the temple Danel lavishes on the gods an abundance of sacrifices and libations, so that they will pray on his behalf to El the father of the gods; whereas Hannah abstains from her portion of the annual sacrifice and addresses God directly, without depending on the intermediacy of the priest who sits nearby. And whereas Danel hopes that El will give him a son who will "be in his house" (1:26) and will honor and serve him and fulfill on his behalf all sorts of ritual obligations in the temple, Hannah vows that the son whom God gives her will serve Him in the sanctuary "and abide there forever" (1:22).

To sum up, even had the prophet Ezekiel (14:12–20) not mentioned Danel by name, in the explicit context of the deliverance of children from death, the many points of contact between the accounts of Aqhat's and Samuel's births would be sufficient evidence that both were written according to a common literary model and can therefore be assigned to a single genre (ignoring the fact that one is in verse and the other in prose). The force of a literary genre is, in part, that it guides the reader to take in the account while relating it to a sequence of events that is more or less anticipated from the outset. The common situation arouses expectations for similar behavior; the implicit comparison between the familiar and the new is one of the ways of shaping the unique attributes of each story that belongs to the genre. The literary affinity is supplemented by a certain commonality of outlook. As we have seen, the gap between the characters of Danel (who sits in judgment at the city gate and rights the wrongs done to a widow) and Hannah does not stem from a principled antithesis of theological and moral norms but rather from the remarkable difference in their refinement.

As we have already observed, the annunciation guarantees that the prospective leader will be aware of the miraculous nature of his birth, and hence (directly or indirectly) also of his destiny. This awareness strengthens and deepens another element found in all the birth accounts (except for that of Samson) and two survival accounts—the *midrashic explanation of the name*.[64] The witty linguistic association between the circumstances of his birth or deliverance and the name given him commemorates the divine grace of the miraculous birth or deliverance (for Isaac, Ishmael, Joseph, Moses, and Samuel), or summarizes the lad's unique traits (for Jacob and Esau, and perhaps also for Samson, if the reader in antiquity associated his name with strength, as Josephus did—"when the child was born they called him Samson, which means strong man" (*Antiquities of the Jews*, 5,8,4).[65]

Thus far we have considered five of the building blocks of our genre, three that are found in almost all the tales and two in the vast majority thereof. This astonishing uniformity stems from the fact that all five serve to erect the basic plot, which is prima facie common to all stories belonging to the genre: the affliction, the annunciation, the destiny, the miracle, and the interpretation of the name. By contrast, a certain flexibility is required to express the various heroes' individuality. With regard to the elements that refer to the heroes' character and conduct, not only is there variety and difference, there is also contrast and opposition. Correspondingly, tables 1.2 and 1.3 devote two columns (positive and negative) to elements where the hero can have alternative reactions ("attitude toward the affliction" and "attitude toward the annunciation") and also to another element ("worthiness of the miracle") that refers to the heroes' conduct and is also divided into two categories ("good deeds" and "prayer"). These three components (or, more precisely, one of the two possibilities in each of them) appear in most of the stories, whereas the two remaining elements, which also have to do with the hero's behavior, are found only in half of them: "the woman's wisdom and resourcefulness" and "thanksgiving."

An integrated scrutiny of the elements associated with the heroes' behavior reveals that the heroes of this genre can be divided into three types. Two are polar opposites—those who acquiesce in their unfortunate situation and those who fight to alter it; in the middle is the third type— those who originally acquiesce but later overcome their resignation. The first group, those who acquiesce in their misfortune and hence are unable to accept the annunciation concerning its miraculous removal, include Abraham, Sarah, Hagar (at first), Rebekah, the widow of Zarephath, and the matron of Shunem (also at first). The internal link between "acquiescence in the misfortune" and "disbelief in the annunciation" is evident in Abraham's ambivalent reaction to the declaration that Sarah will bear him a son. While he keeps his lack of faith inside himself—"Abraham threw himself on his face and laughed, as he said to himself, 'Can a child be born to a man a hundred years old, or can Sarah bear a child at ninety?' "—he openly expresses his acquiescence in his lot—"And Abraham said to God, 'O that Ishmael might live by Your favor' " (Gen. 17:17–18). The other protagonists of this type express their resignation via one of these two elements. On the one hand there is *acquiescence in the misfortune*—Hagar casts the child aside after despairing of his life (Gen. 21:15–16); Rebekah sees the pains of her pregnancy as a threat to her life—"If so, why do I live" (Gen. 25:22); and the widow of Zarephath would evict her lodger Elijah, who has supported her throughout the drought: "What have I to do with you, O man of God?!" (1 Kings 17:18). On the other hand there is *disbelief in the annunciation:* Sarah laughs to herself when she hears the announcement by the three men (Gen. 18:12–15), whereas the Shunammite openly rejects Elisha's words—"Please, my lord, man of God, do not delude your maidservant" (2 Kings 4:16). As already noted, Hagar and the lady of Shunem overcome their initial resignation each in her own way. In her despair, Hagar walks away from her son, "for she thought, '*Let me not look* on as the child dies' " (Gen. 21:16); but when she hears the good tidings of his deliverance and destiny she goes back to him and is no longer afraid to look: "Then God opened her eyes and *she saw* a well of water. She went and filled the skin with water, and let the boy drink" (v. 19). The lady of Shunem, on the other hand, originally rejects Elisha's promise as a vain delusion to which she dare not give credence; but once she does, despite everything, give birth, she knows that she must not acquiesce in his sudden death during the harvest and strives with all her might to get the man of God to restore him to life. While Hagar believes that the promised miracle will indeed come to pass, the Shunammite believes that the miracle already realized by the birth of her son cannot be nullified by his death. The first heeds God's words to her, and the second puts her trust in the promise incorporated in His earlier action on her behalf.

In contrast to the six heroes who are permanently or temporarily resigned to their fate, there is no sign of resignation in the words or deeds of the other five—Isaac, Rachel, Moses' mother, Manoah's wife, and Hannah (Danel the father of Aqhat also belongs to this category). Of Isaac we read only that "Isaac pleaded with the Lord on behalf of his wife, because she was barren" (Gen. 25:21). The heroic refusal of the four women we have mentioned (along with the Shunammite in the second half of her story) to despair of divine salvation is expressed by the combination of two or three elements. The first, *nonacquiescence,* includes a direct reference to the heroine's emotional state: Rachel rebels ("Give me children, or I shall die"— Gen. 30:1); Jochebed is encouraged by the special quality of the newborn ("when she saw how beautiful he was"—Exod. 2:2); Hannah rejects her husband's solace ("in her wretchedness, she prayed to the Lord"—1 Sam. 1:10); and the Shunammite is not afraid to press the man of God ("Let her alone, for she is in bitter distress"—2 Kings 4:27). The second element, *belief in the annunciation,* appears in two accounts (in addition to in the second part of the Hagar story): Manoah's wife strives to persuade her husband of the authenticity of the mysterious herald and the validity of his tidings, while Hannah returns to her composure and family after hearing Eli's blessing. The third element, *the woman's wisdom and resourcefulness,* refers to the vigorous struggle by each of these five women, in the course of which they must overcome the resignation and passivity (and sometimes even the lack of understanding and lack of agreement) of their husband and of other men. Moses' mother conceals the infant and later places him (with his sister's help) in a wicker basket among the reeds; Manoah's wife outdoes her husband in identifying the angel and understanding his message; Hannah exceeds both her husband and Eli in vowing and fulfilling; and the Shunammite excels her husband in recognizing the sanctity of the man of God and, in the second half of the story, surpasses her husband, Elisha, and Gehazi in bringing about the resurrection of her son. Rachel, too, never gives up, but she is the only one whose stubborn efforts—giving Bilhah to Jacob and purchasing the mandrakes from Leah—do not bear fruit; only after she prays to the Lord is she finally answered. In other words, all the men who are described alongside the struggling women fill only supporting roles and clearly belong to the antithetical type—those who acquiesce in the evil decree: Jacob rejects any responsibility for Rachel's barrenness ("Am I in the place of God, who has denied you fruit of the womb?"—Gen. 30:2); Amram takes no part in concealing the child or the efforts to save him; Manoah has difficulty believing the good news and asks for additional clarification ("please let the man of God that You sent come to us again"—Judg. 13:8); Elkanah offers his love as a substitute for ten sons; and the Shunammite doesn't even consider it necessary to tell her husband of the boy's death ("She answered: 'It's all right' " [2 Kings 4:23]).

Thus we see that resignation appears in *all* the scriptural accounts of birth and survival in various forms and at various levels, if not on the part of the main characters—Abraham, Sarah, Hagar (at first), Rebekah, the widow of Zarephath, and the lady of Shunem (at first)—then in the supporting cast—Jacob, Amram (implicitly), Manoah, Elkanah, and the Shunammite's husband (in the second stage). The protagonist who despairs because of his or her childlessness must be an essential component of the literary genre that glorifies the miraculous deliverance from this state, just as the psychological blocks to responding to the good news highlight its wondrous nature.

The birth or miraculous rescue is thus glorified at the expense of the honor of one or both parents. Abraham and Sarah try to internalize their laughter, but it is mercilessly exposed ("[God] replied, 'You did laugh' "—Gen. 18:15) and even imprinted on the memory of the future generations via the child's name, thereby asserting in the most credible fashion that the miracle far exceeds the limits of what could reasonably be expected to occur, that there is no limit to the Lord's power.[66] In those stories where resignation and lack of faith are manifested by a *secondary character*, this weakness is balanced by the fervent struggle of the female protagonist, motivated by her vigorous trust in the Lord who responds to prayers.[67] Even in the stories where acquiescence and despair are the lot of the *main character,* this frailty does not remain unbalanced. In general, these stories too are at pains not only to magnify and exalt the miracle but also to demonstrate *the worthiness of its beneficiary.* In both of the accounts about Abraham and Sarah and in the stories of the women of Zarephath and Shunem there is another major element—an act of loyalty or of loving kindness, which, although not directly linked with the barrenness, nevertheless makes the protagonist worthy of heaven's mercies. In Genesis 17 the commandment of circumcision both precedes and follows the announcement of Isaac's forthcoming birth. First it serves as a sort of premise from which one can infer the essential nature of the annunciation for the fulfillment of the covenant represented by "thus shall My covenant be marked in your flesh as an *everlasting pact*" (17:13). Later it is repeated, as a renewed affirmation that the partner in this covenant will be Isaac, the son who will shortly be born to Sarah: "I will maintain My covenant with him as an *everlasting pact* for his offspring to come" (v. 19). At the end of the story we read that Abraham wasted no time in fulfilling the commandment, and the magnitude of what he did is emphasized: "Abraham was ninety-nine years old when he circumcised the flesh of his foreskin" (v. 24).

Another act of kindness is described in Genesis 18 and in 2 Kings 4—extraordinary hospitality, clearly extended with no expectation of reward. The aged Abraham runs in the heat of the day to meet three anonymous travelers and begs them not to pass by without accepting his hospitality. Similarly, the Shunammite lady urges the man of God to eat in her house and even builds him a small attic chamber on her roof.[68] Similarly, the widow of Zarephath shares her bread with Elijah and accommodates him in the upper room of her house; because of the terrible famine that is raging at the time, however, this is not possible without some sort of recompense. In any case, it is her hospitality toward Elijah that entitles her to his intervention on her behalf—"will You bring calamity also upon this widow whose guest I am, and let her son die?" (1 Kings 17:20). By contrast, we have not read about any act of loyalty or kindness performed by Hagar when, in her despair, she casts her son under a scrub tree. What is emphasized in this account, from the outset, is that it is his father's merit that will protect Ishmael: "As for the son of the slave-woman, I will make a nation of him, too, *for he is your seed*" (Gen. 21:13).

In the other stories where the protagonist is not resigned but fights against the evil decree, we do not hear of any act of kindness. The very refusal to acquiesce, the belief in the good tidings, or the unrelenting struggle to undo the evil decree is considered to be an act of great merit in and of itself. Moreover, the mother's activism and her self-sacrificing devotion receive such great weight in these stories precisely because the miracle is not presented as the exclusive act of God (on the lines of "the Lord will battle for you; you have only to stand still"—Exod. 14:14), but as the interaction of man and God (as in the Amaleqite war, when Joshua fought and Moses aided him by holding up his arms toward heaven). This active partnership in the miracle by its beneficiary is expressed in the prayer for its realization (Isaac and Hannah), in forcefully demanding it from the prophet (the Shunammite), in preparatory deeds (Moses' mother and the Shunammite), in full compliance with the tidings of its advent (Hagar, Manoah's wife,

Hannah), in recognition of its miraculous nature and thanks for having merited it (Sarah, Rachel, Hannah, the Shunammite), and in a readiness to pay for it (Hannah). We may conclude that in Scripture a credible description of a miraculous birth or deliverance must include, in addition to the five elements of affliction, annunciation, destiny, miracle, and interpretation of the name, a sixth component—worthiness of the miracle. This merit, when external to the miracle, need only make the beneficiary worthy of it; when integrated through and through into the fabric of the miracle, it lauds the active participation by human beings in God's deeds on their behalf.

The story of Rachel deviates significantly from this generalization, though. Of all the women who wrestle to achieve motherhood, only her efforts are in vain. She gives her handmaiden to Jacob, in the hope that Bilhah will give birth on her knees and provide her at least with foster-motherhood (Gen. 30:3); as a result Bilhah does indeed bear Jacob two sons, whom Rachel names—Dan and Naphtali. But this act also stirs Leah—who has already borne four sons to Jacob—to give him her handmaiden Zilpah, resulting in two more sons who are named by Leah—Gad and Asher. Rachel does not give up yet and tries to get pregnant by virtue of the mandrakes found by Reuben. But the price is high: "he shall lie with you tonight, in return for your son's mandrakes" (v. 15). The mandrakes do Rachel no good, but Leah has another son—"[Jacob] lay with her that night. God heeded Leah, and she conceived and bore him a fifth son" (vv. 16–17). Only after Leah has borne yet another son, and a daughter to boot, is Rachel, too, finally remembered—"Now God remembered Rachel; God heeded her and opened her womb" (v. 22). She has traveled a long road from her crude demand of *her husband*—"give me children, or I shall die" (v. 1), through her various attempts to extricate herself from her affliction, till the day when God finally responds to her prayer (which is not explicitly mentioned in Scripture and is given the same weight in the story as the prayer of the multiparous Leah—see v. 17). True, Rachel never acquiesces in her barrenness; but neither is her struggle seen as a virtuous deed, nor is there any annunciation before she becomes pregnant. Perhaps the laggard remembrance of Rachel stems from the fact that she suffers more from jealousy of her sister than from barrenness itself and that her main goal is to rid herself of the shame of barrenness, and only secondarily to embrace an infant. This is supported both by the explicit statement at the beginning of the account, "Rachel became envious of her sister" (v. 1), and by the midrashic explanations of the names she gives to her foster-sons and first-born, all of which refer to herself and her struggle: "God has vindicated me; indeed He has heeded my plea" (v. 6); "A fateful contest I waged with my sister; yes, and I have prevailed" (v. 8); "God has taken away my disgrace" (v. 23); and "May the Lord add another son for me" (v. 24). Furthermore, Jacob, in his sharp retort—"Am I in the place of God, who has denied you

fruit of the womb?" (v. 2)—not only disclaims all personal responsibility for
her barrenness, he also indirectly and tacitly directs Rachel to the only address that has the power to help her.[69] But she does not pray to God, as
Isaac had. When finally she does become pregnant it is not in response to
her protracted prayers or some deed of devotion, wisdom, or perseverance.
We read only that God remembered her; perhaps the meaning is that her
suffering had overflowed its destined limits and the time had arrived for
her to bear a child. Hence the main point of the narrative is not to glorify
the miraculous birth of Joseph the dreamer and oneirocritic, but to provide
the foundation for the story of Joseph and his brothers, which hinges on
Jacob's excessive love for the sons of his old age, borne to him by his beloved
wife Rachel after much delay and suffering. If this evaluation is correct, the
story has only marginal affiliation with the other accounts of miraculous
births; that is, the building blocks of the genre serve chiefly as a contrasting
background that arouses expectations and comparisons. The fervent appeal to the Lord is conspicuously absent, as is the annunciation (found in
every other account of a miraculous birth). And since Rachel's refusal to
accept her barrenness stems chiefly from her rivalry with her sister, her
pregnancy is depicted not as a response by God but as His unilateral deed.

It is no wonder, then, that the narrative of Samuel's birth, the fullest
and most detailed instance of the miraculous birth genre to be found in
Scripture, is a sort of antithesis to the account of Joseph's birth. The family
situations from which the plot springs are very similar, although far from
identical. Jacob is married to two sisters, the younger of whom is very beautiful, much beloved, and barren; whereas the older, whom he was forced to
marry by her father's deception, is very prolific. Elkanah, too, has two wives,
only one of whom has children, but the tensions in this family are less acute:
the cowives are not sisters, we are told nothing about their physical appearance, and, although Elkanah loves Hannah more, there is no explicit reference to Peninnah's sufferings. Still, whereas Leah merits divine assistance
(Gen. 29:31) and the reader's sympathy, the more aggressive Peninnah
does not. On the contrary, our sympathies clearly lie with Hannah, who is
oppressed and humble, wretched and unhappy. Both Rachel and Hannah
are loved by their husbands to excess, but the difference between them
is overwhelming. We feel this most acutely when we compare the bitter
dialogue between Rachel and Jacob with Elkanah's comforting words to
Hannah—exchanges that have the same subject and even employ similar
language. Rachel importunes and threatens her husband: "Give me *sons* or
I shall die" (Gen. 30:1); Jacob angrily rejects her demand and ignores her
threat: "Am *I* in the place of God, who has denied you fruit of the womb?"
(v. 2). By contrast, Hannah asks her husband for nothing, while he for his
part does not ignore her weeping and fasting (which to a certain extent
express a decreased will to live). Endeavoring to comfort her, Elkanah inverts two central words in the dialogue between Jacob and Rachel: "Am *I*

not better to you than ten *sons?*" Whereas Jacob's "I" is a disclaimer of responsibility, Elkanah's is an acceptance of it. Whereas Rachel aggressively demands "Give me sons" and Jacob rebukes her that it is God who has denied her any "fruit of the womb," Elkanah holds his tongue with regard to the source of the evil and offers himself to Hannah (contrast "better *to you*" with "give *me*") as a substitute for the "sons" she has not dared to demand. Neither Rachel nor Hannah can accept their misfortune; but whereas Rachel does not ask for divine assistance, despite Jacob's implicit advice, Hannah does pray, despite Elkanah's suggestion that she make her peace with her situation. Hence their struggles are quite different. Rachel, motivated by jealousy of her sister, employs various and sundry stratagems to have children, while Hannah, motivated by her fervent desire to have a son, ignores her cowife and is willing to pay a heavy tax to God in return for the bounty of a male child. Whereas the midrashic interpretations of the names given by Rachel all refer to her struggles and her shame, those given by Hannah refer to her request for the son and his consecration to the sanctuary. When Rachel gives birth to her first-born she immediately asks for another son. Hannah bears additional sons and daughters thanks to Eli's initiative. Jacob perpetuates his excessive love for Rachel in the person of her son—"he made him an ornamented tunic" (Gen. 37:3)—thereby transferring the rivalry of the mothers to their children and engendering a conflict out of which Joseph emerges as the recipient and realizer of bold dreams. Hannah, on the other hand, completes the donation of her son to the service of the sanctuary—"His mother would also make a little robe for him" (1 Sam. 2:19)—thereby continuing to contribute her part to Samuel's destiny to serve as a holy man in Israel.

The pattern that is common to all the stories that belong to a particular genre is sufficiently flexible and varied to allow both full development of the unique nature of every one-time human event as well as variegated and rich development of the alternate possibilities latent in the common basic situation. The paradigm serves as a frame of reference that allows us to examine each component in the context of the expectations aroused by its parallels in the other stories (which the reader and hearer know both from Scripture and from external sources). These analogies and contrasts enrich and deepen the rhetorical possibilities and sharpen and intensify the meaning that can be extracted from each individual account and from all of them taken together.

All these stories exalt the miracle of birth or deliverance. From one perspective, however, they are divided into two groups: those in which the passivity and imperfect faith of their protagonists provide a tangible example of the distance between "Sarah laughed to herself" (Gen. 18:12) and "Sarah said 'God has brought me laughter' " (21: 6); and those that tell us not only that the Lord's power is always sufficient to work a miracle, but also that human beings are never impotent to bring divine salvation nearer and to play their role in this salvation. Within our story itself, Hannah's heroic struggle for motherhood is contrasted with her cowife's enmity, her husband's resignation, and the priest's lack of understanding; within the ambit of the genre as a whole, it is contrasted with the passivity of main and supporting characters and the fruitless activity of Rachel. Both women suffer at the hands of heaven and of mortals, but only Hannah manages to rise above the contention with her cowife and become a full partner in the miracle worked on her behalf. Rachel's legacy to her son Joseph is her beauty and personal charm, along with Jacob's love and the jealousy of Leah's sons. Only by virtue of a long course of pain is his personality tempered and his character purified until the ambitious adolescent who lords it over his brothers becomes their faithful and dedicated provider (Gen. 50:20–21). Samuel, however, serves in the sanctuary from his youth and, like his mother, knows how to win Eli's favor and assistance (1 Sam. 3:8–18). Even before his maturity the Lord appears to him; and when he does reach manhood—"All Israel, from Dan to Beersheba, knew that Samuel was trustworthy as a prophet of the Lord" (3:20). In the light of his miraculous birth, stamped with the double imprint of human prayer and divine response and of divine benevolence and human generosity, his course is plain before him. This two-way donation is the main significance of the account of his birth and is doubly expressed and summarized by the name Samuel, as interpreted by his mother: "I asked the Lord for him"—because the Lord gave him to a barren woman; but also "I, in turn, hereby lend him to the Lord." For her part she gives him back to the Lord, to serve Him all his days.

·2·

YOUNG SAMUEL'S CALL
TO PROPHECY

The Servitor Became a Seer

*But Saul said to David, "You cannot go to that
Philistine and fight him; you are only a youth,
and he has been a warrior from his boyhood!"*

1 Sam. 17:33

On the battlefield in the valley of Elah, victory goes to a shepherd lad,
whose pink cheeks and youthful beauty underscored his newness to warfare; similarly, in the sanctuary of the Lord at Shiloh, prophecy descends
on a young servitor, whose repeated mistakes in identifying the voice of
the Lord bring into relief that he is a novice in hearing the Lord's word.
Saul is wise enough to realize that the Lord, who has rejected him and his
house, may come to the aid of the lad who is throwing his life into the
breach; like that later monarch, Eli understands that the Lord, who is going
to deprive his line of the priestly dignity, may reveal Himself to the boy who
faithfully serves in His precincts. David's miraculous defeat of Goliath
proves to be the first and decisive step on the road to inheriting Saul's
kingdom; hearing the Lord's word, while lying on his bed in Shiloh, is the
first and decisive incident in Samuel's life and prepares him to inherit Eli's
leadership mantle. The two stories—very different with regard to plot, the
protagonists' characters, and literary genre—share a common theme: when
it is impossible to continue as before and the only hope lies in a new beginning, youth is transmuted from a disadvantage to an advantage.

The Literary Genre

There is no great difficulty in defining the compass of the story. It begins
with a reasonably detailed exposition (3:1–3), whose first sentence—"The
boy Samuel served the Lord before Eli" (v. 3:1a)—anchors the events to

51

come in the preceding account of Samuel's birth. Samuel is serving in the sanctuary as a result of his mother's vow—"I will dedicate him to the Lord for all the days of his life" (1:11)—and her irreproachable fulfillment thereof—"she brought him to the House of the Lord at Shiloh" (1:24). The story concludes with verse 21, which, according to all scholars, actually spills over into the beginning of 4:1—"and Samuel's word went forth to all Israel." Syntactically and thematically, this clause is linked to what precedes it; what is more, it has no connection with the second half of the verse (a fact reflected by the "section break in the middle of a verse" found here in a number of medieval Hebrew manuscripts). In addition to these exegetical difficulties, we cannot associate "and Samuel's word went forth to all Israel" with the episode of the battle at Aphek, because Samuel plays no part in that campaign and is not even mentioned in the next three chapters (4–6).

Determining the literary genre to which the story belongs is a rather more difficult undertaking. At first glance it seems perfectly obvious that our story is a call to prophecy. The chapter begins by pointing out that Samuel "*served* the Lord before Eli" (3:1), in an age when "prophecy was not widespread"; it ends with the notice that "all Israel, from Dan to Beersheba, knew that Samuel was trustworthy as a *prophet* of the Lord" (3:20) and that from that time forward the Lord continued to reveal Himself at Shiloh (3:21 and 4:1a). This contrast between the beginning and end of the story defines its subject: the revolutionary change in Samuel's status, from servant to prophet, and, by extension, in the status of prophecy itself, from scarce to widespread. Despite this clear internal evidence, many scholars who have investigated this genre and defined its principal lineaments— Zimmerli (*Ezechiel* 1, pp. 16–20), Kutsch ("Gideons Berufung"), Habel ("Form and Significance of Call Narratives"), and Richter (*Die sogenannten vorprophetischen Berufungsberichte*)—do not classify the story as a call to prophecy.[1] All four attempted to establish a clear literary paradigm, defined by a number of mandatory components that appear in a fixed or nearly fixed order, dictated by a common literary objective.

Habel, for example, saw the calls to prophecy as an application of the fixed form used to commission messengers for secular tasks and found in them the six elements that appear in the account of Abraham's dispatch of his servant to Haran (Genesis 24). The first of these components is the *divine confrontation* between master and messenger: suddenly the Lord (or His angel) appears (often when the recipient of the message is engaged in some routine activity, such as tending sheep or threshing wheat); the description of the miraculous vision usually involves the verb *r[.]h*, 'see'.[2] The second component is the *introductory word*—an introductory vocative addressed to the prospective messenger, followed by an explanation of the background situation: "Moses! Moses! . . . I have seen the affliction of My people in Egypt . . . " (Exod. 3:4–9).[3] Third is the *commission*—the delegation of the task by means of the verbs *h.l.k* ('come', 'go') and *š.l.ḥ* ('send'): "*Come*, therefore, I will *send* you to Pharaoh, and you shall free My people, the Israelites, from Egypt" (Exod. 3:10).[4] The fourth component is the *objection*—the messenger demurs at his appointment and declares his unwillingness to assume it: "Who am I that I should go to Pharaoh and bring the Israelites out of Egypt?" (Exod. 3:11).[5] This is followed by *reassurance and promises of assistance:* "I will be with you" (Exod. 3:12; Judg. 6:16).[6] The sixth element is the *sign* vouchsafed to the messenger, to remove all doubt that he has indeed been sent by the Lord: "That shall be your sign that it was I who sent you" (Exod. 3:12).[7]

Habel found this pattern in its pure form in the calls to Moses, Gideon, and Jeremiah and, with some elaborations and variations, in the calls to Isaiah, Ezekiel, and Second Isaiah (Isa. 40:1–11). Richter, who does not deal with the literary prophets, added to the calls to Moses and Gideon the account of the anointing of Saul (1 Sam. 9–10). He holds that the archetypal form is not the dispatch of messengers but the designation of a savior for Israel. Accordingly he enumerates five elements that are expressed almost identically in these three stories. First is the *description of the crisis* confronting Israel ("I have seen the affliction of My people in Egypt and have heard their outcry because of their taskmasters" [Exod. 3:7]; "I have seen My people [Septuagint: "the affliction of My people"], their outcry has come to Me" [1 Sam. 9:16]). The other four components are essentially similar to those identified by Habel: the commission, the objection, the reassurance, and the sign.

It is clear why these scholars do not include 1 Samuel 3 in the genre of the call to prophecy as they define it. Only the first two of Habel's six features—the *divine confrontation* ("the Lord came and stood there" [v. 10]) and the *introductory word* ("Samuel! Samuel! . . . I am going to do in Israel such a thing . . ." [vv. 10–11])—appear here, while none of Richter's five is in evidence. There is no description of a present danger, only a prophecy of future calamity. No specific task is imposed on the youth; hence he has no reason to refuse his commission and there is no objection to be overcome by means of reassurance or signs. Richter (*Die sogenannten vorprophetischen Berufungsberichte*) describes the scene as Samuel's first prophetic experience rather than his call to prophecy; whether there was such a call, and when it took place, Richter says, is not recorded (p. 175). This strange distinction, which, as noted, contradicts the clear evidence of the narrative itself,[8] illustrates how the methodology of form criticism misses the mark when it is based on the assumption that a literary genre is a rigid paradigm from which only minimal deviation is allowed. Not only does such an inflexible approach lead to the exclusion of unmistakable calls to prophecy, such as those of Joshua, Samuel,[9] and Elisha, it also imposes an excessive uniformity on analogous components and totally ignores motifs that appear in some call narratives but not others. If we abandon this formalistic approach, however, we can appreciate alternative elements that express similar ideas through different means, or even contrasting elements that derive their full significance from their deliberate deviation from the traditional form.[10] In the case of Isaiah's call, for example, Habel understands the prophet's question, "How long, my Lord?" (Isa. 6:11), as expressing his reservations about and even refusal to accept the task of hardening the people's heart.[11] But it is difficult to accept Habel's designation of God's reply, "its stump shall be a holy seed" (v. 13), as the motif of reassurance and encouragement. It seems to me that the purification of Isaiah's lips by the live coal and his volunteering to assume the mission obviate the need for the elements of reassurance and a sign in this particular call.

Furthermore, in order to understand Samuel's call we must broaden the spectrum of components and consider motifs that appear in only some of the call narratives. One of these is the messengers' *initial fitness* for their mission, expressed in their miraculous birth (or deliverance from danger), which marks them for this destiny while still in the womb (e.g., Moses, Samson, Samuel, and Jeremiah), as well as in their positive personal traits: Moses goes out to his brothers, sees their troubles, rescues the Hebrew who is being beaten, attempts to separate his quarreling brethren, and rescues the daughters of Jethro from the shepherds. Gideon, threshing wheat in the wine press, protests against the lot of his people, who are oppressed by the Midianites. Saul stands head and shoulders above the rest of the people, and "no one among the Israelites was handsomer than he" (1 Sam. 9:2). Elisha clings faithfully to Elijah despite the latter's three attempts to evade his company (2 Kings 2:2–6). Similarly, young Samuel is a faithful servant in the sanctuary even before the Lord's word is revealed to him.

But this initial fitness is counterbalanced by another motif, nearly its opposite—the *initial error*: those selected do not anticipate their election and consequently are at first mistaken about the identity of the voice that speaks to them. Moses turns aside to find out "why doesn't the bush burn up," and halts his inquiry only because of the explicit injunction, "Do not come closer. Remove your shoes from your feet, for the place on which you stand is holy ground" (Exod. 3:3–5). Gideon addresses the angel as "my lord" (Judg. 6:13). Saul is reluctant to take his servant's advice to consult the man of God about the lost asses and fails to recognize Samuel when he meets him at the city gate, asking instead, "Tell me, please, where is the house of the seer?" (1 Sam. 9:18). In like manner, young Samuel thrice fails to identify the source of the voice that calls him by name.

The third additional element is the nominee's *apprehension and misgivings* about the confrontation with those to whom he is sent. This is merely another facet of his doubts concerning his fitness for the mission, doubts that motivate his *refusal* to accept it (Habel's fourth element). Moses pleads,

"What if they do not believe me and do not listen to me, but say: The Lord did not appear to you?" (Exod. 4:1).[12] Joshua is promised, "No one shall be able to resist you as long as you live" (Josh. 1:5); Jeremiah and Ezekiel are reassured in almost the same word: "have no fear of them" (Jer. 1:8; cf. also 1:17–19) and "do not fear them" (Ezek. 2:6; cf. also 3:9). Similarly, Samuel "was afraid to report the vision to Eli" (1 Sam. 3:15).

A fourth element is that *the mission is imposed on the messenger* against his will. Though he can dissociate himself from its content and declare, with Jeremiah, "I have not longed for the fatal day" (Jer. 17:16), or ask, like Isaiah, "How long, my Lord" (Isa. 6:11), he cannot release himself from the mission itself. As Amos attests, "a lion has roared, who can but fear? My Lord God has spoken, who can but prophesy?" (Amos 3:8). In the same manner, Abraham makes his servant take an oath to find a wife for his son in Haran. The Lord admonishes Ezekiel not to be mutinous as his brethren have been—"Do not be rebellious like that rebellious breed. Open your mouth and eat what I am giving you" (Ezek. 2:8). Samuel likewise does not tell Eli what he heard during the night until compelled to do so by a fearsome oath (3:17).

The fifth element, the *initial recognition* of the newly consecrated prophet as an authentic messenger of the Lord, supplements the heavenly call with the first acceptance by those to whom the prophet is sent. Joshua, for example, cautiously tests his authority when he asks the two-and-a-half Transjordanian tribes to remember what Moses had commanded them to do (Josh. 1:13). Their response is to accept his jurisdiction: "We will do everything you have commanded us and we will go wherever you send us. We will obey you just as we obeyed Moses; let but the Lord your God be with you as He was with Moses!" (Josh. 1:16–18). The fifty disciples of the prophets accept Elisha as Elijah's successor: "They exclaimed: 'the spirit of Elijah has settled on Elisha!' And they went to meet him and bowed low before him to the ground" (2 Kings 2:15). Similarly, Eli recognizes the authenticity of the Lord's word as spoken by young Samuel: "It is the Lord; He will do what He deems right" (1 Sam. 3:18). Furthermore, the consecration story itself notes that this recognition soon became general: "All Israel, from Dan to Beersheba, knew that Samuel was trustworthy as a prophet of the Lord" (1 Sam. 3:20).

We see, then, that 1 Samuel 3 contains five elements found in many though not all of the call narratives. In itself this fact cannot outweigh the absence of other elements, on which account many form critics have excluded this chapter from the call narratives. For example, Gnuse (*Dream Theophany*, pp. 138–40) sees the absence of the *divine commission*—which he considers to be the crux of call narratives—as decisive evidence that our story should not be assigned to the genre. He goes further, arguing that the *objection*, which involves fear of Eli rather than of the Lord (v. 15), and the *reassurance,* spoken by the priest (vv. 16–17) rather than by the Lord, cannot be considered to be elements of a call narrative, because they do not express its essence—the task imposed by heaven on the neophyte prophet. Perhaps, though, we should associate the unique features of the story with the uniqueness of the situation it relates, since this is the only case in Scripture where the Lord reveals Himself to a child. Here too (see above, p. 33) form criticism must have recourse to a close reading (see below, pp. 61ff.), because that is the only way to properly evaluate whether the significant deviations from the usual call paradigm can be explained by the particular needs of a youngster who assumes the heavy burden of prophecy.

In place of the rejected classification, Gnuse (ibid., pp. 140–49) proposes seeing 1 Samuel 3 as an "auditory message dream," which is well documented in the ancient Near East and in Scripture. Unlike the visual dream (such as Jacob's ladder and the dreams of Joseph and Pharaoh), where the message is expressed through a symbolic vision that must be interpreted, in an aural dream the intent is clear and comprehensible (e.g., the dreams of Abimelech king of Gerar [Gen. 20:3–7] and of Jacob at Beersheba [Gen. 46:2–4]). Gnuse sees 1 Samuel 3 as fundamentally similar with regard to both the specified circumstances of the dream and the revelation itself, paralleling Oppenheim's findings (*Interpretation of Dreams,* pp. 184–245), as well as his own about accounts of dreams in the ancient Near East. The *circumstances* usually include three particulars:

(1) The location is holy ("in the temple of the Lord where the Ark of God was" [v. 3:3b]).
(2) The time is appropriate ("the lamp of God had not yet gone out" [v. 3a]).
(3) The dreamer is asleep ("Samuel was sleeping" [ibid.]).

The description of the *revelation,* too, contains many parallels:

(1) The deity calls the sleeper by name in order to rouse him ("Samuel" [vv. 4, 6, and 8]).
(2) There is divine self-identification (e.g., "I am the God of Bethel" [Gen. 31:13]; in our story, however, there is no need for this, because Eli has already identified the speaker [v. 9]).
(3) The deity makes a (visual?) appearance ("the Lord came and stood there" [v. 10a]).
(4) A message is delivered ("I am going to do in Israel such a thing . . . " [vv. 11–14]).
(5) The dreamer responds (e.g., Abimelech's "O Lord, will You slay people even though innocent?" [Gen. 20:4]; Gnuse [ibid.] hesi-

tatingly finds this in Samuel's words, "Speak, for Your servant is listening" [1 Sam. 3:10b]).

(6)   The dream has a formal termination (e.g., "Then Pharaoh awoke and it was a dream" [Gen. 41:7]; here, "Samuel lay there until morning" [1 Sam. 3:15a]).

The significance of the indications of time and place will be considered below, as part of our close reading. Here we need remark only that the sanctity of the location is not a necessary hallmark of the dream story. True, it is specified in three other dream stories—Jacob at Bethel and at Beersheba (Gen. 28:16 and 46:1) and Solomon at Gibeon (1 Kings 3:4–5); but it also occurs in three call stories that certainly do not involve dreams—the "holy ground" of Moses' consecration (Exod. 3:5), the "Temple" of Isaiah's first vision (Isa. 6:1), and the "mountain of God at Horeb" (1 Kings 19:8 and 13, according to our reading below, pp. 203–204). Just as the sanctity of the location is absent from the other scriptural dream narratives, it is not found in the other consecration stories either.

The verb *š.k.b*, 'lie down', appears seven times in 1 Samuel 3—once with reference to Eli and six times with reference to Samuel. In each place it can be understood as indicating sleep, but this is not imperative, as is attested by what would otherwise be the redundancy of a number of scriptural verses: "he *lay down* and fell asleep under a broom bush" (1 Kings 19:5); "Saul was *lying* asleep within the encampment" (1 Sam. 26:7). It is clear in any case that, unlike other dream narratives, where we are explicitly told that the dreamer is asleep (e.g., Gen. 15:12 and 28:16), wakes up (e.g., Gen. 41:4 and 7:1; Kings 3:15), or dreams (e.g., Gen. 31:10–11 and 37:5 and 9; Judg. 7:13), none of these terms appear here. It seems rather unlikely that the word *dream* would not appear in a story that its readers are supposed to classify as a "prophetic dream," and that neither would there be some other stylistic expression of this affiliation.

The vocative "Samuel" does indeed rouse the lad from his sleep; but instead of listening to the divine words addressed to him, he runs off to Eli. Gnuse offers no parallel for a divine call that occurs three times in a row and in vain, nor does he explain the significance of the misidentification of the voice in the context of a dream narrative. Whereas our approach views this as a legitimate variation on a typical element of the consecration narrative—the *initial error* (see above, p. 54)—Gnuse sees it only as an expression of the "literary artistry of the narrator, for it heightens the suspense and entertains the audience" (ibid., p. 145).

Samuel's reply, "Speak, for Your servant is listening" (v. 10b), cannot be considered a "dreamer's response" to the message that is being vouchsafed to him. It is simply his reaction to hearing his name called, equivalent to the "here I am" that frequently occurs in the *introductory word* element of call narratives. Moreover, the lad's failure to react to the news of the impending catastrophe is an important characteristic of our story, made all the more conspicuous by readers' expectations of an *objection,* which normally intervenes at this juncture.

Similarly, it is extremely forced to understand the narrator's remark that "Samuel lay there until morning" (v. 15a) as the conclusion of the dream, because it is very different from what we normally encounter in dream episodes. What is more, such a designation totally misses the main point, namely, that when Samuel does not run to Eli, as he has already done three times on this fateful night, it is the first manifestation of the profound change that the call has wrought in the mind and conduct of the lad who has in a fateful moment been transmuted from servant to prophet.[13]

The critical assessment of the alternative classification of our story reconfirms its designation as a call narrative that resembles the other call narratives not only in its theme and some elements but also in its objective—legitimizing the prophet as a trustworthy messenger of the Lord, an emissary who did not dare uncover the identity of the one who called him until it was made clear to him through Eli's authority; an emissary who did not seek his mission and even attempted to evade it; an emissary who announced the divine verdict without assuming to judge his superiors.

The Structure of the Story

The narrative of Samuel's call is divided into an exposition, three scenes, and an epilogue.[14] These five subunits are clearly indicated by three markers: (1) a partial change in the dramatis personae; (2) introductory statements (to the three scenes), in each of which Samuel is called (by the Lord or by Eli) and responds; (3) concluding statements (to the exposition and the first two scenes), in all of which we are told that Samuel was lying down, as well as where and/or when. The first scene is divided into three subscenes, which begin and end exactly like the first two main scenes:

Exposition (vv. 1–3)
Characters: Samuel and Eli
Setting: The middle of the night, at two locations in the sanctuary of the Lord
Opening sentence (of the entire story): "The boy Samuel served the Lord before Eli. In those days the word of the Lord was rare; prophecy was not widespread."
Concluding sentence: "The lamp of God had not yet gone out, and *Samuel was lying down* in the temple of the Lord. . . . "

Scene 1, divided into three almost identical subscenes (vv. 4–9)
Characters: The voice of the Lord, Samuel, and Eli
Setting: As in the exposition (Samuel moves between the two locations)

Scene 1a (vv. 4–5)
Opening sentence: "The Lord *called out* to Samuel, and *he said,* 'here I am.' "
Concluding sentence: " 'Go lie down again.' So he *went* back and *lay down.*"

Scene 1b (vv. 6–7)
Opening sentence: "Again the Lord *called,* 'Samuel!' . . . He *said,* 'Here I am.' "
Concluding sentence: " 'Go back and *lie down*' (followed by the narrator's aside that "Samuel had not yet experienced the Lord").

Scene 1c (vv. 8–9)
Opening sentence: "The Lord *called* Samuel again, a third time. . . . He *said,* 'Here I am.' "
Concluding sentence: "Samuel went to his place and *lay down.*"[15]

Scene 2 (vv. 10–15)
Characters: The Lord and Samuel
Setting: Later that same night, in the place where Samuel is lying down
Opening sentence: "The Lord came and stood there, and He *called* as before: " 'Samuel! Samuel!' And Samuel *answered,* 'Speak, for Your servant is listening.' "
Concluding sentence: "Samuel *lay* there until morning; and then he opened the doors of the House of the Lord" (followed by the narrator's aside that "Samuel was afraid to tell the vision to Eli").

Scene 3 (vv. 16–18)
Characters: Eli and Samuel
Setting: The next morning, at an unspecified location in the sanctuary
Opening sentence: "Eli *called* Samuel and said, 'Samuel, my son'; and he *answered,* 'here I am.' "
Concluding sentence: "Samuel then told him everything, withholding nothing from him. And [Eli] said, 'It is the Lord. He will do what He deems right.' "

Epilogue (vv. 19–21, 4:1a)
Characters: Samuel
Setting: A protracted period, in Shiloh
Opening sentence: "Samuel grew up and the Lord was with him: He did not leave any of his predictions unfulfilled."
Concluding sentence (of the entire story): "And the Lord continued to appear at Shiloh: the Lord revealed Himself to Samuel at Shiloh with the word of the Lord; and Samuel's word went forth to all Israel."

Fishbane ("I Samuel 3," p. 193) noted the concentric structure of the story (ABCB′A′). The epilogue (A′) inverts the opening (A), and within this *inclusio* the first scene (B), where Samuel thrice errs and believes that it is Eli who is calling him, is intimately related to the third scene (B′), where Eli really does summon the boy. The second scene (C), in which the Lord appears to Samuel and tells him of the impending downfall of the house of Eli, stands by itself at the center of the story and constitutes its climax.

Juxtaposition of the introduction and epilogue so as to highlight their links (see below) reveals that the three verses of the latter relate to the three statements in the first verse of the introduction. On the other hand, in the epilogue there is no echo of the second and third verses of the introduction, probably because they are really the specific exposition for the first scene (as indicated by the words "one day" that introduce them):

(1a) The boy Samuel *served the Lord* before Eli.

(19–20) Samuel *grew up* and the Lord was with him: He did not leave any of his predictions unfulfilled. All Israel, from Dan to Beersheba, knew that *Samuel was trustworthy as a prophet* of the Lord.

(1b) In those days *the word of the Lord* was rare; prophecy was not widespread.

(21, 4:1a) And *the Lord continued to appear* at Shiloh: the Lord revealed Himself to Samuel at Shiloh with *the word of the Lord;* and Samuel's word went forth to all Israel.

(2–3) One day, Eli was asleep in his usual place; his eyes had begun to fail and he could barely see. The lamp of God had not yet gone out, and Samuel was sleeping in the temple of the Lord where the Ark of God was.

Samuel is present in all five parts, Eli only in the exposition and scenes 1 and 3. He is merely referred to in the second scene and makes no appearance in the epilogue. This absence intensifies the contrast between the beginning of the story, where Samuel is a lad who serves the Lord "before Eli," and its conclusion, where he is an adult accepted as a prophet of the Lord by "all Israel, from Dan to Beersheba." Still, even though the story describes the lad's call to prophecy and the proliferation of prophecy in Shiloh against the background of the priest's old age and progressive blindness and the impending fall of his line, Eli does play an active and essential role in Samuel's consecration. The titles suggested below for the five sub-units should make this very clear:

Exposition: Samuel serves in the sanctuary, where the priest Eli is old and the word of the Lord is rare

Scene 1: The lad misidentifies the voice that calls to him; Eli prepares him to hear the word of the Lord

Scene 2: Samuel hears the Lord's pronouncement of the destruction of Eli's house and fears to report it to the old man

Scene 3: Eli forces Samuel to tell him what the Lord said and confirms its truth and justice

Epilogue: All Israel recognizes Samuel as a trustworthy prophet; the Lord's word is heard frequently in Shiloh.

Samuel has need of Eli's active assistance, both before and after the divine revelation to him, because as a boy he does not have the internal resources to overcome the emotional impediments to his consecration to prophecy. Before the lad can do the two things required of a prophet—*hear* the word of the Lord without awe and *speak* it to its intended recipient without fear—the elderly priest must prepare him for the divine revelation and force him to confront its human object. Thus the unusual structure of this call narrative reflects its unique status as the initiation of an adolescent whose master and teacher—who is not a prophet and has never heard the word of the Lord—is involved in the episode as both distant witness and direct subject of the revelation and can thereby help the lad hear the voice that calls to him and give utterance to its message as a trustworthy emissary.

A Close Reading

Exposition: Samuel serves in the sanctuary,
where the priest Eli is old and the word of the Lord is rare (vv. 1–3)

At the end of the account of Samuel's birth we are told that Samuel fully realized the vocation set for him by his mother in her vow: "Samuel served the Lord as an attendant, girded with a linen ephod" (1 Sam. 2:18). This conclusion is actually the starting point for the present narrative; hence the exposition repeats the essence of that verse, adding that Samuel worked under the supervision and guidance of the priest: "The boy Samuel served the Lord before Eli" (3:1a). The first hint that the theme of the story is prophecy, probably in relation to the lad, appears in the second half of the verse with its emphatic parallelism: "In those days the word of the Lord was rare; prophecy was not widespread." After this initial introduction of the characters and definition of the problem—the absence of prophetic revelation—the exposition proceeds to describe the special circumstances of the night on which the fateful events transpire. At first sight the words "one day" (v. 2a) should lead directly into the plot, but they are in fact followed by a long parenthetical sentence.[16] This temporal indication should be understood in a general sense, with "day" equivalent to "some undefined time" (cf. Gen. 6:5 and Exod. 9:18), since it is followed immediately by the information that "Eli was asleep in his usual place"—that is, on this occasion he is not "sitting on the seat" (1 Sam. 1:9) as he normally does in the daytime. The first part of verse 3, if we understand it literally, in fact indicates that the plot begins in the middle of the night.[17]

Commentators, ancient and modern, are given to a metaphorical understanding of the three statements that follow in the exposition—Eli's advanced blindness, the "lamp of God" that has not yet gone out, and Samuel's lying down in the temple of the Lord. Beyond the inclination to prefer metaphors (which many feel to be richer and more profound than the literal meanings), the specific motive for metaphorization is different for each of the three statements: (1) the irrelevance of Eli's blindness to the plot; (2) the vivid picture of the lamp of God that has not yet gone out (buttressed by the frequent metaphorical uses of "lamp" in Scripture, e.g., "lest you extinguish the lamp of Israel" [2 Sam. 21:17]; "the lifebreath of man is the lamp of the Lord" [Prov. 20:27]; "When His lamp shone over my head" [Job 29:3]); (3) the talmudic prohibition (BT Qiddušin 78b) against sitting, let alone lying down, in the sanctuary.

It is suggested, then, that we understand "he could barely see" as a metaphor for Eli's loss of divine inspiration or as a metonymous expression for his spiritual decline. Yet we certainly encounter elderly blind men who are endowed with a piercing prophetic vision, such as Jacob (Gen. 48:10–19) and Ahijah the Shilonite (1 Kings 14:4–6). What is more, later in our story Eli successfully unravels the perplexing situation in which the lad finds himself ("then Eli understood that the Lord was calling the boy" [1 Sam. 3:8]), evinces a profound intuition that allows him to infer from Samuel's behavior that the Lord has appeared to him during the night (v. 17), and even displays extraordinary religious and moral courage when he accepts the divine verdict against his house (v. 18). All of this is so incompatible with metaphorical blindness that we are forced to a literal understanding of the progressive description, "his eyes had begun to fail and he could barely see," as a concrete manifestation of his extreme old age, which contrasts sharply with Samuel's youth and prepares readers for the changing of the guard. At the same time, Eli's blindness also serves as a backdrop for the lad's anxiety about the old man's well-being, reflected in his immediate response every time he thinks Eli needs his help during the night (vv. 4–9) or day (v. 16).[18]

More common is the interpretation of "the lamp of God had not yet gone out" as a metaphor for Eli's leadership, which had not yet lapsed when the Lord first appeared to Samuel. The aggadist sees this as one manifestation of the divine mercy that grants Israel a continuity of spiritual leadership:

> "The sun rises, and the sun sets" (Eccles. 1:5). R. Abba said: "Don't we know that the sun rises and the sun sets? But before the Holy One Blessed Be He allows the sun of one righteous man to set he causes the sun of another righteous man to rise. . . . On the day that R. Aqiba died, our master [R. Judah the Prince] was born; . . . on the day that our master died, R. Ada bar Ahava was born. . . . Before the Holy One Blessed Be allowed Moses' sun to set he caused Joshua's sun to rise. . . . Before Joshua's sun set, Othniel's sun rose. . . . Before Eli's sun set, Samuel's sun rose. (Genesis Rabba 58,2)

It is rather difficult to see this impressive midrash as the contextual meaning of the present verse. First of all, when the setting is the sanctuary it is reasonable to understand the "lamp of God" literally, as synonymous with the "perpetual lamp" kindled in the seven-branched candelabrum, which burned "from evening to morning" (Exod. 27:21; Lev. 24:3).[19] Second, mention of where Eli and Samuel are lying down requires an accompanying indication of time, to make it clear that the reference is to sleeping at night and not an afternoon siesta (e.g., 2 Sam. 4:5). In addition, we later encounter a temporal cue that makes more sense when it follows the preceding one: "Samuel lay there until morning" (1 Sam. 3:15).[20] It may well be, in addition, that the indication that the revelation occurs in the latter part of the night is intended to reinforce its credibility, as was first suggested by Gersonides: "At this hour, which is ordained for true dreams, prophecy began to reach him." More recently, this idea has been buttressed by classical and Mesopotamian parallels cited by Oppenheim (*Interpretation of Dreams*, pp. 225, 240–41), Gnuse (*Dream Theophany*, pp. 17–18 and 143–44), and Hurowitz ("Eli's Adjuration," n. 17).

It was R. Abraham Maimonides (*Responsa*, §30, p. 39) who first proposed a metaphoric understanding of "Samuel was lying down in the temple of the Lord where the Ark of God was" (v. 3:3b) as a bold solution to a difficult halakic problem: "It is forbidden to sleep in the Sanctuary, but this 'lying down' is not to be understood literally. Rather, it is the first stage in prophecy. In the stages of prophecy there are arcane secrets. With regard to what can be understood of them—it is forbidden to reveal how it transpired—'It is the glory of God to conceal a matter' (Prov. 25:2)." This is a drastic application of the basic principle of legitimate metaphorization accepted by the Babylonian-Iberian school of exegesis: it is *permissible* to understand a verse metaphorically only when we are *compelled* to do so because it cannot be interpreted literally.[21] Whereas he sees no impediment to a literal interpretation of Eli's sleeping (because this was clearly in another place), he finds it absolutely imperative to interpret Samuel's lying down metaphorically, that is, as a mysterious prophetic state (which may not be expounded in public) that descended upon Samuel while he stood in the sanctuary at night.[22] Hardly less daring are the three syntactic solutions proposed by predecessors of R. Abraham Maimonides (of which the last two were probably known to him): (1) detaching the second half of verse 3 from the first half and linking it with verse 4: "in the temple of the Lord where the Ark of God was, the Lord called out to Samuel" (Rashi); (2) rearranging verse 3 to read, "the lamp of God had not yet gone out in the temple of the Lord where the Ark of God was, and Samuel was lying down" (BT Qiddušin 78b; Midrash of the 32 Exegetical Principles, Principle 32; R. Jonah Ibn Ganach, *Sefer Ha-riqmah*, ch. 33, p. 361; this is also the reading of the Authorized Version); (3) filling in the (ostensibly) laconic text of the verse—"Samuel was lying *in the court of the Levites, and the voice was heard* in the Temple of the Lord" (Targum Jonathan).

Rather than this, we may consider a semantic solution, based on the assumption that here the "Temple of the Lord" does not have its restricted sense but refers to the entire Temple compound. We find a similar ambiguity with reference to the term *miškan*, which usually refers to the innermost structure made of boards and covered with draperies of linen (Exod. 26:1; 36:8 and 20; 40:19), but sometimes to the entire enclosure, including the walled-off courtyard surrounding it (Exod. 25:9; Num. 1:53, 31:30).[23] If so, the meaning is not that Samuel lay down in the Holy of Holies, "where the Ark of God was" (though not the seven-branched candelabrum, according to Exod. 26:35 and 27:21), but rather in "his place" (v. 9), which is in the Temple of the Lord—where the Ark of God is—in the broad sense. Since it is clear that this lying down was not an intentional preparation for revelation (see n. 13), the reference to the ark's presence in the sanctuary must be meant to emphasize the extreme devotion of young Samuel, who, like Joshua, Moses' servant (Exod. 33:11), never leaves the sanctuary of the Lord where the ark is—at night he sleeps there, as watchman, and in the morning, as doorkeeper, he opens the gates of the "House of the Lord."[24]

Scene 1: The Lord calls, Samuel errs,
and Eli prepares him to hear the word of the Lord (vv. 4–9)

The first scene is dominated by the dramatic irony produced by the narrator's providing his readers with information concealed from the characters, allowing us to observe from a height their errors and hesitant attempts. Maximum identification with the characters (which would be attained by having us share their indecision and surprises) is sacrificed for the sake of greater awareness of the ironic dissonance between the sublime event and its total misunderstanding. Readers know from the start that it is the Lord who is calling Samuel; they assume that he too is aware of this and that his response, "here I am," is directed to Him who had called. When Samuel runs to Eli, though, we discover that he was responding to his master and not to God. We naturally attribute this astonishing error to the lad's complete innocence and wonder why the Lord did not avert it by calling in a voice clearly not Eli's, or, even better, by identifying Himself as He did to the Patriarchs ("I am the God of your father Abraham" [Gen. 26:24]; cf. Gen. 28:13, 31:13, and 46:3), to Moses (Exod. 3:6), and to the Israelites at Sinai (Exod. 20:2). It must be that the *initial error* (see above, p. 54) is essential here as an element of the call narrative, perhaps all the more so because its hero is a youth.

Samuel responds to the summons like the faithful servant he is. From his couch he immediately cries out, "Here I am," runs to Eli (like Abraham running to greet his guests [Gen. 18:2] and Rebekah running to the well to draw water [Gen. 24:20]); when he reaches him he again says, "here I am" and adds, "for you called me." Nor does he return to his place until Eli dismisses him with the words, "I didn't call you; go lie down again." Samuel's devoted service is a further development of the theme of his *initial fitness* for prophecy (see above, p. 54), since there can be no greater tribute to his character. Yet it is also an external and internal obstacle to the correct identification of the voice that is calling to him from on high.

The call is heard a second time, and Samuel's response seems to be identical to his previous one. Through five slight variations—only one of which is reflected in the Septuagint, apparently because of its general tendency toward uniformity[25]—the narrator adds additional lines to his sketch of the lad and the old man and makes us aware of the delicate relationship between them.

The First Call (vv. 4–5)	**The Second Call (v. 6)**
The Lord called Samuel,	Again the Lord called, "Samuel!"
and he said, "Here I am."	—
He ran to Eli	Samuel *rose* and *went* to Eli
and said, "Here I am; for you called me."	and said, "Here I am; for you called me."
But he said, "I didn't call;	But he said, "I didn't call, *my son;*
lie down again."	lie down again."
So he went and lay down.	—

The switch from reported speech to the vocative "Samuel!" may not be just stylistic variation; it is perhaps intended to make the repeated summons more distinct and tangible. It is clear, however, that the youth's failure to respond "here I am" from where he is lying down reflects a real change in his behavior. When he heard the first call, the devoted servant hastened to respond to his master as quickly as possible. This time, not only does he not announce that he is coming, he does not *run* to Eli as before. Instead, the text clearly indicates that he *rose* from his bed (an action omitted in verses 4–5 in order to convey his quick response) and *walked* to Eli. When he reaches his master's bedchamber he repeats the deferential "Here I am, you called me" exactly as in the first instance. There is, however, a small addition in Eli's response, which indicates that the blind old man has noticed the change in the youth's conduct and understands his feelings. Eli does not interpret Samuel's lack of haste as a sign of laxity in fulfilling his duty but as an expression of the ambivalent situation that the repeated summons has created for the boy. Samuel is torn between his strong desire to obey his master's call quickly and his growing anxiety that he may be disturbing Eli for no reason. Eli puts Samuel's mind at ease with the phrase of endearment "my son," which conveys to us the magnitude of Samuel's devotion to Eli and the depth of Eli's fatherly affection for the lad.[26]

Verse 7 constitutes a short hiatus in the development of the plot. The narrator heightens the dramatic irony by means of an explanatory comment that echoes the explanation in the exposition (v. 1b) with regard both to the topic (the status of prophecy) and the emphatic phrasing (repetition of the same idea in different words). Samuel misidentifies the nature of the voice because at this stage of his life he has not yet experienced the word of the Lord—in other words, because this voice is itself the very beginning of his call to prophecy.[27]

Samuel's reaction to the third call is nearly identical to his response to the second one.[28] This uniformity underscores the fact that Samuel cannot avoid returning and offering his services to Eli, and also that it never even occurs to him that it may be God who is calling him. Only with Eli's help can he even conceive of this possibility. By now Eli has deduced the truth: there have been three successive calls in a place where there is no other living soul, and delusion or error does not seem to be a plausible explanation. Hence Eli counsels Samuel how to respond if he is called a fourth time. Note that it is not a lack of intelligence that prevents Samuel from understanding what Eli does comprehend but rather a profound psychological block. Is it possible that God is calling him rather than Eli the priest? Conversely, Eli apprehends what Samuel fails to see, not because of superior intelligence or experience, but because he lacks the inhibitions generated by self-interest. Nothing deters him from assuming that God might turn to the young servant and pass over the old priest! In this way, Eli's humility compensates for Samuel's.

We are not told that Samuel went and lay down again after the second call, since readers can infer this by analogy with what transpired after the first summons. After the third call, however, this detail is related with particular emphasis; instead of the earlier "he went and lay down," we now read, "*Samuel* went *to his place* and lay down" (v. 9). This damper on the pace of the narrative—four words in Hebrew instead of the two that sufficed

after the first call and the total omission of this detail after the second—
reflects the hesitation with which the youth goes to lie down "in his place"—
the same place where he has already heard the voice three times and can
expect to hear it again. The next time there will be no mistake as to its
source.

Scene 2: Samuel hears the Lord's declaration of the punishment of Eli's house
and fears to report it to the old man (vv. 10–15a)

> *Jeremiah said: "I will tell you what I resemble—a*
> *high priest whose lot came up to administer the*
> *bitter waters. They brought the woman to him; he*
> *uncovered her head and loosened her tresses, took*
> *up the cup to give her to drink—and looked at*
> *her and saw that it was his mother! He began*
> *sobbing, saying: 'Woe is me, my mother!'*
> *(Jer. 15:10)"*

Pesiqta Rabbati 26

In the first scene, the voice seemed to be calling from afar (this is another
reason why Samuel believes it is Eli who is calling). In scene 2, however, the
voice seems to come from close by, because it is accompanied by firm awareness of the Lord's presence: "The Lord came, and stood there" (v. 10a).
The Lord is described as "coming" to Abimelech king of Gerar (Gen. 20:3),
Laban the Aramean (Gen. 31:24), and Balaam (Num. 22:9), whereas in the
description of Jacob's dream at Bethel we read, as here, "the Lord was standing beside him" (Gen. 28:13). In none of these passages is there any indication as to how this divine presence made itself tangible, unlike the case,
for example, of Moses on Mount Sinai: "The Lord came down in a cloud;
He stood with him there" (Exod. 34:5).

From this undefined proximity the Lord again calls to Samuel "as before" (v. 10)—that is, with the same quality of voice as on the earlier occasions. Nevertheless, the lad musters the courage to reply only after his name
is repeated;[29] even then he cannot bring himself to utter the Lord's name.
Eli instructed him to answer: "Speak, Lord, for Your servant is listening."
But he lacks the courage to say more than "Speak, for your servant is listening."[30]

In retrospect, the content of the revelation justifies Samuel's shrinking
from contact with the awesome deity. For even before the Lord discloses
the terrible calamity He is going to wreak on Israel, He warns him that
"both ears of anyone who hears about it will tingle" (v. 11; cf. Jer. 19:3).
This confirmation of the unappealable verdict on Eli's house, which has
already been made known to the priest by the anonymous man of God
(2:27–36), is much more terrible for Samuel. If he was not previously aware
of the divine decree, it is shocking news; and in any case it is terrible for
him because he must listen to its condemnation of his master and teacher

Eli as bearing ultimate responsibility for the moral degradation of his sons.[31] In a single terrible moment the youth is transformed from a servant hurrying to obey the old priest's instructions to a prophet who bears in his heart a double burden—foreknowledge of imminent and irrevocable punishment (v. 14) and awareness of the sin that caused it (v. 13).

Some would emend *wf-higgadti lo* ("I declare to him" [v. 13]) to the imperative *wf-higgadta lo* = "tell him."[32] But there is no justification for this conjectural emendation, which would introduce the motif of the "prophetic commission" into our story. Rather, we should assume that the youth's call to prophecy differs from all other similar accounts in that here the Lord is content merely to reveal His secret to the one He is calling to be His servant. Accordingly, we should read *wf-higgadti* as a conversive future, with the sense "I shall demonstrate to him."[33]

In the absence of an explicit order to convey this message to Eli, readers wonder whether Samuel, in youthful innocence, will run to Eli as before to tell him that the Lord did call him a fourth time, as the old man had foreseen. But not only does Samuel remain in his bed until morning, when he gets up he proceeds to open the doors of the house of the Lord. Again we are astonished: Why should the narrator recount this trivial fact? Evidently Samuel's opening the doors is a further intensification of the motif of the "reluctant prophet." The youth tries to persevere in his servitor's role and conceal the change in his status under the mask of his daily routine.[34] He hopes that Eli will infer from his silent activity that there was no fourth call during the night. This attempt to conceal from his master the momentous event that has befallen him is so out of character for the loyal servant that the narrator feels obliged to intrude and explicitly reveal what is going on inside the youth's soul: "Samuel was afraid to report the vision to Eli" (v. 15).[35] Here the motif of the reluctant prophet is supplemented by another element: an aversion to confronting the subject of the message—a confrontation that is all the more painful in this case because it is his revered guide in the sacred rites, whom he loves as a father, whom the Lord has condemned to suffer such dire punishment.

The boy is unable to put into words his reluctance to become the bearer of the divine message (unlike Moses, who protests, "Who am I that I should go to Pharaoh?" (Exod. 3:11), and Jeremiah, who pleads, "Ah, Lord God! I don't know how to speak, for I am still a boy" (Jer. 1:6). He can only draw some small comfort from the fact that the Lord does not enjoin him to deliver the message to Eli.

Scene 3: Eli forces Samuel to tell him what the Lord said,
and confirms its truth and justice (vv. 15b–18)

The end of scene 2 leaves readers in tense anticipation of what will happen next. Samuel's consecration to prophecy seems to have reached a dead end.

For one thing, it is far from clear why the Lord revealed such unbearable knowledge to the lad as his initiation. Nor is it clear how the Lord's message will be conveyed to its object if the young prophet is not charged with doing so. Much to our surprise, the initiative now passes to Eli, who again displays great insight that is not hampered by anxiety. The elderly priest senses that the lad is avoiding him and has something to hide. He calls him in the morning—in the same manner as during the night—and augments the boy's name with the term of endearment, "my son," thereby indicating that, whatever may have transpired in the interim, it will not come between them: Samuel will continue to be as dear to him as before. Samuel promptly responds, "here am I," hoping that this time—unlike during the night—his old and blind master is calling him only to request some service or other. Instead, the courageous old man firmly demands that Samuel tell him, "What was it that he told you?" (v. 17a), without concealing from him "anything of all that he told you" (v. 17b). Note that just as Samuel omitted the vocative "Lord" from the response that Eli prescribed to him, so now Eli does not mention the Lord, neither at the beginning or the end of his demand, when he knows in his heart that the message refers to him and his house. In this way the narrator expresses one of the central themes of all call narratives: the recoiling from the dreadful encounter with divinity. Moses covers his face because "he was afraid to look at God" (Exod. 3:6); Ezekiel falls on his face (Ezek. 1:28), as does Daniel (Dan. 10:8–9). Young Samuel, who remained on his couch when he sensed the presence of the Lord, buries what he heard deep in his heart, unable to react. Even Eli, who dares to demand that the lad disclose the divine message, cannot bring himself to pronounce the name of the Lord his God.

This indirect language, which reflects Eli's trepidation, is accompanied by a fullness of phrasing that reflects the priest's determination. He does not ask Samuel whether he heard the voice a fourth time but impresses the lad with his utter certainty that he has experienced prophetic revelation and begins straightaway with the demand for information about the content of that revelation: "What was it that he [the Lord!] told you?" Instead of waiting for an answer, he makes plain to the boy that even though he is aware that the divine message is grim and refers to him, nothing should be concealed: "Hide nothing from me." But Eli does not stop with this; he turns his request into a peremptory demand by adjuring the lad with a terrible oath, emphasizing that the disclosure must be full: "Thus and more may God do" to him if he does not do as he is bidden and if he should "hide anything from me of all that he [the Lord!] told you."[36] This wordy and repetitious argument aims at uprooting from Samuel's heart all doubts concerning Eli's unyielding determination to hear everything that the Lord told the lad, however terrible its import (this resembles Boaz's long-winded attempt to persuade Ruth of the unfeigned sincerity of his invitation to glean in his fields until the end of the harvest [Ruth 2:8–9]; something

similar comes through in Abimelech's solicitation of Abraham's good will
[Gen. 21:26]). Readers, for their part, can infer from Eli's wordiness the
extent of his awareness of the incredible difficulty the lad is facing in having
to serve as the bearer of the Lord's message to him and of his obligation
to help the boy by means of a forceful demand that he prophesy (as the
old priest will later help the Benjaminite who fled the rout of the Israelites
to disclose the full severity of the disaster with his gentle words of encouragement, "What happened, my son?" [1 Sam. 4:16]).[37]

Finally the lad succumbs to this pressure and does as requested—"Samuel then told him everything and hid nothing from him" (v. 18a)—obviously unable to anticipate the nobility of the old priest's reaction to the
harsh verdict: "[Eli] said: 'It is the Lord; He will do what seems good to
Him'" (v. 18b). Thus Eli helps Samuel become a prophet not only by compelling him to recount everything he heard, but also by extracting from
the message its double truth: its divine origin ("It is the Lord") and its
justice ("He will do what seems good to Him [*ha-ṭov be-ʿeinaw yaʿaśeh*]").[38]
From Samuel's threefold nocturnal mistake Eli deduced that the lad was
hearing a voice calling to him.[39] And from his profound understanding of
the heart of the boy who has served him with such love that he knows the
terrible things he heard could not come from his soul but only from the
Lord Himself.

At this point, all the other call narratives (except for the consecration
of Joshua) feature a *sign* that confirms to the prophet—and, eventually, to
his public as well—that it is indeed the Lord who is addressing him. Here,
though, this confirmation comes from Eli, who has been involved in the
revelation both as onlooker and subject.[40] When he accepts the divine decree, Eli releases the youth from the burden that always afflicts prophets
of rebuke and destruction: the fear that his listeners may identify the messenger with his message and view the Lord's prophet as a "troubler of Israel." We read in Exodus Rabbah (3,1):

> R. Joshua ha-Kohen said in the name of R. Nehemiah: When the Holy
> One Blessed Be He revealed Himself to Moses, Moses was a neophyte at
> prophecy. The Holy One Blessed Be He said: "If I appear to him in a loud
> voice, I will frighten him. If I appear to him in a soft voice, he will scorn
> prophecy." Said the Holy One Blessed Be He: "What shall I do?" He ap-
> peared to him in the voice of his father Amram. Moses said, "What does
> Father want?" Replied the Holy One Blessed Be He: "I am not your father,
> but the God of your father. I have come to you with a lure in order not to
> frighten you."[41]

This homiletical elaboration on the consecration of Moses is the plain
meaning of the consecration of Samuel. The Lord comes to the youth Samuel using a lure and reveals Himself in the voice of his master and teacher.

Through his misidentification of the speaker Samuel obtains Eli's guidance as to the appropriate way to receive the word of the Lord and his active assistance in conveying the terrible message without fear of inflicting pain. In the end, Eli provides him with direct confirmation of his status as an authentic messenger of the hidden sender.

Epilogue: Samuel is recognized throughout Israel as a trustworthy prophet, and the Lord's word is heard frequently in Shiloh (vv. 19–21, 4:1a)

The epilogue shatters the temporal unity of the story and adds to the day of Samuel's consecration to prophecy a period of undefined duration, during which the lad became a man. The statement that "Samuel grew up and the Lord was with him" (v. 19) resembles, in both content and structure, verses about Moses ("Moses grew up and went out to his kinsfolk" [Exod. 2:11]) and Samson ("The boy grew up, and the Lord blessed him. The spirit of the Lord first moved him . . . " [Judg. 13:24–25]). Here too the intention is evidently not to describe the process of maturation but to note its end— when Samuel grew up he began to function as a prophet, and then it became clear that the Lord was guiding his words, since "all of his words"— counsels, predictions (such as whom the Lord had chosen to be king), and solutions to mysteries (such as the location of the lost asses of Kish)—came to pass. Note that because of Samuel's tender age when he is called, the element of *objection* is expressed only indirectly, through his reluctance; hence there is no need for *reassurance and promises of assistance*, either. This is why the reassuring formula, "I shall be with you," is not spoken by the Lord to His messenger, but related by the narrator to his readers: "the Lord was with him" (v. 19). In consequence of his unbroken chain of successes, Samuel won general recognition as a true prophet: "All Israel, from Dan to Beersheba, knew that Samuel was trustworthy as a prophet of the Lord" (v. 20). How this recognition actually spread is reflected in what Kish's servant tells Saul when they cannot find the missing asses: "There is a man of God in that town, and the man is highly esteemed; everything that he says comes true" (1 Sam. 9:6).

The element of the *commission* is a crux of call narratives. Since consecration to prophecy is not a goal in itself, the commission always includes a definition of the task that the messenger is charged with accomplishing. Moses is entrusted with taking the Israelites out of Egypt (Exod. 3:10); Joshua, with apportioning the land to them (Josh. 1:6). Isaiah is commanded to "harden the people's heart" (Isa. 6:9–10); Jeremiah, "to uproot and to pull down, to destroy and to overthrow, to build and to plant" (Jer. 1:10); and Ezekiel, to speak the word of the Lord to "that nation of rebels" (Ezek. 2:3–5). The story of Samuel's consecration lacks this element and contains no definition of his mission. Because of his youth he assumes the burden of prophecy only gradually; hence he receives no specific commission when he is first called, nor any definition of his prophetic role. But what could not be stated by the Lord can be reported, in the exposition and epilogue, by the narrator. The narrator introduces the story by describing the distress that will be eliminated by Samuel's vocation: "In those days the word of the Lord was rare; prophecy was not widespread" (v. 3:1b). He concludes it with the abundance of prophetic inspiration that descended on Israel through the trustworthy prophet. In the body of the story, between the second and third calls, the narrator notes that "Samuel did not yet know (*yada͑*) the Lord; the word of the Lord had not yet been revealed (*yiggaleh*) to him" (v. 7). In the epilogue he uses the same verbs to underscore the fundamental change that has transpired as a result of Samuel's call: "All Israel, from Dan to Beersheba, knew (*wa-yeda͑*) that Samuel was trustworthy as a prophet of the Lord. And the Lord continued to appear at Shiloh: the Lord revealed himself (*niglah*) to Samuel at Shiloh <with the word of the Lord>" (vv. 20–21).[42] In other words, not only has Samuel come to know the Lord in the meantime, but from this time forward, all Israel, from one end of the country to the other, is aware that Samuel is the faithful emissary of the Lord.[43] Not only did the Lord appear to him on that fateful night, Samuel enjoyed thereafter continual divine revelations.

Hannah intended her son to serve in the Temple "all the days of his life" (1:11) and to dwell in Shiloh "for good" (1:22). But neither mother, priest, nor child could imagine that the temple servitor would become a prophet; that as long as he resided in Shiloh—evidently until its destruction—the Lord would appear to him frequently in His sanctuary; and that this revelation would spread throughout the country: "Samuel's word went forth to all Israel" (4:1a).

•3•

SAUL AT ENDOR

*The Narrative Balance between the Pitiless Prophet
and the Compassionate Witch*

> *Always let your left hand push away and your
> right hand bring closer, not like Elisha, who
> pushed Gehazi away with both hands.*
>
> BT Soṭa 47a

The fatal verdict pronounced by the prophet Samuel—"tomorrow you and your sons will be with me" (1 Sam. 28:19)—paralyzes Saul with fear and causes him to fling himself down full-length on the ground. By contrast, the kind words and generous dinner served by the witch of Endor encourage the king and restore his spirits. We can only wonder at this division of roles between the prophet of the Lord, whose righteousness is unquestioned, and the sinful woman, culpable for a capital crime (Lev. 20:27). Samuel berates Saul for disturbing his rest and castigates him mercilessly with his guilt and weighty punishment. The witch, however, risks her life at the beginning of the story, when she complies with his request, and subsequently becomes a compassionate and generous hostess. How should we understand the startling contrast between these two characters, whose conduct on the human plane seems to be so much at odds with their respective religious stations?

The Structure of the Story and Its Literary Genre

The compass of the story (28:3–25) is self-evident, because it is set in the middle of the account of how David was saved from having to join the Philistine campaign against the Israelite forces (28:1–2 and ch. 29). It can be divided into four parts: an extended exposition and three scenes. The exposition (vv. 3–7) reports the background of the situation—events that transpired over a relatively protracted period and at various places, starting

73

TABLE 3.1: The Structure of the Story of Saul at Endor

Exposition (28:3–7): Anxiety on the eve of the battle, in the absence of a divine response	I. (28:8–14): A desperate act: Getting a medium to raise the prophet
[Opening verse: "Now Samuel had died . . . Saul had put away all the (mediums) who consult *ghosts* from the land."]	[Opening verse: "Saul disguised himself . . . and set out with two men. *They came to the woman* by night."]
Saul in a double affliction:	The medium accuses Saul:
1. "He saw and his heart trembled with fear."	1. "*Why* are you laying a snare for my life, *to get me killed?*"
2. "But the Lord did not answer him."	2. "*Why have you deceived me?* You are Saul!"
Saul surprises his attendants:	Saul verifies the identity of Samuel:
"Find me a woman who consults ghosts, so that I can go to her and inquire through her."	1. "What do you see?"
	2. "What does he look like?"
[Concluding verse (returns to the start of the exposition): "There was a woman in Endor who consulted *ghosts*."]	[Concluding verse: "He bowed low with his face to the ground and did obeisance."]

with Samuel's death and burial in Ramah, through the elimination of mediums and spiritualists from the entire country, and concluding with the order given by Saul, encamped at Gilboa, to locate "a woman who is a medium" (v. 7). The story proper, set entirely in the witch's house, is divided into three scenes, sharply demarcated by a change of protagonists. Scene 1 (vv. 8–14) involves Saul and the witch; scene 2 (vv. 15–20), Saul and Samuel; scene 3 (vv. 21–25), Saul and the witch again.

The exposition presents and explains the story's extraordinary starting point—Saul's decision not to accept the silence of the heavens but instead to breach it unflinchingly, even if this means consulting a medium. In the first scene Saul calms the medium's fears and persuades her to raise Samuel for him. In the second scene, Samuel crushes Saul by bringing him face to face with the bitter truth he had sought to ignore and evade. In the third scene, the medium helps Saul overcome his collapse and gather the strength to set out on his last journey. The antiparallelism between the first and third scenes is marked from their very first verses: "And they [Saul and his men] came to the woman" (v. 8a), versus "and the woman came to Saul" (v. 21a). The borders between the scenes are highlighted and emphasized also by the linguistic and thematic affinities between their closing verses (see table 3.1). The first scene concludes with the king's expression of extreme respect for the prophet, whose succor he hopes to merit in his hour of distress: "he bowed low in homage with his face to the *ground*" (v. 14b;

TABLE 3.1—*continued*

II. (28:15–20): A result too hard to bear— hearing the bitter truth	III. (28:21–25): Unexpected favor—emotional and physical sustenance in advance of the final test
[Opening verse: "Samuel said to Saul."]	[Opening verse: "*The woman went* to Saul."]
Samuel attacks Saul:	The medium coaxes Saul:
1. "*Why have you disturbed me* by raising me up?"	1. "Your handmaid listened to you; I *placed* my life in my hands."
2. "*Why do you ask me,* seeing that the Lord has turned away from you and has become your adversary?"	2. "Let me place a morsel of bread before you."
Samuel prophesies the outcome of the battle:	The medium feeds Saul:
1. "The Lord will deliver the Israelites who are with you into the hands of the Philistines."	1. "He got up from the *ground* and sat on the bed."
2. "Tomorrow you and your sons will be with me."	2. "She set this before Saul and his courtiers and they *ate*."
[Concluding verse: "Saul flung himself prone to the *ground*. . . . *He had not eaten* anything all day and all *night*."]	[Concluding verse (returning to the beginning of scene 1): "Then they rose and left the same *night*."]

cf. 2 Sam. 24:20). The second scene ends with Saul's utter exhaustion and total despair: "Saul flung himself prone on the *ground* . . . for he had *not eaten* anything all day and all *night*" (v. 20). The third scene, and with it the story as a whole, closes with the revival of Saul's physical and spiritual strength, which permits him to return to the point from which the story began: "They *ate* and then they rose and left the same *night*" (v. 25b). This verse links up, antithetically, with the end of the second scene (v. 20). It also constitutes an *inclusio* with the beginning of the first scene (v. 8)—another nocturnal journey by Saul and his two servants, but this time in the opposite direction and with the king's heart, now emptied of all false hopes, filled with determination of a new sort.

Two structural principles reinforce the narrative balance between the prophet, who rejects Saul with both hands, and the witch, who comforts him with equal determination. The first principle has already been mentioned, namely, the bracketing of the devastating confrontation between king and prophet by two scenes in which Saul is heartened by the medium's assistance and human sympathy. The second structural principle is the formal resemblance between how the witch speaks in the first scene and how Samuel speaks in the second scene. Each utters two strong personal indictments of Saul, and all four are phrased as rhetorical questions introduced by the word *lamah*, 'why'. When the medium hears the request put to her by the unidentified stranger, she accuses him of knowingly placing her life in danger, since he is surely aware of what Saul has done to all the mediums and spiritualists in the country: "*Why* are you laying a snare for my life, *to get me killed?*" (v. 9). When she discovers his true identity, she considers his disguise to be proof of his evil intentions: "*Why have you deceived me?* You are Saul!" (v. 12). Similarly, Samuel's first words revile Saul for disturbing his rest among the shades: "*Why have you disturbed me* by raising me up?" (v. 15). Finally, when Saul tries to justify himself and explain his motives, the prophet remonstrates that Saul's very inquiry is senseless: "*Why do you ask me,* seeing that the Lord has turned away from you and become your adversary?" (v. 16). There is a difference, however: the medium's accusations stem from her *fear*, and their sting fades completely after Saul manages to reassure her that she will not come to harm; whereas the prophet's charges stem from *anger*, which, far from being alleviated by Saul's attempt to vindicate himself, is actually intensified. Thus the formal parallel highlights the essential contrast between the medium's initial opposition, which quickly turns into collaboration (in the first scene) and ultimately into generous assistance (in the third scene), and the prophet's conclusive opposition, which leaves open no door for change or hope: "Tomorrow you and your sons will be with me" (v. 19).

The story of Samuel's prophecy of the destruction of the House of Saul resembles, in both theme and plot, that of Ahijah the Shilonite's prophecy of the destruction of the House of Jeroboam (1 Kings 14:1–18). Both belong to a literary genre that might be called "prophetic stories about heavenly decrees concerning a dynastic change." The genre also includes the stories of Saul's transgression in the Amaleqite war (1 Sam. 15) and of Ahab's expropriation of Naboth's vineyard (1 Kings 21), in both of which we find the two main elements that typify the genre—fierce condemnation of the king's trespass and a prophecy that he will lose his kingdom. There are differences between the first two and the last two, which require that they be assigned to different subgenres. The first two stories (1 Sam. 28 and 1 Kings 14) could be subtitled, "a royal attempt to manipulate prophecy results in the *revelation* of a heavenly decree of dynastic extinction"; the latter two (1 Sam. 15 and 1 Kings 21), by contrast, are "prophetic stories about a serious transgression that *causes* a heavenly decree of dynastic extinction." The former do not describe a grave offense by the king, in whose aftermath the prophet is sent to announce that God has rejected him and his house. Instead, both begin with a description of the difficult situation in which the king finds himself, which requires him to consult a prophetic oracle. The king approaches the prophet in a less-than-straightforward manner and learns, not only that there is no escape from this calamity, but also that in fact it betides the end of his kingship. As further evidence that the marked similarity between the stories of Saul and of Jeroboam does in fact stem from their affiliation with the same genre and not from an influence of one on the other or from intentional resemblance between them, we can add to our sample the prophecy of the destruction of the house of Eli delivered by the nameless man of God (1 Sam. 2:27–36). Although this prophecy is not set into an action story and refers to a priestly rather than a royal house, the comparison helps define the subgenre. In addition to castigation of the cumulative sin and the decree of rejection passed on the family, the divine decree against Eli contains another typical element: the tidings of the dramatic death of the heirs as a sign of the Lord's rejection of their father. This triple comparison is summarized in table 3.2, which shows that almost all of the eleven components are found in the stories of Saul and of Jeroboam, and no fewer than six in the story of Eli.[1]

The first and second components are the king's affliction and his consultation with the prophet. Saul's problem is military, that of Jeroboam son of Nebat, medical; both despair of escaping through their own powers and in their distress turn for help to the prophet of the Lord. Since neither of them can do so directly and openly, they feel compelled to conceal their identities (the third element). Saul disguises himself so as not to arouse the medium's fears (and perhaps also her enmity); Jeroboam most likely tells his wife to do so because he wanted to obtain a "neutral" prophecy, not darkened by the heavy shadow of his sins.[2] Saul seeks to evade the silence of heaven by getting a medium to raise the spirit of the dead prophet, whereas Jeroboam hopes to get around the divine anger by sending the child's mother to the prophet in disguise. Even though their motives are quite different, in keeping with the specific circumstances of each story, the deeds themselves—and particularly their literary functions—are extremely similar. This applies in particular to the two functions of the fourth element—the unexpected prophetic disclosure of the disguise—in both stories. The first function is to serve as a bald warning that any attempt to manipulate the prophet's response will fail, expressed in the similar rhetorical questions hurled at the disguised visitors: "Why have you deceived me? You are Saul!" (1 Sam. 28:12); "Come in, wife of Jeroboam. Why are you disguised?" (1 Kings 14:6). The second function is to serve as a preliminary sign of the prophetic validity of the response to their questions (see detailed discussion below, pp. 79–80).

The next two elements—the transgression and the retribution—are also found in the prophecy about the house of Eli (which enters the comparative table here). The two together constitute the distinguishing feature of the genre, although there is also a certain flexibility regarding their order (this is not reflected in the table). Generally the reason (namely, condemnation of the sin) precedes the sentence (namely, extinction of the dynasty). This order prevails in the prophecies of the man of God to Eli and of Ahijah the Shilonite to Jeroboam (as well as in the second subgenre—see 1 Sam. 15:13–29; 1 Kings 21:18–24—and in the mixed genre [Daniel 5:18–28]);

TABLE 3.2: Prophetic Stories about Royal Attempts to Manipulate a Prophecy, Which Lead to the Revelation of a Divine Decree of Dynastic Extinction

The dynasty	Affliction	Consultation with the prophet	Disguise	First sign: Exposure of the disguise	Accusation	
					Election conveys obligations	Breach of obligation
House of Eli (1 Sam. 2:27–36)	—	—	—	—	"I *gave* to your father's house all offerings by fire of the *Israel*ites."	"Why, then, do you maliciously trample upon the sacrifices and offerings? . . . You have honored your sons more than Me."
House of Saul (1 Sam. 28:3–25)	Philistine assault and heavenly silence	Saul . . . set out with two men. They came to the woman by night."	"Saul disguised himself; he put on different clothes."	The witch: "*Why* have you deceived me? You are Saul!"	[In an earlier episode]: "I am the one the Lord sent to anoint you king over His people *Israel*" (1 Sam. 15:1).	"Because you did not obey the Lord and did not execute His wrath upon the Amaleqites."
House of Jeroboam (1 Kings 14:1–18)	Illness of Jeroboam's son Abijah	"[Jeroboam's wife] left and went to Shiloh and came to the house of Ahijah."	"Disguise yourself so that you will not be recognized as Jeroboam's wife."	The blind prophet: "*Why* are you disguised?"	"I *made* you a ruler over My people *Israel*."	"You have acted worse than all those who preceded you."

only Samuel's words to Saul at Endor begin with the sentence, "the Lord has torn the kingship out of your hands"; continue with the reason, "because you did not obey the Lord"; and come back to conclude with a more severe phrasing of the sentence, "tomorrow you and your sons will be with me". Each of these two main elements can be broken down into subelements. In the prophecies to Eli and Jeroboam (and in Samuel's earlier prophecy to Saul [1 Samuel 15]), the prophet begins his condemnation of the transgression of the elect by highlighting the favor of the divine election. As against the tendency of those in power to see divine election as a

TABLE 3.2—*continued*

The dynasty	Retribution		Another sign: Death of the heir(s)	Speedy fulfillment of the sign	Fulfillment of the retribution: Death of the head of the dynasty
	Extinction of the dynasty and election of a successor	Terrible blow against Israel			
House of Eli (1 Sam. 2:27–36)	"I will break your power and that of your father's house . . . and I will *raise up* for myself a faithful priest."	—	"Hophni and Phinehas— they shall both *die* on the same day."	[In a separate episode]: "Eli's two sons, Hophni and Phinehas, were *slain*" (1 Sam. 4:11).	In a separate episode]: "[Eli] fell backward . . . and broke his neck and *died*" (1 Sam. 4:18).
House of Saul (1 Sam. 28:3–25)	"The Lord has torn the kingship out of your hands and has *given* it to your fellow, to David."	"The Lord will *give* the Israelites who are with you into the hands of the Philistines."	"Tomorrow you and your sons will be with me."	[In a separate episode]: "The Philistines struck down Jonathan, Abinadab, and Malchishua" (1 Sam. 31:2).	[In a separate episode]: "Saul grasped the sword and fell upon it . . . and *died*" (1 Sam. 31:4).
House of Jeroboam (1 Kings 14:1–18)	"I will sweep away the House of Jeroboam utterly. . . . The Lord will *raise up* a king over Israel."	"[The Lord] will *forsake* Israel because of the sins that Jeroboam committed and led Israel to commit."	"As soon as you set foot in the town, the child will *die*."	[Part of the story]: "As soon as she stepped over the threshold of her house, the child *died*."	—

natural state of affairs that will endure forever, the three prophets retort that their election was a gift from on high and that its continuation depends on obedience. In all three prophecies, the sentence has two aspects: extermination of the present dynasty on the one hand, and establishment of its successor on the other. In the stories of Saul and Eli another painful aspect is added: the people, too, will suffer for the sin of the king.

The dismal future facing the three dynasties is given dire representation by the prophetic sign whose fulfillment will prevent any possibility of delusion about the inevitability of the sentence pronounced against the dynasty: the dramatic death of Jeroboam's son, of Eli's two sons, and of Saul's three sons. The more moderate sign accorded Jeroboam does not entail his own death as well, whereas the double and triple bereavement of Eli and Saul also involve their own deaths and the extinction of their dynasties.

A literary genre is based on many common elements, found in the same order. Such a pattern has great rhetorical power because it expresses the inner logic of the plot, which epitomizes the meaning of the story. Both Saul and Jeroboam attempt to ignore the profound breakdown of their relationship with the deity who made them king over His people, and they fail to draw the necessary conclusions from the severe admonitions delivered to them: Saul endeavors to overturn the heavenly decree by killing David; Jeroboam continues the cult of Bethel despite the prophecy of the man of God from Judah. Even though their contact with the emissary of divine election is broken off (with regard to Saul and Samuel this is stated explicitly—1 Sam. 15:35), they still rely on him indirectly when they find themselves in severe distress. The failure of this attempt at repression is the common theme of the two stories—the veil is stripped away from the manipulative consultation with the prophet and the temporary adversity uncovers the inevitable final destruction.

A Close Reading

Exposition: Anxiety on the eve of the battle in the absence of a divine response (28:3–7)

> *They shall wander from sea to sea, and from*
> *north to east; they shall run to and fro to seek the*
> *word of the Lord, but they shall not find it.*

Amos 8:12

The exposition, more elaborate than is usual in scriptural narratives, places the story on a solid footing of information. The manner in which the facts are reported—interspersed with a glimpse of Saul's apprehension (v. 5b) and a brief dialogue with the king's courtiers concerning the immediate success in locating a medium (v. 7)—is meant to stir readers to a degree of sympathy for the king in his distress and to a measure of understanding of the highly irregular action he is about to take. The prophet Samuel is dead, buried in his home town; no assistance or guidance, or even admonition and reproof, can be expected from him. Acting on his own initiative, Saul has rid the country of mediums and spiritualists; this certainly redounds to his credit. The Philistines have mobilized their forces and are encamped in battle array in Shunem, in the heart of the Jezreel Valley. Saul meets this challenge by mustering all the Israelite forces and setting up camp opposite the enemy, on the northern slopes of Mount Gilboa. Given the Philistines' overwhelming numerical superiority, Saul is deeply apprehensive. His fear is intensified when he realizes that all the usual avenues for inquiring of the Lord have been closed off: "Saul inquired of the Lord, but the Lord did not answer him, either by dreams [by means of a dream-diviner—see Deut. 13:2] or by Urim [by means of a priest—see 1 Sam. 14:36] or by prophets [other than Samuel]" (v. 6). Thus he feels compelled to consult the spirits of the dead through a medium who somehow escaped the systematic liquidation of her colleagues. He instructs his servants to locate a medium, adding that when they find one he will go to her, probably because her fear of the medium-exterminating king would make it impossible to bring her to the camp, not to mention the embarrassment such an action would cause him.[3] We are not told that the courtiers started searching, but rather that they informed the king, evidently at once, that such a woman could be found in Endor. Saul must have seen this initial success as a hopeful sign.

Scene 1 (28:8–14): A desperate act—getting a medium to raise the prophet

> *Egypt shall be drained of spirit,*
> *And I will confound its plans;*
> *So they will consult the idols and the shades*
> *And the mediums and the spiritualists.*

Isa. 19:3

The first scene opens with shameful disguise in "different clothes" (v. 8a) and nocturnal stealth.[4] His disguise permits Saul to relate openly to the forbidden aspect of the magical technique he asks the medium to apply for him. For when he says to her, "please divine [*qosomi*] for me by a ghost" (v. 8b), he uses the very same term that Samuel had employed to him in his harsh rebuke following the Amaleqite war: "For rebellion is like the sin of divination [*qesem*], defiance, like the iniquity of teraphim" (1 Sam. 15:23). On that occasion, the furious prophet had equated rebellion and defiance with the sin of divination and idolatry; now the equation is inverted, and the sin of divination expresses rebellion and defiance.[5] At this stage, Saul has still not told the medium whom to raise: "Bring up for me the one I shall name to you" (v. 8b). This secretive tone may have heightened the persecuted woman's suspicions. She responds with the grave allegation that his total indifference to the risk to which he is knowingly exposing her is tantamount to scheming to ensnare her in the commission of a capital offense. Her rhetorical question, "why are you laying a snare for my life, to get me killed?" (v. 9), expresses not only her refusal to comply with his request, but also her profound moral disgust at his readiness to imperil her life.

The confrontation is marked by strong dramatic irony. When the medium speaks to the disguised Saul about her fears of Saul, who has exterminated the mediums and diviners, not only has she no inkling that the king could sink so low as to require her services, she believes that he remains true to his path and continues to threaten her existence. The disguised king is accompanied, to his own detriment, by his bygone image as a vigorous monarch whose edicts deter the medium from pursuing her profession. As a result, both he and we realize the extent to which the external step of donning "different clothes" is linked with denying his own inner identity and values.

So as to allay the medium's fears and dispel her suspicions, Saul must guarantee her, in the most persuasive manner possible, that she will come to no harm by fulfilling his request. He takes an oath in the name of the Lord that she will not be punished for violating the Lord's commandment and the king's decree: "*As the Lord lives*, you will not be caught in a transgression over this" (v. 10).[6] In addition to the grave internal contradiction in its content, the oath itself is actually the total inversion of another oath that Saul had sworn in similar circumstances in the past. When the Lord failed to respond to his inquiries about continued pursuit of the Philistines routed at Michmas, he swore to exact the full measure of the law from whoever it was whose sin had caused the oracle to fall silent: "*As the Lord lives* who brings victory to Israel, even if [the transgression] was through my son Jonathan, he shall be put to death!" (1 Sam. 14:39). In that distant time Saul knew that when heaven is silent, it is an expression of divine displeasure, and that it was his royal duty to placate God by uncovering the sin and punishing the transgressor. Now, however, he considers the Lord's silence to be an ordinary "broken connection" that can be mended through magic. Juxtaposition of the two oaths makes plain that the sin of divination is indeed rebellion in the fullest sense of the word: unable to cope with the true significance of the mute oracles, Saul endeavors to compel the Lord to answer him.

Saul's oath satisfies the witch, who expresses her consent by requesting further instructions: "Whom shall I bring up for you?" (v. 11). He replies at once, almost in her own words: "Bring up Samuel for me." The harmonious collaboration is ruptured straight away when the medium sees Samuel (according to the report of the narrator in v. 12)[7] and somehow realizes who her visitor is (precisely how is far from clear to us, although it seems not to have required explanation for readers of antiquity).[8] The penetration of his disguise undercuts his credibility and the validity of his oath. The medium erupts in a heart-rending cry of despair and castigates him crudely, with no respect for his majesty: "Why have you deceived me? You are Saul!" (v. 12). Saul, for his part, discloses no signs of embarrassment and manages to calm her and still her fury by means of a simple, "Don't be afraid," followed by the relevant question: "What do you see?" (v. 13). Throughout the story, its hero is consistently called Saul; only here do we read, "The king answered her." Evidently this emphasis on his majesty is meant to convey to readers the authoritarian tone of voice in which he tells her not to be afraid of him and quickly goes on to ask precisely what she has seen. His interest in what she perceives, but he does not, is evidence of the sincerity of his desire to speak with Samuel. She understands that he really is interested in raising Samuel's ghost, not in incriminating her, and that his disguise was not meant to entrap her, but only to make it easier for him to request her assistance. The fact that the medium provides a matter-of-fact answer to Saul's question demonstrates that the deception no longer frightens her; rather, it has become a pathetic proof of the gravity of her visitor's condition and the honesty of his intentions.

From Saul's point of view, however, this unexpected unmasking is a first proof of the woman's supernatural powers. The fact that her sight of the ghost reveals to her what is hidden beneath the "different clothes" is a striking confirmation that she is speaking the truth when she answers his question and says: "I see a divine being coming up from the earth" (v. 13b). Something similar happens to the wife of Jeroboam son of Nebat when she goes to ask Ahijah the Shilonite whether her son will recover from his illness. Her husband tells her, "Go and disguise yourself, so that you will not be recognized as Jeroboam's wife" (1 Kings 14:2). But when the blind prophet hears her footsteps on the threshold of his house, he greets her by name: "Come in, wife of Jeroboam. Why are you disguised? I have a harsh message for you" (ibid., v. 6).[9] In both texts, the unmasking of the suppliant serves to eliminate a priori any possibility of evading, by calling into question the reliability of the speaker, the harsh prophecy about to be uttered.

The narrator has already informed us that the medium saw Samuel (v. 12). Saul, however, still cannot know this, because she told him only that she sees "a divine being coming up from the earth" (v. 13)—evidently because in her eyes the main thing is to stress the divine qualities of the awesome figure rising from the ground.[10] Her loud shriek and penetration of his disguise have already made it clear to Saul that she is speaking the truth; but it is still crucial for him to know whether she has really succeeded in raising Samuel. So he asks another question—"What does he look like?" (v. 14a)—just as King Ahaziah of Israel asks his emissaries, "What sort of man was it who came toward you and said these things to you?" (2 Kings 1:7). Just as Ahaziah identifies Elijah from the messengers' description of his appearance and garb—"A hairy man with a leather girdle around his loins" (ibid., v. 8)—so too Saul recognizes Samuel from the medium's description of the spirit she has raised: "It is an old man coming up, and he is wrapped in a robe." The validity of the two descriptions of prophets evidently stems from the fact that the medium had never seen Samuel, nor Ahaziah's emis-

saries Elijah; hence the inquisitive kings are impressed by the full corre-
spondence between the description and their recollections of the prophets
in question.

The narrator's report of Saul's certainty—"Then Saul knew that it was
Samuel" (v. 14)—indicates the importance he attached to the establishment
of a reliable connection with Samuel. The entire first scene stands under
the sign of clarifying identities: the medium unmasks the true identity of
her visitor, who had sought to conceal it by discarding his royal garments;
Saul identifies Samuel by the latter's prophetic robes. At the end of this
sequence of events, Saul stands, without his royal vestments, before the
prophet wrapped in his prophetic cloak (cf. 1 Sam. 15:27). The king has
arrived here like a thief in the night, but the prophet has been raised in
his full authority. Saul is quite aware of this disparity and makes no attempt
to obscure it. On the contrary, he displays full respect to the prophet—"he
bowed low with his face to the ground and did obeisance" (v. 14b)—thereby
giving candid expression of his utter dependence on Samuel's words.

Scene 2 (28:15–20): A result too hard to bear—hearing the bitter truth

> The Lord said to Samuel, "How long
> will you grieve over Saul, seeing I have
> rejected him as king over Israel?"

1 Sam. 16:1

Samuel does not tell Saul that necromancy is in itself "abhorrent to the
Lord" (Deut. 18:11–12) and that raising the spirit of a prophet of the Lord
is a particularly abhorrent deed. Instead of employing such objective language, Samuel hurls a distinctly subjective accusation at Saul: "Why have
you disturbed me by raising me?" (v. 15). This very moment Saul has prostrated himself before Samuel, hoping to placate him and enlist his assistance; yet here the prophet castigates him for disturbing his rest in the
underworld and forcing him to rise into the world of the living. It seems
unlikely that this presentation of the sin of necromancy as an act that does
personal injury to the spirit raised is meant to mitigate the severity of the
transgression; since Samuel goes on to speak in caustic personal terms, it
is more plausible to assume that his intention is to add the injury to himself
to the sin of consulting ghosts. In this way he makes it crystal clear that he
is not Saul's ally and that, like the Lord, he too has rejected him as king
over Israel.

Even though Saul already realizes that his hoped-for advocate has
become his accuser, he attempts to blunt the sting of Samuel's rhetorical
question by pretending to understand it as a straightforward request for
information, inviting an explanation in response. Saul's words of self-
justification are meant not only to illustrate the extent of his distress and
of his need for Samuel's guidance but also to present, in the most favorable

light possible, the irregular nature of his appeal to the dead prophet. Saul
resorts to various rhetorical devices to accomplish this twofold task. He
stresses the exigency of his military predicament by referring to the war in
the present tense: "The Philistines are warring against me" (v. 15). On the
other hand, Saul presents the affliction of God's silence as serious but not
fundamental by suggesting that this is a new phenomenon: "God has turned
away from me and answers me *no more*" (v. 15). It is quite likely that Saul's
omission of the fact that he has consulted the Urim (to which the narrator
does refer in verse 6) is not meant to minimize repetition but rather to
avoid an embarrassing reference to the massacre of the eighty-five priests
of Nob, who all "wore the linen ephod" (22:18).[11] Furthermore, Saul employs a euphemism to hide the magical character of consulting Samuel
through a necromancer in his vague "so I have called you" (v. 15b). All
earlier references—by Saul himself (vv. 8, 11), by the medium (vv. 11 and
13), and by the prophet (v. 15a)—employed the specific term *ꜥ.l.h*, 'raise'.
Nor does Saul describe his appeal to Samuel as an inquiry, as do both the
narrator (v. 6) and the prophet (v. 16). Instead, he says, "tell me what I am
to do," which implies a sort of commitment to follow the prophet's instructions. If this is a deliberate echo of Samuel's words when he anointed Saul
in Ramah—"I will tell you what you are to do" (10:8),[12] words that Saul
failed to heed at Gilgal, the king is alluding to the past in order to reinforce
his commitment to obey the prophet this time.

Although there is much less equivocation and evasion in this attempt
at self-justification than in what Saul had said to Samuel after the Amaleqite
war,[13] it is evidently the degree of self-deception it still contains that reig-
nites the prophet's wrath. For his second rhetorical question, "Why do you
ask me, seeing that the Lord has turned away from you and has become
your adversary,"[14] echoes Saul's own words—"God has turned away from
me"—thereby contradicting and refuting the king's comforting illusion
that God's silence is merely contingent and temporary. What is the sense
of asking me about the Lord's intentions for you, Samuel rebukes him,
when His turning away from you is just one more expression of the fact
that He is your adversary, that is, that He has rejected you?

Ever since David's extraordinary victory in the valley of Elah and his
escape from the plots and snares set for him by the jealous king, Saul too
had gradually come to realize that "the Lord was with David" (18:28; cf.
24:20) and "had turned away from Saul" (18:12). Samuel himself had told
him as much when he informed him, after the Amaleqite war, of the Lord's
decision to depose him (15:28). On that occasion the prophet used only
verbs in the perfect (*qaraꜥ . . . u-nᵉthanah*)—"The Lord has this day torn . . .
and has given it to another"—to emphasize, through the prophetic past,
that the Lord's rejection of Saul was irrevocable. Now (v. 17) Samuel uses
the imperfect (*wa-yiqraꜥ . . . wa-yittᵉnah*)—"the Lord has been tearing . . .
and has been giving it to your neighbor"—specifically naming David as that

"neighbor," to reiterate that the word of the Lord is being fulfilled, even if the process has not yet been completed.

Moreover, on the principle of "measure for measure," Samuel identifies the present situation ("this thing . . . this day" [v. 18]) as the just and inevitable punishment for Saul's sin of disobedience at the time of the Amaleqite war: "because *you did not listen* (*lo šamaʿta*) to the voice of the Lord and *did not do* [*uʾ-lo ʿaśita*] His wrath upon the Amaleqites—therefore the Lord *has done* this *to you* [*ʿaśah lʾka*] today" (v. 18). The repetition of the verb ʿ.*ś.h.*, 'do', indicates that this is Samuel's indirect response to Saul's question, "what I am to do?" (*mah ʾeʿeśeh*): nothing can be done to avert the catastrophe, because this is the Lord's way of punishing you for your disobedience. The just retribution of measure for measure may also be implied by the presence of the verb *š.m.ʿ* in the first clause and its absence from the second: because you failed to heed the Lord's instructions then, he does not heed your prayers today: "but the Lord did not answer him" (v. 6); "and [God] answers me no more" (v. 15).

Samuel concludes his rebuke with the terrible announcement of the next day's utter rout—death for Saul and his sons, defeat for the army of Israel. The imminent death in battle of Saul and his sons is expressed in unflinching language that involves Samuel personally: "Tomorrow you and your sons will be *with me*" (v. 19). The clear link between this statement and the prophet's first question, "Why have you disturbed me by raising *me* up?" (v. 15), drives home the bitterly ironic connection between Samuel's unwilling ascent to the land of the living and Saul's and his sons' impending descent to the realm of the dead. Raising Samuel from the underworld today cannot prevent Saul's descent there tomorrow and merely adds one more justification to the sentence passed against him. Thus Samuel adds the personal injury done to himself to Saul's previous sins as one more ingredient contributing to the utter calamity about to strike the king.

The king, doomed to fall in battle on the morrow (the verb *n.p.l.*, 'fall', will occur four times in chapter 31, which recounts Saul's final battle), now falls prostrate on the ground. The enervation of spirit produced by the prophet's ominous words is aggravated by Saul's physical weakness, the result of the fact that "he had not eaten anything all day and all night" (v. 20). That the narrator informs us only now, by way of a flashback, that Saul has not been eating, and that he does not use the word *ṣom*, 'fast', are evidently meant to indicate that Saul had not imposed upon himself a fast to accompany supplication of divine aid (as in Judg. 20:26; 2 Sam. 12:16; Esther 4:16), and certainly not a fast of repentance and submission to the Lord (as in 1 Sam. 7:6; 1 Kings 21:27; Joel 2:12).[15] Saul's abstention from food cannot be considered to be a religious act indicating that he understood his plight, even though his prayers were unanswered ("though they fast, I will not hear their cry" [Jer. 14:12; cf. Isa. 58:5]). Rather, it is a psychological compulsion indicating the extent of his suffering. Saul's abstention from food and drink is an outcome of his anguish and mental distress on the eve of the battle with the Philistines, analogous to the case of Jonathan, who "ate no food on the second day of the new moon, for he was grieved about David, because his father had disgraced him" (1 Sam. 20:34; cf. also 1 Sam. 1:7). If Saul had been unable to eat because of his anxiety as to what the future *might* hold for him, how could he possibly eat now, when the future has been revealed to him in all its horror?

Scene 3 (28:21–25): Unanticipated favor—emotional and physical sustenance in advance of the final test

> *R. Naḥman stated in the name of*
> *Rabbah bar Avuha: "Scripture says,*
> *'Love your fellow as yourself' (Lev. 19:18):*
> *allow him a dignified death."*
>
> BT Sanhedrin 45a

Samuel's part in the story is now ended, although there is no explicit mention of his exit. The reader must infer it from the astonishing fact that assistance comes to the king of Israel, lying prostrate on the ground, worn out and disconsolate, not from the prophet, but rather from the witch of Endor. The expression, "the woman came to [*wa-tavoʾ ʾel*] Saul" (v. 21), seems to mean that she had left the room after Samuel appeared and hence had not heard what the prophet told the king (although it could also be understood in the infrequent sense of "went up to," as in Judg. 3:20). In any case, the narrator clearly describes the scene from the witch's perspective ("she saw that he was greatly horrified" [v. 21]), indicating that she was moved to help Saul by his pathetic appearance, her sympathy with his dismay, and her spontaneous identification with his suffering. Like the angel of the Lord who revives Elijah when he is lying under a broom bush, alone and despondent, wanting only to die (1 Kings 19:4–7), the medium knows that the imperative first step is to fortify the body with food. The angel can *command* the prophet to "arise and eat" and reinforce the injunction by a miracle, which proves to Elijah that in the eyes of God he is indeed "better than his fathers." The witch, for her part, must exert a strong persuasive effort to get Saul to eat.

Clearly she is no longer speaking as a medium who can be informal with her clients but as an ordinary woman who treats her eminent visitor with due reverence. She restores to Saul at least a modicum of his royal dignity by twice referring to herself as "your handmaid." Like other epitomes of hospitality—Abraham (Gen. 18:3), Lot (Gen. 19:3), and the father of the concubine (Judg. 19:6–8)—the woman of Endor represents her guest's acceptance of her invitation as his favor to her. In order to ensure that he will in fact do her this favor, however, she demonstrates that, "measure for measure," it is actually his *duty* to accept her invitation and reciprocate what she has just done for him:

> Your handmaid *listened* to you; I *placed* my life in my hands and *listened* to what you have said to me. Now, therefore, you also *listen* to your handmaid; let me *place* a morsel of bread before you. (vv. 21–22)

The first half of this argument is quite logical: I *listened* to you, and now in exchange you must be so good as to *listen* to me. The second part, however, relies more on linguistic similarity than logical analogy: by acceding to your demand I *placed* my life in my hands, that is, I risked my life. Now you should listen to me and let me *place* a morsel of bread before you (meaning to set the table for a meal: cf. Gen. 43:31–32). This is quite a weak argument, exhibiting a conspicuous asymmetry (as compensation for giving in the past she asks to give again in the present) and disproportion (she gave something great and asks for something tiny in return). But these logical weaknesses contain the very secret of the winning charm of her words; behind the verbal association and far-fetched analogy lies the simple truth that she is not serving a meal to a guest but restoring his life. Moreover, her rhetorical hyperboles cloak her real argument: her willingness to risk her life for him has given her a right to demand that he, too, overcome the dread of death and not give in to his weakness.[16]

The witch concludes her oblique argument with a direct claim that explicitly refers to Saul's welfare: "Eat, that you may have strength when you go on your way" (v. 22). Just as the angel makes it plain to Elijah that his life is by no means over ("Arise and eat, or the journey will be too much for you" [1 Kings 19:7]), so too the witch indicates to King Saul that he cannot end his life lying prostrate on the floor of her house: He has no choice but to fortify himself, physically and mentally, so that he will be able to go on his way. Saul replies, with the stubbornness of the desperate, "I will not eat" (v. 23). Only after further pleading by his two servants and the woman—words that the narrator does not report, probably because their force lay in their expression of concern and sympathy rather than in their content—is the king able to muster his waning strength, rise from the ground, and sit on the bed.

Now the witch has the opportunity to prove not only that she has the insight and eloquence of Abigail and the woman of Tekoa, but also that she is as hospitable as Abraham, who said little (Gen. 18:4–5) and did much—and quickly (Gen. 18:6–8). But whereas the patriarch owned many cattle ("Abraham ran to the herd and took a calf, tender and choice" [Gen. 18:7]), the witch is more like the poor man in the parable of the prophet Nathan, who had only a single ewe-lamb. She slaughters the only fatted calf she has and hastily bakes unleavened bread so as not to unduly delay her guests, thereby allowing them to depart under cover of darkness, as they had arrived.[17]

The Secret of a Story's Greatness: Its Truthfulness

> *It was taught: One angel never performs two*
> *missions, nor two angels a single mission.*

Genesis Rabba 50,2

Confronted by the abundant kindness of the witch, the reader can scarcely help asking two questions about the prophet's stern conduct. First, why does Samuel add the assault on his rest to the roster of Saul's misdeeds while failing to condemn the grotesquerie of having recourse to a medium to raise the prophet's spirit? Second, why doesn't Samuel evince any sympathy or pity for Saul, or at least soften his harsh words so as to keep the king from collapsing to the ground, overcome by guilt and despair? The primary answer to both questions is that all this is indeed to be found in the story: whatever Samuel leaves out is supplied by the *narrator,* on the one hand, and by the *witch,* on the other.

If Samuel had reproved Saul for resorting to necromancy and refused to answer his questions about the future, the prophet's conduct would probably be more in line with our expectations. But then the story would have been less rich and complex. Samuel's questions, "why have you disturbed me?" and "why do you ask me?" voice his bitter disappointment with the king who has failed to comprehend and accept the message implicit in God's unyielding silence. The prophet explicitly condemns Saul's vain desire to force God to answer him, but leaves it to the language of the plot to censure the means by which the attempt was made. In the first scene, Saul reassures the frightened witch with the oath: "As the Lord lives, you will not be punished over this" (v. 10). He certainly has the authority to guarantee that no human court will punish her for necromancy. But readers must wonder whether the king, who has eliminated mediums and spiritualists from the land, ought not to fear that he himself will be accounted guilty according to divine law.

In the second scene, when the very success of raising the spirit of Samuel proves to be his undoing and he collapses under the heavy burden of supernatural knowledge that puts an end to all hope, Saul too realizes that his recourse to necromancy has added yet another sin to his already heavy burden. No prophetic reproof could illuminate the gravity of the sin more clearly than the immediate punishment that is a direct result of this act, namely, the prophet's reply, which is infinitely worse than God's silence, and the absolute certainty that is worse than all doubts and fears.

But why does the prophet allow this sinful woman to be the sole agent of mercy in this episode? The answer seems to be that Samuel's obdurate attitude toward Saul stems from his prophetic duty as the faithful proponent of strict justice. The spirit of Samuel, raised from the underworld, has full and perfect knowledge of what will happen on the morrow and speaks and acts like a living prophet in every respect. At this fateful juncture his role is not only to pronounce the terrible divine verdict, but also to justify it to the condemned man (as well as to generations of readers). The persuasive force of this justification depends mainly on the quality of the prophet's argument, but also on the extent to which he himself is convinced of its validity. Paradoxically, his personal opinion is relatively important, precisely because it reflects a mortal reaction rather than divine discretion. This is why the human emissary of the heavenly court may not exempt himself from passing judgment. Moses, for example, could appease the Lord's wrath against Israel for worshipping the golden calf; but when, himself witnessing the calf and the dancing Israelites, he angrily shattered the tablets of the law, he was unwillingly confirming the essential justice of the heavenly verdict. Thus it is of crucial importance that Samuel is personally affronted by having his spirit raised from the underworld and that Saul's prophetic advocate goes over to the side of the divine accuser.[18]

Whereas strict justice is oriented primarily toward the *past*, inasmuch as it deals with deeds that the defendant has already committed, mercy applies mainly to the *present*, inasmuch as it deals with his suffering. Accordingly, the prophet, vindicating the divine judgment, must apply his "measure for measure" analogy to Saul's sin at the time of the Amaleqite war. The witch, however, is free to relate only to the present situation and ground her "measure for measure" argument on what she has just done for Saul and what he owes her in return. In fact, had she so desired she too could have judged Saul by her own values and extracted vengeance for his liquidation of mediums and spiritualists. But she is innocent of any such tendency and, once reassured by his oath, is willing to carry out his wishes. Readers evidently count this to her credit as early as the first scene. Her luster in our eyes increases even more in the third scene, when she acts out of spontaneous sympathy with what she sees and feels.

Thus in sharp contrast to didactic and moralistic literature, which contends with sin by painting sinners in starkest black and fostering the readers' revulsion for and antagonism toward them, the scriptural narrator has no compunctions about openly confessing the moral virtues of a woman condemned by the ordinance, "you shall not permit a sorceress to live" (Exod. 22:17). Her transgression as a necromancer is one thing, her decency as a sensitive and generous woman quite another.[19] Her extraordinary faithfulness to the truth of life, to the fullness of human experience in all its twists and turns, in all its multifaceted complexity, is quite uncommon in tendentious literature. Such faithfulness is not easily reconciled with a commitment to beliefs and ideology, which by their nature are abstract and all-inclusive. By forgoing to some extent the direct and immediate moral influence that is the ultimate goal of homiletic narratives, our story bears the stamp of truth. Thanks to this truthfulness, readers are brought to reject and detest necromancy and to reinforce their belief that they are duty bound to be "wholehearted" with the Lord (Deut. 18:13)—not because of the "factual" assertion (which real life is apt to disprove) that every medium is wicked and wishes to harm those who consult her.[20] As a result of the honest and generous portrayal of the witch of Endor and her virtues, readers come to understand that her kindness in no way undermines the objection to necromancy, but instead grounds the objection, as it should be, on a fundamental principle.

While moralistic literature does not usually permit itself any display of sympathy for the suffering of sinners, ensnared in their web of sin, the story of Saul at Endor evinces not the slightest trace of gloating over his fall. On the contrary, the narrator makes certain that readers will recognize the guilt of the sinful king but at the same time identify with the bitter fate of a man trapped in a hopeless situation. The narrator achieves this through his deft balancing of the prophet who coldly justifies God's judgment versus the woman who gently aids the condemned man.[21] But why is the narrator not worried that the kindness of the witch will cast a shadow on the character of the prophet and that the prophet's coldness will mitigate our sense that Saul merits his fate?

Samuel's conduct and attitude cannot be evaluated apart from the incident of the Amaleqite war, which is clearly the background to our story (Samuel states this explicitly in verse 18). There, in chapter 15, the prophet reacted to the divine verdict on Saul with shock and protest and made a heroic effort to have the sentence commuted: "Samuel was distressed [*wa-yiḥar*] and he cried to the Lord all night long" (15:11). The use of the root *ḥ.r.h* makes it plain that Samuel was not pleading for mercy but arguing for a more lenient verdict.[22] Even though his prayer was not answered and the prophet had to tell Saul that the Lord regretted that He had made him king, Samuel was not yet reconciled to the decree. Only Saul's denial of the facts and evasion of his royal responsibility gradually led the prophet to identify internally with the justice of the divine decree, and this ultimately led Saul himself to confess his transgression.[23] Samuel's transformation from prophetic advocate to prosecutor had already taken place then and was entirely Saul's fault. Hence, readers can share neither the desperate hopes that Saul pins on raising Samuel's spirit nor his bitter disappointment with the encounter he forces on the shade of the man who had already despaired of Saul during his lifetime (15:35).

The prophet is not permitted to be merciful and show leniency, because any deviation on his part from the letter of the law would be interpreted as a challenge to God's rejection of His chosen king. On the other hand, the witch's compassion does not detract in the slightest from the validity and justice of the divine decree. This is why the balance in this story cannot be *internal* (within Samuel), but must be *external* (juxtaposing the attitudes of the prophet and the witch).

Our story achieves its full realization of both justice and mercy through a clear-cut division of roles between the two nonroyal characters. Despite their diametrically opposed religious positions, they can complement each other because there is no conflict between them, and neither of them impinges on the activity of the other. When the prophet's shade appears, the medium disappears from the scene (and probably has no knowledge of what Samuel tells Saul); when she reappears he has vanished (without having either helped or harmed Saul). Just as the prophet does not seek to vanquish the king in the present, so the medium cannot rescue him from his impending fate. Thus these two characters complement each other in the minds and responses of readers, who, by identifying with each separately, arrive at an honest alloy of rejection and acceptance, of justification of divine judgment and empathy.

This narrative balance between a prophet of the Lord and a necromancer is possible only because, to the scriptural mind, the prophet is a *messenger* of God and never his *representative*. God has many and various messengers, for He alone can execute the full spectrum of divine functions. Because the theme of the story is God's way with His creatures, its perspective is broader than the prophet's view and its truth more comprehensive than the prophet's truth. What is more, the readers, who are not prophets, may not identify exclusively with Samuel and self-righteously assume the prophetic mantle of justice.[24] As spectators from the sidelines, readers can and must do what the prophet was unable to achieve—to see and feel these events from a loftier viewpoint, one that also includes the contribution of the witch as the emissary of divine empathy.[25]

In addition to what human beings do of their own free will, they are also tools in the hands of providence, as Joseph explained to his brothers: "So it was not you who sent me here, but God" (Gen. 45:8). With full awareness of her actions, the witch revives Saul and restores his self-respect and capacity to function. Wittingly and unwittingly she saves him from the worst fate of all—death on the floor of a witch's house, disguised in "other garments" (v. 8), having abandoned his army. More than she could ever know, she enables Saul to rectify, on this last day of his life, the errors of many years. Rather than continuing to run away from the word of the Lord, he will stride bravely to the place where that word will be fulfilled. The king, whose vain fears have moved him to commit terrible crimes, will now go to meet certain death with sublime and desperate heroism. Though he knows that his sentence has already been handed down, he can still pass the supreme test and die at his post, commanding the army of Israel.[26]

The episode of Saul at Endor begins with the king's donning a disguise and denying his own values. It ends with his restoration to his true human identity and authentic self as the king of Israel. Thanks to the compassion that accompanies strict justice, the medium's humanity, together with Saul's restored fortitude, illuminate the morbid darkness of the king's last night on earth.

•4•

"THAT MAN IS YOU!"

A King Sins, a Man Repents, and a Father Is Punished

Thus says the Lord: Have you murdered and
taken possession too?

1 Kings 21:19

Two kings transgressed the Decalogic proscription against coveting: David coveted another man's wife; Ahab, another man's vineyard. The two kings' victims were honest and upright men who refused to violate a sacred principle for the sake of some worldly benefit. Uriah the Hittite refused to go to his house as long as the army was camped in the field and bound himself with an oath: "As you live, by your very life, I will not do this!" (2 Sam. 11:11). Naboth the Jezreelite refused to sell his vineyard and defined his stand as a religious prohibition: "The Lord forbid that I should give up to you what I have inherited from my fathers!" (1 Kings 21:3). David did not hesitate to use the stratagems of war to have Uriah killed by enemy swords; Jezebel went even further and exploited the judicial system to have Naboth stoned as a rebel. The trappings of sovereignty allowed the two monarchs to do their deeds covertly. Through this secrecy each attained what had been denied him: David married Uriah's widow, and Ahab expropriated Naboth's vineyard. This veil of pseudolegality was rent asunder by the prophets of the Lord precisely when the two kings thought that their path—the path of sinners—had succeeded. Nathan reproached David for his double iniquity: "You have put Uriah the Hittite to the sword; you took his wife and made her your wife" (2 Sam. 12:9). Elijah castigated Ahab in similar terms: "Have you murdered and taken possession too?" (1 Kings 21:19). The two kings were taken aback by the prophets' bold and unflinching revelation of their sins and by the terrible punishments threatened by Heaven. Both recognized, each in his own way, the magnitude of their transgression. By virtue of their repentance, the death sentence pronounced on them was commuted, but their punishment was not annulled. Despite the great differences on the personal, moral, and religious planes between David son of Jesse and Ahab son of Omri—differences that led to the difference in the modus operandi of Nathan and Elijah—these two prophetic stories have much in common. The extensive similarity in their plots attests that both belong to a particular literary genre, the prophetic account of a king rebuked for violating a divine ordinance, and even to the same rare subgenre in which a king is rebuked for sins against his fellow man. What is more, the stories of the poor man's lamb and of Naboth's vineyard have a common theme: a king who murders his subject and inherits his prize possession because he has come to act haughtily toward his fellows and because he has been led astray to believe that what is hidden from human beings is also hidden from the Creator.

The Compass and Structure of the Story

The episode of David and Bathsheba is framed by the account of David's war against the Ammonites. The narrative of the war is freestanding (as we see from the version in 1 Chron. 19:1–20:3, where the inner story is missing). By contrast, the story of Bathsheba is intimately linked with that of the war: it is because of the war that Uriah is absent from his house, and it is in that war that he is sent to his death. Whereas David's other wars with the neighboring states, starting from his accession to the throne, are chronicled with extreme brevity in chapter 8, here his war with the Ammonites is narrated at length, evidently because it is the essential backdrop for the story of Bathsheba. Not only do Joab's instructions to Abishai before the battle (10:11–12), and especially Joab's summons to David to come and assume command during the capture of Rabbath-Ammon (12:27–28), give the story life and depth (like everything that is reported in direct speech); they also illuminate the complex relations between the military commander and his king, both in the story of David and Bathsheba and in the other incidents that ensue in its wake.

The story begins in chapter 10, verse 1, with the formulaic "some time afterward," which also leads off the chronicle of David's wars and the list of his ministers (8:1), the story of Amnon and Tamar (13:1), and the account of Absalom's rebellion (15:1). The story concludes before the next introductory formula, that is, at 12:31; in fact this verse presents an obvious closure: "Then David and all the troops returned to Jerusalem," which marks the end of the war and the return of the victor and his army to his capital.

The structure of the frame story

The first part of the story (10:1–19) has three sections that describe the victories over Ammon and Aram in the first year of the war: a prologue that relates the cause of the war, followed by accounts of the first two battles.

The compass of the second and third parts is marked by use of the verb *r*ʾ.*h* 'see, realize', in both their opening sentences (to denote an evaluation of the situation that led to the attack) and their concluding sentences (to denote an evaluation of the situation that led to the retreat or surrender), as follows:

(1) 10:1–5 Hanun humiliates David's messengers—a peaceful gesture is met with a hostile affront.

(2) 10:6–14 Joab escapes the trap and routs the Arameans and Ammonites—a grave situation turns into a great victory.
Opening sentence: "The Ammonites *saw* that they had incurred the wrath of David; so [they] . . . hired Arameans. . . . "
Closing sentence: "When the Ammonites *saw* that the Arameans had fled, they fled . . . and withdrew into the city."

(3) 10:15–19 David routs the Arameans—the Aramean kings' assistance to Ammon leads to their subjugation and neutralization.
Opening sentence: "When the Arameans *saw* that they had been routed by Israel, they regrouped their forces."
Closing sentence: "And when all the vassal kings . . . *saw* that they had been routed by Israel, they submitted to Israel and became their vassals. And the Arameans were afraid to help the Ammonites any more."

That the military initiative remains with the enemy throughout the first year of the war is emphasized not only by the fact that the opening and closing sentences refer to Ammon and Aram but also by the use of extremely similar phrasing in the description of David's response to the challenge posed to him in each of the three subunits, as follows:

(1) 10:5 "When David was told of it . . . "—When he learns of the humiliation of his envoys, he instructs them to stay in Jericho so as to conceal their shame.

(2) 10:7 "On learning this, David . . . "—When he learns that the Ammonites have hired the Aramean armies to assist them, he sends Joab against them at the head of the standing army.

(3) 10:17 "David was informed of it . . . "—When he learns that the Aramean armies have been deployed at Helam, he goes to attack them at the head of "all Israel."

The enemies see, whereas David hears; they act on the basis of what they see in front of them, whereas he acts only pursuant to information that comes from far away. On the surface, this should indicate weakness and a lack of fortitude in evaluating the situation; but the fact that in each section the outcome is in David's favor attests that the initial weakness is described only in order to make the final success stand out more clearly. Just the opposite applies to his enemies. Hanun's humiliation of David's envoys ultimately leads to the subjugation of the Ammonites. The numerical and tactical advantage provided by the alliance between Ammon and Aram does not avail them against the perseverance and bravery of Joab and his warriors; in fact, the massive Aramean intervention on the side of the Ammonites leads to the loss of their kingdoms' independence. The first part of the story thus contains no criticism of David's conduct of the war against the Ammonites; quite the contrary, we marvel that even in a war whose initial campaigns were forced on him, he managed to convert every potential mischance into victory.

In the verse that serves as the link between the history of the war and the episode of David and Bathsheba (11:1), the narrator makes clear that in the second year of the war the initiative passed to David. The temporal setting—"at the turn of the year, the season when kings go out [to battle]"— informs us that this time David is not reacting to an enemy thrust but is guided by the calendar. With the end of the rainy season (during which it is difficult for troops to maneuver and camp in the field), the king once again sends his commander-in-chief to Ammon. Even though, in the wake of the defeat of the Arameans at Helam, there is no longer any fear of Aramean assistance for the Ammonites, the expeditionary force commanded by Joab is reinforced (probably because of information about the strength of the Ammonites and the fortifications of Rabbath-Ammon): "David sent Joab and his servants with him and all Israel" (ibid.). "His servants" (*ᶜavadaw*) refers to "mighty men" (10:7),[1] later referred to as "David's servants" (11:17) or "the king's servants" (11:24), whereas "all Israel" refers to the conscript army (also referred to as "all the people" [12:29]), which David had commanded at the battle of Helam (10:17). Assigning the brunt of the battle to professional soldiers commanded by Joab is neither an innovation nor blameworthy; David had already done so when he was still only king over Judah and residing in Hebron: "Just then David's servants (*ᶜavdei David*) and Joab returned from a raid, bringing much plunder with them" (2 Sam. 3:22; cf. 2:12ff.). Nor was it unusual to give Joab command of the conscript army; this was also the case during the conquest of Edom (whose precise date is not clear): "When David was in Edom, Joab the army commander went up to bury the slain, and he killed every male in Edom; for Joab and *all Israel* stayed there for six months until he had killed off every male in Edom" (1 Kings 11:15–16; cf. 2 Sam. 8:14). Note that the fact that Joab was dispatched at the head of both armies clearly implies that the king stayed behind in Jerusalem. Hence the explicit statement that ends the verse, "David remained in Jerusalem," and perhaps the auxiliary indication of time, "the season when kings go out to battle," with its hint of irony, is part of the episode of David and Bathsheba. This emphasis on a known fact is the first criticism of David. At the same time, it focuses attention on the fateful starting point of this story about the deeds of a king who stays home at the season when kings go out to battle (this exposition will be discussed in its own right below; see p. 103).

Most of the story of David and Bathsheba is set in Jerusalem; some incidents occur at the front. The battle in which Uriah falls is not crucial for the outcome of the campaign, and the end of the war is described separately in the second part of the frame story (12:26–31), which concludes the entire episode with an account of the capture of Rabbath-Ammon during the second year of the war. This part is not broken down into sections like the first one; still, its two main themes parallel the second and third sections of the first part. There, Joab's victory over the Ammonite and Aramean armies (in the second section) paves the way for David's victory over the Aramean armies at Helam (in the third section). Here, Joab takes the "water city" of Rabbath-Ammon, thereby paving the way for the capture of the city itself by David. The contraction of two sections into one reflects the two military advantages of the present situation: this time, the second battle is merely the completion of the first. Nor is it necessary to mobilize the reserves this year, since they are already encamped in Transjordan, as we learn not only from the description of the expeditionary force commanded by Joab (11:1) but also from Uriah's words to David: "The Ark and *Israel* and *Judah* are living in booths [or: located at Succoth]" (11:11).[2] Given these two advantages, we can understand Joab's meaning when he calls on David to complete the capture of Rabbath-Ammon (11:27–28):

> I have attacked Rabbah and I have already captured the water city. Now muster the rest of the troops and besiege the city and capture it; otherwise I will capture the city myself, and my name will be connected with it.

Joab begins by reporting his achievements—the successful assaults on the besieged city and conquest of the fortified compound that contains its water source. Now it is merely necessary to bring up the reserves (in a military context, the verb *ʾ.s.p* is used in Scripture not only in the sense of mobilization but also in the sense of deploying, as in 1 Sam. 13:11 and 17:1) to intensify the siege on the city and reinforce the investing army in anticipation of the decisive assault that will take it. Joab proposes that all of this be done under the direct command of the king, so that he rather than his lieutenant will be credited with the conquest of the city. These tactical particulars (sent in plain language and as an oral message to the king, not in a sealed missive) make it clear that Joab is not proposing an empty show aimed only at bolstering the king's political position. Rather, he is describing what is actually required to take the walled city. At the same time, he makes it plain that given the critical situation of the besieged and the fact that "the rest of the troops" are already encamped in Transjordan, he can carry out the task by himself. Since the conquest will be attributed to the commander who completes it, Joab warns David of the prospective damage to his reputation as a king who goes out before his people and fights its battles (see 1 Sam. 8:20; 2 Sam. 5:2).

David is careful not to yield his glory, assumes command (as he had done in the second stage of the previous year's campaign) and takes Rabbath-Ammon by following the tactics sketched out by Joab (compare verse 29 with verse 28). The war, which began when David's envoys had half their beards shaved off at the order of the king of the Ammonites, concludes with the "crown . . . taken from the head of their king." In addition to the extremely valuable Ammonite crown, which will henceforth adorn the victor's brow, David also carries off a vast amount of booty from the city, subjugates the entire population of Ammon, and returns with his army to Jerusalem. Nothing darkens the military, political, and economic fruits that this great victory provides to David, except for the bitterness in the words of the commander, whose bravery and loyalty made it possible for the king to emerge triumphant. Formally, Joab could have relied on David's command, "Press your attack on the city and destroy it!" (11:25); but he preferred to act with total loyalty and allow the king to overrun the city. All the same, he cannot stifle his implicit protest against the king who stayed behind in Jerusalem, commanded him from there to arrange Uriah's death by Ammonite swords, took Uriah's wife Bathsheba for wife, and can now reap what his servant sowed.

There is no hint in the text that the siege of Rabbath-Ammon lasted beyond "the season when kings go out to war" in the second year. It follows that the city was taken before the birth of David and Bathsheba's son and before Nathan announced his impending punishment to David: "Therefore the sword will never depart from your House" (12:10). The interpolation of the entire story of the sin and its punishment within the frame story of the war requires that later events precede earlier ones; hence we read of the military victory not against the background of the secret transgression (in accordance with the sequence of events) but against that of the anticipated punishment, which thereby casts its terrible shadow on the victory. In this way, the structure of the story hones its response to the riddle of David's kingdom from the day it reached its political and military zenith—the great disparity between might and peace abroad and weakness and dissension at home. The king who sinned in his palace, during and by means of the war, will not be punished by an enemy sword, aimed at a king on the battlefield, but by the sword of his sons, directed at a father in his own house. The first indication of this is Joab's complex stance vis-à-vis his king: even while allowing the latter to reap the full fruits of the victory, he permits himself to give vent to his profound bitterness and thereby express the danger threatened by the sinner's dependence on his emissary. (We will return to this in our close reading. See below, pp. 108–12.)

The structure of the inner story

The episode of David and Bathsheba is divided into two parts of equal length. The first deals with the sin, the second with the punishment. This thematic distinction is reinforced by the prominent antiparallelism of the opening and closing sentences of the two parts (in addition to the *inclusio* that demarcates part 2), as follows:

Part 1 (11:1–27): The king sins—the anatomy of moral-religious decline in the shadow of power.
  Opening sentence, in which David takes the initiative: "At the turn of the year . . . *David sent* Joab and his servants with him. . . . "
  Closing sentence, which foreshadows the impending punishment: "But what David had done *displeased the Lord.*"
Part 2 (12:1–25): A man repents—the anatomy of recognition of the sin and acceptance of the punishment.
  Opening sentence, in which the Lord takes the initiative: "The *Lord sent* Nathan to David."
  Closing sentence, which foreshadows the Lord's favor: "And *He sent* a message through the prophet Nathan; and he was named Jedidiah *at the instance of the Lord.*"

The first part begins with an initiative by David, who dispatches his general to the front. The second part begins with the initiative by the heavenly King, who sends his prophet to the earthly monarch to rebuke him to his face. The concluding sentence of the first part, in which the narrator reveals (only to the reader, for the moment) the divine displeasure with David's transgression, paves the way for this conversion of David from subject to object, from sovereign to accused. Similarly, the second part, too, concludes with Nathan's being sent to David again, this time to notify him (and the reader) that the Lord is pleased by his repentance.

The first part is divided into six smaller units: an exposition (all of it reported), four scenes, and a conclusion (it too reported). These sections are marked off by two indications: (1) a partial change in the dramatis personae; (2) the conclusion of each of the four scenes with direct speech that ends with a letter (or oral message) from David to Joab or from Joab to David. The title assigned here to each section reflects its place in the history of David's religious and moral deterioration:

Exposition (v. 1): "David remained in Jerusalem."
  Characters: David and Joab
Scene 1 (vv. 2–6a): From adultery to machinations
  Characters: David and Bathsheba (and courtiers)

Concluding sentence: (David's first letter to Joab): "Send Uriah the Hittite to me."

Scene 2 (vv. 6b–15): From feigned kindness to stealthy murder

Characters: David and Uriah (and courtiers)

Concluding sentence (David's second letter to Joab): "Place Uriah in the front line where the fighting is fiercest; then fall back so that he may be killed."

Scene 3 (vv. 16–21): From execution of the murderous command to a cynical report

Characters: Joab, Uriah, a messenger

Concluding sentence (Joab's message to David): "Your servant Uriah the Hittite was among those killed."

Scene 4 (vv. 22–25): From using the enemy to kill a loyal servant to indifference to unnecessary losses

Characters: David and the messenger

Concluding sentence (David's message to Joab): "Press your attack on the city and destroy it!"

Conclusion (vv. 26–27): Ostensible conclusion—the path of sinners prospers (in their own eyes)

Characters: David and Bathsheba

The anatomy of the sin begins with the short exposition in which the military background (which, as we have seen, belongs to the frame story) is pulled toward the plot by the prominence accorded to a crucial point: "At the season when kings go out [to battle], David remained in Jerusalem." The king's remaining at home during wartime is not considered to be a sin; but it is a moral flaw that casts a shadow on his devotion to his people and his solidarity with his warriors. What is more, it resembles the hole in the fence that beckons to a thief. Readers are invited to wonder: what is the stay-at-home king about to do?

The four scenes of part I share the same basic structure. Each begins with a *sin* (except for the fourth, which, as a report, depends on the sin recounted in the previous scene), continues with the *complication*, and concludes (except for the fourth) with the *preparation for another sin* that will be committed in the next scene. This uniform structure (schematized in table 4.1) underscores the causal regularity of David's moral decline: "One sin leads to another" because each time unanticipated complications (Bathsheba's pregnancy, Uriah's refusal to visit his wife) pose a new test that David cannot withstand, and he is consequently drawn into a new sin.

By contrast, everything seems to be going smoothly at the conclusion of the first part of the story. Here, too, there are three elements: (1) Bathsheba's mourning for her husband; (2) her marriage to David; (3) the birth of their son. Readers may question the sincerity of the war widow's lament on the death of her husband, a death that freed her from the risk of being

TABLE 4.1: The Structure of the Four Scenes in Part I of the Story of David and Bathsheba

Scene	I,1 (11:2–6a)	I,2 (11:6b–15)	I,3 (11:16–21)	I,4 (11:22–25)
Elements Main Characters	David, Bathsheba	David, Uriah	Joab, Uriah, the messenger	David, the messenger
Sin	"She came to him and he lay with her."	Two attempts to seduce Uriah.	Uriah is stationed in a dangerous position and falls in battle.	—
Complication	"She sent word to David: 'I am pregnant.'"	Uriah twice declines to visit his wife.	Other soldiers are killed.	David learns that Uriah's death involved unnecessary casualties.
Preparation for another sin	Uriah is summoned from the front.	The fatal letter is sent to Joab.	Joab gives his cynical instructions to his messenger: Uriah's death will assuage the king's anger.	David changes his ethical norm: "The sword always takes its toll."

tried for adultery; but at this juncture no real sin is involved, nor is there any new complication. As far as we know, the king's marriage to the widow of one of his heroes who had fallen in battle aroused no astonishment or complaints. Nor are there any suspicions about the legitimacy of their son, who was conceived in a forbidden relationship but is born in a licit one. Almost unwillingly we come to share David's illusion that the path of sinners prospers if they can conceal their deeds. This sense that the end of part I is the conclusion of the entire episode of David and Bathsheba is reinforced by the strong contrast between what was done in secret and hasty sin at the beginning of the story and the very same act, which is now performed legally, openly, and repeatedly: "David sent messengers to fetch her; she came to him and he lay with her . . . and she went back home" (11:4), and "David sent and had her brought into his palace; she became his wife and she bore him a son" (11:27).

But this sense of an ending is shattered when the narrator reveals, at the end of the concluding verse itself, what the protagonists themselves do not yet know: "But what David had done displeased the Lord." This suspenseful ending, concluding one subunit with the crux of the following subunit,[3] is not intended to increase the narrative tension. Rather, it makes a theological statement: the conclusion is spurious[4] because the story cannot conclude in this fashion!

Part II of the story of David and Bathsheba comprises two scenes and an epilogue, marked off by two indications: (1) a partial change in personae; and (2) a contrast between the opening and closing of each scene, creating an *inclusio* structure:

Scene 1 (12:1–15a): From "That man is you!" through "Why then have you flouted the command of the Lord" and ending with "I stand guilty before the Lord!"
Characters: David and Nathan
Opening sentence: "and the Lord sent Nathan to David. *He came to him.* . . . "
Concluding sentence: "*Nathan went* home."
Scene 2 (vv. 15b–23): From the struggle for the child's life to acceptance of his death.
Characters: David and his servants
Opening sentence: "the Lord afflicted the child. . . . David entreated God for the boy; *David fasted.* . . . "
Concluding sentence: "But now that he is dead, *why should I fast?* Can I bring him back again?"
Epilogue (vv. 24–25): The true conclusion—the way of the penitent prospers.

The anatomy of repentance does not need an exposition: the account of the transgression provides an adequate background for it. Whereas part I comprises four scenes with a common structure, here there are two scenes that differ as to content, structure, and, especially, message. The first scene goes through four stages: disguised condemnation, overt rebuke, repentance, and forgiveness; its message is the absolving power of repentance. The second and much shorter scene has two stages: the desperate struggle for the baby's life, followed by the unexpected acceptance of his death; the message is that repentance has only limited power to mitigate punishment. Nathan did indeed tell David that the divine forgiveness of his sin mitigated but did not annul his punishment. Nevertheless, David must learn that his extreme self-abasement cannot avert the evil decree. Thus the two scenes balance each other, together providing a complex view of absolution that does not erase all the results of a sin.

With its three themes and final evaluative sentence, the conclusion of the second part of the story (12:24–25) parallels the epilogue of part I (11:26–27) and, in a manner of speaking, serves to rectify it. Instead of Bathsheba's dubious dirge for the death of her husband, David comforts his wife Bathsheba on the death of their son. Instead of marriage with an illicitly pregnant woman, we now have marital relations that have been strengthened by repentance and bereavement: "he went to her and lay with her." Instead of the birth of a nameless child who soon dies,[5] a viable child is born, with a glorious name, blessed by heaven from his youth ("She bore a son and named him Solomon. The Lord favored him"). Finally, instead of the harsh assessment—"But what David had done displeased the Lord"— that marks the false ending as open to future developments, the episode of David and Bathsheba now reaches its true conclusion as Nathan gives David and Bathsheba's son full legitimacy and explicitly removes him from the influence of the results of his parents' sin: "[The Lord] sent a message through the prophet Nathan; and he was named Jedidiah at the instance of the Lord."

A King Sins

The root *š.l.ḥ*, 'send', occurs twelve times in the twenty-seven verses of chapter 11, a clear expression of David's might—he now rules his kingdom and wages foreign wars through emissaries. The *hapax* "the season when kings go out [to battle]" (11:1) seems meant to open the story on a critical note: "At the season when kings *go out* [to battle], . . . David *remained* in Jerusalem."[6] Years later, when the king had grown old, his warriors had to declare on oath: "You shall not go with us into battle any more, lest you extinguish the lamp of Israel!" (21:17). Similarly, at the time of Absalom's rebellion, his troops insisted that "it is better for you to support us from the town" (18:3). Now, when David is still in his full vigor and has complete control of his men, he has no apprehensions about loosening his direct contact with his army. Who knows better than he the damage to Saul's dominion by the fact that it was his successful commander who "led Israel in war" (5:2)? But this time, it seems, the king is successfully overseeing his general from afar. Joab is careful not to anger the king by tactical lapses (11:20) and invites David to reap what he has sown (12:28). Nevertheless, he inserts into his report on the casualties as well as in his invitation to take the city personally a tinge of irony that implicitly expresses what Uriah had stated explicitly:

> The Ark and Israel and Judah are located at Succoth [or: camping in booths], and my master Joab and my lord's servants are camped in the open; shall I go home to eat and drink and sleep with my wife? As you live, by your very life, I will not do this! (11:11)

The plain meaning of these lines certainly does not allow us to conclude that they were spoken by a rebel (as asserted by the Sages: BT Shabbat 56a and Qiddušin 43a). All the same, they sharply imply the comradeship of the soldiers at the front and their resentment of those who are comfortably ensconced in the rear.

David's oath to the Lord in Ps. 132:1–5 (despite its poetical hyperbole) can help us understand the inner logic of Uriah's oath to David:[7]

> O Lord, remember in David's favor his extreme self-denial, how he swore to the Lord, vowed to the Mighty One of Jacob, "I will not enter my house, nor will I mount my bed, I will not give sleep to my eyes, or slumber to my eyelids, until I find a place for the Lord, an abode for the Mighty One of Jacob."

David vowed to deny himself three pleasures: entering his house, lying down in his bed, and sleeping—until he has found an appropriate place and fitting abode for the Ark of the Lord. Uriah vows that as long as the Ark of the Lord and the army are distant from Jerusalem and encamped in Succoth (see n. 2), and as long as his commander, Joab, and the standing army are bivouacked in the open field outside the walls of Rabbath-Ammon, he will not permit himself to enjoy the three comforts denied to his comrades-in-arms. Both David (in the psalm) and Uriah deprive themselves of what they are entitled to—David, in order to motivate himself to quickly end the disparity between his palatial dwelling and the wanderings of the ark; Uriah, in order to urge the king to curtail the period of his absence from the field conditions in which the troops are living (and David in fact replies, "tomorrow I will send you off" [v. 12]). On the surface, Uriah's demurrer relates only to his relations with his wife and to the soldiers at the front; but one cannot avoid hearing the challenge to David in the rhetorical question that paints David's alluring proposal as unconscionable.

Except for this vigorous maintenance of a different standard of conduct, nothing that Uriah says seems out of place in the speech of a senior officer to his king (compare the speeches of Joab [2 Sam. 3:24–25] and Achitophel [2 Sam. 17:1–3]). Had Uriah said, as might be anticipated, "your servant Joab," he would be respectfully expressing Joab's subordination to David (just as the wise woman of Tekoa does [2 Sam. 14:19–20]); but his reference instead to "my master Joab" emphasizes his particular sense of obligation to his commander at the front. Uriah even balances this statement by referring to the king as "My Lord" when he speaks of the standing army.[8]

The narrator himself uses these terms when he describes Uriah's behavior, both before and after his explanation: "But Uriah slept at the entrance of the royal palace, along with the other servants of his lord (*ʿavdei ʾadonaw*)" (vv. 9 and 13). Through this verbal association between speech and deed, the narrator emphasizes that Uriah is expressing his identification with his master's servants at the front by sleeping among his master's servants in the rear.

The scriptural narrator's characteristic focus on the protagonist (see the appendix, pp. 263ff.) leaves us ignorant of Bathsheba's part in the transgression. We learn absolutely nothing about the nature of her relationship with her husband and the manner of her surrender to David, except for the apparently unnecessary words "she came to him" (v. 4), which make it plain that she was not forced to come to the palace. Hence we should not make too much of the unusual word order—"he saw a woman bathing *from* [*me͑al*] the roof" (v. 2)—and understand the preposition to mean that she was intentionally bathing, immodestly, *on* [*͑al*] the roof. Her guilt may have been substantial; but there is no concrete expression of this, neither in Nathan's parable and in its interpretation, nor in the evaluatory "the Lord was displeased with what David had done" (v. 27). Hence we should assume that the roof in the verse is that of David's palace, from which the king saw the woman bathing inside her house.

Uriah's motives, too, are enshrouded in mist. In vain shall we search for a direct answer to the questions that concern us: did some courtier tell Uriah what had taken place between his wife and the king?[9] Can we hold that he intentionally frustrates the king's plan and interpret his refusal as a partially veiled protest of the injustice done to him?[10] Given the narrator's silence on this matter, however, we can certainly say that the lesson of the story—as the narrator presents it—is heightened if we assume that Uriah acts out of ignorance. David's attempt to conceal his sin is not brought to naught by some flaw in the court apparatus or by the disloyalty of one of his servants. On the contrary, it is precisely the moral superiority of the betrayed husband that frustrates the king's stratagem, and Uriah's guileless-ness that gives his words their force.[11] Nowhere does the story hint that David might suspect that Uriah is acting and speaking out of knowledge of the true situation. It is plausible, then, that David interprets the wine's fail-ure to work its effect as another expression of Uriah's self-control and of his loyalty to his comrades-in-arms. Thus, after failing to exploit Uriah's impulses to get his way, David decides to take advantage of his innocence and extreme loyalty and has no qualms about placing in his hands the very letter that condemns him to death.[12] What we have here is not a desperate if concealed struggle between two men but a scheming rich man who de-spoils an unsuspecting poor man. If, nevertheless, David's stratagem does not succeed[13] and he eventually meets his punishment, it must be because God is watching from on high and nothing is concealed from Him.

David was no Oriental potentate who abducts wives or schemes against husbands to facilitate stealing their wives, along the lines reflected by Abra-ham's fears as he approached Egypt, "If the Egyptians see you, and think, 'She is his wife,' they will kill me and let you live" (Gen. 12:12).[14] True, once smitten by lust after seeing the woman in her bath he was not deterred by the information that she was the wife of Uriah the Hittite (v. 3). It is somewhat astonishing that the narrator does not tell us that this is one of David's warriors (see 2 Sam. 23:39), currently absent at the front (we learn this only in verse 6, when David summons him).[15] After their lovemaking, though, the king sends her back home, hoping that, in the absence of any results, it will be as if nothing had happened (at least so far as the absent husband is concerned). Already at this stage, even before it can be known whether the woman will conceive, the narrator informs us of another aspect of the delicate situation as follows: "he lay with her—*she had just purified herself after her period*—and she went back home" (v. 4). As is emphasized by Driver (*Samuel*, ad loc.), the participial form *mithqaddeǎeth* requires us to understand the words in italics as a subordinate circumstantial clause, meaning that she was just then in the situation of purification after her defilement.[16] Grammatically, then, "purified" cannot refer to purification from the defilement of intercourse (Lev. 15:18), which she performs before going home (i.e., "he lay with her, then she purified herself and went home"), as is suggested by Keil and Delitzsch (*Books of Samuel*, ad loc.). It is also very difficult to accept the view of Rashi and of Kimchi that the clause is meant to clear David of the suspicion of an additional transgression, relations with a menstruating woman. Quite plausible is an interpretation, accepted by many, that goes back to Abravanel: "The narrator states this to indicate that she conceived then, because it is the most appropriate time for this."[17] Most persuasive is the interpretation of two early twelfth-century commentators, the French Joseph Kara—"so that it is impossible to ascribe paternity of the child to her husband Uriah"—and the Spaniard Isaac ben Samuel Alkanzi—"because a woman does not menstruate when she is pregnant."[18] Although the narrator might want to tell us that the odds of Bathsheba's conceiving are high, it is far more important for him to emphasize that when she came to the king she was not pregnant by her husband, so that it will be difficult to conceal her adultery if she does conceive. In addition, this detail is essential for us to understand her utter certainty that she is pregnant by David (v. 5) and his immediate recognition of his responsibility for what has happened and obligation to do something about it (v. 6).

Even when the plot thickens because of Bathsheba's pregnancy, David does not see marriage to her as a realistic way out. Their affair was only a one-night stand. His inclination is to find a way to leave her with her husband, as is demonstrated by the fact that, instead of trying to get rid of Uriah, David immediately summons him to Jerusalem. When the king interrogates Joab's adjutant as to the situation at the front, it is clear to us that the debriefing is merely a cover for the impetuous royal summons to the cuckolded husband. The irony of this deception is highlighted by the fact that the king's questions are reported, but not Uriah's responses. This reminds us that, had Bathsheba not conceived, David would never have asked her husband about "the well-being (*šalom*) of Joab, the well-being of the army, and the well-being (i.e., the state) of the war" (v. 7). At the end of the audience, the king dismisses Uriah and gives him permission to go home to "bathe his feet." In the present context, Abravanel may well be right that this is a euphemism for sexual intercourse. It is clear, in any case, that the king is thereby telling his officer that he will not be sent back to the front immediately and that until he receives further orders he is furloughed to his house. What is more, the royal present sent after him is an expression of the king's satisfaction with his services. Readers, alerted by the echo of "a woman bathing" (v. 2) in "bathe your feet" (v. 8), have no doubt as to David's covert goal in sending Uriah to Bathsheba.

Uriah does not go home, however. We are told this three times in succession in almost identical terms—first by the narrator (v. 9), next by courtiers when they inform David (v. 10a), and finally by David, when he asks Uriah to explain his astounding conduct (v. 10b). This accentuated reiteration tells us that David's scheme has run into an unforeseen impediment, and that the first complication (caused by Bathsheba's pregnancy) is now augmented by another (caused by Uriah's steadfastness in his principles). We have already discussed Uriah's answer above (pp. 103–104); surely it is much more biting if we take it as an unwitting reproach rather than as an open challenge.[19] The sting of these words is felt, then, not by the speaker but by the listener: what Uriah is not willing to do with permission, I did illicitly. Uriah clearly would not dare to apply to the king his self-imposed severity as Joab's subordinate, called from the battlefield but soon to be sent back. But the words surely cut the king to the heart: not only did I behave this way, it was with the beloved wife of my loyal servant!

Uriah's integrity confounds David's scheme and complicates his predicament. As it becomes increasingly clear that there is no easy way to conceal his misdeed, the lure grows to do so by means of an additional transgression. David does not attempt verbal persuasion to sway his servant, but neither does he praise this behavior. Only indirectly does he relate to Uriah's profound identification with his comrades, when he promises him that his stay in the city will not be prolonged: "Stay here today also, and tomorrow I will send you off" (v. 12). But this promise is not kept. Like hosts who detain their guests for longer than the allotted period (an egregious example of this is the father of the concubine of Gibeah, who keeps deferring his son-in-law's departure [Judg. 19:4–9]), David does not dispatch Uriah the next day; instead, on the evening of his third night in the city, he invites him to dine at the royal table. The clear echo of "David remained in Jerusalem" (v. 1) in "So Uriah remained in Jerusalem that day and the next" (v. 12b)[20] tells us that David's reason for putting off Uriah's departure was his hope that a protracted sojourn in Jerusalem would make it more difficult for the husband of such a beautiful woman to adhere to his oath to avoid his house. When night falls, David caps the do-nothing leave in the city with the delights of a royal feast and the intoxicating power of wine.

David manages to get Uriah drunk, expecting that when the latter leaves the palace his feet will carry him home to his wife. We share this expectation as we read, "in the evening [Uriah] went out to sleep"; but then comes the surprise: "on his bed, with his lord's officers" (v. 13). This time, too, David does not attribute the failure of his scheme to the finger of God and does not see it as a warning of what he can expect if he continues in this path.[21] The extreme imbalance of power between king and Hittite subject, David's concern for his good name and authority, and his responsibility for Bathsheba's well-being lead him not to recoil from adding a new sin to the past transgression and sending Uriah to his death by Ammonite swords. Making Uriah the bearer of his own doom seems to be required by the situation—confiding the letter to him makes his summons from the battlefield natural and routine, whereas entrusting it to another envoy might have given Uriah reason to suspect that he has fallen from grace and increase his caution. At the same time, it permits the narrator to juxtapose the king with his victim: Uriah's ethical sensibilities prevent him from doing something he considers to be wrong, even though it would damage no one, whereas David has no qualms about making him the bearer of his own death sentence.[22]

Far more serious is the content of the letter, in which the king orders his general to exploit Uriah's devotion and to reward him for his utter fidelity to his comrades-in-arms by having them abandon him in a situation where he depends on their assistance. The king's commission has two parts: first, to station Uriah in a dangerous salient; second, to see to it that at the height of the battle he is left without cover—"then fall back so that he may be killed" (v. 15). The import of this two-part order is that Uriah be killed by Ammonite hands, without any other Israelite casualties and without the Israelite army suffering defeat. The need for total secrecy, though self-understood, somewhat contradicts the tactic of a planned retreat. Only an extremely talented commander can determine the moment when soldiers can be ordered to fall back without having the command reach the ears of Uriah and without those who retreat being aware that they are abandoning their comrade. David's use of the plural ("Place . . . fall back")[23] apparently allows Joab to assign command of this complex operation to one of his subordinates. Joab, however, prefers not to implement the second and extremely risky part of the order at all; he merely positions Uriah at the most dangerous point on the line (v. 16). Since Uriah falls in company with other soldiers, we may infer that there was no retreat abandoning him; the narrator emphasizes as much by recounting Uriah's death as a sort of appendix to theirs—"some of David's officers among the troops fell; Uriah the Hittite was among those who died" (v. 17). What is more, Joab's report, as conveyed by the messenger he sends back to Jerusalem (vv. 20–21) makes it plain that the casualties resulted when the troops came too near the wall in their pursuit of the force that had sallied out from the city. The slightly more detailed relation by the messenger (vv. 23–24) also implies that the original initiative was taken by the Ammonites ("First the men prevailed against us and sallied out against us into the open"). But in the heat of battle caution was flung to the winds ("we drove them back up to the entrance to the gate") and the casualties multiplied when the force came within range of the archers on the walls.[24]

The severity of the defeat is reflected in Joab's apprehensions about David's wrath and in the encouragement with which David concludes his speech to that messenger, as well as in the king's order to Joab to press the attack until the city is destroyed (v. 25). For reasons that are not hard to imagine (and which the narrator does not specify because they relate to a secondary character), Joab does not implement the complex tactic outlined by David.[25] As a commander concerned for the morale of his troops and for bolstering his moral authority, he clearly prefers the risk of obeying the king's command only in part to giving a secret order for retreat whose base nature would be hard to conceal. Loyalty to his king could not bring Joab to take on himself the risk that David might be willing to accept to get rid of Bathsheba's husband.[26]

The death of the other soldiers cannot be blamed on Joab's deviation from the secret order, just as there is no reason to blame David for their deaths.[27] They were victims of the war, and there is no direct causal link between Uriah's death and theirs. At most one can say that David's words, "where the fighting is fiercest," and his desire that Uriah fall at enemy hands led Joab to excessive boldness and failure to adhere to normal standards of caution.[28] In any case, Joab was duty bound to report on the local setback and explain it. When he prepares an answer for David's anticipated fury that the soldiers came too close to the wall, he appends the death of Uriah as a wondrous remedy—"Then say, 'Your servant Uriah the Hittite was among those killed' " (v. 21). Before we attempt to understand how Joab thought to mitigate one disaster by means of another, we should examine the addition found in the Septuagint between verses 22 and 23:

> The messenger went and came and told David all that Joab had sent him to say [all about the battle. David was angry with Joab and said to the messenger, "Why did you come so close to the city to attack it? Didn't you know you would be smitten from the wall? Who struck down Abimelech son of Jerubbaal? Was it not a woman who dropped an upper millstone on him from the wall at Thebez, from which he died? Why did you come so close to the wall?"] The messenger said to David, "For at first the men prevailed against us. . . . "

This text has two advantages: (1) the messenger's detailed report comes in response to David's criticism; (2) the word "for" (*ki*) with which the messenger begins seems to require a prior question. Hence it is customary to see the Septuagint text as authentic, whether as is (Nowack, Driver), with emendation (Budde), with further expansion (McCarter), or as evidence that the reference to the death of Abimelech belongs here and was spoken by David and not Joab (Caspari, Segal, Hertzberg). The last three are right when they argue that the perfect symmetry between Joab's expectation and their verbal realization is implausible, and that the Septuagint text is an inflated version in which the same passage appears twice.[29] At the same time, we may disagree with their assumption that David is the appropriate source of the tactical lesson to be derived from Abimelech's death. Driver himself acknowledges that the word "for" can be understood in a noncausal sense, as introducing direct address, as in Gen. 29:33 and 1 Sam. 2:16.[30] In the circumstances of a report on a local setback, it is perfectly plausible for a messenger to offer justifications before the commander explodes at him (as in the order of the Masoretic text). What is more, this seems to be the sting in the story. The surprising aspect of Joab's instructions to the messenger is not his ability to foresee the king's angry reaction to the news of a serious tactical blunder, but that he tells the messenger to exclude Uriah's death from the general report and reserve this information to rebut the king's anticipated wrath.

The narrator does not tell us that Joab let his messenger in on the secret of the letter; in light of the incomplete fulfillment of the king's commission it seems likely that he did not. The messenger may have guessed that Uriah's death bound David to Joab in chains of conspiracy and gratitude; or he may have interpreted the general's instructions as intended to cast the blame for the rout alongside the city gate on the much-heralded commander who was present at the spot and paid for his blunder with his life.[31] In any case, he does not follow Joab's instructions. Instead of leaving the matter of Uriah to the end as a trump card, he adds (according to the Masoretic text) the report of Uriah's death to the description of the battle, thereby making the soothing response precede the anticipated anger. The sting of the episode, according to the Septuagint text, is in the rapid transition—but is it not too rapid to be psychologically convincing?—from David's anger at the vain losses to the comforting words that are one hundred eighty degrees removed: "Do not be distressed about the matter. The sword always takes its toll" (v. 25). According to the Masoretic reading, however, the sting lies in the disparity between the expectations of Joab (who knows how much David is normally concerned for the lives of his soldiers) and David's actual response, in the shadow of his lethal commission. Precisely because this time David did not respond as was his wont, the narrator reports Joab's words at length (including the example of Abimelech's death at the hands of a woman, to which David must often have referred) as a means to delineate David's normal approach.[32] All the more astonishing, against this background, is the equanimity the king adopts this time, when he is shackled by his sin.

The superiority of the Masoretic text is evident also in the fine distinction between Joab and the messenger, lost in the Septuagint version. The messenger's failure to report separately on Uriah's death retrospectively illuminates Joab's intention in doing so. Whereas the envoy, standing in person before the king, fears the monarch's ire and does everything to prevent its eruption, Joab's position vis-à-vis David is more complex, both because he can allow himself much more latitude than the envoy can, and also because of the resentment he has accumulated against his king, who on more than one occasion had expressed his revulsion at the ruthless acts of the devoted general. Hence it seems likely that Joab sought to take full advantage of the opportunity afforded him by David's entanglement by embedding a sharp thrust in his embarrassing report: Should the king, safe in his palace, wax wroth at the blood of his servants spilled in vain, this time we have the means to calm him down—for the blood of Uriah was shed with theirs. . . . The author of the reading preserved in the Septuagint has blurred all of this. According to that text, the messenger does precisely as Joab instructed him and reports Uriah's death only after David explodes in anger; but by adding the news to the description of the battle outside the gates, he dispels the dramatic tension with which Joab wished to present Uriah's death. Not only is the Septuagint text implausible as it stands, then; accepting its testimony as to the sequence of events blurs the literary finesse of the episode, detracts from the vitality of the characters, and obscures the hidden struggle between them—a struggle that embodies one of the lessons of the anatomy of the king's sin: When the son of Jesse has recourse to the methods of the son of Zeruiah, he must harden his heart against the unnecessary casualties, knowing full well that this time it was Joab who softened David's command![33]

The city gate was the weak point in the fortifications and was repeatedly the focus of enemy assaults (see Gen. 24:60; Isa. 22:7) as well as of defensive efforts (see Isa. 28:6; Ps. 127:4–5). Since Uriah and his comrades were killed because they came too close to "the entrance to the gate" (v. 23, meaning the open space in front of the gate—see Judg. 18:16; 1 Kings 22:10), the implication of Joab's report is that he expects instructions: should he continue close fighting outside the "entrance to the gate," or should he settle for a passive siege and wait for the city to capitulate from hunger? David's answer is divided into two parts: "Do not be distressed about the matter, for the sword always takes its toll. Press your attack on the city and destroy it! Encourage him!" (v. 25).

The king first makes clear to his general that he must not agonize over the deaths of the soldiers, because it is the nature of war to claim victims. As a strong affirmation that no error was involved in the setback, he instructs him to continue to follow the same tactic, with even more vigor. This perfect cover for both his order and its implementation by Joab is reflected stylistically in the echo of his previous order in the present one. In the secret letter, David wrote: "Place Uriah in the front line where the fighting is fiercest *(ha-milḥamah ha-ḥazaqah)*" (11:15); now he orders that same tactic be pursued: "Press your attack (*haḥzeq milḥamtᵉkha*)" and even gives Joab his full personal backing: "Encourage him! (*uᵉ-hazzᵉqehu*)." This repeated use of the verb *h.z.q* also echoes the encouragement that Joab gave his brother Abishai before the fateful battle on the same field (the open space before the gates of Rabbath-Ammon) a year earlier: "Let us be strong and resolute (*ḥazaq uᵉ-nithḥazzaq*) for the sake of our people and the towns of our God; and the Lord will do what He deems right" (10:12).[34] Joab's statement is an impressive combination of superb dedication to saving one's people and country and humble recognition of dependence on divine judgment. By contrast, David's message, informed by his effort to conceal his reliance on the enemy's sword to bring about the death of one of his heroes, is conspicuous for its moral and religious poverty.[35] Joab bowed his head before the divine judgment—"the Lord will do what He deems right (*ha-ṭov be-ᶜeinav*)"; David pontificates confidently, "Do not be distressed (*ʾal yeraᶜ bᵉ-ᶜeinekha*) about the matter." It is no wonder that David's reply makes no reference to the Lord, who is in fact mentioned nowhere in the episode of the king's transgression (chapter 11), except for the end of the last verse, "but the Lord was displeased (*wa-yeraᶜ ha-davar . . . bᵉ-ᶜeinei YHWH*) with what David had done" (v. 27b). Here the narrator takes David's consolation to Joab and inverts it, preparing us for the restoration of an ethical value system and for the king's return to his God.

The Juridical Parable

The juridical parable is a fictional tale with a realistic plot dealing with an act of lawbreaking, told to someone who has committed a transgression or is intimately involved with the matter, with the aim of getting him to unwittingly pronounce judgment on himself. The addressee of the story will be caught in the snare laid for him only if he innocently believes that the incident being related actually took place and requires his intervention and only if he does not prematurely discover the affinity between the fictional transgression and that in which he is involved. Whereas beast (and tree) fables, by their very nature, refer to something else and thus betray that they are a fabrication, the realism of the juridical parable is intended to conceal the fact that it is a fiction. Just as the teller of the parable must guard against too close a likeness to the actual case, he or she must also avoid excessive deviating from it, lest the force of the analogy be vitiated. At the end of the tale, the narrator whips away the veil, generally by means of some identifying phrase: the true hero of the incident is the listener— "That man is you!" The juridical parable is thus an allegory in disguise, intended to overcome an individual's bias in his own favor so he can measure himself by the same standards he applies to others.[36]

There are three clear examples of the juridical parable in Scripture, and two more that have some attributes of the genre. The three clear examples are all in the historical books (2 Sam. 12:1–14; 2 Sam. 14:1–23; and 1 Kings 20:35–43); the other two are in the prophetic books (Isa. 5:1–7; Jer. 3:1–5). The former are woven into historical events and addressed to kings, whereas the latter are part of the prophet's rebuke of the people. The judicial dilemma—the hallmark of this literary form—is concrete when aired before a king and judge but merely rhetorical when the prophet expounds it to his listeners.[37] The widow who calls out, "Help, O king" (2 Sam. 14:4) and the soldier who "cried out to the king" on the high road (1 Kings 20:39) were seeking a legal remedy from the highest judicial instance, and were answered—the former winning her suit, the latter losing his. By contrast, the complaint of the oppressed poor man is laid before the king by a prophet, not by the ostensible wronged party. Even though Nathan never mentions the names of the two men and the city where they live, David obviously believes that he is hearing a real case requiring him to render a verdict and pronounce sentence: "David flew into a rage against the man, and said, . . . 'As the Lord lives, the man who did this deserves to die! *He shall pay* for the lamb four times over' " (2 Sam. 12:5–6).

The more emphatic his sentence, the more difficult it is for the judge to exempt himself from its implications for himself. David's fury with the rich man who plundered and showed no mercy propels him to give categorical force to his condemnation by means of the oath, "*as the Lord lives.*" The case of the widow's son of Tekoa is more complex, however, so she must press the king for such an asseveration—"Let Your Majesty be mindful of the Lord your God and restrain the blood avenger bent on destruction"—before he consents to utter an oath: "*As the Lord lives,* not a hair of your son shall fall to the ground" (2 Sam. 14:11). Ahab does not render his verdict beyond appeal by an oath in the name of the Lord but produces the same effect by emphasizing that the appellant has already judged himself: "You have your verdict; *you pronounced it yourself*" (1 Kings 20:40). Here the dramatic irony peaks: not only does the king unwittingly judge himself (as in the other juridical parables); in his blindness, he sets a precedent that will quickly return to haunt him—a judgment that is more valid than judgment by someone else.

These two elements—the verdict and its reiteration—are not found in the secondary type of juridical parable, where the demand for justice does not even have a fictional substance. When Isaiah appoints his audience as judges—"Now then, dwellers of Jerusalem and men of Judah, you be the judges between me and my vineyard. What more could have been done for my vineyard that I failed to do in it? Why, when I hoped it would yield grapes, did it yield wild grapes?" (Isa. 5:3–4)—it is merely a literary-rhetorical avatar of an actual appeal to the king for public justice. Because his hearers are not real judges he does not wait for their response. It is enough for the question to penetrate their consciousness and open the way for his response:

"Now I am going to tell you what I will do to my vineyard" (v. 5). Jeremiah does the same thing; he even presents the question in the abstract, without wrapping it in a fable: "If a man divorces his wife, and she leaves him and marries another man, can he ever go back to her?" and answers himself: "Would not such a land be defiled?" (3:1).

These five parables are similar in their reliance on the judicial domain: cases of theft, murder, and negligence by a custodian are brought before David and Ahab; the prophets ask the people about a criminal breach of trust and laws of marriage and divorce. The last two, however, differ from the first group in the degree of realism with which the courtroom situation is endowed. Alongside this formal difference there is a substantive difference: when the appeal is to a king, the facts of the case must justify royal intervention; the prophets can answer their own questions because the legal issue is simple and clear-cut. Isaiah and Jeremiah invoke serious transgressions, moral scandals that arouse instinctive opposition, whereas the negligent custodian and the fratricide who is the only surviving child of his widowed mother constitute more ambiguous cases. We may assume, then, that the case of the rich man who took the lamb of his poor neighbor is not absolutely clear-cut; otherwise, David's suspicions might have been aroused by the very fact that the case was being referred to him.[38]

Various means are used to camouflage the real issue. This ranges from actual disguise—the woman of Tekoa dons widow's weeds, one of the sons of the prophets covered his eyes and ordered his companion to hit him until he was wounded—through linguistic concealment: Nathan sets his case in an unnamed city. Isaiah gives the impression that this time he is not prophesying in the name of the Lord but is reciting a poem about an actual vineyard in a particular place: "My beloved had a vineyard in Qeren Ben-Shemen." Jeremiah merely raises a halakic issue relating to personal status: "If a man divorces his wife. . . . " Just as the means of concealment are similar, so is there great similarity in the modes of disclosure. In three parables, the identification is direct. Nathan charges: "That man is you." Jeremiah says: "You have whored with many lovers." Isaiah provides the key: "For the vineyard of the Lord of Hosts is the House of Israel, and the seedlings he lovingly tended are the men of Judah."[39] In the other two parables, the fictional legal cases are compared with the real situation, accompanied by prominent use of the second person. The man of God accuses Ahab directly: "Because you have set free the man whom I doomed." The woman from Tekoa unveils the analogy indirectly: "Why then have you planned the like against God's people? In making this pronouncement, Your Majesty condemns himself in that Your Majesty does not bring back his own banished one."

Of course, the main point of every parable, especially the juridical parable, where the disguise is intrinsic, is its affinity, tempered by distance, with the real situation. The affinity lies in the analogy between the parable and the incident alluded to, built up from their many lines of similarity. The distance involves a change in the category of crime, diminished gravity, or both of these. Nathan reduces the extent of the crime—one transgression instead of two—and changes its category while mitigating its gravity—the theft of a poor man's lamb instead of adultery and murder. Jeremiah does all of these: his parable speaks of the defilement of the land by the return of the divorced woman who had been married to another man (only one), instead of its incomparably greater defilement by the whoring of a married woman after many lovers. The man of God who reproves Ahab does not need to change the type of misdeed, because he drastically reduces its severity—negligence in guarding an anonymous prisoner instead of the intentional parole of the king of Aram, the man whom the Lord "has doomed." Isaiah, who does not even bother with a full-fledged disguise (see n. 39), is content with modifying the type of offense while leaving the severity of the vineyard's misbehavior—producing sour grapes—on a par with the offense of the Israelites, who do injustice and iniquity instead of justice and equity.

The clear tendency of the juridical parable to present a less severe transgression than actually occurred seems to weaken its application to the situation at hand. But the appearance is deceiving; the parable falls within the scope of the actual event, as Abravanel explains: "The prophet replaced murder of the poor man by the theft of his lamb, so that David would respond that the rich man's life was forfeit merely for the lamb, after which the prophet could draw the a fortiori conclusion" (*Commentary on the Former Prophets*, p. 344).

The juridical parable that Joab plants in the mouth of the wise woman from Tekoa (2 Sam. 14) seems to deviate from this clear and reasonable principle. Here neither the nature of the crime (fratricide) nor its severity are altered. Here, though, the woman's goal is not to get David to convict himself, but to pardon his son. For this, the crime in the parable must be *more severe* than that which really occurred; otherwise, the pardon of the widow's son would not be applicable to the king's son. Indeed, the woman presents the king with a crime that is far more culpable—fratricide in the wake of a quarrel, not as retribution for rape.[40] At the same time, she describes a particularly difficult family situation that, in her opinion, requires that the full severity of the law not be invoked: she is a widow and the fratricidal son is the only one to carry on the name of her late husband. Even though these are not extenuating circumstances (which could detract from the gravity of the crime) but only grave consequences (which might justify commutation of the sentence), they do undermine the a fortiori link between the parable and the real incident. How can the pardon of the widow's only surviving son apply to Absalom, whose father is alive and well and has many other sons? (See 2 Sam. 3:2–5 and 5:13–16.)[41]

Hoftijzer ("David and the Tekoite Woman," pp. 422–24) replies that one must distinguish between the "basic facts" on which the sentence is based and which give it the force of precedent, and "secondary facts" meant to thicken the camouflage and prevent David from discovering prematurely that the reference is really to his son and himself. Similarly, Fokkelman (*Narrative Art* 1, p. 145) and Weisman (*People and King*, pp. 56–57) believe that the theophoric oath the widow manages to extract from David gives his decree the force of binding precedent that also applies to the case of Absalom. These formalistic explanations may be valid, but they do not suffice. The first requires that we totally ignore the judicial and moral weight of the reasons alleged in the request for a pardon. The second requires that absolute validity be accorded to a sacral oath. Hence they should be supplemented by an examination of all the means the wise woman adopts to influence the king.

Joab instructs the Tekoite woman to disguise herself as a "woman *who has mourned a long time* over a departed one" (14:2), emphasizing her firm and unshaken fidelity to her murdered son. He also prompts her with words she is to use in her desperate struggle to save the life of the murderer. These tactics give her a decided advantage over David. True, her mourning is associated with David's by a verbal echo—"he *mourned* over his son [Amnon] *a long time*" (13:37). But whereas she continues to mourn, David's grief for his murdered son has already waned, and his heart has turned to longing for his murderer: "King David was pining away for Absalom, for [the king] had gotten over Amnon's death" (13:39). Joab, aware of this development and of its limits, and estimating that David cannot advance on his own from longing to forgiveness, decides to act behind the scenes to assist him (14:1–2). From the way in which Joab stage-manages the Tekoite woman's appearance before the king, it seems plausible that he felt that a sophisticated juridical parable would not be enough to clarify the judicial and moral complications of the dilemma confronting David. The king also needed the living example of the devoted and brave widow to attain the willingness and courage necessary for escaping his psychological impediments and hesitations.

The narrator does not reveal the extent to which David, hearing the juridical parable and its moral, is conscious of the conspicuous contrast between the woman and himself, whose basic situations are similar though their psychological responses and ability to act are different. It is clear, however, that the woman does not camouflage the affinities between the parable and the real situation with the same care as is done by the other expounders of juridical parables. Nor does she flinch at openly comparing the king's verdict about her son with his avoidance of such a decision regarding his own son (vv. 12–14). Finally, she does not dramatically reveal the fictional nature of her tale; instead, it is discovered by the hearer himself (vv. 18–20). Thus David could have compared her lot with his and her action with his inaction; it seems quite plausible that such a comparison affected his decision.

Both in the parable itself and the long speech that the woman makes afterwards—some of which remains quite incomprehensible despite the best efforts of commentators, both ancient and modern[42]—there seems to be no attempt to defend the murderer or appeal for mercy on his behalf, just as there is no manifestation of maternal love for him. The woman fights for his life, not for his sake, but for hers, that her "last ember not be quenched," and for the sake of her late husband, that he may have "a name and remnant." She asserts that the obligation to avenge the innocent blood of the victim is not on a par with the obligation to avert the terrible consequences of the punishment for his crime. As already noted, David might well believe that Amnon was not as innocent as the widow's dead son and that Absalom's crime was less serious than that of her fratricidal son. Precisely for this reason he is deeply impressed by the devotion of the bereaved mother, who is willing to bear the entire guilt that may be associated with failing to exact the legal penalty: "may the guilt be on me and *on my ancestral house,* Your Majesty *and his throne are innocent*" (14:9). This bold statement reminds us, and perhaps also the king, of the opposite statement, phrased in similar terms, uttered by David himself when he refrained from punishing Joab because of his dependence on him: "Both I and *my kingdom* are forever *innocent* before the Lord of shedding the blood of Abner son of Ner. May [the guilt] fall upon the head of Joab and all *his ancestral house.* May the house of Joab never be without someone suffering from a discharge or an eruption, or a male who handles the spindle, or one slain by the sword, or one lacking bread" (2 Sam. 3:28–29). This time the sin of unavenged blood cannot be on the head of the murderer, since it is he whom she wishes to have pardoned. Since, however, this time too, as with Joab in the past, the king fears that his pardon may return to haunt his throne, she assumes the full responsibility for any possible consequences, just as Rebekah sought to protect her son from the consequences of heeding her words: "Your curse, my son, be upon me!" (Gen. 27:13).

David, who is impressed by the weight of her arguments and the force of her presentation, takes an oath to protect her son against the blood avenger (in verse 11). This is not enough for her; she requests permission to bring another matter before him (v. 12). When this is granted, she vigorously demands that he do for "God's people" the same thing his judgment prevents the blood avenger from doing to her family and pardon his own son as he pardoned hers; otherwise, he will be guilty of injustice (this seems to be the meaning of verse 13). After the king recognizes the validity of the principle that one must not punish a murderer if this would cause irreparable harm to his family, he must apply it to his banished heir as well. True, this is not an a fortiori judicial conclusion, since the severe crime of the widow's son is mitigated only by the grave consequences for his family of his execution. But there is an ethical analogy—Absalom's less serious crime can be mitigated by the less serious consequences that his continued exile would have for the royal house and God's people.

This juridical parable is unique in another way. It seeks not only to oblige David to act in accordance with his ruling but also to persuade him to exert fully the authority and capacity he demonstrates in his judgment. So the woman of Tekoa goes on to explain that in her distress she petitioned the king for help, since only from him could she expect to find an attentive ear, since only the king has the authority and power to spare her from the blood avenger, and since only his judgment can guarantee her "comfort": "for my lord the king is like an angel of God, understanding everything, good and bad" (v. 17). This attempt to bolster David's self-esteem as a righteous judge (and also, perhaps, his authority as the final arbiter) seems evident also in the fact that the woman never explicitly states that her case was fictitious. She wishes to spare David, sorely humiliated by his blind failure to uncloak the evil intentions of Amnon (toward Tamar) and Absalom (toward Amnon), the disgrace of entrapment in a juridical parable. She allows the king to deduce from her long-winded arguments, after she has already been rescued, that in truth she had come not to save her (fictitious) son but his (real) son, just as she enables him to deduce that she did so as Joab's behest.

Thus the motif of "that man is you" is found also in the story of the woman of Tekoa, but inverted. When spoken by Nathan, sent to David to lay bare his sin and abase his pride, these words serve to stun David on two planes, the legal—the incriminating identification—and the psychological—the successful entrapment. But the wise woman of Tekoa, sent to David to give him the fortitude to overcome his doubts and act in accordance with his inclinations, guides him carefully and tactfully to the conclusion that "I am that woman." When she succeeds in this, she effusively lauds his wisdom as discoverer of the parable and its author: "My lord is as wise as an angel of God, to know all that goes on in the land" (v. 20).

The Parable and Its Moral: The Wife of Uriah as the Poor Man's Lamb

The significant mitigation of the severity of the crime, which we found in the four juridical parables related by prophets to incriminate and rebuke (and whose inversion by the Tekoite woman we ascribed to her inverted goal) suffices to explain why there is no parallel to the murder of Uriah in Nathan's parable.[43] Nor are there serious grounds for the opposite question about the addition of a character—the traveler for whose sake the lamb is slaughtered—for whom there is no parallel in the actual episode, given that such supplementary characters are also found in nonjuridical parables in Scripture.[44] The real question is not the addition of a character, but the expressive function of this character in the parable, and this we shall consider below. One should also ask whether Nathan's story contains a genuine legal crux that justifies bringing the case before the king. Isn't this an open-and-shut case of theft? Another question: what parallel does the parable offer for the impulsive passion that overpowered David and led him to sin? If the authors of juridical parables make the fictional incident less grave, we must assume that Nathan, too, is describing an emotional distress similar to that in the real incident, so that David will not be able to dismiss the parable with the argument that, although theft is less serious than adultery, when committed in cold blood it is seven times as despicable.

The apparently superfluous figure of the traveler seems to be the key to all three questions. The parable does not juxtapose a craving for meat to a lust for the bathing woman but rather to the duty of feeding an unexpected guest. *Helekh* in the sense of 'traveler' is found in Scripture only here; evidently it was preferred over other synonyms because it connotes a wayfarer who appears without warning.[45] Indeed, the suddenness with which he appears is highlighted by the threefold repetition of the verb *b.w.ʾ*, 'come, go', in verse 4. The importance of hospitality in Scripture is evident from the Patriarch Abraham's concern for the three wayfarers who pass by his tent (Gen. 18:1–8) and from the willingness of Lot and of the old man who lives in Gibeah to protect their guests even at the price of their daughters' honor (Gen. 19:8; Judg. 19:23–24). The distress of the host who has nothing to offer is reflected by the reason given for the rabbinic prohibition, "a man shall not send his fellow a barrel of wine with oil floating on top. Once someone sent his friend a barrel of wine with oil floating on top, and the latter, relying on it, went and invited guests. But when they came, he discovered that it was a barrel of wine [so that he could not honor them with oil as he had intended] and strangled himself" (BT Ḥullin 94a; see also the other examples there). It is also exemplified by the parable in Luke 11:5–10:

> Which of you shall have a friend, and shall go unto him at midnight, and say to him, Friend, let me have three loaves; for a friend of mine in his journey is come to me, and I have nothing to set before him? And he from within shall answer and say, Trouble me not: the door is now shut, and my children are with me in bed; I cannot rise and give thee. I say unto you, Though he will not rise and give him, because he is his friend, yet because of his importunity he will rise and give him as many as he needeth.

The distress of the host who cannot fulfill his obligation to his guest receives legal status in the hospitality laws of the Bedouin of the Beersheba district. Because this law may help us understand the parable of the poor man's lamb, I quote at length from Aref el-Aref's study of the Bedouins:

> *Adayieh* ('attack') is a Bedouin form of legal theft. If one member of the tribe attacks the flock of his neighbor or a member of the neighboring tribes, and filches one head to make a feast for a guest, this is called *Adayieh* . . . and is legitimate in Bedouin eyes. But they hedged it with certain conditions and restrictions, which if not complied with render the *Adayieh* common theft and punishable. Firstly, the *Adayieh* only applies to small cattle and excludes kine, camels and other livestock. . . . Secondly, the *Adayieh* applies only where the guest is "already on the carpet" and not for one who is expected. . . . The Bedouin may take the sheep if the shepherd is not around, . . . but immediately after the deed is done he must notify the owner. If he fails to notify him then his deed will be accounted stealing. Some tribes do not permit *Adayieh* if the shepherd is not around. It is forbidden to commit *Adayieh* on the flock of a stranger or one who has taken refuge with the tribe (*tenib*). The cattle which are excluded from *Adayieh* comprise: the ram (because it is needed for breeding purposes), the ewe which has a bell or beads attached to its neck (a sign that the owner has a special affection for it), the ewe reared in a tent, and one marked for the payment of a vow. Whoever takes any one of these for *Adayieh* is liable to pay the owner back fourfold. He has likewise to pay the *Zerka*—the fee of the judge before whom the case is brought. . . .
>
> . . .
>
> The *Adayieh* is only to be performed for the honor of the guest when the host is poor.[46]

The parable of the poor man's lamb can be placed in the perspective of the laws of *adayieh* as follows: a visitor arrives unexpectedly at a rich man's house. In order to accord him proper hospitality, the rich man steals a lamb from his poor neighbor,[47] butchers it, and serves it up to the guest. The host acts in this way even though he is not "poor" and does not lack something to feed the guest and even though his neighbor's lamb clearly belongs to the category from which theft in straitened circumstances is not permitted—a pet lamb raised in the tent: "He tended it and it grew up together with him and his children: . . . it was like a daughter to him" (12:3).

Even if we do not assume continuity in the customs of contemporary sheepherders and those of David's time, we may use the *adayieh* law to illuminate two fundamental motifs of the parable: the reality of the man's strong emotional bond to his animal and the urgent need for liberal hospitality.

The first motif—a lamb that is like a daughter—is not so remote from real life. Nathan was not speaking hyperbolically when he skillfully echoed Uriah's reply to David, "how can I go home and *eat and drink and lie* with my wife?" (11:11) in his description of the intimacy between the lamb and its master: "it used to *eat* [of] his bread, *drink* from his cup, and *lie* in his bosom" (12:3).[48] The words "lie in his bosom" bring the parable so close to the real-life situation that it risks dropping its mask. Hence Nathan quickly extracts its sting by effacing the sexual connotations: "it was like a daughter to him."[49]

The second motif is that of the arrival of the traveler, which requires the immediate slaughter of an animal. In the press of events, the rich man snatches his poor neighbor's lamb. The justification offered for this is: "he was loath to take anything from his own flocks or herds to prepare [a meal] for the guest who had come to him" (12:4). If, in fact, something resembling the law of *adayieh* was practiced in Israel in those days, the rich man's action should be understood as wrongful exploitation of the licit category of temporary theft (or, perhaps better, forced loan), motivated by his desire to avoid slaughtering one of his own prized lambs in the guest's honor. If this is an apt interpretation of the situation described in the parable, we can finally answer the ancient question: why doesn't the fine that David imposes on the rich man exceed the fourfold payment set by the Torah for a man who steals a lamb and slaughters it (Exod. 21:37)?[50] The king is simply ruling that, in light of the rich man's ample flocks and the poor man's love for his lamb, the duty of hospitality does not lessen the culpability of the theft.

Even if we assume that in ancient Judah the law did not take the host's distress into account, we must recognize that the parable does not put the accent on the actual theft—that is, the rich man's desire to entertain his guest at the expense of his poor neighbor. The emotional bond between the poor man and his lamb is juxtaposed to the rich man's "compassion" for his herds and flocks, that is, his unwillingness to slaughter one of his own animals to honor the visitor. David is infuriated not by the theft of the poor man's property, but by the insensitivity with which the rich man slaughters the weaker man's darling even though his benefit is negligible compared to the pain he causes his fellow. Hence David goes beyond awarding compensation: "The man who did this deserves to die!" (12:5). Those commentators who[51]—in the interests of symmetry between the parable and real life—assume that this means an actual death sentence are probably mistaken. It seems more likely, following Rashi, Kimchi, and others, that this is hyperbole expressing the magnitude of the sin of hard-hearted disregard of the poor man's love for his only lamb.[52] The phrase "deserving of death" (*ben maweth*) also occurs in David's rebuke of Abner: "As the Lord lives, [all of] you deserve to die, because you did not keep watch over your lord" (1 Sam. 26:16; see also Gen. 31:32 and 44:9).[53] This understanding of "The man who did this deserves to die!" (12:5) holds whether the rich man committed an ordinary theft or stole with the intention of returning what he stole later (as David intended to do with Uriah's wife). By contrast, it is extremely difficult to maintain the Masoretic reading "fourfold" in its literal

sense if the reference is to a theft that can under no circumstances be justified. For if "fourfold" is not a declaration in dry legal language that this
host is no better than any ordinary thief, why did David add a weighty rationale for the normal fine: "because he did such a thing and showed no
pity" (12:6)? Not surprisingly, then, commentators have suggested that we
understand "fourfold" in the sense of "eightfold" (Ibn Ezra and Kimchi),[54]
or in the sense of forty-four times (Ehrlich).[55] No such use of the dual is
found anywhere else in Scripture, though. Hence, as long as we have no
decisive proof that the customary law of *adayieh* prevailed in David's time,
the reading of most versions of the Septuagint—"sevenfold"—is clearly preferable.[56]

When David says *lo ḥamal* he clearly means that the rich man "showed
no pity" (v. 6). But this interpretation requires us to assume that the verb
ḥ.m.l is used with two different senses in close proximity, since *wa-yaḥmol* in
verse 4 means "*he spared* taking anything from his own flocks." Seeking
to avoid this alternation of meaning, several commentators would emend
verse 6 and read *lo* (*lamed-waw*), 'his', in place of *lo* (*lamed-aleph*), 'not',
yielding the sense "he spared his [property]" instead of "he had no pity."[57]
This conjecture should be rejected, however; not only is it far from persuasive, the question itself is unfounded. Scriptural style is not bothered by the
ambiguity caused by using one word with two different significations in a
single context.[58] Hence it sees no problem that the key word in the parable
is repeated in a different sense in its application; in fact, it relies on this as
a stylistic means for linking the two.[59] David does not repeat Nathan's
words; he goes beyond them. He repeats the verb *ḥ.m.l* so as to create an
ironic juxtaposition of the rich man's concern for his property and his lack
of compassion for the poor man, and to strip bare the causal linkage between the two: egoism spawns ruthlessness toward others.

Even before the prophet utters the fateful "that man is you," readers
know (thanks to the dramatic irony) that the king's wrath is rebounding
upon himself. David "showed no pity" for Uriah when he "took" (11:4) his
beautiful wife to his palace; and there was no compassion in his heart when
he gave him the fatal letter. What is more, his eagerness to have Uriah killed
by Ammonite swords caused his lack of compassion to extend to his loyal
soldiers, who fell in the siege of Rabbath-Ammon. The king, whose gorge
would rise (11:20) whenever he heard of unnecessary losses, was totally apa-
thetic when he heard that Bathsheba's husband was among the fallen.
Nathan knew that this insensitivity was temporary and that he could re-
awaken David's moral indignation by recounting a scandal seemingly un-
related to him—"David flew into a rage against the man" (12:5). By virtue
of this psychological continuity,[60] the prophet can use the juridical parable
not only as a means of rebuke, but also as an instrument of repentance.
David recognizes the full severity of his sin when he angrily pronounces
judgment on himself. What is more, this spontaneous reaction is an authen-

tic expression of the sincerity with which he confesses his sin. The words "that man is you" strip the mask of innocence from the royal judge, but the guilty party who is laid bare in this way is not an empty vessel: he still has the faculty to recognize both the magnitude of his sin and the justice of his punishment—"I stand guilty before the Lord!" (v. 13).[61]

The Parable and Its Application: To Despoil a Poor Man Is to Despise God

Too much is too little. It would seem that nothing remains to be said after the four words (two in Hebrew), "That man is you." Similarly, the force of David's reply—"I stand guilty before the Lord!"—is accentuated by its brevity (again only two words in Hebrew). With this in mind, Hertzberg (*I and II Samuel,* p. 258) cautiously suggested that Nathan's drawn-out speech (12:7b–12) is a later addition, whereas in the original version David's reply followed immediately upon Nathan's accusation, with no intervening verbiage. This reconstruction makes the prophet's reassuring "you shall not die" (v. 13b) come immediately after the death sentence that David has unwittingly passed on himself (v. 5), thus annulling it. Granted that brevity is the soul of sublime rhetoric, it cannot serve as a criterion for judging whether Nathan's harangue is original or a later addition. What is more, the prophet adds a new dimension to his rebuke, rather than repeating in explicit terms what he has already expressed indirectly in the parable. Whereas the parable presents the king as a man who had no mercy for his poor neighbor, the rebuke is entirely devoted to castigating his sin against his God: "Why then have you flouted the command of the Lord and done what is evil in his eyes?" (v. 9).[62]

Not only does the overt rebuke add a theological dimension to the king's sin, it heightens its gravity. In the parable of the poor man's lamb, the unrestrained and ruthless submission to one's passions is castigated but there is no hint of evil intent (this perfectly corresponds to the sequence of events in the body of the story). On the other hand, the direct condemnation could well be addressed to a king like Ahab, who murdered and took possession with malice aforethought: "You have put Uriah the Hittite to the sword; you took his wife and made her your wife" (v. 9). The implication here is that Uriah was sent to his death so that the king could marry his wife, whereas he was condemned only when David found no other way to cover up Bathsheba's pregnancy. How are we to explain this disparity between the parable (which corresponds to the actual situation) and its application (which goes far beyond it)?

One could argue that the prophet, blessed with knowledge of hidden motives, knew that at a certain stage a renewed lust for Bathsheba was added to David's need to cover up his sin, and it was this lust that tipped the balance when he wrote the fateful letter. But nothing in the body of the story suggests this; it seems unlikely that such a development would be reported to the reader only here, and only in this roundabout fashion. The problem is resolved, however, if we do not isolate artificially the prophet's open rebuke from the parable and, instead of juxtaposing these two condemnations, view them as complementary. Then it becomes evident that the rebuke does not relate to the transgressor's motives, because they have already been disclosed in the parable. The parable and its application differ, then, not only in their characterization of the sin—between two human beings, in the first, between a man and his God, in the second—but also in their perspective—a focus on causes and motives ("a traveler came to the rich man, but he was loath to take anything from his own flocks") as against a focus on deeds and results (Uriah killed, his wife wedded to the king, God's commandments flouted). If the parable did not precede the rebuke, we might have to rely on the scriptural mentality that does not sharply distinguish between outcome and goal and its tendency to describe end results in terms of original intention.[63] But against the background of the parable, which discloses the motive, it is clear that the prophet is now expounding the "objective" meaning of the king's actions. David did not intend to steal Bathsheba from her husband and certainly did not wish to flout the Lord's commandments; after the fact, however, one can say that he was more concerned for his good name than for the glory of the Lord, and that when he took to wife the widow of a man killed at his order he exacerbated both the murder and the sin that preceded it.

This aspect of the king's transgression is not explained in concepts like ours here but in terms of the scriptural notion of retribution: David returned evil for good.[64] Formally, Nathan's rebuke resembles the complaint of the king of Gerar against Abraham (Gen. 20:9; cf. also 26:29), and the voice of Joseph's conscience warding off the allures of Potiphar's wife (Gen. 39:9). Structurally it corresponds to a pattern frequently found in prophetic chastisements. This pattern has three parts: (1) an enumeration of God's mercies, with repeated emphasis on the pronoun *I* (e.g., Amos 2:9–10 and Hosea 2:10) and verbs of giving (e.g., 1 Sam. 2:28 and Hosea 2:10); (2) an accusation of having repaid good with evil, frequently phrased as a rhetorical question—"why then have you flouted?" (e.g., 1 Sam. 2:29 and Isa. 5:4); (3) a logical conclusion that begins with the word *therefore* (e.g., 1 Sam. 2:30 and Hosea 2:12), stating that God will give the ungrateful one his just deserts and repay him in kind.

The noun *raš* and the verb *r.w.š* occur frequently in the wisdom literature (fifteen times in Proverbs, twice in Ecclesiastes, and twice more in Psalms).[65] Elsewhere in Scripture, though, the noun occurs only in the David narratives—three times in the parable of the poor man's lamb and once in David's reaction to the proposal that he marry into the royal family: "I am but a poor man of no consequence" (1 Sam. 18:23). It seems plausible that Nathan's emphatic use of this rare noun is intended to establish an association with David's self-characterization when he was still only a military commander.[66] Through this association the prophet reminds the "rich man" who ruthlessly despoiled the "poor man" that in the past he himself was "a poor man." What is more, he has gone from being a poor man to a rich man by grace of divine election—"It was I who anointed you king over Israel" (v. 7)—and thanks to the bounty of Heaven—"I gave you your master's house and your master's wives into your bosom" (v. 8). This source of his wealth (that is, his many wives) obliges him to refrain from increasing it in illicit ways: his *master's* wives were given into his bosom, and he may choose "twice as much more" from the unmarried daughters of Israel and Judah;[67] but the wives of his *servants* are forbidden to him. Nevertheless, he was not content with what had been allotted to him, and repaid the Lord's bounty with evil by seizing what was barred to him: "you took the wife of Uriah the Hittite" (v. 10). The theft is followed by murder, which is also castigated in terms of the doctrine of retribution. His survival is a gift from the Lord—"I . . . rescued you from the hand of Saul" (v. 7);[68] but he has taken the life of his servant: "You have put Uriah the Hittite to the sword" (v. 9).

The last part of verse 10 sounds superfluous, as noted by Kimchi: "After he says 'put to the sword,' why does he add 'and had him killed by the sword of the Ammonites'?" He replies that the redundancy is spurious, since the second clause increases the severity of the murder—"he made him fall by the sword of Israel's enemies." Ehrlich and Fokkelman (*Narrative Art* 1, p. 84; *Randglossen* 3, p. 298) proposed that the problematic clause be attached to the following verse. Both solutions are far from satisfactory. Better is Segal's proposal that the clause originally stood at the end of verse 10, after the word "wife" (which also precedes it in its present location in verse 9). In fact, if we move the clause there, the redundant words become meaningful and even complete a striking concentric structure:

The sin (v. 9):
Why then have you flouted the command of the Lord and done what displeased him? You have put Uriah the Hittite to the *sword*, and his wife you took for yourself as a wife. . . .
The punishment (v. 10a):
Therefore the *sword* will never depart from your House
The sin (vv. 10b + 9b):
because you spurned Me by taking the wife of Uriah the Hittite and making her your wife [and had him killed by the *sword* of the Ammonites].[69]

The measure-for-measure association of the punishment with the crime gives the former a moral basis. Thus the word *sword* which appears in the punishment—"Therefore the *sword* will never depart from your House"—

relates to the double accusation of killing Uriah the Hittite "by the sword."
What is more, it strongly echoes what David himself told his messenger to
Joab: "The sword always takes its toll" (11:25).[70] When David becomes en-
tangled with Bathsheba, he totally forgets the lesson that Abigail had stated
so eloquently: "shedding blood needlessly" is liable to be "a cause of stumbling and of faltering courage" to him (1 Sam. 25:31). Consequently, her
long-ago blessing has not been realized either: "The Lord will grant my lord
an enduring house, because my lord is fighting the battles of the Lord, and
no wrong is ever to be found in you" (ibid., 28). Now, though, wrong has
been found in him, and the sword that shed innocent blood will "never"
depart from his house.

The meaning of this prolongation of the term of punishment is not
immediately clear: Does "never" (i.e., forever [*ʿad ʿolam*]) here mean "all
your life," as when Hannah says that Samuel "must remain [in Shiloh] forever" (1 Sam. 1:22); or does it mean "throughout all the generations," as
in Solomon's statement when he orders the death of Joab: "May the guilt
for their blood come down upon the head of Joab and his descendants
forever, and may good fortune from the Lord be granted forever to David
and his descendants, his house and his throne" (1 Kings 2:33)? The second
sense is the more common in Scripture;[71] nor is it plausible that the prophet
means "for the rest of your life," which already implies that David himself
will not be punished by death and renders meaningless the subsequent
commutation of the sentence—"you shall not die" (v. 13).

The question about the duration of the first punishment, which we resolved by having "never" refer to beyond David's lifetime, arises with even
greater force for the term implied by the phrasing of the second punishment: "I will take your wives *before your very eyes* and give them to another
man" (v. 11). At first sight this reinforces the common view that not only
verse 11, which starts with what seems to be a new beginning ("Thus said
the Lord"), but the entire passage (vv. 10–12) is a later addition,[72] since
Nathan's statements in verses 13–14, whose thrust is that David will not die
but the child will, ignore the two heavy penalties pronounced here. This
argument, however, does not apply to the punishment of the sword (v. 10),
since there is certainly a link between the punishment that "the sword will
never depart from your House" and his partial forgiveness—"The Lord has
remitted your sin; you shall not die." Nor does it hold for the sexual punishment (vv. 11–12), since Nathan has no reason to mention explicitly the
death penalty for adultery, which has already been implied by David's self-
incrimination ("the man who did this deserves to die!" [v. 5]), retroactively
confirmed by the fact that intercourse with a married women is a capital
offense (Deut. 22:22; Job 31:9–12). The problem of "before your very eyes"
can perhaps be resolved by adopting the conjectural emendation "from
your bosom."[73] The public punishment for the secret transgression is a clear
reference to the finger of God that is revealed before all in the retribution

that overtakes David when his own son has intercourse with his wives *on the roof* (16:22) at a time when he has been exiled with the rest of his army to Mahanaim (17:24), which is near Succoth![74]

In his application of the parable to the real-life situation, then, the prophet augments the severity of the king's deeds, both in their scope and gravity. When David says, "I stand guilty before the Lord!" he too goes far beyond his original reaction to the rich man's sin against the poor man. His unqualified admission of his guilt before his God—which obviously includes his sin toward his fellow man[75]—is also an acceptance of his punishment when spoken after that has been pronounced. In the wake of this full contrition, the prophet can inform him that his repentance has been accepted, although the consequences of his sin—his flouting of the Lord[76]— can be eradicated only by the punishment: "the child about to be born to you shall die" (v. 14).

The punishment strikes in the verse that immediately follows the rebuke. Its justice is accentuated by the identification of the stricken infant as "the child that *Uriah's wife* had borne to David" (v. 15). How is it possible that someone who heard the rebuke and even accepted its justice does not resign himself and submit to the child's imminent death? Furthermore, David's desperate struggle for his son's life seems to ignore not only the rebuke but also the prophet's declaration that the child's fate has already been determined! These questions led Schwally ("Zur Quellenkritik," pp. 155–56) to the conclusion (accepted by many)[77] that verse 12:15b originally followed directly after verse 11:27, and that everything in between is a later addition. Yet the crux of the problem is not the disparity between Nathan's rebuke and David's actions, but those actions themselves; excising the parable and rebuke do nothing to resolve the difficulty. Note that David's behavior while the infant lies ill surprises even the senior servants of his household. We cannot know what they knew about the sequence of events and Nathan's rebuke; it is clear, though, that the intensity of the king's self-mortification seemed aberrant to them at the time (v. 18) and subsequently quite incomprehensible in light of his rapid return to normal after the child's death (v. 21). The double astonishment of eyewitnesses experienced in the king's ways highlights the extraordinary nature of David's conduct, just as Eli's error regarding Hannah's prayer emphasizes its exceptional nature (see above, p. 19). The servants understand the king's behavior as expressing his pain and grief, and accordingly expect it to be gravely intensified when the grief is exchanged for mourning. David shows them their error: his protracted fast and extreme self-mortification accompany his prayer "for the boy" (v. 16) and express, more than speech possibly could, his pleading: "I thought: 'Who knows? The Lord may have pity on me, and the child may live' " (v. 22). At first sight, such goal-driven self-mortification seems very far from acceptance or comprehension of one's punishment. But it seems clear that David felt that in such a fateful period his duty was not to accept his afflictions submissively, but to deepen his awareness of his dependence on God. His supplications abase his pride more than acquiescence would. The king who sentenced his servant to an unmerited death cannot save the life of his son, who is dying before his eyes. He intensifies this recognition by beseeching the Lord of life for mercy, in word and deed. The hour will arrive for accepting the judgment, but only after David learns that the child has died: "He went into the House of the Lord and prostrated himself" (v. 20). The ritual prostration in the house of the Lord expresses submission, whereas lying on the earth was meant to awaken mercy.

The recourse to supplication in the wake of a seemingly unappealable judgment should not astonish us—consider the reaction of the king and people of Nineveh (which is also phrased with humility: "*Who knows* but that God may turn and relent?" [Jonah 3:9]) and King Hezekiah's prayer (Isa. 38:2–3). David's actions fall into the category of the practices of self-mortification adopted in times of distress to ward off the evil decree: "Yet, when they were ill, my dress was sackcloth,[78] I kept a fast . . . I was bowed with gloom" (Ps. 35:13–14). At the same time, they relate specifically to the previous events that brought this trouble on David's head; his penance is not meant to conceal that transgression and blot out its memory but to recall its full severity so as to uproot it from his heart. When David fasts and lies on the ground (12:16) without washing or anointing himself (12:20), he is belatedly identifying with Uriah's self-restraint when he rejected the equivocal invitation to go home and wash his feet (11:8) and declined to eat and drink and sleep with his wife (11:11). Now the king lies "on the ground," just as his soldiers are camped "in the open" (11:11) and just as Uriah lay "at the entrance of the royal palace" (11:9). David, lying on the ground, is also staying away from Bathsheba; the narrator makes clear that only after the death of the child does David return to her: "David consoled his wife Bathsheba; he went to her and lay with her" (12:24).[79]

Here again the narrator makes a normative statement by means of the terms by which he identifies the characters. She who was called "Uriah's wife" while the child was still alive (12:15) is now called "his [i.e., David's] wife" (v. 24), by virtue of his repentance. One may hypothesize that this bold faith in the power of penance constituted the core of David's consolation to Bathsheba. Her mourning for her dead infant is augmented by the reasonable anxiety that the same fate might await all future children born from her sinful marriage to the king.[80] Perhaps Bathsheba's prayer that this not happen is expressed in the name given to their next child, Solomon. Strong confirmation that David's repentance has been accepted comes from the prophet who had uttered the rebuke: "The Lord favored him, and He sent a message through the prophet Nathan; and he was named Jedidiah at the instance of the Lord" (12:24–25).[81]

Schwally ("Zur Quellenkritik," pp. 155–56) sees irrefutable proof of the secondary nature of 12:1–15a in the contrast between the image of Nathan as a moralist who rebukes the king in the Lord's name and as a scheming courtier who acts on behalf of Bathsheba and her son; this contrast is "so great as make any attempt at harmonization absurd." His schematic picture of the single-track development of prophecy from group ecstasy to literary admonition will not allow the parable and its application to have been composed before the eighth century. Nor can he accept that as far back as David's time there were prophets with entrée to the royal court, deeply involved in worldly interests; hence he sees the designation "prophet" associated with Nathan's name in 1 Kings 1 as an anachronistic interpolation. Ehrlich (*Randglossen*, on 1 Kings 1:23) did not go quite so far; he accepted the authenticity of Nathan's description as court prophet but totally rejected the historicity of Nathan's rebuke of the king. Schwally's arguments, based on a hypothetical line of development, have been totally invalidated by the discovery that as early as the first third of the second millennium BCE there were prophets in Mari—some of whom received financial support from the royal court—who warned the king of personal and political dangers and made material and apparently also ethical demands of him. They addressed the king in the name of the deity and were not afraid to menace him with the withdrawal of divine grace if he did not comply with the deity's demands.[82] As von Rad puts it: "Even if these parallels outside Israel allow us to postulate the historicity of Nathan as both a mantic prophet and a politician at the court of David, yet the internal source, the O. T. itself, does not give a sufficiently clear picture of his office to allow us to differentiate between it and other manifestations of contemporary *nabi*-prophecy" (*Old Testament Theology* 2, p. 11). Yehezkel Kaufmann also dealt with this vagueness: "In the stories about Nathan two figures actually appear—Nathan the prophet and Nathan the royal advisor. But the 'court prophet' is merely the fruit of imagination."[83] Kaufmann bases this sharp distinction between Nathan's deeds as bearer of the Lord's word and his independent actions on 2 Samuel 7, where Nathan initially encourages David in his desire to build the Lord's house, only to return on the next day to deliver the Lord's message that he must not do so.[84] Even if Kaufmann does not clear up all the uncertainties regarding Nathan and his status, he does demolish any basis for denying the historicity of an account in which a king of Israel is rebuked to his face by a prophet of the Lord who ate at his table. David was furious with the rich man who stole the poor man's lamb, but not with the prophet who told him, "That man is you." In fact, the doubts as to the plausibility of such a scene attest to its greatness.[85]

·5·

A PROPHETIC SIGN OVERCOMES
THOSE WHO WOULD DEFY IT

The King of Israel, the Prophet from Bethel,
and the Man of God from Judah

> *For as the rain or snow drops from heaven and*
> *returns not there, but soaks the earth and makes*
> *it bring forth vegetation, yielding seed for sowing*
> *and bread for eating, so is the word that issues*
> *from My mouth: It does not come back to Me*
> *unfulfilled, but performs what I purpose,*
> *achieves what I sent it to do.*
>
> Isa. 55:10–11

In the remarkable story about the man of God from Judah who prophesied the destruction of Jeroboam's altar in Bethel, there is more of the enigmatic than the lucid. It is difficult to put one's finger on the unifying theme of the plot with its multiple reversals; the very elements of the plot are strange and perplexing. The man of God, whom the Lord protected from the king's outstretched arm, soon meets his death at the command of his divine protector and is interred in an alien grave in Bethel. On the day that his prophecy is fulfilled, however, the wheel turns again: the bones of the man of God prevent the desecration of the tomb of the man who had brought about his death. These astonishing vagaries of miraculous immunity, its withdrawal and restoration, are accompanied by no less surprising changes in the identity of the bearer of the word of the Lord. The man of God, who proclaims the Lord's word to Bethel and whose prayer on behalf of the king is answered on high, is easily tricked into believing the false utterance of the old prophet. The latter, for his part, who begins as a liar, becomes the mouthpiece for the authentic word of the Lord, delivered first to the man of God and later to his fellow inhabitants of Bethel. These strange alterations and internal contrasts seem to be the chief motive for the prevalent tendency to question the literary unity and conceptual consistency of the story.[1]

In this chapter I shall attempt to demonstrate, by structural analysis and close reading, that the story is actually a single and well-knit prophetic narrative that extols prophecy while criticizing the prophet. Its theme is the supremacy of the Lord's word over those who speak it and its triumph over those who oppose it.

The Compass and Structure of the Story

It is hard to locate precisely the beginning of our story. The description of the appearance of the man of God in Bethel (1 Kings 13:1–2) depends on the background material in the previous chapter (12:25–33). On the other hand, its style and content are markedly different. The interjectory *wᵉ-hinneh* ("now behold") that introduces 13:1 clearly indicates that the original story could not have begun with this verse since it must refer to a preceding exposition of the circumstances. On the other hand, 12:25–33 cannot be that original exposition, since these verses refer to such key elements as the golden calves (vv. 28–29) and the cult places (12:31), which are not mentioned in the story.[2] It is implausible that the man of God, addressing himself directly to the altar at Bethel (13:2), would totally ignore the golden calves, whose sinful casting features prominently in 12:30. There is a stylistic criterion as well. Not only is the summation of Jeroboam's sins (12:25–33) written in the unmistakable deuteronomistic style of the redactor of the Book of Kings,[3] we can also discern a stylistic affinity between this schematic presentation and the two verses that come right after our story and summarize it (13:33–34).[4] A hallmark thereof is the repeated use of the verb *ᶜ.ś.h*, which appears no fewer than nine times in 12:25–33 to express the essence of Jeroboam's sin—his illegitimate and invalid creation of a cult—and again in the summary (13:33). In the body of the story (13:1–32a), by contrast, it occurs only once (v. 11), with its normal signification rather than the special sense of illegitimate action.

It is likely that the story originally ended with the description of the desecration of Bethel by Josiah king of Judah, now found in 2 Kings 23:16–18.[5] In the first place, it is implausible that it had an open ending that left readers wondering whether the Lord's sentence against the altar would be fulfilled and whether the old prophet's prediction about his tomb would come to pass. In addition, the second half of 2 Kings 23:18—"so they left his bones undisturbed together with the bones of the prophet who came from Samaria"—would be quite appropriate as the conclusion for 1 Kings 13 but has no real meaning in the story of Josiah. In the context of Josiah's campaign against the Samaritan cult, the ancient word of the Lord and the respect shown to the man of God who spoke it are relevant; but what is the incidental fate of the bones of the old prophet doing here? Third, 2 Kings 23:16–18 makes no mention of the golden calves and the cult places, and the verb ʿ.ś.h is used in its normal sense (whereas in verses 15 and 19 it refers to illegitimate action). Fourth, these verses are stylistically reminiscent of our story: they observe the distinction between the "man of God" (23:16 and 17) and the "prophet" (v. 18); they repeat the rare usage of the verb q.r.ʾ with "the word of the Lord" as its direct object (vv. 16 and 17); and they contain the lengthy repetitions that distinguish 1 Kings 13 from similar scriptural tales. On the other hand, the narrative mode of these three verses, which is scenic-dramatic and relies on dialogue, is quite distinct from the reportorial moralizing of the rest of 2 Kings 23 (which has direct speech only in verses 21 and 27 and no real dialogue).

On the basis of the foregoing we may imagine how the redactor integrated the prophetic narrative into the fabric of his deuteronomistic historiography. Since his approach was chiefly historico-didactic, he had no compunctions about dismembering the narrative unit, incorporating the body of the story into the history of Jeroboam and its epilogue into the annals of Josiah. This separation of the prophecy from its fulfillment substantially shifts the center of gravity: the story no longer focuses on prophecy (how the word of the Lord overcomes those who would deny it and is fulfilled three centuries later), but on cult (the illegitimacy of the Bethel altar and its well-deserved destruction). The first theme interested the prophets, their disciples, and their adherents, whereas the second, as is well known, was the main criterion used by the redactor of the Book of Kings for evaluating the conduct of the kings of Judah and Israel.

Moreover, the closing verses of our story, now found in 2 Kings 23:16–18, do not follow smoothly if attached to the end of its main segment (1 Kings 13:32a). This suggests that when the redactor split up the story he omitted a section, preferring to provide the reader with the required information through his own review of Josiah's campaign (we shall return to this point below). He seems to have applied similiar treatment to the original exposition of the story, which he replaced with his own survey of Jeroboam's transgressions. This assumption allows us to account for the discrepancy, in both style and content, between the exposition we have before us and the body of the story, as well as for the linguistic ("and behold") and factual dependence of the story on the missing exposition.[6]

This hypothesis is open to challenge on the grounds of the obvious duplication in 12:33 and 13:1. If 12:33 was indeed written by the person who interpolated the story at this point, why did he not avoid the duplication of "he ascended the altar" and "Jeroboam was standing on the altar"? One possible answer is provided by the redactor's verbose style and his lack of hesitation about repetition and emphases (from this perspective, 13:32–33 are no different from 12:25–31, which precede our story; the same is true of 2 Kings 16:10–12, which also deals with the adoption of an illegitimate cult). Verse 32 is still recounting the long-term and institutionalized transgressions of Jeroboam. The one-time act of mounting the altar deviates from this perspective and also interrupts the syntactic flow of the verse; this supports the common conjecture that the words "he ascended the altar" strayed here from the beginning of the next verse. On the other hand, verse 33 serves as a link between the general survey of Jeroboam's transgressions and the detailed story about what transpired on a particular festival, when the man of God from Judah came to Bethel. As such, it contains the first mention of the specific sin committed on that day. Targum Jonathan renders *wa-ya‘al* at the beginning of the verse transitively—"he offered on the altar"; whereas in the word-for-word repetition at the end of the verse, the Targum renders it intransitively—"he ascended the altar." This is how the first part of the verse is understood by those who assert that the direct object of the verb has dropped out—"he offered [sacrifices] on the altar"—as well as by those who hold that this is a case of idiomatic concision, with the implicit direct object understood. In any case, it seems that the beginning of the verse refers to the king's usurpation of the priestly prerogative of officiating before the altar (as Ahaz does—2 Kings 16:12–14). This is followed by a second reference to the date on which the events to be related occurred, already referred to in general terms in the previous verse, but with added emphasis on the gravity of the deviation from the prescribed season: "in the month which he had contrived of his own mind."[7] The end of the verse relates that Jeroboam ascended the altar and adds the purpose of this act—"to present an offering"—which seems to be taken from the actual story (13:1b) and makes it clear that the king literally ascended the altar ramp. This description is necessary to prepare us for the interjected *w'-hinneh*, 'now behold'. At the same time it generates the tension of anticipating future developments. True, this bridge is not as smooth and even as the integration of the story of Elijah and Ahaziah (2 Kings 1:2–17a) into the redactor's historical survey there.[8] On the other hand, we find similar repetitions in the verses that precede (2 Kings 8:29) and follow (ibid., 10:28) the prophetic account of Jehu's revolt.

Having defined the compass of the story (1 Kings 13:1–32a + 2 Kings 23:16–18), and taking into account our reconstruction of how it came to be interpolated into two different places in the Book of Kings—a process accompanied by the substitution of the redactor's surveys (1 Kings 12:25–33; 2 Kings 23:15) for the original exposition of the entire story and its conclusion—we can now consider its structure.

The story comprises six scenes, five of which take place on a single day— the fifteenth of the eighth month, the festival ordained by Jeroboam for his subjects (12:33). The sixth scene takes place some three hundred years later, in the eighteenth year of Josiah's reign (2 Kings 22:3). The scenes are demarcated by the following indications: (a) a partial or complete change in the dramatis personae (this indication is only partly applicable to scenes 3, 4, and 5, where there is an internal change of characters); (b) introductory sentences that recount the hero's arrival on the scene (using the verbs of motion *b.w.ʾ* or *h.l.k*, supplemented, in scenes 3 and 5, by the verb *m.ṣ.ʾ*);[9] (c) concluding sentences—the first four tell of the hero's departure from the scene (in three of them we are told that he is riding a donkey), whereas in the last two we have direct speech that conveys instructions about the common burial of the man of God and the old prophet; (d) a change of place (this indication, which follows directly from the previous two, applies only partially to scenes 3, 4, and 5, where there is an internal change of place). This pattern can be schematized as follows:

Scene 1 (13:1–10): The confrontation between the man of God and King Jeroboam
  Characters: The man of God, Jeroboam, and the assembled worshippers
  Place: The altar in Bethel
  Opening sentence: "Now behold, a man of God *came* to Bethel from Judah at the command of the Lord."
  Concluding sentence: "So he *left* by another road and did not go back by the road on which he had come to Bethel."
Scene 2 (13:11–13): Astonishing news spurs the prophet to go out
  Characters: The old prophet and his sons
  Place: The home of the old prophet, in Bethel
  Opening sentence: "There was an old prophet living in Bethel; and his sons *came* and told him. . . . "
  Concluding sentence: " 'Saddle the ass for me,' he said to his sons. They saddled the ass for him, and he mounted it."
Scene 3 (13:14–24): The confrontation between the man of God and the old prophet
  Characters: The old prophet and the man of God; at the end of the scene, the old prophet *solus*
  Place: On the road, at the home of the old prophet, and again on the road
  Opening sentence: "He *went* after the man of God. He *found him* sitting under a terebinth."
  Concluding sentence: "He *saddled the ass for him.* . . . He *went*, and a lion found him on the road and killed him."
Scene 4 (13:25–27): Astonishing news spurs the prophet to go out
  Characters: Passersby alone, later joined by the old prophet and his sons
  Place: On the road, and particularly in Bethel
  Opening sentence: "Some men who passed by saw the corpse lying on the road. . . . They *went* and told it in the town."
  Concluding sentence: "He said to his sons, 'Saddle the ass for me,' and they did so."

Scene 5 (13:28–32a): The old prophet and the corpse of the man of God
   Characters: The old prophet *solus,* later joined by his sons
   Place: On the road, and particularly at the family burial site
   Opening sentence: "He *went* and *found* the corpse lying on the road."
   Concluding sentence: "*Lay* (hanniḥu) *my bones beside his.* For what he
   announced by the word of the Lord . . . shall surely come true."
Scene 6 (2 Kings 23:16–18): King Josiah and the sepulchre of the man of
   God
   Characters: Josiah, his ministers, and the people of Bethel
   Place: The cemetery district of Bethel
   Opening sentence: (see n. 9)
   Concluding sentence: " '*Let him be* (hanniḥu lo),' he said, 'let no one
   disturb his bones.' So his *bones* rescued the *bones* of the prophet. . . . "

As noted, there is a change of characters and place in the course of the
third, fourth, and fifth scenes. Both characters and place change in verses
24, 25 and 28–29a, suggesting that we should divide these scenes in two.[10]
Perhaps because of the frequent changes of place in this story, however, the
narrator did not develop these episodes into full-fledged scenes. Instead,
he linked each to the main scene with which it is associated in the unfolding
of the plot. Although to some extent this blurs the division of the story into
scenes, the flexibility of form is repaid by the marked thematic and stylistic
parallelism between the second and fourth scenes. In the second scene
(13:11–13), his sons tell the old prophet about the miracles wrought by the
man of God and the route he took to leave the town. In the fourth scene
(13:25–27), he again acquires information, this time from the passersby
who inform him of the unnatural death of the man of God. The old
prophet's reaction to the two reports is identical: he orders his sons to saddle his ass and sets out hastily, without saying a word as to his intentions.
These are transitional scenes in which the pace of the narrative slows down
and the ground is prepared for the resumption of the plot. These scenes
create this lull by recounting, not action, but the transmission of information that is essentially already known to the reader from earlier scenes. At
the same time, they do maintain the forward momentum of the story: when
the decisive and dynamic old man, who excels at deductive thinking, takes
action, readers are eager to find out what will happen next.

The strict parallelism of the two transitional scenes is only part of the
symmetrical structure of the story. The main plot occupies four scenes, each
of them devoted to one confrontation between the man of God (who continues to act as the bearer of the Lord's word even after his death: see the
titles given above to scenes 1, 3, 5, and 6) and someone else. The thematic
parallels among the four main scenes, and the close similarities between
the two interludes, suggest that the story is divided into four parts, each of
which comprises a relatively short introduction (exposition, link, and

preparation) and a main scene (a stage in the unfolding of the plot). Two of the opening scenes have been dropped from our text, as we have seen, but a conjectural reconstruction of their contents can be based on what has replaced them in the Book of Kings and on their function in the story, as required by their location in its sequential structure.

Table 5.1 is a schematic summary of what we have said thus far about structure. The first conclusion to be drawn from a study of the table is that the allegations about the story's lack of unity and consequent attempts to analyze its component strata stem from a failure to understand the story. Its thematic unity is clearly reflected in its formal cohesive architecture. Formally, the story consists of four parts, which share a uniform basic structure (see table 5.2, below); as for content, there is a clear link between the first two parts on the one hand, and between the third and fourth parts on the other. In the first half of the story (parts I and II), the king of Israel and the prophet of Bethel work to frustrate the word of the Lord and harm its bearer; in the second half (parts III and IV), the prophet and the king of Judah work to honor the man of God and fulfill the word of the Lord.

Because both Jeroboam and Josiah are secondary characters whose actions fuel the plot, the sins of one and the virtues of the other are not psychologically illuminated (at least not in the narrative material that has survived). Nor are the motives of the man of God and of the old prophet elucidated to the extent we are accustomed to find in biblical narratives—a fundamental difficulty that has caused rampant misinterpretation of the story. This is in line with what is truly exceptional about the story, namely, that even the two main characters are subsidiary to its real "hero"—the word of the Lord, which is transformed from word to deed while overcoming its adversaries. A story that focuses on a nonhuman entity like the word of the Lord requires psychological rationales only to lend a measure of verisimilitude and life to the dramatic turning points in the positions of the human actors. These astonishing shifts, the dramatic climaxes of our story, are described in its center (parts II and III), where the initiative is that of the old prophet—although the direction of the action reverses gears when the prophet of Bethel metamorphoses from one who would frustrate the word of the Lord to one who bears and confirms it.

Sign and Portent

In the prophetic context, Scripture seems to use the nouns 'sign' (ʾot) and 'portent' (mofet) synonymously. Even the halakic midrash—with its intrinsic disposition to maximal differentiation—believes that "a sign is a portent and a portent is a sign; the Torah simply uses two words."[11] Nevertheless, I shall use these nouns as *terms* denoting two different means employed by the prophets to give greater weight and substance to their utterance. *Portent*

TABLE 5.1: An Overview of the Structure of the Story of the Man of God

	Part I	Part II	Part III	Part IV
Opening/Link Scene	I,1 [Jeroboam's sins as the background for the journey to Bethel by the man of God]	II,1 (13:11–13) Astonishing news spurs the old prophet to go out	III,1 (13:25–27) *For a second time,* astonishing news spurs the old prophet to go out	IV,1 [Josiah's righteousness as the background for his journey to Bethel]
Main Scene	I,2 (13:1–10) Confrontation between the man of God and King Jeroboam	II,2 (13:14–24) Confrontation between the man of God and the old prophet	III,2 (13:28–32a) The old prophet and the corpse of the man of God	IV,2 (2 Kings 23:16–18) King Josiah and the tomb of the man of God

Note: Because of the addition of two hypothetical expositions (to part I and part IV), the numbering of the scenes has been changed.

will be used for a miracle—for instance Aaron's rod that becomes a serpent (Exod. 7:8–13) and the shadow that runs backward on Ahaz's sundial (2 Kings 20:8–11)—that buttresses the prophet's credibility and confirms the truth of his utterance. *Sign* will refer to a symbolic deed or speech—such as Ahijah the Shilonite's rending of the cloak (1 Kings 11:29–32) and the symbolic names that Isaiah gives to his sons (Isa. 7:3 and 8:3)—that intensifies the word of the Lord and renders it tangible through an actual deed or powerful symbol. Since biblical thinking draws no sharp demarcation between speech and action, between cause and effect, or between potential and actual,[12] a prophetic sign—like the iron horns of Zedekiah son of Chenaanah (1 Kings 22:11)—not only intensifies the impact of an utterance on its hearers; it is also conceived of as anticipating the actual realization of its content. Thus Samuel turns the seemingly accidental tearing of the hem of his robe into a prophetic sign with dire presence and reality: "The Lord has *this day* torn the kingship over Israel away from you and has given it to another who is worthier than you" (1 Sam. 15:28).[13]

The *portent* derives its power from its miraculous nature; its link to the content of the prophecy need not be one of meaning and may actually be merely formal. The power of a *sign,* on the other hand, lies in its content; hence it always has a meaning, transmitted in the language of symbols. Our understanding of this language is scarcely improved by Fohrer's reliance on comparative anthropology to lay bare the magical roots of the prophetic sign and determine the degree to which they have been tamed.[14] The evolution of the magical into the religious may explain how the sign is created, but no more; it is more useful, if we would understand it correctly, to dwell

TABLE 5.2: Detailed Structure of the Story of the Man of God

I,1 [Jeroboam's sins as the background for the journey to Bethel by the man of God]	II,1 (13:11–13) Astonishing news spurs the old prophet to go out
[Conjectured exposition: The breaking of ties with the Temple in Jerusalem. The man of God is sent from Judah. The situation in Bethel on the festival.]	The old prophet's sons tell him about the *portents* and *sign.* The prophet finds out which way the man of God went. The saddling of the ass.
I,2 (13:1–10) The hostility of the king of Israel leads to reinforcement of the word of the Lord	II,2 (13:14–24) The punishment of the man of God reinforces the word of the Lord
The man of God appears when Jeroboam is presenting an offering on the altar. *The word of the Lord:* The altar will be defiled. The king commands: arrest the man of God! *Portents* (The altar collapses): The man of God is protected and the king's arm is healed. The king lures the man of God with promises of food and a gift. Refusal: The *sign* of the threefold prohibition is upheld. The man of God leaves by another route.	The prophet finds the man of God. The prophet lures the man of God by inviting him home. Refusal: The *sign* of the threefold prohibition (recapitulation). The prophet lies: the fabricated word of the Lord. The *sign* is breached: return, eating, drinking. *The word of the Lord:* A disgraceful death will overtake the one who breached the sign. The man of God departs. Fulfillment of the *word of the Lord* and a new *portent:* Death on the way; the corpse is not touched by the lion.

on its affinity to the language of everyday life. Symbolic acts are also to be found in a nonreligious context; for example, the dismemberment of the concubine's corpse by her Levite husband to emphasize the abomination committed in Israel (Judg. 19:29–30), or Shimei ben Gera's throwing of stones and flinging of dirt to add vehemence to his curse of David, who is fleeing his son (2 Sam. 16:5–8). Thus we can better understand Isaiah's going about naked and barefoot (Isa. 20:1–6) in the light of an earlier episode, when the king of the Ammonites slashed the garments of David's emissaries (2 Sam. 10:4; cf. mainly "at the buttocks" with "bared buttocks" [Isa. 20:4]); or Jeremiah's writing down all the evil that will come upon Babylon and then sinking the scroll in the Euphrates (Jer. 51:59–64) in the light of Jehoiakim's earlier burning of the scroll that contained Jeremiah's prophecies (Jer. 36:21–25).[15] The prophetic signs in 1 Kings 13 are to be

TABLE 5.2—*continued*

III,1 (13:25–27) *For a second time,* astonishing news spurs the old prophet to go out	IV,1 [Josiah's righteousness as the background for his journey to Bethel]
Passersby recount the *awesome* death (short recapitulation). The prophet identifies the slain man from a distance and proclaims that his death is a fulfillment of the *word of the Lord.* The saddling of the ass.	[Conjectured exposition: The restoration of the status of Jerusalem. Josiah comes to Bethel. The situation in Bethel on the day of the action.]
III,2 (13:28–32a) The old prophet's initiative confirms the word of the Lord	IV,2 (2 Kings 23:16–18) The word of the Lord is fulfilled by the king of Judah
The prophet finds the corpse of the man of God. *Portent:* The corpse is not touched by the lion (recapitulation). The *sign* is upheld: return, eulogy, burial. A *new sign:* The command of common burial. The prophet confirms the *word of the Lord* about the altar.	Josiah discovers the tombs of Bethel. *The word of the Lord* is fulfilled: The altar is defiled. Josiah notices the tomb marker and asks what it means. The Bethelites explain: This is the tomb of a man of God who foretold what you have done. The king orders that the bones of the man of God be preserved and respected. Fulfillment of the prophet's *sign:* His bones are spared.

identified and decoded in this way, even though (like many other prophetic signs) they are not explicitly designated by this term.

In line with the above definition, the paralysis of Jeroboam's arm and the restoration of its mobility after intercession by the man of God are classic *portents.* They are miracles that bolster the credibility of the stranger from across the border; their content, too—the Lord protects His emissary and responds to his entreaties—relates exclusively to the man of God and has nothing to do with his specific pronouncement. The disintegration of the altar and the spilling of its ashes is also a portent, which clearly demonstrates the truth of the word of the Lord as spoken by this man.[16] Unlike the first two portents, this portent is not merely formal; the collapse of the altar represents and foreshadows its future destruction. Since, however, the two verses about the collapse of the altar (13:3 and 5) do not seem to belong to the original story (both linguistic and thematic arguments support their secondary provenance), in what follows I shall not take this portent into consideration.[17]

Jeroboam changes his tactics as soon as his arm recovers. Rather than trying to subvert the prophecy by laying his hand on the man of God, he now seeks to blunt its sting by embracing him: "Come with me to my house and have some refreshment; and I shall give you a gift" (13:7). The man of God, forewarned against this development by his sender, cannot accept the tempting invitation because of the threefold prohibition imposed by the Lord: "You shall eat no bread and drink no water, nor shall you go back by the road by which you came" (13:9). Here we are dealing with a typical prophetic *sign*, intended to give substance to the prophecy about the total rejection of "this place" (v. 8b) and to start the process of its consummation *today*.[18] Indeed, many have interpreted the ban on eating and drinking as an expression of a total severance of contact with Bethel and as a blatant demonstration that it is impossible to sway the man of God.[19] But what is the meaning of the command to return home by a different route?[20]

To answer this question, we must first clarify how the biblical worldview understands *route* or *way*, both as an experience and as a concept. For our starting point we may cite the injunction against returning to Egypt to buy horses, because "the Lord has told you that you must not go back that way again" (Deut. 17:16). Commentators, both ancient and modern, have had difficulty explaining this rationale; evidently we should understand it in the light of the punishment that concludes the list of retributive catastrophes in the Rebuke Pericope: "The Lord will send you back to Egypt in ships, by a route which I told you you should not see again. There you shall offer yourselves for sale to your enemies as male and female slaves, but none will buy" (Deut. 28:68). Returning to Egypt is the harshest of punishments because it cancels out the Exodus, just as Amos prophesies the exile of the Aramaeans to Qir (Amos 1:5), their land of origin (ibid., 9:7). It is accordingly forbidden to purchase horses in Egypt: returning there voluntarily is tantamount to ingratitude and rejection of the greatest act of grace ever bestowed on Israel. The fact that this conception of returning to one's starting place as the cancellation of the original journey appears as part of a legal proscription indicates that this was the real mental attitude of those who retraced their steps, willingly or otherwise, and not mere rhetoric.

Moreover, just as returning to one's point of departure may be regarded as cancelling out the journey, retracing one's footsteps can be regarded as negating one's mission and abandoning its goal. Failure and frustration are reflected in a return over the very same road, as may be inferred from Isaiah's proclamation about Sennacherib, king of Assyria: "He shall go back by the way he came; he shall not enter this city—declares the Lord" (Isa. 37:34; 2 Kings 19:33). Similar is the case of David's emissaries, sent back empty-handed by Nabal the Carmelite: "David's young men retraced their steps; and when they got back, they told him all this" (1 Sam. 25:12). Again, since retracing one's steps can symbolize a change of mind and reneging on a commitment, Hannah refuses to make the pilgrimage to Shiloh before her son is weaned and can be left there (1 Sam. 1:22–23, as interpreted above, p. 24).

We see, then, that the prohibition on retracing his steps is an integral part of the prophetic sign given to the man of God. Just as the ban on eating and drinking stresses the intensity of the Lord's abhorrence of Bethel, the ban on returning by the same route gives tangible expression to the final and irrevocable nature of the decree. When the man of God "left by another road and did not go back by the road on which he had come to Bethel" (13:10), the entire populace saw that the word of the Lord, as spoken by him, was inviolable. Given the close affinity between messenger and message and between a prophet and his prophecy,[21] it is clear that if the messenger cannot be forced to retreat, his message cannot be withdrawn (cf. Isa. 55:11). Since someone who retraces his steps is conceptually no different from someone who is forced to retreat, the man of God is commanded to return to Judah by a different route than he came by so that his mission will not bear the slightest taint of a retreat.[22]

Violation of the Sign Leads to a New Portent

Because a prophetic sign is conditioned by the human limitations of the person assigned to deliver it, it can be counteracted. When Hananiah son of Azzur breaks Jeremiah's bar (Jer. 28:10–11), the destruction of the sign is understood as an attack on the message it represents. The continuation of that episode teaches us that such an attempt at subversion can be overcome by the re-creation and intensification of the sign: "You broke bars of wood, but you shall make bars of iron instead" (v. 13), as well as by a new portent—the death of Hananiah within a twelvemonth, as predicted by Jeremiah (vv. 16–17). This parallel makes it clear that when the old prophet deceives his colleague from Judah his intention is to undermine the word of the Lord spoken by the latter, by violating the sign that supports it.[23] The old prophet who was "living in Bethel" (13:11) did not participate in Jeroboam's festivities; nor does his sons' account of the words and deeds of the man of God explicitly mention the altar. These two facts seem to indicate that the main concern of the prophet—whose age is emphasized and made even more prominent by his imperious attitude toward his sons—is not for the altar but for his city and its tombs. If he could induce the man of God to retrace his steps and partake of food and drink "in this place,"[24] the man's credibility as a divine messenger might not be impaired; but what would remain of the validity of the sign after its violation by its bearer?

Walking is slower than riding donkeyback; in addition, the man of God stops to rest under the shade of a terebinth. So it is easy for the old prophet to overtake him (v. 14). Given the fact that the old prophet appeared from the direction of Bethel and began by verifying his identity—"Are you the man of God who came from Judah?" (ibid.)—the man of God could conclude that the invitation to return to the prophet's house and "have something to eat" (v. 15) is not a spontaneous gesture of hospitality extended to a chance wayfarer but is intended specifically for him. This realization should have sharpened his awareness of the possibility that someone who was harmed by his prophecy (he might even be fulfilling a royal commission) might be trying to entrap him. Indeed, he rejects the invitation at once, again referring to the triple prohibition imposed on him "by the word of the Lord" (v. 16). But whereas he told Jeroboam, in no uncertain terms, "I will not go in with you" (v. 8), he now tells the man who has taken the trouble to follow his tracks that he would very much like to accept his invitation but is forbidden to do so: "I may not go back with you and enter your home" (v. 16).

Only after the man of God withstands this first test does his interlocutor identify himself—"I am a prophet, too" (v. 18)—and disclose that the invitation is not extended at his own initiative but in accordance with a divine command. Since only the mouth that banned can later give permission, the local prophet stresses that it was the "word of the Lord" that cancelled the threefold prohibition. He even reinforces the credibility of his spurious prophecy by indicating the channel through which he received the divine message: "an angel said to me" (v. 18). At this stage the narrator feels compelled to let the readers in on what is hidden from the man of God— namely, that the prophet is lying. Not only does this revelation spare us the perplexity we might feel later when the disobedience of the man of God is condemned—a condemnation that quite ignores the ostensible abrogation of the threefold ban—but the need for this omniscient aside also indicates that the deception was perfect.

The trusting naivete of the man of God is not chalked up to his credit, evidently because his subjective innocence is of no account when balanced against the objective damage caused when the sign is breached by the one who bore it.

The classic expressions of the weighty responsibility of the prophet to his prophecy are found in the Lord's warnings to Jeremiah and Ezekiel: "Do not break down before them, lest I break you before them" (Jer. 1:17); "If I say to a wicked man, 'You shall die,' and you do not warn him . . . he, the wicked man, shall die for his iniquity, but I will require a reckoning for his blood from you" (Ezek. 3:18; cf. 33:6). The messenger's responsibility vis-à-vis the one who dispatches him can explain the harsh punishment of the man of God who is tricked. Still, we must not forget that the moral and psychological aspects of his punishment are not the core of the narrative, which focuses on the mission rather than on the emissary.[25]

The prophecy of the imminent death of the man of God amazes readers; but even more astonishing is the change of role forced on the old prophet.[26] The very man who sought to undermine the sign by means of a sham divine message now understands clearly, from the genuine revelation visited on him, that his efforts are in vain. Whether he is aghast at the terrible punishment in store for prophets who do not carry out their divinely imposed mission or is impressed by the force of the sign that cannot be negated, he does not conceal the prophecy vouchsafed to him.[27] For in this revelation, which occurs during the fatal meal, the sign begins to be detached from the frailties of the man of God, by making the bearer of the Lord's word into its object.[28] The divine message is taken away from him and directed against him. The hospitality he enjoyed in Bethel is defined as rebelliousness to be punished by an unseemly death (*nivlath⁽e⁾ka*, 'your carcass' [v. 22]) and by burial in an alien grave.[29]

The ambiguity of the text of verse 23 (see n. 26) makes it hard to interpret. Hence we should first try to overcome the problem posed by the phrase "he saddled the ass for him." The question is whether it is the person who eats and drinks in the first part of the verse who saddles the ass *for himself*, or whether we should assume a change of subject, that is, that the old prophet saddles the ass *for his colleague*. In all of Scripture (with the exception of one textually problematic verse [2 Sam. 19:27]), the saddling of an ass by its rider never involves the preposition *l⁽e⁾*- (see Gen. 22:3; Num. 22:21; 2 Sam. 17:23; 1 Kings 2:40; and 2 Kings 4:24). Moreover, in our chapter the dative pronoun *lo* in a similar context clearly refers to the indirect object: the prophet's sons do as he bids them and "saddle the ass *for him*" (13:13). Linguistically, then, it is preferable to assume that in verse 23, as well, the ass is being saddled for someone else. To this we should add a narrative consideration: the close linguistic and thematic parallel between this saddling of an ass and the two occasions on which the prophet's sons saddle an ass for him (vv. 13 and 27) acquires its full significance only through intentional juxtaposition of the cases: here the old prophet, master of his house who relies on his sons for such lowly chores, sets aside his dignity and dirties his own hands to saddle the ass for his guest.[30] There is no reason why we should not understand that it is the old prophet who saddles the ass—either by ignoring this difficult phrase as a marginal gloss or by accepting Ehrlich's conjectural emendation, deleting the problematic preposition, and understanding "the prophet who had brought him back" as indicating the subject of the verb "saddled."

This saddling of the ass is preceded by a rather astonishing temporal indication: "after he had eaten bread and had drunk" (v. 23a). It is astonishing because it is most implausible that the man of God would keep eating and drinking, as if nothing untoward had occurred, after hearing the terrible divine pronouncement. The story provides no psychological justification for such brazen behavior, nor is it compatible with the personality of a man who declined the king's flattering invitation and transgressed the prohibitions only after he was persuaded that they had been withdrawn. It follows that this second mention of the meal does not indicate when the ass was saddled but in what circumstances.[31] In other words, the old prophet, who tricked the man of God into eating and drinking in violation of the word of the Lord, saddles the ass for his guest. On the personal level, this gesture may be regarded as symbolic compensation (albeit meager) of the man of God for the great wrong done to him. On the level of prophecy, it may be interpreted as the old prophet's first inkling of the force of the sign he had sought to abrogate: the prophet who brought back the man of God and plied him with food and drink now treats him with the respect due a master and helps him set out with the shadow of the anticipated punishment hanging over his head. The word of the Lord vouchsafed to him not only tears away the mask of falsehood from the old man, it also propels him to abandon his struggle for his town and the inviolability of its graves. But in order for the adversary to be turned into an adherent, something more is required: a new portent.

The unmistakably miraculous nature of the death of the man of God is strongly emphasized. The sight of the lion and the ass standing sentrylike over the corpse astonishes the passersby. But the significance of the phenomenon is understood only when the old prophet tells them who the dead man is and explains that the Lord was involved in his death. His ability to identify the slain man from afar (v. 26) is not meant to extol his sagacity but to demonstrate his utter certainty that this act is a divine portent and his conviction as to its meaning. The old man, who had kept his thoughts to himself when his sons first told him, in a parallel situation, what the man of God did before the altar (vv. 11–12), now becomes, step by step, the trumpet of the prophecy. The prophecy is confirmed and reinforced by the lion that kills but does not eat and by the very stringency of the punishment meted out to the messenger who violated the sign by partaking of food.[32]

The Inimical Prophet Creates an Additional Sign

Once again the old prophet mounts his ass and follows the trail of the man of God with the intention of bringing him back to Bethel. This time, too, he does not reveal his purpose to his sons. When he reaches the corpse, the lion and the ass are still standing there; thus he sees the portent with his own eyes and is impressed by what was not made explicit, neither by the narrator nor in the wayfarers' report: "the lion had not eaten the corpse, nor had it mauled the ass" (v. 28). The man of God receives full funerary honors in Bethel and his body is interred in the family tomb of the old prophet. In this way the latter is fulfilling the Lord's word to him that the man of God would not be buried in his ancestral sepulchre (that is, in

Judah). In addition, this unusual action reflects reverence and awe for the man with whose life and death such mighty portents were associated. Although "Alas, my brother!" was a common lament at funerals (see Jer. 22:18), its explicit mention in the story makes it plain that the burial of the stranger in the family tomb is an act of public identification with the "brother" prophet from Judah and, implicitly, with his message.

Yet this indirect acknowledgment does not complete the triumph of the Lord's word. After the stranger has been buried, the prophet enjoins his sons to bury him in the same tomb and to place his body alongside the remains of the man of God so that, after the passage of time, it will no longer be possible to distinguish his bones from those of the man of God.[33] His reason: "For what he announced by the word of the Lord against the altar in Bethel . . . shall surely come true" (13:32). In other words, he buried the stranger in his own sepulchre because of his complete faith that his prophecy—that the tombs of Bethel will be desecrated so as to defile the altar—will be fulfilled; only by doing so can he guarantee that his tomb will not be violated in the future. Motivated by selfish reasons, the local prophet unequivocally declares the authenticity of the word of the Lord and its perfect fulfillment and creates a prophetic sign that gives powerful expression to his faith. The man who sallied forth to infringe the sign of the threefold prohibition ultimately creates a sign of his own—the common sepulchre.[34]

If 2 Kings 23:16–18 is part of the original version of our narrative, the story must have been committed to writing only after Josiah's occupation of Bethel. When we read these verses as the conclusion of our narrative, however, we reach the somewhat astonishing conclusion that the narrator was less concerned with telling us that Josiah acted in conformity with an ancient prophecy than in showing that the word of the Lord to Jeroboam was fulfilled in its entirety. The perspective here is not that of the royal court (that is, political), nor of the priestly temple (that is, ritualistic), but distinctly that of prophecy (that is, theological). Josiah is not described as guided by the word of the Lord but as its unconscious executor. Chancing to see the tombs on the hillside outside Bethel, he orders his men to use the bones interred in them to defile the altar; only when he looks up and sees the prominent marker on the tomb of the man of God does he learn from the townspeople who is buried there and what he had prophesied.[35] The king's command not to disturb the bones of the man of God can be understood as a gesture of esteem and recognition for the man whose prophecy is now being realized, or as a considered political act demonstratively adopting the ancient prophecy. On the other hand, there is no contemporary political dimension to the narrator's closing remark, "So they left his bones undisturbed together with the bones of the prophet who came from Samaria" (2 Kings 23:18b), which refers not to the prophecy by the man of God but to the prediction by the old prophet. This seems to have

an importance that goes beyond the ironic aspect of this astonishing sequence of events. The fact that the sign not only impressed the inhabitants
of Bethel in the time of Jeroboam but was also vindicated in the course of
time raises it from the subjective level and gives it an independent objective
status. Saul rent Samuel's cloak unintentionally, but the prophet saw in it a
compelling sign: "The Lord has this day torn the kingship over Israel away
from you" (1 Sam. 15:28). The same holds true for the ostensibly personal
sign of the old prophet. It springs from his clear grasp of the circumstances
and resourceful ability to exploit them for his own needs; but the almost
miraculous fulfillment of his prediction indicates that, from the very beginning, he was only an instrument to reinforce the true prophecy. He uttered
a prophecy but knew not what he uttered.

From Structure to Meaning

Thus far we have discussed the symmetrical structure of the story, the many
reversals in its plot, and the role of the signs and portents in reinforcing
the word of the Lord. All this is summarized in table 5.2 which expands on
table 5.1 and also gives different titles to the main scenes. In table 7 the
titles refer to the characters' actions, whereas here and in table 5.2 the
accent is on what happens to the true "hero" of the story—the word of the
Lord. Scrutiny of the table indicates that the opening scenes of part II and
part III have the same structure; there is reason to assume that the same
structure marked the lost opening scenes of parts I and IV. On the other
hand, the symmetry between the main scenes is less conspicuous. There
are similar and even identical elements in all four, but their internal order
varies as a function of the plot and the changes in the stances of the main
characters.

The striking similarity between the first two main scenes (I,2 and II,2)
highlights, first of all, the paradox that the Lord protects his emissary
against the violence and enticements of the king but leaves him totally exposed to the old prophet's fabrication. The most plausible explanation is
that, even when the emissary is performing his mission, his own personality
still plays a significant role. This is made clear by the internal hierarchy in
I,2 itself. The withering of Jeroboam's arm constitutes miraculous protection extended to the man of God the moment the king attacks him; he
does not have to ask for help. When it comes to healing the king, however,
the man of God changes from the passive object of the miracle to its active
subject: had he not prayed to the Lord, had he not been able to forgo his
honor in favor of giving greater repute to the miracle, the king's arm would
not have regained its power of motion.

Evidently this dilemma is easier than the next one. The man of God
was provided in advance with the sign of the triple prohibition as a shield

against any lure that Jeroboam might dangle before him. The ban on eating, drinking, and returning by the same road guides him as to the correct reaction to the royal invitation; but he retains the power to obey the prohibitions or to breach them. On the symbolic plane, the refusal to accept the king's invitation and proffered gift constitutes a prophetic sign; but his independent decision gives even greater force to the refusal. His compliance with the bans endows the sign with the dimension of a human "testimony," which confirms the word of the Lord by virtue of the emissary's identification with his mission. But free will is a double-edged sword: when the man of God obeys the prohibitions, he is magnifying the Lord's word; when he disobeys them he is diminishing it. This link between the word of the Lord and the human factor seems to be the Achilles' heel of the former. It was this weak link that was targeted by the old prophet.

The second main scene (II,2) opens with a recapitulation of what took place at the end of the previous confrontation (I,2). There the man of God spurns Jeroboam's invitation, basing himself on the bans imposed upon him; here he declines, in the same terms, the almost identical invitation extended by the old prophet of Bethel. As a host, the old prophet has no advantage over the king (except, perhaps, that his hospitality would be more private and less conspicuous). As a prophet, however, he disposes of a powerful weapon—a spurious message from the Lord. The repetition of the motif of invitation and refusal underscores the fact that even though the ability of the man of God to withstand the enticement has not weakened, he is powerless against deceit. Not only is the man of God required to abstain from the pleasures of the proffered hospitality and overcome his desire for honor, he must also apply his best judgment to distinguish between truth and falsehood. Because of weak judgment, the man of God acts the pious fool who believes that he is heeding the word of the Lord when in fact he is breaching the sign confided to him. In order to save the mission from the grave consequences of the emissary's failure, the sender intervenes with a new message that castigates the infringement of the bans (and also implicitly lays bare the old prophet's falsehood). In the ominous shadow of the punishment hanging over the man of God, the two partners in the transgression try to turn back the wheel of the plot. The deceiving host does this by saddling the ass himself, the deceived guest by setting out again. The pathetic attempt to return to the point where the previous main scene ended is of course foredoomed to failure. The scene ends with the violent death of the man of God, in an awful portent in which he is deprived of the heavenly protection he enjoyed when he fearlessly confronted the king.

The clear symmetry between the first scenes of parts II and III (II,1 and III,1) emphasizes the utter reversal in the situation. On the surface, everything is as it was before: the old prophet assembles information, tells his sons what to do, and acts decisively, without explaining what he is doing.

But it is already clear to readers that this time the orientation of his actions has been reversed; for in total contradiction to his original interest as a prophet of Bethel, he identifies the dead traveler from a distance and unravels in public the mystery of his miraculous death as a heaven-sent punishment and the fulfillment of the word of the Lord.

The technique of dramatizing a turning-point by describing contrasting behavior in similar circumstances is found again in the main scene (III,2), which must be read with the second main scene (II,2) in mind. In both scenes, the old man goes out after the man of God: the first time, to offer him hospitality; the second time, to bury him in his own tomb. This symmetry is reinforced by the linguistic parallelism. Scene II,2 opens with the words, "he *went* after the man of God and *found* him . . . " (v. 14); III,2 also begins with the words, "he *went* and *found* the corpse" (v. 28). In II,2, the verb *š.w.b*, 'return', occurs six times,[36] so as to make the infringement of the ban imposed on the man of God to return by the way he came the focus of all the events. In the parallel scene, the same verb is used to make it clear that the punishment meted out to the man of God is one of measure for measure: "he laid [the corpse] on the ass and *brought it back* (wa-yᵉšivehu)" (v. 29). This is supplemented by the antiparallelism between the three elements of the ensnaring hospitality—returning, eating, and drinking—and the three elements of the care lavished on the corpse—bringing it back, the eulogy, and the burial—which demonstrates that the violation of the sign eventually turned into its fulfillment. Just as the old prophet who seduced the man of God into sin becomes "his brother" (v. 30), so too, having set out to nullify the word of the Lord, he eventually confirms it.

The fourth main scene (IV,2) is an inversion of the first main scene (I,2). This *inclusio* structure contributes additional proof of the conjecture that 2 Kings 23:16–18 is the true end of our story. In polar antithesis to Jeroboam, who stood on the altar at Bethel and presented an offering (as stated in 1 Kings 13:1 and repeated in the phrase, preserved in the Septuagint, cited in n. 35), Josiah had "the bones taken out of the graves and burned on the altar" (2 Kings 23:16). The words "bones" and "burned" return the reader to the word of the Lord as spoken at the beginning of the story: "human bones shall be burned upon you" (1 Kings 13:2). This linguistic link is strengthened by the explicit statement at the end of 2 Kings 23:16: "in fulfillment of the word of the Lord proclaimed by the man of God." These words, too, echo I,2: "the word of the man of God who proclaimed against the altar" (1 Kings 13:4). What is more, the people of Bethel describe the man buried in the tomb as "the man of God who came from Judah" (2 Kings 23:17), just as he is designated in the first scene (1 Kings 13:1) and three more times in the course of the story (13:12, 14, and 21). Nor will we be far off if we view "he had the bones taken out (*wa-yišlaḥ wa-yiqqaḥ*) of the graves" (2 Kings 23:16) as an intentional contrasting echo of "Jeroboam stretched out *(wa-yišlaḥ)* his arm above the altar" (1 Kings 13:4).

The unique structure of IV,2 stands out against the background of this close thematic and linguistic affinity. Whereas the three main scenes *begin* with the motif of the "encounter" (that is, the more or less surprising meeting between the man of God and someone else), this motif is postponed to the middle of IV,2, where Josiah first spies the marker on the tomb of the man of God and asks what it is. This deviation from the fixed format is an important means to emphasize that Josiah desecrates the altar even before learning about the prophecy that he would do so. Long ago the word of the Lord had overcome both the king and the prophet who had set out to frustrate it. Now it is realized by the king of Judah, who is not even guided by it. This emphasis attests that the main interest of the narrator is not to extol the king of Judah for his fidelity and obedience to the word of the Lord, but rather to tell us how the word of the Lord was realized, in the fullness of time, even without a conscious decision to do so by the king who fulfilled it. Josiah's lack of conscious intent, when he first sees the tomb, is highlighted by the sentence preserved only in the Septuagint: "He turned and saw the sepulchre of the man of God" (see n. 35). Here the plot returns to the format of the main scenes—the direct confrontation between the man of God and one of the protagonists. After Josiah has unwittingly fulfilled the word of the Lord he is provided with another opportunity to demonstrate his attitude toward the word of the Lord and its bearer. This is not very difficult to do, given the miraculous fulfillment of the ancient word of the Lord, which had so deeply impressed the inhabitants of Bethel, as is evident in their explanation of the tomb marker: "That is the grave of the man of God who came from Judah and foretold these things that you have done to the altar of Bethel" (2 Kings 23:17). The verse draws on the same linguistic building blocks as 1 Kings 13:1–2. The parallel between the words of the "men of the town"—whose altar has just been desecrated before their eyes by the king of Judah—and the dry factual language of the narrator indicates that they indeed grasped what had happened in its true light.[37] Based on their identification of the person buried in the tomb and their account of the prophecy of doom he had pronounced on the altar in the Bethel sanctuary, which had been faithfully handed down from generation to generation, Josiah spares the man of God the terrible disgrace meted out to all those buried around him. Here again the narrator highlights the contrast between Jeroboam, who attacked the bearer of the Lord's word—"Seize him!" (1 Kings 13:4)—and Josiah, who protects the tomb of the man of God—"Let him be" (2 Kings 23:18). The old prophet of Bethel is the bridge between these two monarchs: beginning as a stumbling block to the man of God, he ultimately proclaims his full public identification with him and his prophecy, an identification whose strongest expression is their common grave. Note that Josiah is not told anything about the

old prophet; but when he spares his bones, he is fulfilling—again uncon-
sciously—the ancient sign which the latter had created. He fulfills it, not
knowing that he is doing so.

Our story's reiterated emphasis that the protagonists are not aware of
the full implication of their deeds is reinforced by the narrator's total silence as to the reaction of Jeroboam and the Bethelites to the stern warning
directed against their altar and burial places. True, after the two portents
that Jeroboam experienced in his own body, he did modify his attitude
toward the man of God. Obviously, though, the cancellation of the arrest
order and its replacement by a cordial invitation cannot be equated with
acceptance of the warning and a willingness to derive practical conclusions
regarding the altar. The editor feels obliged to add the evaluation that "even
after this incident Jeroboam did not turn back from his evil way, but kept
on appointing priests for the shrines from the ranks of the people" (1 Kings
13:33); but the original author has nothing to say about the Bethelites' reaction to the prophecies, signs, and portents described in the course of the
narrative. This suggests that, other than what can be inferred from the
continued existence of the altar at Bethel for three centuries, the story is
not concerned with the impression wrought by the signs and portents but
only with their invulnerability—just as the story is concerned not with the
persuasive force of the word of the Lord but with its power of action.

The description of the old prophet's about-face, in both attitude and
actions, is no exception to this rule. On the one hand, nothing is said about
the old prophet's stance with regard to the sinful Bethel cult. On the other
hand, the narrator emphasizes the old man's personal interest in creating
the sign of the common tomb. Thus the change in the Bethel prophet is
not presented as the result of an ideological conviction; rather, it is clearly
assigned to the dimension of succumbing to an overpowering force. The
word of the Lord, with its accompanying signs and portents, is depicted as
possessing an autonomous existence and as endowed with the power to
frustrate the plots of its adversaries, even though it does not force itself on
the consciousness of those who choose to ignore it. Even its ultimate fulfillment does not depend on the consciousness of the one who fulfills it;
centuries may pass, but it will be fulfilled eventually. This tension between
the lofty sovereignty of the word of the Lord,[38] its dependence on human
messengers, and the need to overcome its adversaries, is what lends our
story its unique and strange quality.

The word of the Lord is autonomous but not self-sufficient. It does not
remain in heaven, as a decree that will be implemented some day. It is
uttered on earth, by an emissary; its commission to the hands of a mortal
is one expression of its earthliness. Any attempt to harm the emissary (by
subduing or seducing him), any action against the sign (by attempting to
negate it), *demands* a vigorous reaction. For the sovereignty of the word of
the Lord is not based on its fundamental invulnerability but on its absolute

superiority over anyone who would assail it. The specific lesson of our narrative, read as a prophetic story, is that nothing avails against the word of the Lord; anyone who attacks it will find himself compelled to affirm it, and anyone who betrays his mission will be required to reinforce it, even at the cost of his own life. But does this story have a broader significance, one that retains its validity after the cessation of prophecy in Israel?

It is not easy to uncover such a meaning, chiefly because of this conception of the word of the Lord as a powerful entity that imposes itself on reality—like a blessing or a curse—while overpowering hostile forces. The absence from the story of any hint of the idea of repentance is in keeping with this notion that the word of the Lord acts directly and independently. At first it is addressed to the altar ("O altar, altar" [1 Kings 13:2]), not to the conscience of those present. Quite unlike prophecy as it is usually presented in Scripture, it does not demand a response or compliance. Accordingly, the old prophet makes no attempt to safeguard his tomb by appealing to his townspeople to heed the word of the Lord and tear down the altar. All his actions are based on the self-evident assumption that the illegitimate cult will continue in Bethel. Hence he tries, first of all, to nullify the word of the Lord; failing in this, he tries to escape its consequences for himself. The man of God, the bearer and executor of the word of the Lord, is in no way a "watchman," charged with warning the people against impending disaster and evoking the repentance that could ward off the calamity (Ezek. 3:17–20; 33:1–20; cf. Jer. 36:1–3).

To understand the character of the man of God in our story, then, we need a different model. Perhaps we should have recourse to the *royal messenger,* who proclaims the decrees of the remote sovereign and thereby sets in motion the process of their fulfillment. The word of the Lord spoken to the altar at Bethel is not a warning or rebuke, but a *decree:* the altar has been condemned to eternal defilement at the hands of a king of Judah, who will burn human bones on it (that is, the bones of those who offer sacrifices on it and will be punished by the desecration of their graves). The sentence is irrevocable; the punishment may be commuted, however, if one accepts the decree and implements it voluntarily: destroying the altar could have kept the bones from being burned on it. But the king of Israel and the prophet of Bethel both prefer to attempt to overturn the decree by means of violence, enticement, and deceit, all directed against the emissary.

The fundamental demand made of defendants in a court of law is to acknowledge the authority of the court. Such acknowledgment does not deprive defendants of their right to fight for acquittal. But they are forbidden to display contempt of court, to assault or hinder the work of its agents, or to interfere with execution of the sentence. Accepting the verdict—even justifying it—is not the same as repenting. There is a vast difference between bowing to the authority of the magistrate—even when this is accompanied by an admission of guilt and acknowledgment that the punishment is merited—and repentance, which aims to correct the deviation, abandon the evil path, and espouse the good. What is more, the distinction between acceptance of the justice of the verdict and repentance is not only quantitative. They are two categories that differ in fundamental and substantive fashion, despite the partial overlap between them. The first is an appropriate reaction to a verdict of the celestial court; the second refers to the possibility and obligation to return to the right path. Accordingly there is a vivid tension between biblical texts that focus on rebuke and a call for repentance and those that dwell on the verdict and the demand to accept it. Narratives of the first sort proclaim that when people repent their evil ways they will be answered—the Lord will rescind the evil decree.[39] Narratives of the second type stress the impossibility of eluding the verdict, because it is absolute ("for He is not human that He should change his mind" [1 Sam. 15:29]) and timeless ("but the word of our God is everlasting" [Isa. 40:8]).

There can be no doubt that this disparity reflects different views of the power of repentance on the one hand, and of the absolute nature of the word of the Lord on the other.[40] Yet there is no necessary contradiction between the two notions, as we see, for example, in their dialectic fusion in Jeremiah's prophecy.[41] The total absence of the element of repentance in our story does not necessarily indicate a rejection of the idea in principle. It can be explained as a consequence of the sharp focus on a theme that leaves little room for repentance to begin with—the irrevocable future destruction of the illegitimate altar at Bethel. In order to better understand the conceptual system of our story, then, we must examine it in the light of other stories that also relate to the word of the Lord as a verdict.

The hallmark of these stories is their assumption that a divine decree is irrevocable; hence acceptance of the verdict can do no more than mitigate the punishment or postpone its execution. This unwavering absoluteness is expressed in the divine oath that "the iniquity of the house of Eli will never be expiated by sacrifice or offering" (1 Sam. 3:14) and in Eli's acquiescence in the decree ("He is the Lord; He will do what He deems right" [ibid., 18]), which changes nothing. Similarly, Samuel makes it abundantly clear to Saul that the Lord's rejection of him and his family is final (1 Sam. 15:28–29); hence that monarch's unqualified confession of his sin (v. 30) cannot be the basis for renewed hope ("Samuel never saw Saul again to the day of his death. But Samuel grieved over Saul . . ." [v. 35]). Nor do David's seven days of self-abasement bring about the commutation of the death sentence pronounced on his son conceived in sin (2 Sam. 12:14–23). Similar self-abasement by Ahab, when he hears the annihilation decreed on his dynasty, yields meager results: the evil is postponed to the reign of his son (1 Kings 21:27–29).[42] Even sweeping acts of rectification, such as Moses' destruction of the Golden Calf and slaughter of its worshippers

(Exod. 32:20 and 26–29) or Josiah's eradication of idolatry (2 Kings 23:1–25), cannot annul the disaster to be visited on Israel but only delay its coming (Exod. 32:34; 2 Kings 22:16–20 and 23:26–27).

While submission to the word of the Lord does not guarantee any abatement of the punishment, resistance and disobedience certainly aggravate it. This is as it should be, since the disobedience adds another sin to the reckoning, and the attempt to frustrate the word of the Lord must be converted into a means for reinforcing it. The classic example of this is Pharaoh's refusal to release the Israelites; as a consequence, the Lord multiplies His signs and portents in the land of Egypt (Exod. 7:3–5). The captains of fifty who come to arrest the prophet Elijah pay for their king's rebellion with their lives; their assault on the honor of prophecy provokes a portent that magnifies and glorifies it (2 Kings 1:9–14). As a result of the violent opposition of Amaziah, the priest of Bethel, to Amos's prophecy, and of the priest Pashhur son of Immer and of Jehoiakim king of Judah to Jeremiah's prophecy, the word of the Lord they had tried to stifle becomes more severe and more intense, and they are punished for their own defiance (Amos 7:16–17; Jer. 20:1–6 and 36:19–32).

Our story is a classic example of the category of stories whose theme is the word of the Lord as an irrevocable verdict. But it differs from all the others in that here the punishment that reinforces and vindicates the word of the Lord is visited not on those who rebel against him but on the man of God, who transgresses in a moment of weakness. The king of Israel and the prophet of Bethel, who maliciously attempt to frustrate the word of the Lord, go unpunished, apparently because their intervention is aborted by mighty portents (the paralysis and recovery of Jeroboam's arm, the bizarre death on the road). The disparity between their fates and that of the man of God from Judah is decisive proof that the concept of acceptance of the verdict, too, is only marginal to this prophetic story.

Jeroboam's invitation to the man of God to dine at the royal table could be interpreted as indirect acceptance of the decree. The sign of the threefold prohibition makes it clear, however, that Jeroboam's gesture could not have any effect on the divine decree against the town. The great alteration in the stance of the old prophet also seems to be acceptance of the decree; in fact, he does not go beyond a declaration of his perfect faith that the Lord's word will be fulfilled, with no hint that he recognizes its justice. All the same, three centuries later he is spared from the desecration of the tombs decreed against his town. Like Ahab, Hezekiah, and Josiah, he personally does not suffer the doom that besets everyone else. Our story seems to state, however, that the prophet's bones are not spared as a reward for his extraordinary righteousness but only as a consequence of his mobilizing his selfish motives to create a prophetic sign. One who confirms the word of the Lord only in its formal aspect (that is, with regard to its expected fulfillment) does not acquire any real merit thereby. In the final analysis, his bones are spared disgrace only by the merit of the man of God, which shields their common tomb. Even as he plans their common burial, the old prophet, in his wisdom, understands that he himself deserves no more.

The story of the two prophets and the two kings in Bethel is not meant to extol the virtue of accepting the divine decree any more than it is meant to inspire repentance. From beginning to end the story dwells on a single theme—the fulfillment of the word of the Lord in its appointed time, after it transcends the weakness of its bearer and converts into affirmers those who would violate it.[43] "In its appointed time," because its fulfillment, after the lapse of the three centuries that separate Jeroboam from Josiah, is presented as added proof of its power. Just as the word of the Lord overcomes all who rise against it, it can maintain its power for so many years. Since it was decreed that the altar at Bethel would be destroyed in the reign of Josiah, the longer the interim between prophecy and fulfillment, the greater the glory that "the things once predicted have come" (Isa. 42:9).[44] The fact that Josiah fulfils the Lord's word about Bethel, even though he is not aware of it, is another vindication of the power of the ancient decree.

We do not have adequate historical information on which to base any conjecture as to the religious dilemma that arose some time after the reign of Josiah, a dilemma our story was originally intended to answer in the form of a prophetic narrative about the destruction of the Bethel altar.[45] For this reason we have not gone beyond elucidating the timeless lesson of the story. Our conclusion is that it was meant to stimulate a numinous reverence for the mighty acts of the Lord in history and human life. We may regard as strange and perplexing the fact that there is no relationship between the vigor and immediacy that typify the reaction against those who attempt to breach the word of the Lord, and the slow deliberateness of the centuries required for its fulfillment. In fact, this paradox is one facet of the story's message. The ancient word of the Lord, almost obliterated except for the marker on the tomb of the man of God, reappears and breaks through into history in its full power: "The Lord . . . has carried out the decree that He ordained in the days of old" (Lam. 2:17).

•6•

ELIJAH'S FIGHT AGAINST BAAL WORSHIP

The Prophet's Role in Returning Israel to Its God

> *The Lord your God will raise up for you a*
> *prophet from among your own people,* like
> myself; *him you shall heed.*
>
> Deut. 18:15

The Unity of the Story: Problems and Cruxes

The prophet Elijah fought against Baal worship with all his might but was unable to defeat it. The account of his zeal for the Lord begins with the drought and the prophet's disappearance (chapter 17), continues through the trial on Mount Carmel and the longed-for rainfall (chapter 18), and concludes with the stern vision of the impending destruction and survival of a tiny remnant (chapter 19). These three parts are interlinked with regard to theme and subject matter, follow sequentially in terms of cause and effect, and are set in a reasonably clear continuum of time and place. This frame also includes the description of Elisha's entry into the service of the prophet (19:19–21). By contrast, from the perspectives of time, place, theme, and plot, the subsequent Elijah tales—Naboth's vineyard (chapter 21), his confrontation with Ahaziah's messengers (2 Kings 1), and his ascent to heaven (2 Kings 2)—are not linked to it. Should the narrative unity of chapters 17–19 be seen as the primary unity of a literary creation, or rather as a secondary unity contributed by an editor? It is generally held that our text is a collection of stories, traditions, and anecdotes (at various levels of consolidation), which have been combined with great skill into a single continuous narrative; even their heterogeneity and the seams between them are still manifest. This conclusion is based less on stylistic and structural considerations than on thematic difficulties and tensions. These

155

problems are indeed serious and should be surveyed at the beginning of this reexamination of the unity and structure of the story as a basis for clarifying the prophet's role in returning Israel to its God.

Unlike solutions, which largely depend on the viewpoint of their proponents and the school to which they belong, cruxes have a more autonomous existence. Hence the problems raised by different scholars are linked and can be presented in systematic order, with minimal reference to the assumptions and viewpoints of those who first posed them:

A. Between the announcement to the king of the drought (17:1) and the Lord's command to Elijah to appear before Ahab and herald the renewal of rainfall (18:1), three miracle tales, whose link with the drought seems to be only secondary, are recounted: the sustenance of the prophet by the ravens in Wadi Cherith (17:2–7); the sustenance of the prophet, the widow, and her son in Zarephath (17:8–16); and especially the resurrection of the widow's son (17:17–24). The impression that these three miracle stories were originally independent is strengthened by the frequent appearance of such motives both in Scripture[1] and elsewhere,[2] and by their meager connection with the subject of the main story (the drought) and the personality of its hero (Elijah). There is an additional, formal consideration: the sharp lines of demarcation between the three episodes indicate that they were set down one after the other, with no overlap or integration. They seem to have been interpolated only to serve as "filler" to pad out the three years that elapsed between the two crucial scenes of the real plot. This filler is meant to allow the reader to follow the prophet in his wanderings, to be astonished at the wondrous divine favor that he merited, and to acquire some idea of the seriousness of the drought: the waters of Wadi Cherith dried up because of the lack of rain (17:7), while in Zarephath they were down to their last loaf of bread (17:12). Nevertheless, scholarship has not discovered any substantive integration of these three short accounts into the main plot, beyond the additional information and background they provide.[3] According to Gunkel (*Elias*, p. 11), nothing in these stories—with the exception of Elijah's struggle with the Lord for the life of the widow's son (17:20), which foreshadows his complaint in chapter 19—reflects the essential traits of Elijah the prophet, nor is there any significant development from one miracle to the next.[4] Moreover, the resurrection of the child lacks even the most indirect link with the drought, aside from the purely formal connection that the widow's son was mentioned in the previous anecdote (17:12–13). The main story would lack nothing were the account of the resurrection omitted.

B. Chapter 18 has three parts: the first tells how Elijah encountered Obadiah and then Ahab on the outskirts of the famine-stricken city of Samaria (vv. 1–20); the second is devoted to the trial by fire on Mount Carmel and contains no reference to either the drought or Ahab (vv. 21–40); in the third part, Elijah and Ahab again interact against the background of the great rainfall (vv. 41–46). Some question the originality of the Elijah-Obadiah scene, viewing it as a doublet of the meeting between prophet and king. This doublet introduces an element of tension into the story and allows the relation, in a flashback, of what has been taking place in Samaria in the interim: the outlawing of the prophets of the Lord and the relentless hunt for Elijah. But no one doubts the intimate connection between the dispatch of Elijah to Samaria in the first part of the chapter and his running to Jezreel in its last part, or their relevance to the story of the drought. By contrast with this identity of subject matter and characters, Elijah's failure to mention the drought in his address to the people is most astonishing, as is his total silence about Ahab's deeds during the trial on Mount Carmel: did the king really join the people and fall on his face before the Lord? Did he join the mass descent to Wadi Kishon and passively witness the slaughter of the prophets of Baal (a possible inference from what Elijah says in verse 41—"Go up, eat and drink"—which clearly belongs to the account of the drought)? Also strange—though less so—is the narrator's reticence about what the people did when the skies darkened and the longed-for rains fell on Mount Carmel. It was the people who had proven, by word and by deed, that they merited this blessing; yet not only does the prophet fail to include them in his tidings to Ahab (" 'Hitch up [your chariot] and go down before the rain stops you' " [v. 44]), the narrator does not, for some reason, include the standard concluding formula that the people "returned every man to his house."[5]

These discrepancies, between the account of the trial on Mount Carmel and that of the drought into which it is set, are exacerbated by a number of tensions: (1) The information supplied by the narrator (18:4)—and repeated by Obadiah to Elijah (18:13)—concerning the hundred prophets of the Lord hidden in caves contradicts Elijah's declaration to the people on the heights of Carmel: "I am the only prophet of the Lord left" (18:22).[6] (2) In the actual account of the trial there is no mention of the 400 prophets of the Asherah, mentioned in verse 19, who eat at Jezebel's table. (3) The large quantity of water poured on Elijah's altar (twelve jugs) is most astonishing in view of the terrible drought described at the beginning of the chapter.[7] (4) In the present context, Elijah's words "Eat and drink" (v. 41) are unexplained. Equally astounding is the lack of an explanation as to when and how Elijah was joined by the lad who is suddenly at his side when he crouches on the ground (vv. 43–44).

C. More serious still are the problems involving chapter 19 and its link with what preceded it. First of all, there is no clear continuity between the awesome victory on Mount Carmel and the feeling of utter defeat that overcomes the prophet on the very next day. It is not clear how the threat made by Jezebel (who in any case preferred not to take the risk of killing the prophet and settled for frightening him away) could totally nullify the immense achievement of the day before, and especially the act of repentance by "all the people" (18:39). Furthermore, even if we can find a psychological explanation for the crisis that assails Elijah, the fact that the prophet's assessment of the situation ("The Israelites have forsaken Your covenant, torn down Your altars, and put Your prophets to the sword" [19:10]) is not refuted in the Lord's reply to him is decisive. Quite the contrary: the prophet's complaint is itself the indictment on which the divine punishment is based. To increase the puzzle, this indictment makes no mention of Jezebel and the royal house and ascribes the iniquity to the people alone. This approach, which seems to contradict both the people's response on Mount Carmel and the indictment of Jezebel at the beginning of chapter 19, is also reflected in the sentence: "I will leave *in Israel* only seven thousand" (v. 18).

These cruxes are augmented by other serious problems that hinder our understanding of chapter 19: (1) First there is the astonishing repetition of the question "Why are you here, Elijah?" which comes both before and after the divine revelation (vv. 9 and 13), as well as Elijah's repeated answer ("I have been very zealous for the Lord" [vv. 10 and 14]), as if nothing had transpired in the interim. (2) The significance of the theophany experienced by the prophet remains unclear. Even murkier is the link between the theophany and the broader context in which it appears—the fire that descended on Mount Carmel, which precedes it, and the punishment of destruction, which follows it. (3) Not all scholars are troubled by the fact that Elisha, rather than Elijah, anoints both Jehu and Hazael, leaving a discrepancy between the command to anoint Elisha as his prophetic heir and Elisha's entry into Elijah's service. In any case, the answer to the question as to whether Elisha's nomination belongs to our story depends on the evaluation of these facts.

In my opinion, the available data do not permit a faithful reconstruction of the evolution of the Elijah stories from oral traditions to the written narrative we have before us.[8] Hence we shall not deviate from analysis of the finished story to consider its prior stages unless this is required by some ineluctable exegetical need. I believe that a close reading, attentive to the style and structure of the story, will enable us to resolve most (but not all) of the questions and problems mentioned above. Some of those that remain—especially those relating to chapter 19—seem to have their origin in the prehistory of the story. Only for those may we have recourse to the genetic explanation, which elucidates how the literary anomalies were created even while leaving them unresolved.

In Wadi Cherith and in Zarephath: Hiding and Preparing for the Mission

Elijah's laconic announcement to Ahab of the impending drought (17:1) is incomprehensible without background information about Ahab's sins of

Baal worship. Similarly, the story's reference to Jezebel as a familiar character (18:4, 13, 19; 19:1–2) forces us to assume a prior account of Ahab's
marriage to the daughter of the Phoenician king. In fact, both of these are
found in 16:29–34, but the conspicuous stylistic variance between the summary information of that passage (which bears the distinct stamp of the
Deuteronomic author-editor of the Book of Kings) and the narrative of
chapters 17 to 19 suggests that the original beginning of our story is missing. The common hypothesis that the original exposition was discarded
when the story was incorporated into the Book of Kings, having been rendered superfluous by the parallel information in the editorial framework,
is plausible.[9] Perhaps we may assume that this exposition told not only about
Ahab and his family but also about Elijah and his origins; if so, the author
of the Book of Kings must also be credited with the addition of the words
"the Tishbite, an inhabitant of Gilead" (17:1)[10] as a sort of concise substitute
for the deleted material. On the other hand, it is quite likely that the original story did not include an account of his birth and consecration, as is
found for other prophets. First of all, it is hard to imagine an editor omitting
material of such importance. Second, the three scenes in chapter 17 are a
sort of substitute for a consecration scene since they relate how the prophet
with the unknown past has been made ready for his great struggle.

When we endeavor to show that chapter 17 as we have it is indeed designed as the first part of the account of the drought, we shall have to do
three things: (1) demonstrate the stylistic and structural unity of chapter
17 itself; (2) offer a plausible interpretation of its three scenes as a description of Elijah's gradual ascent of the degrees of prophecy; (3) and show
the stylistic, structural, and thematic links between chapter 17 and chapter
18, which allow us to view the former as the essential introduction to the
latter.

Chapter 17 begins with Elijah's dramatic announcement (v. 1), which
stands by itself but is not an independent scene. This truncated overture is
followed by three full scenes, clearly demarcated by changes in the dramatis
personae and locale, as well as by similarly phrased introductory verses (recounting a direct or indirect divine initiative) and parallel conclusions (indicating the duration and referring to the prophet's words):

Prologue (v. 1): Elijah and Ahab (no location specified)
    Conclusion: "There will be no dew or rain *these years* except at *my word*."
Scene 1 (vv. 2–7): Elijah alone (in Wadi Cherith)
    Opening: "*The word of the Lord came to him:* 'Go from this place; turn
    eastward and go into hiding by the Wadi Cherith, *which is* east of the
    Jordan.' "
    Conclusion: "*After some time* the wadi dried up, because there was no
    rain in the land."
Scene 2 (vv. 8–16): Elijah and the widow (on the outskirts of Zarephath)

Opening: "*And the word of the Lord came to him:* 'Go at once to Zarephath *which is* near Sidon, and stay there. . . . ' "

Conclusion: " . . . she and he and her household had food for a *long time*, . . . just as the *word of the Lord* who had spoken through Elijah."

Scene 3 (vv. 17–24): Elijah, the widow, and her son (in the widow's house)

Opening: "*After a while,* the son of the mistress of the house fell sick. . . . "

Conclusion: " . . . the *word of the Lord* in your mouth is truth."

This sophisticated structure unifies chapter 17 as the first part of the story and defines its scope. Its end is emphasized by the *inclusio*: the circle begun by Elijah's taunting declaration, "except at *my word*," is temporarily closed by the Phoenician widow's recognition that "the *word* of the Lord in your mouth is truth."

The plot begins with Elijah's proclamation to Ahab of the impending prolonged drought (17:1). This fateful confrontation does not receive its own separate scene; the prophet's actual words are related without any indication of where and when the meeting took place and with no description of the circumstances or how the confrontation ended. The narrator's brevity is reinforced by the concision of the prophet, who does not ground his pronouncement on a revelation that had preceded his appearance[11] and does not invoke the prophetic messenger's standard prologue, "Thus said the Lord." This is even more curious given the fact that the text goes on to state explicitly and emphatically that Elijah went to Wadi Cherith (17:2) and from there to Zarephath (17:8) and from Zarephath back to Samaria (18:1) in obedience to divine commands. Are we to infer from this conspicuous contrast that the omission of a divine command to appear before Ahab means that Elijah brought such a severe drought on Israel on his own initiative, and that he was willing to risk so daring an oath on the same basis? The rejection of this hypothesis is more plausible and more in keeping with the personality of Elijah as depicted in the rest of the story, as well as with his explicit statements in his two prayers—one to revive the child (v. 20) and the other for rain (18:36). There are several cases in Scripture where the implementation of a command to deliver a prophecy is not described in so many words (e.g., 1 Kings 21:17–19), and, on the other hand, where the revelatory source of prophetic messages is not recounted (1 Kings 20:22, vis-à-vis verses 13–14).[12] Here too the terse language evidently reflects the narrator's confidence that readers accustomed to elliptical narrative will not draw the wrong conclusions. In any case, it is quite clear that the extreme brevity of this prologue makes it all the more dramatic. The plot is launched with great intensity by the stern proclamation, whose bare relation, with no indication of the circumstances of its delivery, echoes in a way the sudden intrusion of the prophet's words on Ahab's day-to-day routine.

The impression made by the proclamation is intensified by the fact that it is phrased as a personal oath: "As the Lord God of Israel lives, before whom I have stood, there will be no dew or rain these years except at *my word.*" This focus on the prophet's personality is an essential part of the message he delivers: the path to the renewal of rainfall now passes through the prophet of the Lord, without whose word there will be no heavenly blessing. So that its lesson can be learned, the drought, intended to make manifest the impotence of the Phoenician Baal to give rain and dew[13]— must begin and end with the words of the prophet of the Lord. Moreover, making rainfall depend on Elijah's word throws down the gauntlet not only to Baal but to his prophets as well; it is their protracted failure to bring down rain that will open the king's heart to the word of the prophet of the Lord, who dared proclaim the drought before its onset, with an oath from which there can be no retreat.

The drought is depicted in a way that recalls the Ten Plagues; similarly, Elijah's actions to bring and later to put an end to it parallel Moses' actions in Egypt. Here, as there, there is advance warning by the prophet, the impotence of the king's magicians and prophets, the linkage between the end of the plague and a request that the prophet intervene, and specification that the plague is intended to make manifest that "the earth is the Lord's" (Exod. 9:29). It is in this vein that we must understand Elijah's "except at *my word*" as a reference to the prophet's future announcement of the impending rainfall (18:41 and 44), which resembles Moses' declaration to Pharaoh that the plague of frogs will end on the morrow, followed by the notice that "the Lord did according to the *word of Moses;* the frogs died" (Exod. 8:5–9 [AV 9–13]). All this is no more than the first link in the tight parallels that our story weaves between Elijah and Moses, parallels that are stressed by the Midrash: "We find that Moses and Elijah are alike in everything."[14] True, Joshua is described as Moses' heir (based on many analogies in Josh. 1–6), and Samuel makes a similar statement about himself (in his farewell speech, 1 Sam. 12:1–11). But in the case of Elijah, the parallels are more systematic and far-reaching and even constitute a sort of deep structure, both of the three parts of the present story and of the story of his ascent to heaven (2 Kings 2).

The truncated nature of the prologue is also reflected in the narrator's omission of any explicit description of the king's reaction to the prophet's bold challenge.[15] Apparently Ahab refrained from any dramatic move: he neither responded to the prophet nor threatened him.[16] In fact, at the beginning of the first scene (17:2–7), we are not told that Elijah fled to Wadi Cherith because of any imminent danger, but that he went there in response to a divine command. The narrator emphasizes the prophet's obedience in two interlinked ways—through an explicit statement (v. 5a), and through a lengthy parallel between the command and its fulfillment (vv. 2–5):

The word of the Lord came to him:
"*Go* from here; turn eastward and conceal yourself *by the Wadi Cherith, which is east of the Jordan.* . . . "
He went[17] and did according to the word of the Lord:
he went, and he stayed *by the Wadi Cherith, which is east of the Jordan.*

The prophet conceals himself beyond the king's reach, at first sight in order to escape the latter's wrath (cf. Jer. 26:21–23 and 36:26). But in the circumstances as described, his concealment is probably not so much a matter of protecting himself as of simply dropping out of sight (cf. Gen. 31:49; Isa. 40:27 and 45:15). True, when the time comes, Elijah's disappearance will be the practical impediment frustrating Ahab's attempts to end the drought by laying hands on the prophet. But at this point in their confrontation it endows the drought with an additional dimension: the drying up of the heavenly blessing is augmented by the severance of contact.[18] Hence the emphasis that the prophet vanished from public view in obedience to an explicit divine command received immediately after the proclamation of the drought and did not reappear before the king until he had been explicitly commanded to do so shortly before the end of the drought (18:1).

The command to drop out of sight is accompanied by a promise: in the uninhabited wilderness God will be responsible for the prophet's sustenance; ravens[19] will bring him bread and meat, and he will drink from the brook. Thanks to this combination of the miraculous and the mundane, the isolated prophet is not sundered from the fate of his suffering brethren. When the drought intensifies, the wadi too dries up (17:7), teaching us that even in his miraculous milieu the prophet is not cut off from the sphere of human existence. When there is no water left in the wadi, Elijah cannot stay in his hiding place; this concludes the scene with a clear expectation of new developments.[20]

The opening of the second scene—which deals with Elijah's concealment in Zarephath (17:8–16)—is drawn with obvious thematic and stylistic parallels to the start of the previous scene. Verse 8 repeats verse 2 word for word, and the command to go to "Zarephath of (*ʾašer lᵉ-*) Sidon" and stay there is phrased in the same terms as the original command to go and hide in "Wadi Cherith which is east of (*ʾašer ʿal pᵉne*) the Jordan." The Lord, who guided His servant to uninhabited territory, now finds him a second sanctuary in the land of the Phoenicians, the homeland of Jezebel. Here too, in the alleged domain of the queen's own deity, the same drought that the Lord's prophet foretold is raging. Baal's powerlessness in his own country and the Lord's dominion even outside the territory of Israel are stressed both by the fact the Lord has sealed up the heavens over Zarephath and by the fact that He sees to the sustenance of His prophet there. As a sequel to the Lord's command to the ravens to sustain Elijah (v. 4), we have: "I have commanded a widow there to feed you" (v. 9). This time, too, the prophet's obedience is emphasized by phrasing his compliance in the same words as the command: "Arise, go to Zarephath. . . . So he arose and went to Zarephath" (vv. 8–9). Here, though, this is not so conspicuous as in the first scene (perhaps because by now, and particularly against the backdrop of the dried-up wadi, there is no need for this). From this point on there is a great difference between the two incidents, as great as the difference between perfect faith in the Lord and trust in His word, on the one hand, and inspiring others with this faith and trust. Thus we see that the two scenes—marked by the same style and possessing a common central motif (the miraculous sustenance of the Lord's emissary)—are designed as two stages in Elijah's growth as a prophet.

The widow destined to house and feed the prophet is not aware of the divine command.[21] For his part the prophet, who had received it, has to identify the woman among the Zarephathites and make known to her God's word in a manner that will lead her to listen and comply. Consequently, when Elijah reaches the city gate he finds himself in the throes of a typical prophetic situation, albeit on a small scale: the intended recipient of the divine message is not a king or a community but merely a poor Phoenician widow.

Rashi notes that Elijah learned from Eliezer the servant of Abraham (Genesis 24), and their actions are indeed similar in three respects: both decide to identify the woman by means of a test; both apply the test to a candidate who, in their eyes, meets the requirements ("The maiden was very beautiful, a virgin whom no man had known" [Gen. 24:16]; "a widow was there gathering wood"[22] [1 Kings 17:10]); and both are impressed by the good augury of their simultaneous arrival at the well along with the candidate ("He had scarcely finished speaking, *when* [*wĕ-hinneh*] Rebekah came out" [Gen. 24:15]; "*When* he came to the entrance of the town, [*wĕ-hinneh*] a widow was there" [1 Kings 17:10]). On the other hand, their goals are quite different. Abraham's servant, who was seeking a wife for his master's son, put the young woman to a test of *character*, whereas Elijah, seeking a woman who could be persuaded to obey the divine command, sets her a test of *faith*. When Elijah realizes that the woman is willing to interrupt her task of gathering wood in order to give a drink to a stranger, he immediately poses an even more difficult trial—sharing her bread with the hungry in a time of famine. Just as he recognizes by external signs (of no concern to the narrator) that she is a widow,[23] so too does she recognize that he is a prophet of the Lord,[24] or at least an Israelite who serves the Lord. And she swears by his God—while indicating how few twigs she has gathered—that she is reduced to her last loaf of bread so that the duty of hospitality no longer applies to her.[25]

The truth is persuasive, and Elijah does not view her refusal as disobedience. On the contrary, he identifies with her distress and anxiety: " 'Fear not,' said Elijah to her" (v. 13; cf. Gen. 21:17). At the same time, he manages to translate what he had received as a divine command to the destitute widow into a conditional promise: if you accept the command and are stead-fast in performing your duty you will merit having a miracle wrought for you. On the one hand Elijah minimizes the demand in order to make it easier for her to assent ("make me a *small* cake from what you have there"), but on the other hand he emphasizes that the Lord's command entails her recognition of the prophet's priority: "*first* make me a small cake . . . and bring it out to me; *and afterward* make some for yourself and your son" (v. 13). Only if she has enough faith to give him the first portion of her dough, as an expression of her awareness that it is "the Lord, the God of Israel"— not Baal—who "sends rain upon the ground" (v. 14)—only then will she not lack flour and oil as long as the drought persists. This trial of the wid-ow's faith is also a trial of Elijah's prophetic power; when she does as he requests, her success is his as well. That this is in fact the significance of the incident for Elijah is demonstrated by the emphasis on her compliance: "She went and did as Elijah had spoken" (v. 15). The next verse highlights the fulfillment of the miracle of the flour and oil (v. 16), just as the earlier miracle of the ravens had been underscored (v. 6). But whereas in Wadi Cherith the miracle was for the exclusive benefit of the prophet, in Zare-phath it is also for the widow and her son, by means of and for the sake of the prophet. This structural symmetry further illuminates Elijah's transi-tion from passivity to activity and from dependence on the waters of the brook to dependence on the favors of a gentile woman. Furthermore, when the narrator relates that the widow did "as Elijah had spoken *(ki-d'var ʾEli-yahu)*" (v. 15) and that the jar and jug provided flour and oil "just as the Lord had spoken *(ki-d'var YHWH)*" (v. 16), he is echoing the prophet's proclamation to the king, which concludes with "except at my bidding *(l'-fi d'vari)*" (v. 1).[26] This echo directs our attention to the fundamental similari-ties between the two situations and provides the first hint that the encoun-ter between Elijah and the widow is merely a miniature of the fateful con-frontation—which is playing out in the background—between the prophet and the king of Israel. Hence we can say that Elijah in Zarephath found himself in a classic prophetic situation, which moreover resembled his larger mission, both materially and thematically. Ahab will enjoy the bless-ing of rain only when Elijah brings him to the level of the Phoenician woman, that is, only when the monarch recognizes his duty to the Lord God of Israel, who sends rain upon the earth.

The word *yamim*, '[some or many] days', comes at the end of both the first scene (v. 7) and the second: "she and he and her household ate for [many] days" (v. 15). Whereas in the first case the ending was, as noted above, open, here it is closed: like the protagonists, we too expect that this idyllic symbiosis of prophet and widow will continue undisturbed until the end of the drought. Suddenly, however, the angel of death intervenes: "After these things,[27] the son of the mistress of the house fell sick" (v. 17).[28] The severity of the crisis in the relations between widow and prophet stems from the fact that the woman associates her son's death with Elijah's entry into her life.[29] She has the moral courage to acknowledge her sin (which the narrator sees no reason to make explicit), but she cannot accept the harsh verdict because she attributes its cruel fulfillment to the prophet's very presence in her house. She was responsive to the man of God who bore blessings but rebels against the man of God who focused a spotlight on her sin.[30] When she reproaches him, "What is there between you and me, O man of God?" (v. 18), she is severing all ties with him; when she adds, "that you have come here to recall my sin and cause the death of my son?" (ibid.), she is even retroactively abrogating her original compliance—had she known then what she knows now, she would never have admitted him to her house. When they were still standing by the well she had beseeched the man of God to leave her and her son alone since sharing her last loaf of bread with him would only hasten their imminent death. She had said: "we shall eat it and then we shall *die*" (v. 12); and he had replied: "Fear not" (v. 13). That reply is now seen in a terrible light: "you came . . . *to cause the death of my son*" (v. 18).[31]

Conspicuous in Elijah's response, "Give me your son" (v. 19), is not only his practical reaction but also his refusal to dispute her bitter words. This time his manifestations of identification and understanding—parallel to his "fear not" in the previous scene—are not accompanied by a promise. The prophet who had dared to pledge the miracle of the flour and oil in the Lord's name now confronts, like the widow, the naked terror of death; but unlike her he has an opening for hope—the ability to strive with his God for the resurrection of the child. The widow's hostile revulsion and her depiction of the prophet as the bearer of death involve Elijah in his second trial as a prophet, many times more serious than the first. Her scathing words (both parts of verse 18) resonate with indictments similar to those that the people hurled at Moses at the beginning of his career in Egypt (Exod. 2:14 and 5:21), and again during crises in the wilderness (Exod. 14:11–12 and 17:3; Num. 17:6). The reaction of both prophets to the first confrontation in which they find themselves is similar: silence toward the complainants (Exod. 5:22a) and an outcry to God; even the language and content of their prayers are similar:

> Moses: "O Lord, why did You bring harm [*hare'otha*] upon this people? Why did You send me? Ever since I came to Pharaoh to speak in Your name, he has brought harm [*hera'*] upon this people; and You have not delivered Your people." (Exod. 5:22–23)
>
> Elijah: "O Lord my God, why have You brought harm [*hare'otha*] even upon this widow with whom I dwell, by slaying her son?" (1 Kings 17:20)

Both attribute the calamities that beset those under their protection to God who had sent them, while underscoring the causal connection between this calamity and their own mission ("Ever since I came"—"with whom I dwell"). This is the reason for the strongly personal tone that each adopts and for the rhetorical questions that reflect the profound perplexity of the messengers at the consequences to date of their missions. But whereas Moses was not swept away by the panic-stricken "to slay us" of the Israelite foremen's complaint (Exod. 5:21), Elijah expresses his full identification with the widow by using her own words in his prayer: "*by slaying* her son?" (v. 20). Furthermore, Elijah's remonstrance goes far beyond that of his landlady. His use of *ha-gam*, 'even', seems to associate her calamity with the general calamity that has come upon Israel,[32] whereas the words "with whom I dwell" underscore the difference between the other victims of the drought and the tragedy of the woman who deserves a better fate because she is sustaining him. Elijah's prayer can be interpreted as an impersonal protest against the judge of the universe, who fails to distinguish between the righteousness of the widow (whose sin Elijah passes over in silence) and the sins of the Israelites, who are being chastised for worshipping Baal. We should, however, perhaps hear in it an echo of the very personal pain of the prophet who has been cut off from his people and who feels only too strongly—as the drought drags on—the extent to which the Israelites are identifying him with the calamity that followed his proclamation. Now he has been rejected by the widow, too, as a discloser of sin who bears destruction in his wake.[33]

The Lord responded to Moses' prayer with an explanation (Exod. 6:1), whereas Elijah expects reparation for the injustice—the resurrection of the child. Hence he adds action to speech and does everything in his power to bring the child back to life. Three times he stretches himself out on the child; when this proves insufficient, he again prays to his God, but this time in quite a different tone: "O Lord my God, let this child's life return to his body!" (v. 21).[34] This petition totally omits the sufferings of the community, the righteousness of the widow, and the destiny of the prophet; the single focus is the supplication for the life of "this child." It is the word *this*—which on the face of it could have been left out—that gives Elijah's prayer its full intensity. His total concentration on the particular child lying before him casts into shadow his abstract argument about righteousness and its reward and reduces to the proper perspective his personal suffering caused by the indictments leveled against him. His prayer is accepted, and the Lord's compliance with his prophet's request receives strong emphasis, like the prophet's earlier compliance with God's word (v. 5): "The Lord hearkened to the voice of Elijah; and the child's soul returned to his body, and he revived" (v. 22).[35] Nothing is said explicitly about the prophet's emotions following the child's resurrection. But the reader is meant to note the relatively great detail in which ostensibly subsidiary acts are related: how Elijah picks up the child,[36] brings him down from the upper room, gives him to his mother, and says, "See, your son is alive" (v. 23). This demonstrates that, his prayer having been answered, the prophet is concerned only with the child, its mother, and the wonder of life.

Like Moses after the parting of the sea (Exod. 14:30–31), Elijah now attains new recognition as a man of God and His messenger. On the face of it, the widow's " '*Now* I know that you are a man of God' " (v. 24a) is at odds with the fact that even in her grievance she had addressed him as "man of God" (v. 18). But the contradiction is spurious. She had never doubted his superhuman power, not even at that moment of crisis, for she attributed the death of her son precisely to the fact that he was a man of God. Only now, though, has she come to realize that his power is not simply a capacity to harm and that he is in fact a man of God in the fullest sense of the term.[37] The continuation of her declaration—"and that the word of the Lord in your mouth is truth" (v. 24b)—makes it clear that she had not meant that the fulfillment of his promise concerning the flour and oil was insufficient proof that he is the Lord's messenger. Her son's death did not break the prophet's promise of abundant food but revealed it as deceptive, as lacking internal truth. Now, however, after the child has been restored to her, she comes to understand that the Lord's word as spoken by Elijah is indeed true—that is, reliable (cf. Josh. 2:12), abiding (Ps. 19:10), peace bringing (Isa. 39:8; Esther 9:30), kind and full of loving kindness (Gen. 32:11; Exod. 16:6).[38]

The widow's speech brings the crisis to its close; thus this scene, like its predecessor, has a closed ending. On the formal level this link is underscored by the reference to "the word of the Lord" in each conclusion. The restoration of tranquility to the widow's household is not explicitly mentioned, while its duration is covered by the vague word *yamim*, 'days', at the end of the previous scene (v. 15). This situation permits the narrator to end with the declaration of faith by the gentile widow,[39] presented as the zenith of Elijah's achievement at this stage of his prophetic career and as a challenge in advance of his impending return to his own people: will Ahab and Israel also recognize the Lord and His servant Elijah?

Interim conclusion: We have seen that chapter 17 is tightly unified from stylistic, structural, and thematic perspectives. The drought serves not only as its point of departure (v. 1) but also as the backdrop for the three scenes (vv. 7, 14, and 20), and thereby also as the focal point of the reader's expectations: when and how will the drought end? When and how will the next confrontation with Ahab occur? In her two scenes the widow oscillates between obedience and rebellion; this psychological continuum is also found in the depiction of Elijah's empathetic reactions to her doubts. The truth and power of "the Lord's word" and the extent of obedience to it constitute the central motif that unifies the individual scenes (in verses 2, 5, 8, 10, 14, 16, and 24) while also linking them to the main plot (v. 1, as well as 18:1). The three scenes have a common subject: Elijah's growth as a prophet during the years of his concealment. Thus chapter 17, as a

bildungsroman recounting how Elijah was gradually made ready and prepared for his difficult mission to the Israelites, functions as a substitute of
sorts for the missing consecration story. When he announces the drought
to the king he is no more than a courier conveying a message from his
master—like "one of the disciples of the prophets" who was sent by Elisha
to anoint Jehu (2 Kings 9:1–12)—bolstered by a courage and steadfastness
informed by his awareness that the king of Israel is subject to the higher
King whom he serves. When he hides in Wadi Cherith, in accordance with
an explicit command, he is subordinating his personal life to the demands
of his mission, much like prophets before and after him. In Zarephath,
however, he is called upon to be increasingly active and independent. At
first he bears a divine command and must get its recipient to repose her
confidence in the messenger, put her trust in the sender, and obey His word.
Later he is the target of the widow's bitter complaint and her advocate
before his God. When the widow complies with his command, and when
the Lord responds to his prayer, Elijah knows—and so does the reader—not
only that he is a genuine and faithful prophet of the Lord but also that
Elijah in his generation is like Moses in his generation.

On the Outskirts of Samaria, on the Heights of Mount Carmel, and on the Road to Jezreel: Returning and Performing the Mission

The second part of the story (chapter 18), like the first part, begins with a
dramatic statement that starts the plot moving again. Here too it is in the
form of direct address, a freestanding announcement that does not constitute an independent scene (vv. 1–2a). This abrupt and truncated prologue
is followed by seven scenes, distinguished from one another by a partial or
complete change in the characters and by an additional marker, which
changes after the third scene (together with a change of place, from the
outskirts of Samaria to the heights of Mount Carmel). The prologue and
first three scenes all *conclude* with one of the characters on his way to an
impending meeting or confrontation in the next scene. The last four
scenes, by contrast, all *begin* with Elijah's address to his new interlocutor:

Prologue (vv. 1–2a): The Lord and Elijah.
    Concluding sentence: "Thereupon Elijah *went* to appear before Ahab."
Convergence (on the outskirts of Samaria)

Scene 1 (vv. 2b–6): Ahab and Obadiah.
    Concluding sentence: "Obadiah *went* alone in another direction."
Scene 2 (vv. 7–16a): Elijah and Obadiah.
    Concluding sentence: "Obadiah *went* to find Ahab, and told him."

Scene 3 (vv. 16b–20): Elijah and Ahab.
  Concluding sentence: "Ahab . . . *gathered* the prophets at Mount Carmel."

Performance (on Mount Carmel)
Scene 4 (vv. 21–24): Elijah and the people.
  Opening sentence: "Elijah came near to all the people and *said*. . . . "
Scene 5 (vv. 25–29): Elijah and the prophets of Baal.
  Opening sentence: "Elijah *said* to the prophets of Baal. . . . "
Scene 6 (vv. 30–40): Elijah and the people.
  Opening sentence: "Then Elijah *said* to all the people, 'Come near to
  me'; and all the people came near to him."
Scene 7 (vv. 41–46): Elijah, Ahab, and the servant.
  Opening sentence: "Elijah *said* to Ahab. . . . "

The first half is characterized by journeying, because at this stage the
goal is to assemble all the protagonists to converge in one place; the second
half, by contrast, is characterized by speaking, because it is devoted entirely
to Elijah's supreme effort to prove that there is no god other than the Lord
God of Israel. Just as the roots *h.l.k*, 'go', and *q.b.ṣ*, 'gather', in the concluding verses of the prologue and the first three scenes express obedience to
the Lord's will and Elijah's commands, the root *n.g.š*, 'come near', expresses
the change in the balance of forces that takes place on Mount Carmel: scene
4 begins: "Elijah came near (*wa-yiggaš*) to all the people" (v. 21); later, scene
6 begins, "all the people came near (*wa-yigg^ešu*) to him" (v. 30).[40]
  As a counterweight to this breakdown into a stage of convergence and
a stage of performance, the second part of the story is unified by a series
of commands and hortatory speeches, which develops in parallel to the
evolution in the first part. The prologue and first scene present Elijah's
simple and unproblematic compliance with the Lord's command to appear
before Ahab, followed by Obadiah's compliance with Ahab's order to
search for fodder outside the city: these parallel the prophet's immediate
compliance with the divine command to hide in Wadi Cherith and rely on
miracles. Later in chapter 17, Elijah must find a way to overcome the widow's unwillingness to comply with his request; correspondingly, in chapter
18 he encounters an initial stubborn resistance on the part of Obadiah,
Ahab, and especially the people—once again he must eliminate their suspicions and fears, awaken their confidence and belief, and find a way to
conduct the great trial (scenes 2–6). And just as chapter 17 concludes with
the Lord accepting Elijah's prayer and reviving the child, chapter 18 ends
with the Lord heeding his prayer for rain (scene 7). The Lord's messenger
to the people has a personal duty to influence and win them over; when
he succeeds at this, the way is open for him to be the people's emissary to
the Lord.

The first two parts of the story are sharply distinguished from each other by the chiastic parallelism of their introductions:

Part I		Part II
The decree against Israel (17:1): "There will be no dew or *rain.*"		The antithetical command to Elijah (18:1a): "*Go,* appear before Ahab."
	✕	
The command to Elijah (17:2–3): "*Go* from here . . . and hide yourself."		The annulment of the decree against Israel (18:1b): "I will send *rain* upon the earth."

At the beginning of the story Elijah pronounces the decree of drought before Ahab; only then is he told to go into hiding. After three years of drought the Lord commands him to appear before Ahab so that He will be able to renew the rainfall. This clear contrast between his appearance before the king (mentioned also in verses 2, 15, and 17) and the former concealment provides a basis for our hypothesis that when the prophet vanishes, it is not simply a matter of going underground; rather, his disappearance increases the severity of the decree of drought.

Quite a few scholars see the juxtaposition of the vague "many days" with the precise "in the third year" as a clumsy interpolation, the result of glossatory expansion.[41] On the other hand, the juxtaposition may be original, meant by the narrator to precede the precise indication of the objective length of the drought by a strongly subjective expression of its duration as perceived by Elijah (cf. Gen. 29:20 and 1 Kings 2:38–39). In any case it is clear that, just as before, he goes into action in accordance with a divine command, for he returns to his own country only after "many days" when he receives an explicit command to do so. Just as the injunction to go to Zarephath left room for complementary activity by the prophet, so too with this order—and to an even greater extent. From the Lord's words in verse 1 it is clear only that the period of concealment and drought is coming to an end and that the prophet must appear before the king in connection with the rain that is about to be granted. But against the background of Elijah's oath on the eve of the drought, which refers to the prophet's own word as preceding the renewal of rainfall (17:1), it is evident that the purpose of his appearance is to announce the impending rain so that it will in fact be attributed to the Lord. The wording of the announcement and circumstances of its delivery are not specified, however (unlike the situation in the affair of Naboth's vineyard [1 Kings 21:17–19]), nor is there any indication as to whether he is also being enjoined to create the emotional and conscious educational background that will allow his hearers to fully

absorb the message (unlike the instructions that Moses received with regard to the giving of the Torah [Exod. 19:9–13]). In light of our analysis
of Elijah's actions in Zarephath and our distinction between what he did
in response to a divine command and what he added on his own initiative,
it would seem that most of the deeds described in chapter 18 are also the
result of the prophet's fleshing out the laconic message of his master.

The narrator prefaces his description of the tribulations caused by the
drought (which speak for themselves) with the explicit statement, "the famine was severe in Samaria" (v. 2b).[42] Technically speaking, this is a means
to transfer the scene to Samaria even before the protagonist gets there;
thematically, these words prepare the reader for the change that is about
to take place in the stance of the king of Israel. While Elijah is nearing
Samaria—whose pride and rebelliousness have been broken by the severe
famine—Ahab summons the most important of his officers, Obadiah the
majordomo, who is responsible for the royal treasury.[43] Between Ahab's
summons to Obadiah and his speech to the minister we are presented with
a longish characterization of Obadiah, which begins with the judgment that
"Obadiah revered the Lord greatly" (v. 3b) and continues with a tangible
example of this reverence: he had hidden one hundred prophets of the
Lord from Jezebel's wrath and had sustained them (v. 4). Because Obadiah
later recounts all of this to Elijah almost word for word (vv. 12b–13), Gunkel
questioned the authenticity of this exposition (vv. 3b–4). In his opinion,
the narrator effectively used Obadiah's speech to Elijah to convey information about what has been going on in Samaria during the prophet's absence, while providing convincing psychological grounding for the apolo-
gia of the terrified majordomo. But a later reader, who was not brought up
on this sophisticated form of writing and did not understand its advantages,
felt the need to preface the information to the description of the meeting,
thereby producing this detracting repetition.[44] As is so often the case, the
question is better than the answer. The doublet is indeed astonishing, especially given the tendency of scriptural narrators to avoid or truncate long
expositions in favor of integrating essential information into the body of
the plot or relating it through the dialogue of the protagonists. How essential this information is *at this point* in the account, even before the encounter between prophet and minister, depends of course on one's overall interpretation of the encounter scene. (Hence we shall consider scenes 1 and
2 together here.) Gunkel's negative answer is strongly influenced by his
view that the Elijah-Obadiah encounter is a doublet of the main encounter
between Elijah and Ahab (intended to add additional detail and variety to
the plot), and that Obadiah's monologue serves chiefly to convey retrospective information to the reader (*Elias*, pp. 13–14). I believe that this idea is
quite erroneous; it is blind to the meaning of this scene and misses its
unique character.

First of all, we must recognize that Obadiah's reverence for the Lord is the focal point of the scene of his meeting with the prophet. His fidelity to the Lord and His prophets is not mentioned as mere background color; it is not just a matter of bygones but is strongly expressed in the plot itself, in the narrative present. When Ahab's minister descries the prophet he recognizes him (or perhaps recognizes his authority),[45] falls on his face, and addresses him in respectful terms: "Is that you, my lord Elijah?" (v. 7). The comparison with the Phoenician widow cannot be avoided. That gentile woman, it is true, does not worship the Lord; but she trusts His word, feeds his prophet, and recognizes his truth. The deeds of these two are both similar and complementary: the widow gives Elijah water to drink and bread to eat and houses him in her upper room; Obadiah—at the risk of his own life—has concealed one hundred prophets in two caves "and provided them with *bread and water*" (vv. 4 and 13). Moreover, Elijah meets them in extraordinarily similar circumstances. As the famine was gaining ground in Zarephath, the woman had gone out to the city gate and in the vicinity of the spring or well was gathering wood to bake a last loaf of bread for herself and her son. Similarly, when the famine intensified in Samaria the king of Israel and his majordomo left the city, each of them traveling alone,[46] "to all the springs of water and to all the wadis" (v. 5), in the hope of finding fodder to keep the livestock alive! It is difficult to imagine a more glaring depiction of the rulers' cognizance of the terrible nature of the famine than this description of a king and minister who do not stand on their dignity[47] and go out into the country to search for fodder, just like a downtrodden widow.[48] The symmetry between the meeting on the outskirts of Samaria and the meeting at the gates of Zarephath—which will be further intensified and developed as the story progresses—confirms our view that Elijah's experiences in the house of the widow are designed as preparation for his impending mission within Israel.

When we return to the question of whether the exposition (18:2b–3) is truly essential, we must stress that the question is not *whether* the story can be understood without it, but *how* it would be read in its absence. Were we not told of Obadiah's righteousness, we might reasonably assume that the minister is cut from the same mold as his master. We would expect that the prophet, who encounters his adversary when he is reduced to the most dire and shameful straits (cf. 1 Kings 21:20), could subdue the king's servant and even convert him into his own messenger.[49] The initial prostration would be inexplicable, and the unexpected preliminary victory, won even before the imminent duel, would deprive the later triumph of all its glory. As the text stands, though, against the backdrop of the exposition (or at least its core—"Obadiah revered the Lord greatly" [v. 3b]), we are first of all impressed by the astonishing coincidence. The prophet, who is on his way to appear before the hostile king, without knowing where or when he will find him, meets the king's chief minister on the road. Because we have already been introduced to this minister as the clandestine rescuer of the prophets of the Lord, we expect that he will assist Elijah, just as the widow had done. This expectation is reinforced when Obadiah prostrates himself; but it is quickly and rudely disappointed when, incredibly, the minister refuses to do as the prophet bids (vv. 9–14). When Elijah realizes that he is on the right track—thanks to the miraculous encounter with Obadiah, which parallels his encounter with the woman destined to sustain him—the approach he adopts with this man who pays him such reverence is the same he had used with the widow when she agreed to give him water. When he commands him, "Go tell your lord: Elijah is here!" (v. 8), he is putting Obadiah in an extremely difficult position: Obadiah must translate his initial recognition into action and accept great personal danger. The prophet's demand that the minister inform Ahab that "Elijah is here" is tantamount to his declining to accompany Obadiah to the king and insisting that the king forgo his majesty and come to the prophet.[50] The God-fearing minister's vigorous opposition to Elijah's order is quite similar to that of the Phoenician widow in content, phrasing, and emotional attitude toward the prophet of the Lord.

Despite their initial favorable response, both the widow and Obadiah refuse to comply with Elijah's request.[51] The two demurrals are accompanied by explanations whose analogous wording intensifies and underscores the fact that, with Obadiah, Elijah is again facing the same problem:

The widow's speech	Obadiah's speech
	Wherein have I sinned, that you should give your servant into the hand of Ahab to kill me?
As the Lord your God lives, I have nothing baked. . . .	*As the Lord your God lives,* there is no nation or kingdom. . . .
	And now you say, 'Go tell your lord: Elijah is here!'
And now, I am (*wᵉ-hinnᵉni*) gathering a couple of sticks,	When I (*wᵉ-hayah ᵓani*) leave you, the spirit of the Lord will carry you off. . . .
and when I *come* home (*u-vati*) and prepare it for me and my son;	and when I *come* (*u-vati*) and tell Ahab
we shall eat it and then *we shall die.* (17:12)	and he does not find you, *he will kill me.* (18:9–12a)

Both swear by the God of the prophet in order to give maximum credibility to the background information they provide; both narrate the fate in store for them in the immediate future; and both make it dramatically clear that complying with the prophet's request would endanger their own lives. The individual circumstances are different, of course, and hence the Israelite minister's argument is much sharper, both in content and language, than that of the Phoenician widow. She merely describes the penury in which she and her son are about to starve to death, leaving implicit the conclusion that in this situation she cannot share her very last loaf of bread with a hungry stranger. Obadiah, on the other hand, begins with the rhetorical question, "Wherein have I sinned," to which he adds the blunt charge, "that you should give your servant into the hand of Ahab to kill me?"[52] He has no doubt that the prophet's command sends him to his doom, that Elijah is dispatching him to Ahab merely to taunt the king, while the full price will be paid by the minister who thereby assists in humiliating his master. To back up his claim that Ahab's reaction will indeed be fatal to him, he reports on the king's relentless endeavor to lay hands on the prophet, his repeated failures, and his pent-up frustration.[53] In this situation, if the prophet does not go to the king and instead sends him a message concerning his whereabouts, it is only reasonable to conclude that he intends to continue the wearing cat-and-mouse game that has been going on for three years now. The king will have his majordomo executed, not because of impotent rage seeking a scapegoat, but as punishment for permitting Elijah—through unpardonable naiveté or a disloyalty that is tantamount to treason—to escape once again. How, then, can Elijah dispatch to certain death a man who has revered the Lord since his youth and has gone so far as to protect the prophets of the Lord against Jezebel's fury?

This aggressive apology includes abundant information meant to persuade the prophet to take the circumstances into account and spare the life of a man who does not merit punishment as one of Ahab's minions. From Obadiah's tone, however, we see that he is astonished and horrified that such is to be the reward for his righteousness. More than providing information and explanation, he is rebelling and remonstrating. It is clear that his reaction derives from his profound recognition that the prophet of the Lord might indeed bring down disaster and death even on those who fear the Lord. Elijah has already had to counter this monstrous image of himself when the widow's son died and she wanted to evict him from her house. She had ascribed her loss to the presence in her house of the man of God and did not hesitate to voice her bitter indictment of him, just like Obadiah:

> "*What* is there between you and me, O man of God, that you have come here to recall my *sin* (*ʿawoni*) and *cause the death of my son?*" (17:18)

> "*Wherein have I sinned* (*meh ḥaṭathi*), that you should give your servant into the hand of Ahab *to kill me?*" (18:9)

The bereaved widow did not deny her sin, just as she did not mention the good that she had done for the man of God. It was Elijah who raised the issue of justice when he prayed to his God on her behalf: "O Lord my

God, why have you brought harm even upon this widow with whom I dwell by slaying her son?" (17:20). The words "with whom I dwell" are not meant to identify the woman but rather to characterize her as someone who was commanded to sustain the prophet and has in fact done so. This mention of the widow's righteousness is paralleled in Obadiah's speech when he notes that he has hidden one hundred prophets of the Lord and *provided them with bread and water* and concludes with the sharp protest, "And now you say, 'Go tell your lord: Elijah is here,' and he will kill me!" (18:13–14).

We find an internal consistency and great persuasive power in Obadiah's long and emotional monologue,[54] which is unified by the desperate protest of a loyal worshipper of the Lord against the merciless and unjust severity of the prophet's demand. The threefold reiteration that he will face death for complying with the prophet's command (vv. 9, 12, and 14) is not tiresome repetition.[55] Rather, it reinforces the psychological credibility of his speech and deepens our sense of the fear that haunts him.[56] At the same time, however, the reader knows all along that Obadiah's fears are groundless. Elijah is returning to Samaria to bring not death but life; his intention is not to vanish but to appear! Why, then, does the narrator go on at such great length in describing Obadiah's vain terror? Many commentators see this as an expression of the narrator's tendency to highlight the prophet's superior strength vis-à-vis the royal minister (similar to the theme of 2 Kings 1:13–15).[57] However, our reading of the entire scene leads to the conclusion that the emphasis is not on Obadiah's high office but on the fact that he has feared the Lord since his youth. The theme of the meeting is not the panic that the prophet instills in the royal majordomo, but the dread of the prophet that grips even the most faithful of his followers!

We see, then, that the systematic parallels between the Elijah-Obadiah encounter and the two scenes in Zarephath are intended to focus our attention on a chronic problem, which has troubled the prophets of the Lord since Moses—the fundamental alienness of the messenger in the community from which he has sprung and to which he is sent. Elijah's preparation for the moment when the king of Israel will denounce him as "the troubler of Israel" (18:17) began in Zarephath and was completed on the outskirts of Samaria. Given the plaintiveness of "What is there between you and me" (17:18) and "Wherein have I sinned" (18:9), we must not ascribe Ahab's hatred of the prophet merely to the king's wickedness. The sting is that even those who save and sustain prophets are liable to view Elijah as the agent of their doom. The prophet must learn to dismiss the slight to him and to his mission, to feel the terror of those who shrink from him, and even to identify with their demand for justice. When he overcomes his pain at the astounding depth of their suspicion of him, he finds the strength to calm, to strengthen, and to convey blessing and assistance.[58]

So we should not be astonished that the thematic and stylistic parallels between the two stories are continued in the descriptions of how the prophet overcomes the aversion of both the widow and the minister and their unwillingness to comply with his commands:

> Elijah said to her: "Fear not. Go and do as you have said. . . . *For thus said the Lord, the God of Israel:* 'The jar of flour shall not give out and the jug of oil shall not fail until the day that the Lord sends rain upon the ground.' " *She went* and did as Elijah had spoken. (17:13–15)

> Elijah said: "*As the Lord of Hosts lives,* whose servant I am, I will surely show myself to him today." Obadiah *went* toward Ahab. (18:15–16)

Both the widow and Obadiah take oaths in the name of the Lord so as to persuade the prophet of the veracity of their descriptions of the grave situation in which they find themselves (17:12 and 18:10). Elijah, for his part, buttresses the calming information he provides them with a divine promise or an oath in the Lord's name. Elijah does not argue with those who fear for their lives, nor does he reprove them for their suspicions about him; on the contrary, by providing them with additional information which they could not possibly have anticipated he to some extent confirms their original doubts. He manages to persuade them to believe in him and perform the mission with which he charges them, not only by virtue of promises that give his arbitrary command a measure of reasonability, but also by virtue of his human sensitivity, whose presence alongside the prophetic imperative is no less astonishing.

Let us now summarize our findings about the authenticity of the exposition (18:3b–4): (1) Without this exposition, instead of sharing Elijah's astonishment at the unwillingness of this God-fearing man to do as he is bidden, we would be surprised by the respect shown by Ahab's minister to the prophet of the Lord. Hence we must not doubt the authenticity of the second half of verse 3: "Obadiah revered the Lord greatly." (2) This clause remains pallid and unconvincing without the accompanying information that this fear of the Lord was expressed in a clandestine act of resistance, and sounds stylistically truncated if we try to link it directly to verse 5. (3) Verse 4 provides the first hint about a common denominator linking the royal minister and the widow ("bread and water"). The rhetorical effectiveness of the parallel is increased by making the reader aware of it as soon as possible. (4) Verses 4 and 13 are not worded identically. The variations reflect a fine literary sensitivity that is hard to ascribe to a glossator: Obadiah says "when Jezebel was killing (*ba-harog ʾIzevel*) the prophets of the Lord" (v. 13); the use of the root *h.r.g* in his self-justification contrasts with his remonstrative "he will kill me (*wa-haragani*)" (vv. 12 and 14), reinforcing his protest that he does not deserve such a fate. In the exposition, however, the narrator uses the root *k.r.t* (*bᵉ-hakrith ʾIzevel*) (v. 4), foreshadowing Ahab's despondent "so that we are not left (*wᵉ-lo nakrith*) without beasts"

(v. 5), thereby suggesting a situation of measure for measure.[59] A glossator endowed with this level of artistry is in fact a full partner in the telling of the story. And if he is no longer merely a glossator, commentators can no longer blame his stylistic obtuseness for what seem to be difficult or superfluous passages.[60]

The encounter between Elijah and Ahab (scene 3, verses 16b–20), too, involves a trial and falls into the same pattern we have found in the trials that Elijah posed for the widow and for Obadiah: an initial positive response, followed by vehement opposition and finally by cooperation. When Ahab hears from Obadiah that Elijah has reappeared and is willing to meet him (although he adamantly refuses to come to him), he does not refrain from going to the prophet (v. 16). The widow's and Obadiah's respect for the prophet is based on attitudes that antedated their encounter; but when Ahab goes to meet Elijah he is opening a new chapter in their relations. Under the impact of the terrible drought, the monarch in whose kingdom the prophets of the Lord have been annihilated and who has hunted Elijah even beyond the borders of his realm is now willing to present himself before the prophet. The provocative invitation to meet in the open field is not accompanied by explanations or promises; but a sensitive ear might discern a link with Elijah's announcement, before the drought, that the renewal of rainfall will depend on the prophet's word (17:1). Hence Ahab must choose between standing on his dignity and concern for his suffering people; this test he passes with flying colors. When the king finally reaches Elijah, however, he is quick to accompany his sensible action with an aggressive outburst: "Is that you, you troubler of Israel?" (v. 17). From the formal and stylistic perspectives, this challenge is the antithesis of Obadiah's respectful greeting, "Is that you, my lord Elijah?" (v. 7). But from a thematic perspective it parallels the demurring monologue of the God-fearing minister, who, while continuing to address the prophet as "my lord" (v. 13), implicitly accuses him of being his "troubler" (i.e., the cause of his destruction; for this sense of ʿ.k.r, see Josh. 7:25).

The God-fearing royal minister displays respect for the prophet in his speech and by prostrating himself, but the prophet's injunction astonishes and enrages him. By contrast, the idolatrous king gives vent to protest against the drought and enmity toward its instigator but in practice goes to meet the prophet hoping to find a way to cooperate with him. The ordeal of the famine, openly and explicitly attributed to the God of Israel and accompanied by the mysterious disappearance of His messenger, has reduced the gap between the two antithetical positions: it has weakened the apostasy of Ahab and his party, but at the same time has eroded the faith of Obadiah and his fellow believers. As the terror of God's wrath intensified, so too did the enmity toward the man whose intimacy with the Lord brought not peace and tranquility but evil and calamity. But the prophet, who restored the life of the widow's son and now bears tidings of rain, is not deterred or hurt by the king's vehement expression of animosity.[61] He had identified with the widow's plaint and understood Obadiah's perplexity; now, however, he utterly rejects Ahab's indictment: "It is not I who have brought trouble on Israel" (v. 18). But when he hurls the indictment back against the king himself, he softens it both in language and content. Instead of saying "*you* are the troubler of Israel," he speaks more indirectly—"you and your father's House [have troubled Israel]"—and immediately goes on to emphasize the main point: the drought is not an evil desired either by the prophet or by the king (cf. Jer. 17:16), but God's chastisement of his people, who have been led into sin by the royal house—"by [your] forsaking the commandments of the Lord and going after the Baalim" (v. 18b).[62] Elijah does not pause and allow the king's belligerent and vainglorious spirit to prompt him to continue the argument but immediately offers the practical conclusion of his charge—"Now send and gather all Israel to join *me* at Mount Carmel" (v. 19).

With this demand, Elijah is again putting Ahab to the test—one far more difficult than the test he has just passed. Without making any explicit promises of compensation, he demands of the king something similar to what he has previously demanded of Obadiah: to assemble the representatives of the people before the prophet, that is, to send messengers throughout the land announcing the reappearance of Elijah.[63] The king, who has forgone his due honor in the open countryside, with no witnesses, must now do so publicly before the prophets of Baal and Asherah and all of Israel. As a sequel to the conversion of the majordomo into the errand boy of Public Enemy Number One, the king himself is now being asked to be the herald of the "troubler of Israel," the man who is blamed for all the horrors of the drought.[64] Elijah's silence about the purpose of the gathering on Mount Carmel makes it even more difficult for Ahab to comply; on the other hand, his words convey hints that the king obviously manages to understand. Given the prophet's indictment of the royal house for leading the people into sin, it is reasonable that the meaning of "send and gather" is that the prophet will speak directly to "all Israel," while inviting the idolatrous prophets[65] to the well-known cult site on Mount Carmel[66] clearly implies that he intends to stage a confrontation with them. Ahab is faced with a thorny dilemma; his decision to comply testifies that on this occasion, too, the prophet has managed to adapt his demands to the psychological and moral capacity of the individual on trial. When the king had sought to capture the prophet he knew only too well that the key to rain was in the hands of Elijah alone, but he had hoped to wrest it from him by pressure and coercion.[67] Now, however, the unexpected meeting with Elijah (unexpected as to its timing, location, and circumstances) has taught him that the prophet's disappearance was not at all a matter of flight and concealment and that his renewed presence offers no chance of capturing or overpowering him. The appearance of the Tishbite bespeaks dominion and authority but at the same time trust and hope. Even though no explicit promise has been made, Ahab parts from Elijah—like the widow and Obadiah before him—with a strong feeling that the prophet of the Lord is not a "troubler of Israel" but the harbinger of a better future for the nation.

Elijah commands, and the king complies: "Ahab sent to all the people of Israel and gathered the prophets at Mount Carmel" (v. 20). Here too the successful completion of the test is phrased as a repetition of the words of the command (cf. verse 19), stressing the extent of Ahab's obedience. Elijah's method of testing those to whom he has been sent, namely, creating a situation that requires them to make an unambiguous decision, is also applied in his confrontation with "all Israel" on Mount Carmel. The proverb about hopping from branch to branch has never been satisfactorily explained; we can only hypothesize that the people, who adhere at one and the same time to the worship of the Lord and the cult of Baal, are being compared to a bird that keeps hopping from branch to branch but never chooses one to perch on. It is clear, though, that Elijah's appeal to the people as a whole (v. 21) is to be understood as a "call to decision."[68] Initially, though, the prophet goes no further than strong reproof and abstract appeal, unaccompanied by a demand for definitive action. The first indication that this time Elijah's task is much more difficult than were its predecessors is its less favorable circumstances: whereas the widow, Obadiah, and Ahab approached the prophet, here "Elijah approached all the people" (v. 21a). After he finished speaking, though, "the people answered him not a word" (v. 21b). The prophet had indicted Ahab for "going (*wa-telek*) after the Baalim" (v. 18). Here he uses the same language but phrases it much more gently. The Israelites must stop this hopping from branch to branch and decide: "If the Lord is God, follow (*l'ku*) Him" (21). He does not accuse them of causing the drought and refers to it only indirectly: "How long" will they be unable to determine whether it is within Baal's power to save them? "How long" will they fail to understand that the God of Israel demands that they worship Him alone?[69] This leniency toward the people stems from Elijah's evaluation of what can reasonably be demanded of them in the present circumstances. This is why the prophet restrains himself in the face of their sullen silence and does not reprove them further.[70] Instead, he offers them the seductive proposal of staging a test that will free them of their doubts. In order to help the people, who are not yet able to pass their own trial, Elijah will make experience a shortcut to faith.

When Elijah says, "I am the only prophet of the Lord left, while the prophets of Baal are four hundred and fifty men" (v. 22), his principal intention is to define the balance of power in the proposed trial. At the same time, "I am the only [one] left" is also meant to castigate his opponents' brutality. The prophet of the Lord is proclaiming his readiness to contend with the massed power of the 450 prophets of Baal, against the background of their ferocious hostility toward the prophets of the Lord, which has been expressed by the physical annihilation of all of them save himself.[71] His detailed rules for the trial reflect Elijah's great discernment and good sense (we shall discuss this later when we evaluate the narrator's aim). As his first masterstroke he compels his opponents to participate in the trial according to his conditions simply by not discussing it with them[72] and reaching an agreement with the people (his real litigant) over their heads. This initial accomplishment has another aspect: the representatives of the people—who have been converted, by his suggestion, from defendants accused of indecision to jurors charged with reaching a decision—vindicate him unanimously with their enthusiastic response: "And all the people answered, 'Very good!' " (v. 24).

After imposing his own audacious level of faith on the prophets of Baal, he graciously offers them first choice of a bullock (since a tiny blemish is liable to cause a sacrifice to be rejected), as well as the right to slaughter their animal first since they are "the many" (v. 25).[73] The prophets of Baal demonstrate their confidence in their ability to receive a divine portent by agreeing to Elijah's proposal without a murmur of dissent. But whereas they need only prove the substantiality of their deity, Elijah has a double mission to fulfill: he must prove both the reality of the God of Israel and the nothingness of Baal. His insistence on extracting the maximum psychological impact from the two parts of the trial requires that the Lord's speedy response not precede the protracted endeavors of the prophets of Baal nor coincide with them. So that all those present will recognize that the Lord alone is God, Elijah must defer his own prayer until all have witnessed the utter failure of his adversaries' exertions.[74]

Like all their predecessors in this story, the prophets of Baal comply with his words to the letter. Elijah instructs them: "Choose one bull and *prepare* it first . . . and *invoke* your god by name" (v. 25); and they hasten to do as he has bidden: "They took the bull . . . and they *prepared* it, and *invoked* Baal by name" (v. 26a). When their invocation proves to be in vain they begin a ritual dance around the altar,[75] whose construction is mentioned here in a brief flashback: "they performed a hopping dance about the altar that had been set up" (v. 26b). We have evidence from other sources about ecstatic dancing in the cult of the Tyrian Melkart;[76] the designation of this rite as a "hopping" dance may be meant as an ironic gibe: those who "keep hopping from branch to branch" (v. 21) are not only skipping (metaphorically) from one deity to another, they are also putting their trust in the prophets of Baal who desperately (and actually) hop and skip around their altar. When noon arrives and they have not been answered, Elijah spurs them on to increase their efforts: "Shout louder!" (v. 27). Again the prophets of Baal heed him—"So they shouted louder"—and even gash themselves with swords and spears until the blood flows (v. 28).[77] Thus Elijah makes his opponents active partners in proving the nonexistence of Baal,[78] since their unstinting efforts are the best possible warrant for the impotence of their god. Just like the Phoenician widow, Ahab's majordomo, and the king of Israel himself, so too the prophets of Baal implement the prophet's commands; but whereas the former had all complied willingly and knowingly, the last do so unwittingly and under compulsion. Elijah is not fighting for their souls, so he can afford to manipulate them.

If we have correctly understood verses 27 and 28, according to which Elijah intends, first and foremost, to stimulate the prophets of Baal to make a supreme effort, it is hard to agree with the common interpretation (from Targum Jonathan down to the present) that *wa-yᵉhattel* means that Elijah mocked Baal and his devotees. It is true that scorn and humiliation can have the additional effect of spurring their object to added effort; but given the stylistic and structural arguments brought above, it is quite implausible that this response by the prophets of Baal is an unintentional by-product of Elijah's words. Since the trial on Mount Carmel is meant to offer "empirical" proof of the nullity of Baal—his failure to respond to his prophets—it stands to reason that the narrator should stress not only that the prophet does everything in order to increase the credibility of the trial but also that he says nothing that might endanger it. Whereas Jonathan, Rashi, and R. Joseph Kara, on the one hand, and Montgomery, Tur-Sinai (*Plain Meaning*, vol. 2, p. 238), Fohrer (*Elia*, p. 14), and Uffenheimer (*Ancient Prophecy*, p. 204), on the other, read either "he is detained" or "he is on a journey" as coarse allusions to Baal having to attend to bodily functions, Kimchi inaugurated the interpretive current that understands all these mockeries of idolatry as being perfectly realistic from the perspective of the Baal worshippers themselves. This view is carried on in Gersonides' interesting attempt to ascribe to the prophets of Baal astrological views and practices that were considered to be scientific in his time, and by the effort made in our own day to use mythological and cultic texts from the ancient Near East to uncover what Elijah's words meant to his audience.[79] While opinions differ as to the particulars, there seems to be no reason to doubt the basic assumption that Elijah is using the Baal worshippers' own concepts. At the same time, it is clear that in light of Elijah's demand for a decision between the Lord and Baal (v. 21), the words "he is a god" (v. 27) must be understood as being spoken ironically. The question, then, is whether the sense of *wa-yᵉhattel* indeed requires us to assume that Elijah went beyond irony to mockery.

The verse in question is the only scriptural locus where the root *h.t.l/ t.l.l* is generally glossed as meaning 'mock', a gloss that rests exclusively on the conventional understanding of the context.[80] The basic meaning of the root is 'tell a lie' (Judg. 16:10, 13, and 15; Jer. 9:4, where it is parallel to falsehood

[*šeqer*] and lies [*k^ezavim*]); elsewhere it bears the connotation of 'deceive'
(Gen. 31:7 and Exod. 8:25: Laban deceived Jacob by frequently changing
the conditions of his employment; Pharaoh deceived the Israelites by promising, under the pressure of the plagues, to send the people out of Egypt,
only to refuse later to keep his word after the plague had passed). It also
seems to mean 'lead astray' (in the difficult verse Isa. 44:20). Close to this
is the sense 'equivocate' (Isa. 30:10; Job 13:9—referring to insincere speech
motivated by fear of the reactions of one's audience). This sense of lack of
candor seems to fit our verse as well. Hence *wa-y^ehattel* does not indicate that
Elijah is speaking mockingly but is meant to guard the reader against the
serious misapprehension that the prophet truly believes what he is saying
to his rivals in keeping with their beliefs.[81] Elijah cannot say of Baal "for he
is a god" without his tone of voice clearly expressing the sense "according
to you"; *wa-y^ehattel* is thus a narrative device substituting for an ironic tone
of voice.

Hence we can paraphrase Elijah's speech to the prophets of Baal (v. 27)
as follows: intensify your cries to Baal ("Shout louder!"), since—according
to you—he has the power to answer you ("he is a god"); and if he hasn't
answered so far, then it's because he is otherwise occupied ("he may be in
conversation, he may be detained"), or far away ("or he may be on a journey"), or perhaps is sunk in slumber ("or perhaps he is asleep"). But if, as
I said, you raise your voices, he may answer you ("so that he will wake up").
The plausibility of Elijah's words, from the perspective of idolators, guarantees their response: "so they shouted louder" (v. 28).[82] On the other hand,
his ironic distancing allows the prophet of the Lord to address himself simultaneously to the crowd standing round about and to prepare them for
the impending failure of Baal by illuminating his true (non)essence. The
shameful silence of this nongod, to whom 450 of his prophets are crying
with all their might, cannot be explained away by temporary absence or
slumber; whereas the Lord, the true God—who will shortly and before your
very eyes make his fiery response to his lone prophet—neither slumbers
nor sleeps, does not journey or go away,[83] and is the sole source of all the
evils and blessings that come upon you.[84] When the prophets of Baal intensify their prayers in response to Elijah's words, they themselves—once again
quite unwillingly—confirm the truth of this depiction of their vain faith:
Baal, who has not been awakened from his slumber even by the shouts and
cries of his prophets in this hour of fateful trial—has ears but does not hear!

The failure of the prophets of Baal is sealed when the extra time period
elapses with no response. Now Elijah tells "*all* the people, 'Come near to
me' " (v. 30) and receives full compliance: "*all* the people came near to
him" (ibid.). By turning their back on the altar of Baal, all those present
seal the negative verdict as to the divinity of Baal (a verdict that has been
ripening throughout the three years of the drought). There is also a sig-

nificant change in their attitude toward the prophet of the Lord. Earlier in the day, Elijah had to approach them (v. 21); now, in the wake of his opponents' blatant failure, they draw near to him. This compliance with the prophet's call parallels the initial compliance of the widow, Obadiah, and Ahab; but whereas for those three compliance was the first step, followed by opposition, for the perplexed people the order is reversed—having started with silent reluctance, they were enticed to serve as arbiters in the grand trial, and now display the first buds of obedience.

The outcry to Baal, the ecstatic dancing around his altar, and the self-laceration with swords and spears were described at relative length; the construction of the idolatrous altar and the preparation of the sacrifice, however, were alluded to only incidentally (at the beginning of verse 26 and again at its end). These proportions are reversed in Elijah's part of the story. His prayer will impress his hearers not only by its restraint and clarity, but also by its brevity, whereas his preparations are described at great length. This can be seen as a digression intended to increase the tension leading up to the dramatic climax; but it seems to me that this artistic effect is no more than secondary. Elijah, as portrayed, has no anxiety that the Lord might not answer him (hence he is in no hurry to call on Him), but is deeply concerned that the impact of the omen will be diminished by the skepticism of his audience.[85] Then, too, from the perspective of the narrator, who is intent on perpetuating the lesson of the event beyond the moment of its occurrence, it is appropriate to highlight in detail the cautious measures that the prophet adopts to anticipate any possible claims against the credibility of the trial (compare the trial conducted by the Philistine priests and magicians with regard to the Ark of the Covenant [1 Sam. 6:7–12]).[86] Continuing the tactic of letting his adversaries try first and of inciting them to do their utmost, Elijah does nothing until the people have come to him and hundreds of eyes are watching his every move: building the alter, digging the trench, arranging the wood, cutting up the bullock, and laying the pieces on the wood (v. 33). This is evidently why he himself digs a wide trench around the altar but has the onlookers pour the water on the sacrifice and wood.[87] Here too the precise fulfillment of the prophet's command is stressed (v. 34); this time, however, the emphasis is not on their compliance (which is hardly surprising, given the circumstances),[88] but on the extremes to which the prophet goes in his endeavor to avert all suspicion. He is not content with four jugs of water, nor even with eight, and is not satisfied until everything is thoroughly drenched.[89]

Here we might expect the narrator to tell us where the twelve jugs of water came from, or refer to the difficulty of obtaining them in this third year of the drought. Alt ("Das Gottesurteil," pp. 135–49) saw this omission as evidence for detaching the account of the trial (whose focus is the fire from heaven) from the story of the drought (whose focus is the lack of

rain); but it is dangerous to draw such far-reaching conclusions from silence, and especially from the silence of scriptural narrators, who so often
perplex us in this way.[90] As for the fact of the matter, the drying up of Wadi
Cherith (17:7) does not mean that all wells and springs had also dried up.
On the contrary, the description of the horrors of the famine in Zarephath
and Samaria refers to a shortage of flour and fodder, not of drinking water
(17:11 and 18:5). Whether there was a well-known spring in the area (Bir
el Muḥaraq?), or the water came from the flasks, waterskins, and jugs carried by the onlookers, it is quite plausible that the narrator saw obtaining
twelve jugs of water as a purely technical problem that he did not have to
address.

Alongside his concern for buttressing the credibility of the trial, Elijah
is intent on clarifying its meaning. The assemblage around the ruined altar
of the Lord is itself a reminder of past sins, which links up with the indirect
rebuke about the persecution of the Lord's prophets (18:22; cf. also 19:10).
The repair of the ancient altar is intended to demonstrate the title to this
site held by the cult of the Lord God of Israel and to depict its present
neglect as a breach of trust. The construction of the altar from twelve
stones, on the other hand, is intended to symbolize the ancient covenant
between the Lord and the twelve tribes of Israel,[91] and perhaps also to erect
a barrier between the assembled crowd and the possibly foreign prophets
of the Phoenician Baal. This description of the prophet, making his preparations in utter silence while communicating his meaning to those around
him through a set of shared symbols, presents a major exegetical difficulty.
The repair of the ravaged altar (v. 30b) cannot easily be reconciled with
gathering twelve stones and building an altar from them (vv. 31–32a). The
Septuagint attempts to obviate the impression that the reference is to two
different altars by transposing the second half of verse 30 from the beginning to the end of the description and placing it as a summary after the
beginning of verse 32 (while deleting the word "altar" from this first part:
"and with the stones he built in the name of the Lord and repaired the
damaged altar of the Lord"). On the other hand, Rashi, Kara, Kimchi (in
his alternate explanation introduced by "some say"), and Gersonides solved
this problem—along with a problem that must have troubled them much
more, namely, the legitimacy of the original altar in a period when the
Temple is standing in Jerusalem—by an extreme metaphorization of the
"ruined altar of the Lord": by building a new altar or bringing down fire
from heaven, Elijah repaired, not the stone altar, but the neglected worship
of the Lord. Ehrlich, too, adopted this solution. The dominant approach
today, however, is to see the verses as the conflation of two partial descriptions, attempt to determine which of them is the original, and theorize why
the other was added later.[92] I believe that the problem derives from the
conventional image of an altar as made of successive courses of hewn

stones. It is more likely that popular altars, such as the altar of the Lord on the heights of Mount Carmel and the alter that Elijah erected in its place, were made from undressed fieldstone piled up to form a raised platform of greater or lesser height.[93] Such a stone altar would sometimes be built on a base of packed earth (constituting a sort of upper layer on top of an "earthen altar"). In fact, there is an allusion to this mode of construction in the description of the divine fire that fell upon Elijah's altar: "The fire . . . consumed the burnt offering, the wood, the stones, *and the earth;* and it licked up the water that was in the trench" (v. 38). The order here is from top to bottom: hence between the stones of the altar and the trench around it one could see a layer of earth, considered to be part of the altar, and the stones were piled on top of it. The stone "superstructure" of this type of altar is apt to be scattered when the altar is abandoned or purposely destroyed; someone who wishes to restore it will have to gather appropriate stones. Hence if we are right about the structure of the altar, when Elijah repaired the ruined altar he began by fixing the earthen base (making it higher, packing it down, and shaping it), and continued by gathering twelve stones (whether old or new) from which he built the body of the altar, making sure that all could see that the number of stones corresponded to the number of the sons of Jacob.

When the preparations are complete, and before we hear the actual words of the prophet's prayer, we read that "the prophet Elijah approached and said . . . " (v. 36). Since there is no mention of what he approached, we can assume that here the root *n.g.š* has its cultic meaning (cf. Exod. 19:22; Jer. 30:21; and Ezek. 44:13), namely, that Elijah approached the altar. But in view of the prophet's demonstrative care to avoid any suspicion of sleight-of-hand on his part, and because we later read about prayer rather than an offering of incense or some similar ritual, we should rather assume that Elijah "approached" the Lord, and that here *n.g.š* has its common sense of the intensification of a prior contact in order to persuade (Gen. 44:18; 2 Kings 5:13; and Jer. 42:1–2) or to pray (Gen. 18:23). The extreme brevity of "the prophet Elijah approached" heightens the contrast with the lengthy description of the drastic means employed by the prophets of Baal in order to intensify their contact with him. Unlike their frenzied dancing and self-mutilation, the prophet of the Lord has merely to draw near to his God; their ecstatic cries were shouted at the top of their lungs, but he can trust in the power of his words and simply "say" (v. 36).

Elijah's prayer, as a direct and explicit expression of his intentions and expectations, is meant to illuminate the entire story of the trial on Mount Carmel. For us, though, it presents many serious difficulties. The first of these is the evident similarity between its two verses (vv. 36–37), which raises the question of its original scope. Let us begin, then, by juxtaposing them:

Verse 36	Verse 37
O Lord, God of Abraham, Isaac, and Israel!	Answer me, O Lord, answer me,
Let it be known today	that this people may know
that You are God in Israel and that I am Your servant,	that You, O Lord, are God,
and that I have done all these things at Your word.	and that You have turned their hearts backward.

The stylistic parallel of "Answer me, O Lord, answer me" (v. 37a) with "O Baal, answer us!" (v. 26), and that of "that You, O Lord, are God" (v. 37b) both with "If the Lord is God" in Elijah's demand that the people make a decision (v. 21) and with their declaration, "The Lord alone is God" (v. 39), rule out any doubt that verse 37 belongs to the original account. If there is an addition here, it must be verse 36;[94] its purpose might have been to tighten the link between the Carmel incident and the drought. The conspicuous difference between verses 36 and 37 is the reference in the former to the legitimacy of Elijah's mission ("and that I am Your servant"), an issue that, as we have seen, troubled both the widow and Ahab. Moreover, the language of verse 36 is clearly related to what the widow said after the resurrection of her son:

> "Now I know that you are a man of God and that the word of the Lord in your mouth is truth." (17:24)

> "Let it be known today that You are God in Israel and that I am Your servant." (18:36)

Note that the similar phrasing does not blur the significant difference between the Phoenician widow's recognition of the credibility of the man of God and of the truth of the word of God spoken by him, on the one hand, and the greater expectation that the Israelites would recognize the Lord as their God and Elijah as His servant, on the other.[95] Such an evolutionary relationship is far from being a merely mechanical link; moreover, verse 36 is strongly joined to the central theme of chapter 18. The account of the construction of the altar notes that the number of stones in it "correspond[s] to the number of the tribes of the sons of Jacob—to whom the word of the Lord had come: '*Israel* shall be your name'" (v. 31); Elijah, in his prayer, emphasizes the covenant between the Lord and His people, both in the initial vocative—"O Lord, God of Abraham, Isaac, and *Israel*"—and in the body of the prayer—"Let it be known today that You are God in *Israel* (v. 36). But before we can continue to elucidate the meaning and function of verse 36 in the Carmel story itself, we must first consider an exegetical problem that hinders a clear understanding of Elijah's prayer.

The commentators' perplexity over the meaning of the last part of verse 37 (*wf-ʾattah hasibbotha ʾeth libbam ʾaḥorannith*) stems from the fact that, at first glance, "You have turned their hearts backward" implies that it was the Lord who caused Israel to sin—whether by infecting them with the evil inclination (BT Berakot 31b, and Rashi here), or by hardening their hearts as punishment for previous sins (Maimonides in the introduction to his commentary on Mishna Avot, chapter 8, and in his *Mishneh Torah,* Laws of Repentance, 6,3). Alternatively, according to Kimchi's interpretation, God's failure thus far to give a clear sign to His people is tantamount to causing them to sin. This explanation, in its various forms, is indeed very hard to reconcile with the context. Is Elijah really seeking a heavenly sign to make the people realize that it was the Lord who induced them to sin? Nevertheless, Montgomery and Greenberg did adopt this solution. The former merely makes the quasi-theological assertion that attributing the Israelites' backsliding to the providence of the God of Israel (and not to the attractive power of Baal) somehow exalts the name of the Lord. The latter attempts to reconcile the idea that the Lord causes human beings to sin with the particular needs of "an hour of regret and shame":

> Answer me, O Lord, by means of a miracle that will make it clear to the people that You alone are God, and that only Your hidden providence can be responsible for the great sin of their backsliding. — The verse expresses the willingness, in a moment of despair (for such is the moment of entreating for a miracle), to conceive of everything as the work of the deity, so that it will be possible to amend everything through a single triumphant intervention.[96]

Montgomery and Greenberg stretch the constraints of the context because of two linguistic arguments that they consider to be decisive: the perfective form of *hasibbotha* and the meaning of the adverb *ʾaḥorannith* (which in Scripture never has the sense of 'again' or 'returning'). These make it impossible for them to interpret the phrase as "for you are the one who causes them to repent."[97] I do not find these two arguments to be conclusive, however. The verb can be understood as a future perfect, indicating an action that will be completed at some moment in the future: when God responds in fire, "this people will know (*yedʿᵉu*) that You had (previously) turned (*hasibbotha*) their hearts backward."[98] As for the possibility that here *ʾaḥorannith* does imply returning, we should note that in Scripture spatial orientation does not necessarily rely on a fixed point of view. Thus the verb *h.p.k,* in the account of the conquest of Gibeah, serves to indicate both retreat ("the Israelite men *turned about* in battle"—Judg. 20:39) and regrouping to stand fast ("the Israelites *turned about*"—ibid., 41). Similarly, we read that while Shem and Japhet "walked backward (*ʾaḥorannith* = in the direction opposite to that in which they were facing) and covered their father's nakedness, their faces were turned the other way (*ʾaḥorannith* = in the direction opposite to that in which they were moving)" (Gen. 9:23). Similarly, the idiom *hašavath-panim* has the sense of breaking off relations ("*turn your minds away* from all your abominations"—Ezek. 14:6; cf. Ezek. 7:22); but once relations have been severed, *šivath-lev* refers to their renewal ("these people will *turn back* to their master, Rehoboam"—1 Kings 12:27). Hence nothing prevents us from understanding the "turning backward" of Israel's heart as referring to the specific context of their current situation. Because they have already turned their face *away* from their God (cf. 2 Chron. 35:22), "turning their hearts back" now means turning *back toward Him*. What Elijah is saying, then, is: when fire descends on the altar of the Lord, this people will know not only that You are God, but also that You are their God who turned their hearts back to Him.[99]

What concrete event could generate this change of heart? If the reference is to the anticipated descent of fire from heaven, the prophet's words are intended to demonstrate the great interest that God takes in His people and His willingness to work this miracle before their eyes in order to restore His covenant with them. But if we lay the stress on the words "for You" in Elijah's prayer, the meaning is that it is the Lord—not the prophet—who is contending for their allegiance. And this struggle, which is now approaching its climax on Mount Carmel, clearly rests on two elements: the concealment of divine favor during the long drought on the one hand, and the divine grace in the fiery revelation on the other. The advantages of the second interpretation are clear: it is supported by the anaphoric repetition of the pronoun "you," it is more in keeping with the future perfect form of the verb, and it is richer than the first because it incorporates it. Nevertheless, we must acknowledge that no firm decision can be made on the matter. By contrast, I think it clear that the parallel clause in verse 36 refers first and foremost to the three years of chastisement. When Elijah says "Let it be known today . . . that I am Your servant, and that I have done all these things at Your word" (v. 36b), he is clearly referring to his indictment as the "troubler of Israel" and asking his master to refute that charge. Because the words "all these things" come after "that I am Your servant," it is not likely that they relate exclusively to the trial now being conducted on Mount Carmel; it is much more plausible that the reference is to Elijah's entire multistage mission. This mission has been marked by his mysterious disappearance and miraculous return, accompanied by the repeated emphasis on the prophet's authority and role: his declaration that the drought will not end "except at *my word*" (17:1), his request that the widow "first make *me* a small cake (17:13), his injunction to Obadiah, "Go tell your lord: Elijah is here!" (18:8), and his proclamation that he stands alone against his adversaries ("I am the only prophet of the Lord left" [18:22]). But now that his struggle has reached its climax, he solicits God's direct intervention to make it perfectly clear that "all these things" were indeed done at the behest of the Lord and through His power.[100]

The (complete or partial) parallel we have found between the second halves of verses 36 and 37 returns us to our consideration of the authenticity of verse 36, sparked by the surprising repetition in Elijah's prayer. The extended scope of the citation of Elijah's words helps underscore the contrast between the bloody self-mutilation of the prophets of Baal and the oral prayer of the prophet of the Lord. Just as their vain efforts are described in two stages (vv. 26 and 28), separated by their adversary's incitement to intensify their efforts (v. 27), so too Elijah's efforts do not receive an immediate response. In his prayer, too, there are two stages, even though there is no intervening passage that highlights the failure of his first attempt. At the same time, we clearly sense his redoubled spiritual and emotional effort, not only by virtue of the repeated vocative at the beginning of verse 37, but also and chiefly from the repressed terror in its phrasing: "Answer me, O Lord, answer me." His desperate prayer to restore the life of the widow's son, it will be remembered, also has two stages, separated by the description of the prophet's lying on the child three times—an interlude that accentuates the lack of response to the first prayer. His plea was not granted, we recall, because it was chiefly a rebuke directed against Heaven on account of the harm wrought by the hand of the Lord. The second prayer, however, was heeded, because the complaint had been replaced by supplication for the life of the child. Similarly, there is a difference of tone and approach between Elijah's two prayers on the heights of Mount Carmel, although it is not as stark as between the prayers in Zarephath (hence there is no break between them). Whereas the vocative that introduces the first prayer is ceremonious and serene ("O Lord, God of Abraham, Isaac, and Israel!"), that at the beginning of the second is personal and emotional ("Answer me, O Lord, answer me"). Accordingly, in the first prayer the prophet uses impersonal language ("Let it be known today that You are God in Israel"), whereas in the second he refers directly to the throngs standing with him on the mountain ("Let *this people* know that You, O Lord, are God"). The major change, however, is that the second petition contains absolutely no reference to the prophet's own status, which constituted the core of the first prayer: "Let it be known today . . . that *I* am Your servant, and that *I* have done all these things at Your word." In Zarephath, the humble supplication focusing exclusively on the life of "this child" was answered; on Mount Carmel, God responds to the anxious prayer that rises above all personal interest and refers exclusively to repairing the breach between "this people" and its God.

From morning to late afternoon the prophets of Baal called loudly on their god—"but there was no voice, nor one who answered or heeded" (v. 29). Elijah's prayer, however, is answered immediately and vigorously. A divine fire descends from heaven and consumes not only the bullock and the wood on which it is arranged, but also the stones and the dirt of the altar, and it even dries up the water in the trench (v. 38).[101] This extraordinary feat of the fire seems not only to increase the wonder of the miracle but is meant also to provide indisputable foundations for the results of the trial by eliminating any possible doubts about the nature of the fire. All present must realize that the lightning that struck the altar was indeed divine fire (cf. Job 1:16), not only by virtue of the timing, but also because of its uncommon potency. In holy awe all fall on their faces before the unseen God who has answered His servant in fire,[102] loudly proclaiming that He, and none else, is God. Their prostration parallels the honor shown the prophet by the widow, Ahab, and especially Obadiah ("[Obadiah] recognized him and flung himself on his face"—[v. 7]), just as their declaration parallels the widow's confession of faith following the resurrection of her son ("Now I know that you are a man of God and that the word of the Lord in your mouth is truth" [17:24]). This reverence for and recognition of the Lord fulfills their obligation under the conditions of the trial but still offers nothing comparable to the endurance and perseverance shown by the widow, Obadiah, and Ahab in the difficult tests that the prophet had posed for them. Elijah demanded that all three assist him in fulfilling his prophetic mission, overcoming their suspicions and fears by virtue of their trust in him and their faith in his master. Now the time has come to demand a similar response from the assembled Israelites on Mount Carmel.

Elijah told the widow, "Go and do as you have said" (17:13), and her compliance is expressed in the words "She went and did . . . " (17:15). He commanded Obadiah: "Go tell your lord . . . " (18:8), and Obadiah indeed went and told (v. 16). Ahab, too, passed his test and went to meet Elijah (v. 16); moreover, when enjoined, "now send and gather," he complied: "Ahab sent . . . and gathered" (v. 20). In the same fashion Elijah informed all the people, even before the trial, of his essential demand: "If the Lord is God, follow Him" (v. 21); but he was answered by a silent refusal. Hence it is only natural that immediately after their declaration, "The Lord alone is God"— which indicates that they have ceased hopping between the two branches— the prophet demands that they draw the practical conclusion from this theological decision: "Then Elijah said to them, 'Seize the prophets of Baal, let not a single one of them get away' " (v. 40). This enjoins everyone present to participate actively in the prophet's all-out war against Baal worship. We are told that the response of the people, who only that same morning could not or would not abandon it, is complete: "They seized them" (v. 40). It is difficult to estimate how great a risk these individuals ran for helping slaughter the prophets of Baal in a kingdom where the prophets of the Lord had been systematically exterminated by order of the queen (18:4 and 13; cf. 19:2–3). But it stands to reason that the courage and daring required of them was no less than what the prophet had already demanded

of the widow, Obadiah, and Ahab. Despite this mass cooperation, full responsibility for the massacre of the prophets of Baal is ascribed to Elijah:
"*Elijah* took them down to the Wadi Kishon and slaughtered them there"
(v. 40; cf. 19:1).

Rashi, Kara, Kimchi, and Abravanel ignore the ethical and legal aspects
of the slaughter of the prophets of Baal, evidently because they considered
it axiomatic that those who offer sacrifice to other gods have committed a
capital crime (Exod. 22:19) and that this applies all the more to one who
induces others to practice idolatry (Deut. 13:7–12). Only in the commentaries of Ibn Kaspi, Gersonides, and Isaac Aramaa do we find any reference
to the problem of the prophet's zealotry.[103] By contrast, modern commentators such as Montgomery and Gray are strongly repelled by this blood-
shed, judging the deed by the external criterion of freedom of worship.
But our understandable anxiety that the deed might be cited as an example
for our own times must not cause us to adopt an ahistoric perspective. The
essence of a historical perspective is to recognize that times and manners
change, bringing about changes in norms and values. We must not measure
the past by the yardstick of the present or demand that the present adopt
in toto the values of the past. The point of departure for understanding and
evaluating Elijah's deed must be the basic fact that in biblical times the
age of religious tolerance had not yet dawned. Not only were the Israelites
commanded to uproot idolatry from the land (Deut. 12:3), they were also
enjoined to destroy all idolators, whether from the seven nations (Deut.
20:17–18) or Israelites (Deut. 13:13–19), whether isolated individuals (Exod.
22:19; Deut. 17:2–7) or an entire community (Deut. 13:13–19). Given the
utter rejection of idolatry as a religious and moral abomination (Lev. 18:24–
19:4; 1 Kings 21:25–26), it is not surprising that Elijah treated the prophets
of Baal with such severity;[104] we can ask only whether the massacre, without
any semblance of judicial proceedings, is a deviation from scriptural norms.

First of all we must recognize that here too Elijah is following in the
footsteps of Moses; the combination of the demand for a clear decision
("follow him") and the dire command ("seize the prophets of Baal") clearly
echoes Moses' cry in his war against the worship of the golden calf: "Whoever is for the Lord, come here! . . . Thus says the Lord, the God of Israel:
Each of you put sword on thigh . . . and slay brother, neighbor, and kin"
(Exod. 32:26–27). But whereas Elijah does not cite a divine injunction when
he commands the seizure of the prophets of Baal (and will later refer to
the act as an expression of his own great zealousness for the Lord—19:10),
Moses was explicit about this matter: "Thus says the Lord, the God of Israel." It is true that in the account of the golden calf we do not read that
God had so commanded before Moses descended from Mount Sinai; the
Sages were consequently split in their understanding of these words. According to one opinion, Moses derived this command from the law applying
to idolators: "Whoever sacrifices to a god other than the Lord alone shall

be proscribed" (Exod. 22:19) (*Mekhilta*, Bo, 12; ed. Hurvitz, p. 40). According to another opinion, Moses based himself on a particular instruction he received on Mount Sinai that is not explicitly mentioned in the Torah (*Exodus Rabbah*, Ki Thiśśa, 42,4). The inclination reflected by the first opinion—basing Moses' act on standard law—accompanies a tendency to demonstrate that his procedures were also standard—the accused were brought to trial (Jonathan ben Uziel renders "from gate to gate throughout the camp" as "from the gate of the *sanhedrin* to the gate of the court of law in the camp"), judged according to the rules of evidence, and punished according to the extent of their guilt (see BT Yoma 66b). Nachmanides, who could not see this as the plain meaning of the scriptural text, opted for the second opinion; he views the execution of the three thousand who had worshipped the calf as an exceptional deed based on an ad hoc injunction (commentary on Exod. 32:27).

This dispute over Moses' action boils down to an attempt by the proponents of both views to reach a single goal—that the mass slaughter not be viewed as a norm incumbent upon later generations. I am more inclined to the solution offered by Nachmanides, not only because it adheres more closely to the plain meaning of the text and because of its willingness to recognize the extraordinary nature of this ghastly deed, but also because it implies an additional point of contact between Moses' zeal and Elijah's. According to Nachmanides' interpretation, "Whoever is for the Lord, come here" must be understood in the context of the decree of annihilation passed on the people, which Moses had managed to have nullified. This also seems to be how we should understand Elijah's "seize the prophets of Baal"—as an ad hoc commandment that expresses the prophet's anxiety for the survival of Israel. In the retrospective light of chapter 19 (especially verses 10 and 18), Elijah's great zealotry appears not only as a punishment for the great evil that Baal worship had already brought down upon Israel (see 18:18), but also as a shield against the dire threat it posed to the continued existence of the nation. When Elijah is answered in fire and the people once again recognize the Lord their God, he is overtaken by a spirit of zealotry (as we will read in 19:10) and demands, in order to uproot Baal worship from Israel, that those who are prostrating themselves participate in the punishment of those who had led them astray and would have caused their destruction. The third part of the story (chapter 19) is largely devoted to an assessment of the success of Elijah's zeal for God. But no doubt seems to be expressed there as to the legal and ethical justification of his behavior.

The narrator does not explain why Elijah refrained from slaughtering the prophets on Mount Carmel and had to drag them down into the wadi below; we can only theorize about a matter that must have been self-evident to readers in antiquity. Perhaps we can rely on the law relating to a corpse found in an open field. If the point of breaking the heifer's neck is to purify the tilled field from the innocent blood of the murder victim by transferring it, as it were, to "an everflowing wadi, which is not tilled or sown" (Deut. 21:4),[105] it may be that Elijah hesitated to spill the blood of the prophets of Baal in the fields of Mount Carmel and preferred to do this in the nonarable channel of Wadi Kishon.[106] Although this is not a case of innocent blood, caution is nevertheless required to keep the fertile Carmel from being contaminated. The sanctity of human life and the stature of an individual as created in the image of God require extreme caution even in the case of those who are being justly executed (cf. the prohition against leaving the corpse of an executed criminal hanging overnight [Deut. 21:23; cf. 2 Kings 9:34]).[107] The fact that the narrator does not provide a lengthy account of the events in Wadi Kishon, preferring to summarize them in two Hebrew words *wa-yišḥaṭem šam* ("he slaughtered them there"), reflects both his evaluation of the relative importance of the prophet's various deeds on that momentous day as well as his desire to stimulate his readers' imagination about the descent of fire and rain while compelling them to make do with minimal factual information about the punishment of the Baal worshippers.

The narrator has not even alluded to Ahab since telling us that the king had summoned the prophets and the people's representatives to Mount Carmel (v. 20); from this consistent silence readers might conclude that Ahab was not present at the confrontation between Elijah and the prophets of Baal. Suddenly, with no note of explanation, Elijah speaks to him: "Go up, eat and drink, for there is rumbling of [approaching] rain" (v. 41). Is this really the way to inform us that the king of Israel was a witness to the failure of the prophets of Baal and the success of the prophet of the Lord and even joined the people in prostrating themselves and proclaiming the Lord's divinity aloud? Moreover, if the imperative "go *up*" and its fulfillment "Ahab went *up*" relate to "took them *down*" in the previous verse, the implication is that Ahab had joined those who descended to the Kishon, with no apprehension about the far-reaching significance of his presence there—justifying the slaughter of the prophets of Baal. It is hardly surprising, then, that scholars see the absence of any information about Ahab's activities on Mount Carmel and in Wadi Kishon, and about the identity of the servant lad who suddenly appears to assist the prophet at the summit of Mount Carmel (v. 43), as decisive proof of the faulty joining of two independent stories—that of the drought (which breaks off at verse 18 and resumes in verse 41) and that of the trial on Mount Carmel (vv. 21–40).[108] According to this theory, the haziness on these two points stems not only from the joining of the stories, but also from the deletion of a substantial part of the description of the encounter between Elijah and Ahab, in which the prophet's servant was probably mentioned and a reason may have been given for the king's fast. Since, however, we have not yet discerned any substantial indications of a distinction between independent sources in chapters 17 and 18, we should look for another solution to these problems.

Sometimes intensifying a problem makes it easier to solve. The narrator's perplexing failure to refer to Ahab is repeated at the beginning of chapter 19, where it cannot be explained as due to the fusion of disparate sources. When Ahab returns to Jezreel he informs Jezebel about everything that Elijah did on Mount Carmel and in Wadi Kishon (19:1) and then vanishes from the story! The threat against the prophet's life is pronounced by a messenger of the queen; what is more, we never hear anything about Ahab's stand concerning this counterattack by the Baal worshippers. The narrator's silence attains even greater significance when compared with the detailed sketch of the relations of the king and queen and the division of authority between them in the incident of Naboth's vineyard. True, there the narration is scenic, whereas at the beginning of chapter 19 it is merely a report; but this difference in narrative mode seems to be merely one more indication that in the Naboth episode the king's willing complicity in his wife's crimes is a central theme of the story, whereas here the narrator is not particularly interested in Ahab's personal guilt with regard to the sin of Baal worship. When the prophet is engaged in the age-old struggle against Baal worship, he speaks directly to the people; the king is the addressee only for proclamations about the coming and end of the drought and a means for summoning all of Israel and the idolatrous prophets to Mount Carmel.[109] Hence the narrator's silence about Ahab's actions on Mount Carmel and again in Jezreel is intended to convey that in both places Ahab was a passive participant who did not substantially intervene in the course of events. Since Ahab's (contradictory?) reactions to the dramatic actions taken by Elijah and Jezebel have no relevance to the theme of the story, the narrator passes over them in silence. Leaving a central character out of the limelight goes against the literary conventions to which we are accustomed; we are surprised because our expectations and curiosity have not been satisfied. Scriptural narrative, however, must be understood according to its own assumptions, and this is one way in which it differs from the customs of Western storytelling. This question is addressed in the appendix; here we can merely enumerate other manifestations of the elliptical style in our story. Just as we are never told who provided the two perfect bullocks for the altars or the source of the twelve jugsful of water, so too there is no explanation as to when Elijah was joined by his servant who peered out toward the sea for him (18:43)[110] or when the servant catches up with his master after the latter's run to Jezreel. Moreover, just as we did not know that the widow was holding her dead son in her arms until Elijah took him from her (17:19), so too we are not apprised that the servant accompanied Elijah on his flight from Jezreel until we are told that Elijah left him in Beersheba (19:3). Hence the silence about Ahab's behavior during the trial on Mount Carmel is not necessarily the result of inattention by a compiler or editor who fused separate stories; it may very well be a direct result of the mode of biblical narrative, which tends to sacrifice informational clarity in the interest of a sharper focus on the main point.

Just as the narrator ignored Ahab while recounting Elijah's confrontation with the people, he now ignores the people when telling about the renewed interaction between prophet and king.[111] The imperative "go up" that Elijah addresses to Ahab can be understood in a non-topographical sense—motion that does not involve a change of elevation (cf. "go up to the forest country and clear an area for yourselves there"—Josh. 17:15; "Come up with us to our allotted territory"—Judg. 1:3). But right after the description of Ahab's compliance ("Ahab went up to eat and drink") we read, "and Elijah *went up* to the top of [Mount] Carmel" (v. 42), where it is clear that the verb ʿ.l.h indicates the prophet's return from Wadi Kishon to Mount Carmel. The inference is that the prophet spoke to the king below, in the wadi, and perhaps also in close association with what had just occurred there. What, then, is the meaning of "Go up, eat and drink, for there is rumbling of [approaching] rain" (v. 41)? From the rationale given in the second half of the statement, Kimchi, Montgomery, and Gray conclude that a public fast had been proclaimed on the day of the trial (see Joel 1:14) and explain that the prophet is telling the king that he can break his fast publicly, because the rumble of the imminent storm can already be heard. The assumption that we are told about the cancellation of a public fast without having been informed of its proclamation is plausible in and of itself, for it is compatible with the elliptical style referred to above. But another explanation can be offered, one that more strongly links Elijah's words both with the immediate context and with the general structure of the story. Just as we find in Scripture that not eating and drinking on a calamitous day is meant to express profound identification with the victims (2 Sam. 1:12; 3:35), so too we find that obstinately ignoring the suffering of others is expressed by demonstrative feasting: Joseph's brothers sat down to eat after they had tossed him into the pit (Gen. 37:24–25); Ahasuerus and Haman sat down to drink while the city of Shushan was perplexed (Esther 3:15); and Jehu ate and drank immediately after his horses had trampled Jezebel (2 Kings 9:33–34). Thus Elijah's announcement of rain may also be a sort of command to the king to still any doubts concerning his total identification with the slaughter of the prophets of Baal by feasting in public (just as David demanded that Joab join in the mourning and eulogies to acknowledge that his killing of Abner was wrong—2 Sam. 3:31). But instead of linking this explicitly with what has just occurred, the prophet associates his instruction with the reward awaiting those who have returned to worship the Lord alone—the end of the drought. As is his wont, here too the narrator stresses compliance by repeating the words of the command: "Ahab went up to eat and drink" (v. 42); this emphasis reinforces the assumption that this is not a mere announcement of good tidings, but an additional trial of the king's faith. The widow was asked to give her last piece of bread to the prophet and was promised that "the jar of flour shall not give out." Obadiah was asked to bring the king to the prophet and was promised that "I will appear before him this very day." Ahab was asked to summon all of Israel and the prophets of Baal to Mount Carmel, with no explicit promise added; but now, asked to complete the deed by dissociating himself demonstratively from the slaughtered prophets of Baal, he does receive a promise: "for there is rumbling of [approaching] rain."

This fulfills the condition included in the proclamation of the impending drought, whereby dew and rain would not fall "except at my word" (17:1). Now the prophet's word is heard, even though the sky is still cloudless. We might expect that Elijah would join his king in the feast to celebrate the impending rainfall. This expectation is demonstratively disappointed, as expressed by the adversive *waw:* "Ahab went up to eat and drink. *But* Elijah went up to the top of Mount Carmel" (v. 42). While the king is celebrating the promised rainfall—voluntarily or under compulsion—the prophet wanders off to an even higher point on the crest of the mountain and invests all his spiritual resources in beseeching God to quickly fulfill His promise. Now that Israel and its king have passed their test, just as the Phoenician widow had done, Elijah can fight on their behalf wholeheartedly, just as he had struggled for her sake. The narrator reinforces the parallel between these two situations by employing similar motifs and phrasing. In the widow's house, Elijah went off to a high place: "he carried him to the upper chamber" (17:19); so too, Elijah now "went up to the top of Mount Carmel" (18:42); there "he stretched out over the child" (17:21); here "[he] stretched himself (*wa-yighar*) on the ground, and put his face between his knees" (18:42).[112] There the great effort to warm the child's body is stressed by the words "three times" (17:21); here the exertion of his unbroken prostration is expressed by sending the servant to look toward the sea "seven times" (18:43). The words of Elijah's plea for rain are not reported, perhaps because the silent prayer of placing the head between the knees far exceeds the power of words to express total submission to the Lord and total dedication to healing the people's distress.[113] When the servant finally tells him that "a cloud as small as a man's hand is rising in the west" (18:44), Elijah knows that the Lord has answered his prayer, just as he had responded to his voice in Zarephath (17:22). But whereas he had then gone down to the widow and joyfully informed her, "see, your son is alive" (17:23), here he allows his servant to deliver the good tidings of the speedy coming of "a heavy downpour" from that "small cloud": "Go up[114] and say to Ahab, 'Hitch up [your chariot] and go down before the rain stops you' " (18:44). Why didn't Elijah himself deliver this gratifying prophecy, phrased as sound advice? I have no clear answer to this. The analogy with the episode of the widow (who, it will be recalled, reacted to her son's revival with an enthusiastic recognition of the truthfulness of

Elijah's prophecy [17:24]) suggests, however, that the prophet is seeking to avoid a scene of effusive thanks and personal recognition. The cry "the Lord alone is God" is still resonating on the summit of Mount Carmel; total compliance with his commands by both people and king has already given fit expression to their recognition of his prophetic authority. The time has come for him to restore to the king of Israel that very honor he had taken from him when he forced him to come meet him in the open drought-stricken field.[115]

The epilogue of the Elijah-Ahab scene on Mount Carmel (vv. 40–46) contains no direct speech by Ahab. This continues the trend to leave his character and thoughts in shadow. In any case, the king climbs back from the wadi to feast when instructed to "go up," then descends and rides to Jezreel when told to "hitch up and go down." Now the prophet will compensate him by means of a grand gesture. If we remember that Absalom and Adoniahu hired men to run before their chariots and enhance their prestige as heirs to the throne (2 Sam. 15:1; 1 Kings 1:5), it is clear that Elijah's running before Ahab's chariot is intended to honor the king. By this wondrous act Elijah not only generously compensates the king for the lèse-majesté on the outskirts of Samaria, on Mount Carmel, and in Wadi Kishon; he also lets him know, with unparalleled clarity, that nothing the prophet has done was meant to subvert the monarch's rule and undermine his authority. On the contrary, at the sight of the prophet with girded loins running in a heavy rainstorm before the royal chariot "all the way to Jezreel"—a distance of some twenty-five kilometers—we can sense the enthusiasm with which he is restoring to the king that which appertains to the king and the joy with which he is finally returning to his own people.[116]

In the Wilderness, on Mount Horeb, and at Abel-meholah: Flight and Rededication

Like its two predecessors, the third part of the story (chapter 19) begins with a dramatic prologue that is not an independent scene. This is followed by three complete scenes, of which the middle is by far the longest. Four indications clearly demarcate these subunits from one another: (1) a change in setting; (2) a partial change in the dramatis personae; (3) opening sentences that tell us that Elijah arrived at a new place (except for the first scene); (4) concluding sentences that (with one exception) inform us of the decisive inauguration of a long journey:

Prologue (vv. 1–3a)
    Dramatis personae: Ahab, Jezebel, and Elijah
    Setting: Jezreel
    Conclusion: "He was frightened and *arose and went* for his life."

Scene 1 (vv. 3b–8)
   Dramatis personae: Elijah and the angel of the Lord
   Setting: Beersheba and the wilderness
   Opening: "He *came* to Beer-sheba, which is in Judah, and left his servant
   there; he himself *went* a day's journey into the wilderness. He *came* to a
   broom bush and sat down under it."
   Conclusion: "He *arose* and ate and drank; and with the strength from
   that meal he *walked* forty days and forty nights as far as the mountain
   of God at Horeb."
Scene 2 (vv. 9–18)
   Dramatis personae: Elijah and the Lord
   Setting: Mount Horeb
   Opening: "*There* he *went* into a cave, and *there* he spent the night."
   Conclusion: None (the scene ends with the Lord's injunctions to Elijah;
   the absence of an explicit statement that Elijah returned north to in-
   habited territory requires a literary explanation)
Scene 3 (vv. 19–21)
   Dramatis personae: Elijah and Elisha
   Setting: Abel-meholah
   Opening: "He *went* from *there* and came upon Elisha son of Shaphat as
   he was plowing."
   Conclusion: "Then he *arose* and *went* after Elijah and became his atten-
   dant."

We see, then, that the third part of the story is marked by incessant motion: first, Elijah's flight to the wilderness, running from Jezebel, prophecy,
and his life; then his trek to Horeb, which returns him to himself, his God,
and his mission; finally, his hesitant return to settled territory, human society, and his prophetic vocation.
   Chapter 19 is more ambiguous than its two predecessors, and most of
the issues it raises have inspired differing and even conflicting opinions.
This difference between chapters 17–18 and chapter 19 may indicate that
the latter had a different author, whose style was more allusive. In any case,
chapter 19 clearly not only continues the story line of chapters 17 and 18,
it is dependent upon them factually (Jezebel's liquidation of the prophets
of the Lord and Elijah's slaughter of the prophets of Baal), structurally, and
linguistically.[117] If this is indeed the original or even a later sequel to the
story of the drought, we should look into how its author presents the abrupt
transition from Elijah's crushing triumph over Baal worship to his total
despair in the wake of Jezebel's threat, and how he reconciles the contradiction between the people's cry, "The Lord alone is God," and the Lord's
announcement of the impending destruction of the bulk of the people

(19:17–18). We shall attempt to find an answer to this double question in a close reading of the brief prologue.

Like the prologue to chapters 17 and 18, here too a sharp statement sets the wheels of the plot in renewed motion. Elijah's proclamation of the drought is not provided with even a minimal description of the circumstances; similarly, when Jezebel's threat is sent to its recipient, there is no indication of place (from the palace in Jezreel?) or time (the day after Ahab's return, while the long-delayed rains are still falling?). The queen's threat is preceded only by the concise summary of Ahab's report to Jezebel of the events on Mount Carmel. Despite the great brevity and indirect presentation of what he told her, we can discern the spirit of his account. Ahab first told her about "all that Elijah had done" (v. 1), that is, the wondrous miracle of the heavenly fire that descended on the altar and the forecast of the imminent rainfall, and, perhaps, also about the superhuman race before his chariot. Only after this, and separately, did he mention "how he had put all the prophets to the sword" (ibid.). No doubt Ahab adopted this mode of reportage as a way of explaining to his wife how the solitary prophet, only just returned from exile, had the authority and ability to conduct such a massacre. At the same time, it gives him an excuse for his failure to intervene and prevent the slaughter. The king explicitly lays responsibility for the killing of all the prophets of Baal on Elijah. Beyond his quasi-apology for his passivity, implicit in his dry report of the facts, we hear absolutely nothing about his current stance in the ancient struggle between the worship of the Lord and the worship of Baal. From the narrator's silence we can probably infer that Ahab made no attempt to persuade Jezebel that, in view of "all that Elijah had done," there is no alternative to recognizing that "the Lord alone is God," and acknowledge—like the widow in Zarephath—that the word of the Lord in his mouth is truth." Just as Ahab held his peace on Mount Carmel in the presence of Elijah, so too is he now silent before his wife. The narrator does not even report what Jezebel said when she heard the grim tale of the events on Carmel (possibly along the lines of "Now will you show yourself king over Israel?!" [21:7]); instead we read that she declared war, in her own right, on Elijah, as if there were no king (along the lines of "I will get the vineyard of Naboth the Jezreelite for you" [ibid.]). Ahab's weakness, lack of moral fiber, and submission to his wife, which are tangibly and explicitly portrayed in the Naboth episode, are here depicted in meaningful silences that the reader must fill in.

This time Jezebel does not hide behind Ahab's authority (cf. 21:8), probably because she wants to draw on her own credit as the liquidator of the prophets of the Lord (18:4 and 13) and wishes to fend off in advance any possibility of compromise with the softhearted king (as in fact happens in the Naboth affair [21:27–29]). Her forceful stress on her own importance is expressed explicitly in the opening of her message to Elijah, as preserved in the Septuagint: "If you are Elijah, I am Jezebel!" It seems more likely that the Masoretic text has suffered a mechanical deletion here rather than that such an inspired addition was made to the Hebrew text used by the Greek translator. Moreover, as Eissfeldt has shown,[118] the pronouncement is in keeping with Jezebel's flagrant awareness of her own powers when she manages her husband in the Naboth affair—"Now will *you* show yourself . . . *I* will get" (21:7), as well as with the way she uses a personal name when she goads Jehu: "Is all well, *Zimri*, murderer of your master?" (2 Kings 9:31). Perhaps Rofé is right: "The name Jezebel was probably understood as the antithesis to Elijah. Its second element *zebel* is one of the epithets of Baal in Ugarit. The first element probably was *eli* or *avi*. The two names indicated the archetypal conflict between the Tyrian queen and the prophet from Gilead" (*Prophetical Stories*, p. 195 n. 23). Alternatively, we can assume that Jezebel is not presenting her loyalty and zealousness for Baal as on a par to Elijah's for the Lord, but only juxtaposing her own personality to his strong and vigorous personality. Obadiah fell on his face and asked: "Is that *you*, my lord Elijah?" (18:7); Ahab challenged him: "Is that *you*, you troubler of Israel?" (ibid., 17). Jezebel too seems to be ascertaining his identity so that she can measure herself against him: "If (indeed) *you* are Elijah, I am Jezebel!" (cf. 2 Kings 1:10).

When Elijah proclaimed the drought, he endowed the decree with absolute validity by linking it to an oath in the name of the Lord. In just this fashion Jezebel now swears by her own god (in a pagan plural just as that used by Ben-hadad, king of Aram: "May the gods do thus to me and even more" [1 Kings 20:10], and she proclaims that "by this time tomorrow" she will do to him what he has done to each of the 450 prophets of Baal whom he slew.[119] Stipulating a time limit makes the threat more concrete, as in Ben-hadad's ultimatum to Ahab: "tomorrow at this time I will send my servants to you" (20:6). But it also grants a respite during which Elijah can flee, thereby sparing her the task of shedding his blood. Her threat reflects a clear preference for frightening Elijah rather than using force, for threatening to execute him rather than actually implementing the sentence. Jezebel is not depicted as a zealous woman hell-bent on revenge but as a cautious and deliberate stateswoman interested in rolling back the militant prophet's immense achievement by forcing him to run to cover again, an act that all will view as shameful flight.

Unlike previous occasions, when the Lord instructed Elijah when to set out and where to go (17:2–3 and 8–9; 18:1), this time he is left without guidance and must act on his own initiative: "He saw and arose and went for his life" (v. 3). The root *rʾ.h* frequently bears the sense 'understand and recognize' (e.g., Gen. 42:1; Jer. 33:24); but as a transitive verb it really needs a direct or indirect object indicating *what* was understood or recognized (e.g., Gen. 3:6, 6:2). Since no such object occurs in the present verse, we should probably prefer the reading of six medieval Hebrew manuscripts,

namely *wa-yira*ʾ, 'he was frightened' (instead of *wa-yarʾ*), a reading also reflected in the Septuagint and the Peshitta. The prophet who told the widow
not to be afraid (17:13) and calmed Obadiah's apprehension (18:15) now
finds himself confronting the terror of death. With no one to help and save
him he flees (cf. "they fled for their lives" [2 Kings 7:7]) from those who
seek his life.

In the past Elijah was commanded to go "to Zarephath of Sidon" (17:9);
now too he leaves the territory of the kingdom of Israel and goes to "Beersheba of Judah" (19:3). The narrator does not tell us that Elijah's servant
accompanied him in his flight (just as we never learn when and how the
servant joined him on the heights of Mount Carmel—see above, p. 194).
This fact becomes clear to us only when Elijah leaves him behind "there,"
that is, in the southern frontier town of the kingdom of Judah. This separation from his servant is the first indication that Elijah is not merely seeking shelter from the long arm of Jezebel and has already decided to go
much further. During the five or six days of his trek from Jezreel to Beersheba (approximately 165 km), the Lord did not appear to him or tell him
whom he had commanded to sustain him. Did he infer from this that the
Lord had abandoned him? Whatever the case, he now wanders aimlessly
(*we-hu halak* rather than *wa-yelek*) in the wilderness for an entire day, evidently without provisions, until he reaches a broom bush and sits beneath
it. Many have noted the parallel between Elijah's situation and that of Hagar
wandering in the wilderness of Beersheba—her utter solitude after she cast
the child down in the terrible desolation that was bare of everything except
the poor shade of "one of the bushes" (Gen. 21:15), where she has nothing
to hope for but death. If this parallel is intentional (and not simply a result
of the similarity of the circumstances), it means that Elijah intentionally
got himself lost in the wilderness and voluntarily put himself into a situation
that was imposed on Hagar and Ishmael.

It is not easy to reconcile Elijah's journey into the depths of the wilderness, so as to die there, with his previous flight to Beersheba to save his life.
Perhaps the narrator prefaces Elijah's prayer with the seemingly superfluous words, "he . . . prayed that he might die" (v. 4a), in order to persuade
readers of the credibility of Elijah's transition from decisiveness in the political arena (his conflict with the queen) to acquiescence and despair on
the existential plane (his conflict with himself). When he keeps Jezebel
from shedding his blood he has fulfilled his last obligation to his prophetic
mission; that having been done, he has no more reason to live. Even if our
understanding of this phrase is off the mark, its effect is rather that of a
parallelism in prose; we know that the prophet who prays that the Lord
take his life has indeed reached the end of the line.

In the upper room of the widow's house, Elijah stretched himself out
on the body of the child and prayed for his revival: "O Lord my God, let
this child's life return to his body!" (17:21); in the wilderness he starves

and exhausts himself and prays for his own death: "Enough now! O Lord, take my life, for I am no better than my fathers" (v. 4b). This "enough now" (*rav ʿattah*—as in the words of the Lord to the angel to stop destroying Jerusalem: "Enough now! Stay your hand!" [2 Sam. 24:16]) clearly expresses fatigue, despair, and surrender; it may also mean that he has quite exhausted his capacity and should no longer be asked for additional effort (compare Moses' assertion in Num. 11:11–15). By contrast, the reason given, "for I am no better than my fathers," is far from clear, and many have hesitated as to its meaning. I do not believe that Elijah is referring to the nation's forefathers, nor to the generation that left Egypt, nor even to the prophets who preceded him, but rather to his own ancestors. He is no better than they were in that nothing makes him more suited to be a prophet of the Lord. In Scripture, a comparison with one's ancestors frequently invokes a salient characteristic that has not changed with the passage of time and the generations (e.g., "your servants have been breeders of livestock from the start until now, both we and our fathers" [Gen. 46:34]); alternatively, and at the other extreme, it may express a sharp deviation from the customary and expected (e.g., "He will make you more prosperous and more numerous than your fathers" [Deut. 30:5]; "they would again act basely, even more than their fathers" [Judg. 2:19]). The emphasis on the continuity of the generations also lends greater credibility to the speakers' self-definition of their own status: for example, "Your servant, the son of Your maidservant" (Ps. 116:16); "like all my forebears I am an alien, resident with You" (Ps. 39:13). Like Amos's disclaimer, "I am not a prophet, and I am not the son of a prophet" (Amos 7:14), Elijah says, "I am no better than my fathers." Moses asserted his unsuitability for the prophetic mission at the time of his consecration ("Who am I that I should go to Pharaoh and free the Israelites from Egypt?" [Exod. 3:11; see also 4:10 and 13]), whereas Elijah seems to have had confidence, until now, in his ability to serve as God's emissary: he described himself as one who serves the Lord (17:1), did not hesitate to demand that the Phoenician widow give him the first portion of her dough, did not protest when Obadiah described him as someone who may be carried from one place to another by the spirit of the Lord in order to protect him from the wrath of Ahab and Jezebel (18:12), and even asked the Lord for a sign to bolster his status as His servant (18:36). Now, however, in his flight from Jezebel's sword, he decides that all his achievements were spurious. The depth of his fall and despair is in proportion to the height of his expectations and self-confidence. Implicit in his prayer is the idea that he should never have left his forefathers' estate in Gilead; having done so, however, his only refuge now is death.

Elijah lies there in the wilderness, exhausted and emotionally spent,[120] shuts his eyes against the failure of his life, and withdraws into sleep, hoping that the Lord has heard his prayer and will take his soul while he sleeps (for the idea of death as an eternal sleep, see Jer. 51:39; Ps. 13:4). Like the would-be suicide who has taken an overdose of sleeping pills, expecting to close his eyes forever but reawakening to life against his will, a double surprise is in store for Elijah—with regard to the timing (suddenly) and to the fact itself (is it possible?)—as expressed by the extremely rare locution *we-hinneh zeh* (v. 5b; cf. Isa. 21:9). The angel has to touch Elijah to rouse him from his deep sleep; to restore his will to live, he commands him: "Arise and eat." Astonished, Elijah looks around to see what there could be to eat in this desolate place, and again we find the particle of surprise *we-hinneh*: "and there, beside his head, was a cake baked on hot stones and a jar of water!" (v. 6). Enjoined by the angel, and also perhaps moved by his hunger and thirst, he eats and drinks. Nevertheless he demonstratively ignores the Lord's negative response to his entreaty for death and goes back to sleep: "he lay down again."

The resemblance between all of this and what happened in Zarephath is hard to miss: (1) The angel's injunction to rise and eat echoes the Lord's command—"Arise and go to Zarephath . . . ; I have commanded a widow there to feed you" (17:9). (2) "A cake baked on hot stones and a jar of water" recalls "a small cake" (17:13) and "the jug of oil" (17:14). (3) Elijah's spontaneous compliance and subsequent deliberate opposition parallel the widow's willingness to bring him water (17:11) and subsequent refusal to share her last loaf of bread (17:12). The prophet has thus gone from being the bearer of the Lord's word and performer of His miracles to being the recipient of the Lord's word and the beneficiary of His miracles. Just like the Phoenician widow, he too requires further exhortation to overcome his despair and arrive at full compliance. The angel returns, touches him again,[121] and repeats his first injunction, "arise and eat" (we learn incidentally that Elijah did not eat and drink everything he found beside him). This time the angel provides a rationale for his command: "for the journey is too long for you" (v. 7). The difference between Elijah's compliance with the first injunction—external and partial—and his compliance now—internal and comprehensive—is reflected in the difference between "he ate and drank" (v. 6) and "he arose and ate and drank and went" (v. 8). Similarly, the fact that the order comes the first time from "an angel," whereas the second time it comes from "the angel of the Lord," suggests that only now does Elijah see him as the emissary of the Lord.[122] The injunction to eat carries two messages: implicitly it is a rejection of his prayer for death; explicitly it is grounded by the need to gather his strength for the protracted prophetic mission that lies ahead of him. What is more, the angel uses the word *rav*, by which Elijah expressed the feeling that he has reached the end of his road, but in the opposite sense: not as "enough," but as "too long" (see Josh. 19:9; and see Zakovitch, "Still Small Voice," p. 334). Elijah complies with the angel's directive and sets out on his journey; but instead of returning northwards, to the arena of his mission, he continues his flight into the depths of the wilderness in order to reach the site of the Lord's appearance to His people and His prophet: "with the strength from that meal he walked forty days and forty nights as far as the mountain of God at Horeb" (v. 8).

Elijah was the beneficiary of two kinds of food-related miracles during the drought—bread and meat in Wadi Cherith, and flour and oil in Zarephath. In the wilderness, two more food-related miracles are worked for him—the cake and water underneath the broom bush, and his ability to go without eating and drinking during his long trek to Mount Horeb. In the earlier stage when he was being readied for his mission, Elijah's greater personal involvement in the second miracle distinguished it from the first. Now, as he returns to his mission, he is equally passive in both miracles; the difference between them is that the second miracle is incomparably more wondrous than the first. The provision of his needs in the wilderness attests to the Lord's continued concern for His servant and makes him aware that his mission is not over yet. But the second miracle constitutes a triumphant answer to his assertion, "I am no better than my fathers." Moses, alone of all human beings, was freed from dependence on physical needs and could go for forty days and forty nights without bread and water (Exod. 34:28; Deut. 9:9 and 18); now the Lord persuades Elijah, through personal experience, that he is as on a par with Moses with regard to his capacity to serve as His messenger. That Elijah is drawn to "Horeb, the mountain of God" (as it is called in Exod. 3:1) indicates that more is required than merely renewing the sense of mission and nurturing the messenger. The prophetic crisis has not yet passed, evidently because Elijah has received no instructions as to the nature of the long journey he must undertake. He seeks the answer at the very same spot where Moses received the boon of the greatest intimacy with God that a human being can endure.[123]

At the beginning of the second scene (vv. 9–18), Elijah reaches Mount Horeb and enters the cave which, according to all circumstances,[124] "is the cleft in the rock where Moses stood" (Rashi). Some hold that he enters the cave in order to sleep; but it seems likely that the miraculous journey has already delivered him from the emotional state in which he had sought sleep and death under the broom bush. Indeed, with Abravanel, we should note the narrator's precise language: "The verse does not say that he slept there, but that he spent the night (*lan*) there" (for *l.i.n*, "spend the night," see Gen. 19:2; Exod. 23:18; and Lev. 19:13). The Lord placed Moses at the opening of the fissure in the rock to protect him from His uncommon proximity; it is plausible that Elijah, too, is seeking this combination of intimacy and shelter. In the first part of the story, we twice read that "the word of the Lord came to him" (17:2 and 8); similarly, the second part of the story begins with "after many days, in the third year, the word of the Lord came to Elijah" (18:1). Here, however, the accent is on his surprise at hearing the Lord's word: "And lo (*wᵉ-hinneh*), the word of the Lord came to him" (v. 9).

Abravanel may be going too far when he glosses *wᵉ-hinneh* as an expression of the Lord's satisfying Elijah's thirst for His word; still, it is clear that the word creates an interval of suspense. Unlike all the previous incidents, this "word of the Lord" is not a unilateral edict but the beginning of a dialogue.

The idiom *mah lᵉka* (here = "why") can be part of a genuine question (as when Caleb asks his daughter, "what is the matter?" [Judg. 1:14]; see also 2 Sam. 14:5); it can also appear in a rhetorical question that is actually a rebuke (e.g., "How can you be sleeping!" [Jonah 1:6; see also Judg. 18:23–24]). Hence it must always be interpreted according to context. Some read into the word "here" divine displeasure that Elijah is here and not in the place where he is supposed to be fulfilling his commission.[125] But this does not strike me as plausible against the background of Jezebel's threat and the absence of any specific directive from the Lord. "Why are you here?" is more likely to be a real question,[126] one that invites Elijah to define his situation and explain why he is continuing his flight after the Lord has manifestly demonstrated that he *is* better than his fathers. Thus far the narrator has concealed the motives for Elijah's conduct, probably so that we will feel the depth of the crisis before we ponder the degree to which it is justified.[127]

Elijah's answer (v. 10) is phrased in a lofty style full of literary echoes. Its three sentences are built of parallel clauses, as in poetry, and it even has a quasi-poetic rhythm. Hence we should read and gloss it in accordance with the structure and flow of its sentences:

> I have been zealous for the Lord, the God of Hosts, for the Israelites have forsaken Your covenant.
> They have torn down Your altars, and put Your prophets to the sword.
> I alone am left, and they are out to take my life.

The introductory words, in the first person, make it plain that the personal question "Why are you here, Elijah?" is answered with a distinctly personal response—"I have been zealous." This zeal for the Lord refers to his part in the eradication of Baal-worship from Israel, that is, the slaughter of the 450 prophets of Baal, and perhaps also to the trial by fire, which took place at his initiative[128] (but not to the decree of drought, which is not represented in the story as a direct result of the prophet's zeal). This conclusion is strengthened by the strong affinity between the entire first sentence and the Lord's statement to Moses after the act of zealousness against those who worshipped Baal-peor: "Phinehas, son of Eleazar son of Aaron the priest, has turned back My wrath from the *Israelites* by displaying among them his zeal for Me (*bᵉ-qannᵉʾo eth qinʾathi*), so that I did not wipe out the *Israelites* in My zeal" (Num. 25:11). Moreover, it seems that Elijah addresses the Lord as "the God of Hosts" to hint that, like Phinehas, whose zeal was intended to appease the Lord's wrath and put an end to the plague, his own zeal is meant to appease the wrath of the great and terrible deity, who reacted to the abandonment of His covenant with a three-year drought.[129]

In the second sentence, Elijah offers tangible examples of the flagrant breaching of the covenant, citing two grave acts mentioned in chapter 18: "they have torn down Your altars" alludes, both thematically and linguistically, to "He repaired the damaged altar of the Lord" (18:30); "they have put Your prophets to the sword" refers to "when Jezebel was killing the prophets of the Lord" (18:13). The third sentence, too, is replete with verbal resonances that give it greater weight: the first part, "I alone am left," is an almost exact quote of Elijah's complaint on Mount Carmel, "I am the only prophet of the Lord left" (18:22); the end, "they are out to take my life (*wa-y^{e}vaqq^{e}šu eth nafšî*)," is a double echo—both of Ahab's systematic pursuit during the years when he was in hiding—"there is no nation or kingdom to which my lord has not sent to look for you (*l^e-vaqqeška*)" (18:10), and of the renewed threat against his life (*nefeš*), which caused him to flee once again: "if by this time tomorrow I have not made you (*nafš^{e}ka*) like one (*k^e-nefeš*) of them" (19:2).

Elijah's response is not presented chronologically. It begins with the slaughter of the prophets of Baal; then, to justify this act, he goes backward in time and enumerates the sins that preceded it. In the third sentence, however, Elijah skips without warning from causes to effects. The first effect—"I alone am left"—still relates to the situation that preceded the revelation on Mount Carmel; but the second effect—"they are out to take my life"—jumps to after that event. This unexpected fusion of remote and recent past has two rhetorical consequences: Jezebel's threats against his life are presented as a direct sequel to the systematic annihilation of the prophets of the Lord; by contrast, the slaughter of the prophets of Baal, wrenched out of its chronological sequence by its placement at the beginning of his speech, is left with no practical results. His failure to mention the proclamation of the drought, the descent of heavenly fire, and the gift of rain stems directly from the distinctly personal nature of Elijah's response. He begins with "I have been zealous for the Lord, the God of Hosts" (expressing the extremism inherent in his prophetic endeavor) and concludes with "they are out to take my life" (expressing the gravity of his prophetic failure). Between these two poles he presents a well-documented indictment of Israel's betrayal of its God (expressing the magnitude of his prophetic task). The prophet's response inextricably interweaves Israel's extreme breach of the covenant and his own appalling failure to return them to the Lord. Phinehas's zeal put an end to the plague, whereas Elijah's zeal turned him into a fugitive. He may indeed be better than his fathers, and his great zealousness for his God may be evidence of this; but in view of its paltry results, what task can remain for him in Israel?

This interpretation of Elijah's reply remains incomplete without answers to three difficult questions: (1) Why does the prophet indict the Israelites for Jezebel's transgression? (2) How can he totally ignore the proclamation by all those present on Mount Carmel that "the Lord alone is God" (18:39) and their active participation in his slaughter of the prophets of Baal? (3) Doesn't this explicit decision against Baal worship renew the covenant with the Lord? In fact, these three questions are merely different facets of a single crux—the reader's compelling sense that the information provided at the opening of chapter 19 is insufficient to explain the rapid fall from the heights of triumph on Mount Carmel to the abyss of despair in the wilderness. Many hold that verses 1–3a of chapter 19 are the work of an editor who joined two separate stories (chapters 17–18 with chapter 19) by means of an excessively narrow bridge.[130] By contrast, I attempted to understand these verses as an integral part of the story (see above, p. 198) and attributed their concision to the particular narrative mode adopted in the opening of each of its three parts. Our close reading has shown that with a few bold strokes of the brush, Ahab is depicted as hesitant and submissive whereas Jezebel is decisive and forceful. When her messenger conveys her threat to the prophet (a meeting the narrator preferred to leave off-stage), Elijah has no difficulty assessing the true state of affairs—the weak king has been shunted aside by the foreign queen. Elijah indeed flees Jezebel's sword, but his mortal despair is nourished chiefly by the implications of Ahab's failure to act and Jezebel's boldness.

Ahab had been present on Mount Carmel; his eyes had seen the fire fall from heaven and his ears had heard the proclamation of the renewal of rainfall, delivered only minutes before its fulfillment. But when he told his wife about "all that Elijah had done," the persuasive force of these tangible signs melted away and he went back to his previous hopping from branch to branch. Ahab's behavior could be attributed to his weak character and perplexity, but for Elijah the king's recidivism is a painful demonstration that tangible signs and wondrous miracles are an inadequate foundation for belief in the unseen God. Perhaps Elijah (and the narrator with him) generalizes this conclusion to all those present on Carmel and sees the king as an embodiment of the collective personality of the people.[131] Such bitter disappointment at the rapid dissipation of the experience of the miracle was also Moses' lot when the Israelites made the Golden Calf only a few short weeks after witnessing the voices and flames on Sinai. There is also an extremely painful interpersonal aspect—which the narrator leaves entirely to the reader's imagination: all of the lofty hopes that Elijah had pinned on Ahab during his enthusiastic run before his chariot go up in smoke; to increase the pain and humiliation, that very race now seems to have been rash and absurd. The depth of the despair is in proportion to the magnitude of the frustrated hope.

What we have said about Ahab applies to Jezebel too. The audacity of Jezebel, who does as she wishes in the kingdom and demonstratively swears a pagan oath, intimate to Elijah that the foreign influence continues, un-abated by the Lord's actions (the protracted drought) and his own deeds (the trial by fire and the public slaughter of the prophets of Baal). If the verbal echoes in Elijah's words are meant to associate him with Phinehas, the entire story of the foreign queen's introduction of Baal worship to Israel (16:30–33) must be read in close connection with the story of the Israelites' whoring after Baal-peor because of their attraction to the Moabite women (Num. 25:1–9). Elijah's zeal is as drastic as Phinehas's and did indeed make the end of the drought possible; but the influence of the contemporary avatar of Cozbi daughter of Zur has not been weakened and she can still put the Lord's prophet to flight. Phinehas's success casts a dark shadow on Elijah's failure.

This argument may explain Elijah's despair and the expression of it; but as a realistic assessment of the people's guilt at the hour that Elijah speaks his indictment it has at most *potential* validity. Perhaps ancient readers did not feel a problem here: familiar with the actual situation during the reigns of Ahab (the affair of Naboth's vineyard), Ahaziah (the dispatch of emis-saries to Baal-zebub the god of Ekron), and Jehoram (who persisted in the sins of his parents), they knew that Elijah's assessment of the situation was right on the mark and by no means hysterical and that his pessimistic con-clusions were quickly verified on the national level. But as a matter of literary criticism, our present attempt to endow a potential situation with contemporary plausibility by relying on information about the historical circumstances that was available when the story was written down, instead of relying exclusively on the literary text, seems not quite valid. We shall have to return to this issue later.

Instead of a direct response to his bitter complaint, Elijah receives instructions concerning the impending theophany. The first words of the Lord's response, echoing Elijah's customary oath—"As the Lord God of Israel lives, before whom I have stood" (17:1, 18:15)—hint at the link be-tween this revelation and the prophet's personal distress: "Come out and *stand* on the mountain *before the Lord*" (v. 11). Elijah applied the metaphor of a servant standing before his master to his status as the Lord's messenger; now the Lord tells him to go out of the cave and stand before Him, literally. While metaphorization of the concrete is a frequent stylistic and literary phenomenon,[132] reconcretization of a metaphor is extremely rare and con-sequently comes as somewhat of a surprise and intensification.[133] Elijah's standing before the Lord is about to change from a metaphor for the rela-tionship to an actual situation. Decisive proof of the magnitude of this metamorphosis is the very need to give instructions—an indication that Elijah has not yet undergone this experience and must be warned against possible errors.

The prophet who could not overcome his despair without signs and won-ders and is still finding it difficult to stand before his master as before, in the metaphorical sense of this expression, is now called to stand before Him in the literal sense. This standing before his master is a reconsecration of his prophetic vocation that renders it deeper and more intense.[134] In fact, the well-defined literary genre of "calls to prophecy," (see pp. 51–58) includes a subgenre of reconsecration. Thus far we have encountered three pronounced components of this subgenre in chapter 19: (1) the prophet's complaint that he is tired of his life; (2) his declaration that he has failed in his mission; (3) his scathing indictment of the people, which is incompatible with unalloyed devotion to his mission. Later in our chapter we will find an additional element of the subgenre: (4) the Lord's response, which renews the prophet's vocation by giving him new strength and sketching out his future path. These four elements are found, more or less in this sequence, three more times in the prophetic books: (1) Jer. 12:1–6; (2) Jer. 15:10–21; (3) Isa. 49:1–6. The prophetic complaint that most closely resembles our story is that in Jeremiah 15. A brief review of its content can help us decide whether, despite the basic formal difference between a first-person poem and a third-person prose account, they belong to the same literary genre, since both make a similar rhetorical use of the prophet's personal experience—the concretization of Israel's stiff-neckedness in the crisis undergone by the prophet who is sent to them.

Jeremiah starts with a bitter *complaint:* Would that he had never been born—"Woe is me, my mother, that you ever bore me" (v. 10)—because he has totally *failed* as a prophet—"a man of conflict and strife with all the land." He has no personal dispute with anyone—"I have not lent, and I have not borrowed"; nevertheless, "everyone curses me." This general hostility has reached the point of dangerous plots by his enemies; his *indictment* of their wickedness is implicit in his *prayer that God take vengeance* on them: "O Lord you know [the truth; or perhaps the gravity of my situation]—remember me and take thought of me, avenge me on those who persecute me; do not yield to your patience, do not let me perish! Consider how I have borne insult on your account" (v. 15).[135] Elijah stresses his perfect devotion to the fulfillment of his mission—"I have been zealous for the Lord"; Jeremiah does the same thing, but prefaces it with a reference to his enthusiastic response to his original consecration: "When Your words were offered, I devoured them; Your word brought me the delight and joy of knowing that Your name is attached to me, O Lord, God of Hosts" (v. 16; cf. Isa. 49:1b–3). In the next verse we find an extremely close parallel to Elijah's zeal for his God: "I have not sat in the company of revelers and made merry! I have sat lonely because of your hand upon me, for You have filled me with rage" (v. 17). Jeremiah then returns to his initial *complaint,* expressing his disappointment at the lack of adequate support from his master (evidently Elijah was too desperate to even mention this): "Why must my pain be endless, my wound incurable, resistant to healing? You have been to me like a spring that fails, like waters that cannot be relied on" (v. 18). Now he hears the

Lord's response, which is a call to resume his mission, a demand for greater effort, a promise of success and assistance, and even confirmation from on high of the people's guilt:

> Assuredly, thus said the Lord: If you turn back, I shall take you back and you shall stand before Me; If you produce what is noble out of the worthless, You shall be My spokesman. They shall come back to you, not you to them. Against this people I will make you as a fortified wall of bronze: they will attack you, but they shall not overcome you, for I am with you to deliver and save you—declares the Lord. I will save you from the hands of the wicked and rescue you from the clutches of the violent. (vv. 19–21)

Unlike Elijah in our story, Jeremiah does not attain a theophany; he is reinforced chiefly by the divine promise to protect him, save him from his enemies, and help him in the struggle against the wicked and the violent. Leaving aside this difference, however, there is great similarity between the Lord's promises to Jeremiah and His declaration to Elijah that He is about to intervene vigorously in the struggle against Baal worship (19:15–18). There are also verbal affinities: (1) In both cases the overcoming of the prophetic crisis is characterized as a *return:* to Jeremiah—"If you *turn back*, I shall take you back"; to Elijah—"*Go back* by the way you came" (v. 15). (2) The reconsecration is described as renewed standing before the Lord, in metaphorical language to Jeremiah—"you shall stand before Me"—and in concrete terms to Elijah—"Come out and stand on the mountain before the Lord."[136]

The threefold warning against the mistaken expectation that the Lord will be revealed in wind, earthquake, and fire, and the mystery-laden revelation of the Lord's presence in a "still, small voice" have been the subject of an impressive array of theological exegesis. But a literary interpretation must be contextual; we must interpret the Lord's appearance to Elijah as it is woven into the plot and in a manner that is compatible with the prophet's spiritual world and his personal situation in the cave on Mount Horeb. Hence we cannot accept the interpretation which holds that this warning is a second stage in the polemic against Baal worship. According to this view, in chapter 18 the Lord's superiority over Baal was demonstrated in the realm that Baal worshippers believed to be in his dominion—bringing down fire and rain. In chapter 19, however, the struggle is on the level of principle: in utter contrast to Baal, the Lord is not immanent in the three awesome manifestations of storm, but in something quite different—a "still, small voice."[137] Yet it is hardly plausible that Elijah, as he is described in chapter 18, needs these warnings, as if he too holds to the mythological concept he has been fighting against. Chapter 18 offers no substantive basis for the idea of fire as a manifestation of the godhead, neither in Elijah's words ("the god who responds with fire, that one is God" [v. 24]) nor in the narrator's description ("the fire from the Lord descended and consumed the burnt offering" [v. 38]). Moreover, the multitude who fall on their face and proclaim that "The Lord alone is God" (v. 39) are not struck by a sacred awe and fear of death, as the Israelites were when the Lord revealed Himself to them in His great fire (cf. Exod. 20:18–21; Deut. 18:16–17).

Another interpretation we must reject is that the peculiar nature of this revelation is meant as a criticism of Elijah's fierce zeal for the God of Israel.[138] Some of the proponents of this view[139] base themselves, on the one hand, on the impressive parallel between the three violent natural manifestations and the still, small voice that follows them and, on the other, on the three military catastrophes that will beset Israel and the survival of the seven thousand. They see this parallel as the key to understanding the unspoken meaning of the Lord's words to His zealous prophet. Just as the Lord avails Himself of destructive forces but Himself appears in the stillness, so He will continue to smite His people as Elijah has done, but the purpose of His acts is to save the loyal remnant. Although the Lord judges His people according to the full severity of strict justice, His true attribute is mercy. This is an attractive reading, but incompatible with the fact that chapters 17 and 18 describe Elijah not as a single-minded zealot but as a prophet who is personally devoted to helping individuals and the community—reviving the widow's son and hastening the fall of rain. Moreover, I do not believe that we can see the destruction of the vast majority of the people and the survival of such a tiny remnant[140] as a manifestation of heavenly mercy. True, both the theophany and the Lord's declaration that the war against Baal worship will continue are presented in the literary format of "three-and-four." Yet this formal parallel cannot establish a substantive link between the still, small voice and the survival of a tiny remnant; it is also most doubtful whether there is any association between the three natural forces and the three swords that will smite Israel. More than criticism of Elijah's zeal for the Lord, chapter 19 provides major sanction for the systematic and protracted struggle against Baal worship in Israel, until the final and utter destruction of all idolators.

Elijah is enjoined to "come out and stand on the mountain before the Lord" (v. 11); the Lord will not be revealed to him within the cave but only when he is standing at its entrance. Similarly, the Lord instructed Moses, "station yourself on the rock" (Exod. 33:21), probably because the cave was too narrow to contain the immense sight. In the present, as in the past, the revelation is a dynamic rather than a static phenomenon. Moses was told: "I will make all my goodness *pass* before you" (ibid., v. 19); Elijah is told: "And lo, the Lord *passes by*" (v. 11).[141] Moses was forewarned of the fundamental impossibility of getting too close: "You can *not* see My face, for man may *not* see Me and live. . . . I will shield you with My hand until I have passed by. Then I will take my hand away and you will see My back; but My face must *not* be seen" (Exod. 33:20–23); whereas Elijah is forewarned of

the special nature of the particular revelation being vouchsafed to him—
the Lord will not speak to him "from the whirlwind" (Job 38:1 and 40:6),
but from what follows it. Even though the two warnings are phrased in
strongly negative terms (the word *lo*, 'not', occurs three times in each passage), and even though Moses was warned against *danger*, whereas Elijah is
cautioned against *error*, neither warning seems to imply criticism. Both
prophets are about to come closer to the deity than all other mortals have
done, and this intimacy necessarily involves certain precautions. The warnings are not intended to detract from the prophets' self-understanding but
to prepare them for the new experience that far exceeds normal prophetic
experience (the Lord's revelation on Sinai was also preceded by a severe
warning: "warn the people not to break through to the Lord to gaze"
[Exod. 19:21–25]).

Because of a theological impulse there is a tendency to understand the
three warnings as correcting a fundamental error that Elijah made in his
presentation of the exclusivity of the Lord in chapter 18. On Mount Carmel
the Lord's might was manifested in the fire that consumed the sacrifice and
thereafter (and separately) by the long-needed rainfall; there is no mention
of destructive winds or earthquakes. The attempt by Cross (*Canaanite Myth*,
pp. 163–69 and 194) to see the theophany in storm (typical of Baal) as a
common denominator of what occurred on Sinai and Carmel and what is
denied at Horeb is not persuasive, because there is no real correlation between the fire and rainfall of chapter 18 and the wind, earthquake, and fire
(which comes last) of chapter 19. More to the point, we do not find here a
rejection in principle of the Lord's appearance in wind, earthquake, and
fire but only Elijah's preparation for a unique revelation, of which these
three are an inseparable part in that they precede the appearance of God
Himself: "And lo, the Lord passes by, and a great and mighty wind, splitting
mountains and shattering rocks, *before* the Lord" (v. 11).[142]

Sometimes wind, earthquake, and fire are emissaries of the Lord that
perform His will (e.g., Ps. 97:3–4, 104:4 and 32), and sometimes He Himself
is embodied in them (for example, Ps. 18:7–16) and even speaks from their
midst (e.g., Exod. 19:18–19; Deut. 4:11–12). Here, however, they go before
Him, like the runners before the king's chariot (2 Sam. 15:1; 1 Kings 1:5),
announcing his arrival and preparing bystanders for his appearance. It is
obvious that an earthquake shakes, shocks, and appalls body and soul, and
that a blazing conflagration has an immense power to terrorize and inspire
panic, to enchant and exalt. But even an uncommonly strong wind is far
below those in terrifying sublimity; hence the verse must underscore the
power of this storm to shatter mountains and rocks (cf. Job 1:19). Even the
strongest tempests fall short of this destructive force; nor do hurricanes
and tornadoes occur in the land of Israel and its neighbors. Kimchi (commentary on verse 12) sought to bring the verse closer to natural phenomena: " 'splitting mountains and shattering rocks' is an exaggeration." But

the language of the verse suggests that the reference is to a phenomenon never seen or heard (like the divine fire on Mount Carmel that consumed earth and stones and water). Elijah stands exposed to the awesome wind that upsets the order of creation; after that comes the earthquake that shakes the mountain (cf. Exod. 19:18) and the man standing on it; and this is followed by the fire that consumes everything in its path. The Lord is introducing Elijah to the various facets of His might and majesty—not only to amaze and overwhelm him but also to encourage and strengthen the prophet, who has been defeated as a result of his zeal for the invisible God. He is warned in advance that these three manifestations of the Lord's might are merely a prelude to the revelation of the Lord Himself in the "still, small voice" that will follow them.

The expression "still, small voice" (v. 12) is extremely difficult.[143] It is clear that it is not meant to be a paradoxical description of divine speech as a combination of silence and sound, since immediately thereafter Elijah does hear aural "speech": "Then a voice addressed him and said . . . " (v. 13), and, subsequently, "The Lord said to him" (v. 15). Hence we must conclude that before Elijah hears the word of the Lord he is apprised by the "still, small voice" of the very presence of the Lord (cf.: "The Lord came and stood there, and He called" [1 Sam. 3:10]).

The verb *d.m.m* generally means "be silent" (e.g., Lev. 10:3; Amos 5:13); accordingly the noun *d⁽e⁾mamah* is understood in the sense of "silence, quiet," just as in modern Hebrew.[144] Given the manifest difficulty of linking the adjective *daqqah*, 'thin', with silence, it seems more plausible to understand *d⁽e⁾mamah* as 'murmur', as it is rendered by the Septuagint and Targum Jonathan and as the phrase seems to be employed in the *Songs of the Sabbath Sacrifice* scroll from Qumran.[145] In fact, the verb *d.m.m* apparently appears with the sense of "keening softly" ("Moan [*domu*], you coastland dwellers" in Isa. 23:2 parallels "Howl, you ships of Tarshish" in the previous verse). Accordingly, it has been suggested that, in two other verses where it appears, we take the noun *d⁽e⁾mamah* as referring to the whistling of the wind as the storm dies down: "He reduced the storm to a *whisper*, the waves were stilled" (Ps. 107:29); and especially in the description of the theophany in Job 4:15–17: "A wind passed by me, making the hair of my flesh bristle. It halted; its appearance was strange to me; a form loomed before my eyes; I heard a *murmur*, a voice, 'Can mortals be acquitted by God? Can man be cleared by his Maker?' " A terrifying wind had passed before Eliphaz (as here before Elijah). It stopped, and an uncommon sight was revealed before his eyes (as happened to Moses in the cleft in the rock). Finally, a voice was heard speaking from the stillness that followed the storm (again as here).[146]

The Lord's address to Elijah begins, "*Come out and stand* on the mountain before the Lord" (v. 11a). Following the detailed instructions we are now told how he obeyed them: "When Elijah heard [i.e., as a direct reaction to what he had been told; cf. Gen. 39:15–19], he wrapped his mantle about his face [just as Moses hid his face when he realized that the Lord was appearing to him in the burning bush (Exod. 3:6)] and *went out and stood* at the entrance of the cave [just as he had been commanded to do]" (v. 13a). At this juncture we are astonished that there is no description of the fulfillment of the Lord's word; at the very least we would expect a short phrase along the lines of "and it was so" (cf. Gen. 1:9 and 11; Judges 6:38). However, since the episode of Moses in the cleft of the rock (Exod. 33:17–23), the model for the scene of Elijah in the cave, concludes with the Lord's announcement of what is about to happen rather than with a description of the event itself, it seems likely that here too the narrator felt that his readers, accustomed to the extreme ellipses of scriptural narrative, would not even miss the absent element (just as they do not notice it in 1 Kings 21:17–20: the Lord tells Elijah what to say to Ahab; without a pause we read Ahab's response, having never been told that the prophet did indeed go to Naboth's vineyard and deliver the message).

As Elijah leaves the cave he covers his face with his mantle, knowing that after the wind, earthquake, and fire have passed he will stand before the Lord Himself. With the "still, small voice," which makes the deity's presence tangible, in the background, he now hears a voice that, to our great astonishment, merely repeats the question he has already answered inside the cave: "Why are you here, Elijah?" (v. 13b). Many theorize that the word-for-word repetition of both question and answer (vv. 13b–14) is merely a mechanical doubling of the question and answer in verses 9b–10. However, it is certainly possible to understand the repetition of the question as providing an opportunity for Elijah to redefine his wishes and expectations, or perhaps his very status as an emissary of the Lord, in the wake of his prophetic reconsecration. By repeating his original answer word-for-word, though, Elijah declares that the theophany that has been granted him at Horeb has no impact on the failure of his war against Baal worship, Israel's betrayal of its God, his solitary survival as prophet of the Lord, and his flight for his life.

There is stylistic confirmation that only now does the Lord speak to Elijah directly and immediately; here for the first time we read, "The *Lord* said to him" (v. 15). Previously we have encountered expressions that attest to greater distance: "the *word of the Lord* came to him" (v. 9); "a voice addressed him" (v. 13b). Furthermore, when the angel of the Lord provided Elijah with physical and emotional sustenance he told him, "the journey (*derek*) is too long for you" (v. 7). Now the Lord Himself says, and with greater specificity, "go back on your way (*dark'ka*)" (v. 15)—that is, return to your prophetic vocation. (The injunction is even more pointed by its echo of the Lord's instruction to Moses in Midian, to which he had fled from Pharaoh's sword: "Go back to Egypt" [Exod. 4:19].) In his response to Elijah's complaint, the Lord adopts all of the postulates on which it is based and derives far-reaching conclusions from them: (1) The Israelites have indeed breached their covenant with their God; hence the zeal for the Lord must continue and even intensify. (2) Elijah is indeed unable to wage single combat against Baal worship; hence he must designate two kings and one prophet to complete the job that he has begun. (3) Not only have the Israelites destroyed the Lord's altars, they have also put His prophets to the sword. Their dire punishment is that the Lord will loose three swords against them until only a pitifully tiny remnant remains in Israel. Contrary to the common opinion, not only is there nothing in the Lord's response that explicitly or implicitly demurs at Elijah's zeal, the prophet's ardor is ratified by being carried much further: whereas Elijah put to death only the most wicked (that is, the 450 prophets of Baal), the Lord proclaims almost total annihilation, after which Israel will be left with only the most righteous (that is, the seven thousand who have never worshipped Baal).

Elijah fled southward as far as Mount Horeb, where the Lord commands him to go back the way he has come, both geographically and biographically: "The Lord said to him, 'Go back on your way, to the wilderness of Damascus' " (v. 15). It is hard to decide whether we should expand the concision of this verse with a second predicate—"*and go* to the wilderness of Damascus"—or with an adjectival phrase modifying "way"—"the way *that goes toward* the wilderness of Damascus" (cf.: "So Esau started out that day on his way to Seir" [Gen. 33:16]). If the three anointings are enumerated in chronological order, the journey to Damascus, in the far north, is first on the list. It seems, however, that the order in which the three "swords" are presented corresponds to the severity of the blows they will strike against Israel; as Kimchi notes: "The Lord listed them in the order of their vengeance: Hazael will be first, and after him Jehu, and after him Elisha, just as He said, 'Whoever escapes' " (commentary on verse 15). Just as the doom of the three swords clearly moves from the most severe (Hazael) to the lesser (Jehu) and then to the least (Elisha), their direct parallel with the three anointings requires that the latter be enumerated in the same order: first setting up the external enemy who is destined to conquer large swaths of Israelite territory, then erecting the domestic enemy who will destroy the house of Ahab, and finally anointing the prophet who will continue Elijah's war against Baal worship.

The anointing of Hazael must not be understood literally, for an Israelite prophet had no authority to anoint a usurper in the kingdom of Damascus. The metaphoric sense also applies to Elisha, since no prophet was ever consecrated for his mission with anointing oil. Only Jehu's anointing is real; the extension by metaphor to the other cases[147] unites these three fateful initiatives into a single act with a common purpose. Perhaps this bent for stylistic and thematic unification also explains the fatal sword to be wielded by the prophet, since nowhere in Scripture do we read that Elisha, following his master's example, kills idolators.[148] In any case, the string of disasters that will overtake Israel is not described from a political and military point of view (since Jehu's sword will destroy the House of Ahab and the Baal worshippers, whereas Hazael's sword will smite all Israel during the reign of the House of Jehu [2 Kings 13:3–7]), but from a demographic perspective—all three swords will be wielded against the people of Israel.

In his complaint Elijah indicted Israel for the systematic annihilation of the prophets of the Lord: "the Israelites have . . . put Your prophets to the sword. I alone am left, and they are out to take my life" (v. 10). The Lord responds that, measure for measure, they will be punished by decimation upon decimation: "Whoever escapes the sword of Hazael shall be slain by Jehu, and whoever escapes the sword of Jehu shall be slain by Elisha. I will leave in Israel only seven thousand—every knee that has not knelt to Baal" (vv. 17–18). This sequence of onslaughts recalls the systematic action of the three avengers described in Isa. 24:17–18: "Terror, and pit, and trap upon you who dwell on earth! He who flees at the report of the terror shall fall into the pit; and he who climbs out of the pit shall be caught in the trap" (see also Jer. 48:43–44). But whereas the passage in Isaiah does not mention survivors, here the Lord says, in the first person, "I will leave in Israel only seven thousand." Zakovitch ("Still Small Voice," p. 344) sees here the three-four pattern, highlighting the contrast between the havoc wreaked by the three swords and the salvation that will come from by the Lord Himself. In the end, the Lord's mercies will overcome His strict justice; unlike Elijah, then, He is not seeking vengeance on His people. Indeed, were the number of survivors not so tiny, one could understand the catastrophe as a severe punishment that will purify Israel of its dross and that will be applied with full caution to avoid sweeping away the righteous with the wicked. But leaving only seven thousand from the entire population of the kingdom of Israel is another expression of the ghastly extent of the punishment, not a counterweight to its gravity. The three swords will be wielded by persons anointed by the Lord's mandate; they are clearly His emissaries, executing His will (just like Assyria, "rod of my anger" [Isa. 10:5], and Nebuchadnezzar, "My servant" [Jer. 25:9]). The narrator does not focus on the deeds of the three swordsmen but on the fate of the remnant that each will leave behind:

> Whoever escapes the sword of Hazael shall be slain by Jehu,
> and whoever escapes the sword of Jehu shall be slain by Elisha.
> And thus I will leave in Israel only seven thousand. . . . (vv. 17–18)

The three statements describe a continuous action directed from on high, in which the second sword completes the work of the first, and the third devours the leavings of the second, until only those who never served Baal remain unwinnowed. "I will leave" does not express a countervailing divine grace but the full and just application of the letter of the law.

This sharp focus on the remnant signifies a major escalation of the

Lord's war against Baal worship. In the past Elijah was enjoined to return "all Israel" (18:19) to the Lord by means of a protracted drought; to this the prophet added, of his own accord, the ordeal by fire and the massacre of the prophets of Baal. Now, however, the Lord commands him to inaugurate a new epoch, in which the arena of the struggle will be transferred from nature to history, and the attempt to influence the people will be replaced by the annihilation of almost all of them. A series of political and military catastrophes—a bloody war with a foreign enemy, a bloody conspiracy at home, and prophetic combat—will eliminate all the sinners, until only the seven thousand who have never worshipped Baal survive.[149]

Elijah does not plead for mercy for Israel when he hears this gruesome verdict. If the significance of "anoint Elisha son of Shaphat of Abel-meholah to succeed you as prophet" (v. 16b) is indeed that Elijah's mission will end when his heir assumes his vocation, we can understand his silence as yet another indication that he has lost his vitality as a prophet with the capacity to be zealous for the Lord while at same time praying on behalf of sinners. This is how the encounter is interpreted in the Midrash (see n. 134) and again recently by Zakovitch: "Form and content are linked in our chapter to show us that Elijah did not behave as he should have; he was a tired and exhausted prophet, too wrapped up in himself, setting aside his mission and slandering his people Israel" ("Still Small Voice," p. 344). For Zakovitch, the gravity of Elijah's silence is underscored by the implicit contrast with Moses' heroic struggle against a similar sentence: "Now, let Me be, that My anger may blaze forth against them and that I may destroy them, and make of you a great nation" (Exod. 32:10). Moses successfully warded off the evil decree (ibid., v. 14) and reawakened divine mercy (ibid., 34:6–7); but the zealous Elijah, through his silence, loses his prophetic vocation (Zakovitch, ibid., pp. 344–46).

Yet there is no need to understand that Elisha will be the Lord's prophet "instead of" Elijah (although this is the sense of the preposition *taḥath* in many passages; e.g., Gen. 22:13 and 2 Sam. 17:25); we can take it in the sense of "after you" (as David says of Solomon: "he shall succeed me as king [*yimlok taḥtai*]"—1 Kings 1:35). If so, nothing in the anointing of Elisha expresses a lack of confidence in Elijah; at most, the nomination of a successor rebuts his belief that the extraordinary efforts of a single prophet could uproot Baal worship from Israel in a single generation. Nor need we contrast Elijah's failure to defend Israel with Moses' altruistic devotion to his people at the time of the Golden Calf; it seems more appropriate to compare Elijah's despair and grievance with those of Moses in the affair of the complainers (Numbers 11).

Many themes are common to these two episodes: the prophet's despair that the people are being led astray by outside agitators (the Egyptian rabble—the Phoenician Jezebel); the view of the prophetic mission as an impossible burden ("Why have you dealt ill with your servant?"—"Enough now, O Lord"); the appeal against the obligation to continue bearing it ("Did I conceive all this people?"—"for I am no better than my fathers"); the preference for death over life ("kill me"—"take my life"); and a bitter complaint about prophetic isolation ("I cannot carry all this people by my-self"—"I alone am left"), to which an answer is immediately forthcoming—the appointment of assistants (the drawing of the spirit onto the seventy elders—the anointing of Hazael, Jehu, and Elisha). Moreover, in the conflict between the Lord and His people, both prophets identify unequivocally with the deity: Moses' response to the complaints of the gluttons was like his master's reaction ("The Lord was very angry, and Moses was distressed" [v. 10]); Elijah's response to Israel's forsaking of the covenant with its God is to be zealous for Him ("I have been zealous for the Lord"). True, the magnitude of the punishment decreed is vastly different in the two epi-sodes: at Kibroth-hattaavah only a small minority of the people succumbed to the plague ("the people who had the craving" [v. 34]), whereas the pres-ent decree is that only a tiny minority will survive ("seven thousand"). But neither prophet fears that his words will fan the divine wrath, because the severe backsliding has caused them to despair of their people and of them-selves. In this way the prophet's despair serves as a sort of human endorse-ment of the rightness of divine justice.

Hence we should not understand Elijah's repeated indictment and his thundering silence when he hears the verdict as meaning that his zeal for the Lord has hardened his heart toward his brethren but only that his fail-ure in his war against Baal worship has dried up his capacity for prayer (such as that in 18:42–43). When Israel's advocate becomes its accuser, the reader is persuaded that there is indeed no escape from the terrible pun-ishment.[150]

It is rare, but not unheard of, for a scriptural scene to conclude with direct address (e.g., Gen. 14:24, 28:22, 34:31; 1 Kings 21:29; Jonah 4:11). So there is no formal impediment to taking the Lord's speech to Elijah as the end of the third part of story and of the story as a whole. However, since odysseys should conclude with the return of the hero (classic examples are Gen. 22:19 and 1 Sam. 26:25), and since the main point of the reconsecra-tion is the command, "Go back on your way" (v. 15), readers notice that this scene—unlike its predecessors—does not end with a phrase like "Elijah went back on his way" (see above, p. 198). Instead of an explicit and full expression of Elijah's compliance with his instructions, we find only a par-tial substitute for this in the words "he went from there" (v. 19), which introduce the short scene of Elisha's selection. Clearly one can see these words as referring to Elijah's journey northward and as indicating that Eli-jah wholeheartedly complied with the command only if this scene is an intrinsic and original part of our story.

Two main reasons have been advanced for viewing this episode as origi-nally part of the corpus of Elisha stories, moved here by an editor:[151] (1)

Going to Abel-meholah does not fulfill the divine command to proceed to the wilderness of Damascus (v. 15); hence the original sequel to our story— which, it is presumed, related Elijah's anointing of Hazael, Jehu, and Elisha—has been replaced by an episode about Elisha's becoming Elijah's attendant (1 Kings 19:19–21) and separate stories of Elisha's "anointing" of Jehu and Hazael (2 Kings 8:7–15, 9:1–13). (2) The Lord's command to Elijah to anoint Elisha as prophet in his place in 1 Kings 19:16 is quite incompatible with Elijah's attempts to avoid Elisha's company on his last day in 2 Kings 2:1–6 and his refusal to accede to his faithful disciple's request to bequeath his prophetic vocation to him on the pretext that it is not in his province to transfer the divine spirit to him (ibid., v. 10). On the other hand, Elijah's conduct at Abel-meholah is in keeping with his conduct on his last day; here too Elijah refrains from anointing Elisha as prophet and merely takes him on as his attendant.

The first argument is based on an excessively literal understanding of the Lord's command—that the three anointings must be with oil, must take place in the order in which they are enumerated, and must be performed by Elijah himself. But it does not hold water when we realize that we must understand the anointings as metaphoric and as enumerated in thematic rather than chronological sequence (see above, p. 215) and assume that Elijah was merely enjoined to begin a multistage process that would be completed by his successor. The second argument is based on the assumption that the words "and became his attendant" (v. 21), which conclude the Abel-meholah scene, illuminate its significance retrospectively; it requires that we understand the casting of the mantle as the appointment of Elisha as the prophet's attendant. If we examine this action more closely, though, we reach a totally different conclusion—namely, that by this act Elijah did fulfill the injunction to "anoint" Elisha as his successor.

In Scripture, one's garment is viewed as part of one's being; to a certain extent, one's clothing is like one's body. The Torah proscribes any assault on the wholeness of the body as an expression of mourning (Deut. 14:1–2), but it *is* permissible to manifest one's pain and even intensify it by tearing one's clothes (it may also have been licit to pluck out the hair of the head and the beard; see Ezra 9:3). When one wishes to taunt and humiliate without striking and wounding, one cuts off half the garment and shaves off half the beard (2 Sam. 10:4–5). The garment is imbued with a portion of its owner's essence: when Jonathan removes his cloak and gives it to David he is expressing his deep love for him (1 Sam. 18:3–4); when the army commanders spread their clothes on the stairs under Jehu they are declaring their submission and loyalty (2 Kings 9:13). Ceremonial garb adds majesty and authority to the office holder, while the particular garment "which the king has worn" (Esther 6:8), in addition to being royal raiment, also contains within it some of the personal virtue of the king. The transfer of the high priesthood from Aaron to Eleazar is underscored by the son's being clothed in the same priestly vestments that his father has just removed (Num. 20:25–28; cf. Isa. 22:21). Elijah's cloak, like Samuel's (1 Sam. 15:27 and 28:14), is the badge or uniform of his prophetic office (1 Kings 19:13; 2 Kings 2:13–14; Zech. 13:4) as well as his distinctive mark of identity (2 Kings 1:8). When he throws his mantle over Elisha it clearly signifies that Elijah is calling him to assume the mantle of prophecy "in his stead." Hence it is most implausible to understand "and became his attendant" as a retrospective clarification that Elijah had not called on Elisha to be the heir of the vocation embodied in the mantle, but merely appointed him as his servant. It is, however, quite reasonable to understand this statement as concise information about how Elisha prepared himself for prophecy during Elijah's lifetime.

The close reading that follows will demonstrate that there is no stylistic reason not to see the Abel-meholah episode as the concluding scene of chapter 19 and that with regard to content and structure it fulfills that task admirably. As we have already noted, there is no explicit mention of Elijah's compliance with the injunction to return north at the end of the previous scene; we learn this indirectly, from the first words of this scene: "He went from there [i.e., Horeb] and came upon [evidently after a search; see the similar opening of a similar story: 1 Kings 11:29 as well as 1 Kings 21:20] Elisha son of Shaphat" (v. 19a). The understated language that conveys the first stage of Elijah's return to the field of action foreshadows the minimalism that typifies all his actions in Abel-meholah and that evidently expresses the reticence of the persecuted and routed prophet to impose his dangerous and frustrating mission on someone else. By contrast, Elisha's reactions are marked by an opposing maximalism, by the sweeping youthful enthusiasm and total devotion of the young man who bends his shoulder to receive the mantle that is cast on him.

We are not told how Elijah identified the man to whom he was sent, but we are treated to the detail that twelve yoke of oxen are plowing the field "ahead of" Elisha, who is following the twelfth plow. Kimchi suggests a symbolic interpretation: "This is a sign that he will oversee the twelve tribes of Israel as prophet and guide." But a prophet is not a king reigning over twelve tribes, nor is twelve always a typological number (cf. 2 Sam. 2:15). Gersonides, for his part, advances a concrete interpretation that closely links this information with the purpose of Elijah's arrival: "I think that this is mentioned to show that Elisha's father was extremely wealthy, but Elisha nevertheless left his father's house to attend Elijah." A field that is being plowed by twelve plows at the same time must be quite large and its owner a very wealthy landowner. The prepositional phrase "ahead of him" clearly suggests that Elisha, in addition to guiding the twelfth plow, is also the overseer of the others plowing in the field. This initial impression is confirmed when Elisha slaughters the yoke of oxen, indicating that he is the owner's son and not a hired foreman.

The apparently superfluous words, "Elijah came over to him" (v. 19b), seem to tell us that Elijah does not call to Elisha from a distance—unlike his conduct with the Phoenician widow (17:10–11) and Ahab (18:8)—but goes to him through the broad field. Just as he does not call him from afar, neither does he say anything to him when he approaches him but casts his mantle on him without a word. Elisha immediately understands the full significance of this symbolic act and responds with great decisiveness: he abandons the oxen in mid-furrow and runs after Elijah. This pursuit juxtaposes Elijah's minimalism and Elisha's maximalism: it implies that Elijah continues to walk without stopping, while the immediacy and rapidity of Elisha's compliance attest that it was done wholeheartedly. This disparity between Elijah's reserve and Elisha's commitment also characterizes the ensuing dialogue between them. Elisha requests Elijah's permission to take leave of his parents before he joins his new master, thereby proclaiming that he has already accepted Elijah's authority and depends upon his word. Elijah, for his part, not only accedes to his request and lets him "go back," he also makes it plain that he has no authority to stop Elisha from doing as he wishes ("What have I done to you?"). In this way Elijah denies, at least on the surface, the mandatory force of the act of casting his mantle and makes Elisha's decision to follow him a voluntary act.

Elisha requests permission to kiss his parents goodbye (cf. Gen. 31:28). Elijah agrees with the words "go back," and Elisha complies precisely in this fashion: "He turned back from him" (v. 21a). Clearly this turning back from Elijah includes Elisha's farewell to his parents. But it is noteworthy that the narrator avoids depicting this scene (evidently to keep it from becoming the focal point of the episode), just as he passes over in silence another event that must surely have taken place—the return of the mantle to its owner (to ensure that it remain a purely technical act and not acquire any symbolic meaning).[152] Instead of recounting what we can supply on our own, the narrator focuses on something new—Elisha's total break with agricultural labor, as a prerequisite for his full adherence to his new vocation (for the opposition between these two careers, see Zech. 13:5). Like Saul, who was called from "driving the cattle" (1 Sam. 11:5) to rescue Jabesh-Gilead, and whose devotion to his national mission was also expressed by his use of the yoke of oxen to mobilize the army ("he took a yoke of oxen and cut them into pieces" [ibid., v. 7]), so too Elisha is called from behind the plow and takes leave of the laborers with the grand gesture of a magnificent farewell banquet: "He took the yoke of oxen and slaughtered them" (19:21). Like Araunah the Jebusite, who did everything in his power to help David halt the great plague and offered him not only the oxen for a sacrifice but also the "threshing boards and the gear of the oxen for wood" (2 Sam. 24:22), so too Elisha, by using the implements of his labor as firewood for the sacrifice, proclaims that he is abandoning it without a second thought, forswearing agriculture forever without looking back (cf. Gen.

19:17). Like Hannah with Samuel, who expressed her wholehearted and generous fulfillment of her vow in the abundant gifts that she sent along with her son (1 Sam. 1:24; see above, pp. 25–26), Elisha makes known to all that he is following the prophet into the unknown with a willing heart and no reservations, by including all those present in his joy: "he gave it to the people, and they ate" (cf. 2 Sam. 6:19).

When Elijah fled to the wilderness from Jezebel's threats, one expression of his despair with his life and mission was his inability to bring his servant with him—"he came to Beer-sheba, which is in Judah, and left his servant there" (19:3b). Now, in a simultaneous *inclusio* and *inversio* at the end of the story, when he returns to inhabited country, he is joined by Elisha: "Then he arose and followed Elijah and became his attendant" (v. 21b). What is more, when Elijah, sitting underneath the broom bush in the wilderness, prayed for death, he grounded his entreaty in the statement, "I am no better than my fathers" (v. 4), undoubtedly meaning that, in the hindsight of his failure as a prophet, he ought to have stayed in his ancestral home in Gilead and followed in his forefathers' course. Now, as his mission is renewed, he hears Elisha say, "Let me kiss my father and mother good-by, and I will follow you" (v. 20)—an expression of the young man's desire to forsake his parents and everything they would one day bequeath to him and cleave to the man who destines him, when the day comes, to don the mantle of prophecy.

As a finale that balances the prelude, the Abel-meholah episode is an effective conclusion to the third part of the story. It is also an epilogue to the entire story, since a number of its themes reach their full development in it.

As we have seen, Elijah's method, from Zarephath to Mount Carmel, was to put the recipients of his message to a test of faith by posing them a difficult challenge: the widow was asked to feed him during the drought; Obadiah, to overcome his fear and bring the king to him; Ahab, not to stand on his dignity and to go meet the prophet; and the people, to seize the prophets of Baal and drag them down to their deaths alongside the Kishon. In the same fashion he now calls on Elisha to follow him, employing a wordless gesture whose obligatory force he immediately negates in order "to test whether he was saying yes with a full heart" (Kimchi commentary on v. 19). Of course the similarity—the imposition of a trial—is offset by a vast difference in the extent of compliance and even more so in the circumstances. All the previous tests of faith involved overcoming an initial resistance. All were conducted under the duress of the drought, a pressure that was augmented, on Mount Carmel, by a miraculous tangible sign. By contrast, not only does Elisha take up the gauntlet spontaneously, immediately, and decisively—in utter contrast to the gate of Zarephath, the outskirts of Samaria, and the heights of Mount Carmel—the trial in the fields of Abel-meholah takes place against the background of affluence—

"he was plowing. There were twelve yoke of oxen ahead of him, and he was with the twelfth"—and abundance—"he gave it to the people, and they ate." The significant detail concerning the scope of the agricultural property, and the focus on the farewell sacrifice, are intended to highlight the antithesis between this trial and its predecessors, namely, that Elisha is not responding to outside pressure and does not require signs and portents: he is motivated by an inner impulse, total confidence in the prophet, and unalloyed faith in his master.

There also seems to be an intentional contrast between Elisha's running after Elijah, which concludes the third part of the story, and Elijah's race before Ahab's chariot, which concludes the second part. That expression of accord with and loyalty to the king ended in disillusionment and black despair. By contrast, when Elisha sprints after the prophet to join him it is the first stage in the restoration of Elijah's personal status and a gate of hope that this allegiance, which does not stem from distress, is real and will not vanish when the affliction does.

Thus a sort of equilibrium is created between the grim prospect of Israel's future entrusted to Elijah on Mount Horeb and the personal recovery caused by Elisha's uncommon assent. Not only is Elijah rescued from his isolation as human being and prophet, his labor of influence and persuasion is crowned with extraordinary success. As happened at the beginning of his career, in Zarephath, so now, at the first stop on his return to his vocation, his success on the interpersonal level has implications for what can be anticipated between the nation and its God.

Conclusion: The Three Parts of the Story—A Retrospective

The overall story of Elijah's war against Baal worship has two separate objectives. The episodes of the drought and the trial on Mount Carmel demonstrate the nothingness of Baal. The second objective is to explain Jehu's revolt and Hazael's victories as condign punishment for the continuation of Baal worship in Israel even after its vanity was proven. The first two parts of the story (chapters 17 and 18) deal with the Lord's exclusive control over "nature" as a means of demonstrating His exclusivity. The third part (chapter 19) sketches out the ways of His direct providence in history so as to prove His justice. These two objectives are different; but not only are they complementary, the second is built upon the first.

When the story was first set down, the war against Baal worship was probably not yet past history but a real-life struggle in which Elijah, through his story, continued to play an active role. To this end the narrator depicted the horrors of famine in Zarephath and Samaria, described at length the strict attention to the conditions of the trial on Mount Carmel, and highlighted the intense astonishment of all those present when the Lord's fire descended on His altar. However, since Baal worship continued in Israel despite all this, the crux of the story is not the *victory* (which was ephemeral) but the *portent* (whose validity endures). That "all the people" fell on their faces, calling out, "The Lord alone is God," and, in obedience to the prophet of the Lord, proceeded to kill the prophets of Baal—these testify to the truth and power of the miracle, a wonder that those of later generations ignore at their own peril. Their acceptance of the events on Mount Carmel depends decisively on the story's capacity to bring the past alive with such intensity that the readers, too, stand on the heights of Mount Carmel on that fateful day and cry out, as part of the great throng, "the Lord alone is God." This cannot be achieved unless the prophet is depicted as the man who battled the prophets of Baal out of his zeal for the Lord, and as a man whose love for his people moved him to grant them the portent of fire and the bounty of rain. Von Rad is right that "the subject of the Elijah stories is basically not the prophet himself but the Lord" (*Theology* 2, p. 24), since the literary portrayal of the prophet's personality and deeds is intended to endow the signs and portents with full reality by anchoring them in historical circumstances and human situations.

Hence there is no foundation to the argument, frequently advanced, that there is no real link between the Mount Carmel episode and the personal miracles of chapter 17, which involve the prophet and other individuals and make no reference to Baal worship. The assertion that the story of the drought and the trial by fire can be understood without the background of Elijah's experiences in Wadi Cherith and Zarephath is valid only at first glance. Such an understanding can be only partial and external, because it is the analogy between private and public events that links the latter to the prophet's strong personality, endowing them with biographical depth and ethical continuity. Our close reading of chapter 18 showed that Elijah's method of posing challenges of faith to Obadiah, Ahab, and the people of Israel can be traced back to his testing of the Phoenician widow, just as the confrontation between the prophet and the widow lays the groundwork for Obadiah's recoiling from the prophet as a bringer of calamity and Ahab's antagonism toward him as "troubler of Israel." This analogical link is credible because it is valid not only for the reader but also for the protagonist. The prophet's actions in chapter 17 not only shed light on his deeds on Mount Carmel, they actually make them possible. Elijah's successful revival of the widow's son allows him to accept and understand the manifestations of suspicion and hostility on the part of those to whom he brings the blessing of rain. He who was answered with flour and oil in Zarephath will be answered with fire and rain on Mount Carmel; he who stretched out on the child and overcame death will stretch out on the soil of Mount Carmel and bring a speedy end to the drought; and he who could move the Phoenician woman, who was on the verge of evicting him from her house, to declare that "the word of the Lord in your mouth is truth" will move the Israelites, after their earlier sullen refusal to respond to him, to proclaim that "the Lord alone is God, the Lord alone is God."

In chapter 19 Elijah plunges from the zenith of surpassing personal achievement and public victory to the abyss of renewed, mortal despair and loss of his way as both man and prophet. Even if we cannot see Jezebel's threat on his life as sufficient explanation for this fall, we must admit that on Mount Horeb Elijah's zealousness for his God receives full backing, the culpability for his failure is laid squarely on the shoulders of the people, and his indictment of Israel provides additional justification for the drastic severity with which the Lord will henceforth judge His people. Despite all that has been done to return Israel to its God—the plague of drought, the portent of fire, and the bounty of rain—Baal worship has not been uprooted; there is no alternative to subjecting them to three swords of destruction, from which only the faithful remnant will escape.

The narrator's unwavering focus on the prophet's personal involvement in returning Israel to its God has two facets—theological and literary. From the theological perspective, it is of fundamental importance that there be a clear and sharp distinction between master and messenger, between the divine injunction and its human execution. So that we do not forget that the man of God remains flesh and blood—even if he goes without food and water for forty days and forty nights—we should know that the trial by fire takes place at his own initiative; and we should hear the three warnings he receives before the Lord is revealed to him in a still small voice, his face covered by his mantle. So that we do not attribute divine force to mortal actions, we should be aware of the truncated nature of the Lord's message to him and the obligation imposed on him to understand and interpret it correctly (on the order of "you have seen well" [Jer. 1:12]). Furthermore, the prophet's presence before the Lord does not dehumanize him—not only because the abyss that separates him from the Lord cannot be bridged, but also because he is not simply an angel who says only what he has heard and does only what he has been commanded. Elijah is depicted as a distinct and strong personality: he hesitates to obey the command to eat when he wishes to die, and he responds minimalistically to the injunction to anoint a prophet to succeed him when he finds it difficult to wholeheartedly accept the renewal of his vocation. His contemporaries could see him in his full humanity, and the narrator depicts him in the same vein—in prayer for assistance and entreaty to die, in desperate resurrection and zealous massacring, in surpassing resourcefulness and loss of orientation, in vigorous steadfastness and frenzied running.

From the literary perspective, everything we learn about the relations between the prophet and his master, between the prophet and those to whom he is sent, and between the prophet and his own emotions, constitutes an integral part of the prophetic message. Not only are the deeds that Elijah performs by the explicit command of the Lord or on his own initiative prophetic signs; his unique personality, which informs his struggles with God, with Israel, and with himself, is also an instrument for implementing his mission. The sharp transition from his enthusiastic race before the king's chariot to his despairing prostration under the broom bush in the wilderness adds a human perspective to a divine judgment whose justice is hard to fathom. Elijah's fervent desire to help the Phoenician widow and assist the Israelites on Mount Carmel gives credibility and force to his profound despair with a people that has forsaken the covenant with its God. We lack the capacity to identify either with the Lord's mercy toward His creatures or His wrath against them; but we can experience the emotions of the human prophet of flesh and blood, whose spiritual torments and moral judgments are in principle similar to our own. Elijah differs from us, for he alone stood before the Lord and heard Him speak from a still small voice; but he resembles us as well, for he is flesh of our flesh, and the word of the Lord was addressed to him as it is addressed to us. Thanks to the literary portrait of the prophet's soul, readers can hear the Lord's word through Elijah's ears.

•7•

ELISHA AND THE WOMAN OF SHUNEM

The Miracle Worker Needs Guidance from the Beneficiary of his Miracle

> *But Moses' hands grew heavy; so they took a stone, put it under him and he sat on it, while Aaron and Hur, one on each side, supported his hands; thus his hands remained steady until the sun set.*
>
> Exod. 17:12

The Compass and Genre of the Story

Any determination of the compass of this story is bound up with defining its literary genre. There is no doubt that the story begins at 2 Kings 4:8, since it is demarcated from the previous story by three clear signs: change of place—Elisha's arrival in Shunem; change in heroinc—from the widow of the son of the prophets to the grande dame of Shunem; and change of genre. The miracle of the jug of oil (4:1–7) is one of the short Elisha stories, which Rofé (*Prophetical Stories,* pp. 13–22) designated "short *legenda*." Such stories have a number of characteristics: each recounts a single miraculous deed; they stand independently and are not anchored in a temporal sequence of events; their plots are simple, with only three or four stages; their heroes are anonymous and nonindividuated; and their focus is astonishment at the miracle and reverence for its worker. By contrast, the account of the woman of Shunem is a long story with narrative elaboration (recognizable from its very first words, "one day," which anchor the event in a particular unit of time), a developed plot, a sophisticated structure, and three-dimensional characters (cf. Rofé, ibid., pp. 27–33).

Indeed, the two miracles described here—the birth of the Shunammite's son and his resurrection—constitute a single unified story, not only

227

because the second is anchored in the first (with regard to the characters) and flows from it (with regard to the plot), but also because the first does not stand by itself and is designed to serve as an introduction to the second. If we try to read the story of the miraculous birth as an independent *legenda*, we realize that the description of the miracle itself (v. 17) is too short to serve as a fitting conclusion for the lengthy description that has preceded it (vv. 8–16) and sense that the Shunammite's disquiet at the annunciation of her forthcoming pregnancy (v. 16) is not simply a matter of weak faith but an expression of some profound truth whose nature, it stands to reason, will be clarified later. In fact, when she reminds Elisha, after her son's death, of her words on that occasion, as a sort of promissory note that he must now redeem (v. 28), the reader realizes that she was right to say, "do not delude your maidservant."

The story is also unified by the threefold use of the temporal indication "one day," which relates the main events of the plot to three nonconsecutive days, two described in the first part (vv. 8 and 11) and the other in the second part (v. 18). The story concludes at verse 37, the end of the story of the boy's resurrection, when the woman leaves the stage with her son. In stark contrast to the (temporary) conclusion of the birth story—which is narrated with great concision as a matter-of-fact report, without the birth's meriting its own day on stage—this is a true closure, in the form of the detailed and drawn-out description of how the beneficiary of the miracle displays her gratitude: "She came and fell at his feet and bowed low to the ground; then she picked up her son and left" (v. 37).

The story is over, but not necessarily complete, for in 8:1–6 we encounter a sequel: Elisha saves "the woman whose son he revived" (8:1) from famine by a timely warning of the ensuing seven years of drought; and when she returns from the land of the Philistines, the king of Israel returns her house and fields to her, and even the revenue of the harvests gathered during her absence, because she was the beneficiary of the miracle that Gehazi has been telling him about. The question as to how this epilogue is related to the body of the story has significant exegetical implications, because all of the Elisha stories—short and long alike—extol his greatness, except for our story, in which the praises lavished on the woman of Shunem imply criticism of the man of God.[1] This is clearly the case only with regard to the story itself and not to its sequel. To correctly understand the significance of this change in point of view and judgment we must determine whether the sequel is an organic part of the story, detached and inserted elsewhere in the Book of Kings by the editor (as we found in the story of Samuel's birth and in the story of the man of God from Judah),[2] or whether it is a separate story about the same characters.

Those who view 8:1–6 as the original continuation of the story of the Shunammite (see the commentaries by Kittel, Šanda, Montgomery, and Cogan and Tadmor) rely principally on two items: the continuity of plot and characters (Elisha and Gehazi, the woman of Shunem and her son, plus the king of Israel who listens avidly to Gehazi's recounting of the story of the resurrection); and the presence of vestiges of the north Israel dialect in both the body of the story and its continuation (the second-person feminine singular pronoun ʾatti appears in 4:16 and 23 as well as in 8:1). They supplement this with two hypotheses: perhaps the famine about which Elisha warned the Shunammite is that described in the story of "death in the pot," which immediately follows the story of the Shunammite (4:38); perhaps Gehazi's conversation with the king indicates that this occurred before he was stricken with leprosy, as is described in the story of Naaman (5:27). Šanda tried to explain its present location in chapter 8 on chronological grounds: only a later king who did not know Elisha personally would want to hear about him from his servant. Cogan and Tadmor ascribe its placement to the associative linkages favored by the editor of the Elisha stories: both in the story of the salvation of Samaria (6:24–7:20) and in the epilogue of our own story, which immediately follows it, Elisha foresees the future with great precision and a distressed woman cries out to the king for help.

On the other hand, Gunkel (*Geschichten von Elisa*, pp. 29–30) believes that the epilogue was written by a later author (who twice refers to "the woman whose son he revived" [8:1 and 5] instead of to "the Shunammite," as she is called in the body of the story) and suggests two reasons why he did so: first, to buttress belief in the miracle of resurrection through the testimony of the beneficiary herself, which was accepted by a later king after investigation and inquiry; second, to add a final fillip to the story in the form of an ironic sequel to the Shunammite's declaration that "I live among my own people" (v. 13)—because of her destitution she does indeed require Elisha's intervention with the king, albeit after the prophet's death.

According to Rofé, however (*Prophetical Stories*, pp. 32–33), we are not dealing with a later addition but with a different and earlier written version of an oral tradition about the resurrection of the boy. This story is not as artistically well developed as the longer account of the lady of Shunem and more closely resembles the *legenda* in its miniature compass, cutout characters, and, principally, its message: "Even after Elisha's death, his memory and fame alone are capable of carrying out acts of kindness on behalf of his believers" (ibid., p. 33).

We can agree that 2 Kings 8:1–8 does not seem to be the original continuation of the story of the woman of Shunem or its later completion—not only because its narrative mode is totally different but also because it bears no sign of any attempt to emulate its style. Whereas the mise-en-scène of every subunit of the story of the woman of Shunem is defined with regard to place (Shunem or Carmel) and time ("one day"), 2 Kings 8:1–8 offers no indication of where Elisha warned the mother of the boy or where the king conversed with Gehazi; nor is there any specification of time ("one day") in the two places in the story where we might expect it according to the narrative mode of the story of the Shunammite, at the beginning of verse 1 and in the middle of verse 3.

On the other hand, 2 Kings 8:1–6 is not an independent and freestanding story that can be understood on its own. Not only is its heroine identified and characterized by information known to the reader from another place; all the elements of its plot refer to the story of the woman of Shunem. Unlike the short *legenda*, in which Elisha always responds to a challenge posed by someone else (generally a request for assistance, and once a mocking curse), this account begins with an initiative by Elisha, which is not to be understood divorced from the two themes of the story of the Shunammite—his desire to recompense her for her hospitality and his special responsibility for the well-being of her son. What is more, the plot of this account relates ironically not only to the woman's confidence that she does not need to have the man of God intervene with the king on her behalf, but also to her vigorous opposition to Gehazi's involvement and to a "remote-control" rescue worked through Elisha's staff. Finally, it also offers an answer to the delicate issue of the limits on the prescience of the man of God.

We may conclude that 2 Kings 8:1–6 is utterly different from the story of the woman of Shunem in its narrative mode but totally dependent on it for its content. Hence it must not be read as part of our story but as an intrascriptural response to it. Its textual separation from the body of the story is probably not the result of an editorial decision; rather, it was a priori intended to be read at some remove, as a sort of rectifying afterword, presented not as an immediate sequel to and direct result of what happened in Shunem and Carmel but as another opportunity afforded Elisha to take care of the woman and her son and a chance for the readers to see him in quite another light.

Both the story of the woman of Shunem itself and the incident that serves as its completion and counterweight are prophetic stories that deal with the "great things that Elisha has done" (8:4), while focusing on the interrelations between the worker of the miracle and its beneficiary. Both stories make secondary use of familiar literary genres: the first combines the story of a miraculous birth with the story of a miraculous survival, while the second combines two *legenda*—about foreknowledge and about help from afar. The anonymity of the child, whose birth and resurrection are both miraculous, tells the reader that the first story deals not with the child but with the man of God.[3] The overt and implicit links between the body of the story and the sequel indicate that the latter is not an independent story in praise of two other wonders performed by Elisha but a polemic meant to refurbish the tarnished prestige of the man of God.

Since all the signs indicate that the story of the Shunammite ends with the resurrection of the child (4:37), a commentator who would understand it as an independent narrative must avoid relying on the sequel in 8:1–6, and we shall do this here. After we have completed our reading of the story, however, we shall deal separately with the other narrative as well because of great interest aroused by the tension between the two and because the light cast by this tension on the story of the woman of Shunem highlights its unique features.

The Literary Function of the Minor Characters

Alongside the two main characters—Elisha and the woman of Shunem—there are two supporting characters who reflect the social milieu in which the story takes place—the servant of the man of God and the woman's elderly husband. There would seem to be a fifth character as well—the child, given that almost the entire plot hinges on his birth and resurrection. But as the passive object of events he lacks any individuation and is permitted only one line, crying to his father: "My head, my head" (4:19). Similarly inconsequential are the two servants who silently do as bid by their master and mistress and whose literary function is to contrast the father's relative serenity in the face of his son's illness—he merely sends the child back to its mother (vv. 19–20)—with the mother's alacrity—she orders the servant to proceed as fast as possible (vv. 22–24).

The first sentence of the story introduces the two protagonists and mentions the wealthy woman's initiative in the invitation to the man of God. We do not learn of the existence of her husband, however, until she decides to augment her hospitality by building an upper chamber. Another indication of his secondary status, in both life and story, besides this delay in introducing him, is the fact that we never hear of any direct intercourse between him and his important guest; throughout the narrative, all the contacts of the man of God are with the woman rather than her husband (this is particularly conspicuous in verse 13). However, since the Shunammite is married (not a widow able to come and go as she pleases, like the heroine of the previous *legenda*), she does not have freedom of action and must either involve her husband in her deeds or neutralize him. Thus, in normal times, she asks his consent to build the upper chamber on the roof of their house; in time of crisis, she conceals the death of their son from him. The narrator tells us these things not only so that her behavior will strike us as socially plausible, but also so that her husband's normal and correct behavior can serve as a contrasting background for her own individuality, both as the leading hostess in Shunem and as a desperate fighter for her son's miraculous resurrection.[4]

Similarly, the reader learns that the man of God is accompanied by a servant only when Elisha requires his services. This accords with the typical pattern of scriptural narrative, which focuses attention on the protagonist by providing scant information on secondary characters. For example, we are not told where Gehazi slept when Elisha went to his upper room and slept on the only bed there; only when Elisha effusively praises the Shunammite's hospitality do we realize, from his use of the plural, that the hospitality included his servant as well: "He said to him, 'Tell her, "You have gone to all this trouble for *us*" ' " (4:13). In normal times, having a servant raises the prophet's prestige, for it exempts him from having to do things that are below his dignity; in crisis situations, however, when he is tempted to impose on the servant tasks that only he himself can perform it is liable to become an impediment to him. In normal times the servant, as go-between for the high-ranking guest and the hostess concerned for his comfort, makes it possible for the two main characters to give full expression to their punctilious concern for good manners. The man of God does not have to descend from the upper room to the house of his hostess, maintains a distance from her private affairs (to the point that he does not even realize that she is childless), and does not go out to meet her when she arrives at his home unexpectedly. The Shunammite, for her part, does not receive his instructions directly (v. 12); even when she is invited to enter his room she prefers to stand at the door (v. 15). In an emergency, however, she conveys the seriousness of the situation by a dramatic breach of etiquette—adamantly refusing to speak to Elisha through his servant and even daring to clasp his feet. Gehazi, who rushes forward to push the woman away from her excessively intimate contact with the man of God, must not be seen as the literary type of the attendant who crassly and bureaucratically "protects" holy men from their admirers and devotees (so presented by Rofé, *Prophetical Stories*, pp. 34–35), but rather as a faithful representative of norms applicable in normal times, which are breached and invalid when the angel of death is on the prowl. For Gehazi the servant on Mount Carmel is like Eli the priest at Shiloh: the latter would expel the barren woman who is praying for a child because he takes her for a shameless drunkard; while the former would send away the bereaved mother who has come to plead for the life of her child because she is impetuous and unmannerly. The crass mistakes of both these good men are meant to underscore the extraordinary and radical conduct of Hannah and the Shunammite, whose wretchedness is described in similar terms (Hannah as *marath nefeš*, the Shunammite as *nafšah marah lah*). Conspicuous against the background of Gehazi's expected behavior is the totally different conduct of Elisha, who displays a broadness of mind, sensitivity, and humility that enable him to sense, even before she tells him what has happened, the great tragedy of this woman who is breaching all rules of etiquette.

Supporting characters help adumbrate main characters not only through contrast (as when the main character rises above or falls below the level of the supporting character), but also by complementing them (when there is no contrast or tension). When Gehazi reveals to Elisha that the Shunammite is childless and her husband is old, he is not merely providing the prophet with essential information. He is also broadly hinting that the miracle of childbirth would be an apt reward for her hospitality. And when Gehazi takes Elisha's staff with no fear or reservations and goes off to place it atop the dead child, he shares his master's expectation that he has the power to work the miracle from afar. The delicacy of the allusion about the birth of a child, and the tacit consent with regard to the resurrection, seem to rule out ascribing to Gehazi any far-reaching personal initiative in the performance of these two miracles (as proposed by Sabbato,[5] who sees him as a negative protagonist who draws Elisha after him). It is more reasonable to see the servant's confident expectation that his master can work the miracles of birth and resurrection as a faithful reflection of the latter's own self-image—Elisha saw himself as his servant saw him. In this way the supporting character helps to clarify for the reader that the theme of the story is how the man of God became prisoner to his own self-image, and how the wealthy woman of Shunem was able to comprehend what master and servant did not and restore to Elisha his independence and full power as a man of God.

The Structure of the Story

The temporal indication "one day" marks the start of the three main scenes (all of which occur in the same place), while a change of location marks the start of the other two (which occur later on the same day as the scenes that immediately precede them).[6] Scene one (4:8–10) begins on the day when the Shunammite first played hostess to Elisha and thereby established her prior right to invite him to dine with her on his future visits to Shunem. The scene continues with her crowning her hospitality by having an upper room built for him. This second act goes much farther than the first, so that it would have been appropriate for the Shunammite's conference with her husband to be introduced, too, with the indication "one day." Such an emphasis on the passage of time, however, would have split the scene of hospitality in two and would have breached a major structural principle that will become evident as the story proceeds, namely, that each scene describes two actions by one of the main characters, aimed at a single goal.

The second scene (4:11–17) is distinguished from the previous one in three ways: a change in time—on one of the days when Elisha visited Shunem; a slight change in place—from the woman's house to the attic room; and the conspicuous transfer of the initiative from hostess to guest— Elisha, with the help of Gehazi, seeks to reward the Shunammite for her hospitality and makes her *two* generous offers. The relatively slow pace of the description of this fateful day is supplemented by the summary narration of its outcome, which lasted for an entire year: as promised, the woman became pregnant and gave birth to a son at the appointed time.[7]

The third scene (4:18–24) opens with the death of the child on one of the days of the harvest season, followed by *two* preparatory actions taken by his mother in order to restore him to life: closing him up in the upper room and her hasty departure to the home of the man of God. The fourth and fifth scenes transpire, as already noted, on that same day. This compression of time expresses the feverish activity to save the child: in the morning he goes out to the harvesters, at noon he dies on his mother's knees, at the end of a nonstop journey of some twenty-five kilometers she reaches Carmel (evidently toward evening), and Elisha races back to Shunem with her and revives her son (evidently around midnight).[8]

The fourth scene (4:25–30) takes place at a new location, the home of the man of God on Mount Carmel. Just as in the second scene, Elisha, with the assistance of Gehazi, seeks a way to help the Shunammite woman. These *two* attempts—to obtain information from afar and to save the child from afar—encounter vigorous opposition on the part of the Shunammite. The scene concludes with Elisha's acquiescence in her demand that he himself return with her to Shunem. The fifth scene (4:31–37), too, is parallel, like its predecessor, to the second scene. The plot returns to the former setting, the upper room in Shunem, where *two* attempts are made to revive the child, the first by means of the staff carried there by Gehazi, the second by Elisha himself. In the end the Shunammite woman is invited to carry out her son, now restored to life.

The fifth scene, and with it the entire story, concludes with Elisha's telling the women, "Pick up *(śeʾi)* your son" (v. 36), and her doing so: "she picked up *(wa-tiśśaʾ)* her son and left" (v. 37). These verses contain a strong echo of what the child's father told one of the harvesters, "Carry him *(śaʾehu)* to his mother" (v. 19), which is also followed by the implementation of the command: "He picked him up *(wa-yiśśaʾehu)* and brought him to his mother" (v. 20). The contrast between the servant's carrying the dying child to his mother and the mother's carrying the resurrected child signifies that this is the miraculous conclusion to the crisis that erupted with the child's sudden illness and death. Thus the end of the story does not return to its beginning but to the start of the third scene. Indeed, there is a plot cadence at the end of the second scene (as we noted earlier): a son is born to the Shunammite woman exactly at the time fixed by Elisha (v. 17). In retrospect this temporary relaxation can be seen as the end of the first part of the story, also underscored by an *inclusio:* the name Elisha, which appears at the beginning of the story (v. 8a) but is thereafter absent from the body of the first part, returns as its very last word (v. 17b). Thus the story is divided, formally and thematically, into two parts: the first devoted to the miraculous birth, the second to the miraculous resurrection.

The two parts of the story are of quite unequal length: the miraculous birth is described in ten verses, divided into two scenes, whereas the miraculous resurrection receives twenty verses, divided into three scenes (see table 7.1). This deflection of the center of gravity to the second part makes it abundantly clear to the reader that the story is not meant to laud the pious hospitality of the wealthy woman of Shunem toward the man of God, but rather to exhibit her extraordinary ability to treat him with profound reverence and at the same time to contend with him as to the way he can restore her son to life. Similarly, the story is not meant to extol Elisha's two great miracles but rather to investigate the interaction between his ability to work miracles and his human limitations. This objective is expressed by means of another structural principle: the contrast between the first and third scenes—in which the Shunammite is the initiator and actor—with the second, fourth, and fifth scenes—in which it is Elisha who takes the initiative and acts. In the first scene, the Shunammite's two initiatives to extend hospitality to the man of God are successful, and in the third scene she performs two acts essential to the resurrection of her son; these actions impress upon us her broad-minded generosity, independence, and resoluteness. By contrast, Elisha's actions reflect inadequate information, insufficient understanding, and ineffectual involvement. In the second scene, he makes two attempts to repay the Shunammite woman; the first is rejected out of hand, and only the second succeeds (temporarily), despite her qualms. In the fourth scene, his two attempts to assist her encounter her adamant opposition. Finally, the fifth scene recounts his two attempts to revive the child. As in the second scene, the first attempt fails and only the second is successful (this time permanently).[9] This sophisticated structure—with its underlying format of five scenes, alternation of the active character, and contrasting success of the action—faithfully serves the paradoxical theme of the story: the Shunammite woman has greater understanding, but Elisha has exclusive power to work miracles. Hence the man of God can successfully apply his full ability only when he recognizes that she is right and he is wrong: "So he arose and followed her" (v. 30).[10]

A Close Reading

I,1: The Shunammite Woman Extends
Perfect Hospitality out of Profound Respect (4:8–10)

The story begins with a brief exposition in the first half of the first verse (v. 8a). We are informed that the plot is set in Shunem, to which Elisha comes as a wayfarer. Nothing is mentioned about Elisha except his name, which indicates that the narrator (or the compiler of the Elisha stories) assumes the reader knows him as a wandering man of God (2 Kings 2:18, 23, and 25) and has already been introduced to him with his full name and

TABLE 7.1: The Structure of the Story of the Woman of Shunem

I. Hospitality toward the Man of God and Its Reward: The Miraculous Birth	
I,1 (in Shunem): The Shunammite Woman—doubly successful hospitality (4:8–10)	I,2 (in Shunem): Elisha fails and then succeeds in finding a fit reward for the Shunammite (4:11–17)
[Opening sentence: "One day Elisha visited Shunem."]	[Opening sentence: "One day he came there."]
1. Food: "Whenever he passed by, he would stop there for a meal."	1. Elisha's offer of social assistance is declined: "I live among my own people."
2. Lodging: "Whenever he comes to us he can stay there."	2. The promise of miraculous succor arouses anxiety—"Do not delude your maidservant"—but the child is born at the appointed season.

place of origin (1 Kings 19:16 and 19). The other main character—who remains anonymous, evidently because her name had been forgotten (see n. 14)—is presented as a great lady residing in the town. The adjective *gadol*, 'great', is applied in Scripture both to the propertied and affluent (such as Nabal the Carmelite, 1 Sam. 25:2) and to those of high rank and social status (e.g., Naaman, the commander of the army of Aram, 2 Kings 5:1). Later in the story it becomes clear that this Shunammite is indeed both wealthy and prominent. The plot gets under way with her success in getting Elisha to come and dine at her table: "she urged him (*wa-yaḥazeq bo*) to have a meal." The verb *ḥ.z.q* in the *hifᶜil*, followed by the prepositional *bet*, is found one other time in the context of hospitality: "His father-in-law pressed him (*wa-yaḥazeq bo*) and he stayed with him for three days" (Judg. 19:4). It seems likely that in both instances it indicates detaining a traveler from continuing his journey (by verbal persuasion rather than force). The reader may infer how the Shunammite woman did this from the descriptions of the exemplary hospitality of Abraham and of Lot, who invested great effort in persuading wayfarers of their intense desire to entertain them in their homes and to promise that the delay would not be excessive (Gen. 18:1–5 and 19:1–3a; see also 24:56). Just as the narrator provides no concrete description of what the woman of Shunem did to win over Elisha,

TABLE 7.1—*continued*

II. The Miracle-worker Is Called on to Restore It: The Miraculous Revival		
II,1 (in Shunem): The Shunammite performs two actions necessary to restore her son to life (4:18–24)	II,2 (in Carmel): Elisha's two attempts to help from a distance meet the Shunammite's vigorous opposition (4:25–30)	II,3 (in Shunem): Elisha fails and then succeeds in reviving the boy (4:31–37)
[Opening sentence: "One day, he went out to his father."]	[Opening sentence: "She went on until she came to the man of God."]	[Opening sentence: "Gehazi went on before them."]
1. The Shunammite lays her dead son in the bed of the man of God and closes the door.	1. Gehazi does not receive the information he asks for: "It is well."	1. The staff fails to revive the child: "The boy has not awakened."
2. The Shunammite sets out and hides the reason from her husband: "It is well."	2. The dispatching of Gehazi does not satisfy the Shunammite: "As the Lord lives and as you live, I will not leave you!" Elisha acquiesces and goes with her.	2. Elisha succeeds in reviving the child as a result of an extraordinary effort—"The boy opened his eyes"—and receives the woman's full esteem—"She came and fell at his feet and bowed low to the ground."

merely noting her success, he says nothing about the content of the hospitality itself. Only its extraordinary outcome attests to its uncommon nature: thereafter, every time he passed through Shunem, Elisha went to dine at her house at his own initiative.

Only after we have been impressed by the intense nature of her hospitality does the narrator disclose her motives, through the device of her conversation with her husband. Whereas Abraham and Lot fed total strangers, she invites Elisha to her house because he is a man of God; she is explicitly motivated by her reverence for him. To persuade her husband that they ought to enhance their hospitality from meals to include accommodations, she argues that Elisha is "a holy man of God" and that they have a certain commitment to him because he "comes our way (ʿover ʿaleinu) regularly" (this seems to be an intentional echo of Abraham's remark that "you have come your servant's way [ʿavartem ʿal ʿavdᵉkem]"—Gen. 18:5). She proposes that they build a separate room on the roof of their house, fully furnished, which will always be ready for him—"so that whenever he comes to us he can stay there." (This contrasts with normal hospitality, based on finding room in the house for the guest; see Gen. 24:31.) But why does she stress that a "small" attic is all that is required?

In the light of what we have been told about her generosity, it makes no sense that this is an expression of thrift on her part. Rather, taking into account that she says this to her husband, it seems that she is trying to help him overcome his disinclination to extend hospitality that goes beyond the normal limits.[11] Her husband's response is not reported, but it is clearly in the affirmative; in scriptural narratives consent is almost always given tacitly. Nor are we told about the construction of this upper room, because readers can be counted on to fill in this detail on their own.

The Shunammite's hospitality is described through allusive analogy to that of Abraham and explicit contrast to the account of Elijah's residence in the upper room of the widow of Zarephath (1 Kings 17:8–24).[12] Here we are told about a grande dame who seeks to honor the man of God by profuse hospitality; there, a poor widow who gathers wood responds to a request by the man of God to feed him, in return for his promise that she and her son will not lack for flour and oil until the end of the drought. Moreover, the *conclusion* reached by the widow of Zarephath after the miracle of her son's resurrection is precisely the Shunammite's point of departure:

> The widow of Zarephath: "Now I know that you are a man of God and that the word of the Lord in your mouth is truth." (1 Kings 17:24)
> The woman of Shunem: "For certainly I know that it is a holy man of God who comes this way regularly." (2 Kings 4:9)

Not only the location of these remarks in the respective stories (at the end for the widow of Zarephath, at the beginning for the woman of Shunem), but also their phrasing indicates that the widow is referring to the miracle that Elijah has wrought for her and the truth of the Lord's word spoken through him, whereas the woman of Shunem is relating to Elisha's very being. Scripture does not apply the adjective *holy* to the ability to prophesy and work miracles but to the affiliation of the priests (Num. 16:3–7), nazirites (Num. 6:5, 8), and the entire people of Israel, as a "nation of priests" (Exod. 19:6), to the domain of the sacred. Whereas the widow's demonstrative *ʿattah zeh* is clearly an indication of time—"now"—pointing to her changed awareness in the aftermath of the miracle, the demonstrative+particle *hinneh naʾ* used by the Shunammite can be taken in two ways. It may be a temporal adverb meaning 'now' (this is the sense when Naaman says, after he is healed of his leprosy, "Now [*hinneh naʾ*] I know that there is no God in the whole world except in Israel" [2 Kings 5:15]); if so, the woman of Shunem is making a statement based on what she has learned about Elisha since he began frequenting her house (this is how it is rendered by Targum Jonathan and explained by Rashi, Kimchi, Gersonides, and Abravanel). It is more likely, however, that here *naʾ* is an emphatic particle (as when Abraham tells Sarah, "I certainly [*hinneh naʾ*] know what a beautiful woman you are" [Gen. 12:11]); in this case, the Shunammite's statement is based on what she has clearly known for some time.[13] In either case, the contrast with the story of Elijah and the widow underscores all the more strongly that the woman of Shunem expects no reward, just as she does not have to have a miracle take place before her eyes to know with full confidence that Elisha is a holy man of God and to find a tangible and appropriate expression of her reverence for him.

I,2: Elisha Tries to Find a Fit Reward for her Reverence (4:11–17)

The previous scene concluded with a sketch of the Shunammite's plans: "Let us make a small enclosed upper chamber and place a bed, a table, a chair, and a lampstand there for him, so that whenever he comes to us he can stay there" (v. 10b). This scene begins with their exact realization: "One day he came there [to the house of the Shunammite and her husband]; he retired to the upper chamber [which had been built in the interim] and lay down there" (v. 11). According to the Shunammite's remarks to her husband, the construction of the upper room is intended to offer the man of God the full respect he merits. However, the adjacent accommodations could in practice remove barriers and lead to greater intimacy; hence the narrator makes clear that both sides—guest and hostess—took great pains that this not happen. Elisha avoids getting involved in the life of the family (to the point that he does not know what is going on in the house below). When he wishes to reward the Shunammite for "all this trouble," he has his servant Gehazi invite her to the upper room,[14] and she complies respectfully: "she stood before him" (v. 12).

It is not clear whether "before him" refers to Elisha, who is the subject of verse 12a ("He said to his servant Gehazi"), or to Gehazi, who is the subject of the second half of the verse ("He called her"). The verse is similar, in both content and equivocal phrasing, to verse 36; but there the context makes it perfectly clear that she stood before Elisha: "[Elisha] called Gehazi and said, 'Call the Shunammite woman,' and he [Gehazi] called her. When she came to him [Elisha], he said, 'Pick up your son.' " To our perplexity, however, the context of verse 12 requires us to draw the inverse conclusion, namely, that the Shunammite stood before Gehazi: in the next verse Elisha instructs Gehazi what reward to offer her. When she turns it down, they consult as to a suitable alternative. Finally, in verse 15, Elisha tells Gehazi to call her again, but even now she refrains from actually entering the prophet's room: "He called her, and she stood in the doorway."

Gersonides and Abravanel concluded from this that she stood in front of Gehazi, but Abravanel was not happy with this until he had inquired whether the data would also permit some alternate interpretation:

> We can also say that the first time Gehazi called her she entered the room and sat near Elisha. But the prophet did not want to speak to her [directly],

because she was a woman. So even though she was there he spoke to Gehazi and told him to ask her whether he should speak to the king on her behalf, etc. From the fact that he avoided speaking to her directly she realized that he did not want such intimacy with a woman. When he called her the second time, then, she stood in the door and did not enter the room, because of his sanctity. The prophet, for his part, when he saw that she was keeping a proper distance, spoke directly to her: "At this season next year. . . . "

This explanation was adopted by David Altschuler (the author of the *Metzudot* commentary) and accepted by Rofé (*Prophetical Stories*, p. 30). But is it plausible that Elisha would speak to the Shunammite through Gehazi while utterly ignoring that she is in the room with them, whether because she is a woman (as Abravanel suggests) or because he "insists on proper respect for his person" (as Rofé believes)?

Another way to resolve the problem is to assume that the text has been corrupted by the interpolation of several words. For example, Kittel (*Biblia Hebraica*, ad loc.) would delete the bracketed words from verses 12–13: "He said to his servant Gehazi, 'Call that Shunammite woman.' [He called her, and she stood before him. He said to him,] 'Tell her. . . . ' " Šanda (*Bücher der Könige*, p. 30) would delete only two [three in Hebrew] words from verse 13: "He said to [him, 'Tell] her." According to the first of these proposed emendations, the story does not tell us whom the Shunammite stood before, and we are to understand implicitly that Elisha spoke to her through Gehazi. According to the second proposal, there is no mention of Gehazi as a go-between in the dialogue, and Elisha spoke directly to her. Paradoxically, the smaller emendation has the greater impact on the sense of the narrative.

The problem remains and must be more clearly defined. The problem is not *thematic*, since the context makes it perfectly clear that Elisha spoke to the Shunammite through his servant. Nor is it *syntactic*, since nothing prevents us from construing the text as "he [Gehazi] called her, and she stood before him [Gehazi]." The difficulty is essentially *stylistic:* if the narrator really means to say that even though Elisha sent for her to come to the upper room she avoided doing so, why doesn't he make this clear by adding a single word—"and she stood before *Gehazi*"? Perhaps we may assume that the narrator means to tell us not that the Shunammite did not enter the bedchamber of the man of God (as this would go without saying for his readers), but rather that she stood (even before Gehazi) as a servant before her master, awaiting his instructions. (Compare: "Then King David answered: 'Call Bathsheba to me!' So she came into the king's presence and stood before the king" [1 Kings 1:28]; and, in the story of Naaman, "Then he returned to the man of God, he and his entire retinue, and he came and stood before him . . . " [2 Kings 5:15].)

Elisha's words of gratitude do not refer to what the Shunammite has actually done for him but to the attitude that her deeds express: "You have gone to all this trouble for us" (v. 13). The primary signification of the root *h.r.d* is fear and trembling ("all the people who were in the camp *trembled. . . .* the whole mountain *trembled* violently" [Exod. 19:16 and 18].) Its secondary meaning refers to vigorous activity motivated by anxiety and concern ("The elders of the city went out *in alarm* to meet him and said, 'Do you come on a peaceful errand?' " [1 Sam. 16:4]; see also 1 Sam. 21:2) or by awe of majesty ("The Lord will roar like a lion, and they shall march behind Him; when He roars, His children shall come *quivering* out of the west" [Hos. 11:10]; see also Isa. 66:2 and 5). Elisha wants to reward the Shunammite for her reverence but does not know what she lacks. He asks her, by way of example, whether she needs his intervention with the civil or military authorities, to whom he is known and with whom he has influence. The Shunammite, however, rejects his offer of assistance with vigorous confidence, saying, "I live among my own people" (Rashi: "among my own people—among my relations: no one harms me and I have no need of either the king or the commander of the army"). What is more, she totally ignores his question, "What can be done for you?" Both her response and her silence are meant to underscore the fact that she lacks nothing, that she expects no reward, and also perhaps her feeling that accepting anything for what she has done out of reverence for the prophet would constitute post factum evidence that it was not a disinterested gift.

Elisha pays no heed to all of this and repeats to Gehazi the very same question that the Shunammite had left unanswered: "What then can be done for her?" (v. 14a). Whereas in every other scriptural story of a miraculous birth the narrator reports the fact of the woman's barrenness at the very outset (Sarah: Gen. 11:30 and 16:1; Rebekah: Gen. 25:21; Rachel: Gen. 29:31; the wife of Manoah: Judg. 13:2; Hannah, 1 Sam. 1:2 and 5–6), here we learn that the Shunammite is childless only in the course of the story, and from Gehazi: " 'The fact is,' said Gehazi, 'she has no son, and her husband is old' " (v. 14b). Had we known this earlier we might have made a connection between her family situation and the construction of the upper room and attributed an ulterior motive to her. By contrast, our astonishment when we learn of her barrenness reinforces our prior impression both as to her motives and to the credibility of her negative response to Elisha's offer of a reward.[15] Gehazi's answer is based on reliable information as to what she truly lacks (she is like Sarah, who says of herself, in similar terms, "my husband is old" [Gen. 18:12]) and on a sound assessment of the miracles his master can work. According to the biblical mode of thought, the difference between natural and supernatural deeds is one of degree rather than kind. Hence we should not be astounded at the ease with which Gehazi passes from a nonmiraculous social reward to an existential miraculous one. Elisha enthusiastically adopts his servant's suggestion, as is evident from the fact that now he wants to speak directly to the woman so that he can himself announce the good news to her. It would seem that Gehazi's proposal captures his fancy in that it enables him not only to supply her need, as she had provided his, but also to reward her for her reverential attitude toward him by doing something that is a direct result not of his social prestige but of his being "a holy man of God." What is more, because her invitation to the man of God to eat and lodge in her house, motivated by her profound respect for him, is the antithesis of his mocking expulsion by the lads of Jericho ("Go away, baldhead! Go away, baldhead" [2 Kings 2:23]), we ought not to be astonished that in both cases Elisha's reaction is so vigorous and so extreme. Those who curse the wandering man of God, whose influence depends on the recognition given him, merit a terrible punishment, and those who show him public honor, like the Shunammite, deserve an extraordinary reward. They referred to his ridiculous appearance—his baldness—and were condemned to death; she related to his exalted inner essence—his sanctity—and is blessed with the gift of life.

Because of the extremely elliptical style of the story, which focuses on the essential and leaves much for readers to comprehend on their own,[16] it is not exactly clear where the woman of Shunem is when Gehazi summons her the second time. It does not stand to reason that she returned to her house while Gehazi was conveying her response to Elisha and the two continued their consultations, for such a display of displeasure with his offer of a reward is clearly out of keeping with her restrained conduct and good manners. It is preferable to assume that she remained standing on the flat roof in front of the upper room and waited. When Gehazi goes to call her again, the idea clearly is not that she climbs up to the roof a second time but that she enter the room of the man of God and hear what he has to say from his own mouth. In her modesty, however, she still prefers to stand in the doorway (v. 15).

With great ceremony Elisha conveys the good tidings to her: "And Elisha said, 'At this season next year, you will be embracing a son' " (v. 16a). He not only promises that she will bear a son as soon as possible and uses picturesque language to give tangible expression to the full maternal joy of embracing a child; he also uses the term *ka-ʿeth ḥayyah*, 'at this season next year' (found only here and in Gen. 18:10 and 14), evidently drawing an analogy between her reward for hospitality to the man of God and the reward received by Abraham and Sarah for their hospitality to the three angels.

Despite the sublime content and form of the annunciation, the Shunammite's reaction resembles her response to his first offer. She cannot deny the information on which the good tidings are based, namely, her barrenness and husband's age, but she has reservations concerning the annunciation itself: "Please, my lord, man of God, do not delude (*ʾal tkazzev*) your maidservant" (v. 16b). At first sight this is merely skepticism that such a wondrous miracle can actually occur, similar to the laughter of Abraham and Sarah (Gen. 17:17 and 18:12), Naaman's anger (2 Kings 5:11–12), and the sarcasm of the king's adjutant (2 Kings 7:2). But it hardly seems plausible that when the Shunammite woman says *t'kazzev* she means 'not fulfill' (as in Num. 23:19: "God is not a man to be capricious [*wi-ykazzev*], or mortal to change His mind. Would He speak and not act, promise and not fulfill?") or 'deceive' (as rendered by Targum Jonathan and the commentaries of Kittel and Montgomery). It is more likely that here the verb *k.z.b* has the sense of 'arousing false hopes' (as in Job 41:1—"any hope . . . must be disappointed [*nikz'vah*]") or of "doing something that cannot last" (as in Isa. 58:11—"You shall be like a watered garden, like a spring whose waters do not fail [*lo y'kazz'vu*]"). The second interpretation is more in keeping with the combination of exaggerated propriety—"my lord, man of God . . . your maidservant" and emphatic determination—"do not delude."[17] Rather than as skepticism concerning Elisha's desire or ability to work the miracle, deriving from a lack of trust or smallness of faith, we should understood her reaction as an expression of profound doubt that she is worthy of such a miracle, a doubt whose source lies in pious humility. Against the confident prophecy of the man of God, who foresees the accomplishment of his word, she juxtaposes the prophecy of her heart, which fears the terrible disappointment to be expected from a miracle that cannot last. We must not hear her words as criticism that Elisha is acting in a quasi-magic fashion and failing to invoke the name of God, as when Naaman says: "I thought . . . he would surely come out to me, and would stand and invoke the Lord his God by name" (2 Kings 5:11).[18] However, we may well perceive the narrator's implicit criticism of Elisha, who acts on Gehazi's suggestion and fails to examine the matter any more deeply than his servant does, who is determined to work the miracle and pays no attention to the Shunammite's reluctance and who makes no attempt to dispel her anxiety.

Despite all this, the narrator hastens to inform us that Elisha's word was indeed accomplished in full and at the appointed time (like the angel's promise to Abraham and Sarah [Gen. 21:2]). This is not the end of the story, however, but only the end of its first part.

II,1: The Woman of Shunem Refuses to Accept Her Son's Death (4:18–24)

Several years pass, and the child is old enough to go out to the fields by himself and watch the harvesters at work. One day, however, his head suddenly starts to hurt. As any small child would, he goes to his father for help and complains: "My head, my head" (v. 19). We should not hear this complaint as a realistic transmission of childish speech; for as Kimchi notes, in scriptural style "those in pain or mourning tend to repeat themselves, for example, 'My entrails, my entrails' (Jer. 4:19)" (see also "my eyes, my eyes flow with tears" [Lam. 1:16]). The child's extreme youth is reflected in his appeal to his father (which is missing in a similar description of a sudden death of an adult during the harvest (see Jth. 8:2–3) and in the fact that, on his father's instructions, one of the servants carries him home and his mother places him on her lap to comfort him (v. 20). The picturesque description of the child rocked in his mother's arms until he dies, more than it is intended to depict the maternity of the woman of Shunem as an intimacy of body and soul, is a bitterly ironic manifestation that Elisha's pledge has indeed proved a disappointment: she is embracing a son, as promised, but the son who sits on her lap is dying. The miraculous gift of a child has been annulled by its swift withdrawal.

Now readers have a great surprise in store for them: the woman who accepted her barrenness and whose acquiescence in that state has been retroactively validated by the premature death of her child does not accept her bereavement. The woman who did not ask the man of God to work a miracle that would enable her to bear a child, despite her husband's old age, and who even tried to deter him from working such a miracle for her, will henceforth fight like a lioness to obtain a much more wondrous miracle—the resurrection of her dead son. Although this turnabout is not explained or justified, neither by the narrator nor by the heroine, it is embodied in a series of vigorous actions from which the reader can infer what the woman of Shunem is thinking and feeling.

In total contrast to the widow of Zarephath, who accepted the fact of her son's death, blamed Elijah for causing it, and demanded that he leave her house (1 Kings 17:18), the woman of Shunem refrains from any expression of pain or sorrow (evidently because that would be acknowledgment of the child's death). All her actions are intended to bring the man of God to her house, in full confidence that he has the power to restore the dead to life. Whereas the widow responded passively to Elijah's instruction, "Give me the boy," and the prophet himself had to do everything—"he took him from her arms and carried him to the upper chamber where he was staying, and laid him down on his own bed" (v. 19), here the man of God is absent, and it is the Shunammite who makes all these preparations: "She went up and laid him on the bed of the man of God" (2 Kings 4:21). We are not told that Elijah closed the door of the upper room behind him (probably because this is self-evident), but Elisha explicitly told the widow of the son of the prophets to do this—"Then go in and shut the door behind you and your children" (v. 4), and the Shunammite does likewise (v. 21). The symbolic, mystical, or magical significance of these acts is rather obscure,[19] but there is no doubt that she does the very best thing she could. She seems to have two objectives when she carries the child's corpse to the upper room: first, to introduce him into the sphere of influence of the man of God; second, to conceal the body from her husband and everyone else in the house—in fact, to prevent those of little faith from accepting the child's death as incontrovertible fact and manifesting this in expressions of grief and mourning and preparations for his burial. This is why she cannot tell her husband the reason for her precipitate trip to the man of God; any explanation might lead her to a statement that in some sense acknowledges the child's death and thereby seals his fate. Here too she acts just as Elisha himself had done in similar circumstances, when the sons of the prophets were speaking freely of Elijah's imminent passing: "I know it, too; be silent" (2 Kings 2:3).[20]

The woman cannot simply leave the house without informing her husband (especially when her son is ill), nor can she travel without an escort (cf. Gen. 22:3; Num. 22:21; 1 Sam. 28:8). Hence she calls her husband and explains that she must pay an urgent call on the man of God ("that I may quickly go to the man of God and come back" [v. 22]); to this end she asks him: "Please [*na⁾*], send me [from the fields] one of the servants and one of the she-asses" (ibid.). Since at harvest time everyone, man and beast alike, is busy working, she stresses that she needs only one servant and one she-ass. And because such concerns are irrelevant when there is an emergency, this minimal request hints that her trip is not linked to the boy's condition but is rather something that she must do for the man of God (note that she again adopts the means of persuasion she had used in normal times—"Let us [*na⁾*] make a *small* enclosed upper chamber" [v. 10]). The husband must catch her soothing signals, for he does not inquire about the boy's illness; but he does ask why she is going to the man of God now, when the normal custom is to visit him on Sabbath and New Moon. Perhaps we should overhear displeasure with her excessive piety in his question. But her laconic answer, "It's all right," which on the one hand indicates that there is no cause for worry and on the other that the urgency of the matter leaves her no time to explain what it is all about, shows that she understands his query not as a rhetorical question expressing reproof but as a serious question requesting information. We may conclude that the fundamental condition of the woman of Shunem is like that of Hannah. Both had loving husbands who filled all their needs and requests; but in their desperate struggles for motherhood they were alone. Hannah went alone to pray and make her vow, because Elkanah would not have believed that her prayer would be heard and her vow accepted; so, too, the woman of Shunem sets out alone and conceals the reason for her journey, because her husband would not have believed that the man of God could do anything for their dead son.

Abigail, too, rode on a donkey with her five serving girls attending "her on foot" (1 Sam. 25:42); here the servant is not only an escort but also guides the ass by walking in front holding its reins or by prodding it from behind (the verb *n.h.g* has both meanings; cf. Gen. 31:18 and Songs 8:2). During the course of the five- or six-hour ride to Mount Carmel there would be a need for several rest stops. However, the Shunammite tells the servant not to halt out of concern for her comfort and ease but to keep going until she gives him an explicit instruction to the contrary (v. 24). Saving the child depends on the speed of her journey, and the narrator leaves it for the reader to understand that such an instruction was never given. In parallel to the first scene, here too every one of the woman's actions—from rocking her son on her lap to riding swiftly to Elisha—are marked by devotion, faith, understanding, determination, and energy. The correctness of her course will become clear in the subsequent scenes.

II,2: Elisha—First by Proxy and then in Person (4:25–30)

The situation when the fourth scene opens is analogous to that at the start of the second scene: then Elisha was in the upper room and asked the Shunammite to come up from her house; now Elisha is at his own home on Mount Carmel and she goes there on her own initiative. In Shunem, Elisha sent Gehazi to the woman to find out how he can repay her; in Carmel, he sends Gehazi out to her to learn the reason for her unexpected visit. In the second scene she told Gehazi that she lacked nothing and dwelt in the midst of her own people; in the fourth scene she tells him that everything is all right: "It is well" (v. 26).

The reader is astonished: why does she not disclose the reason for her journey to the servant of the man of God, who has come running out to meet her? Why does she put him off with spurious cheer, as she had previously done with her husband? Gersonides sees this as a continuation of her previous circumspection: "She did not want to open her mouth to speak evil tidings." Gunkel explains it as a continuation of her fear of losing time in lengthy explanations (*Geschichten von Elisa*, p. 24). Given the close analogy with the opening of the second scene, however, it seems more likely that in addition to and beyond these practical considerations, she refuses to expose her motives to the emissary when she realizes that once again the man of God is groping in the dark with regard to her situation. Elisha's threefold question—"Is it well (*šalom*) with you? Is it well with your husband? Is it well with the child?" (v. 26)[21]—is much closer to the reason for her coming than was her husband's more general query. But the fact that the last question asks after the child's health clearly attests that Elisha has no prophetic knowledge of the calamity that has befallen her (as noted by Šanda, *Bücher der Könige*, p. 32). Her offhand reply to Elisha's questions, as relayed by Gehazi, is in fact part of her message to the man of God: the crisis that has brought her to his doorstep is so grave that it cannot be dealt with by proxy; secondhand information will not be an adequate basis for his intervention.

When the woman of Shunem reaches Elisha's abode on Mount Carmel, the similarity with the second scene abruptly turns into strong antithesis. In her house the Shunammite took great pains to maintain the maximum distance between herself and her eminent guest; even when invited, she did not enter the upper room: "she stood in the doorway" (v. 15). Here, how-

ever, she goes right up to the man of God and breaches all decorum: "she
clasped his feet" (v. 27). Gehazi, shocked by this violation of reverence and
good manners and by the astonishing decline of the woman of Shunem—
from *wa-taḥazeq* with words, when "she urged him to have a meal" (v. 8), to
wa-taḥazeq physically, when "she clasped his feet"—starts to push her away.
But Elisha has understood what she is trying to express through her extraordinary conduct, namely, that a terrible catastrophe has befallen her,
the total opposite of the *šalom* she has uttered, and that she expects him to
come to her assistance and rescue her. That Elisha rises above the conventional reaction and emotional insensitivity of his servant clearly opens a
door of hope for the Shunammite. When she hears Elisha explain to Gehazi
that he forgoes the respect due him and that he should "let her alone,"
because her extraordinary and passionate conduct clearly reflects the extraordinary and passionate situation in which she finds herself: "she is in bitter distress." (This description does not mean that she is bitter and wretched
but that she is performing an act of desperation because her situation
is desperate, much like the Danites in the house of Micah [Judg. 18:25],
Hannah at Shiloh [1 Sam. 1:10],[22] and the men of David's troop at Ziklag
[1 Sam. 30:6].)

The man of God is not embarrassed to avow candidly that he is judging
by appearances only, for he has not merited a prophetic revelation of what
has befallen her: "the Lord has hidden it from me and has not told me" (v.
27). The duplication here can be understood as emphatic variation; scriptural prose has many examples of such synonymous parallelism meant to
highlight and emphasize (e.g., Gen 22:12; Josh. 2:15; Judg. 13:2–3; 1 Sam.
3:1 and 7, 20:1, 21:2). In this case, the narrator wants to focus our attention
on this sentence, the first mention, in our story, of God's name by the man
of God. But it can also be understood as two independent statements: not
only has the Lord blocked Elisha's autonomous prophetic vision (that is,
his much-acclaimed power to see from afar [e.g., 2 Kings 5:26; 6:9, 12, and
32]); He has also given him no prophetic revelation of the Shunammite's
calamity.[23] Whichever explanation we accept, Elisha humbly states that he
must listen to what she has to say because he senses the intensity of her
tragedy but has no prophetic knowledge about it.[24]

The nature of the change that now begins to take place in Elisha's soul
is elucidated by the juxtaposition of his present awareness with his former
insensibility at the end of the second scene. On that occasion he did not
attribute his lucid knowledge of future events to the Lord: "At this season
next year, you will be embracing a son" (v. 16). Now, however, he ascribes
his ignorance to divine intervention: "the Lord has hidden it from me." In
Shunem he acted on the advice of Gehazi and did not react to the woman's
apprehension; now, aware of his limitations as a man of God, he understands the situation immeasurably better than his adoring servant and is
ready to hear what the woman of Shunem refused to tell Gehazi.

Even when she is finally speaking with the man of God, the woman of Shunem does not explicitly mention her calamity and makes no overt supplication. Her rhetorical question, "did I ask my lord for a son?" (v. 28a), hints that her calamity is linked to her son. By citing her original reservations about the promised miraculous reward, she implies to him that her fears have indeed been realized: "Did I not say: 'Do not mislead me'? [Or: 'do not try to allay my concern'—see the discussion in the next paragraph]" (v. 28b). This second half of her statement closely resembles Reuben's protest to his brothers: "Did I not say to you, 'Do not harm the boy'? But you paid no heed" (Gen. 42:22). Nevertheless, she prefers to avoid an explicit accusation that the man of God did not listen to her and leaves this charge to be inferred from the reference to her earlier reaction, which she quotes not literally but interpretively.[25]

Then she had said to him, "do not delude (*ʾal tᵉkazzev*) your maidservant" (v. 16b); now she paraphrases that as "do not mislead [?] (*lo tašleh*) me." In Aramaic, the root *š.l.h* means 'err or make a mistake'; relying on this, many commentators interpret it as does Kimchi: "*tašleh* is like *tašgeh*—the Aramaic for *šᵉgagah* is *šalu* [e.g., Onkelos on Lev. 4:2]; that is, 'do not lead me astray. What use is a son if he doesn't live?' " If, however, *tᵉkazzev* means 'arouse false hopes', as suggested previously (pp. 242–43), then perhaps we should derive *tašleh* from the Hebrew root *š.l.h*, 'be tranquil or at ease', found elsewhere in the *qal* ("Why are the workers of treachery at ease [*šalu*]" [Jer. 12:1]) and in the *nifʿal* ("Now, my sons, do not be slack [*ʾal tiššalu*]" [2 Chron. 29:11], where the meaning is, "do not allow yourselves to be seduced into false tranquility"), but in the *hifʿil* only here. What is clear is that she repeats only the respectful term of address, "my lord," and not the humble "your servant," as she describes Elisha's part in the sequence of events that has brought her to her present straits: she did not ask him to repay her largesse with a boon, but he did not heed her warning and gave her an ephemeral blessing which has proven to be in truth a great misfortune. As on that prior occasion in Shunem, now too she does not request his assistance as an obligation to herself but states his responsibility to his own words and deeds. Had he not worked the miracle, she would have no claim upon him. Now, however, that his miracle has been undone, she expects him to rectify the situation and restore it.

Elisha at once grasps the implications of her harsh declaration, spoken while she clasps his feet. No further questions are needed for him to understand what has happened. He orders Gehazi to "take the staff of the man of God" and proceed to Shunem with the greatest possible alacrity ("tie up your skirts"), while avoiding any act or conversation that might delay him on the way or divert his attention from his mission; once there he is to place the staff on the boy's face (v. 29).[26] Hearing this, the Shunammite realizes that the man of God agrees with her in two respects: first, that the onus is on him to perpetuate the miracle he worked and that he has the power to do so. Second, his travel instructions to Gehazi resemble her own to the servant who brought her to Mount Carmel, as well as her repeated refusal to answer questions by hiding behind a laconic *šalom*. This provides retrospective confirmation of her assessment of the importance of the time factor: the man of God can revive a person who has passed away quite recently, but not necessarily a long-dead corpse (the dead man revived by contact with Elisha's bones was just being placed in his grave [2 Kings 13:21]).

At first glance it seems that Elisha has done everything that could be expected of him; nevertheless, the woman of Shunem is utterly dissatisfied. Just as at the end of the second scene she had reservations about the annunciation of the miracle of childbirth, now too she demurs at the manner in which the man of God has chosen to work the miracle of resurrection. Once again she is confident that she knows better than he when it comes to miracles that involve her. She vows, "as the Lord lives and as you live," that she will not leave him and will not go home unless he accompanies her and sees personally to the restoration of her child. We should not understand this as rejection in principle of the magical quality of resurrection by proxy, relying on one of the man of God's intimate possessions; she herself had laid the child down on Elisha's bed, no doubt in the belief that contact with items that had absorbed his power and sanctity could be of assistance. Nor should her stubborn insistence that Elisha do more than merely send Gehazi with his staff be compared with Naaman's anger that Elisha does not come out of his house to greet him and merely sends a messenger with instructions to bathe in the Jordan (2 Kings 5:11–12). For whereas Naaman had to overcome his arrogance and expectations, there is no suspicion that her pride might erect a barrier between her and the miracle. In fact, there is a great difference between the two: Naaman rages and starts for home, viewing the prophet's intention of acting from afar as a sign of apathy and contempt. The woman of Shunem, however, sees Elisha's desire to operate at a distance as an indication that he has failed to comprehend that his full personal involvement is imperative; fearing failure and loss of time, she refuses to leave his house until he agrees to come with her. As previously with the miraculous birth, here too they disagree as to the appropriate balance between his power to work the miracle and the degree to which she merits it. His prophetic overconfidence has misled him to believe that dispatching his staff is quite enough, whereas her exaggerated pious humility causes her to believe that the child, who has been given and taken back, will not be given a second time unless the man of God personally fights to perpetuate the miracle that has been recalled by heaven.

Elisha does the Shunammite's bidding in this matter, too, even though it is not yet clear to him whether the staff, carried by Gehazi, will revive the child. In the face of her self-confidence and determination, he probably begins to fear a mistake that cannot be rectified. Moreover, he may also be deeply impressed by the fact that the oath with which she binds herself to him—"As the Lord lives and as you live, I will not leave you!" (v. 30) is the very same oath with which he cleaved to Elijah when he knew that his master was about to leave him forever without naming him as his successor (2 Kings 2:2, 4, and 6). The servant who dared so unrelenting an expression of his expectations from the man of God and ultimately had his request filled by his master, now himself become the man of God, is able to evaluate the astonishing combination of tenacity and insistence and understand that pious awe does not always entail passive obedience, because there are situations in which the beneficiary of a miracle will not obtain it unless he himself has the courage to guide the hand of the miracle worker.[27]

Although the Shunammite's oath overtly and intentionally links our story with that of Elisha's consecration to prophecy,[28] the same cannot be said of the striking similarity between the description of Elisha's compliance with the Shunammite's instructions—"So he arose and followed her" (v. 30b)—and that of the compliance by Manoah, Samson's father, with his wife's bidding—"Manoah arose and followed his wife" (Judg. 13:11). In the first place, Elisha is unaware of this likeness, and certainly not motivated by it; second, the reader clearly perceives the full import and weight of Elisha's following the Shunammite without comparing his situation to that of Manoah. All the same, it is evident that the linguistic similarity is not a coincidence but a direct result of thematic affinity on the one hand, and of the designing force of the literary genre on the other. In stories of miraculous births and miraculous survivals of a child (which are generically very close), there is frequently an element of the superior wisdom of the wife and mother, who is not only wiser than the male protagonist but even manages to persuade him of the rightness of her path and gets him to follow her.[29]

II,3: Elisha—First by Proxy and Object and then by Prayer and Physical Contact (4:31–37)

The failure of the attempt by proxy to revive the child is recounted with great brevity, but it is made clear that Gehazi had followed Elisha's instructions to the letter. First, he started out as soon as he was sent (that is, before Elisha agreed to go himself).[30] Second, Elisha had told him, "place my staff on the face of the boy" (v. 29), and indeed Gehazi "had placed the staff on the boy's face." Third, when the child fails to respond, he takes the responsible initiative of rushing back to report to his master that "the boy has not awakened" (v. 31). The juxtaposition of the term *awakening* to the idiom "there was no sound or response (*wǝ-ʾeyn qol wǝ-ʾeyn qašev*)" also appears in Elijah's goading of the prophets of Baal to arouse Baal to respond with fire from heaven: "perhaps he is asleep and will wake up" (1 Kings 18:27); this is followed, at the conclusion of their abysmal failure, by the identical Hebrew idiom, slightly expanded: "but there was no voice, nor one who answered or heeded (*wǝ-ʾeyn qol wǝ-ʾeyn ʿoneh wǝ-ʾeyn qašev*)" (v. 29). At first glance this verbal echo of a pagan rite should lend an idolatrous hue to the reliance on the staff. However, because Gehazi was merely executing Elisha's instructions and because reviving the child with the help of Elisha's staff is not essentially different from splitting the Jordan with the help of Elijah's cloak (2 Kings 2:13–14), we should probably assume that the allusion to the prophets of Baal invokes not their mode of action but their lack of results. Just as the prophets of Baal were disappointed by Baal's silence, which Elijah had foreseen, so too Elisha and Gehazi's expectations that the child could be revived by proxy and an object prove false, whereas the Shunammite's prediction is confirmed.

Extreme brevity is appropriate to the account of Gehazi's attempt (v. 31) for another reason: his failure will be understood through contrast with the success of Elisha's actions, which are related in great detail (vv. 32–35). We are never told that Gehazi entered the house or what he saw there, whereas Elisha's arrival is described in two separate stages, each of which begins *wa-yavoʾ*, 'he came' (or 'went in'). Elisha is not surprised by the sight of the dead child, for he knew about this by inference from what the Shunammite had told him and explicitly from Gehazi's report. Hence the statement that "Elisha came into the house, and there was the boy, laid out dead on his bed" (v. 32) should be understood as describing the acute transition from abstract knowledge about the child's death to immediate sense perception of his body.[31] The reference to the fact that the child is "laid out dead on his bed" and the description of Elisha's closing himself up in the room—"He went in, shut the door behind the two of them" (v. 33)—reaffirm the correctness of the Shunammite's preparatory actions (v. 21).

Elijah, too, began his act of resurrection with prayer; there his actual words are cited, along with those of his second prayer, whereas his magico-medical actions are presented only in précis: "Then he stretched out over the child three times" (1 Kings 17:21). Here, by contrast, the proportions are reversed. Elisha's actions are described at length, but the narrative does no more than report the fact of his prayer: "he . . . prayed to the Lord" (v. 33b). This difference attests that despite the similarity of the two stories in subject and genre, they focus on different themes, evidently as a function of the different roles that the incidents play in the individual development of the two prophets. For Elijah the contrast is between his first prayer, which is not answered, and the amended prayer, which is;[32] for Elisha, however, the contrast is between the dispatch of his staff, which fails, and the direct personal effort that combines prayer with action and is crowned with success.

By prefacing prayer to action, Elisha is in a certain fashion continuing his humble submission to God, which began with the explicit admission that the Lord had concealed the Shunammite's calamity from him (v. 27). He is also expressing his awareness of the limitations on the independent operation of his prophetic power (which worked so wonderfully in the miracles of the birth of the Shunammite's son and Naaman's cure). On the other hand, we should not understand his lying atop the child's corpse as a contrast to Gehazi's placing of the staff there but as an intensification of that action. Only maximum contact between Elisha's body and the child's corpse—"his mouth on its mouth, his eyes on its eyes, and his hands on its hands"—can restore the boy to life. The inclusion of the eyes shows that the reference is not to artificial resuscitation. The description of the outcome—"the body of the child became warm" (v. 34)—indicates that the intention is a transfer of "the natural warmth emitted from his mouth and eyes, because most miracles are performed using a small natural stratagem" (Kimchi), or perhaps the "transfer of the vital force to the child from Elisha's limbs" (Gersonides).[33]

When the first vital sign—the warming of the body—appeared, Elisha stopped lying atop the child and "walked once up and down the room" (v. 35); then he returned and lay on him a second time. Kimchi, Gersonides, and Abravanel, who wished to limit the magico-medical element of Elisha's actions and enhance the religious aspect, strained to interpret this walking up and down as a sort of prayer. More plausible, however, is the explanation offered by Gunkel (*Geschichten von Elisa*, p. 27) and by Montgomery, namely, that Elisha walked back and forth in the small room in order to recover from the exertion of lying atop the child's body. In the story of Elijah and the widow's son, too, we are told that he stretched himself out on the child "three times," but not what he did in the intervals. Here, however, we have a concrete description of how Elisha stretched his muscles or gathered new strength before returning to lie atop the Shunammite son a second time. The inference to be drawn is that in this story the accent is on the great effort that the man of God must invest to perform the miracle of resurrection.

Elisha's persistence in his difficult mission is also highlighted by the enumeration of the classic vital signs that marked the child's return to life: "the boy sneezed seven times, and the boy opened his eyes" (v. 35). In the case of Elijah, by contrast, we are told only that "the child's life returned to his body, and he revived" (1 Kings 17:22). Thus Elisha did not desist from his efforts at resuscitation until he had counted no fewer than seven sneezes and had seen the child open his eyes. Then and only then did Elisha know that the miracle would not be again snatched from between his fingers. He summons Gehazi (who had been waiting outside the room) and tells him to call the Shunammite.

The Shunammite's entry into the room is also recounted in two stages, each of which begins *wa-tavoʾ*, 'she came'. First we read, "she came to him" (v. 36), evidently stopping just inside the threshold of the room, where

Elisha meets her and says, "pick up your son." The cold and matter-of-fact statement is in stark contrast to Elijah's warm and joyful cry to the widow of Zarephath: "See, . . . your son is alive" (1 Kings 17:23). Elijah carried the child down from the upper room himself; when he handed the boy to his mother he called on her to wonder at the miracle of her son's resurrection. Elisha, however, returns to his prior reliance on his servant to summon the Shunammite. Like a craftsman who has finished a job, he tells her to "pick up (*śᵉᵓi*)" her son, unaware that he is using the same dry and practical language employed by the boy's father when he told one of the harvesters, "Carry him (*śaᵓehu*) to his mother" (v. 19). All of this makes plain that in this great hour Elisha's thoughts are on reinstating his correct relations with the landlady. In a moment of crisis, when he heard her desperate oath, he did not stand on his dignity but complied with her demand and followed her back to Shunem. In retrospect, she was right and he wrong. All the same, now that he has succeeded in healing her affliction, he summons her and tells her, with classic understatement (which makes no reference to the miracle he has wrought), that the problem is solved.

For her part, the woman of Shunem fully accepts Elisha's desire to restore their relations to the previous situation: "she came and fell at his feet and bowed low to the ground" (v. 37a). By falling at his feet, she seeks to amend her assault on his dignity when she clasped his legs.[34] Her prostration before him returns her to the condition of the humble maidservant of the holy man of God, who has not only renewed his miraculous gift of life, but who also compassionately heeded her distress and done everything in his power to help her. When the disparity between his prophetic powers and personal limitations is overcome, the Shunammite ceases to guide Elisha. The supreme expression of this is her silent obedience when she picks up her son and leaves the prophet's room without saying a word.

Between This Story and Earlier Stories

Our close reading has shown that, in addition to the web of internal associations that link the various elements of the story, its rhetorical abundance is also supported by a network of external associations with earlier stories. We should now examine, from a broader perspective, the intimate links we have already noticed between the first part of the story of the woman of Shunem and the narrative of the birth of Isaac (Gen. 18:1–16 and 21:1–8), and between the second half of the story and the account of Elijah's resurrection of the son of the widow of Zarephath (1 Kings 17:8–24). In addition, we should consider something we have not discussed previously, namely, the nature of the relationship between our story and the short *legenda* that immediately precedes it at the beginning of chapter 4—the miracle of the jug of oil (vv. 1–7).

The main elements of stories that belong to the same genre are in any case quite similar; hence such parallels are not necessarily intentional. As a "miraculous birth story," the account of the birth of a son to the woman of Shunem (vv. 8–17) uses the same building blocks as the story of the birth of Isaac: a barren women with an elderly husband, meriting divine help as a reward for uncommon hospitality, a prophetic annunciation of the birth of the son, a reaction of skepticism or demurral at the annunciation, and, finally, the birth of the son at the promised time.[35] It is clear, though, that beyond their common generic affiliation, these two stories are also linked on the stylistic level and that the link is clearly intentional and rhetorically significant. In addition to mild but conspicuous linguistic echoes concerning the cause of the problem ("her husband is old" [v. 14] echoes "my husband is old" [Gen. 18:12]) and the reason for the hospitality ("who comes this way [ʿover ʿaleinu] regularly" [v. 9] closely resembles "you have come your servant's way [ʿavartem ʿal ʿavdᵉkem]" [Gen. 18:5]), the two central verses in our story are phrased like their parallels in the story of Abraham and Sarah:

The Annunciation:
I will return to you at this *season next year,* and Sarah shall have a *son.* (Gen. 18:14; cf. also v. 10)

At this *season next year,* you will be embracing a *son.* (v. 16)

The Fulfillment:
Sarah *conceived and bore a son* to Abraham in his old age, *at the season* of which God *had spoken.* (Gen. 21:2)

The woman *conceived and bore a son* at the [same] *season* [the next year] of which Elisha *had spoken* to her. (v. 17)[36]

Elisha evidently phrased his good tidings to echo the angel's proclamation to Abraham, so as to hint to the woman of Shunem that her magnanimous hospitality merits a miraculous reward similar to that received by the patriarchs for their exemplary hospitality. Contrary to what the thematic analogy and linguistic borrowing might lead us to expect, however, the Shunammite does not laugh inside or give verbal expression to skepticism that the good tidings can be realized. Instead, she attempts to deter the man of God from working a miracle that she may not deserve. Sarah's lack of faith retroactively exalts the wondrous miracle, whereas the pious humility of the Shunammite shifts the focus of the story from the prophet's ability to work a miracle to the permission given him to do so. Elisha is not aware of this shift; his lack of response indicates that he prefers to continue measuring the Shunammite according to Sarah's dimensions and to allow the impending fulfillment to refute her arguments and allay her fears. Superficially the narrator seems to share this perspective, since he reports the birth of the

Shunammite's son in language obviously borrowed from the story of Abraham and Sarah, language that highlights the full realization of Elisha's promise. Hence the child's death comes as a complete surprise not only to Elisha but also to the reader, who has been misled into ignoring the distinction between Sarah's skepticism and the Shunammite's humility and to attribute the same force to "as *Elisha* had spoken to her" as "of which *God* had spoken" to Abraham and Sarah. The Shunammite, however, clearly aware that she is not equal in stature to the nation's ancestors and cognizant that there must be some limit on the permission granted the man of God to modify the natural order, is not astonished by the death of her son and even manages to return Elisha to the pious humility that is the wellspring of his restored and intensified power to grant life.

As a story about the "miraculous survival of a boy," the second half of the story of Elisha in Shunem (vv. 18–37) is built of the same basic elements as the second half of the story of Elijah in Zarephath (1 Kings 17:17–24): a woman deserves assistance from the man of God by virtue of having hosted him (in the first half of the story); the child dies suddenly; the mother informs the man of God of the disaster (albeit in very different ways); the man of God locks himself up with the child's corpse in the upper room, prays for him, and treats him; and, finally, the child revives and is returned to his mother. To this we can add the strong stylistic affinities between the two stories, which we noted earlier (see above, pp. 238–39, and 251), and which disclose a two-edged contrast within the analogy. Elisha, like his great mentor, does manage to revive the dead; but Elijah is superior to Elisha in all respects, whereas the woman of Shunem is clearly superior to the widow of Zarephath. This alternation stems from the fact that the two prophets worked similar miracles at quite different stages in their careers. Elijah came to Zarephath at the beginning of his prophetic mission, a refugee in need of sustenance and shelter; every manifestation of opposition by the widow (from her initial refusal to feed him to her charge that he is responsible for the death of her son) was a challenge that stimulated him to develop his full prophetic capacity.[37] By contrast, Elisha, when he passed through Shunem from time to time, was among his own people, honored by his king, and accompanied by his servant. Already a prisoner of his earlier successes and public image, he required guidance from the beneficiary of his miracle to regain his vocation as a man of God. This difference between the tyro and mature prophets must be supplemented by their different characters and by Elisha's depiction as a member of the second generation of prophecy, confronted by the typical dangers of establishment and professionalization. Proof of sorts for the foregoing is that one can understand every detail in the story of Elijah and the widow without recourse to the story of Elisha and the Shunammite, whereas the second story requires the first as a contrasting background, which brings out Elisha's remoteness and restraint vis-à-vis Elijah's enthusiastic identification and overinvolvement, and the religious stature of the Shunammite vis-à-vis the positive but not exemplary character of the Tyrian widow.[38]

In summary, the narrator uses the story of Elijah's resurrection of the child the same way he uses the story of the miraculous birth of Isaac: allusions to an analogous incident in an earlier generation highlight the special problems of the later generation.

There is no such historical perspective between the story of the Shunammite and that of the miraculous jug of oil (4:1–7), because they deal with the same hero in the same period of his life, when he is already recognized as a prophet in Israel (the mentor of the sons of the prophets in one story, a "holy man of God" in the other). The two stories are written in the same idiom; both contain relics of the north Israel dialect (the second-person feminine with the suffix -*ki* in verses 2, 3, and 7). They also share stylistic elements: in the first story, too, Elisha is called "the man of God" (v. 7). Both the Shunammite (v. 10) and the widow, addressing him, call themselves "your maidservant" (v. 2). The widow says "you well know (*we-attah yadaʿta*)" (v. 1) just as the Shunammite says, "I well know (*hinneh naʾ yadaʿti*)" (v. 9). Elisha asks the widow, "what can I do for you?" (v. 2), just as he asks the Shunnamite, through Gehazi, "what can we do for you?" (v. 13).

As miracle stories they belong to a single genre but to two different subgenres: the first is a short *legenda* recounting a wondrous miracle, whereas the second is a long and complex narrative of the problems raised by a miracle that is withdrawn and then renewed. Furthermore, nowhere in the story of the Shunammite is the reader directed to the story of the miraculous jug of oil; it is not required as a necessary backdrop for understanding the story or spotlighting a particular theme. The only exception to this general rule is perhaps the Shunammite's closing the door of the upper room, an action thematically and stylistically identical with Elisha's instructions to the widow that is confirmed by the analogy as the appropriate step in the circumstances. This solitary link may be the result of a common theme; it certainly does not associate the two stories together in literary terms. Hence it seems likely that the sequential placement of the two stories is due to the editor. Rofé explained the juxtaposition by the principle of association, since the heroines of both stories ask the man of God to save their children, the first from slavery and the second from death (*Prophetical Stories*, p. 50). An ancient tradition—which can be traced back at least to Josephus (*Antiquities of the Jews* 9,4,2) and Targum Jonathan and then continues through various aggadic midrashim (*Pesiqta de Rab Kahana* 2,5)—intensifies this resemblance by identifying the widow as the wife of Obadiah, Ahab's majordomo, who at great risk to himself had concealed a hundred prophets in two caves and supplied them with bread and water: his merit as a sustainer and protector of the prophets exceeds even that of the Shunammite. We may also hypothesize, though, that the stories were placed one after the other not only because of their slight thematic affinity but also because on some deep level they provide *contrary* answers to two related questions: first, does the personality of the man of God limit his ability to work miracles? Second, what part does the beneficiary of the miracle play in the working of the miracle?

The similarity between Elisha's question to the widow—"What can I do for you?"—and his question to the Shunammite—"What can we do for you?"—is merely stylistic. Their functions in the plot are quite different: the widow is asked whether she knows of a way in which her wish can be fulfilled, whereas the Shunammite is asked what her wish is. Furthermore, whereas the Shunammite knows how to resurrect her son better than Elisha does, the widow is at pains even to understand his question and Elisha has to be more explicit: "What can I do for you? Tell me, what have you in the house?' " (v. 2). Long-winded redundancy of this sort is also found in his instructions to her: " 'Go,' he said, 'and borrow vessels outside, [i.e.] from all your neighbors, [more explicitly:] empty vessels, and not too few' " (v. 3). She indeed does precisely as she is told, as is highlighted by the repetition of the very terms of his instructions—"Then go in and shut the door behind you and your children" (v. 4) in the description of their execution—"She . . . shut the door behind her and her children" [v. 5]). Even now she does not grasp what the houseful of oil is meant for (or perhaps she is not sure she has the right to use it for profane purposes) and goes to tell the man of God about the miracle. Once again he gives her detailed instructions, which the reader could have foreseen: to sell the oil, pay off her debt, and support herself on the balance (v. 7).

Clearly the utter dependence of the beneficiary of the miracle on the man of God is recounted to praise her; in light of his immediate consent to help her and his wondrous ability to work a miracle from a distance, it is appropriate that she have full trust in him. Elisha did not accompany the widow to her house, because there was no need for this. The jug of oil began to give its bounty when she tipped it over the first vessel, kept doing so as long as her two sons continued to bring her empty vessels, and stopped on its own when the last vessel was full. The narrator makes this wondrous event more concrete through the short exchange between the widow and one of her sons, " 'Bring me another vessel.' He answered her, 'There are no more vessels,' " and through the explicit statement that "the oil stopped" (v. 6). Clearly he means to extol Elisha's full control over the miracle, which takes place in his absence: it begins and ends by itself, just at the appropriate times. We also learn about the obligations of the beneficiary of the miracle: to merit it ("your servant revered the Lord"), to trust in the prophet's ability to elicit a great miracle and heed his directive to gather many vessels ("and not too few"), to faithfully fulfill the instructions of the man of God ("she . . . shut the door behind her and her children"), and not to act without further guidance ("she came and told the man of God").

It is hard to imagine a more appropriate antithetical background to the story of the woman of Shunem than this short *legenda*. First of all, it buttresses Elisha's confidence that his own prophetic promise, omitting all reference to the Lord, can produce a miraculous birth and that his staff can work the miracle of resurrection. Second, it provides a tangible example of the naive pious devotion that Elisha and Gehazi could expect to receive from those loyal to the man of God and eager to honor him. The story of the woman of Shunem presents Elisha and his servant as captives of the concept of prophecy depicted in the *legenda*, a concept that was clearly prevalent and accepted. It reveals the grave and latent danger to the man of God posed by excessive confidence in his own powers and the imperative nature of his admirers' awareness that his sanctity is no barrier to human weaknesses. The widow cried out to Elisha, whereas the woman of Shunem clasped his feet. Both had implicit confidence in his ability to rescue them, but the Shunammite, unlike the widow, knew that she would enjoy the fruits of the miracle only if she were bold enough to guard its worker from error by listening to her own innate religious sensitivity and maternal intuition.

This dialectic tension between the two stories is not sufficient proof that the story of the Shunammite was intended a priori to present an alternative view to that of the story of the jug of oil. What is clear, however, is that their inclusion in the corpus of Elisha stories and the Book of Kings and their sequential arrangement reflects a broad view that legitimizes both of these remote positions. Even though we generally assume that the simpler position is earlier in time than the more complex one, we should take into account that the view presented in the *legenda* continued to have sworn partisans in later generations as well: for the corpus of Elisha stories includes another short *legenda*, meant to provide an overt counter, in the form of a corrective epilogue, to the position depicted in the story of the woman of Shunem.

The Story and Its Sequel: A Corrective Epilogue

The literary genre of the sequel to the story of the Shunammite (2 Kings 8:1–6), as well as its relationship to the story itself, have been discussed above (pp. 228–31). Here we shall read the epilogue closely and then consider its structure and meaning as a corrective epilogue.

The story begins with Elisha's instructions to "the woman whose son he had revived" to leave her house and land and go sojourn elsewhere so as to be spared the seven-year famine that the Lord has decreed on the land. In this opening, Elisha's manner differs from what we saw in the second half of the story of the Shunammite in three ways: first, he takes the initiative, because of his special concern for the welfare of the family of the child whom he had brought back to life; second, he mentions the name of the

Lord and attributes to Him the imminent climatic change; third, his prophetic power is not expressed by some rectification of the situation (for
example, by miraculously multiplying their food) but in clear and confident
foresight and wise counsel of how to be spared from the impending catastrophe. The narrator feels no reason to inform the readers whether the
Shunammite's old husband was still alive; evidently it is understood that
Elisha's dealings would be with the woman, just as in the story itself. Even
though her status within her family has not changed, her conduct now is
quite different—she silently does as she is told. In addition to the explicit
statement, "the woman had done as the man of God had spoken" (v. 2),
her absolute obedience is highlighted by what seems to be the superfluous
repetition of the terms of his instructions in the description of their implementation (just as in the story of the jug of oil):

The instruction: "*Arise* and *go with your household* and *sojourn* wherever you
can . . . for *seven years*" (v. 1).
The implementation: "The woman *arose,* and did in accordance with the
word of the man of God, and *went with her household* and *sojourned* in the
land of the Philistines for *seven years*" (v. 2).

Elisha's "sojourn wherever you can" left the selection of the place to her
own discretion; she chose the land of the Philistines (like Isaac, who went
to live there during the famine in the land, and "stayed there a long time"
[Gen. 26:1–3 and 8]). The narrator notes the length of her stay in the land
of the Philistines for a third time when he speaks of her return: "*At the end
of seven years* the woman returned from the land of the Philistines" (v. 3).
The purpose of this prolixity is evidently to tell us that just as she trusted
in the word of the man of God and left her house immediately (unlike Lot's
hesitancy, for example), so too she returned immediately at the end of the
seventh year without waiting to find out whether the drought had indeed
broken. With typical concentration on the main point, the narrator skips
over the intervening stages (Did she first go to her estate and discover that
it had been taken over by others? Had she heard about this in the land of
the Philistines?) and reports that she went to the king to request his assistance in amending the unfortunate result of her compliance with the advice of the man of God, namely, her dispossession from her house and land.
Readers who have surely asked themselves, seeing her quiet obedience, "is
this the woman of Shunem?" gain the impression that when she returns to
live among her people she is still imbued with her former trust in her capacity to petition the king of Israel for legal remedies on her own behalf.

Here the continuity of the plot is broken. To our great astonishment,
we learn that even though the woman has not asked Elisha for help (is he
still alive?), precisely at the moment of her arrival Gehazi is with the king,
responding to the latter's request that he tell him "all the great things that

Elisha has done" (v. 4). The emphatic notice taken of this extraordinary simultaneity indicates that, precisely at the moment when she appeared with her son, Gehazi was recounting the greatest of all great miracles—the resurrection of a dead child. Thus the presence of the Shunammite and her son provides tangible affirmation of this wonder; Gehazi declares with emotion: "My lord king, this is the woman and this is her son whom Elisha revived!" (v. 5). The king, exploiting the unexpected opportunity to verify the incredible story through this independent and reliable witness, interrogates the woman as to the details of the deed and hears about the miraculous resurrection for a second time, this time from the beneficiary of the miracle herself.

The woman had stated her complaint when she first arrived (v. 5), so after he hears her story the king can respond immediately: "she told him [the story]; so the king assigned an officer (*saris*) to her and instructed him . . . " (v. 6). This makes it clear that his response is not necessarily based on the justice of her suit but is principally a gesture toward the miracle and its worker and a reaction to what he has seen with his own eyes. The king further expresses this sentiment by appointing one of his officers to handle her affair,[39] ordering him to restore to her not only all her property but even what she had not requested: "all the produce of the fields from the time she left the land until now" (v. 6)! With this royal generosity the short story reaches its dramatic conclusion. The heroine of the story (and its readers) realize that, in addition to the first miracle that Elisha had worked at his own initiative, a second miracle has now been worked in his absence but through his power.

This is another way in which the epilogue differs from the main story: not only does Elisha (with no need for advice from Gehazi) help the Shunammite save herself from the famine; his miraculous protection is effective from afar even when he is not present (this time with effective reliance on Gehazi), in a sphere in which, ostensibly, she has no need of his help—speaking on her behalf to the king. As in the story of the jug of oil, where the miracle that the oil stops flowing completes the miracle that it started flowing, here too prophetic assistance is completed in a double miracle: the woman is saved from famine on the one hand and saved from the results of being saved on the other.

Even though the style of the epilogue is not that of the story of the woman of Shunem (see above, p. 229), it resembles it formally in one way: its structure is identical to the uniform structure we found in the five scenes of the main story (see table 7.2). Just as we are told, in each scene, about two actions performed by one of the protagonists, here too we learn of two deeds (this time extremely successful) that Elisha executed on behalf of the Shunammite. In the first part of the *legenda* he counsels her to find sustenance during the years of famine; in the second half, her house, fields, and the revenues of the seven years are returned to her on his account.

TABLE 7.2: The Structure of the Epilogue of the Story of the Woman of Shunem

The Persistent Prophetic Concern Yields Another Reward: Food and a House
(Somewhere): Elisha succeeds twice, with good counsel and succor from afar (8:1–6)
1. Food during the famine, thanks to Elisha's advice—"Arise and go with your household"— and the woman's compliance—"The woman did in accordance with the word of the man of God."
2. The house, fields, and produce of her fields are returned to her, thanks to the miraculous coincidence of Gehazi's account to the king: "This is the woman and this is her son."

The parallelism between these two gifts and what she had done for him in the first scene—she fed him and built an upper chamber for him—means that the present action is not only due to an enduring prophetic concern for beneficiaries of miracles (lest the child die a second time), but also to his gratitude for what the woman gave him when she was rich: food and lodging.

In sum, then, the epilogue is meant to amend the main story by tying together what remains separated in it. In the story, the prophetic ability of the man of God is impeded by the limits of his personality, whereas here no aspersions are cast on his astonishing ability or his philanthropic personality. As a barrier against any criticism, the reader is here clearly shown that the miracle worker does not need to be prodded by the beneficiary of the miracle, and certainly does need not her guidance. On the contrary, by virtue of her humble obedience she merits the miracle, even in that very sphere in which she had totally rejected his assistance.

Thus the corpus of the Elisha stories depicts two different paradigms for a man of God and the correct attitude toward him. One is realistic: the man of God is described as a great and wonderful man but susceptible to human frailties; his devotees must be aware of and balance these frailties by taking an active role in the implementation of the miracle. The second model is idealistic: the man of God is described as the perfect bearer of the word of God who fully exhausts his prophetic potential. In 2 Kings 8:1–6, the alternate paradigm is not represented by an alternate story intended to replace the story of the Shunammite with a different version of the same events (as was done by the author of Chronicles with a number of stories from the books of Samuel and Kings),[40] but by the addition of an epilogue. The original story is not cast aside, but its sting is removed by a sequel that moves in a different direction and represents a different paradigm. This is not a naive harmonizing attitude that throws out of court the very possibility that the man of God might suffer human weaknesses, but a harmonizing effort that restores the situation to its correct state. Looking from the epilogue back to the beginning, what happened in Shunem and on

Mount Carmel is not a typical situation but a temporary lapse, which Elisha managed to overcome when he became aware of it. Elisha's greatness was not only that he got up and followed the woman of Shunem when he realized that this was necessary, but also that, at some later date, he spoke to her in such a fashion that, without questioning his instructions, she got up and left her house for seven years.

Those who lean toward one or the other of the two paradigms remain at loggerheads till this very day. The advocates of the realistic position view human frailties as a direct result of the sharp distinction between the Creator and His creatures; in the critical attitude to every individual, *qua* human being, they see a necessity that is not to be condemned; and they consider the image of the grande dame of Shunem to be an extraordinary depiction of reverence for sanctity that is not blind, and of shared responsibility accompanied by a true humility that is intended to serve as an example for the generations.

APPENDIX

Minor Characters in Biblical Narrative

The number of characters who appear in biblical narrative, of every period, is extremely small. Even in narratives with a long, involved plot, such as the story of Joseph or the Book of Esther, no single scene has more than two or three active characters. Only rarely does the dialogue develop into a three-way conversation. Not only are there few characters; the focus is always on the deeds of the protagonists, while the fate and character of the minor personages is neglected. We hear, for example, a great deal about Joseph, very little about Reuben, and nothing about Naphtali. In effect, the sons of Jacob are fused into a collective character whose actions, travels, and reactions are sketched in general terms only. About David's younger sons we know nothing other than their names and the fact that they participated in two fateful banquets (2 Sam. 13:27–36; 1 Kings 1:9 and 25). Only from indirect hints can we infer that they fled Jerusalem with their father during Absalom's rebellion (2 Sam. 15:16). Scripture has nothing to say as to whether they participated in the war against their brother (or perhaps sat out the conflict), their reaction to David's lamentation for his dead son, or their stance in the ongoing struggle between David and Joab. The intriguing question of why the raw material for so many fascinating stories was never exploited will be addressed here.

Gunkel explained it as reflecting a primitive level of social development, in which the individual is not sharply distinguished from the collective. In addition, he held that the narrators of antiquity were unable to appreciate and delineate individual traits or handle scenes with many actors. Nonetheless, Gunkel believed that there was some compensation for these social, psychological, and literary limitations in that the focus on the protagonist endows biblical narrative with greater clarity.[1] This type of explanation rests on the assumption that the storytellers of all ages and cultures aspire to the same artistic goal; hence, to understand and evaluate a work properly we need only locate it along the line of evolution from the primitive to the highly developed. However, just as it is impossible to consider a relief to be a primitive form of sculpture, or opera to be a more highly developed form of drama, neither can we judge a medieval statue according to the criteria appropriate for a Renaissance sculpture. Every art form is governed by its own specific norms, conditioned by its possibilities and limitations; every age has its own unique modes of expression, which are in keeping with its goals and means. Only the assumption that fundamentally different forms of expression can legitimately exist side by side can enable us to uncover the formal uniqueness of biblical narrative and to understand the message embodied in this specific form.

Instead of attempting to explain the extremely limited cast, we must first recognize it as a literary fact, determine its scope, and try to understand its artistic uses by the narrator. Unless we do so, we will ask the wrong questions and tend to over-interpretation, as happened to Hertzberg, a sensitive commentator who was amazed that only two verses are devoted to the description of Michal's restoration to David. "So Ish-bosheth sent and had her taken away from her husband, Paltiel son of Laish. Her husband walked with her as far as Bahurim, weeping as he followed her; then Abner said to him, 'Go, return,' and he returned" (2 Sam. 3:15–16). Hertzberg interprets the narrator's silence about Michal's reaction to her parting from Paltiel and restoration to David as an expression of the fact that "she is merely a pawn in the political game."[2] However, the fact that Abner's decisiveness, in the face of Paltiel's grief at parting from Michal, is described, whereas the narrator abandons Michal at Baḥurim, near Jerusalem, and leaves it for the reader to assume that she reached Hebron where she met David, indicates that the narrator focuses on the political gesture made by Ish-bosheth and Abner; the feelings of the woman who is Saul's daughter and Paltiel's wife, as well as the feelings of the husband of her youth, who is now king, are irrelevant to his purpose.[3]

To be sure, the account of Michal's restoration to David is especially brief, but it is by no means exceptional. Hence it is a good example of what Kaufmann termed the "elliptical character of the biblical narrative," or of what Alter called "the drastic selectivity" of the ancient Hebrew narrator.[4] All narrators, in every time and place, select and reject, lengthen and abbreviate, illuminate and obscure in keeping with their own rhetorical intent and the literary conventions of their audience. The tendency of the biblical narrators to skip a stage in the plot and let readers fill in the gap[5] disturbed readers as early as the Septuagint translators[6] and Josephus. Their additions to the body of the narrative reflect not only their anxiety that a Hellenistic reader might otherwise misunderstand the text,[7] but also his literary taste and expectations of a plausible and lucid sequence of events.[8] Since modern readers share these expectations, Kaufmann and Alter try to dissuade us from imitating the Septuagint translators and Josephus by imposing our own literary assumptions on the text. Kaufmann does this by noting the prevalence of such lacunae in the plot, Alter, by trying to uncover the aesthetic meaning of this method.[9]

This elliptical quality is especially evident in the appearance and disappearance of minor characters from the narrative. We are told how Moses' sister keeps an eye on the reed boat from afar and gives sage advice to Pharaoh's daughter, even though her own birth (and that of her brother Aaron) are never mentioned (Exod. 2:1–8). Similarly, Elijah sends his servant on various errands while he is praying for rain on Mount Carmel, but nothing is said about where, when, and how the servant entered his service, what the young man was doing during the prophet's miraculous run to Jezreel (1 Kings 18:42–46), or when and where he rejoined his master (ibid., 19:3). This freedom to focus on or ignore minor characters is displayed in the last sentence of the story of the binding of Isaac, which tells of Abraham's return to Beersheba with his two servants but makes no mention of Isaac: "Abraham then returned to his servants, and they arose and went together to Beer-sheba; and Abraham stayed in Beer-sheba" (Gen. 22:19). The midrash concluded from this omission that Isaac did not go back with them,[10] while the literal exegetes stressed that the self-evident fact that he accompanied his father does not have to be stated explicitly.[11] We modern readers share both the exegetical conclusion of the literalists and the stylistic sensitivity of the homilists. We shall not attempt to explain here why Abraham's departure with the servants is stressed but Isaac's presence is ignored. Suffice it to say that this is clearly a formal expression of the subordination of the secondary to the chief character.[12]

The elliptical style obscures the nonessential but does not always totally eliminate it. Job's wife is not mentioned in the last chapter of the book, but if we insist on knowing what happened to her we may infer from this very silence that the Lord restored her as he restored her husband. More drastic is the lacuna that neither conjecture nor imagination can fill, because of a basic lack of information. What was the marital background to the attempts by Potiphar's wife to seduce Joseph? Why did Achitophel betray David? What were Bathsheba's feelings about her husband Uriah? What was Ahab doing on Mount Carmel from the morning until after the massacre of the prophets of Baal? In general, then, the actions and feelings of secondary characters are described only when they are required to advance the plot or to shed light on another actor, and not out of a genuine interest in these characters themselves. Protagonists are subject to a different rule. Their personality is an organic part of the theme of the story; hence the narrator paints them in greater detail—not only what is essential to an understanding of the plot, but also what is necessary for a fuller knowledge of their distinctive nature. The deeds of the forefathers can serve as a guide to posterity only if the narrative depicts the doers as well as their deeds. For this reason the criterion for identifying protagonists is not how many of their deeds are recounted in the narrative, but the extent to which they themselves are described. In most stories, only one main character is portrayed in detail, although quite a few narratives do have two or even three main characters: Judah and Tamar; Samuel and Eli; Naomi, Ruth, and Boaz.

A primary function of some minor characters is to move the plot forward; others endow the narrative with greater meaning and depth. The supporting cast in the story of the birth of Samuel (1 Samuel 1) numbers three: Peninnah, whose cruel scorn gives the plot its initial impetus; Elkanah, who retards its progress with vain words of consolation; and Eli, who first retards the plot with his rebuke and later, having recognized his error, pushes it toward its climax with his blessing of Hannah. Elkanah also provides a contrast to his wife, the heroine of the story, thereby contributing to her well-realized portrait. With regard to minor characters who further the plot, commentators need only determine that they are secondary characters and explain their part in the sequence of events. By contrast, when it comes to supporting characters who add a third dimension to the story, commentators must uncover their expressive function in the narrative context. We shall try, therefore, to define and classify the *expressive* auxiliary roles played by the minor characters.

Biblical narrative is meant to instruct and motivate rather than to impress and delight. It appeals more to the will and the intellect than to the senses and the sentiments. As Erich Auerbach has so convincingly shown, the biblical narrator strives for a meaningful presentation rather than for a visual one. It is not joy in a description that "imitates" life, in all its variety, that motivates the biblical narrator, but the drive to uncover relationships and to illuminate connections and to give narrative form to a particular conception of life.[13] Hence the biblical narrator prefers to shine the spotlight on the main lines of development rather than provide "uniform illumination" of the entire situation. Peninnah, Elkanah's other wife, is not mentioned as participating in the yearly pilgrimages after the birth of Samuel, because the narrator sees no need to magnify the miracle bestowed on Hannah by humbling her rival. On the other hand, a minor character's opposing stance may serve to clarify the hero's dilemma at a particular crossroads and lend force and significance to his decision. Joshua's advice to Moses ("My lord Moses, arrest them!" [Num. 11:28]), and the confidential advice of King Ahab's messenger to Micaiah son of Imlah ("speak favorably" [1 Kings 22:13]) provide the two prophets with an opportunity to articulate their unconventional values. Such prompting of the protagonist may also provide a post factum explanation of events. Michal's contempt for the king's leaping and whirling before the slavegirls and his servants' fear of revealing the death of Bathsheba's son to their master enable David to explain his exceptional and unexpected acts (2 Sam. 6:20–23 and 12:17–23)

More than prompting the hero to an explanation of his actions (an explanation intended for readers as well), though, minor characters help clarify situations by serving as background. The story of Elijah's attempt on Mount Carmel to bring Israel back to its God begins with two introductory scenes. In the first, the severity of the famine is illustrated by the description of how the king and his majordomo go in search of fodder for the starving livestock (1 Kings 18:1–6). The second scene contains a relatively lengthy depiction of the terror that strikes the God-fearing Obadiah when he hears Elijah's demand that he go summon his royal master (ibid., 7–15). This meeting teaches both Elijah and the reader how terrifying and threatening is the prophet's image in the eyes of his own people, who blame him for the tribulations of the raging famine.

In the story of Naaman's leprosy, which focuses on the double miracle that proves that "there is a prophet in Israel" (2 Kings 5:8), the supporting cast is particularly large: the young girl from the land of Israel, Naaman's wife, the king of Aram, the king of Israel and his ministers, and Naaman's servants. They do not all fit into the same category, from the standpoint of narrative art, but can obviously be divided into two camps with regard to their attitude toward the prophet—which runs counter to our expectations. All the Arameans (from page to king) are willing to believe in the prophet's ability to perform miracles; it is the Israelites who resist, except for the young captive. Thus the contrast between Naaman, the commander of the enemy army, and Gehazi, the servant of the prophet of the Lord, is underscored by applying their attitudes to their respective national groups. This prepares the ground not only for the merciful healing of Naaman, but also for the terrible affliction visited on Gehazi.

Irony is another way to illuminate the situation or the main character: a sage and true remark by a servant or adviser casts the vacillations and blunders of his master or his king in an ironic light. The sensible response by Jonadab son of Shimeah, when he points out the implausibility of the rumor that all the king's sons have been murdered, dramatizes how David's guilt feelings deprived him of his common sense (2 Sam. 13:30–35). Similarly, in the story of the Levite's concubine, the servant's suggestion that they spend the night in the Jebusite city lends a retrospective irony to his master's preference for Israelite Gibeah: it is the Levite's naive assumption of the moral superiority of his own people that brings him to the Sodom-like town (Judg. 19:10–13). The narrator exploits this servant for other ends as well; to understand them correctly, we must note precisely where the narrator mentions him (vv. 3, 9, 11–13, and 19) and where he ignores him (vv. 4–8, 10, 14–18, and 20–30).[14] On this point, though, another example of a servant who is wiser than his master will better serve our purpose: the story of Saul's search for the asses (1 Samuel 9). Here the servant's superiority over Saul is emphasized: he provides his master with both advice and money. On the one hand, the servant is the providential messenger who unwittingly brings together God's chosen leader and the prophet who has been commanded to anoint him king. At the same time, the servant who guides his master serves to highlight the naiveté, simplicity, and humility of the country boy who is destined to rule over the people of Israel. Later, when Saul is transformed into "another man," he must send the servant away and face the prophet and his mission alone. Finally, at the end of the episode, he again makes use of the servant to conceal the fateful change that has overtaken him: "Saul's uncle asked him and his servant, 'Where did you go? . . . What did Samuel say to you *[plural!]?*' Saul answered his uncle, 'He certainly told *us* that the asses had been found.' But he did not tell him anything of what Samuel had said about the kingship" (1 Sam. 10:14–16).

We shall conclude with the use of minor characters as a device for the moral evaluation of the protagonist. This evaluation, which is one of the chief concerns of the biblical authors of every period, is almost never expressed explicitly, but only indirectly, in the language of deeds and their consequences. Goitein showed that it would have been possible to omit the characters of Orpah and the kinsman who refuses to redeem Ruth without doing violence to the plot, and that their sole purpose is to emphasize the merit and praiseworthiness of Ruth and Boaz.[15] Indeed, an encounter with a *positive* minor character, whose values and conduct reflect the prevailing norms, enables the narrator to depict the hero's exceptional virtue without explicitly praising him. In this way, the confident faith and calm wisdom of Samson's mother is contrasted, to her credit, with the lack of faith and limited understanding of her husband, Manoah (Judges 13). Similarly, David rises above his men's reasonable fear of going to save Keilah (1 Sam. 23:3–5), their infectious despair after the raid on Ziklag (1 Sam. 30:6), their simplistic morality when their enemy Saul is within their reach in the cave (1 Sam. 24:4–7), and their selfish desire to divide up the spoils only among the men who had fought (1 Sam. 30:22–25). To David's men one should add his eldest brother, Eliab (1 Sam. 17:28–30), his wife Michal (2 Sam. 6:20–23), and, above all, his cousins and generals Joab and Abishai, from whose violence he so often dissociated himself (1 Sam. 26:8–11; 2 Sam. 3:28–39, 16:9–12, 19:22–24; 1 Kings 2:5–6). On the other hand, his confrontation with Uriah the Hittite, who refuses to go home, implicitly condemns David's sin with his officer's wife (2 Sam. 11:11). And Joab's modification of David's treacherous secret order to arrange for Uriah's death indicates that David's sin has made him sink even lower than the sons of Zeruiah (ibid., vv. 16–25).

The condemnation of the hero may be intensified by contrasting him with a positive character or by comparing him with a negative character. Saul is castigated for his moral decline by his bodyguards' refusal to obey his command to murder the priests of Nob, and by his recourse to his unscrupulous foreign servant, Doeg the Edomite (1 Sam. 22:16–19). The heroes of the biblical narrative and its audience shared the belief that foreigners have no fear of God and hence no hesitations about sinning. As is usual in the case of minor characters, the extraordinary righteousness of the sailors on the Tarshish-bound ship does not receive a full-fledged literary explanation. Their conduct is described in detail in order to give ironic perspective to the Hebrew prophet's flight from his God: while they pray, Jonah sleeps! Given the biblical tendency to identify the character of a messenger with the contents of his message (2 Sam. 18:27), Joab's choice of a *Cushite* servant to convey the news of his victory over Absalom indicates his desire to blur the painful personal aspect of the death of the rebellious son while stressing the military achievement (ibid., 21–32).[16]

We began by emphasizing how little attention biblical narrative pays to minor characters, only to end by expounding their great importance to the biblical narrator. It is precisely the option of saying so little about them that makes them such an effective means for accenting the main issue. Given the tendency of biblical narrative to theological understatement and its eschewing of pronounced ethical value judgments, it is frequently the minor characters who provide the key to the message of the story. Beyond their function of furthering the plot (by providing advice and assistance, or through acts of interference and resistance), they have a definite expressive role—the indirect characterization of the protagonist and the implied evaluation of his or her deeds. This is done mainly through comparison and contrast: the unexpected is set against the expected and conventional, the exceptional against the norm, and conscience against utilitarian calculations. Minor characters can also participate in the ironic reversal of social conventions: the confident and resourceful activity of a woman versus her husband's passiveness and resignation; the error of king and master versus the prudence of their servants; and even the defiance of a Hebrew prophet versus the obedience of gentiles. The fact that the biblical narrator does not sanctify the social order but only religious and ethical values enables him to use minor characters to express criticism of the protagonist or to make a low-ranking person the hero of the story. For the basic intention of biblical storytelling is not to glorify important persons and institutions, or even to reinforce adherence to abstract beliefs and concepts, but to depict flesh-and-blood characters whose rises and falls serve us as models and as warnings.

NOTES

1. The Birth of Samuel

1. Segal (*Books of Samuel*, pp. 18 and 26 [introduction] and p. 20 [commentary] suggests that the "Birth and Youth of Samuel" (1:1–2:11, 2:18–21, and ch. 3) was written by the author of the Book of Samuel, who incorporated passages from the "Eli and Ark of the Covenant Source" into his story. Noth ("Samuel in Silo," pp. 391–93) hypothesizes that the author of chapter 3 is responsible for all of the complex narrative in the first three chapters, making use of two sources, "The Birth of Samuel and his Early Service in Shiloh" and the "Sins of the Sons of Eli," which he wove together and continued.

2. The unexpected references to the sons of Eli ("Hophni and Phinehas, the two sons of Eli, were priests of the Lord there *[šam]*" [1:3b]) in chapter 1, and to the Ark ("where *[šam]* the Ark of God was" [3:3b]) in chapter 3 may have been added to reinforce the melding of the two strands. The first seems to be meant to anticipate the sins of Hophni and Phinehas, related in chapter 2, while the second anticipates the Philistine's seizure of the Ark in chapter 4. Both clauses seem to draw on the language of 4:4—"there *[šam]* Eli's two sons, Hophni and Phinehas, were in charge of the Ark of the Covenant of God." In any case, there is no substance to Eslinger's suggestion (*Kingship of God*, pp. 70 and 76) that 1:3b should be understood as contrasting the ritual activity of Elkanah, who makes the pilgrimage to Shiloh to offer sacrifice to the Lord, and the passivity of Hophni and Phinehas, who are "simply there." Eslinger's proposal ignores the highly stereotypical phrasing of this aside (another example of the paradigm: "where *[šam]* (lived) Ahiman, Sheshai, and Talmai, the Anakites"—Num. 13:22), which makes it impossible to attribute such a specific meaning to it. This attempt to resolve a thematic difficulty by considering it to be a sophisticated rhetorical device is characteristic of the exegetical price that Eslinger pays for his harmonizing reading of 1 Samuel 1–12. Similarly, the impressive endeavors to uncover the common aspects of this large literary unit made by Willis—who draws analogies between the House of Eli and the House of Saul ("An Anti-Elide Narrative Tradition"); by Polak, who focuses on the narrative method ("Main Strand," pp. 64–93); and by Polzin, who presents chapters 1–3 as a sort of parable for the rise and fall of the House of Saul (*Samuel*, pp. 19–54)—fail, in my opinion, to do justice to the stories that constitute it. Reading each story separately is a condition for understanding its individuality; hence such a reading must precede interpreting it as a component of the larger unit.

3. See above, pp. 51ff.

4. In the story of Job, too, the opening prose scenes are organized into two parts distinguished by formal indications. The prefatory exposition (1:1–5) is followed by two parts, each comprising two scenes, the first set in heaven and the second on earth. The heavenly scenes conclude with Satan taking leave of the Lord (1:12, 2:7a); those on earth end with statements concerning Job's steadfastness in

the face of his trials: "For all that, Job did not sin nor did he cast reproach on God" (1:22); "For all that, Job said nothing sinful" (2:10).

5. The translators and commentators split into two camps—those who assign all of verse 19 to the previous scene, and those who align it with the following scene. Both camps seem to share the latent assumption that the break between the two parts cannot fall in the middle of the verse. But midverse scene changes are fairly common in scriptural narrative. See, for example, 2 Sam. 12:15; Jon. 3:3; Job 2:7; Ruth 1:19; and perhaps also Exod. 2:15.

6. The compound source reference reflects the fact that Hannah's prayer intervenes between the two parts of the sentence in both the Masoretic text and the Qumran Samuel scroll (4QSam^a). In the Septuagint, though, the entire sentence follows the prayer (2:11). I have bracketed the second half of the sentence because I believe it to be secondary (see above, pp. 3–4). If I am right, these concluding statements were much more similar to each other in the original text than they are in the text now before us.

7. The discrepancy in number found in the Masoretic text here—literally, "then *they* would return to *his* place"—is not in the Qumran text, which reads, "the man would return to his place"; nor is it in a number of medieval Hebrew manuscripts—"they would return to *their* place."

8. The verbal root is missing from the Qumran text and has been supplied from the parallel Septuagint version. The superfluous "there" of the Masoretic text—"they bowed low there before the Lord"—may well attest that it was originally preceded, in this textual tradition as well, by the verb *leave*.

9. The correlation is not impaired by the fact that the first homiletical explanation of the name is at the beginning of part II and not in part I; such explanations are not meant to demarcate the sections of the story but only to give the narrative an additional dimension by focusing its three themes in a single name with three corresponding interpretations.

10. As was previously noted, the epilogue is not really a scene in the literary sense. For simplicity's sake, however, it is so designated here and below, whenever we are dealing with its content and structure rather than its narrative mode.

11. The alternation of scenes of preparation and implementation is fairly frequent in scriptural narrative. The story of Job's tribulations devotes the scenes in heaven to discussions of Job's righteousness and the permission received by Satan to put him to the test, while the scenes set on earth describe Satan's actions and Job's reactions to them. Each of the four parts of the Book of Ruth is divided into three scenes, of which the first describes preparations, the second reports implementation, and the third evaluates the new situation. Each of the four parts of the story of the man of God from Judah (1 Kings 13) has two scenes, of which the first serves as an opening and bridge and only the second moves the plot forward (see above, pp. 135–36).

12. Scriptural narrative found many ways to satisfy the desire to avoid delaying the start of the plot until after the exposition is complete. The story of Micah's idol (Judg. 17) opens with a minimal exposition—"There was a man in the hill country of Ephraim whose name was Micah"—and continues immediately with Micah's confession to his mother that he stole the money. Only after we are told that his mother consecrated the money to "the house of Micah" (v. 4) do we encounter the bulk of the exposition—information about Micah's house of God and about the period and its nature (vv. 5–6). The story of the battle at Michmas (1 Samuel 14) opens with Jonathan's direct speech, proposing to his attendant that they cross over to the Philistine garrison, continues with a four-verse exposition, and then, because of the length of the exposition, repeats Jonathan's words to his attendant. Similarly, in the prophecy about the two baskets of figs (Jeremiah 24), the information about

the historical situation is in a parenthetical statement (v. 1b) inserted into the description of the vision, which begins in verse 1a and continues in verse 2.

13. Driver's prooftext (*Notes*, pp. 5–6) for the alternation of the future (*yiqṭal*) and inverted perfect (*wᵉ-qaṭal*) to express a habitual or repeated action is Exod. 17:11—"whenever Moses held up (*yarim*) his hand, Israel prevailed (*wᵉ-gavar*); but whenever he let down (*yaniaḥ*) his hand, Amalek prevailed (*wᵉ-gavar*)"—along with Exod. 18:26 and Judg. 2:18–19. A detailed description of repeated action is also found in the passage dealing with the iniquities of Eli's sons (1 Sam. 2:12–17). In the first and last verses of this passage, which constitute an *inclusio*, we find the simple past (*qaṭal*) and inverted future (*wᵃ-yiqṭol*), whereas in the actual description the verbs are consistently in the habitual forms (except for the unexpected *wa-yomer* at the beginning of v. 16). By contrast, in the description of Absalom's stealing of the hearts of the Israelites (2 Sam. 15:1–6), the habitual forms occur at the start and end of the passage (vv. 2 and 5), while the dialogue between Absalom and the litigant is reported as a one-time event (all the verbs of speech are in the inverted future), which is generalized by the expression "any [or every] man" and the vague identification "from one of the tribes of Israel" in verse 2. Less straightforward is the alternation of habitual and one-time forms in Judg. 6:1–6, 1 Sam. 27:7–11, and Job 1:4–5.

14. Joüon and Muraoka, *Grammar of Biblical Hebrew* (§171f.) gives the following examples of *waw* denoting causal contrast ("even though"): Gen. 18:27 and 48:14; 1 Sam. 12:12.

15. Driver (*Notes*, pp. 7–8) surveys the various views; this survey was brought up to date by McCarter (*I and II Samuel*, pp. 51–52). The right answer may well be that of Sarfatti, "Arithmetical Fractions," p. 5), whose hypothesis was unknown to McCarter. According to Sarfatti, *ʾappayim* means "double" or "twofold," and is derived from *pim* (1 Sam. 13:21), with the addition of a prosthetic *alef*. The expression *manah aḥath ʾappayim* would thus mean, "twice a single portion." This was also the gloss of R. Joseph Kara. Aberbach in "Manah 'achat 'appayim," pp. 350–53, also derived *ʾappayim* from *pim*, but his rather forced interpretation is "a single portion worth one *pim* of silver." The objections raised by Deist in " 'appayim' (1 Sam. 1:5) < *pym?*," pp. 205–208, to viewing the *alef* of *ʾappayim* as prosthetic had already been answered by Sarfatti. Deist's proposed emendation—*ʾavusah*, 'fat'—seems very farfetched.

16. Midrash Samuel 1,8 imaginatively supplements the text and reports Peninnah's crude taunts: "What did Peninnah say to her? 'Did you buy your son a scarf, and your second one a tunic?' "

17. On the superiority of the Peshitta text, see Driver and Segal ad loc.

18. The prevalent attitude of a patriarchal society, namely, that the husband's love depends to a large extent on his wife's fertility, was expressed by Leah after she was delivered of her first-born son, Reuben: "The Lord has seen my affliction, and now my husband will love me" (Gen. 29:32).

19. As was pointed out by Adar, *Biblical Narrative*, p. 18.

20. For the first five verses Elkanah is the main character, both as the principal actor and as the head of the family, and all the other characters are defined with reference to him: "He had two wives" (v. 2); "his wife Peninnah" (v. 4). Starting in verse 6, though, the story focuses on Hannah and her destiny. This is indicated formally by the reference to Peninnah as "her cowife" (v. 6) and to Elkanah as "her husband" (v. 8).

21. *ʾaharei ʾoklah bᵉ-šiloh:* The Septuagint's "after *they* had eaten," referring to the entire family except for Hannah, seems preferable, although Driver believes that the Masoretic reading can be explained by taking *ʾoklah*, with no *mappiq* in the final *heh*, as an infinitive construct with the feminine termination, as in Jer. 12:9,

"bring them to devour (*l^e-ʾoklah*)." This is also the gloss offered by Rashi, Kimchi, and Gersonides. The indication of place, "in Shiloh," is surprising, since it would seem obvious that until they go home to Ramah (v. 19) the action is set in Shiloh. Responding to this difficulty, Wellhausen (*Der Text der Bücher Samuels*, p. 38) proposed modifying the word division and reading *ʾaharei ʾakol ha-b^ešelah* ("after the eating of the boiled [meat]"), on the basis of Num. 6:19, "the shoulder of the ram when it has been boiled"). Klostermann (*Die Bücher Samuelis*, p. 2), for his part, suggested the reading *ba-liškah* instead of *b^e-šiloh* (i.e., "after the eating in the chamber"), relying on the expanded Septuagint version of verse 18 ("she came to the chamber (*ha-liškathah*) and ate." Even though this emendation is more radical than Wellhausen's, it may be preferable on literary grounds: to clarify Hannah's movements, it is reasonable to assume that the narrator would tell us not only where she went ("near the doorpost of the temple of the Lord") but also where she came from and returned to (the chamber).

22. A midrash offers a radical expression of Hannah's isolation, though I believe it deviates from the norms of contextual interpretation: " 'The heart alone knows its bitterness' (Prov. 14:10a)—this refers to Hannah, who was very sad, as we read: 'she was desperate' (1 Sam. 1:11)—all by herself. When she was remembered, God remembered her all by herself, as we read: 'no outsider can share its joy' (Prov. 14:10b). Furthermore it is written, 'My heart exults in the Lord . . . I rejoice in your deliverance' (1 Sam. 2:1–2)—I rejoice all by myself, but no one else will share my joy" (*Exodus Rabbah* 19,1).

23. In this context, the argument advanced by Kaufmann (*Religion of Israel*, p. 309) is most apt: "Ordinarily, the individual prays for himself. When, on occasion, an intercessor appears, he is not a priest, but a righteous man or prophet (Gen. 20:7 and 17; Num. 12:13; Deut. 9:10; Jer. 15:1). Greenberg ("Patterns of Prayers," pp. 47–55) modifies this far-reaching assertion by noting (p. 51) that in at least one passage (Joel 2:17) priests are mentioned as praying in the Temple on behalf of the people, and by including blessings as prayers on behalf of others (p. 52). Accordingly we must view the threefold priestly benediction in Num. 6:22–27 as the specific form of the priests' prayer on behalf of the people; its sublime phrasing attests that it was an integral part of the divine service. Indeed, it is through a blessing that Eli ultimately helps Hannah (1:17). It follows that Hannah's failure to ask Eli for assistance does not necessarily stem from the nature of the institution of the priesthood; hence we should explain her attitude in the context of her independent personality and desperation (see above).

24. The quasi-poetic nature of the exchange between Elkanah and Hannah is blurred in the Septuagint version because of its interpolations and omissions (some of which preceded the translation, as is indicated by the Qumran Hebrew text). The first half of Elkanah's speech, in the Septuagint, reads: " 'Hannah!' She said to him: 'Here I am, my lord!' He said to her: 'What is the matter, that you are weeping, / and *why* aren't you eating, / and *why* is your heart so sad? . . . ' " The vocative (which parallels that in Hannah's vow) is absorbed into the dialogue (which follows the pattern of Gen. 22:7), and one member of the *anaphora* has been replaced by another expression. Hannah's vow, in the Vatican MS of the Septuagint, runs as follows: "O Lord of Hosts, if You will look upon the suffering of Your maidservant and remember me, / and if You grant Your *maidservant* a male child, / I will dedicate him as a nazirite before you until the day of his death; / he will not drink wine or strong drink, / and no razor shall ever touch his head." The omission of "and not forget Your *maidservant*" mars the *epiphora*, pattern, and meter, while the expatiation upon the laws relating to a nazirite spoils the meter and pattern (instead of AAABB, which resembles the pattern of Elkanah's speech, we have AABBB). The second half of Hannah's vow is preserved in the Qumran scroll,

though more is missing than extant. The text is presented by Ulrich (*Qumran Text*, p. 39), who filled in the long lacuna from the Septuagint, because the two versions are of similar length: "I will dedicate him [as a nazirite before you until the day of his death; / he will not drink wine or strong drink, / and] no razor shall ever touch [his head]."

25. Dus ("Die altisraelitische amphiktyonische Poesie," pp. 45–54) pointed out the lyrical nature of Judg. 21:3 and 2 Sam. 7:7. Not only does he find full metricality in the latter verse, he considers verses 5b–6 to be poetic as well. Relying on the threefold repetition of "Israel" in 1 Sam. 2:28–29, he claims to be able to reconstruct the original poem by eliminating the appositional phrases and constructing a unified stanza out of these verses plus verse 30.

26. See Shoshany, "Studies in the Prosody of the Old Testament," pp. 150–52.

27. Another example of a quasi-poetic dialogue whose two parts have a close formal link is Samuel's call to the people to attest to his honesty (1 Sam. 12:3) and the people's compliance with his request (v. 4).

28. In a similar vein, the Israelites in the wilderness vowed to waive in advance all benefits that might accrue from victory over the Canaanite king of Arad: "If You deliver this people into our hand, we will proscribe their towns" (Num. 21:2). See Parker, "Vow in Ugaritic and Israelite Narrative," p. 697. Indeed, the full gravity of Hannah's vow can be appreciated only in the context of parents' expectations of their sons in biblical society. Sons are supposed to live at home, at least in their youth ("Your wife shall be like a fruitful vine within your house; your sons, like olive saplings *around your table*" [Ps. 128:3]—and its antithesis, "*He will take your sons* and appoint them as his charioteers and horsemen . . . his chiefs of thousands and of fifties; . . . they will have to plow his fields . . . and make his weapons . . . " [1 Sam. 8:11–12]). But Hannah vows that her son will "remain there for good" (1:22). A son is supposed to help his father ("I will be tender toward them as a man is tender toward a son who works with him" [Mal. 3:17]; but Samuel will be "in the service of the Lord" (2:18). A son is supposed to help his mother and support her in her old age ("She has none to guide her of all the sons she bore; none takes her by the hand, of all the sons she reared" (Isa. 51:18); but Samuel will minister to the aged Eli (1 Sam. 3:1–16). On filial duties in Ugarit and as stipulated in the Talmud, see above, p. 35.

29. Willis ("An Anti-Elide Narrative Tradition") blames Eli's mistake on the priest's age and failing vision and cites this as evidence for the unity of chapters 1–7. This forces him to saddle Eli with both moral blindness (he does not see his sons' transgressions but only hears about them [2:22]) and intellectual blindness (manifested in his slow realization that it is the Lord who is calling Samuel [3:8]), and to move both shortcomings forward to chapter 1, even though it says nothing about the priest's advanced age. Willis's harmonizing approach prevents him from understanding the literary function of the priest's plausible misconception of Hannah's conduct, and it keeps him from seeing the positive aspect of his complex personality, which allots Eli a key role in the stories about the birth and consecration of Samuel (see further pp. 19–22, 29–30, 61–71).

30. As a matter of their contextual meaning, Hannah's "Oh no, my lord!" and "your maidservant" attest to her great humility. Nevertheless, the Sages gave them a homiletical interpretation that emphasizes that, objectively, the woman is right and the priest wrong; this interpretation is to serve as a warning to future generations of religious functionaries against a moralizing haughtiness lacking in empathy. As is their practice, building on the legitimate (if slightly strained) rendering of *lo adoni* as '*not* my lord', they put in the heroine's mouth words they did intend to be taken as an authentic report of how she actually addressed the priest: "Ula—some say R. José son of R. Hanina—said: 'she said to him: "You are not a lord [or master]

in this matter, and the Holy Spirit does not rest upon you, if you suspect me of this." ' Others say, 'This is what she said to him: "You are not a lord, there is no Divine Presence or Holy Spirit behind you, if you have judged me guilty and have not judged me innocent. Do you not know that I am a very unhappy woman and have drunk no wine or strong drink?!" ' " (BT Berakot 31b).

31. On the other hand, Seeligmann (*Studies in Biblical Literature*, pp. 305–306) suggests understanding the expression here, as well as its parallel in Job, in the sense of 'panting' or 'short of breath.'

32. According to Zalevsky ("Vow of Hannah," p. 314 n. 35), the words "go in peace" are meant as a counterweight to the ostracism of "go away from the presence of the Lord" found in the Septuagint text of Eli's rebuke (v. 14). This antiparallelism is evidence in favor of the Septuagint reading; nevertheless I cannot accept it as genuine because of my sense that these words are too harsh for Eli to have spoken. More plausible is the assumption that the interpolation was inspired by the prohibition on the consumption of wine and strong drink in the holy precincts (Lev. 10:8–9) and that it is yet another example of the tendency to reconcile the story with Pentateuch ordinances, a tendency evident in other interpolations found in the Septuagint and Qumran texts (see Grintz, *Biblical Introductions*, pp. 128–29).

33. Jepsen ("Amah und Schiphchah," pp. 293–97) holds that a *šifḥah* is inferior to an *ʾamah*, citing, inter alia, Abigail's declaration to David, "Your handmaid (*ʾamah*) is ready to be your maidservant (*šifḥah*), to wash the feet of my lord's servants" (1 Sam. 25:41). If he is correct, then here we should interpret Hannah's substitution of *šifḥah* for *ʾamah* as an expression of increased deference to Eli. But it would seem that Ch. Cohen ("Studies in Extra-Biblical Hebrew Inscriptions," pp. xxv–liii) is right when he argues that the two words are synonymous, as can be demonstrated, for example, by what the woman of Tekoa says to David: "Your maidservant (*šifḥah*) thought I would speak to Your Majesty; perhaps Your Majesty would act on his handmaid's (*ʾamah*) plea" (2 Sam. 14:15; also in vv. 16, 17, and 19; and cf. Ruth 2:13 and 3:9).

34. Instead of the Masoretic "and she ate," the Septuagint here reads, "and she came to the chamber, where she ate and drank with her husband." Weingreen ("A Rabbinic-Type Gloss," pp. 225–28) considers this to be an exegetical interpolation, like that which intruded into the Masoretic text of verse 9—"and after they had drunk." I believe, though, that the latter is no interpolation at all, since it is essential as the background for the fact that Hannah has drunk nothing. Hence we should see the Septuagint's expansion as the result of its characteristic tendency toward greater clarity and uniformity (see below, ch. 2, n. 25, and appendix, nn. 6–8).

35. The Masoretic text here is extremely problematic: "the Lord remembered her" is separated from "Hannah conceived" by the temporal indication "at the turn of the year." This disrupts the immediate connection between her remembrance by Heaven and its tangible results on earth (compare Gen. 30:22–23); furthermore, the indication of time loses its meaning since it refers to conception rather than the usual time of birth (see following discussion). Driver (*Notes*, p. 16), who presented the problem in this fashion, notes that R. Jacob Reifmann hypothesized that "at the turn of the year" should follow "she bore a son," and that this hypothesis is supported by the Septuagint text (see J. Reifmann, *Or Boqer* [Berlin, 1878], p. 28 [Hebrew]). From Reifmann's twenty-five proposed readings of this nature, it is clear that he is not referring to the traditional exegetical mode of "rearrange it and understand thus" but to emendation of the text.

36. Parker ("Vow in Ugaritic and Israelite Narrative") reinforces the understanding of Hannah's reply as an answer to an implicit suspicion that she has forgotten her vow, now that her situation has improved, by a parallel from Keret (KTU

1.15 III 20–26 = *ANET*, p. 146, III 20–26)—After his children were born, King Keret forgot to fulfill his vow to Asherah.

37. Even a sacrificial animal must not be offered before the appropriate time: "When an ox or a sheep or a goat is born, it shall stay seven days with its mother, and from the eighth day on it shall be acceptable as an offering by fire to the Lord" (Lev. 22:27; cf. Exod. 22:29). The Mishna (Bekorot 4,1) asks, "How long must a first-born animal be tended [before it is given to the priest]?" The reply: "Small animals, 30 days; large animals, 50 days. R. José says: small animals, three months." The Gemara (BT Bekorot 26b) explains R. José's view: "because its teeth are soft." Rashi comments (ad loc.), "it cannot eat grass, so if it is not with its mother it will die."

38. This is the view of R. Joseph Kara, who cites Hannah's subsequent action— once she brought Samuel to Shiloh she never brought him home again to Ramah— as proof. Gersonides independently arrived at the same conclusion. Just as Abravanel ignored Gersonides' contribution, so too Driver, Segal, Hertzberg, Stoebe, and McCarter ignored Ehrlich (*Randglossen* 3, 167), who took note of the internal logic of the verse and understood it correctly.

39. In the chapter on the man of God from Judah (pp. 140–41) we shall discuss and give examples of the concept, prevalent in the Bible, that when you retrace your footsteps you have to some extent nullified your original journey and have, as it were, changed your mind and abandoned your goal.

40. Elat ("History and Historiography," p. 11) notes that, according to an ancient Babylonian document, children were weaned at age three. In the story of Hannah and her seven sons (2 Macc. 7:27), the mother says to her youngest child: "My son, have mercy on me who carried you in my womb for nine months and suckled you for three years." In Midrash Samuel (2,9 and 3,3), R. José son of R. Avin says that Samuel was nursed for two years; the Gemara (BT Ketubot 60a), however, records a dispute among the Mishnaic sages: according to R. Eliezer, "a baby continues to nurse until 24 months"; whereas according to R. Joshua, it is "as long as four or five years," or, according to another phrasing (which the Gemara equates with the latter), "until his pack is on his back."

41. I believe that the two readings are merely textual variants of the same idea. But Walters ("Hannah and Anna," pp. 385–412) sees them as quite different statements, incorporated into two separate stories that have altogether different messages. The farfetched glosses on which his interpretation is based (one of which is explicitly homiletical [see p. 411]) attest to how forced it is.

42. On positive minor characters who embody the good mean against which the protagonist stands out in relief, see above, pp. 268–69.

43. The Masoretic text here—"three bulls (*bᵉ-farim šᵉlošah*)"—is problematic, since verse 25 speaks of only a single bull. Hence almost all commentators read "a three-year-old bull (*bᵉ-far mᵉšullaš*)," on the model of "a three-year-old ram" (Gen. 15:9), and assume that the Masoretic text stems from improper word division and the interpolation of vowel letters. This emendation is supported by 4QSamᵃ, the Septuagint, and the Peshitta. Speiser ("Nuzi Tablets") cited extrascriptural examples of the omission of the noun specifying a unit of time, of mentioning the age of animals in legal and economic documents, as well as of the legal principle that the term *šor*, 'ox', applies to an animal that is at least two years old. On the other hand, Grintz (*Biblical Introductions*, p. 128 n. 8) upheld the authenticity of the Masoretic text, arguing that the Qumran text (reconstructed on the basis of the Septuagint) speaks of the slaughter of two bulls, one by Elkanah and the other by the lad—evidence that the original text spoke of "bulls" in the plural. But 4QSamᵃ does not state that Elkanah sacrificed another bull; rather, he offered "the annual

sacrifice." It follows that the interpolation was motivated by the desire to make this pilgrimage correspond to the earlier ones; just as the start of the story does not specify what kind of animal Elkanah offered, here too the text says only "a sacrifice."

44. Tsevat, "Assyriological Notes," pp. 77–86.

45. There is no reason to prefer the Septuagint's "and the lad was with them." We have already been told that "she took him up with her," so the Septuagint is merely replacing a tautology of form with a tautology of content.

46. The frequent assertion that the original story dealt with the birth of Saul rather than Samuel, since the former's name corresponds to the root *š.ʾ.l* used in Hannah's explanation of the name, has been forcefully rebutted by Zakovitch, "Study of Precise and Partial Derivations," pp. 41–42; by Tsevat, "Die Namengebung Samuels," pp. 250–54; and by Garsiel, *Biblical Names*, pp. 17–19 and 244–45.

47. On the secondary nature of 2:11b, and on the similarity between this concluding line (1:28b + 2:11a) and the conclusion of part I (1:19a), see above, pp. 3–5.

48. As long as Samuel was not consecrated as a prophet, the robe he received from his mother had no connection with the one that marked him as a seer (as attested by the description given by the witch of Endor—"he is wrapped in a robe" [1 Sam. 28:14; cf. also 15:27]). On the other hand, the robe is clearly associated with the *ephod:* "You shall make the robe of the ephod of pure blue" (Exod. 28:31); "he clothed him with the robe, and put the ephod on him" (Lev. 8:7). It is true that both of these verses are speaking of the high priest and of the "ephod of gold, of blue, purple, and crimson yarns, and of fine twisted linen, worked into designs" (Exod. 28:6). But we know that ordinary priests wore "the linen ephod" (1 Sam. 22:18), as did David when he brought the Ark of the Covenant to Jerusalem (2 Sam. 6:14). Since the little robe is mentioned here in the same breath with a "linen ephod," it stands to reason that Samuel, too, wore his ephod on top of his robe.

49. The symmetrical contrast between the epilogue and the first scene has already been discussed.

50. On the scriptural narrators' practice of focusing on the protagonist and telling about minor characters only as long as their presence is required by the plot or in order to illuminate the hero, see above, pp. 264–66.

51. The Masoretic text here is problematic; on the better readings of other versions, see above, n. 7.

52. On our hypothesis that the latter half of this verse is secondary, see above, pp. 3–4.

53. A similar tension between Hannah as she is depicted in the story and her character as reflected in the psalm is generated by the view that she was a prophet— a view intended to resolve the anachronistic reference to "His king" in the last verse of the psalm. Kimchi (on 2:10) offered an alternative explanation that avoids this tension by means of the unlikely assumption that even before the establishment of the monarchy the verse could have been uttered without prophetic inspiration: "Hannah said this either prophetically *or on the basis of a tradition,* since the tradition had come down to her that in the future there would be a king in Israel. She concluded her song with a reference to the king because she mentioned the downfall of the wicked, who are the enemies of Israel, and said that God would give power to the king of Israel by whom Israel would be rescued from their enemies. But if she did say it prophetically, she was alluding to the fact that it would be through her son Samuel that Israel would receive a king, and he would anoint him." A similar attempt was made by Willis ("Song of Hannah," pp. 139–54), who sees the kings of the Canaanite city-states and Abimelech who reigned in Shechem as a possible background for a paean of royal victory that might have been sung in Shiloh, if indeed the psalm refers to such a local monarch.

54. When we examine the function of Hannah's psalm in the broader context of the Book of Samuel it takes on another meaning in addition to that it possesses in the limited ambit of the story of Samuel's birth. Thus Childs (*Introduction*, pp. 272–73), Polzin (*Samuel*, pp. 30–36), and Cook ("Song of Hannah," pp. 154–84) all argue that the conspicuous parallels between Hannah's song and David's link the poems that stand at the beginning and end of the book, and that they can be seen as a sort of introduction and conclusion that cast a distinctly theological light on the age of the protomonarchy—the Lord casts down and also lifts up high priest, prophet, and king:

Hannah	David
(1 Sam. 2)	(2 Sam. 22)
10a	14
10b	51
8–9	26–29
6	17–20

55. Knierim ("Old Testament Form Criticism," pp. 458–63), offers a strong justification for preceding "form-critical" inquiries by a "close reading" so that we can properly evaluate the interactions between the conventional (the characteristics of the genre) and the specific (the uniqueness of the story in question). The necessity of using both these disciplines is discussed and further exemplified below with regard to stories of prophetic consecration.

56. Here *miracle* does not denote only a supernatural event but any action described as due to specific divine intervention. The birth of Joseph, after Rachel has endured many years of barrenness, does not necessarily depart from the laws of nature (unlike the case of Isaac's birth to nonagenarian parents). But Scripture does depict it as the result of the Lord's intervention: "God remembered Rachel; God heeded her and opened her womb" (Gen. 30:22). The same applies to the other childless women: Rebekah (Gen. 25:21), Manoah's wife (Judg. 13:3, 6–7, and especially 23–24), and Hannah (1 Sam. 1:11, 19–20, and 27). In fact, even Leah's first pregnancy, which is not preceded by prolonged barrenness, is described in almost the same language: "The Lord saw that Leah was unloved and he opened her womb; but Rachel was barren" (Gen. 29:31); for divine Providence oversees the normal course of the world as well. In other words, just as Scripture presents the difference between a "supernatural" miracle and a "natural" miracle as one of degree rather than of kind, this too is the difference between a "natural" miracle (i.e., special divine intervention) and "providence" (normal divine intervention).

57. Gordon, *Ugaritic Textbook*, pp. 245–50; H. L. Ginsberg, "The Tale of Aqhat," in Pritchard, *ANET*, pp. 149–55; Obermann, "How Daniel Was Blessed"; Spiegel, "Noah, Danel, and Job," pp. 305–55.

58. Rank, *Myth of Birth*, pp. 3–96; Ackerman, "Literary Context of the Moses Birth Story," pp. 74–119; Fisher, *Ras Shamra Parallels*, vol. 2, pp. 133–52 and 155–214; Irvin, *Mytharion*; Zakovitch, *Life of Samson*, pp. 74–84; Rudin-O'Brasky, *Patriarchs in Hebron and Sodom*, pp. 48–74; Alter, "How Convention Helps Us Read," pp. 115–30.

59. The many points of similarity between the stories of the widow of Zarephath and the matron of Shunem, on the one hand, and the other stories under consideration here justify our assumption that those two stories make a secondary use of the birth/survival genre within the context of a prophetic story. This is why the children who owe their lives to prophetic intervention lack any specific individual destiny and are not even dignified with names. (The aggadists may have had

the same view, for they restored these narratives to their ostensible original genre by supplying information omitted by Scripture and providing the children with names and biographies: "R. Eliezer taught: 'Jonah son of Amittai was the son of the widow of Zarephath' " (*Yalquṭ Shimoni* 2,550; *Pirqe Rabbi Eliezer* 33). "Why was he called Habakkuk? Because the verse says, 'at this season next year you will be embracing (*ḥoveqet*) a son' (2 Kings 4:16), and he was the son of the Shunammite. He received two embraces—one from his mother, and one from Elisha, as it is written, 'he put his mouth on its mouth (ibid. 34)' " (*Zohar*, Introduction, I 7b). On the secondary use of a literary genre, see Tucker, *Form Criticism*, pp. 15–16 and 51–54.

60. Obermann ("How Daniel Was Blessed") disagrees. He views these filial obligations as a description of a "model son" (p. 24) and presents Danel's desire for an exceptional son as a parallel to Baal's desire for an exceptional temple (p. 30). Koch ("Die Sohnesverheissung," pp. 211–21), goes even further. He holds that Danel, the sacral king, needs a son to see to the continuation of the cult of his fathers' gods, since the stability and order of the regime depend on the unbroken continuity of the rites. Koch accordingly sets aside the plain meaning of the classic family duties—guarding the father's house at night, holding his hand when he is intoxicated, repairing his roof and laundering his clothes in the winter—and interprets them as ritual obligations. The extent to which this interpretation is detached from reality is demonstrated by the talmudic parallels cited by Spiegel ("Noah, Danel, and Job," p. 317 n. 17) in the name of Saul Lieberman: "What is meant by honor? Providing with food and drink, clothing, covering and shoes, and guiding in and out of the house" (JT Qiddušin 1,7); or, in another version, "giving food and drink, clothing and shoes, and guiding" (ibid.). See also Cassuto, "Daniel and His Son," pp. 199–205; Y. Avishur, " 'Duties of the Son,' " pp. 50–60.

61. See also Isa. 49:1 and 5. Compare also the seven parallels from Assyrian and Babylonian royal inscriptions in which the kings declare themselves to be destined from the womb for their royal role; cited by Paul, "Deutero-Isaiah," pp. 108–86. (I would like to thank Professor Moshe Garsiel, who brought this article to my attention.)

62. Something similar is found (twice) in the story of the binding of Isaac: Abraham conceals the purpose of his ascent of Mount Moriah from his servants and tells them, "*we* will worship and *we* will return to you" (Gen. 22:5); and so it did indeed turn out. He calms Isaac with the words, "God will choose the sheep for His burnt offering" (v. 8); and this too came to pass. Another answer to this problem was offered by Elat ("History and Historiography," pp. 16–17); he suggests that Samuel served, by virtue of his mother's vow, first in Shiloh and later in Mizpah, Gilgal, Bethel, and Ramah, all of which were cult centers during his lifetime.

63. There is no annunciation in the story of Moses' birth and rescue. The aggadist evidently felt a need to supply this lack by placing words of wisdom in the mouth of Miriam, Amram, and Jochebed's daughter: " 'Father, your decree [abstaining from relations with Jochebed or divorcing her] is harsher than Pharaoh's. Pharaoh has decreed [death] only on the males, but your decree is on both males and females. Pharaoh's decree applies only to this world, but yours, to this world and the world to come. There is doubt whether the decree of the wicked Pharaoh will be fulfilled; but you are a righteous man, so your decree will certainly be fulfilled, as it is written: 'You will decree and it will be fulfilled' (Job 22:28). At once he returned to his wife" (BT Soṭa 12a).

64. Compare Garsiel, *Biblical Names*, pp. 172–73, 186, 239–40, 244–45.

65. Zakovitch (*Life of Samson*, pp. 70 and 78) explains the absence of any explanation of Samson's name as a consequence of the struggle against the mythological tradition. Because of his apprehension that the name might be associated

with the god Shamash (who must have been worshipped in Bet Shemesh, the town not far from Zorah), the narrator preferred to leave out the homiletical explanation altogether. As Zakovitch himself notes, though, it is precisely the omission that invites the forbidden gloss; had the author really been afraid of it he should have sealed up the lacuna with a nonmythological derivation of the hero's name. It seems more plausible to assume that to the extent that the name Samson is intuitively associated with the power of the sun (Hebrew *šemeš*), the author left it to his readers to make the connection, as Zakovitch explicitly suggests regarding the name Delilah (pp. 182–83).

66. In a similar vein, Moses' despair and skepticism magnify the miracle of the provision of meat for the 600,000 who wandered in the desert (Num. 11:11–15).

67. This rule also seems to apply to the story of Isaac and Rebekah, which differs from the other examples of the genre not only in that the two characters with the contrasting attitudes are of more or less equal importance, but also, and chiefly, in that the theme of a miraculous birth is presented with a concision that borders on the merely schematic. This is because the story does not focus on Rebecca's barrenness (that this lasted for twenty years is indicated only after the fact and indirectly, when we read that "Isaac was sixty years old when they were born" [Gen. 25:26], rather than as the necessary background for Isaac's prayer), but on the birth of the twins and their contention for the status of first-born. This is evidently why, in this story, the element of "acquiescence" applies not to the childlessness but to the difficult pregnancy that followed it.

68. Rudin-O'Brasky (*Patriarchs in Hebron and Sodom*, pp. 72–74) is probably correct when she says that in the framework of the entire Abraham complex of stories, which begins with the promise of progeny (Gen. 12:2–3), "hospitality cannot serve as a sufficient cause for the promise of a son." Nevertheless, the lavish detail with which this scene is described clearly indicates that his extremely liberal hospitality is an indication of Abraham's worthiness of a miracle and that this excellence is *added* to both the divine promise and his other merits. The causal link between hospitality and the promise of a son is explicit in the story of the Shunammite (Elisha asks what recompense he can make his hostess), but even in its implicit form is understood by readers. The proof is that in the story of the destruction of Sodom it is perfectly clear that Lot's hospitality augments and makes tangible his worthiness to be saved, just as the Sodomites' mistreatment of strangers emphasizes the townspeople's guilt—even though the angels make no statements linking Lot's rescue and his fellow citizens' annihilation to their respective conduct (see Gen. 19:12–13). Consequently I see no basis to the idea that the causal link was deleted from Genesis 18 when the incident was incorporated into the Abraham complex so as not to overshadow the divine promise motif. The silence about the causal link makes no difference if it is evident to readers in any case.

69. On the lack of prayer and annunciation in this story, and on the great similarity between Rachel's demand that Jacob give her sons (in the plural) lest she die, and Esau's demand that Jacob give him some stew to eat since "I am at the point of death, so of what use is my birthright to me?" (Gen. 25:32), see Alter, *Art of Biblical Narrative*, pp. 186–88.

2. Young Samuel's Call to Prophecy

1. A useful survey of scholarship since call narratives were first recognized as a literary genre (by H. Schmidt in 1915) can be found in Killian, "Die prophetischen Berufungsberichte," pp. 356–76, and in the monograph by Gnuse, *Dream Theophany*, pp. 133–42.

2. E.g., "An angel of the Lord *appeared* to him in a blazing fire out of a bush"

(Exod. 3:2); "the angel of the Lord *appeared* to him" (Judg. 6:12); "I have *seen* an angel of the Lord face to face (ibid., v. 22); "I beheld (*wa-ʾerʾeh*) my Lord seated on a high and lofty throne" (Isa. 6:1); "the heavens opened and I *saw* visions of God" (Ezek. 1:1). In the first two *r.ʾ.h* is used in the passive ("appeared"), while in the other three the prophet actively sees.

3. See also "The Lord is with you, valiant warrior!" (Judg. 6:12); "O mortal, stand up on your feet that I may speak to you" (Ezek. 2:1).

4. See also "*Go* in this strength of yours and deliver Israel from the Midianites. Behold I am *sending* you" (Judg. 6:14); "Whom shall I *send*? Who will *go* for us?" (Isa. 6:8).

5. See also "How can I deliver Israel? Behold my clan is the humblest in Manasseh, and I am the youngest in my father's household" (Judg. 6:15); "I don't know how to speak, for I am only a youth" (Jer. 1:6).

6. See also "For I am with you to deliver you" (Jer. 1:8); "do not fear them and do not fear their words" (Ezek. 2:6).

7. See also "Give me a sign that it is You who are speaking to me" (Judg. 6:17–23); "The Lord put out his hand and touched my mouth" (Jer. 1:9); "Open your mouth and eat what I am giving you" (Ezek. 2:8–3:3).

8. Gnuse (*Dream Theophany*, pp. 155–56), who also rejects the classification of our tale as a call to prophecy, admits that 3:19–4:1a reveal that what preceded them was such. In order to undercut their testimony he holds that these verses are not part of the original story but were added by the editor.

9. 1 Samuel 3 has been recognized as a call narrative mainly by scholars who focus on the content of the chapter rather than on the definition of its genre. See Segal, *Books of Samuel*, p. 32; Hertzberg, *I and II Samuel*, pp. 29–31; von Rad, *Old Testament Theology*, vol. 2, p. 55; Henry, *Prophet und Tradition*, pp. 17–18; Stoebe, *Das erste Buch Samuelis*, p. 125; Baltzer, *Die Biographie*, pp. 67–69, and McCarter, *I and II Samuel*, p. 100.

10. On the need to base Form Criticism on a more flexible and open method than Richter's, see Knierim, "Old Testament Form Criticism," pp. 447–48 and 458–67.

11. Berridge (*Prophet*, pp. 26–27), disagrees. He argues that the words "How long, My Lord?" express opposition to the content of the mission but not to the call itself. Since, however, the nature of his mission is revealed to Isaiah only after he expresses his willingness to accept it, his reservations and reluctance must relate to its content.

12. Prophets are prey to this suspicion even when their position is firmly grounded; see Moses in Num. 16:28; Elijah in 1 Kings 18:36; and Jeremiah in Jer. 43:2–3.

13. Gnuse (*Dream Theophany*, pp. 149–52) does not attempt to buttress his classification of the story as a "message dream" by means of the common argument that it describes an "incubation" (i.e., an intentional effort to attain a prophetic dream by virtue of sacrifices, preparatory rites, and sleeping in the sanctuary), like that related in 1 Kings 3:4–15 and perhaps also in Gen. 46:1–4, which is quite common in descriptions of prophetic dreams in the ancient Near East. In fact, he rejects this possibility out of hand because we do not read of any preparations made by the boy and especially because his repeated misidentification of the voice that is calling him indicates beyond a doubt that he has not expected or prepared himself for a nocturnal epiphany.

14. This is Fishbane's division of the story ("I Samuel 3," pp. 193–94), which I accept in all particulars.

15. In this concluding sentence, at the end of scene 1, the location is indicated again, as in the concluding sentences of both the exposition and scene 2.

16. Such anticipation of the beginning of the plot within the body of the exposition is also found in the story of Samuel's birth. See above, p. 12.

17. The story of the binding of Isaac, too, begins with a general indication of time—"After these things" (Gen. 22:1); only from the text of verse 3—"early next morning"—does it become clear that the revelation took place during the night.

18. Compare the commentary of R. Joseph Kara: "*[Eli's] eyes had begun to fail and he could not see*—so when he needed something he did not go to the person he needed, but stayed where he was and called him. This is why Samuel thought, when [the Lord] called him, that it was Eli calling him, even though he didn't see Eli standing near him."

19. Telling time by reference to the sacrificial rituals is found in a number of places in Scripture: "in the morning, when it was time to present the meal offering" (2 Kings 3:20); "when noon passed, they prophesied until the hour of presenting the meal offering" (1 Kings 18:29; see also verse 36); "about the time of the evening offering" (Dan. 9:21); see also BT Berakot 2a–3a.

20. This argument, put forward by Kimchi, is strengthened by the fact that in many stories the plot advances through a clear sequence of temporal indications. For example: the creation (Gen. 1:5, 8, 13, 19, 23, and 31); Jacob's dream (Gen. 28:11 and 18); the concubine at Gibeah (Judg. 19:5, 7, 8, 9, 11, 14, 25, and 26); the four lepers at the gates of Samaria (2 Kings 7:5, 7, 9, and 12); and Ruth on the threshing floor (Ruth 3:8, 13, 14, and 18).

21. See Saadya Gaon, *Book of Beliefs and Opinions*, 7,1; Abraham Ibn Ezra, introduction to the long commentary on the Pentateuch, "The Third Path," vol. 1, p. 137 (Weiser's edition).

22. Abravanel, too, gave a metaphorical interpretation to the verse, while attempting to anchor it both in biblical usage and the narrative context: "The *beth* prefixed to 'the temple' is not locative [i.e., 'in'], as the commentators believed, but instrumental, as in '*from* the mirrors of the women' (Exod. 38:8) or '*in* gold and silver' (Exod. 35:32). [The verse] says that Samuel . . . was lying and concentrating on the theme of the Lord's Sanctuary, where the Ark of God is, and because his thoughts were on the subject of the ark the prophecy of how the ark would be exiled descended on him. 'Lying' refers to the fact that he was thinking deeply about the subject, as in 'even at night his mind has no respite (*lo šakav libbo*)' (Ecc. 2:23) or 'upon my couch at night' (Cant. 3:1), which refers to thought."

23. On this sort of semantic flexibility, see Cassuto, *Commentary on the Book of Exodus*, pp. 347–48. On the entire passage, see Batten, "Sanctuary at Shiloh," pp. 29–33.

24. "House of the Lord" has the restricted and expanded senses in two successive verses—1 Kings 8:63–64. Here too it may be used in the broader sense and refer to the opening of the Temple compound to the public.

25. Some favor the smoother and uniform version of the Septuagint and tend to see its readings as original. See Driver, *Notes*, p. 42; Segal, *Books of Samuel*, p. 34. By contrast, those who see these variants as the result of consummate literary art view their systematic removal as yet another example of the conspicuous tendency of the Septuagint translators (as well as of the scribes of the Samaritan version) to reduce repeated passages to the same phrasing for the sake of comprehension and clarity. On this tendency see Frankel, *Vorstudien*, pp. 77–80; Cassuto, *Commentary on the Book of Genesis, Part I*, pp. 265, 266, and 288; idem, *Commentary . . . Genesis, Part II*, pp. 113–14; and Sternberg, *Poetics*, pp. 365–440 (esp. pp. 371–74). Sternberg attempts to provide a theoretical basis for the assumption that elegant variation is not practiced merely for the sake of stylistic variety but as an intentional and precise rhetorical strategy. Even those who do not agree with all the literary interpretations offered in the article must admit that his attempt to extract meaning from vari-

ations is justified. The first to do this in any systematic way seems to have been Abravanel, who phrased the question neatly: "Why didn't Samuel and Eli act the same way each time the voice called?" (his sixth question on the episode). He noted these variations closely (ibid.) and dealt with their literary implications (in his commentary on vv. 5–10).

26. For the use of "my son" as a phrase of encouragement to one who is not really the speaker's son, see also 1 Sam. 4:16 and 2 Sam. 18:22.

27. With this explanatory interjection, which is meant to forestall any misunderstanding by the reader, compare Judg. 16:20: "And [Samson] awoke from his sleep, and said [to himself]: 'I will break loose and shake myself free as I had the other times.' For he did not know that the Lord had departed from him." Since readers already know that Samson's strength left him while he was asleep, they are likely to wonder about Samson's vain attempt to muster his strength. Hence the narrator intervenes to tell us that the hero himself was still unaware of what had transpired. There the narrator asks his readers to ignore information he has just provided them, whereas in our narrative we are dealing with external knowledge that readers may be assumed to bring with them, namely, that Samuel was an Israelite prophet.

28. The only difference is that in the second subscene we are told that "Samuel rose and went *(wa-yaqom Š^emuel wa-yelek)* to Eli" (v. 6), whereas in the third subscene "he rose and went *(wa-yaqom wa-yelek)* to Eli" (v. 8). In the second subscene, the name "Samuel" is inserted between the two verbs, probably to slow down the pace of the narrative. The third time, however, the narrator increases the tempo somewhat, perhaps to avoid tiring the reader with repetitions.

29. In the Septuagint, the doubled "Samuel, Samuel" appears the first two times, only a single vocative the third time (haplography?), and none whatsoever the fourth time (except in the recensions of Origen and Lucianus, who read, with the Masoretic version, "Samuel, Samuel"). Double vocatives occur in the epiphanies granted to Jacob (Gen. 46:2) and Moses (Exod. 3:4). These passages probably influenced the Greek translators to double the name not only in our narrative but also in the first divine call to Abraham in the story of the binding of Isaac (Gen. 22:1).

30. Samuel's unwillingness to utter the name of the Lord is parallel (as we shall see shortly) to Eli's in verse 17. A similar meaningful omission occurs in the episode of the binding of Isaac—the lad Isaac leaves out the knife when he asks his father, "Here are the firestone and the wood; but where is the sheep for the burnt offering?" (Gen. 22:7).

31. The context requires that we understand *w^e-lo kihah bam* (v. 13b) as "he did not prevent them" or "he did not rebuke them." Since this is the only passage where the root *k.h.h* has this sense, there is, in my opinion, insufficient basis for the various attempts to link this definition of Eli's blindness with the description of his affliction in the exposition—"his eyes had begun to fail *(kehoth)*" (v. 2b).

32. Driver (*Notes*, p. 43) makes this proposal, following Klosterman and Bude. R. Joseph Kara says much the same thing, but in accordance with the stylistic principle of "eliptical speech," which allows him to fill out the text rather freely: "this is why I have appeared to you, to tell him that I am sentencing his house to endless punishment."

33. As was proposed by Ehrlich (*Randglossen* 3, p. 179). The root *n.g.d* has this sense in the confession over the first fruits—"You shall go the priest in charge at that time and say to him, 'I *acknowledge* this day before the Lord your God that I have entered the land' " (Deut. 26:3)—as well as in Joab's rebuke of David—"by showing love for those who hate you and hate for those who love you . . . you have *made clear* today that the officers and men mean nothing to you" (2 Sam. 19:7). That

the verb *wᵉ-higgadti* is accented on the penult is no sure indication of the past tense, since the enclitic *lo* that follows it entails a recessive accent in accordance with the principle of *nasog aḥor*.

34. In Pharaoh's court the majordomo was charged with opening the gates of the palace every morning, thereby inaugurating the official day. See de Vaux, *Ancient Israel*, p. 130. It may be, however, that in addition to fleeing to his routine occupations (this was Kimchi's interpretation), Samuel opens the gates and admits the public into the sanctuary in an attempt to avoid meeting Eli alone.

35. The root *r.ʔ.h* indicates an auditory rather than visual disclosure in 2 Kings 8:10 and 13, too.

36. See Janzen, "Withholding the Word," pp. 97–114. Janzen explains the recurrent demand that prophets conceal nothing of what they have heard (e.g., "the king said to Jeremiah, 'I want to ask you something; don't hide anything from me' " [Jer. 38:14]) as associated with the suspicion that they report messages they have in fact not received ("You are lying! The Lord our God did not send you . . . " [Jer. 43:2]). He sees adjuring the prophet to stick to what he has heard (such as the oath imposed on Samuel by Eli, or that imposed by Ahab on Micaiah son of Imlah [1 Kings 22:16]) as part of the formal procedure he hypothesizes was followed by the Israelites as a means of guaranteeing the credibility of prophets. Hurowitz ("Eli's Adjuration") attempts to buttress this hypothesis with extremely interesting parallels from Mari, of which the most important is the oath of trust imposed on the haruspex, who swears before King Zimri-Lim "to relate and not to conceal" everything he may spy in the entrails of the sacrificial animal, for good or evil. Hurowitz proposes that we see Samuel's adjuration by Eli as evidence of an initiatory oath required of neophyte prophets, or, alternatively, as an authoritative demand that he uphold the oath he took when he completed his preprophetic training. But Samuel's three errors indicate that he had no expectation of receiving the word of the Lord; similarly, his silence in the morning attests that he never sought to be a prophet. Hence we do better to assume that the Mari oath and Eli's adjuration of Samuel represent a similar response to a common problem—the reluctance to give vent to prophecies of evil out of fear of the reaction of their objects (see Jer. 1:17; Ezek. 2:6–7), or out of pity for them (somewhat analogous to the nonprophetic messenger who conceals some of what he knows, like Ahimaaz, who cannot bring himself to tell David of Absalom's death [2 Sam. 18:29]). The Lord, entrusting Jeremiah with His message, commands the prophet: "Do not omit anything" (Jer. 26:2); Jeremiah, as the faithful emissary, promises in advance: "I will withhold nothing from you" (Jer. 42:4). But the oath that Eli imposes on Samuel stems from the right of the object of a prophecy to hear the Lord's message in full, just as Ahab adjured Micaiah (1 Kings 22:16) and David demanded of the wise woman from Tekoa: "Do not hide from me anything I ask you!" (2 Sam. 14:18).

37. Hurowitz ("Eli's Adjuration") discerned a clear concentricity (ABCBA) in Eli's speech, with the oath at the center, immediately preceded and followed by the demand that Samuel conceal nothing (BB) and the two questions about the content of the revelation (AA). He sees this sophisticated structure as evidence of ritual-formulaic speech; but it seems more likely that it results from the internal logic of the vigorous effort of persuasion required to stir the lad from his silence and is also a realistic manifestation of Eli's own excitement (compare the lengthy argument of the wise woman from Tekoa; there too the verb *d.b.r* occurs repeatedly [2 Sam. 14:12–16]).

38. David, fleeing from Absalom, accepts the divine judgment in similar terms: "If He [the Lord] should say, 'I do not want you,' here I am; He will do to me what seems good to Him *(yaʿaśeh li ka-ʔašer ṭov be-ʿeinaw)*" (2 Sam. 15:26).

39. This was made clear by Abravanel (commentary on v. 9): "Why did this

prophecy come to Samuel in this fashion? The reason in my opinion is that Eli should know about it and ask about it in the morning, so that Samuel would be forced to tell it to him. This would not have been the case had the prophecy come to Samuel in the manner of other prophets, for then he might have been too bashful and ashamed to relate it to his master. Even as it was he said nothing to him until after he adjured him to do so."

40. Consecration is always an individual manner, and no stranger can be present when the prophet stands in the presence of the Lord. There can be only external and indirect testimony that the epiphany did in fact take place. In addition to the present story, this is found in the revelation to Moses, both on Mount Sinai (Exod. 24:15–18) and in the tent outside the camp (Exod. 33:8–11); in the consecration of Elisha (2 Kings 2:7 and 15); and in the Lord's appearance to Daniel (Dan. 10:7).

41. *Midrash Exodus Rabba, Chapters 1–14*, ed. Avigdor Shinan (Jerusalem, 1984), pp. 119–20 (Hebrew).

42. The words in angle brackets complicate the sentence and blur its meaning. Perhaps they originally constituted a marginal note, referring to "Samuel's word" in the next verse (4:1a) and were intended to eliminate the misconception that he spoke on his own account rather than the Lord's.

43. "Prophet *to* the Lord" (the literal Hebrew reading here) is synonymous with "prophet of the Lord" (see 1 Kings 18:22, 22:7; 2 Kings 3:11). "Trustworthy prophet" means one who is reliable and authoritative (see Isa. 8:2; Jer. 42:5; Ps. 19:8).

3. Saul at Endor

1. Another story about a heavenly decree concerning the impending extinction of a dynasty—Daniel 5:1–30—has been excluded from this comparison because it is not a prophetic story (the hero is a savant, not a prophet) and because it is a mixed kind with traits of both subgenres. On the one hand, there is a detailed description of a grave transgression—drinking from the sacred vessels of the Temple to honor pagan idols; but there is also a troubling mischance or affliction—the hand that writes a mysterious inscription on the wall, which arouses great dread and leads to the summons to Daniel when it becomes clear that none of the sorcerers and magicians can decipher the inscription. King Belshazzar has no reason to disguise himself. Furthermore, the story totally lacks the signs—both that of seeing through the disguise and that of the announcement of the impending death of the heir (evidently because it ends with the death of the father of the dynasty himself: "That very night, Belshazzar, the Chaldean king, was killed" [v. 30]). I would like to thank my student, Amihai Nahshon, who pointed out this partial parallel to me.

2. Kimchi expounds the passage thus: "Because he knew that Ahijah hated him for having gone away from the Lord, he said in his heart: 'If Ahijah knows that she is my wife he is certain to prophesy misfortune' (based on Ahab's remarks about Micaiah ben Imlah [1 Kings 22:8]); hence he told his wife to disguise herself so that he would not recognize her as the wife of Jeroboam."

3. When Saul ordered his servants to find a musician to play for him, he explicitly ordered that he be brought to the royal court (1 Sam. 16:17).

4. According to Ehrlich (*Randglossen* 3, p. 263), the visit takes place at night because witches work only in the dark. Josephus (*Antiquities of the Jews* 6,14,2 [p. 333]), however, ascribes the timing to the king's desire to conceal his departure from camp: "Saul, without the knowledge of any in the camp, stripped off his royal robes and, accompanied by two servants whom he knew to be quite trustworthy, came to Dor." Abravanel interprets the nocturnal visit in the same way, though with

an allusion to Saul's military responsibilities: "They went by night so that no one in the camp would see and be aware of his absence." Indeed, the fact that the narrator considers it necessary to emphasize that they also returned by night (v. 25) shows that, whether or not the medium needed darkness, it was certainly necessary to conceal the king's humiliating visit to her.

5. This association is noted by Fokkelman, *Narrative Art* 2, p. 602.

6. Generally speaking, after the phrase "he swore by the Lord," the divine name is not mentioned in the oath itself (see 2 Sam. 19:8; 1 Kings 1:17 and 30; 2:8 and 42), while the form "as the Lord lives" is not accompanied by the stipulation that the oath was in the name of by the Lord (see Judg. 8:19; 1 Sam. 19:6, 26:10; 1 Kings 1:29; Jer. 4:2, 38:16). By contrast, the emphatic repetition in verse 10, "Saul swore to her *by the Lord*: 'As *the Lord* lives . . . ' " is very rare (see 1 Kings 2:23, and to some extent also 1 Sam. 20:42; Jer. 12:16). Presumably this emphasis is intended to underscore the internal contradiction in Saul's action. R. Simeon ben Lakish pointed this out through an apt simile: "What did Saul resemble at that moment? A woman who is with her lover and swears by her husband's life. So too Saul was inquiring of the necromancer and medium and swore to her by the Lord, 'As the Lord lives, you won't get into trouble for this' " (*Leviticus Rabba* 26,7, vol. 3, ed. Margoliouth [Jerusalem, 1958], p. 600).

7. Ben-Sira numbers among Samuel's praises his prophetic presence at Endor: "Moreover after he died he was enquired of, he declared unto the king his way. And he lifted his voice from the earth, to blot out iniquity by prophecy" (Sir. 46:20). The Sages, too, accepted the testimony of the verses as given and did not question the ability of mediums to create a real link with the dead. They even formulated a careful description of the invocation of the dead, based on our chapter: "Three things have been said about one who raises the dead by magic means: the one who raises him sees him but does not hear his voice [based on v. 21]; the one who asks the question hears his voice but does not see him [v. 13]; the bystanders [like Saul's two attendants] neither hear nor see" (*Tanḥuma*, Emor, §2; cf. Mishna Sanhedrin 7,7; BT Sanhedrin 65b). The doubts on the matter began in the Geonic period. Saadya Gaon denied the possibility that the medium resurrected Samuel but also rejected the anonymous opinion that one could interpret the words "Samuel said to Saul" (v. 15) as expressing—against their plain meaning—Saul's subjective impressions. He preferred to assume that it was God who brought back Samuel (cited by Samuel ben Hofni Gaon in his responsum concerning the story of the medium [L. Ginzberg, *Ginzei Schechter* (New York, 1929) 1, pp. 299–300 (Hebrew)]; see also Abravanel's commentary on v. 8). Samuel ben Hofni Gaon agreed that it is contrary to reason for a medium to raise the dead but disagreed with Saadya's reluctance to accept metaphorization of "Samuel said" and with Saadya's solution. Instead, he interpreted the entire scene as a sham: everything that Saul heard was spoken by the medium of her own accord (ibid.). Hai Gaon returned to Sa'adiah's approach without rejecting the legitimacy, in principle, of Samuel ben Hofni's interpretation (see his truncated response in Simḥa Assaf, *From the Geonic Literature* [Jerusalem, 1932/33], pp. 156–58 [Hebrew]), as was later done, in acerbic language, by the Spanish exegete Isaac ben Samuel Alkanzi (in his *Arabic Commentary on the Book of Samuel*, ad loc., MS Firkovitch II 3362, which is being prepared for publication by Maaravi Peretz). Abraham Ibn Ezra forcefully rejected the possibility that there could be anything real in the acts of mediums and spiritualists: "The empty-headed said: 'Were mediums not genuine, as well as sorcerous practices, Scripture would not have banned them. I say precisely the opposite: Scripture does not ban what is true, but only what is false, as is attested by idols and graven images! I do not wish to go on at length, otherwise I would provide clear proofs to explain the matter of the medium" (commentary on Lev. 19:31). In his long com-

mentary on Exod. 22:3, Ibn Ezra comes very close to the approach of Samuel ben Hofni: "Samuel's words, 'Why have you disturbed me?' report, not what Samuel said, but what Saul heard: the verse is speaking from Saul's perspective." From his commentary on "one who inquires of the dead" (Deut. 18:11), however, it follows that he saw this as autosuggestion rather than as trickery perpetrated by the medium: "It is like when one goes to the cemetery and takes the bone of a dead person; his thoughts and folly will show him an image in a dream or even awake. All of these are abominations to the Lord." (In his commentary on Lev. 19:31 and 20:27, Isa. 29:4, and Job 32:19, he calls necromancy "an art.") Maimonides has similar things to say on the subject (*Commentary on the Mishna*, Sanhedrin 7,7; *Sefer Hamitzvot*, negative commandments 8, 9, 38; *Laws of Idolatry* 6:1, 11:14 and 16). So does his son Abraham (*Responsa*, §27, p. 37). On the other hand, Kimchi and Abravanel are convinced that mediums really do raise the dead. The former follows the Sages, whereas the latter has his own approach: "as it is said, it was with the force of the demon and did not apply to Samuel's soul, Heaven forfend, but only to his body. It is the demon that knows what will happen in the future and tells them. Samuel's soul was not vouchsafed a prophecy after his death" (*Commentary on the Former Prophets*, ad loc.).

8. Readers were perplexed by this as early as the Second Temple period. The Septuagint renders verse 14 as "an upright man" (reading *zaqef*, 'upright', in place of the Masoretic *zaqen*, 'old'). Frankel (*Vorstudien*, p. 188) suggested that this may have been what the Midrash had in mind: "How did she know? The Sages said: The shade of a king does not rise the same way as the shade of a commoner. For a king, his face is above and his feet below, like people in the world, whereas for a commoner, his face is below and his feet above" (*Tanhuma*, Emor §2). Josephus, however, explains that it was Samuel who identified himself (*Antiquities of the Jews* 6,14,2). Kaufmann's explanation (*Collected Papers*, p. 214) involves reconstructing the biblical view of the mantic nature of invoking the dead: "She 'sees' Samuel through the power of sorcery and through the power of sorcery she 'knows' what he knows. The prophetic afflatus from the world of spirits is drawn down on her, and through this power she also recognizes Saul." Whereas Fokkelman (*Narrative Art* 2, p. 606) explains the scene by invoking contemporary parapsychological theory.

9. This comparison was pointed out by Kaufmann, *Collected Papers*, p. 215. In the annunciation of the birth of Isaac (Gen. 18:1–16), too, the miraculous disclosure of what is concealed in the present lends greater veracity to the prediction of the future. Not only was Sarah inside the tent and hidden from the eyes of the visitors, who sat outside under the tree, she laughed inwardly and even sought to deny the fact. Nevertheless, her laughter was exposed by the angelic guest, a fact that embarrassed her at the moment but at the same time served as solid proof of the truthfulness of the announcement.

10. Kaufmann (ibid., p. 210) explained that the first axiom of invoking the dead is "that the souls of the dead are 'divine beings' [*elohim*]" (1 Sam. 28:13; Isa. 8:19), nonearthly beings from another sphere of existence; they have a mantic ability to know and reveal what is hidden in the future."

11. "R. Isaac ben Hiyya said, 'The heart alone knows its bitterness' (Prov. 14:10). Why didn't [Saul] say to [Samuel], 'or by urim and thummim'? Because if [Saul] had said to him, 'or by urim and thummim,' [Samuel] would have replied, 'You did evil when you destroyed Nob, the city of the priests' " (*Leviticus Rabba* 26,7, vol. 3, ed. Margoliouth, p. 604). See also BT Berakot 12b.

12. This possible link was suggested by Kiel, *Book of Samuel*, vol. 1, p. 285, and by Fokkelman, *Narrative Art* 2, p. 611.

13. See the excellent literary analysis of this story by Sternberg, *Poetics*, pp. 482–515.

14. With the Masoretic reading, ʿareka 'your enemy', compare Ps. 139:20 and Dan. 4:16. The Masoretic reading is to be preferred to the *vorlage* of the Septuagint, ʿim reʿeka 'with your fellow', which seems to be influenced by the text of the next verse, "and has given it to your fellow, to David."

15. Gunn (*Fate of King Saul*, p. 109) compares Saul's fast, which began at least twenty-four hours before the battle, with the ban on eating that he imposed on his soldiers in the middle of the battle at Michmas (1 Sam. 14:24). The fact that Jonathan did not know about that strict prohibition, as well as his sharp criticism of the damage done by the oath, criticism that he voiced for all to hear (vv. 27–30), shows that this was no sacral fast (supposed—on the basis of these very same verses—to have been practiced during holy wars). Presumably, then, Saul's imposition of the fast at Michmas was a disciplinary and tactical measure, meant to press the pursuit of the fleeing Philistines to its utmost potential.

16. The rhetorical use of "measure for measure" by both the witch and the prophet intensifies the formal resemblance in their manner of speaking, examined at the beginning of this chapter.

17. Kimchi discussed the significance of baking matzoh in his commentary on verse 25: "This is said in order to tell us that she rushed to bake it and did not wait for it to leaven so that she could feed him quickly, because she saw that he was extremely upset."

18. The same applies to the personal condemnations uttered by several prophets: Elijah—"the Israelites have forsaken Your covenant, torn down Your altars, and put Your prophets to the sword. I alone am left, and they are out to take my life" (1 Kings 19:10); Hosea—"Give them, O Lord—give them what? Give them a womb that miscarries, and shriveled breasts" (Hos. 9:14); and Jeremiah—"For I was like a docile lamb led to the slaughter; I did not know that it was against me they devised their plots. . . . O Lord of Hosts, O just Judge, Who tries the hearts and the mind, let me see Your vengeance upon them, for I lay my case before You" (Jer. 11:19–20; cf. 17:14–18 and 18:21–23).

19. Josephus emphasizes the narrator's extremely positive portrayal of the witch: "Here it is but right to commend the generosity of this woman, who . . . bore him no resentment for having condemned her profession nor turned him away as a stranger and as one with whom she had never been acquainted; but instead she gave him sympathy and consolation, exhorted him to do that which he regarded with great unwillingness [i.e., to eat], and offered him with open friendliness the one thing which in her poverty she possessed. . . . It is well, then, to take this woman for an example and show kindness to all who are in need, and to regard nothing as nobler than this or more befitting the human race, or more likely to make God gracious and ready to bestow upon us this blessing (*Antiquities of the Jews*, 6, 14,4 [p. 339]).

20. Rahab, too, is described in generally positive moral terms. She wins the reader's sympathy not only on account of her kindness to the spies sent by Joshua but also, and chiefly, on account of her resourcefulness, courage, and profound theological discernment. Bird ("Harlot as Heroine," pp. 110–39) demonstrated how the story of the Jericho spies is built on the surprising reversal of readers' expectations about the negative heroine.

21. The idea that the story itself is balanced does not seem plausible to those who refuse to credit scriptural narratives with complexity and sophistication. Where we find a consciously elaborated balance, such readers find only an editorial patchwork of conflicting biases. Hertzberg (*I and II Samuel*, p. 220), for example, hypothesizes that our narrative is composed of two layers: the first, reflecting the attitude of Saul's contemporaries, is sympathetic to the king and aware of the tragic element in his personality and fate. The second layer, he holds, represents the Deu-

teronomistic school, which judges Saul and represents his recourse to necromancy as decisive proof of the justness of God's rejection of him.

22. See the thoughtful and sensitive analysis of Samuel's intercession offered by Muffs, *Love and Joy*, pp. 25–27.

23. All this is deftly illuminated by Sternberg in *Poetics*, pp. 505–15.

24. An extreme measure of excessive moralizing can be found in Beuken, "1 Samuel 28," pp. 3–17. According to Beuken, Saul initially refuses to eat because he understands that it is forbidden for him to gain restored vitality from a woman whose profession is based on death. When, out of weakness, he does give in to her urging that "now you also listen to your handmaid" (v. 22), this merely intensifies the rebuke of Samuel's earlier "you did not listen to the Lord" (v. 18). Thus Saul reaches the nadir of obeying the medium instead of obeying the Lord.

25. Only through bold homiletical interpretations could the Midrashists find any balance between strict justice and mercy in the soul of the prophet himself. For example, they ascribed Saul's recovery of fortitude to Samuel's counsel: "[Saul] said to him, 'Can't I escape?' [Samuel] answered, 'If you run away, will you be saved?' [Saul] asked him, 'Can't I draw up my troops in battle array?' [Samuel] said to him, 'If you array your troops for battle, will you win? If, however, you accept the [divine] verdict, then "tomorrow you and your sons will be with me." ' R. Yohanan said, ' "With me" means "in my company" ' [i.e., in Paradise!]" (*Leviticus Rabba* 26,7, vol. 3, ed. Margoliouth, pp. 605–606).

26. Saul's valor is praised by three persons with experience in the ways of kings and their battles: David (2 Sam. 1:17–27), Josephus (*Antiquities of the Jews* 6,14,2), and Isaac Abravanel, who writes, in his commentary on verse 25: "After they ate they made their way back to camp. This is the great heroism of Saul, that he 'put forth more strength' [Eccles. 10:10], knowing for certain that he and his sons would die in that battle, for he defied death 'on the heights of the field' [Judg. 5:18] like 'the mighty men that were of old, the men of renown' [Gen. 6:4]."

4. "That Man Is You!"

1. The reading of 2 Sam. 10:7, *ha-ṣavaʾ ha-gibborim*, presents both linguistic and semantic difficulties. The reading of 1 Chron. 19:8, *ṣ̌vaʾ ha-gibborim*, is to be preferred. In fact, Jonathan, the Lucianic version of the Septuagint, and the Peshitta all render the phrase in 2 Samuel as if this were the reading.

2. Yadin ("Valley of Sucoth," pp. 170–76) proposed that we understand the word *sukkoth* here not in the sense of temporary structures but as a place name. The assumption that "the Ark and Israel and Judah" were not bivouacked in the field with the professional army that was besieging Rabbath-Ammon but instead remained in the base camp in the Valley of Sukkot is compatible with the rest of the military information provided in the story. We should add that Joab's language in his message to David, "Now muster *the rest of the troops*" (12:28) does not indicate a further mobilization of reserves but refers to the rear echelon encamped in the Valley of Sukkot, as is indicated by the use of the term employed by the narrator in the first part of the frame tale: "*the rest of the troops* he put under the command of his brother Abishai" (10:10).

3. See Gen. 39:6; Exod. 2:24–25; Judg. 19:30; 2 Kings 5:19, and other references given in chapter 6 n. 20.

4. A false ending, followed by a sequel that takes both protagonist and reader by surprise, can be found in: "As he finished speaking, he threw the jawbone away; hence that place was called Ramath-lehi" (Judg. 15:17). Samson celebrates his strength in a secular song of victory, throws down his ad hoc weapon, confident that no further dangers are lurking, and commemorates his bare-handed triumph

over 3000 enemies by naming the place Ramath-lehi. Many scriptural stories end with an etiological note of this sort (e.g., Num. 11:3 and 34; 20:13; 21:3; Josh. 22:34). But here, to our great astonishment, this is not the end of the story. Almost at once Samson again finds himself in mortal danger, threatened by terrible thirst. Now he has the wisdom to call on the Lord, thanking Him for His great salvation and asking Him to save him from death by dehydration. The story reaches its true conclusion with an additional etiological note: Samson commemorates the prayer that was answered by giving the place the name *Ein ha-qore* (v. 19).

5. Veijola ("Salomo," pp. 230–41), who is mining the story for cruxes that will allow him to distinguish sources and conjecturally reconstruct the evolution of the story, is unable to discern the rhetorical function of the child's anonymity. He arrives at the extravagant hypothesis that *this* child was originally named Solomon, since (he contends) the original continuation of "she bore him a son" (11:27a) has to be "and named him Solomon" (12:24b), and everything between these two phrases—the infant's death and Nathan's rebuke—is only a later interpolation. See below, n. 60.

6. Smith (*Books of Samuel,* ad loc.) suggests this possibility but prefers the *kethib* "the messengers" *(ha-mal'akhim)* to the *qere* "the kings" *(ha-mᵉlakhim)*. But even without the unequivocal testimony of the parallel text in 1 Chron. 20:1, of the ancient versions, of the Aleppo Codex, and of a number of medieval manuscripts, the *qere* seems more plausible since it relates the temporal setting to the season of the year appropriate for warfare rather than to the previous dispatch of messengers which, timewise, is quite irrelevant to the present context. Particularly sensitive is the rendering of the Targum on 1 Chron. 20:1: "At the season when kings leave their palaces—in the month of Nisan." Perry and Sternberg ("King through Ironic Eyes,") developed at length the hypothesis that verse 1 is meant ironically (see pp. 267–69); but they, too, believe that the irony has been tempered and even concealed by the factual chronicle style.

7. McCarter pointed out this parallel (*I and II Samuel,* p. 286).

8. "My master's servants" cannot be taken to mean "Joab's servants" (i.e., troops), since the royal army is consistently referred to as the king's *servants,* whereas a local commander's troops are his *men*: "David said to Abishai: . . . 'Take your lord's *servants* (*ᶜavdei ʾadonekha*) and pursue him. . . . Joab's *men* (*ʾanšei Yoʾav*), the Cherethites and Pelethites, and all the warriors, marched out behind him" (2 Sam. 20:6–7; cf. 1 Sam. 29:10–11; 2 Sam. 2:12–13 and 29–32).

9. *Contra* Garsiel ("Story of David," pp. 256–59) who argues that the story does contain sufficient hints that, along with the historical information available to us, make it possible to reconstruct the process of Uriah's dawning awareness of David's betrayal.

10. This is the tack of Adar (*Biblical Narrative,* p. 201), who views the protest by the injured party as complementary to the prophet's rebuke: "David is brought low first by the courage of Uriah, and second by Nathan's rebuke; he is brought low because there are free men under the king and because there is a God over the king."

11. Perry and Sternberg ("King through Ironic Eyes") disagree. They believe that the uncertainty as to whether Uriah knows about his wife's infidelity is intentional and serves to intensify the ironic perspective on the sinful king by means of two carefully balanced sets of lacunae to be filled in. For criticism of their view, see Arpali, "Caution," and Simon, "Ironic Approach." For Perry and Sternberg's rebuttal, see "Caution," pp. 608–63.

12. Perry and Sternberg ("King through Ironic Eyes," p. 277) hypothesize that David did suspect that Uriah knew, suggest that he entrusted him with the letter anyway because, in the pressure of the situation, he had lost his better judgment

and did not realize the attendant danger. But the humiliation that would ensue from disclosure of the contents of the letter is so extreme, and the consequences of Uriah's survival are so fateful, that the assumption that David's wits failed him to the point that he did not foresee all of this seems absurd—especially since he could easily have dispatched the letter by another messenger. Perry and Sternberg (ibid., p. 274) think Uriah's conduct suspicious because it was too idealistic: why didn't he visit his home for even a few minutes? Could such a brief visit be interpreted as disloyalty to his comrades? We may reply that, given Bathsheba's exquisite beauty, her husband might act according to the principle, "Tell the Nazirite to walk around the vineyard and not come near it" (BT Šabbat 13a). Even were Uriah not afraid of his own impulses, he might be apprehensive about the tongue-wagging of those who saw him entering or leaving his house. The bottom line, though, is that the narrator provides not the slightest hint of any such suspicion on David's part.

13. That David was well known for his machinations is demonstrated by Saul's apprehensions, "I have been told he is a very cunning fellow" (1 Sam. 23:22).

14. One of Ehrlich's arguments (*Randglossen* 3, pp. 295–96) for the historical implausibility of the Bathsheba episode is that, in those days, a king of Israel would not have had to kill a husband in order to wed the wife. His proof is that Saul took Michal from David's house and gave her to Paltiel ben Laish; David, when he reigned in Hebron, took her back from Paltiel. But the two cases are not really parallel, and Michal's vicissitudes say nothing about the normal custom in Israel. With regard to Egypt, Gressmann (*Die älteste Geschichtsschreibung*, p. 157), offers an extrascriptural proof: the spell engraved on the pyramid of the pharaoh Onas includes the phrase: "Then he will take the wives away from their husbands whereto he wishes, whenever his heart desires them."

15. The addition, "Joab's arms-bearer," appended to verse 3 in 4QSam[a] and also documented by Josephus (*Antiquities of the Jews* 7,7,1) (see Ulrich, *Qumran Text*, p. 173), resolves both problems.

16. See also *Gesenius' Hebrew Grammar*, §141e, where our verse is cited as an example of the circumstantial *waw*, along with other verses, including Judg. 13:9 and 2 Sam. 4:10.

17. This interpretation is adopted by Nowack, Driver, Smith, Segal, and Hertzberg in their commentaries ad loc. Smith notes that the Arabs of antiquity knew that this is the most favorable time for conception; compare the Sages' observation that "a woman conceives only near the time of her immersion" (BT Niddah 31b).

18. This exegetical triumph is unknown to the modern commentators I have checked, except for Ehrlich (*Randglossen* 3, p. 296). Perry and Sternberg ("King through Ironic Eyes," p. 270) and Fokkelman (*Narrative Art* 1, p. 52) reached the same conclusion independently.

19. Compare the irony created by the unconscious echo in the words of Job's wife ("Blaspheme God and die" [2:9]), of what Satan had said to God ("he will surely blaspheme You to Your face" [2:5]); or again, in what the captain tells Jonah ("Arise, call upon your god!" [1:6]), of the Lord's instruction to His prophet ("Arise and go to Nineveh and call out against it" [1:2]). Only the reader is aware that Job's wife's counsel echoes Satan's words. Job's ignorance thereof gives additional force to his vigorous refusal: "You talk as any shameless woman might talk" (2:10). By contrast, Jonah and David could have heard the voice of God speaking to them from the mouths of the captain and Uriah; but they were determined not to do so.

20. In the Peshitta and the Lucianic version of the Septuagint, "the next day" is part of the following verse. Nowack, Driver, Ehrlich (*Randglossen* 3, p. 297), Fokkelman (*Narrative Art* 1, p. 57) and McCarter prefer this text, also according to which Uriah spent three days in Jerusalem. I prefer the Masoretic division, however,

because it highlights the contrast between David's promise to dispatch Uriah on the morrow and his failure to do so.

21. This represents a deviation from his remarkable sensitivity to God's providential intervention in the course of his life: 1 Sam. 24:10; 25:32 and 39; 26:23; 2 Sam. 5:20; 6:21.

22. Gunkel (*Das Märchen*, p. 132) offers two European literary parallels to Uriah's letter, which has become a catchword. One comes from *Iliad* VI, 168–90; the second from *Hamlet*, V, ii. For a possible Sumerian parallel, see B. Alster, "A Note on the Uriah Letter in the Sumerian Sargon Legend," *Zeitschrift für Assyriologie* 77 (1987), pp. 169–73. Abravanel sees it as one of Uriah's virtues that "he did not look at the letter, did not read it, and gave it to Joab." But for the narrator (who focuses, as we have seen, on the protagonist), the main thing is David's manipulation of this fidelity. The letter was undoubtedly sealed with the royal signet (cf. Isa. 29:11), as Josephus confidently states (*Antiquities of the Jews*, 7,6,1). Nevertheless, it is clear that David would not have entrusted it to Uriah had he not been entirely certain of the latter's trusting innocence.

Using victims as the means of their own destruction is so repugnant to Nachmanides that he found a prooftext in the Pentateuch that this must not be done even to animals. He notes, on "two of each kind shall come to you to stay alive" (Gen. 6:20): "He told [Noah] that they would come to him in pairs of their own accord, so he would not have to hunt them in the mountains and islands. . . . But later (7:2) He commanded him to *take* seven pairs of each clean species. He did not say that these would come to him, but that he should take them. Those coming to be saved and produce offspring after them come of their own volition; but [God] did not decree that those who would be sacrificed as burnt offerings *come on their own to be slaughtered;* rather, Noah must take them."

23. David's two other orders to Joab in this chapter (vv. 6 and 25) use the singular imperative.

24. The addition that follows here in the Lucianic text of the Septuagint (v. 24), namely, that the number of those slain was "around 18," is of great literary interest. The phrasing echoes that with regard to the casualties at the fall of Ai— "about 36 of them" (Josh. 7:5). In both places we encounter a typological number based on twelve, which is a round number in the sexagesimal system. Around "three dozen" fell at the gates of Ai, and around "a dozen-and-a-half" outside the gate of Rabbath-Ammon.

25. Joab's dilemma is vividly portrayed in the Midrash. " 'Put Uriah in the thick of the battle.' So David wrote to Joab. He complied and Uriah was killed. *All* the commanders attacked Joab, as we read: 'Uriah the Hittite: thirty-seven in *all*' (2 Sam. 23:39). He showed them his commission. This is why David says: 'what Joab son of Zeruiah did to me' " (1 Kings 2:5)" (*Yalqut Shimoni* 2,148).

26. The narrator tells us nothing about the relations between Joab and Uriah.

27. Nevertheless, such an accusation is made in the Midrash, which aims to demonstrate the power of repentance: "Rabbi Yohanan said: 'David was sorry about three things, and the Holy One, blessed be He, forgave him for them. . . . and for the wife of Uriah the Hittite, on account of whom the Israelites maligned him: Is it possible that David, who stole the lamb and killed the shepherd and caused *Israel to fall by the sword*, can have any victory?—'There is no deliverance for him through God' (Ps. 3:3)! But He did forgive him: 'The Lord has remitted your sin; you shall not die' (2 Sam. 12:13)" (*Yalqut Shimoni* 2,148).

28. Relying exclusively on tactical considerations, Garsiel ("Story of David," pp. 259–60) reconstructs Joab's plan of attack on the city by means of a suicide squad that included Uriah. The story's silence about this first stage of the battle he ex-

plains as due to the fact that the scriptural historiographer has an ethical rather than a military perspective. The narrator conceals what really happened because he does not wish to justify Joab's actions as militarily plausible, and especially because he wants to teach us the lesson that killing one person may cause the death of many more. This example of Garsiel's method of "the integration of the disciplines, literature and historiography" (ibid., p. 248) casts doubt on its legitimacy, since the attempt to offer a literary explanation for the narrator's silence about a totally hypothetical historical incident offends the canons of both disciplines.

29. As proof of this, note the duplication in the Septuagint text—"all that Joab had sent him to say / all about the battle"—created by the combination of what Joab said above (v. 18) and what the narrator says here (v. 22).

30. See *Gesenius' Hebrew Grammar*, §157b.

31. This interpretation is suggested by Keil and Delitzsch, *Books of Samuel*, ad loc.

32. In the opinion of Fokkelman (*Narrative Art* 1, pp. 60–69), this loquacity, centered on the question, "Who killed Abimelech?" is meant to create an analogy between the shameful and unnecessary death of Abimelech at the hands of a woman and the similar death of Uriah because of a woman. Joab could only have guessed that Uriah died on account of his wife. In David's ears, however, the analogy rings with great force and reinforces his guilt.

33. Perry and Sternberg ("King through Ironic Eyes," p. 277), who assess David's order as undercutting its own purpose, ascribe the improvement of the plan to Joab the "doer": "So he plans the suicide attack in which many are killed, *among* them Uriah" (p. 279). They emphasize the word "among" so they can rely on the verse, "Uriah the Hittite was *among* those who died" (v. 17). But they ignore the fact that nothing the narrator says in that verse suggests that it was Joab who initiated that skirmish. Because the envoy explicitly says that the initiative was that of the Ammonites and that Uriah and his men approached the wall only in hot pursuit, Perry and Sternberg assume that one must not rely on his words because he spoke out of fear of the king's anger and, similarly, that when the narrator says, "The messenger went and came and told David all that Joab had sent him to say" (v. 22), it is an expression of the feigned naiveté (p. 280) that they are seeking throughout their analysis. This approach suffers not only from implausible interpretations and arbitrary assumptions but also from ignoring the ethical dimension given to the story of the battle by the ironic reversal in the status of David and Joab regarding conscientious self-control.

34. Fokkelman (*Narrative Art* 1, pp. 63–64) understands the echo in the same way.

35. The acceptance of the local setback on the battlefield is a direct result of the stratagem of using the enemy's sword to eliminate an important man whom the king wants out of the way. David should have remembered how morally repugnant and militarily questionable is such a stratagem, since Saul had intended to apply it to him when he was a commander in the latter's army: "Saul said to David, 'Here is my older daughter, Merab; I will give her to you in marriage; in return, you be my warrior and fight the battles of the Lord.' Saul thought: 'Let not my hand strike him; let the hand of the Philistines strike him' " (1 Sam. 18:17; reiterated in vv. 21 and 25).

36. Gunkel (*Das Märchen*, p. 133) found something like a juridical parable in Herodotus: after Cambyses murdered his brothers, his sister rebuked him indirectly by stripping the leaves from a lettuce and asking whether the denuded plant was more attractive than the full one. When he replied that it was prettier when the leaves were on, she said, "But thou has done as I did to the lettuce, and made bare the house of Cyrus!" (Herodotus 3,32, trans. G. Rawlinson [London, 1880]). This

is not a legal suit to be adjudicated, however, but only a picturesque exemplification of a contemptible deed. From the perspective of the listener's surprise, the dramatic irony, and the sudden revelation of the real culprit, there is some resemblance to the juridical parables found in Scripture.

37. According to Abraham Ibn Ezra, there is another juridical parable in Haggai 2:11–19: "This was a parable like Nathan's parable to David, where he caught him and said to him, 'That man is you' " (commentary on Haggai 2:14, emended according to MS London-Montefiore 49). There Haggai asks the priests a halakic question concerning the difference between the transmission of sanctity through indirect contact and the transmission of impurity. He applies their unequivocal answer as to the greater infective power of impurity to the impurity of the sacrifices offered by "this people." It does not seem, though, that this is a juridical parable meant to trap the judges in self-incrimination, since it is not the priests who are ensnared by their judgment and their response is merely intended to provide, in dramatic form, halakic information that can serve as a basis for indicting others.

38. See the discussion above, pp. 118–21.

39. As was shown by Hoffman ("Song of the Vineyard"), the parable of the vineyard differs from the classic juridical parable in that there is no attempt at hermetic camouflage from the outset and that various hints are strewn through the body of the parable to make the audience wonder whether the prophet is really referring to a vineyard, to a beloved woman, or perhaps to Judah and Israel. Furthermore, the identification of the vineyard with the House of Israel does not strike the hearers without warning, since the owner of the vineyard has already been identified indirectly: "I will command the clouds to drop no rain on it" (Isa. 5:6b).

40. *Contra* Weisman (*People and King*, pp. 45–47), who believes that the crime of the widow's son is less severe because it was a case of manslaughter rather than murder. He reads the words, "there was no one to come *between them*" (v. 6) as indicating that the widow used a neutral term so as not to incriminate the surviving brother of premeditated murder. Were this her intention, though, she should have used the phraseology of scriptural law and said that the assailant had not "been hostile to [the victim] in the past" (Deut. 4:42) or that he "did not seek his harm" (Num. 35:23). What is more, the ostensible close reading has no standing without a far-fetched and unsupported emendation of the text: instead of "and killed him (*wa-yameth ʾotho*)," Weisman proposes that we read "and he died (*wa-yamoth*)."

41. In spite of this difference, David was able to empathize with the widow, because the initial rumor of Absalom's murder of Amnon included the (false) report that "he had killed all the king's sons and that not one of them had survived" (2 Sam. 13:30). This was pointed out in a term paper by one of my students, Ilana Goldstein.

42. This applies also to the innovative glosses proposed by Hoftijzer ("David and the Tekoite Woman," pp. 424–42). Despite their philological underpinnings, they are no more persuasive than the accepted intuitive glosses.

43. Daube ("Nathan's Parable," pp. 275–88) holds that this difficulty is so serious as to entail the conclusion that the parable of the poor man's lamb originally referred to an incident in which the husband was not murdered. He hypothesizes that it was intended to castigate Saul for taking Michal, David's only wife at the time, away from him and giving her to Palti ben Laish (the traveler in the parable). When David sinned with Bathsheba, the parable was redirected against him, in part to rebuke him for doing to Uriah what Saul had done to him. Such a secondary use of the parable would have been possible, even though it is more appropriate to the former circumstance because, according to Daube, patriarchal society views theft and adultery as kindred crimes (p. 285). Yet this explanation applies equally to the original use of the parable; the very need to rely on it for a hypothetical

reuse indicates that the doubtful reconstruction of the history of the parable has not resolved the problem.

44. See Simon, "The Parable of Jotham," pp. 1–34, esp. pp. 11–14.

45. Another possible reason for the use here of the rare word *helekh* is to create an association between the primary cause of the real-life sequence of events and its reflection in the parable. At the beginning of the story of David's sin, we read "David . . . strolled (*wa-yithhallekh*) on the roof of the royal palace" (2 Sam. 11:2); at the beginning of the rich man's sin we read: "a traveler (*helekh*) came to the rich man." I cannot provide a suitable literary answer, other than the scriptural vogue for elegant variation (e.g., both *ʾiš* and *baʿal* for husband [2 Sam. 11:26]; *selaʿ* and *ṣur* for rock [Judg. 6:20–21]; *naʿar* and *ʿelem* for lad [1 Sam. 17:65–68]), to the Sages' question (BT Sukka 52b): "At first he is called *helekh* (traveler), later *ʾoreah* (guest), and finally *ʾiš* (man)." In their reading, the traveler stands for the evil inclination, and the verbal progression from the traveler passing through to the guest who stays a while to the man who has settled down in the household expresses a moral lesson: "The Evil Inclination starts out like a spider's web but ends up like the ropes of a wagon" (ibid., 52a).

46. *The Beduin Tribes in the District of Beersheba* (Hebrew translation, Tel Aviv, n.d.), pp. 66–67, 123. Because this paragraph is rendered in non-technical language in the later English version of this book (Aref, *Beduin Love, Law, and Legend*, pp. 146–47), I have deviated slightly from the text presented there. Compare: "It is lawful in case of need to requisition another man's sheep for the purpose of entertaining a guest" (Murry, *Sons of Ishmael*, p. 60). In a personal communication, Professor Emanuel Marx (author of *Bedouin of the Negev* [New York, 1967]) wrote me that he had encountered a similar case in his fieldwork among the Negev Bedouin: "Salem Abu Gwe'id had agreed to buy two sheep from Wefi Abi ʿAroz ten years ago, for IL 3.5 (IL 1.75 each), but had not yet paid. Came a guest and he slaughtered one of the sheep. Then Wefi became angry and swore to divorce his wife if he ever sold the sheep to Salem, and refused to accept payment. He dragged Salem to the qadi, first to Sheikh Abu Qrenat who wanted him to return the one sheep and also pay IL 3. But Salem refused to comply, claiming that double payment was due only where custom had been infringed, but here this was not the case. Then it was agreed that Salem was to pay IL 2.5 for the second sheep, so that Wefi would get a slightly higher price. Wefi for quite some time refused to take the awarded amount, but in the end submitted." Professor Marx explained that the dispute stemmed from the fact that only the buyer was a Bedouin, whereas the seller was a fellah "who was not concerned about the custom of slaughtering a sheep to entertain a guest. The verdict represented a compromise between the customs of the two sides."

47. The verb *l.q.ḥ*, 'take', is used for theft (Judg. 17:2) and for armed robbery (Prov. 27:13). Nathan probably used this verb to indicate that the rich man treated the poor man's property as if it were his own: "he was loath to take (*laqaḥath*) anything from his own flocks or herds . . . so he took (*wa-yiqqaḥ*) the poor man's lamb" (12:4).

48. See G. Gerleman, "Struktur und Eigenart der hebräischen Sprache," *Svensk Exegesik Arbok* 22/23 (1957/58), p. 256. Gerleman rightly argues that the poor man's relationship with his lamb is described metaphorically and emotionally rather than literally. Even if this were a literal description, "drink from his cup" does not mean that they drank from the same vessel but, as Ehrlich demonstrated, that they drank the same beverage (parallel to partitive sense of "ate [of] his bread"). Something similar is found in the Assyrian myth of "The Debate between the Shepherd and the Farmer": when they importune the goddess to marry the

shepherd, they promise her: "his goodly repast he will eat with you" (Pritchard, *ANET*, p. 41).

49. Readers in antiquity, much closer to the daily life of shepherds, understood that there is nothing "absolutely unnatural" (Stolz, *Das erste und zweite Buch Samuel*, p. 240) or any "exaggerated sentimentality" (Lasine, "Melodrama as Parable," p. 103) in the fact that one small lamb might be so dear to its poor owner that he raises it with himself and his sons (that is, in his house and not in the sheepfold) and that it might even nestle in his bosom like a daughter (see 1 Kings 3:20), with the same sort of intimacy that the devoted shepherd treats his flock: "He gathers the lambs in his arms and carries them in his bosom" (Isa. 40:11).

50. R. Judah bar Ḥanina solved the problem by understanding the dual form *ʾarbaʿtayim* not as "fourfold" but as "four times four": "The Holy One, Blessed be He, said to David: 'You committed adultery once; sixteen adulteries will be committed against you. You killed once; sixteen of yours will be killed.' Fourfold—four times four is sixteen" (*Yalquṭ Shimoni* 2,148).

51. Like Abravanel, Caspari (*Die Samuelbücher*, p. 533), Hertzberg (*I und II Samuel*, p. 313), and Fokkelman (*Narrative Art* 1, p. 77).

52. A poor man's means of sustenance are compared to his very life: "A hand-mill or an upper millstone shall not be taken in pawn, for that would be taking someone's life in pawn" (Deut. 24:6; cf. 24:15). See also the peasant's appeal to the chief steward in the Egyptian story, "The Protest of the Eloquent Peasant": "Do not plunder of his property a poor man, a weakling as thou knowest him. His property is the (very) breath of a suffering man, and he who takes it away from him is one who stops up his nose" (Pritchard, ANET, p. 409).

53. According to Phillips ("Interpretation of 2 Sam XII, 5–6," pp. 242–44), *ben maweth* and the synonymous *ʾiš maweth* (2 Sam. 19:29; 1 Kings 2:26) are terms used to express extreme culpability that cannot be rendered in the language of the criminal code and leave the court powerless to pronounce judgment.

54. Ibn Ezra's commentary on the Former Prophets has not survived. But he deals with this question in *Yesod Mispar* (p. 152), where he states, rather cautiously, that "it may mean eight, and this means double [the fine] specified in the Torah, and this [fine] is according to royal judgment." In his two commentaries on Gen. 4:15, however, he states that *šivʿatayim*, 'sevenfold', is not a dual, and he holds the same position in his commentary on Isa. 30:26 (see also his vacillation on this question in *Yesod Mispar*, pp. 160–61).

55. This view should be compared with the reading "forty for one" which Kimchi cites as the reading of Targum Jonathan. A. Sperber's edition (*The Bible in Aramaic*, Part II [Leiden, 1959]) has the reading "four for one," but the textual apparatus there documents two textual traditions with the reading "forty."

56. This is the reading of all manuscripts of the Septuagint except for the Lucianic version, which corresponds to the Masoretic text, as well as of the Peshitta and Josephus (*Antiquities of the Jews* 7,7,3). A similar expression, "sevenfold" (Prov. 6:31) parallels "all he owns"; but this has no bearing on our text, since it is clearly hyperbolic rather than a precise legal formula. Since the judicial nature of David's response is obvious, it stands to reason that a copyist, troubled by the reading "sevenfold," revised the verdict to match the stipulation in the Pentateuch. On the other hand, the reading "sevenfold" can be explained as intended to solve the fundamental problem raised in the main text, analogous to the "emendation" of Targum Jonathan mentioned in the previous note.

57. Ehrlich, Driver, Hertzberg, and McCarter.

58. In the parable itself, the verb *l.q.ḥ* has both its primary sense as well as its secondary meaning of robbery (see above, n. 47). Compare "the people who were

at the entrance of the house (*pethah ha-bayit*) . . . they struck with blinding light, so that they were helpless to find the door (*pethah*)" (Gen. 19:11); "Be not afraid [i.e., panic-stricken]; for God has come only in order to test you, and in order that the fear [i.e., awe] of Him may be ever with you" (Exod. 20:17 [AV 20:20]); "How long will you judge perversely, showing favor to the wicked? Judge [i.e., save] the wretched and the orphan . . . " (Ps. 82:2–3).

59. The parable of Jotham ends with the sentence, "if you are acting honorably (*be-ʾemeth*) in anointing me king over you," followed closely by its application, which begins with the words, "if you acted rightly and justly (*be-ʾemeth u-ve-thamim*)" (Judg. 9:15–16). Just as in our story the verb *h.m.l* tightens the link between the parable and the real event, so the verb *h.w.s* at the end of the book of Jonah (4:10–11) serves to reinforce the link between the symbol and what it represents: "You cared about [were distressed by the fate of] the plant. . . . And should I not care about [have mercy on, prevent the destruction of] Nineveh . . . ?"

60. This continuity, evidence that the parable is an integral part of the story, answers those who question the authenticity of the parable, including Schwally ("Zur Quellenkritik," pp. 155–56), Smith (*Books of Samuel*, p. 322), Nowack (*Richter,* p. 194), Ehrlich (*Randglossen 3*, pp. 255–56), Gunkel (*Das Märchen*, pp. 35–36), Seeligmann (*Studies in Biblical Literature*, p. 211, n. 16), and Veijola ("Salomo," pp. 233–34). There are other linking motifs as well: (1) the clear echoes of Uriah's refusal to go home (11:11) in the description of the intimacy between the lamb and its master (12:3); (2) the possible echo of *wa-yithhallekh,* 'strolled' (11:2) in the rare noun *helekh*, 'traveler'; (3) the expression "he took (*wa-yiqqah*) the poor man's lamb" (12:4), which returns us to "he fetched her (*wa-yiqqaheha*) and she came to him" (11:4); (4) "the Lord sent Nathan" (12:1 and 25), which reflects the many messengers sent out by David during the course of the story.

61. According to Lasine ("Melodrama as Parable," pp. 110–12), what Nathan tells David is not a juridical parable meant to trap him into self-incrimination but a sentimental melodrama whose lack of realism conceals its link to David's sins and allows its use as an allegory of sorts. Its open ending prompts David's emotional moralizing outburst, which Nathan then redirects at him. But nothing in his reaction to the fictional injustice can rehabilitate his ability to distinguish between reality and fiction (as attested by the future successes of Amnon and Absalom in deceiving him) or amend his moral powers of judgment (as attested by his failure to punish those wayward sons). As I understand it, though, Nathan's story is perfectly realistic by scriptural standards (see above, pp. 120–21, and especially nn. 48 and 49), and it has all the hallmarks of the juridical parable (see above, pp. 112–115). There is no reason to burden it with therapeutic goals that go beyond the classical purpose of the juridical parable—getting a transgressor to recognize the seriousness of his deed and the justice of his punishment. Just as David's acknowledgment of his sin does not exempt him from punishment but only commutes the adulterer's death sentence, neither does it repair the many flaws that his vices have wrought in his soul and personality. This is the moral and theological lesson of the story of David and Bathsheba, which is set within the story of the war against the Ammonites: when David reached the zenith of his power as king, his precipitous descent as human being and father began.

62. This is also the relationship between the parable of Jotham (Judg. 9:8–15) and its application (ibid., 16–20). See Simon, "Parable of Jotham," pp. 29–30.

63. Outstanding examples of this are 2 Sam. 14:7 and Jer. 27:10.

64. Cf. Gen. 44:4–5 and Prov. 17:13.

65. See Hurvitz, *Wisdom Language*, pp. 69–70.

66. This link was pointed out by Carlson, *David*, p. 160.

67. The meaning of "I gave you the House of (*beith*) Israel and Judah" is rather

vague; hence many prefer the reading of the Peshitta: "The daughters of (*b͡e noth*) Israel and Judah." It is perfectly clear, in any case, that the second part of the verse is referring to women: "if that were not enough, I would give you twice as much more."

68. Cf. "For every first-born is Mine: at the time that I smote every first-born in the land of Egypt, I consecrated every first-born in Israel, man and beast, to Myself, to be Mine, the Lord's" (Num. 3:13).

69. This structure of transgression/punishment/transgression is very common in Jeremiah (2:5–11; 23:14–15; 35:16–17), as was pointed out by Bole, *Jeremiah*, p. xvi, n. 12.

70. Cf. Carlson, *David*, p. 158.

71. See Jenni, "Das wort *olam*, pp. 232–36.

72. This is the opinion of Wellhausen, Smith, Nowack, Gressmann, and Segal. Fokkelman (*Narrative Art* 1, p. 85) and McCarter disagree.

73. This was proposed, for totally different reasons, by Joüon, "Notes philologiques," p. 306.

74. According to Garsiel (*Biblical Names*, p. 115), this measure-for-measure linkage is intensified by the direct allusion to Penuel and Mahanaim in the homiletic derivation of names he finds in Uriah's speech: "The Ark and Israel and Judah are located at *Succoth*, and my master Joab and Your Majesty's men are camped in the open (*'al p͡e nei ha-śadeh ḥonim*)" (11:11).

75. See the fine remarks on this in Weiser's commentary on Psalms (*Die Psalmen*), on the verse "against you alone have I sinned" (Ps. 51:6 [AV 51:4]).

76. As to whether the euphemism "you have spurned the *enemies* of the Lord" is the original reading, see the commentaries of Ehrlich, Hertzberg, and Fokkelman (*Narrative Art* 1, p. 451). For parallel euphemisms in an Egyptian ordinance of the Thirteenth Dynasty and an Akkadian letter from Mari, see Yaron, "Coptos Decree," pp. 89–91; Anbar, "Un euphémisme 'biblique'," pp. 109–11. Nevertheless, McCarter (*I and II Samuel*, p. 296) has a point when he alleges the presence of a different euphemism in the Qumran text (4QSam^a)—"the Lord's word"—as evidence that the softening is of editorial origin.

77. See above, n. 60.

78. David, too, wore sackcloth, as we learn after the fact from "he changed his clothes" (12:20), from the explicit statement in some versions of the Septuagint, from Josephus's account (*Antiquities of the Jews* 7,7,4), and from the Qumran text 4QSam^a: "he came and lay on the ground in sackcloth" (Ulrich, *Qumran Text*, p. 100).

79. The words "lay with her" indicate that "he went to her" and do not have a sexual connotation. There is nothing out of line in the fact that we are told that David comforted her before he went to her; biblical narrative frequently states the intention and goal of a sequence of events before it presents them in detail (see Gen. 27:27, 37:21–22; 1 Sam. 25:39–40).

80. See the midrash cited by Kimchi in his commentary on verse 24 (I have been unable to locate the source), according to which Bathsheba was avoiding intercourse with David.

81. In the Lucianic version of the Septuagint, the reading is "by the Lord's word."

82. See A. Malamat, "Prophetic Revelations in New Documents from Mari and the Bible," *VT* suppl. 15 (1966), pp. 207–27.

83. Y. Kaufmann, "Nathan the Prophet," pp. 64–68.

84. We find a similar turnabout in Jeremiah's transition from silence, when challenged by Hananiah son of Azzur (Jer. 28:11), to his message delivered, some time later, in the name of the Lord (ibid., vv. 12–17).

85. Readers persuaded by the arguments presented here will find a sublime expression of the greatness of the man who recognizes his sin and the king who esteems his chastiser in the fact that the third son of David and Bathsheba was named Nathan (1 Chron. 3:5).

5. A Prophetic Sign Overcomes Those Who Would Deny It

1. See the critical survey of the history of scholarship on this story (through 1975) in the earlier, separately published version of this chapter (Simon, "1 Kings 13," pp. 81–85).

2. The "cult places" are mentioned in 13:32b, but that is clearly a secondary expansion. For those who assign an early date to the composition of the story, the historical argument is decisive: the geographical reference "in the towns of Samaria," uttered here by the old prophet, is anachronistic; only after 734 BCE (or, more likely, after 720) could the name of the city of Samaria be applied to an entire region (cf. 2 Kings 17:24 and 26; 23:19). For me, the verse is clearly secondary for literary reasons: in the body of the narrative the man of God delivers the word of the Lord against the Bethel altar only. It seems unlikely that the extension of its force to "all the cult places in the towns of Samaria" should be an appendix at the end of the story, and spoken by the old prophet, of all people.

3. Cf. 1 Kings 11:1–13; 14:19–24; 16:29–33; 21:25–29; 2 Kings 8:16–27; 13:1–13.

4. Similar transitions from story to redactor's summary are found in 1 Kings 21:25 and 2 Kings 10:28.

5. This is the opinion of Gressman (*Die älteste Geschichtsschreibung,* pp. 246–49), Montgomery (*Books of Kings,* p. 261), Jepsen ("Gottesmann und Prophet," pp. 171–72), Rofé (*Prophetical Stories,* p. 171), and Eynikel ("Prophecy," pp. 235–36).

6. The redactor treated the Elijah stories in similar fashion. This is evident from both the truncated form of the opening (17:1) and their dependance on an exposition we no longer possess (see pp. 158–59).

7. This is exactly how the redactor of the Book of Kings handled the verses that he appended to the end of the main portion of the story (13:33–34), where he notes that, after this incident, Jeroboam was not influenced by the signs and portents and remained steadfast in his sin. To emphasize this fact, he repeats the words he had used earlier, "he appointed priests from the ranks of the people . . . and stationed at Bethel the priests of the shrines" (12:31–32), in almost the same phrasing: "he kept on appointing priests for the shrines from the ranks of the people," adding, to underscore the severity of this deed, "he ordained as priests of the shrines any who so desired" (13:33).

8. See Rofé, "Baal," pp. 222–23.

9. The one exception to this rule is the last scene (2 Kings 23:16–18). Here, as we have conjectured, the original opening sentence, that told of Josiah's coming to Bethel, has been replaced by the redactor's survey of the purification of the cultic site there (v. 15).

10. Van Dorp ("Wat is die steenhoop daar?" pp. 67–68) does treat them as separate scenes, and accordingly divides chapter 13 into nine scenes (instead of our five), demarcated clearly by changes of place (house to high road and back again) and by a partial change in the personae. This division produces a concentric structure, which both begins and ends in Bethel; its central scene, too (vv. 20–22)—the forbidden meal in the house of the old prophet—also takes place in Bethel. Methodologically, there is a certain advantage to strict adherence to the conventional markers. But although the concentric structure may be formally impressive, it con-

tributes nothing to our understanding of the story and even prevents us from seeing its symmetrical structure and division into four parts.

11. *Sifre on Numbers*, Naso 23 (ed. H. S. Horvitz [Leipzig, 1917], p. 27). This is also the opinion of Ibn Ezra and D. Z. Hoffmann in their commentaries on Deut. 13:2. On the other hand, Rashi, Nahmanides, and S. D. Luzatto (in their commentaries, ad loc.) do distinguish between the two terms.

12. See J. Pedersen, *Israel, Its Life and Culture* (London, 1926), vols. 1–2, pp. 167–70; von Rad, *Theology* 2, pp. 93–108.

13. For the sign as implementing the word of the Lord, cf. especially 2 Kings 13:15–19; Jer. 28:10–11 and 51:61–64. As for premature realization as an expression of this implementation, see Jer. 28:13–14, 32:9–15, and 43:9–10. See also Robinson, "Prophetic Symbolism," pp. 1–17; Guillaume, *Prophecy and Divination*, pp. 169–80; Rowley, "Nature of Prophecy," pp. 1–38; Fohrer, *Die symbolischen Handlungen;* Fishbane, "Biblical *ot*," pp. 213–34. Fohrer's monograph and Fishbane's article make no reference to 1 Kings 13.

14. Fohrer, *Die symbolischen Handlungen*, pp. 20–70 and 94–107.

15. Jeremiah 36 sheds light on several aspects of 1 Kings 13. The writing of the scroll is a prophetic sign, intended to reinforce the spoken word of the Lord by rendering it in a physical, written form (cf. Jer. 30:2 and 51:60; Isa. 8:1–2). On the other hand, Jehoiakim's decree that the scroll be torn up and burned is a *countersign*, intended to violate the word of the Lord—that is, to prevent its consummation. The countersign was to have been complemented by an assault on the person of the prophet who speaks the word of the Lord, but the attempt to imprison Jeremiah and Baruch is frustrated by *heavenly protection:* "But the Lord hid them" (36:26). Subsequently the countersign, too, is nullified by the *renewal and reinforcement* of the prophetic sign: the new scroll contains everything recorded in the burnt one, "and more of the like was added" (36:32). All these stages are paralleled in 1 Kings 13, though not in the same order.

16. Cf. the commentary of R. Joseph Ibn Kaspi (*Adnei Kesef* on 1 Kings 13:5): "Scholars err when they translate the noun *mofet* as *merveille* 'marvel'; its correct translation is *démonstratio*. [Maimonides] explained that a *mofet* is what is possible in nature." This interesting linguistic precision—based on the classification of miracles in chapter 10 of the *Treatise on the Resurrection of the Dead*, in which Maimonides argues that "buildings may naturally develop cracks, especially new construction,"—has nothing to do with my distinction between *sign* and *portent*. In my classification both marvel (which totally deviates from the natural order) and *mofet* (which subjugates nature to the needs of the prophetic demonstration) are subsumed under the category of portent.

17. The linguistic difficulty is that the perfect *we-nathan* clashes with the imperfects that precede and follow it; it can refer to the past (as the context demands) only if it is an Aramaism added by a later hand (see *Gesenius' Hebrew Grammar*, §112). Moreover, the temporal indication "on that day" is awkward if contributed by the author but perfectly understandable in a later interpolation. Noth's attempt (*Könige*, pp. 290 and 297) to understand *we-nathan* as referring to the future seems extremely forced and artificial. Thematically, the collapse of the altar is not well integrated with the portent of the paralyzed arm. In verse 4 Jeroboam stretches out his arm "above the altar" to fend off the man of God; it withers. In verse 5 the altar disintegrates, but we are not told what happens to the king who is standing on it (or at least on the steps or ramp attached to it). Verse 6 then returns to the arm and its recovery of mobility; the impression is that the king is still standing on the altar.

18. The anticipatory aspect is particularly marked in the three prohibitions

laid on Jeremiah—not to marry, not to enter a house of mourning, and not to attend a house of feasting "in this place" (Jer. 16:1–13). For how can one father children, comfort mourners, and take part in rejoicing in a city that is doomed to destruction?

19. This interpretation, with slight variations, was advanced by R. Joseph Ibn Kaspi (*Adnei Kesef*, p. 56), Šanda (*Die Bücher der Könige*, 1:352–353), Jepsen ("Gottesmann und Prophet," pp. 174–75), and Klopfenstein ("I Könige 13," p. 656). The last-named author, hypothesizing that the king invited the man of God to eat and receive a gift in a chamber adjacent to the altar, attempts to make the shared meal into a sacred feast associated with the conclusion of a treaty. By analogy, he applies this idea also to the meal in the home of the prophet (p. 657). Not only is there no mention of any chamber near the altar, the chapter is replete with emphases on the word *bayith* ('house/home'), which recurs five times: in Jeroboam's invitation *ha-baytah* ("to my house" [v. 7]); in the refusal—*haṣi beitheka* ("half your house" [v. 8]); in the invitation extended by the old prophet—*ha-baytah* ("come home with me" [v. 15]); in the fictitious word of the Lord—*ʾel beitheka* ("to your house" [v. 18]); and in the narrator's explanation—*be-veitho* ("in his house" [v. 19]). Hence it is clear that the reference is to the private homes of the king and the prophet and that the proscriptions apply to "this place" in its entirety. Rashi, Kimchi, and Ehrlich (*Randglossen* 7, pp. 248–49) understood the bans in the light of the rabbinic laws applying to a city that is home to idolatry and the prohibitions concerning heathen festivals (see BT ʿAboda Zara 11b). Abravanel compared them to the scriptural ban on an "idolatrous city" (Deut. 13:13–19). Montgomery (*Books of Kings*, p. 262) regarded the two proscriptions as an expression of the complete and exclusive dedication that the prophet must tender to his mission.

20. All the answers that have been offered are unsatisfactory. Ibn Kaspi explains that "it was [God's] wish that he not tarry in Bethel at all" (*Adnei Kesef*, p. 56). This interpretation is shared by Šanda and Noth. The latter views this third prohibition as supplementing those on social contact: the man of God is to go home by another route so that he will be unknown on his return as he was unknown on his arrival. Gray conjectures that this is a precaution to protect him against a possible attack as he leaves Bethel. Alternatively, he suggests that *derekh*, 'road' or 'way', be understood as a metaphor for his mission; the proscription expresses the duty of avoiding any delay or interruption in its execution. Montgomery, Klopfenstein, and Jepsen do not address themselves to this point, while Ehrlich rejects the originality of verses 9b–10 because there is no way to interpret "the ban on returning to Judah by the same way." He holds that there is sense only to a ban against *returning* to Bethel after the man of God has already set out for home, since such a prohibition is clearly linked to the prohibition on receiving benefit from an idolatrous city. Hence, according to Ehrlich, verses 9b–10 are the result of a misunderstanding by an interpolator who, failing to properly understand the third ban, moved it to an earlier place in the story and joined it with the other two prohibitions, a context in which it makes no sense. This opinion is shared by Würthwein ("Die Erzählung vom Gottesmann," p. 183).

21. Bearing a message is regarded as being identified with its tenor: "He is a good man, and he comes with good news" (2 Sam. 18:27; see also Joab's remark to Ahimaaz, ibid. 20). Hence the bearer of good tidings merits a reward, while the bearer of evil tidings deserves punishment (2 Sam. 4:10), unless he can demonstrate his complete detachment from them (1 Sam. 4:12 and 16–17). Similarly, the prophet is identified with his prophecy: when Zedekiah son of Chenaanah strikes Micaiah son of Imlah on the cheek, the blow is meant to abrogate the word of the Lord he spoke (1 Kings 22:24); Elijah (2 Kings 1:10) and Elisha (2 Kings 2:23–25) regard assaults on them as undermining their mission.

22. To the best of my knowledge, only Gersonides offers a similar (albeit inverted) interpretation of this prohibition: "He bade him not to return by the way he had taken to Bethel, as if to suggest that the way by which he had come to Bethel, to deliver the words he had to say, was of no benefit, since his words there were to no avail, because of the magnitude of Jeroboam's rebellion" (on v. 9).

23. The text is silent as to the motives of the old prophet in issuing his fatal invitation to his colleague, so we must infer them from his actions. Three main explanations have been offered. (1) *Altruistic:* The old prophet wants to help the man of God. Abravanel, who rejected the assumption that the Bethelite is a false prophet, conjectured that he wanted to lighten the burden borne by the man of God by inviting him home to rest. (2) *Egoistic:* The old prophet wants to increase his own prestige. Šanda (*Die Bücher der Könige,* p. 353) assumes that the old man sought to gain esteem through contact with the wonder-worker. Josephus (*Antiquities of the Jews* 8,9) attributed to him a greater ambition—to blacken his competitor from Judah in the eyes of the king by causing him to sin, thereby revealing him as one who does not keep his word. (3) *Prophetic or public:* The old prophet wants to test the validity of the word of the Lord by investigating whether the man of God will obey the ancillary prohibition associated with it. This is the opinion of Gray (*I and II Kings,* p. 322). Klopfenstein ("I Könige 13," p. 657) expanded on this idea by emphasizing that the purpose was not merely to test but to tempt and lead astray. For if the word of the Lord can be altered in one case, why should it not be subject to revision with reference to the fate of Bethel as well? Jepsen offers a similar view ("Gottesmann und Prophet," p. 178), and my own interpretation is not very far removed from it.

24. That the ban on food and drink applies to all of Bethel is stressed by the three mentions of "in this place" (13:8, 16, and 22), plus the locative "there" in verse 17.

25. The attempts by Samet ("1 Kings 13," pp. 70–71) to answer the question as to why the man of God should even imagine that the Lord had repealed His injunction ignore the rule that lacunae left by the narrator without a shred of material to fill them are simply not to be filled in. This also applies to the attempt by Van Winkle ("I Kings XIII," pp. 40–42) to view the unsaid as the crux of the story. He holds that the sin of the man of God derives from his forgetting the principle that a true prophecy always encourages observance of the Lord's commands (Deut. 13:5); hence the man of God fails to realize that a prophecy aimed at getting him to infringe a divine injunction (v. 21) must be false.

26. The second half of verse 20 is ambiguous, since "prophet" can be either the subject or object of "brought him back": the verse can be rendered, "the word of the Lord came to the [old] prophet [of Bethel] who had brought him [the man of God] back"; but it can also be rendered, "the word of the Lord came to the prophet [i.e., the man of God] whom he [the old prophet] had brought back." The first rendering is adopted by Targum Jonathan, R. Johanan (BT Sanhedrin 103b), Rashi, Ibn Kaspi, and Gersonides; the second by Josephus (*Antiquities of the Jews* 8,9), Kimchi, and Abravanel. All modern commentators accept the first possibility, influenced by the stylistic point noted so clearly by Ibn Kaspi: "Both of these men were prophets and are always mentioned together in this story, so the first is always called 'the man of God' and the second is called 'the prophet' " (commentary on v. 20). The one exception to this clear-cut distinction is at the end of verse 23: "he saddled for him the ass, for the prophet whom he had brought back." Ehrlich (*Randglossen* 7, p. 249) suggests the conjectural emendation of *la-navi*ʾ, 'for the prophet', to *ha-navi*ʾ, 'the prophet', which allows us to understand the last words as an internal clarification: the saddling was performed by the (old) prophet who had brought him back. On the other hand, Kittel, Šanda, Montgomery, and Noth

rely on the fact that the last part of verse 23—everything after "he saddled the ass"—is missing in the Septuagint. They assume that the problematic phrase was originally a marginal gloss to explain that the ass belonged to the old prophet (Šanda and Noth) or to clarify that this time the old prophet (rather than his sons) saddled the ass, "for the prophet whom he had brought back" (Kittel and Montgomery). On this point, see p. 143.

27. Samet ("1 Kings 13," p. 73) rightly points out that the old prophet could have concealed this authentic prophecy and pretended that nothing had changed. But it overpowers him, not he it.

28. Something like this happens to Jonah in his flight from the Lord. The lots cast by the sailors identify Jonah as the cause of the storm. When he is thrown into the water the storm abates, and this portent inspires the seamen with a great fear of the Lord. In this way Jonah, the prophet who refused to proclaim the word of the Lord, becomes its object and as such also its unwilling subject!

29. There is clear link between the Lord's verdict on the man of God—"your carcass shall not come to the grave of your fathers" (v. 22)—and the verdict pronounced against the altar of Bethel: "human bones shall be burned upon you" (v. 2). This indicates that the infraction of the word of the Lord by the man of God resembles in some measure the transgression of Bethel and that the similarity of the punishment is intended to reinforce the word of the Lord, which he has violated. At the same time, we must not overlook the disparity between desecration of a corpse (cf. 1 Kings 14:10–13, 16:4, 21:19 and 23–24; 2 Kings 9:10, 25–36, and 33–37; Isa. 14:19–20; Jer. 22:19) and the honorable burial of the man of God, flawed only in that he is not interred in his ancestral sepulchre (see 2 Chron. 21:19–20, as against 2 Sam. 19:38 and 21:12–14).

30. Šanda (*Die Bücher der Könige*, p. 355) rightly notes that the words "he went (*wa-yelek*) by another way" (v. 10) do not necessarily mean that the first time he left Bethel the man was on foot. Even when he is clearly riding an ass, the narrator uses the same verb: "he went (*wa-yelek*)" (v. 24; cf. also vv. 14 and 28). It may well be that the ass of the man of God is not mentioned earlier simply because it is irrelevant to the story. Cassuto ("Journey of Ashera," pp. 1–7) assumes that the repetition of the old man's instructions to his sons to saddle his ass for him is merely a prose descendant of a poetic formula prevalent in the ancient literary tradition. He found two interesting parallels in the Ugaritic texts: Daniel orders his daughter to saddle his ass for him (1D, 49–60), and Ashera orders her servants to do so (2AB IV, 1–18). Cassuto makes no reference to other scriptural passages about saddling an ass, probably because in those cases the ass was saddled by the rider himself. To me it seems that this motif, in its two forms, should not be dismissed simply as a literary convention. Rather, every time it appears we should look for the internal demands of the narrative that explain its use. Indeed, the Ugaritic parallels reinforce the impression that the saddling of the ass by someone of inferior status emphasizes the authority and preeminence of the rider. The full significance of the saddling of the ass for the man of God by the old prophet becomes apparent against this background.

31. For such use of the preposition *ʾaḥarei*, 'after', with a circumstantial meaning, see: "And the Lord said to Abram, *after* Lot had parted from him" (Gen. 13:14; cf. Lev. 16:1); "So Pharaoh said to Joseph, '*After* God has made all this known to you, there is none so discerning and wise as you'" (Gen. 41:39; cf. Judg. 11:36 and 2 Sam. 19:31). Compare also "*after* he has shaved his consecrated hair" (Num. 6:19), which does not mean that the shaving is completed while the Nazirite is standing at the altar, but rather defines his condition when the priest places the ram's shank on his palms. This is also how we should understand circumstantial uses of the verb *k.l.h*, that is, as indicating the situation after the completion of an act, as noted by

Ibn Ezra in his commentary on Gen. 2:2 ("the completion of an act is not an act [itself]"), and by Cassuto in greater detail (*Commentary on the Book of Genesis, Part I*, pp. 61–62).

32. The lion's superiority to the man of God, with regard to obedience to the divine command, is cited by Gunkel (*Das Märchen*, pp. 32–33) as characteristic of animal parables, both in general and among the Israelites: animals are more sensitive than humans to the suprasensory world and to the divine word. Nevertheless, it would seem that Jonah's fish, Elijah's ravens, and Elisha's two bears do not confirm that Scripture presents the Lord's control of animals as an essential advantage of the animal over the human emissary. It is true, however, that the lion's not feeding on the carcass seems to be an intentional contrast to the failure by the man of God to observe the ban on eating in Bethel. When the lion does not devour the corpse or kill the ass, the meal enjoyed by the man of God in Bethel is put in the spotlight, just as the blindness of Balaam, the "open-eyed prophet," is accented when his ass perceives the angel of the Lord.

33. Secondary reinterment of bones in an individual niche does not seem to have been practiced during the First Temple period. Burial caves from this period generally comprise a number of chambers. In each chamber a ledge was carved the length of each of the three walls, along with a sunken pit for collecting the bones. On most of the ledges there was a horseshoe-shaped depression for the head of the dead person. Thus each ledge was meant for a single corpse. But after time had passed the bones could be transferred to the sunken pit and another body placed on the ledge. See G. Barkai, A. Mazar, and A. Kleiner, "The Northern Jerusalem Cemetery in the First Temple Period," *Qadmoniot* 8 (1975), pp. 71–76 (Hebrew). The wording of the injunction to bury the two men together is a bit difficult: "lay my bones beside his" (13:31b). Evidently he did not say "lay me" (which is the Septuagint rendering) because he wanted to stress the purpose of the command—the intermingling of their bones. But it is also possible to understand his words literally, that is, that when they collect his bones they should put them in the same pit with the bones of the man of God.

34. Samet ("1 Kings 13," pp. 80–84) argues that the prophet's charge to his sons to bury him alongside the man of God is self-evident (and therefore superfluous) on the practical level; hence we must understand it as an ethical will, "as an explicit instruction to his sons that he has repented the course of his entire life and as an acknowledgment of his full partnership with the man of God in the rejection of Jeroboam's cult" (p. 81). In fact, not only are the practical instructions necessary (see the previous note), the bold symbolism cannot conceal the fact that the old prophet never condemns the sin of offering sacrifices in Bethel, explicitly or implicitly; his injunction to his sons merely expresses his perfect faith that the word of the Lord will be fulfilled and the altar will be defiled. The assertion that the practical goal of the injunction—to protect his bones—makes no sense when uttered by someone who does not know that the man of God prophesied that "human bones shall be burned upon you" (13:2) is astonishing, given the fact that it was from his sons, whom he instructs to bury him alongside the man of God, and that the old prophet found out what the man of God had said (v. 11). What is more, if the old prophet really did sincerely repent, why, in 2 Kings 23:18, does the narrator emphasize that his bones are spared by the merit of the man of God and not by his own merit?

35. The Septuagint version of 2 Kings 23:16 adds the bracketed words to the Masoretic text: " . . . in fulfillment of the word of the Lord foretold by the man of God [when Jeroboam stood on the altar on festival day. He turned and saw the grave of the man of God] who had foretold these happenings." The assumption that the Masoretic text reflects a deletion due to homoeoteleuton ("the man of

God") is plausible in and of itself, and is further supported by the fluency of the version preserved in the Greek translation.

36. There is a seventh occurrence at the end of verse 23, but it is of doubtful authenticity (see above, n. 26).

37. The significant phrase "by the word (*bi-dᵉvar*) of the Lord" (1 Kings 13:2) is not repeated in the account of the townspeople, who instead refer vaguely to "these things (*ha-dᵉvarim ha-ʾelleh*)." Were it not for the fact that these same words (*ha-dᵉvarim ha-ʾelleh*) are also used by the narrator (2 Kings 23:16), I would be more confident of my hunch that this is an intentional understatement expressing the limits of what the Bethelites could accept: they could not help acknowledging the miraculous realization of "these words" uttered by the man of God, but cannot yet bring themselves to admit that this was indeed "the word of the Lord."

38. On the independent and direct action of the word of the Lord, see Isa. 55:8–11; Ps. 147:15.

39. For example, Isa. 1:18–20; Jer. 18:1–11; Ezek. 18:1–32 and 33:10–20; Jonah 3:10. See also Deut. 30:1–3; 1 Kings 8:33–40.

40. The intensity of the disagreement is reflected also in the explicit attitude toward those who express doubts about the power of repentance: Ezek. 18:25 and 33:17–20; Jonah 4:2.

41. We may infer from Jeremiah's prophecy that the concept of repentance accords significant weight to the element of time. As the time fixed for the punishment draws nigh, the opening for repentance becomes progressively narrowed. The gates of repentance, initially wide open (Jer. 18:1–11), to the point of complete abrogation of the impending calamity (Jer. 7:3–7; 17:24–26; 25:3–5; 26:3 and 13), swung to when it was decreed that Judah, along with "all the nations," would be subjugated by Nebuchadnezzar (25:9–13; 27:9–13). The only option left was to surrender to Babylonian rule and avoid destruction (27:7–13; 38:17–18; but see also 21:8–10).

42. According to 2 Chron. 32:26, this was also Hezekiah's fate: thanks to his submission to the Lord, the catastrophe decreed for Jerusalem will not take place in his lifetime. On the other hand, according to 2 Kings 20:19 and Isa. 39:8, the postponement of the destruction is merely a hope uttered by Hezekiah when he acknowledges the justice of the divine decree.

43. This definition of the theme of the story suggests that it be categorized, thematically, with the Book of Jonah, as a "prophetic theological story" (see above, n. 28, and Simon, *Jonah*, pp. 10–15). This is what Rofé did (*Prophetical Stories*, p. 173), classing it, along with *Jonah*, as a "prophetic parable" and noted that in both criticism is aimed at the prophet of the Lord. Neither the man of God from Judah nor Jonah remain loyal to their missions; the lion and the great fish are more compliant messengers than they are; and the Lord deals harshly with his prophets. With regard to the narrative mode, however, our story is very different from Jonah, as well as from the frame tale of Job, which is also very close to the latter. Unlike Jonah and the Job frame tale, the story of the man of God from Judah is not written in a nonrealistic and suprahistorical style. Even its miracles are naturalistic (except for the cracking of the altar, which clearly does not fit in with the rest of the story [see above, n. 17], and the lion watching over the dead body), and its historical anchors are stressed by the reference to two kings by name.

44. Cf. 1 Kings 8:56 (God's word to Moses is fulfilled in Solomon's days) and 1 Kings 16:34 (the word of the Lord, spoken so long ago by Joshua, smites the rebuilder of Jericho in the reign of Ahab). Von Rad noted the centrality of the idea of the power and vitality of the word of the Lord in the deuteronomic theology of the Book of Kings (see "Die Deuteronomistische Geschichtstheologie," pp. 189–204).

45. One conjecture is that of Jepsen ("Gottesmann und Prophet," p. 176), who believes that the story was written to combat any possible revival of the Samaritan cult in Bethel after the death of Josiah. Jepsen ignores the fact that neither in the body of the story nor in the editorial framework is there any attack on the syncretism typical of the Samaritan cult.

6. Elijah's Fight against Baal Worship

1. Food-related miracles are recounted about Moses (see chiefly Exod. 16:11–13) and Elisha (2 Kings 4:1–7 and 38–44). There is also the story of how Elisha restores the life of the son of a hospitable hostess (2 Kings 4:8–37).

2. Gunkel (*Elias*, p. 12, nn. 7–12) offers a number of comparisons.

3. An exception is the instructive article by R. L. Cohen ("Literary Logic," pp. 333–50), which reached a number of conclusions similar to my own, independently of the first version of the present chapter (published in 1980). His article did not have a great impact on criticism of the Elijah stories, aside from its auspicious influence on Long, *First Kings* (pp. 170–207). Brichto, in his *Toward a Grammar of Biblical Poetics*, pp. 122–66, also adopted an integrative approach, but his preference for a radical metaphorization of Elijah's miracles and struggles forced him to discover a vast number of cruxes, which he interprets as signs left by the narrator to tell readers not to understand the story literally. Overemphasizing cruxes is a well-known way of dismissing them.

4. This problem seems to have bothered the aggadists as well, leading them to link the separate incidents into a single continuous plot: the key of rainfall was given to Elijah so that he could punish Ahab for blaspheming during his visit of consolation to the house of Hiel the Bethelite. The prophet was required to return it, however, when he needed the key of resurrection to revive the widow's son. This opened the way for the renewal of rainfall (see BT Sanhedrin 113a; *Yalquṭ Shimoni* 2,207).

5. Cf., for example, Josh. 24:28; Judg. 21:24; 1 Sam. 8:22.

6. This problem is made worse by the content of Elijah's complaint to the Lord on Mount Horev, namely, that the Israelites have "put Your prophets to the sword. I alone am left" (1 Kings 19:10). There the explanation that on Mount Carmel Elijah could call himself the last remaining prophet of the Lord, since the others had been forced underground, is not applicable.

7. Eissfeldt (*Der Gott Karmel*, p. 34), tries to resolve this contradiction by assuming that every possible effort was made to supply what was required at events of supreme political importance. But Steck (*Überlieferung*, p. 9, n. 3) seems to be right in arguing that Eissfeldt's explanation may be satisfactory from a factual point of view but not from a literary perspective: the problem is not the practical difficulty of where so much water was found but the narrator's failure to address it.

8. A detailed and documented foundation for this assessment can be found in the critical survey of the history of scholarship on 1 Kings 17–19 included in the earlier, published version of this chapter (Simon, "Elijah's Fight," pp. 55–63).

9. This was first suggested by Wellhausen (*Die Komposition*, p. 287), and taken over by Gunkel (*Elias*, p. 9) and many others. Contrary to their view, Rofé (*Prophetical Stories*, p. 184) holds that 16:29–17:1 does constitute the beginning of our story; this requires viewing the verse on the rebuilding of Jericho (16:34) as a later interpolation.

10. For the problem presented by *mi-tišbi*, see Montgomery and Gray, ad loc.

11. The expression *ʾašer ʿamadti lᵉ-fanaw*, literally "before whom I have stood," does not necessarily refer to any particular earlier revelation. This is evident from the context of the other loci in which it appears (cf. 1 Kings 18:15; 2 Kings 3:14

and 5:16), from its sense, "whose servant I am" (cf. 1 Sam. 16:22; 1 Kings 1:2 and 12:6; Jer. 52:12), and from its application to the angelic host (1 Kings 22:19) and to the prophetic role (Jer. 15:19).

12. See W. Baumgartner, "Ein Kapitel vom hebräischen Erzählungsstil," *Eucharisterion: Gunkel Festschrift* (Göttingen, 1923), pp. 148–49.

13. Given the consistent ascription of responsibility to Jezebel, the daughter of the king of Sidon, for the introduction to Israel of the Baal cult (1 Kings 16:31–33, 18:4 and 19, 19:1–2; 2 Kings 3:13, 9:7 and 22), the reference seems to be to Baal Melkart, the Phoenician rain god. In addition, the ritual and mythological allusions in chapter 18 correspond quite well with what we know about Baal Melkart and about Baal Hadad, the chief god of the Ugaritic pantheon, lord of life, vegetation, and fertility, god of the storm and thunder, lightning and fire, who dispenses rain and dew to the earth. See the critical historical surveys of the extensive study of this topic in Uffenheimer (*Ancient Prophecy*, pp. 192–206) and Fensham ("A Few Remarks," pp. 227–33). Uffenheimer presents weighty arguments against identifying the Baal of our story with Baal Carmel or Baal Shamayim. Fensham emphasizes that any characterization of Baal on the basis of nonscriptural sources may rely only on attributes that appear consistently from Ugaritic writings down to Hellenistic times.

14. *Pesiqta Rabbati*, ed. Ish-Shalom (Vienna, 1900), ch. 4, p. 13.

15. Similarly, we read nothing explicit about Ahaziah's reaction to Elijah's prediction of his imminent death and must fill in the details on our own (2 Kings 1:16).

16. Cf. Pharaoh's reaction to the first plague: "Pharaoh's heart stiffened *and he did not heed them,* as the Lord had spoken. Pharaoh turned and went into his palace, *paying no regard* even to this" (Exod. 7:22–23).

17. Ehrlich and Montgomery correctly interpret the first "he went" as a preparatory verb to "and did," rather than as indicating a change of place. Montgomery identified this usage later in our story as well (17:15). For other examples, see Gen. 35:22; Exod. 2:1; Deut. 17:2–3; 1 Kings 16:31; 2 Kings 3:7. It seems likely that this "superfluous" word is actually another way of accentuating that Elijah did not proceed on his own initiative but in obedience to the divine command.

18. For various forms in which king and prophet sever all relations between them, see 1 Sam. 16:1–2, 28:6 and 15–16; 1 Kings 13:7–10; 2 Kings 3:13–14.

19. Skinner (*Kings*, p. 224) hit the nail on the head when he described the attempts to play down this miracle by interpreting the "ravens" metaphorically as "rationalistic absurdity." On the other hand, Ginzberg (*Legends of the Jews* 6, p. 317, n. 6) tried to find this rationalist approach in *Genesis Rabbah* 33,8 and in BT Ḥullin 5a, where the opinion that "the ravens were real ones" is cited alongside opinions that the reference is not to birds but to persons of this name or so called after their town. It seems, though, that the background for this Talmudic disagreement is not the problem of the extraordinary miracle but the question of the source of the meat and whether it was kosher. On the other hand, Kimchi, Gersonides, and Abravanel all returned to the literal sense, "ravens." This does indeed seem to fit the plain meaning of the story; the narrator's silence as to what motivated the *ʿorʿvim* to feed the prophet constitutes *literary* evidence that the reference is to birds and not human beings. Here we read, "I have commanded to feed you"; later we read, "I have commanded a widow to feed you" (v. 9). Given the identical phrasing, the difference between the birds' blind obedience and the necessity of persuading the widow to implement the Lord's bidding stands out.

20. For examples of similar "open" endings, which leave the reader expecting a sequel, see Gen. 37:36; Exod. 1:22; Judg. 13:20, 15:8, 16:22; 2 Sam. 11:27, 13:22 and 39, 14:24; Ruth 3:18. The fact that this conclusion relates both to the account

of the drought ("because there was no rain in the land") and to the scene with the ravens (because of his dependence on the waters of the wadi) indicates that the continuity between verses 2–7 and verses 8–16 is not secondary and the work of an editor, but inherent to the story. Hence Gunkel's claim (*Elias*, p. 11) that the scenes in chapter 17 are connected by weak links and sharply differentiated from one another cannot be valid for more than the preliterary stage. For further discussion, see below.

21. For the use of the root *ṣ.w.h* in the sense of "designate," see 2 Sam. 17:14; Isa. 23:11.

22. Here "widow" evidently indicates not only marital status, but also, and chiefly, social status. She is an extremely poor woman with no one to protect her (cf. Exod. 22:21–23; Deut. 24:17–22, 26:12–13; Isa. 1:17 and 23; Job 29:13), and thus particularly vulnerable to the ravages of the drought. Almost at once we discover that she and her son are down to their last meal. Fensham ("A Few Remarks," p. 234) sees this as an additional facet of the anti-Baal polemic: Baal, who ought to be seeing to the well-being of the widow and orphan, is incapable of doing so since, in a time of drought, he is believed to be dead and in the Underworld. The fact that the widow is gathering wood may be another expression of her poverty, but it may merely be an indication to the prophet that she is getting ready to bake bread. All of this will be further illuminated in the retrospective light of chapter 18.

23. On the subject of widow's weeds, compare Gen. 38:14; 2 Sam. 14:2 and 5. Similarly, in Exod. 2:6, we are not told how Pharaoh's daughter determined that Moses was a Hebrew child.

24. On Elijah's prophetic appearance, see 2 Kings 1:8; on his prophet's cloak, see 1 Kings 19:19 and 2 Kings 2:13–14.

25. In normal times, there is a duty to supply travelers and the needy not only with water (drink) but also bread (food). See Deut. 23:5; 1 Kings 18:4; 2 Kings 6:22; Prov. 25:21; and Job 22:7.

26. This link with the central theme of the story—which will be reinforced at the end of the next scene ("the *word* of the Lord in your mouth is truth" [v. 24])—is further underscored by the phrasing of the second part of verse 16, "just as the *word* of the Lord who had spoken through Elijah." I have not mentioned this in the main text because the latter may have been added by the editor-compiler of the Book of Kings. Not only does the expression, "like the word of the Lord who had spoken through X" appear previously (16:34), in the Deuteronomistic preface to our story, all its other occurrences seem to belong to the editorial stratum of the Book of Kings (see 1 Kings 14:18, 15:29, 16:12, 22:38 [without the concluding "through X"]; 2 Kings 14:25, 24:2). In light of this, all of verse 16 could be considered an editorial addition. However, taking into account the close links between its first half and verse 6 (the emphasis on the fulfillment of the promise) and the resonance with verses 1 and 24 of the phrase "like the word of the Lord," it seems more likely that only the words "who had spoken through Elijah" were added by the editor. Verses that conclude with "like the word of the Lord" and definitely belong to the body of the stories in which they appear are found in the Book of Kings (see 1 Kings 12:24; 2 Kings 4:44 and 9:26).

27. The expression "after these things" (*wa-yʰhi ʾaḥar ha-dʰvarim ha-ʾelleh*) is used in Scripture both as a secondary editorial linkage between independent stories (see 1 Kings 21:1; Josh. 24:29) and to denote the transition from one stage to another within a continuous narrative, as seems to be the case here (see also Gen. 39:7 and 40:1). Similarly, *wa-yʰhi ʾaharei ken* is found in both usages: 2 Sam. 21:18 is a classic example of an editorial link (see also 2 Sam. 8:1), whereas the beginning of 2 Sam. 15:1 (and apparently also 2 Sam. 2:1) belongs to the main body of the story.

28. Here the widow is called "the mistress of the house." Clearly, though, this

should not be understood as a vestige of an original independence of the resurrection tale, which, according to many, did not involve the widow: later in the story, too, she is referred to as "the widow" (v. 20). The subsequent references to "his mother" (v. 23) and "the woman" (v. 24) evidently indicate that the narrator employed stylistic variation for its own sake. This also seems to be how we should understand the variant terms *maṭar* (v. 1) and *gešem* (v. 7), as well as *maʿog* (v. 12) and *ʿuggah* (v. 13), in the previous scene.

29. What the widow says here about the prophet's presence in her house, the Lord says about His own presence in the midst of the Israelites: "But I will not go in your midst, since you are a stiff-necked people, lest I destroy you on the way" (Exod. 33:3).

30. This sense of "recalling sin" as making it more substantial and real, is found in the definition of the meal offering brought by the jealous husband who suspects his wife of adultery as "a meal offering of remembrance which recalls wrongdoing" (Num. 5:15). Just as the ritual intensification of the clandestine sin of the woman who has gone astray is a precondition for her punishment, so Israel was commanded to remember in perpetuity what Amalek had done to it, so that the living memory of this wrong could lead to the annihilation of its perpetrator (Deut. 25:17; cf. Ezek. 21:29). The prophets who rebuke Israel for its sins and announce its imminent punishment recall its sins by means of their words, whereas Elijah is supposed to have done this by his mere presence in the widow's house, as the midrash explains: "Two people, Lot and the woman of Zarephath, said the same thing. The woman of Zarephath said: 'Until you came to my house, the Holy One Blessed Be He saw my deeds and the deeds of my city, and my deeds were superior to those of my city. But now that you have come to stay with me you have recalled my sin and caused the death of my son!' Lot said: 'Until I went to live with Abraham, the Holy One Blessed Be He saw my deeds and those of my city, and my deeds were superior to those of my city. But now that I am traveling with Abraham his deeds are superior *and I cannot stand his flame*' " (*Genesis Rabbah*, ed. J. Theodor and Ch. Albeck [2nd ed., Jerusalem, 1965], 50,11).

31. The widow's words (17:18) contain the overtone of the ghastly accusation that the whole purpose of the prophet's stay in her house was to cause the death of her son. However, given the lack of discrimination between purpose and result in scriptural thinking, we would do better to interpret her remarks in the following context: the result of the prophet's arrival is that the child whom he saved from death by famine died from illness because of him.

32. It is astonishing that scholars who separate this scene from the story of the drought pay no attention to the word *hagam*, which clearly refers to the general calamity, whether its sense here is "in addition to" or "even" (compare Isa. 1:15). Only with great difficulty can the rare sense of "precisely this and no other" be accepted here (cf. Num. 22:33).

33. The personal interpretation of Elijah's prayer is reflected in the following Midrash: "Elijah stood and prayed before the Holy One Blessed Be He and said: Master of the Universe, have I not suffered woes enough, that I must also suffer this woman, whom I know spoke to deride me out of the distress over her son?!" (*Pirqe Rabbi Eliezer* [Warsaw, 1852 (repr. Jerusalem, 1963)], ch. 33). This approach is also reflected in the Septuagint version, "Woe is me, O Lord" (instead of the Masoretic, "O Lord, my God").

34. The prophet's two petitions are separated not only by his attempt at a practical remedy but also by the narrator's repetition of the words, "he cried out to the Lord and said," and the prophet's repetition of the vocative, "O Lord my God" (v. 21). The difference between Elijah's two prayers becomes starker when we compare Moses' complaint, "O Lord, why did You bring harm upon this people?" (Exod.

5:22) with his outcry when he sees his sister stricken by leprosy: "O God, pray heal her!" (Num. 12:13).

35. This structural link between these two verses by virtue of the drawn-out repetition is clear evidence of the superiority of the Masoretic text of verse 22 over the truncated Septuagint version: "And it was so and the boy lived."

36. The Septuagint text lacks the words "Elijah picked up the boy" (v. 23a). It is difficult to assume that they have been added in the Masoretic text since no reader would be bothered by the omission of this information.

37. In scriptural language it is not at all rare for one word to appear twice in the same context with a significant variation in meaning—once with its primary meaning, and the second time with an expanded, intensified, or metaphoric meaning. For example "Perhaps the Lord your God will hear (*yišmaᶜ*) [i.e., "take note of"] all the words of the Rabshakeh . . . and will mete out judgment for the words that the Lord your God has heard (*šamaᶜ*)" (2 Kings 19:4; cf. 19:16 and 20). Or again: "Moses said to the people: 'Do not *fear* [i.e., be terrified]; for God has come only in order to test you, and in order that the *fear* of Him [i.e., religious awe] may be ever with you, so that you do not go astray'" (Exod. 20:17 [AV 20]). This semantic fluidity is also reflected in usages that strike us as tautological: "But the *boy* [i.e., young man] did not draw his sword, for he was timid, being still a *boy* [i.e., untried]" (Judg. 8:20; cf. 1 Sam. 1:24). Our verse, which adopts this rhetorical device, means: "you are truly and sincerely a Man of God." Similarly, the captain of fifty, when he comes to arrest Elijah, calls him "Man of God" (2 Kings 1:9); the prophet responds, "If I am a man of God [in the fullest sense of the term], let fire come down from heaven and consume you with your fifty men" (v. 10).

38. On the biblical conception of truth, see J. Pedersen, *Israel, Its Life and Culture* (London, 1926), vol. 1, pp. 336ff. Rofé, who believes that "the *legenda* (17:12–24) which relates the resurrection of the Zarephathite widow's son is not an integral part of the narrative" (*Prophetical Stories*, p. 184), questions the above interpretation: "But these characteristics of the word of the Lord were already known to the widow from the miracle of the flour and oil. What then is the meaning of her statement that 'Now I know these things'?" (ibid., n. 3). This question can also be posed with regard to the angel who tells Abraham, "now I know that you fear God" (Gen. 22:12), even though Abraham's fear of the Lord has already been proven repeatedly in the past. Just as the binding of Isaac is the most difficult ordeal, attesting to a sublime degree of fear of God, so too Elijah's resurrection of the boy indicates that he is a man of God of a far higher degree than the widow had previously thought. What is more, in the interim the child had died because of Elijah and she had attacked him in the frenzy of her disappointment and anger. This link is intensified by the sophisticated structure of the scene, pointed out by R. L. Cohen ("Literary Logic," pp. 336–37): her expression of faith in the Man of God (which concludes this scene) is a fitting response to her challenge to him (which begins the scene), and this *inclusio* is reinforced and emphasized by the chiastic parallel between "Give me your son" (A) and "See, your son is alive" (A') and between "he took him from her arms" (B) and "Elijah picked up the child and brought him down from the upper room" (B').

39. From the perspective of both content and phrasing, her remark resembles the profession of faith made by Jethro, the priest of Midian, before Moses: "Now I know that the Lord is greater than all gods" (Exod. 18:11). Compare Long, *First Kings*, p. 186.

40. Indications of time and place do not serve to mark change of scene in chapter 18 because many scenes occur in the same place and in immediate succession. Except for the prologue, which takes place in Zarephath, scenes 1–3 take place on the outskirts of Samaria on a single day, and scenes 4–7 on Mount Carmel

and in Wadi Kishon, also on a single day. The interval that elapses between the Lord's appearance to Elijah in Zarephath and his encounters on the outskirts of Samaria, and then between these encounters and the trial on Mount Carmel are not specified. On the other hand, four temporal cues bring to the fore the rapid passage of time on the day of the trial on Mount Carmel and thereby help build up the dramatic tension. Two of these temporal indications occur in the fifth scene: "When noon came" (v. 27) and again "when noon passed" (v. 29). The third comes shortly thereafter, in the sixth scene, when the trial is as its height: "When it was time to present the meal offering" (v. 36). The fourth indication of time is in the seventh scene, where it underscores that the great rainfall came right after the announcement of its coming: "Meanwhile the sky grew black with clouds" (v. 45).

41. See Ehrlich (*Randglossen* 7); Kittel (in *Biblia Hebraica*); Eissfeldt (*Der Gott Karmel*, p. 27, n. a); Fohrer (*Elia*, p. 7, n. 6); Steck (*Überlieferung*, p. 10, n. 1); Würthwein; and DeVries. Disagreeing are Šanda, Montgomery, and Gray.

42. Cf. 2 Kings 6:25, where a similar statement is incorporated into the body of the description.

43. Compare de Vaux, *Ancient Israel*, pp. 129–31. See also S. Yeivin, s.v. *pᵉqiduth*, *Biblical Encyclopedia* 6 (Jerusalem, 1971), p. 547 (Hebrew).

44. See Gunkel (*Elias*, p. 15) and, following him, Gressman (*Die älteste Geschichtsschreibung*, p. 58), Fohrer (*Elia*, p. 9, n. 9), Steck (*Überlieferung*, p. 11, n. 4), Würthwein, and DeVries.

45. Daube (*Studies in Biblical Law*, p. 65, n. 25) convincingly demonstrated that in Scripture the verb *n.k.r* also has a distinctly legal sense. He offers the current verse as a borderline case, and finds it hard to decide whether it refers only to identification or also to taking a position.

46. That king and majordomo split up and searched separately is plausible from a practical perspective—"they divided the country between them to explore it" (v. 6)—for it doubles the efficiency of the survey. But at the same time it increases the disgrace of the situation—"Ahab went alone in one direction" (v. 6)—something not done even by those of less august rank than a king: Gen. 22:3; Num. 22:22; 1 Sam. 9:3 and 21:2. Finally, it also serves the purposes of the plot, by allowing the encounter between Elijah and Obadiah to precede that between Elijah and Ahab.

47. Compare the parallel description of the king's helplessness in the face of the horrors of famine in the time of Elisha (2 Kings 6:24–31). Ahab's statement to Obadiah, according to the Masoretic text, begins in a tone of command: "Go through the land, to all the springs of water and to all the wadis" (v. 5a). The Septuagint text (according to the persuasive reconstruction by Orlinsky, "On the Commonly Proposed Lek Wena'abor," pp. 515–17), however, replaces the imperative with the jussive: "Come, let us explore." This reading is compatible with the plural that the king employs thereafter ("perhaps we shall find some grass to keep horses and mules alive"), as well as the fact that Ahab too participates in the survey: "They divided the country between them to explore it" (v. 6). Another indication of Ahab's dejection is his expression of doubt, "*perhaps* we shall find some grass" (cf. Jon. 1:6 and 3:9). But the reader, who already knows about the Lord's command to Elijah, sees, in addition to all this, that the king of Israel is unwittingly doing the Lord's will. The Lord commanded His prophet: "*Go (lek)*, appear before Ahab" (v. 1); correspondingly, Ahab said to Obadiah: "*Go (lek or lᵉkah)* through the land" [or: "Come, let us explore"] (v. 5). It is as a result of these two statements that the confrontation will take place (for similar convergences of two strands of a plot, cf. Exod. 4:18–27; 1 Kings 21:15–18).

48. Supplementing the parallels between the drought and the plagues of Egypt

mentioned above (p. 161), we can add now the affront to the king and his ministers and their humiliation. The frogs, wild animals, and locust attacked Pharaoh's ministers and Pharaoh himself ("your bedchamber and your bed" [Exod. 7:28–29; 8:17 and 20; 10:6]), while the boils assailed the magicians (from whom Pharaoh expected magical countermeasures) to the point that they were forced to desert their post alongside Pharaoh (Exod. 9:11).

49. This is similar to the neutralization of the king's messengers by Samuel (1 Sam. 19:20–21) and by Jehu (2 Kings 9:17–20), and the conversion of Ahaziah's messengers to Elijah's emissaries in the account of the king's consultation of Beelzebub (2 Kings 1:3–6).

50. This demand for recognition of the prophet's superior status parallels the ostensibly arbitrary demand of the widow, "but *first* make me a small cake" (17:13). Compare to this the bitter struggle between Moses and Dathan and Abiram as to who will go to whom (Num. 16:12–15 and 25), as well as the manifest respect that the three kings showed Elisha when they went to consult him (2 Kings 3:12).

51. R. L. Cohen ("Literary Logic," p. 339, n. 14) also noted this parallelism.

52. Obadiah calls both Elijah and Ahab "my lord"; his distress as the servant of two masters is unbearably exacerbated by Elijah's injunction, for he believes that fulfilling it will gain him a death sentence from his king. A similar situation confronted the Israelite foremen at the beginning of the careers of Moses and Aaron; their vigorous protest that they are caught between a rock and a hard place resonates in Obadiah's complaint here: "May the Lord look upon you and punish you for making us loathsome to Pharaoh and his courtiers—*putting a sword in their hand to kill us*" (Exod. 5:21); "What wrong have I done, that you should *give your servant into the hand of Ahab to kill me?*" (1 Kings 18:9).

53. On the basis of an inappropriate Germanic parallel, Gressman (*Die älteste Geschichtsschreibung*, p. 264), followed by Fohrer (*Elia*, p. 34) and Würthwein (*Die Bücher der Könige*, p. 222), viewed requiring neighboring peoples to take an oath as a legendary motif. A. F. Rainey ("Administration in Ugarit and the Samaria Ostraca," *IEJ* 12 [1962], pp. 62–63) anchored our verse in the solid ground of reality, finding parallels in the clause on the extradition of fugitives in the Alalaḫ documents. There, too, we find that the party demanding extradition may require the local authorities to swear by the gods that the fugitive is not in their jurisdiction.

54. Fohrer (*Elia*, pp. 34–35) sees verses 10–11 and 13 as expansions; but Steck (*Überlieferung*, pp. 11–13), refuting this argument and train of reasoning, demonstrated the logical structure of Obadiah's speech. He too views verse 13 as an addition, however, but for another reason: Obadiah's assertion of innocence can rest on the end of verse 12 alone. In Steck's interpretation, the mention of Jezebel belongs to a later stratum, that of the editor. Clearly the motif of providing bread and water to the prophets is too strongly anchored in the close analogy between Obadiah and the widow for this to be the work of an editor.

55. As a result of the mechanical elimination of repetitions in Obadiah's speech, Würthwein retains only verses 9–11, and DeVries, verses 9–12.

56. In biblical narrative, direct speech relies on repetitions of this sort, inter alia: (1) to express the speaker's emotional tension, deep perplexity, or frenzy (e.g., 1 Sam. 3:17, 4:16, and 21:15–16; 2 Kings 5:18); (2) as a persuasive rhetorical device (e.g., 2 Sam. 13:31–32 and 15:19–20; 2 Kings 1:13–14). Obadiah's emotional speech reflects both of these factors.

57. Compare Gunkel (*Elias*, p. 51), Gressman (*Die älteste Geschichtsschreibung*, p. 261), Fohrer (*Elia*, p. 34), and Würthwein (*Die Bücher der Könige*, p. 219).

58. In this he followed the example of Moses and Aaron, who shunted aside their humiliation at the most monstrous indictment possible—"You have brought

death upon the Lord's people!" (Num. 17:6)—and went forth to protect their accusers against the Lord's wrath: "[Aaron] stood between the dead and the living until the plague was checked" (v. 13).

59. The double mention of "prophets of the Lord" in verse 13, as compared to the single appearance of the phrase in verse 4, may be an additional means of depicting Obadiah's tension. A third difference is in the characterization of Obadiah. The narrator himself tells us that "Obadiah revered the Lord greatly" (v. 3), whereas in his testimony about himself Obadiah says, "Yet your servant has revered the Lord from my youth" (v. 12). This variation, too, seems deliberate: the narrator, relying on his narrative authority, can tell us, in absolute terms, how much Obadiah revered the Lord ("greatly"), whereas the character can speak only of the unbroken duration of his faith in the Lord.

60. The question can be turned on its head: why did the narrator decide to weary us by repeating in Obadiah's speech the information already provided in the exposition? To this we can offer two answers. First, he does intend to weary us, that is, to make us cognizant of the excessive length of Obadiah's account: the majordomo even tells the prophet what the latter must already know ("My lord has surely been told . . . " [v. 13]). Hence readers, like the prophet, are hearing known facts. Second, Obadiah's contention would be quite different if he went no further than asserting that he has revered the Lord since his youth and failed to express his shock that Elijah, totally ignoring his complete identification with the prophets and their mission, intends to harm him, just like his master Ahab.

61. Ibsen's *Enemy of the People* (1882) is a sort of secular avatar of the prophetic "troubler of Israel." The text makes no reference to Elijah; nor do I know whether Ibsen was aware of the affinities of character and fate between the biblical prophet and his Dr. Stockmann. Of particular interest is the people's hatred for the physician, who holds fast to his honesty and refuses to subordinate it to the economic interests of his resort town. Elijah's conflict is different, but the ugly manifestations of mass psychology are quite similar.

62. The Septuagint text lacks "commandments"; that reading is preferred by Kittel (*Biblia Hebraica*), Montgomery, Eissfeldt (*Der Gott Karmel*, p. 28), and Gray, because in this context the word has the distinct ring of a later era. There is a similar problem with 19:10, where the Septuagint reads, "for they have abandoned you" instead of "they have abandoned your covenant" (although in the corresponding verse—19:14—some Septuagint manuscripts agree with the Masoretic text). The phrasing of 18:21 and 39 would seem to tip the balance in favor of the shorter text, which focuses the problem on the actual acceptance of the yoke of heaven, which, as is known, comes before the acceptance of the yoke of the commandments.

63. Moses put Pharaoh to a similar test of faith. The damage caused by the plague of hail can be reduced if the king of Egypt believes the warning of the Lord's prophet and displays this in public: "Therefore, send and get your livestock and everything you have in the open brought under shelter. . . . Those among Pharaoh's courtiers who feared the Lords' word brought their slaves and livestock indoors to safety" (Exod. 9:19–20). This is not merely good advice (as Cassuto held in his commentary, ad loc.), but another link in the chain of trials that Moses posed for Pharaoh. In fact, the similarity is linguistic as well as thematic: corresponding to Moses' "Therefore send and get . . . under shelter (*wᵉ-ᶜattah šᵉlaḥ haᶜez*)," Elijah says, "now send and gather (*wᵉ-ᶜattah šᵉlaḥ qᵉvoṣ*)."

64. The question of the literary unity of chapter 18 depends to a large extent on our evaluation of the reliability of verses 17–19, which link the drought story to the account of the trial on Mount Carmel. Alt ("Das Gottesurteil," pp. 2–3), who first expressed doubts as to the unity of the chapter, saw the end of verse 18 as a Deuteronomistic addition meant to bridge between the two stories by providing a

theological rationale for the drought. Eissfeldt (*Der Gott Karmel*, p. 34) answered that even without this clause there is a link in the body of the story, since the indictment of Ahab as troubler of Israel (18a) is meaningful only in connection with the disastrous drought. To which Steck (*Überlieferung*, p. 9, n. 3) retorted that the indictment of Ahab as the cause of the drought and troubler of the people contradicts Elijah's own accusation, on Mount Carmel, that the people are responsible for that calamity (vv. 21 and 39); furthermore, all of verse 19 is "clearly secondary." This assessment is in keeping with his radical hypothesis that, in the original account of the drought, verses 18:1–2a were followed by a detailed description of the encounter between Elijah and Ahab, and immediately thereafter came the episode of the granting of rain (vv. 40–46). He holds that the interpolation of the meeting between Elijah and Obadiah and of the trial on Mount Carmel caused the relation of the encounter between Elijah and Ahab to be truncated and reworked as a bridging passage. In verses 17–20 he accordingly finds only vestiges of the original account, covered over by the versions of later editors (p. 13). To this we may answer as follows: (1) Even if—and there is no need to do so—we interpret Elijah's challenge to the people in verse 21 as an indirect statement of their responsibility for the drought, this does not contradict the accusation that it was Ahab who caused the people to sin. (2) Given the thematic and formal continuity between the injunction to Obadiah and the injunction to Ahab, the ungrounded assertion that verse 19 is secondary seems quite out of line.

65. Since Wellhausen (*Die Komposition*, p. 279, n. 1), it has been commonly held that the reference to the 400 prophets of the Asherah should be stricken from verse 19, given that they are not mentioned later in verses 22 and 40 (the fact that the Septuagint mentions them in verse 22, but not in verse 40, invalidates its testimony), and given the awkwardness of the omission of the accusative particle *'eth* before they are mentioned. I feel that Kimchi's alluring suggestion that they are absent from the rest of the story because Jezebel vetoed their going to Mount Carmel places too great a burden on the narrator's silence as a method of indirect expression, especially given the unmodified "the prophets" in verse 20. On the other hand, it is hard to understand why an interpolator who wanted to magnify the dimensions of Elijah's triumph would add the prophets of the Asherah only in verse 19 and refrain from doing so in the crucial passage (v. 40). A more plausible assumption, then, is that the prophets of the Asherah were accidentally deleted from the later verses rather than intentionally added to the earlier one.

66. The evidence concerning Mount Carmel as a cult site—going back to an Egyptian text of the mid-third millennium BCE and continuing as late as the remains of a statue bearing a dedicatory inscription to Zeus Heliopolites "Carmel" (or "the Carmelite") from the third century BCE, discovered by M. Avi-Yonah on Mount Carmel—were surveyed by Eissfeldt (*Der Gott Karmel*, pp. 1–25); cf. Z. Kla'i, *s.v.* "Carmel," *Biblical Encyclopedia* 4 (Hebrew), and Uffenheimer, *Ancient Prophecy*, pp. 192–98 and 206. It is going too far to conclude from this that Elijah chose a pagan cult site in order to defeat Baal on his own ground (Montgomery, *Books of Kings*, p. 301), even though this idea fits in well with the symmetrical parallel with the miracles of food and resurrection in Zarephath in Phoenicia. In light of the phrase, "he repaired the damaged altar of the Lord" (18:30), we should probably stick with the hypothesis that the trial was conducted in a place sacred to both parties.

67. Many believed that harming a prophet impaired his prophecies. See 1 Kings 13:4 and 22:24; 2 Kings 1:9ff.

68. In the words of Eichrodt, *Theology* 2, p. 277.

69. Whether the episode of the trial in verses 20–40 refers to the drought is a question of crucial importance for the issue of the unity of the chapter. Verse 21

is not decisive evidence, because "how long" is a regular feature of prophetic rebukes; there it expresses the fact that persisting in a sinful action increases its gravity (e.g., 1 Sam. 1:14). On the other hand, it is also used in the context of deriving conclusions from an ongoing phenomenon (e.g., Exod. 10:7). Hence it is possible, but not necessary, that "how long" refers to the three-year drought, if we assume that the drought is a fundamental given of the situation and does not have to be explicitly mentioned.

70. Moses, too, encountered this kind of passivity on the part of the Israelites in Egypt—"they would not listen to Moses, because of their broken spirit and cruel bondage" (Exod. 6:9)—and he too made few demands on them as long as he was still contending with Pharaoh.

71. Of all of the solutions proposed to resolve the contradiction between "I am the only prophet of the Lord left" and Obadiah's rescue of a hundred prophets of the Lord, Ehrlich's is the best, taking account of the context of Elijah's speech and its goal. According to Ehrlich, Elijah did not mention them because, driven underground, they could not function as active prophets. We can add that not only did the hidden prophets play no part in the balance of forces on Mount Carmel, the very fact that they had had to flee to caves increased the sin of their persecution. Accordingly, Elijah's indictment is that, until his sudden return, the active presence of the prophets of the Lord had for all practical purposes been driven out of public life in the country.

72. In Elijah's speech to the people (vv. 22–24a), the words "you will then invoke your god by name" (v. 24a), which seem to be addressed to the prophets of Baal, constitute a difficult crux. The change in interlocutor, in the middle of the speech, is both astonishing and implausible. For as soon as the people agree (v. 24b), Elijah turns to the prophets of Baal and says the very same words to them, this time in the imperative: "invoke your god by name" (v. 25b). All the ancient versions reflect the Masoretic text. Nevertheless, I see no alternative to the conjecture that in verse 24a we should read in a third person: "let them invoke their god by name."

73. The demonstrative scorn at the uneven balance of forces and the chivalric attitude toward the opponent recall Samson's behavior in his contest with the thirty friends (Judg. 14:12–13 and 18).

74. Elijah did not propose this two-stage process at first, when he spoke to the people (vv. 22–24), because he preferred to represent his going second as a concession made directly to his opponents. This clever act of camouflage attests not only to Elijah's wisdom and resourcefulness, but also to the importance he attached to keeping the onlookers' attention from being divided between the two altars and to guaranteeing that the Lord's response come against the background of Baal's silence.

75. The preposition ʿal has the sense of "around" in Gen. 19:4: "the men of Sodom . . . gathered around (ʿal) the house."

76. See Montgomery (*Books of Kings*, pp. 301–302) and Uffenheimer (*Ancient Prophecy*, pp. 203–204).

77. On self-laceration as a custom of prophets in Ugarit, see J. J. M. Roberts, "A New Parallel to 1 Kings 18:28–29," *JBL* 89 (1970), pp. 76–77. On the significance of shedding blood, considered to be the vital force, in order to rouse Baal to life, see Fensham, "A Few Remarks," p. 235.

78. Like the Egyptian magicians who tried to compete with Moses and Aaron in bringing the plagues, but in practice managed only to intensify them. Their initial successes increased, ironically, the suffering of the Egyptians, whereas their failure from the third plague on proved the absolute superiority of the God of the Hebrews.

79. See Cassuto, *Goddess Anath*, p. 51; de Vaux, "Prophets of Baal," pp. 243–51; Montgomery; Gray; Gaster, *Myth*, pp. 308–309; Rowley, "Elijah on Mount Carmel," pp. 51–53; Uffenheimer, *Ancient Prophecy*, pp. 204–206; Bronner, *Stories*, pp. 134–37; and Saint-Laurent, "Light from Ras Shamra," pp. 129–35.

80. The sense of derision and laughter is common in medieval Hebrew. It can be found earlier in Targum Jonathan on the present verse (*wa-hik*).

81. To this anticipation of a possible misunderstanding by readers, compare the opening sentence of the story of the binding of Isaac (Gen. 22:1a). See also the narrator's note as to the true intentions of Jehu when he gathered all prophets, worshippers, and priests of Baal to offer sacrifice to Baal (2 Kings 10:19b) and, in the story of the man of God from Judah, the aside, "he was lying to him" (1 Kings 13:18), intended to clarify that the Lord had not made contradictory statements to the two prophets.

82. In order to reconcile the conventional gloss of *wa-yᵉhattel* in the sense of ridicule with the fact that the prophets of Baal complied with Elijah's urgings, Preuss (*Verspottung*, p. 88) was forced to assume that they related seriously to his derisive suggestion, thereby revealing their absurdity, just like that of their god.

83. Just as the fact that the Sages applied the term "Baal's field" to arable land watered by rain (e.g., BT Baba Batra 3b) is evidence that Baal worship had disappeared from Israel by their age, so too the use of metaphors that attribute sleep and travel to the God of Israel (Ps. 35:22–23, 44:24, 59:5–6, and 78:65) should be seen as a reflection of the intensity of monotheistic belief.

84. Attributing both evil and good to the Lord is a logical complement to the denial of pagan relativism. Elijah will later state this explicitly in his prayer (vv. 36–37), at least according to the interpretation I shall propose for verse 37b.

85. Pharaoh, too, tried to call into question the validity of the wonder of the staff that metamorphosed into a serpent by exposing its magical nature. This is why he commanded his "wise men and sorcerers" to do the same thing through their spells (Exod. 7:11). In that test, the wonder wrought by Moses and Aaron manifested only a relative advantage: "Aaron's rod swallowed their rods" (v. 12). This made it easier for Pharaoh to stiffen his refusal—"Pharaoh's heart stiffened and he did not heed them" (v. 13). Elijah, however, wants an absolute decision, a total failure that will be extremely difficult to explain away, juxtaposed to a manifest and carefully monitored miracle that is almost immune to skepticism. This, in fact, is the format of the trial of the twelve staffs that concludes the affair of Korah's rebellion. Aaron's staff, which blossomed and produced almonds, as well as the other staffs, which remained as before, were put on view before the people: "Moses then brought out all the staffs from before the Lord to all the Israelites; each identified and recovered his staff" (Num. 17:24). This is also how Josephus understood the emphatic public nature of Elijah's actions: "He bade them retire and the others draw near to watch that he should not secretly apply fire to the wood" (*Antiquities of the Jews* 13,18,5).

86. Of course the credibility of the trial also depends on the historical credibility of the story. Montgomery (*Books of Kings*) cautions against rationalization of the miracle, such as the suggestion that Elijah had someone pour naphtha on the altar and set it alight by means of solar rays focused by a mirror: "such rationalizing would preserve the historicity of the story at the cost of its morality" (p. 307). Sensible remarks concerning the historical credibility of miracle tales and the possibility of verifying them scientifically can be found in Würthwein, "Die Erzählung vom Gottesurteil," pp. 137–39.

87. The idea that pouring water is a form of sympathetic magic meant to bring down rain (see Raphael Patai, *Water* [Tel Aviv, 1936], pp. 56–57 [Hebrew]; Ap-Thomas, "Elijah," pp. 153–56; Gaster, *Myth*, pp. 509–10; and Tromp, "Water and

Fire," p. 495) is refuted by the fact that it was not the prophet who poured it. Relying on other hands makes good sense as a matter of caution against deception on the part of the prophet; but why should Elijah refrain from performing a miracle or ritual act with his own hands? Quite the contrary: the virtue of such an action depends directly on who performs it (cf. 2 Kings 4:29–30). To this we should add Montgomery's point (*Books of Kings*, p. 308) that on Mount Carmel water was poured on the *sacrifice*, a phenomenon that has no parallel in the water-libation rituals of Israel or its neighbors.

88. According to the Masoretic text, verse 34 notes only the fulfillment of the second and third commands; the Vatican MS of the Septuagint, however, includes the performance of the first command—"and they did so." In any case, the elliptical phrasing of the Masoretic text is perfectly clear and understandable as it stands; furthermore, it is compatible with the narrator's inclination to avoid making this compliance into the main thing. The tendency to fill in too much is quite evident in the Septuagint version of our chapter, as in many other places.

89. Rashi, Kara, Kimchi, Gersonides, and Abravanel, on the one hand, and Gunkel (*Elias*, pp. 18–19), Fohrer (*Elia*, p. 15), and Rowley ("Elijah on Mount Carmel," p. 56), on the other, explain the pouring of the water as a means of increasing, by contrast, the miracle of the fire.

90. We shall return to this phenomenon later (pp. 193–95). Here we note only that nothing in our story explains how the two bullocks (unblemished, of course) required for the trial came to be found on the upper slopes of the Carmel, either.

91. As many have noted, in this too Elijah resembles Moses: "He set up an altar at the foot of the mountain, with twelve pillars for the twelve tribes of Israel" (Exod. 24:4b); cf. also Josh. 4:1–9 and 19–24.

92. Gunkel (*Elias*, p. 18), Gressman (*Die älteste Geschichtsschreibung*, p. 259), Eissfeldt (*Der Gott Karmel*, p. 29), Smend ("Das Wort," pp. 527–28), Fohrer (*Elia*, p. 17, n. 22), and Steck (*Überlieferung*, p. 17, n. 2) retain the last part of verse 30 and see verses 31–32a as an addition. The two last-named adopt what might be called a scientific version of the halakic concept of ad hoc legislation (see *Talmudic Encyclopedia* 8 [Jerusalem, 1957], cols. 513–14 [Hebrew]). They hold that an interpolator wanted to present Elijah's altar as a new one, built for the current trial only and swiftly destroyed by the heavenly fire at its conclusion; they accordingly maintain that the words "the stones, and the earth" (v. 38) are from the same hand. By contrast, DeVries (*1 Kings*) retains verses 31–32a and views verse 30b as an "ideological interpolation," whereas Würthwein (*Die Bücher der Könige*, p. 216) sees both statements about the altar as later additions. Montgomery prefers the assumption that we have before us two parallel traditions: the narrator, rather than choosing between them, attempted to reconcile them. Only Šanda and Gray try to reconcile the descriptions. They believe Elijah's altar consisted of two levels with a combined height of at least two and a half cubits. Only the lower stage of the ancient altar had survived; the prophet repaired it first, then built the upper level atop it, using twelve stones.

93. There are few archaeological vestiges of this type of altar, so we must rely on internal textual evidence and reason only. Cf. M. Haran, *s.v.* "altar," *Biblical Encyclopedia* 4 (Jerusalem, 1962) (Hebrew).

94. This is the opinion of Gunkel (*Elias*, p. 18, and p. 70, n. 20), Smend ("Das Wort," pp. 256–57), and Würthwein. Eissfeldt (*Der Gott Karmel*, p. 29), Fohrer (*Elia*, p. 15), Gray, DeVries, and Montgomery retain the two verses. Montgomery bases his choice on the fact that liturgical language naturally tends to be long-winded.

95. Just as the splitting of the Red Sea brought the Israelites to believe in the Lord and in His servant Moses (Exod. 14:31).

96. Greenberg, "You Have Turned Their Hearts Backward," p. 66.

97. This is the interpretation, in different variations, of Saadya Gaon (*Book of Beliefs and Opinions*, end of ch. 4; also cited by Kimchi), Menahem Ḥelbo (cited by

Joseph Kara), Joseph Kimchi (cited by David Kimchi, *Sefer Hashorashim*, s.v. *a.ḥ.r*), Ehrlich (who emends *ʾaḥorannith* to *ʾaḥareḵa*), Gunkel (*Elias*, p. 18), Šanda, Eissfeldt (*Der Gott Karmel*, p. 29), Fohrer (*Elia*, pp. 15–16), Gray, Würthwein, and DeVries.

98. See Driver, *Treatise*, p. 17. His examples include Lev. 14:48; 1 Sam. 20:22; 1 Chron. 14:15.

99. If the text read, "You caused their hearts to return to You," all would be clear and simple. Perhaps we should assume that this phrasing was avoided as being too extreme. The Lord will sunder their attachment to Baal, but the responsibility for returning to Him remains theirs, as Isaiah would later assert: "For the people has not turned back to Him who struck it and has not sought the Lord of Hosts" (Isa. 9:12).

100. Verse 36 seems to echo Moses' words before the earth splits open to swallow up Dathan and Abiram; this intensifies the self-justificatory tone of Elijah's prayer: "And Moses said, 'By this *you shall know* that it was the Lord who sent me *to do all these things;* that they are not of my own devising' " (Num. 16:28).

101. It is doubtful whether *l.ḥ.k* is found in Scripture with the restricted meaning of "lick" (Isa. 49:23; Ps. 72:9); clearly, though, it does occur with the broader meaning of "consume" ("as an ox licks up the grass of the field" [Num. 22:4]). If we assume that in verse 38 *liḥekah* has the more restricted sense, we obtain an implausible opposition between the consumption of the sacrifice, wood, stones, and earth, in the first part of the verse, and the "licking" of the water by tongues of fire in the second part. Since water is no more fireproof than stones or earth, understanding the word in the restricted sense would force us to move the caesura from "earth" to "the wood." The Septuagint's different word order (the fire "consumed the burnt offering, the wood, and the water that was in the trench; and it licked the stones and the earth") cannot serve as reliable evidence for such an understanding of the verse. Hence we ought to assume that in our verse *liḥekah* is used as a parallel for "consumed"; rather than limiting the miracle, it intensifies its wonder: not only did the fire consume the altar, it also consumed the water, the antithetical element that had been poured around the altar to protect it from alien fire.

102. The verbal similarity between "When they saw this, all the people flung themselves on their faces and cried out" (v. 39) and the Israelites' reaction to the miraculous fire that culminated in the dedication of the Tabernacle by Moses and Aaron—"When they saw this, all the people shouted and flung themselves on their faces" (Lev. 9:24)—seems to be intentional. Cf. also 2 Chron. 7:3.

103. "He slaughtered them" in verse 40 can be understood in one of two ways: they were slaughtered by others, at Elijah's command, or he personally killed them (cf. Abraham Ibn Ezra's indecision concerning the erection of the Tabernacle by Moses in his standard commentary on Exod. 26:30 and 40:2).

104. Cf. von Rad (*Theology* 2, pp. 31–32), who emphasizes that the killing of the prophets of Baal must not be seen as an act of vengeance or zeal enthusiastically executed by Elijah but as the implementation of an ancient law (Exod. 22:19) whose enforcement had lapsed.

105. Cf. Rofé, "Breaking of the Heifer's Neck," pp. 119–43.

106. Gersonides, in his commentary on 19:1, writes as follows: " 'He slaughtered them there'—as if he did not want their blood to defile the land; this is why their blood was spilled in the wadi, which would carry it to a distant place." However, in the present century the length of the westernmost segment of the Kishon, where water flows year-round, is never more than a few kilometers, and it significantly diminishes after a long drought.

107. Even a totally unscrupulous murderer like Ishmael son of Nethaniah was probably careful about this (Jer. 41:7 and 9).

108. This is the opinion of Alt ("Das Gottesurteil," pp. 1–3), Fohrer (*Elia*, pp.

34–36), Steck (*Überlieferung*, pp. 9–19), Würthwein ("Die Erzählung vom Gottesurteil," p. 132), Tromp ("Water and Fire," pp. 489–91), and DeVries.

109. Note that whereas in the incident of Naboth's vineyard the liquidation of the House of Ahab is declared to be punishment for this sin by the king and queen (21:19 and 21–24), in our story the destruction of the royal house is presented as punishment of the *people:* "Whoever escapes from the sword of Hazael shall be slain by Jehu, and whoever escapes the sword of Jehu shall be slain by Elisha. I will leave in Israel only seven thousand" (19:17–18).

110. Those overcome by curiosity about this detail can assume that the lad attached himself to Elijah after the fire fell from heaven, just as Saul was joined by "the men of valor whose hearts God had touched" (1 Sam. 10:26) right after he was singled out by lot at Mizpah.

111. It cannot be denied that this screaming silence perplexes even those totally at home with the elliptical style of Scripture, since incorporating a simple phrase like "and the people returned every man to his home" in verse 45 would satisfy our desire for informational balance. Transferring the question from the author to the editor is of no utility here, given the impressive literary and aesthetic unity we have discovered in chapter 18. An editor who intervenes to such an extent in the presentation and phrasing of the traditions available to him assumes the status of a storyteller and should pay attention to the omission of minimal information about the protagonists. The only possible answer is that he knew that his readers, whose literary conventions were different from ours, would not be disturbed by what bothers us. Edwin Muir clearly described the necessary one-sidedness of those conventions: "Their limitations . . . are legitimate ones, not the limitations of any particular author, but of the human mind. This mind, trying to see life whole, has to narrow its focus, or instinctively does so; it renounces in order to gain" (*The Structure of the Novel* [London, 1928], p. 114).

112. Given that in the story of Elisha's resurrection of the Shunammite's son we read "he stretched himself (*wa-yighar*) over him" (2 Kings 4:34), it is surprising that the root *g.h.r* is not used in the description of Elijah's revival of the Phoenician widow's son. Had the narrator done so, the same verb would be used both in the account of the struggle for the boy's life and in the account of the struggle for rain, strongly reinforcing the parallels between them. The narrator's avoidance of this association suggests that he wanted to avoid this aspect of similarity. When the prophet stretches himself out on the child's body he is trying to revive him through physical means; but when he stretches himself on the earth he is prostrating himself in prayer before the Lord. In other words, the narrator wanted to deflect any association of this action with a physical action directed at the earth (sympathetic magic of some sort).

113. The various parallels from the Talmud and from Jewish and Muslim mystical literature cited by Fenton ("La 'tête entre les genoux,' " pp. 413–26) clearly indicate that placing the head between the knees is done while seated on the ground, with the knees bent up and held together. This posture is quite incompatible with lying stretched out on the ground. Hence we must say that two separate actions of Elijah are being described, as was noted by Kimchi (in his first gloss): "At first he fell on his face and stretched himself out on the ground and prayed; after that he sat up and placed his face between his knees and would not get up from praying until he knew that there was a sign of rain." Precisely this interpretation was offered a generation before Kimchi by R. Hananel ben Samuel the Dayyan, the father-in-law of Abraham Maimonides, in his Arabic-language commentary on the *haftaroth,* cited by Fenton: "Après quoi, Élie s'assit et *posa son visage entre ses genoux,* visant ainsi à détourner son attention de toute la création et de consacrer sa méditation uniquement à sa préoccupation présente. Les nations (= les Soufis)

nous ont emprunté cette pratique. Ils en ont hérité et s'en sont ornés (= ils préten-dent qu'ils l'ont initiée). Ainsi, ils s'asseoient dans cette posture toute une journée. Ils appellent cela *tayziq*, c'est-à-dire 'cacher son visage dans son col', à savoir le bord de son vêtement" ("La 'tête entre les genoux'," p. 422). This intercreed rivalry about who first devised the method blurs the fact that neither the Bible nor the Talmud describe a meditative posture aimed at attaining mystic enlightenment but a petitionary posture whose objective is to obtain an answer. The Talmudic parallel to such complete and unceasing devotion to prayer, until one receives an answer, is the story of Ḥoni Ha-meʿaggel: "I swear by Your great name that I will not move from this spot until You have mercy on Your children" (BT Taʿanit 19a).

114. Since we have already been told that Elijah and his servant were at the top of Mount Carmel, here the imperative ʿaleh must be understood in the sense of "go" (as mentioned previously in connection with v. 41). The use of a verb in two different senses in a single context is quite common in Scripture (see above, n. 37). Here, though, it is most disturbing, since it causes confusion about the char-acters' whereabouts.

115. The relationship between Elijah's running before the king's chariot and the encounter with Obadiah is underscored by the appearance in both episodes of the motif of the prophet's miraculous powers of locomotion. Obadiah was afraid that Elijah would disappear miraculously—"*the spirit of the Lord* will carry you off I don't know where" (18:12); now the narrator, describing Elijah's miraculous race before the chariot, says, "*the hand of the Lord* had come upon Elijah" (v. 46).

116. Abravanel, ad loc., demonstrates that here "the hand of the Lord" indi-cates supernatural capacity rather than a prophetic mission.

117. Compare Steck (*Überlieferung*, p. 23), Smend ("Das Wort," pp. 542–43), and Zakovitch ("Still Small Voice," p. 330).

118. Eissfeldt, " 'Bist du Elia,' " p. 69.

119. In the assertion that Elijah merits death for having shed innocent blood we hear an echo of his indictment, in the wake of the drought, as "troubler of Israel" (18:17), as well as of the accusation that Moses and Aaron "have brought death upon the Lord's people" (Num. 17:6).

120. Almost all agree that the repetitive "he fell asleep (*wa-yišan*) under a broom bush" (v. 5a) is merely an inexact dittography of "he sat down (*wa-yešev*) under a broom bush" in the previous verse. As for the possible rebuttal that the repetition is meant to underscore the extent to which the prophet, sleeping in the wilderness, lacks everything (as in "taking one of the stones of that place, he put it under his head" [Gen. 28:11]), if this were the case we would expect the definite article in the repetition: "under the [= the aforementioned] broom bush."

121. On the surface, "the angel of the Lord returned a second time (*wa-yašov . . . šenith*) and touched him" (v. 7a) means that the angel returned to the place where Elijah was lying and touched him. But the tautology "return a second time" is not found in Scripture; furthermore, given the proximity to "he lay down again (*wa-yašov wa-yiškav*)" (v. 6b), it seems likely that here *wa-yašov* is used as an auxiliary verb indicating repeated action rather than as an independent verb indicating re-turn. What remains unusual is that the adverb *šenith* comes between the auxiliary and main verbs rather than at the end of the sentence, as in Josh. 5:2.

122. For variation in the designations of characters as one of the most impor-tant techniques for expressing changes in the point of view—from that of the nar-rator to that of the protagonist and vice versa—see Berlin, *Poetics*, pp. 59–61 and 87–91. Cf. also above, ch. 1, n. 20.

123. It is difficult to accept Kimchi's opinion that "he did not know where to go, but simply kept going for forty days and forty nights until Mount Horeb. The way was made straight for him as for the ark, as it is written 'the cows went straight

ahead,' etc. (1 Sam. 6:12)." In the first place, the text reads "he walked . . . as far as the mountain of God at Horeb"; second, it is hard to imagine that Elijah was simply roaming in the wilderness without a destination; third, because there is no hint in the text of the miraculous experience of reaching an unexpected destination; fourth, because the Lord goes on to ask him, "why are you here, Elijah?"

124. The fact that the text employs the definite article—"*the* cave ⟨*ha-m^e^{c}arah*⟩"—is meaningless; compare *ba-m^e^{c}arah* with regard to Obadiah's protection of the prophets of the Lord (18:4 and 13), which certainly is not intended to indicate a particular cave.

125. See Malbim (*Mikrae Kodesh*); von Nordheim ("Ein Prophet," p. 161); and Zakovitch ("Still Small Voice," p. 335).

126. Seybold ("Elia am Gottesberg," p. 8, n. 30) remarks that the interrogative *mah l^{e}ka* is common in Scripture, especially in audiences with a king. See 2 Sam. 14:5; 1 Kings 1:16; 2 Kings 6:28; Esther 5:3.

127. In the Book of Jonah, too, the narrator does not disclose the motives of the prophet's flight until chapter 4, which resembles the present chapter in many ways. Perhaps its use of this uncommon narrative device is borrowed from here.

128. Here, in my opinion, the perfect *qanno^3 qinne^{3}thi* has the sense of completed past action (as, e.g., "I was sure [*^{3}amor ^{3}amarti*] that you had taken a dislike to her [*sano^3 s^{e}ne^{3}thah*], so I gave her to your wedding companion" [Judg. 15:2]; see also 1 Sam. 22:9 and 22) and is not, as proposed by Zakovitch ("Still Small Voice," p. 336), the progressive perfect of an act begun in the recent past and still in progress. This is chiefly because *qanno^3 qinne^{3}thi* is not "a call for vengeance" but the characterization of a deed, as is evidenced even by what Zakovitch cites as his proof text: "Come with me and see my zeal for the Lord" (2 Kings 10:16), which does not refer to the proclamation that Jehu is about to issue but to a deed he is about to perform and which can be seen.

129. Apart from here, the expression "forsake the covenant" (*^{c}azov b^{e}rith*) is found only in Deut. 29:24, and there too the meaning is that "they turned to the service of other gods and worshipped them" (v. 25). When used by Elijah, this rare locution echoes his rebuke of Ahab: "by *forsaking* the commandments of the Lord and going after the Baalim" (18:18).

130. See Gunkel, *Elias*, pp. 20–21; Fohrer, *Elia*, p. 37; Stamm, "Elia am Horeb," pp. 327–28; Steck, *Überlieferung*, pp. 20–21; Würthwein, *Die Bücher der Könige*, p. 229; Seybold, "Elia am Gottesberg," p. 5; and Hentschel, *Die Elijaerzählungen*, p. 65.

131. Such a view is reflected in the three consecutive years of famine visited on all Israel as punishment for Saul's slaughter of the Gibeonites (2 Sam. 21:1–9) and the plague that struck the people from Dan to Beersheba because of the census conducted by David (2 Sam. 24:10–17).

132. A striking example of literary metaphorization is found in Jeremiah 38. In verse 6 we read that "Jeremiah sank into the mud." In verse 22, Jeremiah warns Zedekiah of what is in store for him by means of the derisive song that the women being led off into captivity will sing about him, which includes the image, "your feet are sunk in the mire."

133. A good example of such surprise and intensification is the negotiations between Ben-hadad and Ahab (1 Kings 20:1–12). The king of Aram begins by setting the terms of surrender: "Your silver and gold are mine, and your beautiful wives and children are mine" (v. 3). The king of Israel accepts them, but restates the terms in a way that on the one hand is less specific and on the other hand goes even further, clarifying, by including himself, that the dominion spoken of is in the nature of political and economic rule rather than title or possession in the full sense of the word: "As you say, my lord king: I and all I have are yours" (v. 4). But Ben-hadad refuses to accept this and repeats his original wording while unambig-

uously stressing that he means concrete and not metaphorical mastery: "When I sent you the order to give me your silver and gold, and your wives and your children, I meant that tomorrow at this time I will send my servants to you and they will search your house and the houses of your courtiers and seize everything you prize and take it away" (vv. 5–6). Ahab, astonished by the concretization of the original terms, sums up the failure of the negotiations in his report to the elders of the land: "See for yourselves how that man is bent on evil [i.e., unconditional surrender that will be exploited limitlessly]! For when he demanded my wives and my children, my silver and my gold, I did not refuse him" [i.e., I agreed to this as a metaphor for limited submission] (v. 7). When he receives the elders' vigorous support for his refusal to surrender, he presents his negative reply as a return to the first (metaphorical) sense of the surrender terms: "All that you first demanded of your servant I shall do, but this [concrete] thing I cannot do" (v. 9).

134. A contrary opinion, which is based chiefly on verse 16 (to be discussed shortly), sees chapter 19 not as a renewal of consecration but as its abrogation, that is, as the termination of the prophet's mission. This view goes back to the *Mekilta* (*Petiḥta*, ed. H. S. Hurvitz and I. A. Rabin [Frankfurt am Main, 1931], p. 4): " 'A prophet in your stead' means 'I do not want your prophecy.' " Following this midrash, Rashi, too, sees Elijah's dismissal as a punishment: "I do not want your prophecy, because you impeach my children" (Rashi on v. 16). Kimchi (ad loc.), who categorizes this gloss as "homiletic," views the dismissal as the Lord's reply to Elijah's yearning for death. Gersonides took this over from him, adding that Elijah despaired of being able to influence Israel, "to the point of revulsion from his life because of their evil ways" (commentary on verse 15). Nordheim ("Ein Prophet," pp. 167–68) and Zakovitch ("Still Small Voice," p. 343) combine the two rationales—punishment and acceding to his wish—as a double explanation for Elijah's replacement by Elisha. By contrast, Baltzer (*Die Biographie*, pp. 95–96) and Macholz ("Psalm 29 und 1 Könige 19," p. 331) see the episode as a reconsecration; Macholz compares it with Jer. 12:1–6 and Isa. 49:3–6.

135. Whereas here the indictment of the people is only implied by the prayer for vengeance, in chapter 12 Jeremiah states it separately and more explicitly: "You are present in their mouths, but far from their thoughts" (v. 2). There too, however, the emphasis is not on the gravity of their sins but on the terrible nature of the requested punishment: "Drive them out like sheep to the slaughter, prepare them for the day of slaying!" (v. 3). By contrast, the prophet of consolation (Isa. 49:1–6)—by the very nature of the circumstances—does not assail the people and does not seek vengeance on them. But his efforts at consolation have proven fruitless and he too gives vent to his despair: "I thought, 'I have labored in vain, I have spent my strength for empty breath' " (Isa. 49:4a).

136. Hentschel (*Die Elijaerzählung*, pp. 99–104) suggests classifying the episode of Elijah at Horeb as a "prophetic complaint," modeled on the "complaint songs" in Psalms and Jeremiah. It is true that the element of complaint is conspicuous in stories of prophetic reconsecration; but their distinguishing mark is that the Lord's response to the complaint, while promising assistance and rescue, also demands or ensures renewal of the prophetic mission with greater vigor and greater success. This element is found not only in 1 Kings 19 and Jeremiah 15, but also in Jer. 12:5–6 and Isa. 49:5–6.

137. See Cross (*Canaanite Myth*, pp. 148–94, esp. pp. 190–94); cf. also Jeremias (*Theophanie*, pp. 112–15), and Bronner (*Stories*, p. 63).

138. Gersonides underscores the ineffectiveness of zealousness: "The evils occasioned by moral zeal are of no benefit to them. You see that the cessation of dew and rain for three years did not make them submit to the Lord" (commentary on v. 12); and Uffenheimer—its immorality: "In the narrator's account of the still small

voice there flowers the first prophetic self-criticism of the violent path of the militant prophets" (*Ancient Prophecy*, p. 233).

139. See Malbim (*Mikrae Kodesh*, on verses 11 and 14), Stamm ("Elia am Horeb," pp. 333–34) and especially Zakovitch ("1 Kings 19," pp. 341–45).

140. Stamm ("Elia am Horeb," p. 344) himself computes that 7000 families represent about ten percent of the 60,000 landowners from whom Menahem ben Gadi levied the tribute he paid to Assyria (see 2 Kings 15:19–20). Rofé (*Prophetical Stories*, p. 158) compares "I will leave in Israel only seven thousand" (19:18) with the report that Hazael left Jehoahaz with "a force of only fifty horsemen, ten chariots, and ten thousand foot soldiers" (2 Kings 13:7), and notes that "seven and ten are interchangeable typological numbers" (n. 11). There, however, the reference is to remnants of the army and not to the survivors among the people at large.

141. Almost all commentators, starting with Targum Jonathan and running through the most recent (the salient exceptions are Abravanel and Zakovitch, "Still Small Voice," p. 341) assume that the Lord's words to Elijah include only the injunction to leave the cave and stand on the mountain before Him. They understand the rest of verse 11, beginning with "and lo," not as an advance warning of what is about to take place but as a report of the actual occurrence, and accordingly render the participle *ʿover* as a past tense ("passed"). The advantage of the traditional interpretation is that the text includes a description of the theophany, whose omission would seem quite strange (but see below). Nevertheless, it has many significant deficiencies: (1) There is no indication in verse 11 of a transition from the Lord's words to the narrator's voice; moreover, the combination of the interjectory "and lo" with the present participle is often employed in instructions and directions about impending events (e.g., "Lo, I will come *[hinneh ʾanoki baʾ]* to you in a thick cloud" [Exod. 19:9]; see also Gen. 24:13; Exod. 3:13, 4:14). (2) If we assume that the Lord's speech continues through the end of verse 12, it is perfectly clear why verse 13 opens with a report of the fulfillment of the injunction: "When Elijah heard [the Hebrew text does not contain the accusative pronoun *it!*], he wrapped his mantle about his face and went out and stood at the entrance of the cave." By contrast, it is quite difficult to refer this sentence to Elijah's response to hearing the still, small voice. (3) It is not at all clear why Elijah does not go out of the cave as soon as he is told to do so but remains inside until he hears the still, small voice. How could he know in advance that the Lord would not appear in the wind, earthquake, and fire?

142. Zakovitch brings out this point very strongly ("Still Small Voice," p. 338).

143. [Note that in Hebrew the construction is not noun plus two adjectives but rather two nouns (the second in genitive relationship to the first) plus an adjective modifying the second noun—"a voice of small (or thin) silence (or murmur)."—Trans.]

144. Gersonides glosses: "A low voice from the Lord, composed as if it were of sound and silence." Ehrlich argues that the genitive construction—a voice *of* still silence—is like "knee-deep water" [lit. "water of knees"] (Ezek. 47:4) and that it means a low sound that can be heard only when absolute silence prevails.

145. See Newsom, *Songs*, pp. 303, 314–15. Cf. Schiffman, "*Merkawa* Speculation," pp. 36–37.

146. This is the interpretation of Zakovitch ("Still Small Voice," p. 340), relying on Tur-Sinai, *Job*, pp. 48–49.

147. Compare Abravanel (on v. 18); Ehrlich (*Randglossen* 7, on v. 15); and Gray (*I and II Kings*, on v. 16).

148. Elisha instigates Jehu's plot against the house of Ahab (2 Kings 9:1–9) and speaks with extreme sharpness against Jehoram's adherence to the prophets

of Baal (2 Kings 3:13). With these exceptions, there is no evidence that he actively pursued Elijah's war against Baal worship. Rashi (on v. 17) glosses this to his credit: "We find that he was responsible for the death only of the 42 children killed by the bears at Jericho." Rofé (*Prophetical Stories*, p. 188) would infer from this gap between the historical Elisha and his depiction here as Elijah's successor in the war against Baal worship that our story was not composed until at least two generations after Elisha's death, evidently at the time of the reintroduction of Baal worship by King Manasseh of Judah. Skinner (*Kings*, p. 241), however, sees the disparity between the prophecy and history as decisive proof for the priority of our story since the prophecy is related with no thought for the extent to which it was later fulfilled.

149. Von Rad (*Theology* 2, pp. 21–22) disagrees with the view that the idea of the remnant, from which the nation will sprout once again ("a remnant shall return," in the language of Isa. 10:21; see also Isa. 11:11–16) originated with the prophets. It was a political reality—the kings of Assyria boasted that they left alive only a tiny remnant of certain nations, and in Scripture, too, we read about "the remaining Rephaim" (Josh. 13:12) and "a remnant of the Amorites" (2 Sam. 21:2); but it was also a religious concept—Noah and his family were the remnant of mankind, Lot and his daughters, the remnant of Sodom. To this can be added what the Lord says to Moses after the sin of the Golden Calf (Exod. 32:10).

150. For the similar significance of the prophetic indictments of Israel by Samuel, Hosea, and Jeremiah, see above, pp. 89–90.

151. See Alt, "Die Literarische Herkunft," pp. 123–25; Eissfeldt, "Die Komposition," pp. 51 and 53–55; Zakovitch, "Still Small Voice," p. 330.

152. These gaps may perhaps run a little deeper than is customary in scriptural narrative, but not to the point of perplexing readers who are used to its conventions of elliptical expression (see in the index, "Ellipses and gaps"). Thus, for example, we are never told that Moses removed his shoes from his feet (Exod. 3:5), whereas in the parallel story about Joshua we read that "Joshua did so" (Josh. 5:15).

7. Elisha and the Woman of Shunem

1. In the story of Naaman, too, Zakovitch found an attitude critical of Elisha, but one much more moderate than that found in the story of the Shunammite (*Every High Official*, pp. 50–51, 54–55, 61–63, 80, 92, and 133–36).

2. See above, pp. 1–4 and 131–36.

3. See above, p. 35.

4. On this function of a minor character, see pp. 268–69.

5. See Sabbato, "Story of the Shunammite," p. 49.

6. A similar use of the temporal indication "one day" is found in the first part of the frame story of the Book of Job. The first scene (1:1–5) is an exposition describing habitual actions. This is followed by three scenes that begin with "one day," set alternately in heaven and on earth (1:6–12, 1:13–22, and 2:1–7a); the fifth scene (2:7b–10) is distinguished only by the change of location (from heaven to earth), because it occurs on the same day as the previous one. This vividly depicts how avid Satan is to wound Job physically, on the very day he received permission to do so. Savran (*Telling and Retelling*, pp. 97–102) and Long (*Second Kings*, pp. 51–59) both ignored the fact that the temporal indication "one day" serves to mark the beginning of scenes. As a result, the structures proposed by them differ from that proposed here.

7. The division of the story into three days of action and the different pace of each has been established by Rofé (*Prophetical Stories*, pp. 27–28).

8. With this we should compare Saul's excursion from Mount Gilboa to Endor

(a distance of 5–10 kilometers) and back in the course of a single night (1 Sam. 28:8 and 25) and the nocturnal expedition of the men of Yabesh Gilead to Beit She'an (23 kilometers) and back (1 Sam 31:12).

9. On the cumulative impression of Elisha's failures, see Samet, "Double Embrace," p. 74.

10. The desire to discover toeholds in the story for reconstituting the process of its creation led H.-C. Schmitt (*Elisa*, pp. 93–99) and A. Schmitt ("Die Totenerweckung," pp. 1–8 and 13–15) to view Elisha's two proposals to reward the Shunammite and two attempts to resurrect the child as duplication resulting from the patching together of two parallel traditions. But eliminating the two failures—the failure to help the Shunammite on the social level and to resurrect her son by means of the staff—from the plot hardly seems plausible in and of itself (see the section on a close reading in this chapter) and undermines the sophisticated structure of the story, thereby preventing us from grasping the rhetorical significance of this structure.

11. On the use of contrast in the presentation of characters, see above, pp. 268–69.

12. Rofé, who believes that the story of the widow of Zarephath depends on the story of the Shunammite, argues, inter alia: "How could such a needy woman have an attic, unless this detail was also borrowed from the story about the Shunammite?" (*Prophetical Stories*, pp. 133–34). I would reply that the fact that, in a time of drought, the widow is starving because she has no one to support her and no source of income, is easily reconciled with her ownership of a house (which she must have inherited from her late husband) large enough to have an upper room. The upper room is mentioned in the story because it is essential to it: both to prevent scandal (Elijah is living in the widow's house) and because the miraculous resurrection requires complete solitude.

13. Both linguistically and thematically, her remarks resemble the reliance of the widow of the son of the prophets on Elisha's perfect and confident knowledge: "Your servant my husband is dead, and *you know* how your servant revered the Lord" (2 Kings 4:1).

14. Another apparent manifestation of the preservation of distance between Elisha and the woman is the way in which he speaks about her—"call that [*ha-zoth*] Shunammite woman" (v. 12), which Gunkel (*Geschichten von Elisa*, p. 19) characterizes as "cordial condescension." In fact the demonstrative *zeh* does often express disdain, as we find twice in the story of Naaman: the king of Israel says of his neighbor, the king of Aram: "*this one* [*zeh*] writes to me" (2 Kings 5:7); Gehazi refers to the Aramean commander as "that [*ha-zeh*] Aramean Naaman" (5:20). Given, however, that Elisha refers to her in this manner throughout the story—when he means to reward the Shunammite for her hospitality (v. 13), when he is troubled by her sudden appearance at Mount Carmel (v. 25), and when he calls her to take her son, restored to life (v. 36)—this form of speech cannot be meant to reflect his opinion of her. We ought rather to assume that her name had been forgotten (see also vv. 19–20 and 8:1 and 5), forcing the author to place this anonymous expression in Elisha's mouth, without any understanding that this deviation from realistic speech might impair the story's verisimilitude. The reader is assumed to understand that Elisha knew his hostess's name and used it when addressing her, just as Boaz certainly knew the alternate redeemer and called him by name, although the text of Ruth has him say, "come over and sit down here, So-and-so" (Ruth 4:1).

15. Compare Sternberg, *Poetics*, pp. 309–10.

16. Here are several examples of the narrator's skipping over self-evident intermediate stages and concealing information that we deem essential: we are not told that Gehazi conveyed Elisha's words to the Shunammite and relayed her re-

sponse to Elisha (v. 13). It is not clear how the woman, who was at home, conversed with her husband, out in the field with the harvesters: if she bid him return home (in her own voice or through a messenger), the narrator has failed to describe his arrival there (v. 22). We are told that Elisha followed the woman to Shunem (evidently both traveled on foot), but there is no mention of when the serving lad and ass returned (v. 30). See also Rashi's commentary on verse 26.

17. The word *ʾal* must be repeated in combination with the vocative (see Judg. 19:23; 2 Sam. 13:12). Hence it does not intensify the force of the negation, as is demonstrated by David's remark to Absalom: "No, my son, no, we must not all come or we will be a burden to you" (2 Sam. 13:25).

18. See Zakovitch, *Every High Official*, pp. 61–62.

19. Rashi comments on Elisha's instruction to the widow of the son of the prophets in verse 4: "Close the door—it is the honor of miracles to come in secrecy."

20. Rofé (*Prophetical Stories*, p. 47, n. 18) compares this enforced silence with what is told about the day on which Rabbi Judah the Prince died: "The rabbis decreed a fast and prayed for mercy, saying: Anyone who says, 'Rabbi has passed away,' will be stabbed with a sword" (BT Ketubot 104a).

21. The threefold repetition is an expression of great concern, much as a similar repetition by David is an expression of abundant blessing: "Peace to you, and peace to your household, and peace to all that is yours" (1 Sam. 25:6).

22. See above, p. 15.

23. This combination of two types of prophecy is found in the description of the meeting between Samuel and Saul (1 Sam. 9:15–20): although it is emphasized that God directly informs Samuel of the election of Saul as ruler of Israel as well as the identification of Saul son of Qish with the man spoken of, there is no indication that He told Samuel where Saul could find his asses; evidently we are meant to understand that Samuel knew this through his own far-seeing powers.

24. Uffenheimer (*Ancient Prophecy*, p. 275) sees the account of Elisha's need for music in order to fall into a divine trance (2 Kings 3:15) as an expression of the same sober and critical attitude to prophetic ability found here.

25. Cf. Savran, *Telling and Retelling*, pp. 69–70, 96–97, 101. In his opinion, however, this is not a mere interpretive quotation but a quotation that reinterprets the original statement (p. 110): he considers the discrepancy between the original statement and its quoted version to be much greater than I do.

26. In the annunciation and description of its fulfillment, the word used is *ben* (vv. 16 and 17). From the time he goes out to the field (v. 18), however, until Elisha asks after his health (v. 26), he is called *ha-yeled*. From there until verse 32 he is referred to as *ha-naʿar* five times in succession—by Elisha (v. 29), the narrator (vv. 31a and 32), and Gehazi (v. 31b). In verse 34 the narrator twice refers to *ha-yeled*, whereas in verse 35 he again says *ha-naʿar* (twice). At the end of the story, Elisha says, "Pick up your son [*bᵉnek*]" (v. 36), and the narrator accordingly notes that "she picked up her son [*bᵉnah*]" (v. 37). The presence of the first cluster of *ha-naʿar* in verses 29–32, which deal with Gehazi's unsuccessful attempt, has been offered as stylistic evidence that this section derives from a parallel source (see H.-C. Schmitt, *Elisa*, p. 95; A. Schmitt, "Die Totenerweckung," p. 3; Stipp, *Elischa*, pp. 284–94). The clustering may astonish even those who view Gehazi's attempt to revive the child as an essential part of the plot. In Scripture, *naʿar* can refer to an infant (1 Sam. 4:21) and so can *yeled* (1 Kings 3:25); both nouns designate the three-month-old Moses ("When she opened it, she saw that it was a child [*yeled*], a boy [*naʿar*] crying" [Exod. 2:6]). There are alternations of *naʿar* and *yeled* that seem to be a matter of elegant variation, with no semantic distinction and not even meant to reflect the different points of view of various protagonists (see 1 Kings 14:3, 12, 17; 2 Kings 2:23–24). On the other hand, there are also conspicuous clusters of one

noun, almost to the exclusion of the other (2 Sam. 12:15–23: *ha-naʿar* once, as opposed to twelve occurrences of *ha-yeled*). In light of all this, the only conclusion that can be drawn is that this variation is indeed a stylistic phenomenon, but we do not understand the rules that govern it.

27. Just how daring is this yoking of opposites is attested by the fact that Rashi, Kimchi, Gersonides, and Abravanel all ignored the story's implicit criticism of Elisha and preferred to adopt, to one degree or another, the midrash that blames Gehazi for the failure of the staff to revive the child (JT Sanhedrin 10,2; *Pirqe Rabbi Eliezer* 33). This approach is possible, however, only if one ignores verse 30, which indicates that the Shunammite foresaw the failure and that Elisha followed her to Shunem only because of her oath. Hence it is not astonishing that the four commentators mentioned above pass over this verse in silence. Modern exegesis, too, has not given appropriate recognition to this verse's importance for the plot and has not noted its theological significance in the context of the biblical concept of prophecy. This is chiefly because many moderns are still unable to ascribe a mature and complex view to the scriptural story and tend to assume that our story seeks only to exalt and glorify Elisha the miracle-worker. An exception is Long ("Figure at the Gate"), who emphasizes the tension between the two contradictory impulses he finds in the story—lauding the man of God versus praising the Shunammite. However, since Long's is a deconstructivist reading ("Metaphorically speaking, the text undermines itself, that is, the story bears two contrastive but coherent readings" [p. 174]), he evinces a strong tendency to intensify the contrasts and avoids any attempt to embed them in a single dialectic view.

28. On the close literary links among the various Elisha tales, see Zakovitch, *Every High Official,* pp. 145–48.

29. See above, pp. 44–45.

30. To make this clear the narrator resorts to the pluperfect, expressed by the *qaṭal* form with subject preceding predicate (v. 31).

31. Jacob, too, gained extraordinary strength only when he actually saw Rachel with Laban's sheep (Gen. 29:10); the witch of Endor had to use every means in her power to strengthen Saul after she had seen the depth of his fall (1 Sam. 28:21).

32. See above, pp. 166–67.

33. Wislicki provides a medical rationale for Elisha's actions and suggests that Elisha was warming the child's body ("Revival of the Child," pp. 876–78). It should be stressed, however, that Wislicki's assumption that the child had not actually died, based on the opinion of one Talmudic sage (BT Niddah 70b), clearly contradicts the plain sense of verse 32.

34. In this her conduct is similar to Elijah's with Ahab: running before his chariot (1 Kings 18:46) is meant to restore the royal honor taken from him when it was necessary to arouse him to participate in the eradication of Baal worship from Israel (see above, p. 197).

35. On this literary genre and its various components, see above, pp. 133–50.

36. The similarity between the two verses is even greater if we delete the bracketed words, which intrude on the syntactical structure of the Hebrew verse and seem to be attracted from the previous verse (as proposed by *Biblia Hebraica,* Šanda, Montgomery, and Gray).

37. See above, pp. 163–68.

38. Uffenheimer, too, believes that the Elisha stories are later than the Elijah stories and depend on them, but most of his arguments and proofs are different (*Ancient Prophecy,* pp. 270–72). On the other hand, H.-C. Schmitt (*Elisa,* pp. 153–54), A. Schmitt ("Die Totenerweckung," pp. 454–74), and Stipp (*Elischa,* pp. 451–58) all believe that the Elijah resurrection story is a reworking with theological expansion of the Elisha story. Finally, Killian takes a complex intermediate position

("Die Totenerweckungen," pp. 44–56). Their arguments are based on problems I consider to be more imaginary than real, which bother them because they fail to perform a close reading that is alert to the rhetorical wealth and theological profundity of these stories.

39. The situation here is superficially identical to what we read about Ahab: "So the king of Israel summoned an officer [*saris*] and said, 'Bring Micaiah son of Imlah at once' " (1 Kings 22:9). If so, a *saris* is merely a junior functionary delegated to implement the king's explicit instructions. It is possible, however, that here the reference really is to a eunuch (the primary sense of *saris*), whom the king delegates to accompany the Shunammite out of concern for her feminine modesty (Montgomery). If so, this continues the theme of modesty found in the body of the story as well (see above, pp. 239–40, 246–47, 253).

40. See Fishbane, *Biblical Interpretation*, pp. 380–88, 392–97, 401–403.

Appendix

1. See Gunkel, *Genesis*, pp. xxxvi–xxxviii.

2. Hertzberg, *I and II Samuel*, p. 239.

3. Similarly, we are told about Moses' meeting with his father-in-law, Jethro, but nothing about his meeting with his wife and two sons (Exod. 18:1–8). Nor does Abraham figure in the meeting between his servant and Isaac after the former's return from his successful mission in Haran (Gen. 24:66–67).

4. Kaufmann, *Joshua*, pp. 74–76; Alter, *Art of Biblical Narrative*, p. 126.

5. For example, in 2 Kings 5:3 we read that the girl captive from the land of Israel suggested to Naaman's wife that he turn to Elisha. In the next verse Naaman is relating this recommendation to the king: the narrator saw no need to include the intermediate phase, when Naaman's wife tells her husband about the girl's suggestion. In the story of the miracle of the jug of oil (2 Kings 4:1–7), Elisha directs the widow to borrow vessels from all her neighbors and to shut herself up in her house; the next thing we read is that "she went away and shut the door behind her and her children" (v. 5). Readers must imagine on their own the actual borrowing of the vessels.

6. See, for example, the Septuagint's explanatory additions to 1 Sam. 3:15 ("and rose up early in the morning") and to 1 Sam. 5:3 ("they came to the Temple of Dagon and saw").

7. Josephus accounts for Elijah's ability to identify the widow who was to feed him by inserting a missing link: "Then God informed him that this is the woman who would take care of him" (*Antiquities of the Jews* 8,13,2). Compare the more plausible answers of Rashi and David Kimchi, who preferred not to assume another revelation.

8. See the Septuagint's addition to 2 Kings 4:5 ("she did so") and Josephus's addition to 1 Kings 1:28 ("who left the room at the prophet's arrival" [*Antiquities of the Jews* 7,14,5]). Josephus illuminated the vague circumstances of Samson's binding by Delilah (Judg. 16:8) by supplying "while he was lying drunk" ("while he was sleeping" in another version) (ibid., 5,8,11).

9. Kaufmann, *Joshua*, pp. 74–76; Alter, *Art of Biblical Narrative*, pp. 114–30. Going further, feminist criticism seeks to redeem biblical women from their subordinate status in society and in the stories by uncovering the dependence of the mode of narrative on the patriarchal worldview and the tendentious buttressing of its norms, and by a vigorous filling-in of lacunae aimed at completing what the narrator left out about the suffering and exploitation of the female characters. Even when this brand of criticism is not overtly subjective in its approach or quasi-homiletical in its methods, and even when it does attempt to remain within the

strict confines of scholarly methodology, it is liable to offer a specifically feminist explanation for more general phenomena and to explain a character's place in the narrative shadow by her gender rather than by the fact that she is a minor character. For example, Exum views the narrator's silence as to Michal's feelings as "literary murder," intended to punish her for daring to go beyond the role allotted to her in patriarchal society, in addition to the cruel sanction imposed upon her by David after she dares reprove him in public—avoiding sexual relations with her ("Murder They Wrote," pp. 46–47, 49–57, and 60–61). But Exum ignores the fact that Michal did not have children by Paltiel, either (which casts doubt as to whether her lifelong childlessness was the result of an intentional sanction by David), as well as the perfectly reasonable possibility that her rebuke of David provoked so sharp a rejoinder not because a woman should keep quiet in public but because David heard Saul's voice speaking through his daughter's mouth.

10. See, for example, *Genesis Rabbah* 56,11 and *Midrash Hagadol*, ad loc. For a comprehensive and profound analysis of all midrashim on this verse, see S. Spiegel, *The Last Trial*, trans. Judah Goldin (New York, 1967).

11. Abraham Ibn Ezra, Kimchi, and Ibn Kaspi stressed that these homilies have no real basis in the text. Rashi, Nachmanides, von Rad (*Genesis*) and Speiser (*Genesis*) simply did not comment on the failure to mention Isaac in this verse.

12. Another example is in 1 Kings 22, which contains a detailed account of fulfillment of the prophecies of Micaiah son of Imlah to Ahab but ignores his fate and that of his rival, Zedekiah. Was Micaiah soon released from prison? Did Zedekiah really hide "in the innermost room" (v. 25)? This silence is an indication of the theme and direction of the narrative.

13. Licht counters that "the mimetic disposition is characteristic of the basic approach of the biblical narrators to their material, although this disposition cannot be expressed everywhere" ("Mimesis in the Bible," p. 139). However, almost all the examples he puts forward to support this cautious principle can be given an alternative interpretation that links what Licht presents as a mimetic jewel with the main point of the story and its message.

14. In some secondary manuscripts of the Septuagint this differentiation was blurred by a clarifying expansion at the end of verse 10: "and his servant" is added.

15. See Goitein, *Bible Studies*, p. 53.

16. Similarly, the conscience-stricken and humane attitude of the king's Cushite eunuch toward Jeremiah serves to spotlight the heartless cruelty of the princes of Judah who cast the prophet into a muddy pit and left him there to die (Jer. 38:1–13).

BIBLIOGRAPHY

Aberbach, D. "Manah 'achat 'appayim (1 Sam. 1:5): A New Interpretation." *VT* 24 (1974): 350–53.

Abravanel, Isaac. *Commentary on the Former Prophets.* Jerusalem, 1956 (Hebrew).

Ackerman, James S. "The Literary Context of the Moses Birth Story." In Kenneth R. R. Gros Louis et al., eds., *Literary Interpretation of Biblical Narratives*, pp. 74–119. Nashville, 1974.

——. "Knowing Good and Evil: A Literary Analysis of the Court History in 2 Samuel 9–20 and 1 Kings 1–2." *JBL* 109 (1990): 41–64.

Adar, Zvi. *The Biblical Narrative.* Jerusalem, 1957 (Hebrew).

Alkanzi, Isaac ben Samuel. *Arabic Commentary on the Book of Samuel.* 1 Samuel: MS Petersburg-Firkovitch II, 3362; 2 Samuel: MS London-British Library Or. 2388.

Alster, B. "A Note on the Uriah Letter in the Sumerian Sargon Legend." *Zeitschrift für Assyriologie* 77 (1987): 169–73.

Alt, Albrecht. "Das Gottesurteil auf dem Karmel." *George Beer Festschrift*, pp. 1–18. Stuttgart, 1935 (repr. in *Kleine Schriften* 2, 135–49. Munich, 1953).

——. "Die Literarische Herkunft von I Reg 19:19–21." *ZAW* 32 (1912): 123–25.

Alter, Robert. *The Art of Biblical Narrative.* New York, 1981.

——. "How Convention Helps Us Read: The Case of the Bible's Annunciation Type-Scene." *Prooftexts* 3 (1983): 115–30.

Anbar, M. "Un euphémisme 'biblique' dans une lettre de Mari." *Orientalia* 48 (1979): 109–11.

Ap-Thomas, D. R. "Elijah on Mount Carmel." *PEQ* 92 (1960): 146–55.

Arama, Isaac. *Akedat Yizchak* (commentary on the Torah). Lemburg, 1708 (Hebrew).

Aref, Aref el-. *Beduin Love, Law, and Legend.* Trans. from Arabic in collaboration with the author by H. W. Tilley. Haifa, 1944.

Arpali, Boaz. "Caution: A Biblical Story! Comments on the Story of David and Bathsheba and on the Problems of Biblical Narrative." *Hasifrut* 2 (1970): 580–97 (Hebrew).

Avishur, Y. "The 'Duties of the Son' in the Story of Aqhat and Ezekiel's Prophecy on Idolatry (ch. 8)." *Ugarit-Forschungen* 17 (1986): 49–60.

Baltzer, Klaus. *Die Biographie der Propheten.* Neukirchen, 1975.

Batten, L. W. "The Sanctuary at Shiloh, and Samuel's Sleeping Therein." *JBL* 19 (1900): 29–33.

Ben Sira. In R. H. Charles, ed., *The Apocrypha and Pseudepigrapha of the Old Testament in English*, vol. 1, pp. 268–517. Oxford, 1913.

Berlin, Adele. *Poetics and Interpretation of Biblical Narrative.* Sheffield, 1983.

Berridge, J. M. *Prophet, People and the Word of God.* Zurich, 1970.

Beuken, W. A. M. "I Samuel 28: The Prophet as 'Hammer of Witches.'" *JSOT* 6 (1978): 3–17.

Bird, Phyllis A. "The Harlot as Heroine: Narrative Art and Social Presupposition in Three Old Testament Texts." *Semeia* 46 (1989): 110–39.

331

Bole, M. *Jeremiah.* Jerusalem, 1984 (Hebrew).

Brichto, Herbert Chanan. *Toward a Grammar of Biblical Poetics: Tales of the Prophets.* New York, 1992.

Bronner, Lea. *The Stories of Elijah and Elisha as Polemics against Baal Worship.* Leiden, 1968.

Budde, Karl. *Die Bücher Samuel.* Tübingen, 1902.

Carlson, R. A. *David, the Chosen King.* Uppsala, 1964.

Caspari, D. W. *Die Samuelbücher.* Leipzig, 1926.

Cassuto, U. "The Journey of Ashera in II AB, IV 1–18 from Ugarit." *Tarbiz* 20 (1949): 1–7 (Hebrew).

———. *A Commentary on the Book of Genesis, Part I: From Adam to Noah.* Trans. Israel Abrahams. Jerusalem, 1961.

———. *A Commentary on the Book of Genesis, Part II: From Noah to Abraham.* Trans. Israel Abrahams. Jerusalem, 1964.

———. *A Commentary on the Book of Exodus.* Trans. Israel Abrahams. Jerusalem, 1967.

———. *The Goddess Anath.* Trans. Israel Abrahams. Jerusalem, 1971.

———. "Daniel and His Son in Tablet IID of Ras Shamra." Trans. Israel Abrahams. *Biblical and Oriental Studies* 2 (Jerusalem, 1975): 199–205.

Childs, Brevard S. *Introduction to the Old Testament as Scripture.* Philadelphia, 1979.

Cogan, Mordechai, and Hayim Tadmor. *II Kings* (Anchor Bible). Garden City, N.Y., 1988.

Cohen, Ch. "Studies in Extra-Biblical Hebrew Inscriptions I: The Semantic Range and Usage of the Terms *amah* and *shifchah*." *Shnaton: An Annual for Biblical and Ancient Near Eastern Studies* 5–6 (1983): xxv–liii.

Cohen, Robert L. "The Literary Logic of 1 Kings 17–19." *JBL* 101 (1982): 333–50.

Cook, Joan E. "The Song of Hannah: Text and Contexts." Ph.D. diss., Vanderbilt University, 1989. Ann Arbor: University Microfilms, 1991.

Crenshaw, James L. *Prophetic Conflict: Its Effect upon Israelite Religion.* Berlin, 1971.

Cross, Frank Moore. *Canaanite Myth and Hebrew Epic.* Cambridge, Mass., 1973.

Daube, David. *Studies in Biblical Law,* 2nd ed. New York, 1969.

———. "Nathan's Parable." *Novum Testamentum* 24 (1982): 275–88.

Deist, F. " ʾappayim (1 Sam. 1:5) < *pym?" *VT* 27 (1977): 205–208.

DeVries, Simon. *1 Kings* (*Word Biblical Commentary,* vol. 12). Waco, Texas, 1985.

Dorp, J. van. "Wat is die steenhoop daar? Het graf van de man Gods in 2 Koningen 23." *Amsterdamse Cahiers voor Exegese en Bijbelse Theologie* 8 (1987): 64–79.

Driver, S. R. *A Treatise on the Use of the Tenses in Hebrew.* 3rd ed. Oxford, 1892 (repr. 1969).

———. *Notes on the Hebrew Text and the Topography of the Books of Samuel.* 2nd ed. Oxford, 1913.

Dus, J. "Die altisraelitische amphiktyonische Poesie." *ZAW* 75 (1963): 45–54.

Ehrlich, Arnold B. *Randglossen zur hebräischen Bibel.* Vol. 3 (1 and 2 Samuel). Leipzig, 1910. Vol. 7 (Kings). Leipzig, 1914.

Eichrodt, W. *Theology of the Old Testament.* Trans. J. A. Baker. 2 vols. London, 1961–1967.

Eissfeldt, Otto. *Der Gott Karmel.* Berlin, 1953.

———. " 'Bist du Elia, so bin ich Isebel' (1 Kön. 19:2)." *VT* suppl. 16 (1967): 65–70.

———. "Die Komposition von 1 Reg 16:29–2 Reg 13:25." *BZAW* 105 (1967): 49–55.

Elat, Moshe. "History and Historiography in the Story of Samuel." *Shnaton: An Annual for Biblical and Ancient Near Eastern Studies* 3 (1978/79): 8–28 (Hebrew).

Eslinger, Lyle M. *Kingship of God in Crisis: A Close Reading of 1 Samuel 1–12.* Sheffield, 1985.

Exum, J. Cheryl. "Murder They Wrote: Ideology and the Manipulation of Female

Presence in Biblical Narrative." In Alice Bach, ed., *The Pleasure of Her Text: Feminist Reading of Biblical and Historical Texts,* pp. 45–67. Philadelphia, 1990.

Eynikel, Erik. "Prophecy and Fulfilment in the Deuteronomistic History: 1 Kgs 13; 2 Kgs 23:16–18." In C. Brekelmans and J. Lust, eds. *Pentateuchal and Deuteronomistic Studies,* pp. 227–37. Leuven, 1990.

Fensham, F. C. "A Few Remarks on the Polarization Between YHWH and Baal in I Kings 17–19." *ZAW* 92 (1980): 227–36.

Fenton, Paul B. "La 'tête entre les genoux': contribution à l'étude d'une posture méditative dans la mystique juive et islamique." *Revue d'histoire et de philosophie religieuses* 72 (1992/94): 413–26.

Fishbane, Michael. "The Biblical *ot*" *Shnaton: An Annual for Biblical and Ancient Near Eastern Studies* 1 (1975): 213–34 (Hebrew).

———. "I Samuel 3: Historical Narrative and Narrative Poetics." in Kenneth R. R. Gros Louis, ed., *Literary Interpretation of Biblical Narratives,* vol. 2, pp. 191–203. Nashville, 1982.

———. *Biblical Interpretation in Ancient Israel.* Oxford, 1985.

Fisher, L. R. *Ras Shamra Parallels.* 2 vols. Rome, 1975.

Fohrer, George. *Elia.* Zurich, 1957.

———. *Die symbolischen Handlungen der Propheten.* 2nd ed. Zurich, 1968.

Fokkelman, J. P. *Narrative Art and Poetry in the Books of Samuel.* 4 vols. Assen, 1981–1993.

Frankel, Z. *Vorstudien zu der Septuaginta.* Leipzig, 1841.

Garsiel, Moshe. *Biblical Names: A Literary Study of Midrashic Derivations and Puns.* Ramat-Gan, 1991.

———. "The Story of David and Bathsheba: A Different Approach." *CBQ* 55 (1993): 244–62.

Gaster, Theodore Herzl. *Myth, Legend, and Custom in the Old Testament: A Comparative Study.* New York, 1969.

Gersonides. *Commentary on Former Prophets* (Hebrew) [in all Rabbinic Bibles].

Gesenius' Hebrew Grammar, ed. and enlarged by E. Kautzsch. Trans. G. W. Collins, rev. A. E. Cowley. 2nd ed. Oxford, 1910.

Ginzberg, Louis. *The Legends of the Jews.* Trans. Henrietta Szold. 7 vols. Philadelphia, 1928–1966.

Gnuse, R. K. *The Dream Theophany of Samuel.* Lanham, Md., 1984.

Goitein, S. D. *Bible Studies.* 3rd ed. Tel Aviv, 1967 (Hebrew).

Gordon, C. H. *Ugaritic Textbook.* Rome, 1965.

Gray, John. *I and II Kings* (Old Testament Library). 2nd ed. Philadelphia, 1970.

Greenberg, Moshe. "You Have Turned Their Hearts Backward (1 Kings 18:37)." In Jakob J. Petuchowski and Ezra Fleischer, eds., *Studies in Aggadah, Targum, and Jewish Liturgy in Memory of Joseph Heinemann,* pp. 52–66. Jerusalem, 1981 (Hebrew).

———. "The Patterns of Prayers of Petition in the Bible." *Eretz-Israel: Archaeological, Historical and Geographical Studies* 16 (1982): 47–55 (Hebrew).

———. *Ezekiel 1–20* (Anchor Bible). Garden City, N.Y., 1983.

Gressman, Hugo. *Die älteste Geschichtsschreibung und Prophetie Israels.* Göttingen, 1921.

Grintz, Joshua M. *Biblical Introductions.* Tel Aviv, 1972 (Hebrew).

Guillaume, A. *Prophecy and Divination among the Hebrews and Other Semites.* London, 1938.

Gunkel, Hermann. *Genesis.* Göttingen, 1902.

———. *Elias J. und Baal.* Tübingen, 1906.

———. *Das Märchen im Alten Testament.* 2nd ed. Tübingen, 1921.

——. *Geschichten von Elisa.* Berlin, [1922].

Gunn, David M. *The Fate of King Saul: An Interpretation of a Biblical Story.* Sheffield, 1980.

Habel, Norman. "The Form and Significance of the Call Narratives." *ZAW* 77 (1965): 297–323.

Henry, M.-L. *Prophet und Tradition.* Berlin, 1969 (= *BZAW* 116).

Hentschel, Georg. *Die Elijaerzählungen.* Leipzig, 1977.

Hertzberg, Hans Wilhelm. *I and II Samuel, a Commentary.* Trans. J. S. Bowden. London, 1964.

Hoffman, Yair. "The Song of the Vineyard." In J. Licht and G. Brin, eds., *Studies in Bible Dedicated to the Memory of Israel and Zvi Broide,* pp. 69–82. Tel Aviv, 1976 (Hebrew).

Hoftijzer, J. "David and the Tekoite Woman." *VT* 20 (1970): 419–44.

Hurowitz, Victor Avigdor. "Eli's Adjuration of Samuel (1 Sam. 3:17–18) in Light of a 'Diviner's Protocol' from Mari (AEM I/1,1)." *VT* 44 (1994): 483–97.

Hurvitz, Avi. *Wisdom Language in Biblical Psalmody.* Jerusalem, 1991 (Hebrew).

Ibn Ezra, Abraham. *Yesod Mispar,* ed. S. Pinsker. Vienna, 1863 (Hebrew).

——. *Torah Commentary,* ed. A. Weiser. 3 vols. Jerusalem, 1976 (Hebrew).

Ibn Kaspi, Joseph. *Adnei Kesef,* vols. 1–2 (commentary on the Prophets), ed. J. Last. London, 1911–1912 (Hebrew).

Irvin, D. *Mytharion: The Comparison of Tales from the Old Testament and the Ancient Near East.* Neukirchen, 1978.

Janzen, Waldemar. "Withholding the Word." In B. Halpern and J. D. Levenson, eds., *Traditions in Transformation,* pp. 97–114. Winona Lake, Ind., 1981.

Jenni, Ernst. "Das Wort *olam* im Alten Testament." *ZAW* 64 (1952): 197–248.

Jepsen, Alfred. "Amah und Schiphchah." *VT* 8 (1958): 293–97.

——. "Gottesmann und Prophet (Anmerkungen zum Kapitel 1 Könige 13)." In H. W. Wolf., ed., *Probleme Biblischer Theologie* (G. von Rad Festschrift), pp. 171–82. Munich, 1971.

Jeremias, Jörg. *Theophanie: Die Geschichte einer alttestamentlichen Gattung.* Neukirchen, 1965.

Josephus, Flavius. *Antiquities of the Jews,* trans. H. St. J. Thackeray and R. Marcus, vols. 4–9: *Josephus.* London, 1930–1937.

Joüon, Paul. "Notes philologiques sur le texte hébreu de 2 Samuel." *Biblica* 9 (1928): 302–15.

Joüon, Paul, and T. Muraoka. *A Grammar of Biblical Hebrew.* 2 vols. Rome, 1991.

Kara, Joseph. *Commentary on the Former Prophets,* ed. S. Eppenstein. Jerusalem, 1972 (Hebrew).

Kaufmann, Y. "Nathan the Prophet in the Royal Court." *Beit Mikra* 2 (1957): 64–68 (Hebrew) (repr. in *Collected Papers,* pp. 180–84).

——. *Joshua.* Jerusalem, 1959 (Hebrew).

——. *The Religion of Israel.* Abridged and trans. by Moshe Greenberg. Chicago, 1960.

——. *Collected Papers.* Tel Aviv, 1966 (Hebrew).

Keil, Carl Friedrich, and Franz Delitzsch. *The Books of Samuel.* Trans. J. Martin. Edinburgh, 1872.

Kiel, Judah. *The Book of Samuel.* 2 vols. Jerusalem, 1981 (Hebrew).

Killian, Rudolf. "Die Totenerweckungen Elias und Elisas." *Biblische Zeitschrift* 10 (1966): 44–56.

——. "Die prophetischen Berufungsberichte." In *Theologie im Wandel,* pp. 356–76. Munich, 1967.

Kimchi, David. *Commentary on the Former Prophets* (Hebrew) [in all Rabbinic Bibles].

——. *The Book of Roots.* Berlin, 1847 (Hebrew).

Kittel, Rudolf. *Die Bücher der Könige* (Handkommentar zum Alten Testament). Göttingen, 1900.

Kittel, Rudolf, and Martin Noth, eds. *Regum I & II.* In R. Kittel and P. Kahle, eds., *Biblia Hebraica.* Stuttgart, 1937.

Klopfenstein, M. A. "I Könige 13." In *Parrhesia* (Karl Barth Festschrift), pp. 639–72. Zurich, 1966.

Klostermann, A. *Die Bücher Samuelis und der Könige.* Nördlingen, 1887.

Knierim, Rolf. "Old Testament Form Criticism Reconsidered." *Interpretation* 27 (1973): 435–68.

Koch, K. "Die Sohnesverheissung an den ugaritischen Daniel." *Zeitschrift für Assyriologie,* n.s. 24 (1967): 211–21.

Kutsch, Ernst. "Gideons Berufung und Altarbau, Jdc. 6, 11–24." *Theologische Literaturzeitung* 81 (1956): 76–84.

Lasine, Stuart. "Melodrama as Parable: The Story of the Poor Man's Ewe-Lamb and the Unmasking of David's Topsy-Turvy Emotions." *Hebrew Annual Review* 8 (1984): 101–24.

Licht, Jacob. "Mimesis in the Bible." In J. Licht and G. Brin, eds., *Studies in Bible Dedicated to the Memory of Israel and Zvi Broide,* pp. 133–42. Tel Aviv, 1976 (Hebrew).

Long, Burke O. *First Kings* (The Forms of the Old Testament Literature Series, vol. 9). Grand Rapids, Mich., 1984.

———. "A Figure at the Gate: Readers, Reading, and Biblical Theologians." In G. M. Tucker et al., eds., *Canon, Theology, and Old Testament Interpretation* (B. S. Childs Festschrift). Philadelphia, 1988.

———. *Second Kings* (The Forms of the Old Testament Literature Series, vol. 10). Grand Rapids, Mich., 1991.

Macholz, Christian. "Psalm 29 und 1 Könige 19." In R. Albertz et al., eds., *Werden und Wirken des Alten Testaments* (Claus Westermann Festschrift), pp. 325–33. Göttingen, 1980.

Maimonides, Abraham. *Responsa,* ed. A. H. Freimann. Jerusalem, 1937 (Hebrew).

Malbim, M. L. *Mikrae Kodesh* (commentary on the Prophets and Hagiographa). Warsaw, 1875 (Hebrew).

McCarter, Peter Kyle. *I and II Samuel* (Anchor Bible). Garden City, N.Y., 1980, 1984.

Medan, Y. "Bathsheba's Story." *Megadim* 18–19 (1993): 67–167 (Hebrew).

Montgomery, James A. *The Books of Kings* (ICC). New York, 1951.

Muffs, Yochanan. *Love and Joy: Law, Language and Religion in Ancient Israel.* New York, 1992.

Murry, G. W. *Sons of Ishmael (A Study of the Egyptian Bedouin).* London, 1935.

Newsom, Carol. *Songs of the Sabbath Sacrifice: A Critical Edition.* Atlanta, 1985.

Nordheim, Eckhard von. "Ein Prophet kündigt sein Amt auf (Elia am Horeb)." *Biblica* 59 (1978): 153–73.

Noth, Martin. "Samuel in Silo." *VT* 13 (1963): 390–400.

———. *Könige.* Neukirchen, 1968.

Nowack, Wilhelm. *Richter, Ruth, und die Bücher Samuels* (HKAT). Göttingen, 1902.

Obermann, J. "How Daniel Was Blessed with a Son." *JAOS* suppl. 6 (1946): 1–30.

Oppenheim, A. Leo. *The Interpretation of Dreams in the Ancient Near East.* Philadelphia, 1956.

Orlinsky, H. M. "On the Commonly Proposed Leḵ Wena'abor of 1 Kings 18:5." *JBL* 59 (1940): 515–17.

Parker, Simon B. "The Vow in Ugaritic and Israelite Narrative Literature." *UF* 11 (1979): 697.

Paul, Shalom M. "Deutero-Isaiah and Cuneiform Royal Inscriptions." *JAOS* 88 (1968): 180–86.

Perry, Menakhem, and Meir Sternberg. "The King through Ironic Eyes: The Narrator's Devices in the Biblical Story of David and Bathsheba and two Excursuses on the Theory of the Narrative Text." *Hasifrut* 1 (1968): 263–92 (Hebrew).

———. "Caution, A Literary Text! Problems in the Poetics and the Interpretation of Biblical Narrative." *Hasifrut* 2 (1970): 608–63 (Hebrew).

Phillips, A. "The Interpretation of 2 Sam. XII, 5–6." *VT* 16 (1966): 242–44.

Polak, Frank. "The Main Strand in the First Book of Samuel 1–15." Ph.D. diss., Hebrew University of Jerusalem, 1984 (Hebrew).

Polzin, Robert. *Samuel and the Deuteronomist*. San Francisco, 1989.

Preuss, H. D. *Verspottung fremder Religionen im Alten Testament*. Stuttgart, 1971.

Pritchard, James B. *Ancient Near Eastern Texts Relating to the Old Testament*. Princeton, 1963.

Quell, G. *Wahre und falsche Propheten*. Gütersloh, 1952.

Rad, Gerhard von. *Genesis, das erste Buch Mose*. Göttingen, 1956. [Trans. into English by J. H. Marks. London, 1961.]

———. "Die deuteronomistische Geschichtstheologie in den Königbücher." *Gesammelte Studien zum Alten Testament*, pp. 189–204. Munich, 1958.

———. *Old Testament Theology*. Trans. D. M. G. Stalker. 2 vols. New York, 1962–1965.

Rank, Otto. *The Myth of Birth of the Hero and Other Writings*. New York, 1959.

Rashi. *Commentary on the Former Prophets* (Hebrew) [in all Rabbinic Bibles].

Richter, Wolfgang. *Die sogenannten vorprophetischen Berufungsberichte*. Göttingen, 1970.

Roberts, J. J. M. "A New Parallel to 1 Kings 18:28–29." *JBL* 89 (1970): 76–77.

Robinson, H. W. "Prophetic Symbolism." In D. C. Simpson, ed., *Old Testament Essays*, pp. 1–17. London, 1927.

Rofé, Alexander. "The Breaking of the Heifer's Neck." *Tarbiz* 31 (1962): 119–43 (Hebrew).

———. "Baal, the Prophet, and the Angel (2 Kings 1): A Study in the History of Literature and Religion." *Beer-Sheva* 1 (1972/73): 222–30 (Hebrew).

———. *The Prophetical Stories*. Jerusalem, 1988.

Rowley, Harold Henry. "The Nature of Prophecy in the Light of Recent Research." *HTR* 38 (1945): 1–38.

———. "Elijah on Mount Carmel." In *Men of God*, pp. 37–65. London, 1963.

Rudin-O'Brasky, Talia. *The Patriarchs in Hebron and Sodom (Genesis 18–19)*. Jerusalem, 1982 (Hebrew).

Saadya Gaon. *The Book of Beliefs and Opinions*. Trans. Samuel Rosenblatt. New Haven, 1948.

Sabbato, Mordechai. "The Story of the Shunammite." *Megadim* 15 (1992): 46–52 (Hebrew).

Saint-Laurent, George E. "Light from Ras Shamra on Elijah's Ordeal upon Mount Carmel." In Carl D. Evans et al., eds., *Scripture in Context*, pp. 123–39. Pittsburgh, 1980.

Samet, Elchanan. "1 Kings 13: The Story and Its Meaning." *Megadim* 6 (1988): pp. 55–85 (Hebrew).

———. "The Double Embrace." *Megadim* 13 (1991): pp. 73–95 (Hebrew).

Šanda, Albert. *Die Bücher der Könige* (Exegetisches Handbuch zum Alten Testament). 2 vols. Münster, 1911–1912.

Sarfatti, G. B. "Arithmetical Fractions in Biblical and Mishnaic Hebrew." *Tarbiz* 28 (1959): pp. 1–17 (Hebrew).

Savran, George W. *Telling and Retelling: Quotation in Biblical Narrative*. Bloomington, 1988.

Schiffman, Lawrence H. "*Merkawa* Speculation at Qumran: The 4Q Serekh Shirot

'Olat ha-Shabbat.' " In J. Reinharz and D. Swetschinski, eds., *Mystics, Philosophers and Politicians* (A. Altmann Festschrift), pp. 15–47. Durham, 1982.

Schmitt, Armin. "Die Totenerweckung in 2 Kön. 4, 8–37: eine literarwissenschaftliche Untersuchung." *Biblische Zeitschrift* 19 (1975): 1–25.

———. "Die Totenerweckung in 1 Kön. XVII, 17–24." *VT* 27 (1977): 454–74.

Schmitt, Hans-Christoph. *Elisa*. Gütersloh, 1972.

Schwally, F. "Zur Quellenkritik der historischen Bücher." *ZAW* 12 (1892): 153–61.

Seeligmann, I. L. *Studies in Biblical Literature*. Jerusalem, 1992 (Hebrew).

Segal, M. H. *The Books of Samuel*. Jerusalem, 1964 (Hebrew).

Seybold, Klaus. "Elia am Gottesberg." *Evangelische Theologie* 33 (1973): 3–18.

Shoshany, Ronit. "Studies in the Prosody of the Old Testament." M.A. thesis, Tel Aviv University, 1986 (Hebrew).

———. "A Prosodic Explanation for a Textual Alteration in Bialik and Rawnitsky's *Sefer Ha-agadah*." *Hebrew Computational Linguistics* 25 (1987): 71–83 (Hebrew).

Simon, Uriel. "The Parable of Jotham: The Parable, Its Application, and Their Narrative Framework." *Tarbiz* 34 (1964/65): 1–34 (Hebrew).

———. "An Ironic Approach to a Bible Story: On the Interpretation of the Story of David and Bathsheba." *Hasifrut* 2 (1970), pp. 598–607 (Hebrew).

———. "1 Kings 13: A Prophetic Sign—Denial and Persistence." *HUCA* 47 (1976): 81–117.

———. "Elijah's Fight against Baal Worship: Unity and Structure of the Story (1 Kings 17- 18)." In U. Simon and M. Goshen-Gottstein, eds., *Studies in Bible and Exegesis*, vol. 1, pp. 51–118 (Hebrew). Ramat-Gan, 1980.

———. *Jonah*. Tel Aviv, 1992 (Hebrew).

Skinner, John. *Kings* (Century Bible). London, ca. 1893.

Smend, Rudolf. "Das Wort YHWH's an Elia: Erwägungen zur Komposition von 1 Reg. XVII–XIX." *VT* 25 (1975): 525–43.

Smith, H. P. *The Books of Samuel* (ICC). Edinburgh, 1899.

Speiser, E. A. "The Nuzi Tablets Solve a Puzzle in the Books of Samuel." *BASOR* 72 (1938): 15–17.

———. *Genesis* (Anchor Bible). Garden City, N.Y., 1964.

Spiegel, Shalom. "Noah, Danel, and Job." In *Louis Ginzberg Jubilee Volume*, ed. A. Marx et al., pp. 305–55. New York, 1945.

Stamm, Johann Jakob. "Elia am Horeb." In *Studia Biblica et Semitica* (T. C. Vriezen Festschrift), pp. 327–34. Wageningen, 1966.

Steck, Odil Hannes. *Überlieferung und Zeitgeschichte in den Elia-Erzählungen*. Neukirchen, 1968.

Sternberg, Meir. *The Poetics of Biblical Narrative*. Bloomington, 1985.

Stipp, Hermann-Josef. *Elischa—Propheten—Gottesmänner*. St. Ottilien, 1987.

Stoebe, Hans Joachim. *Das erste Buch Samuelis*. Gütersloh, 1973.

Stolz, Fritz. *Das erste und zweite Buch Samuel*. Zürich, 1981.

Tromp, N. Y. "Water and Fire on Mount Carmel: A Conciliatory Suggestion." *Biblica* 56 (1975): 480–502.

Tsevat, M. "Assyriological Notes on the First Book of Samuel." In J. M. Grintz and J. Liver, eds., *Studies in the Bible Presented to Prof. M. H. Segal*, pp. 77–86 (Hebrew). Jerusalem, 1964.

———. "Die Namengebung Samuels und die Substitutionstheorie." *ZAW* 99 (1987): 250–54.

Tucker, G. M. *Form Criticism of the Old Testament*. Philadelphia, 1971.

Tur-Sinai, N. H. *The Plain Meaning of Scripture*. 2 vols. Jerusalem, 1964/65 (Hebrew).

———. *The Book of Job*. Jerusalem, 1972 (Hebrew).

Uffenheimer, B. *Ancient Prophecy in Israel*. Jerusalem, 1973 (Hebrew).

Ulrich, Eugene C. *The Qumran Text of Samuel and Josephus*. Missoula, Mon., 1978.

Van Winkle, D. W. "I Kings XIII: True and False Prophecy." *VT* 39 (1989): 31–42.

Vaux, Roland de. *Ancient Israel: Its Life and Institutions*. Trans. J. McHugh. London, 1961.

———. "The Prophets of Baal on Mount Carmel." In *The Bible and the Ancient Near East*, pp. 238–51. London, 1972.

Veijola, T. "Salomo: Der Erstgeborene Bathshebas." *VT* suppl. 30 (1979): 230–50.

Walters, S. D. "Hannah and Anna: The Greek and Hebrew Texts of 1 Samuel 1." *JBL* 107 (1988): 385–412.

Weingreen, J. "A Rabbinic-Type Gloss in the LXX Version of I Samuel 1:18." *VT* 14 (1964): 225–28.

Weiser, Arthur. *Die Psalmen*. Göttingen, 1959.

Weisman, Zeev. *People and King in Biblical Jurisdiction*. Tel Aviv, 1991 (Hebrew).

Wellhausen, Julius. *Der Text der Bücher Samuels*. Göttingen, 1871.

———. *Die Komposition des Hexateuchs und der historischen Bücher des Alten Testaments*. Berlin, 1889.

Willis, John T. "An Anti-Elide Narrative Tradition from a Prophetic Circle at the Ramah Sanctuary." *JBL* 90 (1971): 288–308.

———. "The Song of Hannah and Psalm 113." *CBQ* 35 (1973): 139–54.

———. "Samuel versus Eli." *Theologische Zeitschrift* 35 (1979): 201–12.

Wislicki, L. "The Revival of the Child by Elisha: A Case of Hypothermia." *Koroth* 5 (1972): 876–78 (Hebrew).

Würthwein, Ernst. "Die Erzählung vom Gottesurteil auf dem Karmel." *ZThK* 59 (1962): pp. 144–51.

———. "Elijah at Horeb: Reflections on 1 Kings 19:9–18." In J. I. Durham and J. R. Porter, eds., *Proclamation and Presence* (G. H. Davies Festschrift), pp. 152–66. London, 1970.

———. "Die Erzählung vom Gottesmann aus Juda in Bethel: Zur Komposition von 1 Kön. 13." In H. Gese and H. Rüger, eds., *Wort und Geschichte* (K. Elliger Festschrift), pp. 181–89. Neukirchen, 1973.

———. *Die Bücher der Könige* (Das Alte Testament Deutsch, vol. 11, pt. 2). Göttingen, 1984.

Yadin, Yigael. "The Valley of Sucoth in the Campaigns of David and Ahab." In Jacob Liver, ed., *The Military History of the Land of Israel in Biblical Times*, pp. 170–81. Jerusalem, 1964 (Hebrew).

Yaron, R. "The Coptos Decree and 2 Sam. XII:14." *VT* 9 (1959): 89–91.

Zakovitch, Yair. "A Study of Precise and Partial Derivations in Biblical Etymology." *JSOT* 15 (1980): 31–50.

———. *The Life of Samson*. Jerusalem, 1982 (Hebrew).

———. "A Still Small Voice: Form and Content in 1 Kings 19." *Tarbiz* 51 (1982): 329–46 (Hebrew).

———. *Every High Official Has a Higher One Set Over Him: A Literary Analysis of 2 Kings 5*. Tel Aviv, 1985 (Hebrew).

Zalevsky, Saul. "The Vow of Hanna (1 Samuel 1)." *Beit Mikra* 23 (1978): 304–26 (Hebrew).

Zimmerli, Walther. *Ezechiel* (Biblischer Kommentar). 2 vols. Neukirchen, 1955–1968.

INDEX OF BIBLICAL AND RABBINIC CITATIONS

Rabbinic Citations

INDEX OF SUBJECTS

INDEX OF AUTHORS

361

URIEL SIMON is Professor of Bible and Director of the Institute for the History of Jewish Bible Research at Bar-Ilan University, Israel. He is the author of *Abraham Ibn Ezra's Two Commentaries on the Minor Prophets; Four Approaches to the Book of Psalms;* and *The Book of Jonah—A Commentary.*